This book highlights one of the most important trends in understanding consumer behavior, and from some of the leading international scholars in the field. They explore the concept of consumer behavior analysis from different perspectives, this is a must read if you want to truly understand consumer behavior.

Sir Cary Cooper, *CBE, the 50th Anniversary Professor of Organizational Psychology and Health at Manchester Business School, University of Manchester, UK and President of the British Academy of Management*

This book presents a comprehensive coverage of consumer behavior analysis. It will introduce behavior analysts to how the science of behavior can be applied in this area and to the Behavioral Perspective model of consumer choice (BPM). Among the many topics it offers an excellent and readable introduction to operant behavioral economics and how this can be applied to consumer behavior. The writing is supported throughout by examples from the research and it addresses the application of laboratory research findings to consumer behavior. It will be a useful book and I recommend it.

T. Mary Foster, *Professor, University of Waikato, New Zealand*

I highly recommend this book to academics, researchers, organizational leaders and policy makers whose goals are to predict and influence consumer behavior. Most consumer research disregards the effect of the consumer setting on behavior and is often not grounded in empirically demonstrated principles. Fortunately, emerging ideas offered by Foxall et al. lay substantial groundwork for an advanced analysis of consumer behavior with workable implications for changing consumptive behaviors.

Ramona Houmanfar, *Editor of the* Journal of Organizational Behavior Management *and Associate Professor and Director, The University of Nevada, USA*

The Routledge Companion to Consumer Behavior Analysis

The Routledge Companion to Consumer Behavior Analysis provides a unique and eclectic combination of behavioral, cognitive and environmental perspectives to illuminate the real-world complexities of consumer choice in a marketing-oriented economy. Edited by a leading authority in the field, the contributing authors have created a unique anthology for understanding consumer preference by bringing together the very latest research and thinking in consumer behavior analysis.

This comprehensive and innovative volume ranges over a broad multi-disciplinary perspective from economic psychology, behavioral psychology and experimental economics, but its chief focus is on the critical evaluation of consumer choice in the natural settings of affluent, marketing-oriented economies. By focussing on human economic and social choices, which involve social exchange, it explores and reveals the enormous potential of consumer behavior analysis to illuminate the role of modern marketing-oriented business organizations in shaping and responding to consumer choice.

This will be of particular interest to academics, researchers and advanced students in marketing, consumer behavior, behavior analysis, social psychology, behavioral economics and behavioral psychology.

Gordon R. Foxall is Distinguished Research Professor at Cardiff Business School, Cardiff University, where he directs the Consumer Behavior Analysis Research Group (CBAR), and he is also Visiting Professor in Economic Psychology at the University of Durham, UK.

Routledge Companions in Business, Management and Accounting

Routledge Companions in Business, Management and Accounting are prestige reference works providing an overview of a whole subject area or sub-discipline. These books survey the state of the discipline including emerging and cutting edge areas. Providing a comprehensive, up to date, definitive work of reference, Routledge Companions can be cited as an authoritative source on the subject.

A key aspect of these Routledge Companions is their international scope and relevance. Edited by an array of highly regarded scholars, these volumes also benefit from teams of contributors which reflect an international range of perspectives.

Individually, Routledge Companions in Business, Management and Accounting provide an impactful one-stop-shop resource for each theme covered. Collectively, they represent a comprehensive learning and research resource for researchers, postgraduate students and practitioners.

Published titles in this series include:

The Routledge Companion to Fair Value and Financial Reporting
Edited by Peter Walton

The Routledge Companion to Nonprofit Marketing
Edited by Adrian Sargeant and Walter Wymer Jr

The Routledge Companion to Accounting History
Edited by John Richard Edwards and Stephen P. Walker

The Routledge Companion to Creativity
Edited by Tudor Rickards, Mark A. Runco and Susan Moger

The Routledge Companion to Strategic Human Resource Management
Edited by John Storey, Patrick M. Wright and David Ulrich

The Routledge Companion to International Business Coaching
Edited by Michel Moral and Geoffrey Abbott

The Routledge Companion to Organizational Change
Edited by David M. Boje, Bernard Burnes and John Hassard

The Routledge Companion to Cost Management
Edited by Falconer Mitchell, Hanne Nørreklit and Morten Jakobsen

The Routledge Companion to Digital Consumption
Edited by Russell W. Belk and Rosa Llamas

The Routledge Companion to Identity and Consumption
Edited by Ayalla A. Ruvio and Russell W. Belk

The Routledge Companion to Consumer Behavior Analysis

Edited by Gordon R. Foxall

Routledge
Taylor & Francis Group

LONDON AND NEW YORK

First published 2016
by Routledge
2 Park Square, Milton Park, Abingdon, Oxon OX14 4RN

and by Routledge
605 Third Avenue, New York, NY 10017

First issued in paperback 2021

Routledge is an imprint of the Taylor & Francis Group, an informa business

Publisher's Note
The publisher has gone to great lengths to ensure the quality of this reprint but points out that some imperfections in the original copies may be apparent.

British Library Cataloguing in Publication Data
A catalogue record for this book is available from the British Library

Library of Congress Cataloging in Publication Data
The Routledge companion to consumer behavior analysis / edited by Gordon R. Foxall.
pages cm. — (Routledge companions in business, management and accounting)
Includes bibliographical references and index.
1. Consumer behavior. 2. Marketing research. I. Foxall, G. R.
HF5415.32.R677 2016
658.8'342—dc23
2015008848

Typeset in Bembo
by Swales & Willis Ltd, Exeter, Devon, UK

ISBN 13: 978−1−03−224246−0 (pbk)
ISBN 13: 978−0−415−72992−5 (hbk)

DOI: 10.4324/9781315850696

To Jean

Contents

Contents

PART III
Behavioral interpretation of consumer choice 229

Figures

Tables

Tables

Contributors

Ioanna Anninou is currently a Teaching Fellow in Marketing at Surrey Business School, University of Surrey. She received a BSc in Marketing and Communication from Athens University of Economics and Business and holds MSc degrees from Cardiff University, in Strategic Marketing and in Social Sciences Research Methods. She has held marketing-related roles which have advanced her practical knowledge of marketing.

Erik Arntzen holds a PhD on stimulus equivalence from the University of Oslo in Norway, a degree in clinical psychology, and has an interest in ethics relating to behavior analysis. He is currently Professor in Behavior Analysis at Oslo and Akershus University College (OAUC), researching memory in dementia patients. He serves on the editorial board of several journals.

Jordan Belisle is a doctoral student in the Behavior Analysis and Therapy program at Southern Illinois University, and a member of Dr. Mark Dixon's gambling laboratory. His research focus is in the area of language development and the effects of contemporary technology on addiction formation.

Nguyen Bui Huynh has lectured at Danang University, Vietnam and holds an MBA from Humboldt State University in the USA and an MSc from Cardiff University in the UK, where he is currently working towards a PhD studying individual differences in terms of motivation and emotion in a variety of consumer situations.

Paulo R. Cavalcanti is a doctoral student at the University of Brasília and is currently investigating phenomena related to judicial behavior of collegial magistrates based on the BPM. He also holds a master's degree from the University of Brasília where he investigated individual differences in consumer behavior. He is also interested in conceptual analysis in psychology.

John Desmond is Reader in Management at the University of St Andrews working mainly in the area of consumer behavior, with an interest in alternative theoretical perspectives to mainstream accounts of consumer behavior, particularly psychoanalytic and sociological accounts and also in marketing ethics. His interest in the general social significance of marketing is reflected in a current study of obituaries.

Mark R. Dixon, BCBA-D, is a Professor and Coordinator of the Behavior Analysis and Therapy Program at Southern Illinois University. For the past five years he has also served as the Director of an SIU initiative (Behavioral Consultant Group) to infuse behavior analysis within schools, alternative education, and residential facilities serving individuals with autism and other developmental disabilities. He also runs a behavioral therapy clinic (Project HEALTH) for persons suffering from problem gambling or obesity. He has published three books and over 100 peer-reviewed journal articles, and delivered over 300 presentations nationally and internationally.

Asle Fagerstrøm has an MSc in Marketing, and Diploma in Education. In 2010, he received a PhD in Marketing from BI Norwegian Business School. He is Associate Professor at Westerdals - Oslo School of Arts, Communication and Technology and also at Oslo and Akershus University College. His research focuses on behavioral economics, consumer behavior analysis, online consumer behavior, and human–computer interaction.

Gordon R. Foxall is Distinguished Research Professor at Cardiff Business School, Cardiff University where he directs the Consumer Behaviour Analysis Research Group (CBAR), and Visiting Professor in Economic Psychology at the University of Durham. He holds PhDs in industrial economics and business (University of Birmingham) and in psychology (University of Strathclyde), and a higher doctorate (DSocSc), also from the University of Birmingham. He is the author of over 300 refereed papers and some 25 books. He has held visiting appointments at the Universities of Michigan and Oxford. A Fellow of the British Psychological Society (FBPsS) and of the British Academy of Management (FBAM), he is also a Fellow of the Academy of Social Sciences (FAcSS). His research includes the role of neuroscience in the explanation of consumer choice and the behavior of the marketing firm. This work has inaugurated a new area of research, *Consumer Behavior Analysis*.

Paul M. W. Hackett is currently at Emerson College, Boston. During 2015–16 he will be a visiting academic in the Department of Philosophy at the University of Oxford. He holds PhDs in both psychology and fine art and graduate qualifications in fine art and religious studies and has a particular interest in facet theory as applied to consumer behavior.

Donald A. Hantula is Associate Professor of Psychology, Director of the Decision Laboratory at Temple University and Associate Editor of the *Journal of Organizational Behavior Management*. He takes an evolutionary/behavioral approach to research in behavioral economics, human decision making in dynamic environments and technological applications.

Wooyang Kim is currently Assistant Professor of Marketing at Paseka School of Business at Minnesota State University Moorhead, and Chief Analyst at Marketing & Research Strategists. His research interests focus mainly on the consumer decision process, emphasizing the perceived behavior and the resultant outcomes in response to the immediately encountered information and environments. The topic also deals with examining the role of socio-demographic characteristics, such as ages, genders and cultures. The concerned research topics divide into three facets in response to consumer decision process: ecological information foraging, consumer innovativeness, and consuming healthcare services. Related to his research interests, he has published in several journals including Advances in Consumer Research, Asia Pacific Journal of Marketing and Logistics, Journal of Accounting & Marketing, Journal of Global Scholars of Marketing Science and among others. He also presented his research at several conferences such as Association for Consumer Research, Atlantic Marketing Association and Society for Consumer Psychology. He holds Ph.D. in Business of Administration from Temple University, MBA from Pepperdine University, and MS in Marketing, Strategy and International Business from Konkuk University, Seoul, Korea.

Sumana Laparojkit (PhD, Cardiff University) is the Director of the IMBA program and a lecturer at the Faculty of Management Sciences, Prince of Songkla University, Thailand. Her research interests are in the behavioral aspects of consumer behaviour, consumer behaviour in the brand community, marketing communications, social media marketing, and branding.

Nils Magne Larsen is an Associate Professor at Harstad University College and The Arctic University of Norway (UiT). He holds a PhD from Brunel University, London, an MBA from the University of Wisconsin-Madison, and a Lic.rer.pol. from Universität Mannheim, Germany. He has published widely and is the author of several books.

Patrícia Luque Carreiro is a PhD candidate in the Behavioral Sciences department at the University of Brasília. She holds a Master's degree in Psychology, and BAs in Psychology and Business Management. Presently, she works in the Federal Court of Accounts, in Brasília, Brazil.

José Paulo Marques dos Santos is Assistant Professor of Marketing and Neuroscience at University Institute of Maia (ISMAI), and Lecturer in the Department of Experimental Biology of the Faculty of Medicine, University of Porto, Portugal. Originally a Chemical Engineer, he now has a PhD in Neuroscience in Marketing and his main interests are related to behavioral neuroscience, social neuroscience, and brands.

Iván Felipe Medina is a psychologist and holds a Master's degree in Consumer Psychology. He is a PhD candidate in Education with an emphasis on environmental and urban pedagogy. He is currently an associate researcher in the Consumer Psychology Master's Program of Fundación Universitaria Konrad Lorenz.

R. G. Vishnu Menon is a PhD student in Marketing at Reykjavik University, with a Bachelor of Technology degree in Mechanical Engineering and a Post Graduate Diploma in Business Management. He has both engineering and marketing experience with international organizations. His overall research interests are digital marketing, use of eye-tracking in marketing, and online consumer behavior from a behavioral perspective.

Peter Morgan is Reader in Quantitative Analysis at Cardiff Business School. Originally a Physical Chemist, he has a degree in Industrial Chemistry and a PhD in Polymer Physical Chemistry. Co-author of a textbook on computational methods for the chemical sciences, his current research interests include methodologies such as neural networks, evolutionary computation, and exploratory data analysis. His recent publications are in the areas of sampling for price index construction, trends in UK violent assault rates, and pruning techniques for neural networks. He is a member of the Violence and Society Research Group and the Centre for Price and Inflation Studies, both at Cardiff University.

Luiz Moutinho is the Foundation Chair of Marketing at the Adam Smith Business School, University of Glasgow in Scotland. His areas of research interest encompass biomarketing, neuroscience in marketing, evolutionary algorithms, human-computer interaction, the use of artificial neural networks in marketing, modeling consumer behavior, marketing future-cast, and tourism marketing. He has published widely and is Editor-in-Chief of the *Journal of Futurecast in Marketing and Management* and Founding Editor-in-Chief of the *Journal of Modeling in Management*.

Jorge M. Oliveira-Castro is a professor at the Institute of Psychology, University of Brasília, responsible for teaching and research on conceptual issues in psychology, consumer behavior analysis, and behavioral economics and is also an Auditor at the Federal Audit Court in Brazil. He has an MSc in psychology and a PhD in experimental psychology. His main research interests are in the behavioral economics of choice, particularly when applied to consumer and judicial situations, and its conceptual underpinnings.

John G. Pallister was until recently a senior member of the Marketing and Strategy Section of Cardiff Business School, Cardiff University.

Rafael Barreiros Porto is Professor of Marketing and Competitive Strategy at the Business Administration Department, Universidade de Brasília, Brazil. He holds a PhD of Behavioral Sciences, a Master of Work and Social Psychology, a Bachelor of Advertising, and an MBA in Corporate Strategy. He has conducted research mainly on branding, strategy performance, and consumer behavior.

Andrew Rogers has some 20 years' experience working within consumer marketing analytics functions of FTSE100 and Fortune500 organizations and is currently studying for a PhD at Cardiff Business School in consumer behavior. He holds a BSc in Mathematics, an MBA, an MSc in Social Science Research Methods, and CStat through the Royal Statistical Society.

Marithza Sandoval-Escobar specializes in consumer psychology; she also holds a Master of Psychology in Experimental Analysis of Behavior and a PhD in Education with emphasis in environmental and urban pedagogy. She is currently director of the Master's Program in Consumer Psychology at Fundación Universitaria Konrad Lorenz, developing scientific research projects and consulting processes for public and private companies in the region.

Valdimar Sigurdsson is Associate Professor in Marketing and Consumer Psychology and Head of Marketing at the School of Business of Reykjavik University in Iceland. He also chairs the Professional Program in Digital Marketing at Reykjavik's Open University. His research interests include consumer behaviour analysis (consumer psychology), in-store experiments (retailing), and experimental analysis in digital marketing, and he has published widely.

Kevin J. Vella is currently in the final stage of writing a PhD in the application of reinforcement learning psychology to develop an evolutionary understanding of the competitive market behavior of firms through the principle of Selection by Consequences and within the framework of the Marketing Firm. Prior to this, he has had a twenty-year career in the marketing of technology products.

Ji (Karena) Yan is a lecturer in Marketing at Durham University Business School. She holds a PhD in Marketing (University of Cardiff). Her research interests fall into consumer behavior and economic psychology.

Preface

Consumer behavior analysis brings behavioral economics and behavioral psychology to the marketplace of human purchase and consumption activities. To date, it has been principally concerned with the behavior of consumers in affluent marketing-oriented economies, though the research it has generated has been international and there is no inherent reason why it should not apply to any economic system. The work of the Consumer Behavior Analysis Research Group at Cardiff Business School is methodologically based on the application of behavioral economics to the marketplace and, in particular, to the analysis of consumer and marketer behavior in natural settings.

Behavioral economics describes several subdisciplines which seek to unite economics and psychology. The term is applied, for instance, to Simon's tempering of neoclassicism with the cognitive limitations of real-world economic actors, to Kahneman and Tversky's demonstrations of the boundaries of economic rationality, and to Ainslie's picoeconomics of intertemporal conflict among the competing interests of hyperbolic discounters. Nor are these schools of behavioral economics discrete subdisciplines in themselves but approaches that overlap and impinge upon one another. As a consequence, behavioral economics is one of the most exciting and potentially fruitful spheres of intellectual activity currently available to those who strive to understand economic behavior.

One source of behavioral economic thought and practice derives from the confluence of operant psychology with microeconomics over the last forty years. Behavior is economic to the extent that it involves the allocation of a limited number of responses to produce an array of benefits; at the same time, this allocation incurs costs. This covers all that behavior analysts study as operant choice: it is not that the behavior itself is inherently economic but that certain tools can be brought to bear in its analysis. The benefits and costs relate ultimately to biological fitness and are seen most graphically in the acquisition of primary reinforcers in the course of which potentially fitness-enhancing alternatives are forgone. But secondary reinforcers also play a central role in the relationship of individual conduct to biological fitness via economic choice.

Operant choice is economic behavior: the allocation of limited responses among competing alternatives; hence the definitions of rewards found in biology and neuroeconomics which casts them as things "for which an organism will work." Both matching analysis and behavioral economics, which are at the heart of this research program, lead to the conclusion that all behavior is choice and can, therefore, be analyzed in economic terms. Consumer behavior analysis has a more restricted sphere of application: human economic and social choices which involve social exchange.

In examining this contribution in its potential to illuminate consumer behavior in situ, this volume ranges over broad economic psychology that derives from Herrnstein's discovery of matching, Baum's formalization of laws of matching, and the ensuing interaction of behavioral psychology and experimental economics pioneered by Hursh, Rachlin, Baum, and others. Its chief focus is on the critical evaluation of behavioral economics in this tradition, the findings and theories of which stem mainly from experimental analyses of the behavior of non-humans, to consumer choice in the natural settings of affluent, marketing-oriented economies.

The unifying framework for this *Routledge Companion* is the Behavioral Perspective Model (BPM), a critical elaboration of the three-term contingency of behavior analysis, as it embraces complex economic choice in the marketplace. Our work has involved translating the techniques underlying matching analysis to real-world economic situations, and the consequences of our findings for economic issues such as the substitutability, complementarity, and independence of commodities. We have also investigated the elasticities of demand for consumer goods using behavioral economic techniques adapted to consumer behavior analysis, and the role of essential value in understanding consumer choice in the marketplace. The results support the BPM as a means of investigating consumer behavior in the marketplace but we have not been concerned only with the behavior of consumers. Our analysis of the Marketing Firm (TMF) brings economic and psychological thought to bear on understanding the role of the modern marketing-oriented business organization in shaping and responding to consumer choice. Our research also involves issues relating to evolutionary psychology and temporal discounting, addiction, the neuroeconomics of consumer behavior, and the philosophical and theoretical aspects of explaining consumer choice.

This volume represents many of these themes and others which arise not only in consumer behavior analysis itself but which also throw light on this nascent discipline from viewpoints in the behavioral and social sciences such as psychoanalysis, neuroscience, ethnography, and information foraging. I believe that the result reflects a stimulating intellectual framework of conceptualization and analysis and hope that this collection proves interesting and useful for all who seek to understand human economic and social behavior.

Gordon Foxall
Cardiff
28 February 2015

Acknowledgements

I am delighted to have been asked to edit *The Routledge Companion to Consumer Behavior Analysis*. I am most grateful to Jacqueline Curthoys and Sinead Waldron from Routledge for commissioning the work and for the encouragement and help they have given me along the way. I must also express my thanks to the authors whose cooperation has made this book a joy to edit. Especially, I owe a great debt to my wife, Jean, for her encouragement, support, and practical help in bringing this volume to completion. The book is justly dedicated to her.

Chapter 15 is reproduced from *Analysis of Gambling Behavior* 6, 5–22, 2012, by kind permission of the publisher.

Chapter 22 is to appear in *Qualitative Research Methods in Consumer Psychology; Ethnography and Culture* (ed. P. Hackett, New York: Routledge, 2015) and is reproduced by kind permission of the publisher.

Part I
Introduction

Consumer behavior analysis comes of age

Gordon R. Foxall

Consumer behavior analysis

Consumer behavior analysis combines behavioral psychology, behavioral economics, and marketing science to increase understanding of the behavior of consumers. Its principal focus has until now been on consumer behavior in affluent, marketing-oriented economies but there is no inherent reason why it should not concern itself with the study of consumption in any context. It has also tended toward the analysis of human economic behavior in natural settings, though this is far from inimical to experimental analyses which are in fact essential to the evaluation of the approach. In this chapter, I should like to introduce the research program that stems from consumer behavior analysis, describe its central model, and discuss its evaluation through empirical research, and the applications and interpretations to which it has led.

A primary objective of the *Consumer Behavior Analysis Research Program* (Foxall, 2001, 2002) has been to ascertain the contribution that behavioral psychology, also known as behavior analysis, behaviorology, and radical behaviorism, can make to the study of consumer choice (Foxall, 1994, 1998). A second objective, equally important, has been to discover the "bounds of behaviorism" as a means of explicating consumer choice, the point, if any, at which a behaviorist explanation breaks down, and therefore the point at which we have to resort to intentional, including cognitive, explanation. The first endeavor in either case has been the development of a behaviorist model of consumer choice and its testing, to destruction if necessary, in the process of defining and determining the role of behaviorism in making consumer choice more intelligible. The second of these objectives, the development of an intentional model of consumer choice, has been the subject of other works (Foxall, 2004, 2007a, in preparation). It is the first stage in the research program, the generation and evaluation of the *Behavioral Perspective Model of consumer choice* (BPM; Foxall, 1990/2004), with which this volume is predominantly concerned.

The current chapter presents the behaviorist depiction of consumer choice, the BPM, that is the primary vehicle for the intellectual inquiry I have briefly described, and describes the scope of the research that has been concerned to test it and to establish the behaviorist explanation of consumer choice. In addition, the chapter introduces the chapters that follow, which provide state-of-the-art discussions of the most recent research. This research has two interconnected strands: behavioral-economic investigations of consumer choice, and interpretive analyses of complex consumer behavior that is not directly amenable to experimental or correlational research. While some of the chapters involve both facets of the research program, Parts II and III of the volume comprise contributions that, for the most part, deal respectively with these themes.

The Behavioral Perspective Model

Consumer behavior is influenced by both the economic and technical properties of goods on one hand and the social meaning of acquiring, owning, and using them on the other. People drive cars to get around *and* to be seen getting around, wear clothes for protection from the elements *and* to signal to everyone how well they are doing as earners and consumers, adorn themselves with jewelry *not only* to impress their fellows or fit in with social expectations *but also* to raise or confirm their own self-esteem. To the extent that consumption is influenced by consequences such as these, it is operant; to the extent that it reflects both the functional and the social, it is under the influence of a complex of utilitarian and informational reinforcers. Businesses meet these consumer wants by offering marketing mixes that stress product attributes of both kinds, advertising and distribution channels that complement and enhance them, and price levels that are consonant with both the technical-economic purposes and the social-psychological meanings that the resulting brands address. Both sources of reinforcement must be included in a behavior-analytic model of consumer choice. So must the punishing consequences associated with each, for every economic transaction meets with aversive outcomes as well as those that reward. These consequential causes of behavior are depicted on the right-hand side of the BPM (Figure 1.1).

The BPM is essentially an elaboration of the "three-term contingency" that is the basic explanatory device of operant behaviorism:

$$S^D \rightarrow R \rightarrow S^r$$

in which a discriminative stimulus, S^D, is an element of the environment in the presence of which a response, R, has been rewarded by the appearance of another environmental element, S^r, which because of its "strengthening" effect on the behavior is known as a reinforcer.

Behavior setting scope

The consumer behavior setting comprises the stimuli that set the occasion for these causal consequences should particular acts of purchase and consumption be enacted. The consumer behavior setting is composed of stimuli that signal the outcomes of behavior – the availability of particular brands, for instance, within a supermarket – and stimuli that motivate the behavior – say, a point-of-sale advertisement that emphasizes the unique taste or value-for-money that buying the item will generate. The stimuli that compose the consumer behavior setting are, first, *discriminative stimuli*, elements of the environment in the presence of which the individual discriminates behaviorally by performing only those behaviors that have been previously reinforced in similar circumstances; and, second, *motivating operations*, aspects of the environment that enhance the value of a reinforcer. For instance, while the wording of an advertisement for a washing powder that promises "Our brand produces whiter clothes!" may be a discriminative stimulus for buying this product, the accompanying picture of a child wearing pristine, clean clothes might enhance the efficacy of the reinforcer if this symbol has previously been associated with sound parenting: i.e., it acts as a motivating operation (Fagerstrøm et al., 2010).

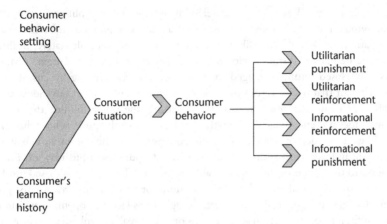

Figure 1.1 Summative Behavioral Perspective Model

Note that the essence of the model is the *consumer situation* → *consumer behavior* link. At the initiation of any particular instance of consumer behavior the only relevant behavioral consequences (reinforcement and punishment) are those that have occurred in the past when similar behaviors were enacted within similar situations. These are now embedded in the consumer's learning history and the consumer behavior setting (comprising discriminative stimuli and motivating operations), the interaction of which comprises the consumer situation

Motivating operations are, like discriminative stimuli, pre-behavioral stimuli under the control of which behavior may fall: specifically, a motivating operation enhances the relationship between a response and its reinforcing consequences (Michael, 1993). Motivating operations have been discussed in the literature of consumer behavior analysis by Fagerstrøm, (2010; see also Fagerstrøm et al., 2010; Fagerstrøm et al., 2011). Sigurdsson et al. (2013) integrate motivating operations with utilitarian and informational reinforcement in an examination of the appropriateness of the BPM to managerial decision-making in e-mail marketing. The addition of this source of stimulation expands the three-term to the four-term (and, indeed, the *n*-term) contingency (Sidman, 1994).

The *scope* of the consumer behavior setting is of prime importance in gauging its likely influence on consumer choice (Schwarz & Lacey, 1988). Relatively *open* settings permit a wider range of behaviors to be enacted – they offer more choices – than relatively *closed* settings in which just one or a few behaviors are possible. Consumer behavior settings can be described on a continuum from relatively open to relatively closed. This conceptualization is especially relevant to the study of consumer behavior, and particularly, retail research. Generally, though not inevitably, in the relatively closed setting, persons other than the consumer arrange the discriminative stimuli that compose the setting in a way that compels conformity to the desired behavior. The open setting, however, is marked by a relative absence of physical, social, and verbal pressures to conform to a pattern of activity that is determined by others (what ecological psychologists call a behavior program; see Schoggen, 1989); it is comparatively free of constraints on the consumer, who, thus, has an increased range of choices. He or she has some ability to determine personal rules for choosing among the products and brands on offer, which stores to visit, and so on. A typical open setting is represented by a departmental store in which the consumer can move from section to section, browsing here, considering there, making a purchase or leaving altogether to find another store, or even giving up on shopping and going home.

In contrast, extremely closed consumer behavior settings are exemplified by the dental surgery or the gymnasium where only one course of action is reinforced and removing oneself from the situation, while not impossible, is fraught with social and, ultimately, health-related costs. Less extreme but still distinctly closed for the consumer behavior context, a bank is usually a physically closed setting, arranged to encourage orderly queuing by customers and to discourage behavior that detracts from the efficient execution of transactions. Social and verbal elements also enter into the closed nature of the setting: the single-file line that leads to the teller window does not encourage conversation, at least not to the point where the business of the bank is likely to be delayed. Social and regulatory aspects of the consumer behavior setting are also apparent in less formal contexts such as having to purchase a birthday gift for a friend, which is closer to the center of the open-closed continuum. The setting is closed insofar as the consumer conforms to social rules that describe moral or material rewards for reciprocity or punishments for ignoring generosity in others, though it has facets of openness stemming from the capacity of friends to depart from social norms or even break the rules on occasion, not only without censure but with a strengthening of the relationship.

Consumer situation

Also on the left of the BPM shown in Figure 1.1 is the consumer's learning history for this and similar products, what he or she has done in the past, and the reinforcing and punishing outcomes this has had. The learning history primes the discriminative stimuli (S^D) and motivating operations (MO) that make up the consumer behavior setting and evokes the behavior that will generate or avoid the consequences on offer.

The term "contingencies of reinforcement" refers to the setting in which behavior occurs, the behavior itself, the rewarding and punishing consequences of the behavior, plus the relationships among them. These determine the *rate* at which the behavior is performed, the basic datum of behavior analysis (Skinner, 1950, 1963): for now it is enough to note that rewards or reinforcing consequences have the effect of increasing the rate at which it occurs while punishers reduce it.

It is the consumer situation that results from the interaction of learning history and consumer behavior setting that is the immediate precursor of consumer behavior. The consumer situation induces or inhibits particular consumer behaviors depending on whether the consumer behavior analysis is relatively open or relatively closed. In this non-intentional construal of the BPM, the consumer situation thus amounts to the scope of the setting, i.e., its degree of openness or closedness, weighted by the individual's consumption history, which directly impacts upon the probability that particular consumer behaviors will occur.

Patterns of reinforcement

The stimuli that comprise the consumer behavior setting and that enter into the consumer situation prompt the consumer to discriminate his or her behavior by purchasing or consuming certain products and services, marques, and brands rather than others. The behaviors performed are those that have been reinforced in the past, and the discriminative stimuli, motivating operations, and learning history that interact to form the consumer situation are associated with utilitarian or functional and informational or symbolic reinforcements that will result from current behaviors. These consequences of behavior, shown on the right-hand side of the model in Figure 1.1, may be positive or aversive, reinforcing or punishing in their effects on future consumer choice. Utilitarian reinforcers, which are mediated by the products themselves,

	Low utilitarian reinforcement	High utilitarian reinforcement
Low informational reinforcement	MAINTENANCE	HEDONISM
High informational reinforcement	ACCUMULATION	ACCOMPLISHMENT

Figure 1.2 Patterns of reinforcement and operant classes of consumer behavior

Source: Foxall, G. R. (2010). *Interpreting Consumer Choice: The Behavioral Perspective Model*. New York: Routledge

are associated with the technical and operational qualities of the item bought and consumed. Informational reinforcers are socially mediated, however, and consist in performance feedback on the consumer behavior in question or other behaviors instrumental in making it possible. Almost any car will provide the utilitarian benefits of "getting from A to B." But a Porsche usually delivers the performance feedback that comes from recognition of the owner's occupational status, social position, and other sources of honor and prestige. Like other socially constructed, symbolic outcomes of behavior, informational reinforcers are relative to the values of the community: in a social system conscious of CO_2 emission or fossil fuel consumption, a prestige car might not confer the positive social feedback just assumed.

Consumers acquire combinations of utilitarian and informational benefits in the course of buying and using products, represented as a *pattern* of low/high utilitarian reinforcement and low/high informational reinforcement. The idea of a pattern of reinforcement replaces that of a schedule of reinforcement, something applicable more to the precision of the laboratory than interpreting complex choices in the marketplace. Defined in terms of a pattern of reinforcement, consumer behavior falls into one of four operant classes: maintenance, accumulation, hedonism, and accomplishment (Figure 1.2).

Patterns of consumer behavior

The BPM contingency matrix (Figure 1.3) comprises eight distinct categories of contingencies, the outcome of combining consumer behavior setting scope and reinforcement patterns (Foxall, 2010). The following chapters reveal that the generic BPM shown in Figure 1.3 can be construed in both extensional and intentional forms and that these offer different levels of explanation of consumer behavior. Thus far, empirical work has emphasized the extensional construal of the model; this chapter argues for an intentional construal based on research into the role of emotionality in consumer choice.

Behavioral economics meets marketing science

Summary of research

A large volume of empirical research which has had the dual purposes of testing the predictive capacity of the BPM and of elucidating the nature of consumer choice by viewing it through the lens of behavior analysis has been inspired by the model.[1]

This work has increasingly incorporated techniques pioneered in behavior analysis and, especially, behavioral economics (Hursh, 1984; Hursh & Roma, 2015; see also Foxall, 2015a) to investigate behavior in the non-intentional terms that are the hallmark of operant psychology

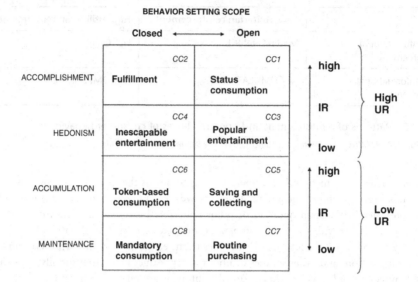

Figure 1.3 The BPM contingency matrix

CC = contingency category, each of which locates a class of consumer situations defined functionally in terms of a unique combination of *pattern of reinforcement* and *consumer behavior setting scope*

Source: Foxall, G. R. (2010). *Interpreting Consumer Choice: The Behavioral Perspective Model.* New York: Routledge. Reproduced by permission

and experimental economics. Defining economic choice as the allocation of behavior within a framework of costs and benefits (Staddon, 1980), this perspective adopted matching and maximization techniques to the study of consumers' brand and product choices (Fagerstrøm et al., 2011; Foxall, 1999a; Foxall & James, 2002, 2003; Foxall & Schrezenmaier, 2003; Wells & Foxall, 2013; see also Curry et al., 2010).

Experimental research based on testing predictions and applications suggested by the BPM has involved both food retailing and offline and online marketing (Sigurdsson et al., 2011; Sigurdsson et al., 2013; Sigurdsson et al., 2015; see also Foxall & Sigurdsson, 2013). An important facet of this research has been the use of field experiments, typically in retail organizations, which allow the full force of the marketing mix to be investigated in its effect on consumer behavior. Sigurdsson et al. (2013), for instance, tested the BPM in the context of Norwegian retailing with an econometric analysis of the effects of the pattern of reinforcement specified in the model. The predictability of each individual predictor (utilitarian, informational, and pricing) was tested and compared with multiple regression models, based on all three predictors, and to previous findings. This was done based on the analysis of buying behavior of brands for ten different product categories. The results revealed that informational level was the best individual predictor for consumer buying behavior, but the combination of the three behavioral consequential predictors together (relying on the BPM) tended to give the best prediction.

Matching and maximization. This translational research program has demonstrated that the matching phenomena explored by Herrnstein (1961, 1970, 1997) provide insights into the psychological measures of standard microeconomic variables such as product and brand substitutability, complementarity, and independence (Foxall et al., 2010; Romero et al., 2006) which also serve to define product categories, sub-categories, and brands (Foxall et al., 2010). In a significant development, Oliveira-Castro et al. (2010) integrated matching with the BPM variables of utilitarian and informational reinforcement as well as price.

Price elasticity of demand. Further behavioral economics research has involved the operational measurement of utilitarian and informational reinforcement and the estimation of price elasticity of demand coefficients for brands that feature varying combinations of these elements of reward (Foxall et al., 2004; Foxall et al., 2007; Foxall et al., 2010; Oliveira-Castro et al., 2006; Oliveira-Castro et al., 2008; Oliveira-Castro et al., 2008). This work underpins the BPM approach by showing that consumer demand is a function not only of price but also of the pattern of reinforcement delivered by goods. Of particular interest is the empirical research which demonstrates that changes in consumer behavior, measured as elasticity of demand for fast-moving nondurables, is a function of the pattern of utilitarian and informational reinforcement (Foxall et al., 2004; Foxall et al., 2013; Oliveira-Castro et al., 2011; Yan et al., 2012a, b).

Consumers' utility functions. Consumers' utility functions demonstrate that consumers maximize measurable combinations of these goods: Oliveira-Castro et al. (2015) show that consumers maximize selected combinations of utilitarian reinforcement and informational reinforcement in accordance with the following Cobb-Douglas utility function:

$$U\,(x_1, x_2) = x_1^a \, , \, x_2^b \tag{1}$$

where U is the total amount of utility obtained by consumption of x^1 and x^2, x_1 is the quantity of utilitarian reinforcement consumed, x_2 is the quantity of informational reinforcement consumed, and a and b are empirically determined parameters such that a + b = 1. The implication is that consumers maximize the utility that derives from particular combinations of utilitarian and informational reinforcement subject to the constraint imposed by their budget for the goods in question.

The chapters that follow are divided into two sections, *Behavioral economics meets marketing science* and *Behavioral interpretation of consumer choice*. Both of these are concerned with the first of the two issues mentioned in my opening to this chapter: the determination of the contribution of behavior analysis to understanding in consumer research.

Chapters in Part II: Behavioral economics meets marketing science

The first chapters that form Part II are concerned principally with experimental analyses of consumer choice and they gradually elide with chapters that employ time-series analyses of consumer behavior based on panel data.

Chapter 2: Experimental analysis of consumer choice (Fagerstrøm and Sigurdsson)

This chapter argues that experimental analysis is the most fundamental element in consumer behavior analysis because it links other research with the explanatory basis of natural science. Without an experimental research program to generate and test the ideas on which behavioral explanations and interpretations are founded, consumer behavior analysis might indeed descend into speculation. It is important, however, in the quest to understand consumer behavior in natural settings that consumer behavior analysts work within a progression of experimental styles, from the laboratory to the field. This chapter expands on the nature of experimentation at all these levels, from those of the closed setting of the lab to those that feature more open settings provided by in-store contexts and consumer brand choice.

Chapter 3: Behavior analysis of in-store consumer behavior (Sigurdsson, Larsen, and Fagerstrøm)

The authors explore in greater depth the methodologies involved in in-store consumer behavior analysis. The authors show how in-store experimental consumer behavior analysis differs from conventional marketing research, the importance of establishing and maintaining rapport with retailers, and the relevance of particular experimental methods to research questions and available retail contexts.

Chapter 4: Behavior analysis of online consumer behavior (Sigurdsson, Larsen, and Menon)

This chapter addresses the paucity of studies of online consumer behavior from a behavioral point of view which is anomalous given the vast opportunities this area of research offers for experimental work in the operant tradition. The chapter discusses the methods in use for research into online consumer behavior, comparing and contrasting it with more mainstream behavior analytical research. Online studies of consumer behavior form an intermediate position between traditional laboratory investigations and field studies: the settings are relatively closed, an experimental research design is readily achieved, and yet the results provide a rigorous examination of consumer behavior as the outcome of the entire marketing mix which is normally available only in more open retail settings.

Chapter 5: Equivalence classes and preferences in consumer choice (Arntzen, Fagerstrøm, and Foxall)

This chapter extends research on the phenomenon of stimulus equivalence and transfer of function to the realm of consumer and marketing research. Individuals who are trained to respond with stimulus B when stimulus A is presented, and then with stimulus C when A is presented, show a tendency to respond with C when presented with B. This emergent relationship has never been trained: the individual's selection of C has never been reinforced in the presence of B. Research on equivalence class formation and transfer of function has not yet been conducted within the context of consumer behavior and marketing communication. This chapter indicates, on the basis of experimental analysis, that this is a promising line of investigation for consumer behavior analysts and that it has important implications for marketing research, brand extension, and new product development.

Chapter 6: Experimental analyses of choice and matching (Sigurdsson and Foxall)

The possibility of applying microeconomic analysis in the operant-psychological study of behavior arises from the fact that both disciplines involve the allocation of scarce resources to competing ends (Foxall & Sigurdsson, 2013). The matching paradigm, inaugurated by Herrnstein (1997), is based on the finding that when faced with alternative behaviors that have different payoffs, both nonhuman and human animals allocate their available responses in the same proportion that marks the reinforcements received from each choice. This behavioral outcome, known as matching, has important parallels with the ways in which consumers allocate their brand purchases over a series of shopping trips. This chapter traces the evolution of matching research from animals behaving in the closed confines of the operant chamber to consumer choice in the open settings of the modern marketplace. It also marks the range of methodologies available and indeed necessary for such research, from experimental studies to correlational studies based on panel data, a theme that is characteristic of several of the ensuing chapters in Part II.

Chapter 7: Consumer store choice (Bui Huynh and Foxall)

This chapter builds on the large volume of research into matching and maximizing in the purchasing of nondurables by extending the work into the field of retail choice. It makes use of the concept of the *scope of the consumer behavior setting* by comparing consumption patterns for large supermarkets (representing *open* settings on the basis of their having a wide range of products and brands) with those for smaller convenience stores (representing relatively *closed* settings because of their restricted ranges). The findings are consonant with earlier research on product and brand matching, showing that consumers' store patronage exhibits amount matching, upward sloping relative demand curves, and a tendency toward maximization.

Chapter 8: Dimensions of demand elasticity (Oliveira-Castro and Foxall)

A major impetus for the matching research we have pursued has been the identification of the effects of the market's mix (variously represented by differences in utilitarian and informational reinforcement, and in price) on the quantities of products and brands purchased by consumers. Research on aggregate patterns of consumer brand choice had previously assumed that the price differentials exhibited by competing brands would have little effect, but the matching research showed this emphatically not to be the case. This chapter develops this theme by examining research on the price elasticity of demand for consumer goods. It summarizes the results of the research on price elasticity inspired by the BPM: that consumers buy larger quantities when paying prices that are lower, both within and across brands; that consumers who buy larger quantities tend to pay lower prices, both within and across brands; that purchase quantities vary with the magnitude of informational and utilitarian benefits provided by the brands; and that intra-brand price variations, especially those associated with consumers switching across package sizes, account for the largest portion of changes in quantity bought across shopping occasions. The chapter also describes the application of a behavior-economic approach to the conceptualization of demand elasticity in terms of essential value to consumer behavior for nondurables.

Chapter 9: Essential value in the BPM (Yan and Foxall)

This chapter develops further the idea of essential value in the context of the BPM by showing how the patterns of contingencies presented by the model impact the behavior of consumers relative to changes in price. Utilitarian and informational reinforcement, and the open-closed scope of the consumer behavior setting, all influence consumption when price changes. The studies on which this chapter is based have extended research on essential value to human consumers of nondurables in natural settings in the face of competing brands that differ in terms of the pattern of reinforcement they offer. The inclusion of informational reinforcement as well as utilitarian benefits introduces a social dimension to the analysis of essential value, while the comparison of open and closed consumer behavior settings (represented by supermarkets and convenience stores, respectively) demonstrates the centrality of behavior setting scope to any study of consumer behavior. The results are highly confirmatory of the BPM variables, showing their relevance to the study of human consumer behavior in natural settings.

Chapter 10: Triple jeopardy in a behavioral perspective (Rogers, Morgan, and Foxall)

The phenomenon of double jeopardy (DJ) in the marketing context reflects the fact that small brands not only attract fewer consumers than larger ones but that those scarcer customers buy less of the brand. This finding has implications for the notion of brand equity, as a measure of brand performance, of which it is potentially undermining. This chapter reveals that the utilitarian and informational reinforcement provided by brands enters significantly into their equity, over and above the effects of price elasticity of demand and DJ. A conclusion, which helps reconcile the concepts of DJ and brand equity, is that the BPM-defined pattern of reinforcement is the basis of a triple jeopardy effect; brands with larger market shares prosper by providing increased utilitarian and informational benefit compared with brands with smaller market shares (over and above the effects of price or DJ). The reconciliation is suggested by the view that this triple jeopardy might constitute a source of brand equity.

Chapter 11: Consumer purchase and brand performance (Porto and Oliveira-Castro)

This chapter draws attention to the difficulties of determining how firms' market shares are established. Even though consumers' past behavior and the firm's use of the marketing mix explain sales to a large degree, there remains the task of understanding market shares in a competitive marketplace. The authors describe two experiments designed to elucidate the role played by these behavioral antecedents, the interactive effect of which represents the consumer situation, the interaction of learning history and current setting stimuli. The initial experiment, which had the advantage of taking place in a natural environment, showed the importance of the magnitude of the pattern of reinforcement in influencing sales. In the second experiment, the proposition was tested that this consumer situation would forecast day-to-day sales. That it did so enables the authors to argue that the mechanisms that comprise the consumer situation are crucial to the definition of brand market structure.

Chapter 12: What do consumers maximize? (Oliveira-Castro, Cavalcanti, and Foxall)

An intriguing possibility is that what consumers maximize is a combination of utilitarian and informational reinforcement. This likelihood is inherent in the original formulation of the BPM, and is supported by research into consumer behavior as matching and maximization, by the research on price elasticity of demand and other behavioral economics work reviewed in this volume, and from the discussions of market structure and brand equity in the preceding two chapters. Yet the evidence from this research, while indicative, does not clinch the matter. The discussion of utility functions in this chapter takes us an important stage further. A utility function embodies the satisfaction gained via consumption as a function of the quantities of the goods consumed. This chapter examines the proposition that what consumers maximize is the quantities of utilitarian and informational reinforcement that they can consume within the limitations of their budgets. The results demonstrate that consumers do maximize utilitarian and informational satisfactions, that each product category exhibits an optimum benefit bundle that is peculiar to itself, and that individual differences in utility are consistent over time, which suggests that each pattern of consumer satisfaction derives from a specific indifference curve.

Chapter 13: The BPM in the Latin-American context (Sandoval-Escobar and Medina)

Chapter 13 is an account of research testing the BPM which was undertaken in Latin America, notably Colombia. Three areas of study are featured. First are analyses of consumer panel data concerned with inter- and intra-consumer consumption patterns, revealing relations between consumers' matching behavior and the levels of utilitarian and informational reinforcement provided by brands. Second are two panel-data analyses for various product categories, and with a specific focus on "green" or "eco purchase" consumption, and the variables that influence this choice. Finally, the authors undertake a review of the conceptual basis of the BPM. The empirical studies are particularly welcome for their extension of the theme of environmental conservation, which has long been a feature of the Consumer Behavior Analysis Research Program (see, most recently, Foxall, 2015b) to a new context.

Behavioral interpretation of consumer choice

Radical behaviorists have for many years proposed that behavior that lies beyond the confines of an experimental analysis can be the subject of an interpretive analysis in which the principles of behavior established in the laboratory are employed to disambiguate observed environment-behavior relationships (Skinner, 1969). The obvious problem with such an approach is that the contingencies that control the behavior cannot be isolated with the precision that is possible in the experimental space which provides the investigator with considerable capacities to control dependent and independent variables. As Skinner (1957) noted in his interpretive analysis of verbal behavior, one can generate a "plausible" account of complex behavior of this kind, but as an interpretation rather than an explanation such an account would be "merely useful, not true or false" (Skinner, 1988, p. 364). Interpretations of this kind mark an advance on mere specula-tion conducted in the absence of an underlying experimental analysis. Even though knowledge cannot be gained with the aid of definite means of identifying uncontentiously the stimuli under whose control the behavior in question falls, nor even the behavior itself defined as rigorously as the operant chamber allows, the principles derived from the experimental analysis can be directed toward the purpose of plausibility (Foxall, 1996, pp. 339–345; Lee, 1988).

Unfortunately, neither Skinner nor any other practitioner of behavioral interpretation has specified just what such plausibility consists in. Skinner's own interpretation of verbal behavior has been criticized for its substitution of "vague, analogic guesses" for scientific knowledge (Chomsky, 1959), and for ignoring the empirical knowledge on language generated by other scholars (Staats, 1996). The interpretive account of human verbal behavior provided by Skinner (1957) was therefore largely an extrapolation based on the behavior principles acquired from the animal laboratory, the basic notion of contingency-shaped behavior being a function of discrim-inative and reinforcing stimuli employed in the control of the limited food-producing behavior of hungry rats and pigeons. I am not here making the widespread criticism of radical behavior-ism that it seeks to explain human behavior by experiment results obtained from nonhuman animals, though that view is not without force. Rather, I would point out that very few years after the publication in 1957 of *Verbal Behavior*, on which work had begun three decades earlier, Skinner announced that behavior was not only subject to direct contact with the contingen-cies of reinforcement: it might also be the outcome of rules (Skinner, 1966). The admission of rule-governed behavior to the canons of scientific analysis available to behavior analysts reveals the vast limitations of a behavioral interpretation that fails to comprehend the scope of its subject matter. Some greater effort to understand the range of phenomena one is attempting to deal with must surely precede its behavior-analytic interpretation.

The interpretations of complex human behavior provided by Skinner in the last section of his *Science and Human Behavior* (1953) also reveal a somewhat imperialistic approach that is not sufficiently in touch with the details of the behavior they seek to deal with or with the disciplines that got there first. They tend to be vague and lacking in conviction, hardly acknowledging that other intellectual communities had made progress in studying economic behavior, political behavior, religious behavior, and many more aspects of human activity, contributions to these spheres that must be counted as vast by comparison with those of behavior analysts.

The problem of behavioral interpretation has been at the heart of the Consumer Behavior Analysis Research Program since its inception and the BPM was envisioned initially as primarily an interpretive tool (Foxall, 1990/2004, 1996). The initial phase of the research program was involved with the generation of behaviorist interpretations of such aspects of consumer behavior as attitude-behavior relationships (Foxall, 1983), the adoption and diffusion of innovations (Foxall, 1986), environmental conservation (Foxall, 1984), purchase and consumption (Foxall, 1990/2004), saving and domestic asset management (Foxall, 1994), consumers' emotional reactions to consumer environments (Foxall, 1997), and marketing management (Foxall, 1999b). All of these continue to be foci of interpretive research. However, just as important as the execution of a program of interpretive research aimed at elucidating complex consumer behavior is the accompanying refinement of the nature of behavioral interpretation itself. Three volumes have been devoted to the nature of behaviorist interpretation: *Consumers in Context: The BPM Research Program* (Foxall, 1996) describes the origins of the research program and the early approaches to interpretation; *Context and Cognition: Interpreting Complex Behavior* (Foxall, 2004) deals with general issues arising from the need to interpret in behavior analysis; and *Interpreting Consumer Choice* (Foxall, 2010) discusses the way in which the nature of behaviorist interpretation is relevant to consumer behavior analysis.

What seems essential to the behavioral interpretation of complex behavior is the generation of models of the focal human activity in terms that span the fundamentals of behavior analysis (such as the three-term contingency) and the disciplines primarily concerned with the study of that activity. In the case of the behavior-analytic interpretation of consumer behavior this would entail a model that combined the conceptual and methodological purviews of behavior analysis on the one hand and economics and marketing on the other. The aim of this integration is to increase investigators' awareness of any elaboration required for an operant interpretation that is not apparent from consideration of the three-term contingency itself. The development in due course of the BPM made clear that human economic behavior is a function of both utilitarian and informational reinforcement, for instance; that emphasis must be placed on the interaction of the consumer's learning history and the current consumer behavior setting he/she is facing to form the consumer situation; and the role of the consumer behavior setting itself as the repository of a field of discriminative stimuli and motivating operations rather than the simpler configuration of antecedent stimuli that are manipulable within the operant laboratory. The *scope* of the consumer behavior setting emerges also as a determinant of consumer behavior, as do the eight categories of contingency that are uniquely associated with particular patterns of consumer behavior. The BPM appears to be the sort of model of the middle range required to make behavioral interpretation an activity that is grounded in both an underlying methodology and explanation, and a level of understanding of consumer behavior that is in touch with its discernable characteristics.

Chapters in Part III: Behavioral interpretation of consumer choice

The chapters that form Part III are concerned with the critical exploration of these theoretical and methodological extensions of behavior analysis in the field of interpretive consumer choice.

Chapter 14: Gambling behavior (Dixon and Belisle)

Dixon and Belisle provide a general context for the study of gambling in the context of behavior analysis, drawing on a large volume of experimental and survey evidence on disordered gambling. Their review is of interest for its coverage not only of gamblers' public behaviors like buying a scratch ticket or pressing a spin button, but also of their private events such as neurochemical changes and covert verbal behavior. It also brings the analysis of gambling into contact with the understanding of the contextual nature of gambling made available by Relational Frame Theory (RFT; Hayes et al., 2001). RFT builds on the phenomenon of stimulus equivalence (Chapter 5), and offers a unique approach to the analysis of disordered gambling behavior, decision-making, and choice, which has far-reaching implications for consumer behavior analysis in general.

Chapter 15: When loss rewards (Foxall and Sigurdsson)

A particular aspect of gambling is the subject of this chapter, namely the tendency of a "near-miss" in slot machine gambling (scoring, say, two matching symbols when three are required for a win) to motivate rather than suppress further play. This contradicts orthodox reinforcement theory where failure punishes behavior. This chapter comprises a critical review which examines neurophysiological correlates (and perhaps causes) of this effect, revealing that near-misses recruit similar reward-oriented brain regions to those implicated in wins. Two additional research traditions complicate this picture. So-called cognitive distortions that may also motivate play following the experience of a near-miss are also reviewed, as is the possibility that contextual factors, inherent in the programming of the machines and the physical arrangement of gambling milieux, modify responses to near-miss outcomes. A recurring theme in all research traditions is the role of a possible source of reinforcement separate from the effect of monetary wins and a potential link between this secondary reinforcement and arousal in players. The authors argue that informational reinforcement can account well for the near-miss effect as a result of the sounds and sights generated by slot machines in the wake of gambling outcomes that apparently come close to genuine successes.

Chapter 16: A functional analysis of corruption from a behavioral-economic perspective (Luque Carreiro and Oliveira-Castro)

Luque Carreiro and Oliveira-Castro argue that the capacity of the BPM to explicate human behavior transcends its original application to consumer behavior. Their chosen vehicle to illustrate this is the interrelationship of officials and bribers in the course of corrupt behavior. They discuss models of crime and corruption developed by important economic theorists, and then suggest a model of corruption on the basis of typical cases of these phenomena. They go on to describe corruption in terms of the BPM approach, showing the multiple consequences of corrupt behavior. Hence, contingencies are analyzed in terms of their effects on operant classes of behavior, including the behavior setting and learning history as antecedents, and the utilitarian and informational consequences of the crime, in a model that permits the systemic analysis of corruption.

Chapter 17: From consumer response to corporate response (Vella)

It is comparatively rare in the marketing literature for explanations of consumer behavior to be conducted in similar terms to explanations of marketing management, yet there ought to be an intellectual context in which their interdependence is more readily understood. The BPM and the model of the *marketing firm* that follows from it (Foxall, 1999b) provide this continuity of explanation. Previous empirical research (Vella & Foxall, 2011) establishes that the explanatory variables proposed by the Marketing Firm Model can be operationalized for the interpretation of corporate behavior. The idea of bilateral contingency between the firm and its customers is particularly valuable in analyzing corporate behavior on the basis of its effects on customer choice (Foxall, 2014, 2015b). This chapter suggests how further refinement of the variables might proceed in light of the requirements of further research on the firm.

If the process of behavioral interpretation is to remain a reflexive activity, maintaining a spirit of self-awareness and self-criticism to avoid the stagnation that can accrue when alternative perspectives are not taken into consideration, it is important that it be viewed in an informed but critical manner by practitioners of a variety of approaches, both within and beyond consumer behavior analysis. The remaining chapters were commissioned with this in mind.

Chapter 18: Motivating operations and consumer choice (Fagerstrøm and Arntzen)

Critics of behavior analysis frequently seem to assume that it is a system that was fixed in the mid-twentieth century, since when it has failed to show any sign of innovativeness. The huge contributions made by the analysis of verbal behavior in the last twenty years give the lie to this, as does the contribution of operant behavioral economics. Some developments may be smaller but they too are significant. The idea of motivating operations (Michael, 1993) drew attention to the capacity of some stimuli to alter the reinforcing effect of another stimulus event, and/or to influence the emission of the behavior related to that event. As such, motivating operations form a significant element of the consumer situation. The concept has numerous ramifications for the analysis of consumer choice and marketing activity, which this chapter discusses on the basis of empirical evidence.

Chapter 19: Consumers as inforagers (Kim and Hantula)

This chapter is based on the observation that consumers do not acquire goods alone: they search for and acquire information, too. That is, consumers can be regarded as "inforagers." As such, their relationships with their environments may be represented in Darwinian terms as "ecologically rational." Such a perspective can compensate for the limitations of consumer information-processing models based on rational choice assumptions. The implication is that "information is a communication between minds and immediate environments from an organismic perspective." Consumer information search can be depicted as foraging, and the process can then be understood in terms of biology and evolution.

Chapter 20: Decision-"making" or how decisions emerge in a cyclic automatic process, parsimoniously modulated by reason (Marques dos Santos and Moutinho)

The biological theme is continued in this chapter whose authors state, refreshingly, that "We just do not believe in Psychology apart from Biology." They contrast the "given view" which assumes decision-making to be a straightforward procedure, based on the simplifying notion that decision-makers take informational outputs and transform them into behavioral outputs. But this is not the sole possibility. Marques dos Santos and Moutinho argue that the idea of decision-making is biased in its assumption that reasoning is inevitably involved. The model they introduce in place of the familiar computer metaphor eschews systematic reasoning but yields nevertheless decisions and actions that can be described as purposeful. This model is a hybrid of the S–R (stimulus–response) and the S–O–R (stimulus–organism–response) theories, which they discuss in the light of empirical research findings, notably in neuroscience, before producing a further theory through the incorporation of the BPM, with which they argue their original hybrid has overlapping elements.

Chapter 21: Consumer behavior analysis (Desmond)

In a wide-ranging chapter, John Desmond looks at consumer behavior analysis from the viewpoint of psychoanalysis, a psychological perspective which he has successfully exploited in furthering the understanding of consumer behavior. Arguing that the behaviorist and psychoanalytical perspectives on consumer behavior can act as foils not only to one another but also to cognitive psychology, he reminds us that these disciplines offer linkages to the evolutionary- and neuro-sciences. The foils they offer to each other are basic components of the clash of paradigms that some philosophers see as essential to scientific progress: behaviorism repudiates mentalism but psychoanalysis takes psychic causation as foundational; behaviorism explains behavior in terms of situational determinants; while, for the psychoanalyst, subjective experience is all-important. This chapter is an erudite and humorous contribution to the debate concerning the relative contributions that the psychologies can make to understanding the balance between biological, contextual, and psychic influences on behavior.

The remaining chapters, even where they have quantitative aspects, are primarily concerned with qualitative interpretation of consumer behavior.

Chapter 22: Ethnographical interpretation of consumer behavior (Hackett)

Hackett proposes using the BPM alongside consumer ethnography, and develops a mapping sentence (MS) framework, based on the statistical technique of facet analysis, for combining them. The proposed MS offers one possible way of conducting, analyzing, and bringing together research on consumer choice that uses the insights provided by the BPM framework for understanding consumer behavior. The MS offers a unique conjoint understanding of how elements of the BPM are related to aspects of ethnographic consumer research. The chapter defines and explains examples of consumer ethnography to demonstrate that ethnography used together with the BPM produces information that allows both behavioral understanding and prediction.

The next two chapters are concerned with the exploration of an approach to consumer behavior analysis that involves intentional interpretation along lines suggested by Foxall (2004, 2007a). Although this has not been a major theme of this volume, the development, where it is required for purposes of explanation, of an intentional interpretation of consumer choice is a major theme of consumer behavior analysis (Foxall, 2013). These chapters are included to elaborate the contribution of intentional behaviorism (Foxall, 2007b, 2007c, 2008) to consumer research.

Chapter 23: Collective intentionality and symbolic reinforcement (Laparojkit and Foxall)

The advent of internet-based consumer clubs provides a unique environment in which to examine the role of symbolic stimuli (both antecedent and consequential) in the analysis of consumer choice. Comparatively little impetus for such research derives from the behavioral aspects of car consumer clubs, the reinforcers they offer, and the effects of the consumer situations they provide on consumer behavior. The study we describe aimed to establish whether, and if so how, the rewards received from brand community participation account for members' sustaining participation in virtual brand communities. This chapter shows how the rewards of participation in car consumer communities can be identified and how they affect members' behavior. The empirical investigation we describe is based on the intentional model of consumer choice (Foxall, 2013) and appeals to Searle's (2010) conception of *collective intentionality* as a principal means of interpreting club membership over time.

Chapter 24: Consumer confusion (Anninou, Pallister, and Foxall)

The complexity of modern shopping environments means that consumers are more frequently than ever afflicted by anomy and confusion. The research described in this chapter is concerned with understanding consumer confusion in terms of the subjective experience of buyers: their desires and beliefs as well as their individual consciousness of how it feels to be shopping in a puzzling context. Anomy is a lack of rules; hence, the analysis of choice in terms of rule-governed behavior is inadequate. The extensional model of consumer choice (now known as BPM-E) is useful but limited in this regard, as is orthodox behavior analysis in general: the language of explanation must be enlarged to include intentional terms. The resulting intentional model of consumer choice (BPM-I) is then available to make sense of the customer's experience.

The concluding chapter seeks to integrate the qualitative approaches to the interpretation of consumer choice that have characterized some of the preceding chapters with the behaviorist agenda that characterizes the BPM. Dennett's heterophenomenology suggests a methodology for the incorporation of consciousness into a framework of analysis that explains behavior by means of its situation (including the current stimulus field and the consumer's history) and its potential pattern of reinforcement.

Chapter 25: Consumer heterophenomenology (Foxall)

This chapter considers a novel route to qualitative research into consumer behavior that derives from a suggestion made by Dennett (1991) for obtaining verbal reports that relate to subjective consciousness, capturing first-personal experience (which is not scientifically admissible) into third-personal texts that can be used in scientific investigations. A serious problem in the study of consciousness is that the third-personal stance taken by science cannot easily accommodate the first-personal phenomena in which the subjective, possibly ineffable, experience of personal consciousness consists. Dennett proposes *heterophenomenology* as a means of approaching first-personal experience through transcribing verbal reports of thoughts and feelings into texts which can be analyzed by investigators. The chapter proposes that this methodology might be employed in Consumer Behavior Analysis, and suggests that the Behavioral Perspective Model of consumer choice might aid the interpretation of heterophenomenological texts.

Note

1 Research is very actively underway in each of the areas mentioned and others. Several special issues of academic journals in behavior analysis, economic psychology, retailing and marketing management, and managerial economics have been devoted to this research: see the *Journal of Economic Psychology* (volume 24, numbers 5 and 6, 2003), the *Journal of Organizational Behavior Management* (volume 31, numbers 2 and

3, 2010), the *Service Industries Journal* (volume 31, number 11, 2011), and *Managerial and Decision Economics* (2015, in press).

References

Chomsky, A. N. (1959). A review of Skinner's *Verbal Behavior, Language*, 35, 26–58.

Curry, B., Foxall, G. R. and Sigurdsson, V. (2010). On the tautology of the matching law in consumer behavior analysis, *Behavioural Processes*, 84, 390–399.

Dennett, D. C. (1991). *Consciousness Explained*. Boston, MA: Little Brown.

Fagerstrøm, A. (2010). The motivating effect of antecedent stimuli on the web shop: a conjoint analysis of the impact of antecedent stimuli at the point of online purchase, *Journal of Organizational Behavior Management*, 30, 199–220.

Fagerstrøm, A., Foxall, G. R. and Arntzen, E. (2010). Implications of motivating operations for the functional analysis of consumer behavior, *Journal of Organizational Behavior Management*, 30(2), 110–126.

Fagerstrøm, A., Arntzen, E. and Foxall, G. R. (2011). A study of preferences on a simulated online shopping experiment, *Service Industries Journal*, 31, 2609–2622.

Foxall, G. R. (1983). *Consumer Choice*. London: Macmillan; New York: St. Martin's Press.

Foxall, G. R. (1984). Environment-impacting consumer behaviour: a framework for social marketing and demarketing. In Baker, M. J. (Ed.) *Perspectives on Marketing Management, Volume 4* (pp. 27–53). Chichester: Wiley.

Foxall, G. R. (1986). The role of radical behaviourism in the explanation of consumer choice, *Advances in Consumer Research*, 13, 195–201.

Foxall, G. R. (1990/2004). *Consumer Psychology in Behavioral Perspective*. London and New York: Routledge. (Reprinted 2004 by Beard Books, Frederick, MD.)

Foxall, G. R. (1996). *Consumers in Context: The BPM Research Programme*. London and New York: Routledge.

Foxall, G. R. (1997). Affective responses to consumer situations, *International Review of Retail, Distribution and Consumer Research*, 7, 191–225.

Foxall, G. R. (1998). Radical behaviorist interpretation: generating and evaluating an account of consumer behavior, *The Behavior Analyst*, 21, 321–354.

Foxall, G. R. (1999a). The substitutability of brands, *Managerial and Decision Economics*, 20, 241–257.

Foxall, G. R. (1999b). The marketing firm, *Journal of Economic Psychology*, 20, 207–234.

Foxall, G. R. (2001). Foundations of consumer behaviour analysis, *Marketing Theory*, 1, 165–199.

Foxall, G. R. (Ed.) (2002). *Consumer Behaviour Analysis: Critical Perspectives in Business and Management*. London and New York: Routledge.

Foxall, G. R. (2004). *Context and Cognition: The Interpretation of Behavior*. Reno, NV: Context Press.

Foxall, G. R. (2005). *Understanding Consumer Choice*. London and New York: Palgrave Macmillan.

Foxall, G. R. (2007a). *Explaining Consumer Choice*. London and New York: Palgrave Macmillan.

Foxall, G. R. (2007b). Explaining consumer choice: coming to terms with intentionality, *Behavioural Processes*, 75, 129–145.

Foxall, G. R. (2007c). Intentional behaviorism, *Behavior and Philosophy*, 35, 1–56.

Foxall, G. R. (2008). Intentional behaviorism revisited, *Behavior and Philosophy*, 37, 113–156.

Foxall, G. R. (2010). *Interpreting Consumer Choice: The Behavioral Perspective Model*. New York: Routledge.

Foxall, G. R. (2013). Intentionality, symbol, and situation in the interpretation of consumer choice, *Marketing Theory*, 13, 105–127.

Foxall, G. R. (2014). The marketing firm and consumer choice: implications of bilateral contingency for levels of analysis in organizational neuroscience, *Frontiers in Human Neuroscience*, 8, 472, 1–14. doi: 10.3389/fnhum.2014.00472.

Foxall, G. R. (2015a). Operant behavioral economics, *Managerial and Decision Economics*, in press.

Foxall, G. R. (2015b). Consumer behavior analysis and the marketing firm: bilateral contingency in the context of environmental concern, *Journal of Organizational Behavior Management*, in press.

Foxall, G. R. and James, V. K. (2002). Behavior analysis of consumer brand choice: a preliminary analysis, *European Journal of Behavior Analysis*, 2, 209–220.

Foxall, G. R. and James, V. K. (2003). The behavioral ecology of brand choice: how and what do consumers maximize? *Psychology and Marketing*, 20, 811–836.

Foxall, G. R. and Schrezenmaier, T. C. (2003). The behavioural economics of consumer brand choice: establishing a methodology, *Journal of Economic Psychology*, 24, 675–695.

Foxall, G. R. and Sigurdsson, V. (2013). Consumer behavior analysis: behavioral economics meets the market place, *The Psychological Record*, 63, 231–237.

Foxall, G. R., James, V. K., Oliveira-Castro, J. M. and Ribier, S. (2010). Product substitutability and the matching law, *The Psychological Record*, 60, 185–216.

Foxall, G. R., Oliveira-Castro, J. M. and Schrezenmaier, T. C. (2004). The behavioral economics of consumer brand choice: patterns of reinforcement and utility maximization, *Behavioural Processes*, 65, 235–260.

Foxall, G. R., James, V. K., Chang, J. and Oliveira-Castro, J. M. (2010). Substitutability and complementarity: matching analyses of brands and products. *Journal of Organizational Behavior Management*, 30(2), 145–160.

Foxall, G. R., Oliveira-Castro, J. M., James, V. K. and Schrezenmaier, T. C. M. (2007). *The Behavioral Economics of Brand Choice*. London and New York: Palgrave Macmillan.

Foxall, G. R., Yan, J., Oliveira-Castro, J. M. and Wells, V. K. (2013). Brand-related and situational influences on demand elasticity. *Journal of Business Research*, 66, 73–81.

Hayes, S. C., Barnes-Holmes, D. and Roche, B. (2001). *Relational Frame Theory: A Post-Skinnerian Account of Human Language and Cognition*. New York: Kluwer/Plenum.

Herrnstein, R. J. (1961). Relative and absolute strength of response as a function of frequency of reinforcement, *Journal of the Experimental Analysis of Behavior*, 4, 267–272.

Herrnstein, R. J. (1970). On the law of effect, *Journal of the Experimental Analysis of Behavior*, 13, 243–266.

Herrnstein, R. J. (1997). *The Law of Effect: Papers in Psychology and Economics* (Ed. by Howard Rachlin and David I. Laibson). Cambridge, MA: Harvard University Press/New York: Russell Sage Foundation.

Hursh, S. R. (1984). Behavioral economics, *Journal of the Experimental Analysis of Behavior*, 435–452.

Hursh, S. R. and Roma, P. G. (2015). Behavioral economics and the analysis of consumption and choice, *Managerial and Decision Economics*, in press.

Lee, V. L. (1988). *Beyond Behaviorism*. Hillsdale, NJ: Erlbaum.

Michael, J. (1993). Establishing operations, *The Behavior Analyst*, 16, 191–206.

Oliveira-Castro, J. M., Foxall, G. R. and James, V. K. (2010). Consumer brand choice: allocation of expenditure as a function of pattern of reinforcement and response cost, *Journal of Organizational Behavior Management*, 30(2), 161–175.

Oliveira-Castro, J. M., Cavalcanti, P. and Foxall, G. R. (2015). What consumers maximize: brand choice as a function of utilitarian and informational reinforcement, *Managerial and Decision Economics*, in press. doi: 10.1002/mde.2722.

Oliveira-Castro, J. M., Foxall, G. R. and Schrezenmaier, T. C. (2006). Consumer brand choice: individual and group analyses of demand elasticity, *Journal of the Experimental Analysis of Behavior*, 85, 147–166.

Oliveira-Castro, J. M., Foxall, G. R., James V. K. (2008). Individual differences in price responsiveness within and across food brands, *Service Industries Journal*, 28, 733–753.

Oliveira-Castro, J. M., Foxall, G. R., James V. K., Pohl, R. H. B. F., Dias, M. B. and Chang, S. W. (2008). Consumer-based brand equity and brand performance, *Service Industries Journal*, 28, 445–461.

Oliveira-Castro, J. M., Foxall, G. R., Yan, J. and Wells, V. K. (2011). A behavioural-economic analysis of the essential value of brands, *Behavioural Processes*, 87, 106–114.

Romero, S., Foxall, G. R., Schrezenmaier, T. C., Oliveira-Castro, J. and James, V. K. (2006). Deviations from matching in consumer choice. *European Journal of Behavior Analysis*, 7, 15–40.

Schoggen, P. (1989). *Behavior Settings*. Stanford, CA: Stanford University Press.

Schwarz, B. and Lacey, H. (1988). What applied studies of human operant conditioning tell us about humans and about operant conditioning. In Davey, G. and Cullen, C. (Eds.) *Human Operant Conditioning and Behavior Modification* (pp. 27–42). Chichester: Wiley.

Searle, J. (2010). *Making the Social World: The Structure of Human Civilization*. Oxford: Oxford University Press.

Sidman, M. (1994). *Equivalence Relations and Behavior: A Research Story*. Boston, MA: Authors Cooperative.

Sigurdsson, V., Hinriksson, H. and Menon, V. (2015). Operant behavioral economics for e-mail marketing: An experimental analysis of database segmentation, *Managerial and Decision Economics*, in press.

Sigurdsson, V., Larsen, N. M. and Gunnarsson, D. (2011). An in-store experimental analysis of consumers' selection of fruits and vegetables. *The Service Industries Journal*, 31, 2587–2602.

Sigurdsson, V., Khamseh, S., Larsen, N. M., Gunnarsson, D. and Foxall, G. R. (2013). An econometric examination of the Behavioral Perspective Model in the context of Norwegian retailing, *The Psychological Record*, 63, 277–294.

Sigurdsson, V., Menon, V., Sigurdarson, J. P., Kristjansson, J. S. and Foxall, G. R. (2013). A test of the behavioral perspective model in the context of an e-mail marketing experiment, *The Psychological Record*, 63, 295–308.

Skinner, B. F. (1950). Are theories of learning necessary? *Psychological Review*, 57, 193–216.

Skinner, B. F. (1953). *Science and Human Behavior*. New York: Macmillan.

Skinner, B. F. (1957). *Verbal Behavior*. London: Methuen.

Skinner, B. F. (1963). Behaviorism at fifty, *Science*, 140(3570), 951–958.

Skinner, B. F. (1966). An operant analysis of problem solving. In Kleinmuntz, B. (Ed.) *Problem Solving: Research, Method, and Theory*. New York: Wiley. Reprinted in Skinner, B. F. (1969). *Contingencies of Reinforcement: A Theoretical Analysis* (pp. 133–171). Englewood Cliffs, NJ: Prentice-Hall.

Skinner, B. F. (1969). *Contingencies of Reinforcement: A Theoretical Analysis*. Englewood Cliffs, NJ: Prentice-Hall.

Skinner, B. F. (1988). Comment on Stephen P. Stich: "Is behaviorism vacuous?" In Catania, A. C. and Harnad, S. (Eds.) *The Selection of Behavior. The Operant Behaviorism of B. F. Skinner: Comments and Consequences* (pp. 361–364). Cambridge: Cambridge University Press.

Staats, A. W. (1996). *Behavior and Personality: Psychological Behaviorism*. New York: Springer.

Staddon, J. E. R. (1980). (Ed.) *Limits to Action: The Allocation of Individual Behavior*. New York: Academic Press.

Vella, K. J. and Foxall, G. R. (2011). *The Marketing Firm: Economic Psychology of Corporate Behaviour*. Cheltenham, UK and Northampton, MA: Edward Elgar.

Wells, V. K. and Foxall, G. R. (2013). Matching, demand, maximization, and consumer choice, *The Psychological Record*, 62, 239–257.

Yan, J., Foxall, G. R. and Doyle, J. R. (2012a). Patterns of reinforcement and the essential value of brands: I. Incorporation of utilitarian and informational reinforcement into the estimation of demand, *The Psychological Record*, 62, 377–394.

Yan J., Foxall, G. R. and Doyle, J. R. (2012b). Patterns of reinforcement and the essential value of brands: II. Evaluation of a model of consumer choice, *The Psychological Record*, 62, 361–376.

Part II

Behavioral economics meets marketing science

Experimental analyses of consumer choices

Asle Fagerstrøm and Valdimar Sigurdsson

Introduction

Marketing can be seen both as a sub-discipline of economics, the science of how organisms use scarce resources, and psychology, the science of overt and covert behavior. Traditionally, marketing has been described as an area for application for its main disciplines (Foxall, 1999). It has been seen as a business philosophy concentrating on how the organization can work as one entity to maximize revenue by fulfilling consumers' current and future wants (e.g., Jaworski & Kohli, 1993; Kohli & Jaworski, 1990; Narver & Slater, 1990). This entails the use of consumer behavior analysis in marketing management.

Marketing is based on behavioral function, which is interested in the effects of incentives and penalties in the form of the fulfillment of needs and wants. As such, it can be defined as "the study of the behavior of consumers and marketers, especially as they interact" (Foxall, 2001, p. 165) and the research of their bilateral workings on each other. The functional school involves enquiring about the consequences of behavior that make behavior analysis particularly relevant to marketing research. If theories of consumer behavior are used, they are most often taken from one of the basic disciplines (for example, psychology and economics) and applied to a particular marketing theme. It could, however, benefit marketing and its application if the environmental–behavior laws and principles of the behavior of marketers and consumers could be found, analyzed and made clear. By focusing on description, prediction and control of behavior, different theories, methods and applications can be compared in the search for economical and comprehensible descriptions of the behavioral classes of marketing.

Behavior analysis has its strongest roots in experimentation and inductive research methods, and by the rejection of dualism it can be defined as a natural science (Baum, 2005). It is also a selection science (Pierce & Cheney, 2004), and research must be framed to encompass the dynamic complexity associated with evolving systems, whether the systems are biological, behavioral or social. The unified conceptual framework of behavior analysis and selection sciences may provide a way to integrate data from several disciplines. One obvious discipline that is of interest to behavior analysis is psychology. However, other disciplines that are of legitimate scientific interest are biology, education, sociology, general networks theory, political science, anthropology, medicine, psychiatry, social work and economics. Within economics, relevant research programs are behavioral economics (e.g., Bowles, 2004), behavioral ecology of consumption (Rajala & Hantula, 2000) and consumer behavior analysis (Foxall, 1990/2004, 2007).

This chapter focuses on how to design experiments to understand, predict and influence consumer choices. The focus is mainly consumer behavior analysis, but its presentation of experimental analysis of consumer choice is also relevant for behavioral economics and behavioral ecology of consumption. An introduction to both laboratory and field experiments will be given together with examples from the behavioral perspective model research program. Some specific issues related to microworlds, the use of technology in designing and administering laboratory experiments, and the use of in-store experiments of consumer brand choice will be discussed in more detail.

Consumer behavior analysis

Consumer behavior analysis takes behavior analysis as its initial foundation (Foxall, 2010). The choice of behavior analysis stemmed from its minimal deployment of theoretical terms, its avoidance of cognitive terminology, and its insistence on describing behavioral responses exclusively by reference to environmental stimuli. The behavioral perspective model is a consumer behavior model that is based on the principles from behavior analysis. The model was first described in *Consumer Psychology in Behavioral Perspective* (Foxall, 1990/2004), and was recently reviewed in *Explaining Consumer Choice* (Foxall, 2007).

The dependent variable

The behavioral perspective model accounts of purchase and consumption conceptualize behavior at a molar level rather than that of the individual response (Foxall, 2010). Figure 2.1 shows that the main perspective of the behavioral perspective model is the consumer situation which exerts a direct influence on the shaping and maintenance of consumer behavior (the dependent variable) in specified surroundings (Foxall, 2007).

The dependent variable in consumer behavior analysis is the rate of response. However, consumer behavior analysts do not talk about behavior as if it is composed of discrete responses. They consider consumer behavior as a performance that follows a specific stimulus and/or

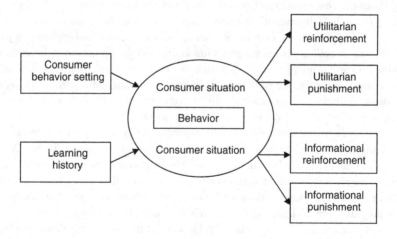

Figure 2.1   The Behavioral Perspective Model

Source: Foxall (2010). *Interpreting Consumer Choice: The Behavioral Perspective Model.* New York: Routledge. Reproduced by permission

results in a particular consequence. When a response is strengthened or weakened by the events or stimuli that follow the consumer's response, it is called operant behavior (Catania, 2013).

The independent variables

Consumer choice produces consequences which, in the behavioral perspective model, are classified as reinforcers (utilitarian or informational) and punishers (utilitarian or informational) (Foxall, 2007). Reinforcement, as a process, represents the consequences of consumer behavior that increase the probability of similar responses being repeated in the future. Utilitarian reinforcement is the tangible functional and economic benefits which stem from purchasing products, ownership and consumption. Informational reinforcement is a consequence of consumer behavior that is more likely to involve a lifestyle statement by which the consumer is reinforced by social attention or appreciation. Punishment, as a process, entails those consequences of consumer behavior that reduce the probability of similar responses being repeated in the future. Utilitarian punishments are the cost of consuming: relinquishing money; time-consuming registration before payment; forgoing alternative products; and so forth. Informational punishment is an aversive consequence of consumer behavior mediated by the social network. The key independent variable incorporated in the behavioral perspective model related to the consequences of consumer behavior is thus reinforcement (utilitarian or informational) and punishment (utilitarian or informational).

Shopping and consumption produces consequences which consist in reinforcement and punishment and, in this manner, the consumer acquires a learning history with respect to acts of this kind. For a consumer in a novel shopping situation, the neutral stimuli are transformed by this learning history into discriminative stimuli that signal the probable outcomes of a particular behavior in the setting by their intersection with the consumer's pertinent history of reinforcement (utilitarian and informational) and punishment (utilitarian and informational). It is this learning history that adds meaning to otherwise neutral-setting stimuli by investing them with the consequences of previous approach-avoidance behaviors in similar circumstances (Alhadeff, 1982). Therefore, the consumer behavior setting scope is the extent to which the current consumer behavior setting compels a particular pattern of behavior (for example, shopping online requires that the consumer must log on to the web, find the web shop, select products, put them in the shopping basket, and go through the confirm-order procedure). The consumer behavior setting consists of the current discriminative stimuli that signal reinforcement and punishment contingent upon the process of a purchase or consumption response. These settings of consumer behavior comprise the stimuli that form the social and physical environment (Barker, 1968). Stimuli that compose the consumer behavior setting may be: (1) physical (e.g., point-of-purchase promotion, store brand), (2) social (e.g., the salesperson, other customers in the shop), (3) temporal (e.g., opening hours, festivals like Halloween) or (4) regulatory (e.g., self- and other-rules that specify contingencies) (Foxall, 2005). The consumer's learning history is, in the behavioral perspective model, manifested within a particular behavior setting: prior learning establishes what will act as a discriminative stimulus in that setting by embodying the consequences, reinforcing and punishing, of earlier behavior in the presence of the relevant setting elements. So, if for example previous shopping online has produced consequences such as economic fraud, the consumer will probably establish a rule that the Internet is not a safe place to shop.

The central explanatory component of the behavioral perspective model is the consumer situation, represented by the interaction of learning history and the current consumer behavior setting which exerts a direct influence on the shaping and maintenance of consumer behavior in specified surroundings (Foxall, 2007). The consumer situation is more specific than a setting: the consumer situation is defined and circumscribed not only by the consumer setting variables that signal utilitarian and informational consequences of behavior, but also by the salience of those discriminative stimuli as determined by the consumer's learning history. Thus, the consumer behavior setting, learning history and consumer situation are antecedents that function as independent variables in the behavioral perspective model.

Behavioral and social scientific research can be categorized into four major areas (Kerlinger & Lee, 2000): laboratory experiments, field experiments, field studies and survey research. This categorization is based on the assumption that there is a distinction between experimental and non-experimental research, and a distinction between laboratory and field research. The following section gives a presentation of laboratory experiments and field experiments in consumer behavior analysis.

Laboratory experiments

According to Kerlinger and Lee (2000), a laboratory experiment is "a research study in which the variance of all, or nearly all, of the possible influential independent variables not pertinent to the immediate problem of the investigation is kept at a minimum" (p. 579). A typical consumer behavior laboratory experiment aims to analyze the behavior-environment relationships. The experimenter can isolate the consumer situation from life outside the laboratory by eliminating the many extraneous influences that may affect antecedents and consequences (the independent variables) and consumer behavior (the dependent variable).

Several studies within consumer behavior analysis have investigated consumer brand preferences. For example, studies based on supermarket till receipts for weekly grocery shopping (Foxall & James, 2002, 2003) and studies based on panel data for fast-moving consumer goods (Foxall et al., 2004; Foxall & Schrezenmaier, 2003) have accumulated comprehensive knowledge about consumers' preference. However, due to the use of aggregated data, these studies do not acquire data about how individual consumer purchase patterns are developed, as requested by Hennig-Thurau and Klee (1997).

One way to study individual consumers' preferences toward a brand is to arrange different reinforcement contingencies for two or more choices in the laboratory (Fagerstrøm et al., 2011). Reinforcers can be organized according to different arrangements in which responses in a class that are followed by reinforcers are specified, i.e., schedules of reinforcement. Such arrangements can either be continuous or intermittent. Every correct response in a class is reinforced on a continuous reinforcement schedule, while on intermittent reinforcement schedules some of the responses in a class are reinforced. According to Catania (2013), there are four main types of simple schedules of reinforcement. These are arranged according to number of responses (R) or an interval plus a response (I) in combination if the interval or number is fixed (F) or variable (V). Hence, in fixed-interval (FI) schedules the interval remains constant from trial to trial, while in variable-interval (VI) schedules the interval varies from one reinforcement to the next. In fixed-ratio (FR) schedules the arrangement is that the number of responses required before reinforcement is constant from trial to trial, while in variable-ratio (VR) schedules the number of required responses changes. A number of studies have shown that VR schedules relatively produce the highest response rates and also that behavior maintained on such schedules is quite resistant to extinction. Extinction is the discontinuation of any reinforcement that once maintained a given response. Extinction, as a behavioral process, refers to a decline in the rate of response caused by withdrawal of reinforcement (e.g., Catania, 2013).

In a laboratory experiment by Fagerstrøm et al. (2011), the authors investigated to what extent manipulation of environmental contingencies could contribute to the understanding of how consumer brand preferences develop. A laboratory experiment with two different schedules of reinforcement was arranged to study participants' choice in an online shopping context. Preference was studied by arranging different schedules of reinforcement simultaneously for two responses. When one of the alternatives was chosen more frequently than the others, it was denoted as a preference for an alternative source of reinforcement (Pierce & Cheney, 2004). Results from the experiment show that (Fagerstrøm et al., 2011) responses in nine out of 40 participants were not under the control of the experimenter-defined contingencies, one had an equal preference for the two alternatives and three participants showed color-sensitive behavior. For the remaining 27 participants, 18 showed preference according to the experimenter-defined contingencies (shop most frequently on the alternative with the highest number of programmed reinforcements), and nine were not under the control of experimenter-defined contingencies (shop most frequently on the alternative with the lowest number of programmed reinforcements). In general, the laboratory experiment by Fagerstrøm et al. (2011) found that 18 out of 27 participants showed preferences according to the experimenter-defined contingencies. In the first phase of the experiment, during the first part of training, it was observed there was more switching between the alternatives than later in the maintenance phase. In addition, choice time decreased as a function of the number of trials.

The laboratory experiment by Fagerstrøm et al. (2011) demonstrates that it is possible to study consumer preference on concurrent ratio schedules, where the researcher controls the reinforcement. The study expanded knowledge about consumer behavior when having a closed-setting experiment with control over reinforcement. Moreover, the study extended knowledge about how customer brand preference develops by studying environmental contingencies that shape and maintain consumer choices, and it represents one of only a few attempts to apply laboratory experimental analysis to understanding consumer preferences from observing individual behavior.

Another laboratory experiment by Fagerstrøm and Hantula (2013) investigated credit card use in a consumer choice setting. Building on the hyperbolic discounted utility model (see Green & Myerson, 2004), the study aimed to understand credit card use by students. Hyperbolic discounting is the tendency for people to increasingly choose a smaller-sooner reward (a temptation) over a larger-later reward as the delay occurs sooner rather than later in time. A simulated shopping experiment was prepared where 21 participants were asked whether they would save money for a new model of their favorite mobile phone brand, or buy the product on credit and get it immediately. The results showed (Fagerstrøm & Hantula, 2013) that the participants were willing to pay a high interest charge (nearly 40%) rather than waiting, saving money and purchasing the phone interest-free. However, these results were moderated by student experience with credit card purchases. Those who did not normally use a credit card did not opt to buy the phone immediately on credit, but preferred to delay purchase until the money was saved. These data demonstrate that in some cases, immediate availability of a much desired product such as a mobile phone may induce credit spending with extremely high interest rates.

Microworlds

Laboratory experiments, as a method for pursuing research, have pros and cons, as evidenced by the debate they have given rise to within behavioral and social scientific research. According to Brehmer and Dörner (1993), one could relate this discussion to the difficulties posed by complexity: the uncontrollable complexity of the field experiment creates problems of inference, while the controlled laboratory experiment may generate weak external validity. DiFonzo et al. (1998) contend that computer-simulated microworlds offer a solution to this dilemma.

The term "microworlds" appears to be used for the first time by Turkle (1984), who describes it as the carefully constructed, graphically rich and complex rule-governed worlds of video games. Further, within the field of decision-making studies, Brehmer (1992) and Brehmer and Dörner (1993) define microworlds as computer-generated simulation environments that participants interact with and that possess, to varying degrees, a dynamic, complex and opaque character. The ability to simulate dynamic decision systems using computer-simulated microworlds offers a level of experimental realism not often experienced in traditional laboratory research (DiClemente & Hantula, 2003; Hantula et al., 2008; Hantula & Bryant, 2005; Omodei & Wearing, 1995; Smith & Hantula, 2003). Furthermore, microworlds offer the researcher a high degree of experimental control, thus incorporating the benefits of experiments – effects due to experimental manipulation.

The consumer brand preference experiment by Fagerstrøm et al. (2011) can be categorized as a type of computer-simulated microworld study in which the dynamic aspect is only partly present. Based on a simulated shopping situation made in MediaLab, participants interact with the environment by browsing between two web shops and deciding which option to choose. MediaLab is software developed by Empirisoft for the creation of psychological experiments in a computer lab which makes possible multi-stimuli experiments and the recording of data on each individual participant. MediaLab made it possible to set up the experiment and automatically record data. Thus, microworlds bring useful features to consumer behavior analysts including realism and high levels of control, and MediaLab is software that can be used to administer the study.

Field experimentation

Marketing needs to have a theoretical and/or empirical foundation to account for the situational influence of the marketing mix on consumer choice. The matching law (Herrnstein, 1961, 1970) is a mainstream behavior analysis of choice behavior and has been studied for several decades (e.g., Baum, 2002; Davison & McCarthy, 1988). The matching law's research history, indeed the history of the whole of behavior analysis, has mainly been conducted in a systematic experimental framework where knowledge is built by constantly putting more factors under experimental control. Most of the research has been done on animal behavior in the behavioral laboratory. The few experimental studies that have been conducted on human behavior have all been done in a rather closed setting.

The subject matter of consumer behavior analysis is also the exploration of the possibility of using the concepts and methods of behavior analysis applied in research, on a simpler level, for the study of consumer choice in open settings. As such, it studies the impact of important variables on consumer choice in natural situations. Some of these variables have already been identified from research on matching at a simpler level. To deal with the influences of the marketing mix on consumer choice, behavior analysis needs to find the sole effects of the most important variables to determine its importance in accounting for complex consumer behavior. The experimental method, where the effect of each independent variable is found to keep the others constant, is a necessary step in exploring the ability of behavior analysis to describe, predict and control consumer choice in open settings. This brings us to the open experimental question of the research program, which is important for both consumer marketing and behavior analysis: How can online and in-store behavioral experiments help to accumulate valid and reliable knowledge of the effects of marketing mix factors on consumers' choices in natural and open settings?

This entails behavior analytical evaluations (see, e.g., Johnston & Pennypacker, 1993) and comparisons of the legitimacy of different outcomes from consumer choice and matching analysis of sales data obtained with in-store experiments. The Consumer Behavior Analysis Research Program (e.g., Foxall & Sigurdsson, 2013) uses behavioral economics as a paradigm and explores the relevance of in-store (e.g., Sigurdsson et al., 2014) and online behavioral experiments (e.g., Sigurdsson et al., 2013) on such metrics as relative sales and matching analysis to the study of consumers' brand choice in natural open settings.

In-store experiments

The in-store experimental settings have consisted of different store types, such as convenience, supermarkets and discount stores. The research attempts to elucidate to what extent within-group in-store experiments, with relative responses and matching analysis, are relevant to consumer choice exploration. Different methods of data analysis are used on the sales data generated from the in-store experiments. This includes relative sales analysis and reinforcer-cost matching analysis (also known as relative demand analysis). The relative sales analysis has its predecessors in previous behavior analytical work in the concept of relative response rate (Herrnstein's dependent variable, e.g., 1961) and visual inspections of moment-to-moment changes in response rate (Skinner's dependent variable, e.g., 1974). In fact, relative sales analysis is a combination of these, as it represents momentary changes in relative sales of a particular target brand (analogs to the experimental key in the behavioral laboratory) as a function of particular environmental contingencies. It is considered important for the evaluation of different matching analyses to have an assessment of consumer choice (relative sales analysis) to make a comparison. The reinforcer-cost matching is mostly known from previous consumer behavior analysis research as relative demand analysis (see, e.g., Foxall & James, 2001, 2003; Foxall et al., 2004; Oliveira-Castro et al., 2005) but it is here represented within the framework of matching.

In sum, the in-store experiments have been designed to explore whether consumer choice and the substitutability of brands (matching) are affected by an experimental manipulation of important marketing mix factors such as *1 Place,* the placement of brands in store layouts (Sigurdsson et al., 2011b), *2 Price,* pricing of fast-moving consumer goods or brands (Sigurdsson et al., 2011a), and *3 Promotion,* in-store advertisements of a brand's benefits (Sigurdsson et al., 2010).

In-store experimental methodology

The program is a methodological exploration of the relevance of in-store behavioral experiments. It is part of the consumer behavior analysis agenda of investigating the relevance of behavioral economics in the context of marketing. It studies how important marketing factors affect consumer choice in complex, real, affluent and competitive retail environments. More precisely, traditional marketing mix factors are manipulated to explore their effects on consumers' buying behavior. The main question is to what extent the behavior analytical methodology can answer what effects certain periodical changes in such factors as Place, Price and Promotion have on consumers' buying behavior in the natural environment.

Similarities and deviations from characteristic behavior analysis

Behavior analysis is built on the method of single-subject experimental designs, where the term "single" refers to the experimental comparison but not the few subjects generally used (e.g., Perone, 1991). According to Johnston and Pennypacker (1993): "[an] experiment is a series of actions that result in a set of special observations that would not otherwise have been possible" (p. 8). The main purpose of an experimental design is to avoid threats to internal validity by trying to exclude the effects of other variables under study on the dependent variable. This is ideally done by controlling both the variables under study (the independent variables) and other important variables (extraneous variables) thought to affect the dependent variable and make the effects of the independent variables unclear. This allows the researcher to examine what effects different conditions have on behavior. Without the ability to intervene, behavioral control is bound to be based on speculations.

When evaluating the behavioral perspective of consumer behavior research, and marketing in general, it is important to understand how much effect, or control, of consumer behavior can be attributed to the environment. Experiments are the best way to explore this. But unlike the laboratory experimenter, who can control most or all important variables in the laboratory – like deprivation, reinforcement schedules etc. – the field experimenter studying consumer choices unfortunately does not have that option; studying, as he/she does, consumer behavior in natural settings. There are both strengths and weaknesses in experimental work in consumer behavior analysis. This is because external validity and the analogous interpretations, built on the findings, are much more related to the actual reality than interpretations built on experimental findings with lower animals as subjects, without wanting to diminish their value. We here propose, in line with the Behavior Perspective Model, a continuum of open to closed settings, where the aim for consumer behavior analysis is to have the most control possible in open natural settings (Figure 2.2). This shows how the research, listed here, tries to apply experimental control to study consumer behavior in open settings, within the framework of matching theory.

This research tries to retain the rigorous methods and concepts used and developed in the behavioral laboratory, but obviously this can be hard to attain. It is important to be patient in the search for greater control over consumer behavior, as there are many stepping stones. Table 2.1 shows, in a simplified manner, how this study differs in an important way from general laboratory research in behavior analysis, in that it shares some familiarity to experimental work in general psychology and related disciplines.

Table 2.1 compares the experimental analysis of behavior with more traditional experimental psychology. The bold items best correspond to this research. The in-store experiments have many participants, consisting of the consumers in the stores during the experiments. The research uses within-subject experimental design, to the extent that the consumers (in each store) can be looked at as a group. The main point is that the experimental comparison is made within each store's consumer group, but not with some other independent group (between-group comparison). The study uses direct, repeated measures of consumer choice behavior

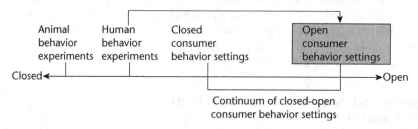

Figure 2.2 Continuum of consumer behavior settings and the transfer of experimental control from closed to open environments

Source: Adapted from Foxall (1993)

Table 2.1 A comparison of behavior analytical and traditional experimental psychology research

Dimension	Experimental analysis of behavior	Traditional experimental psychology
Number of subjects	Few	Many
Research design	Within-subject	Between-subjects
Data collection	Direct, repeated measures of behavior	Various methods, often indirect and nonrepeated measures of behavior
Data analysis	Graphic	Statistical
Approach to variable data	Consider the variability as imposed; isolate and control the responsible extraneous variables	Consider the variability as intrinsic; use statistics to detect effects of the independent variable despite the variability

Source: Adapted from Poling et al. (1995)

(e.g., relative sales). This is different from dividing a large number of subjects into two groups, experimental and control groups, where the behavior of the two groups is generally compared using the rules of inferential statistics (Johnston & Pennypacker, 1993).

Regarding analysis of data, the results are presented in graphic form showing consumers' choices during the baseline and interventions for each store. The data are not entered into a database for the ease of an inferential statistical analysis; nor for data from each experiment (e.g., the Price experiment) or for the same types of stores (e.g., budget stores), as would be expected from a social science perspective. This is an exploration of the relevance of behavior analysis, as represented in the work of, e.g., Skinner (1938) and Herrnstein (1961, 1970, 1997), and their followers (e.g., Sidman, 1960). As characteristic for behavioral analytical research, the results present descriptive statistics such as measures of central tendency, variation and association (e.g., mean, range and regressions with slope and intercept) but no inferential statistics (for the pros and cons of the use of inferential statistics in behavior analysis, see an introduction to six articles in Baron (1999); see also Hopkins et al. (1998)). Instead, visual inspections are used to interpret whether there is a difference between conditions (see a critical discussion of this approach in Fisch, 1998). It is important to remember that although the dissertation puts behavior analysis forward in the realm of consumer behavior research, it is first and foremost a critical exploration of the behavioral perspective (matching), and those methods advocated by the behavioral research community (e.g., visual inspections, repeated measures, behavioral control). As such, in this case, these factors are tested (like visual inspections) but others, although being worthy of exploration (especially inferential statistics), are omitted.

Field experiments rely on experimental techniques by controlling important extraneous variables, such as the prices of the competing brands, extra line-ups and other stimuli in the stores. This is obviously a field experiment, meaning that it is impossible to control the environment in the way done in the closed setting of the behavioral laboratory. However, this study deals with the behavior to be interpreted: real consumer behavior in the modern marketing system.

Group analysis

Traditionally, behavior analysis has emphasized the study of individual organisms; analyzing the interrelationship between a behaving organism and its environment. The field owes much of its success to the individual behavior approach since it, among other things, reduces behavioral variability when compared to studying groups. Strictly speaking, "Behavior is a biological function of organisms, and a group is not an organism" (Johnston & Pennypacker, 1993, p. 81). Lots of valuable information is lost (e.g., individual patterns of behavior) when researchers study only the behavior of a number of people. When data are put together, it can hide functional relationships. That can also be asserted whenever data are grouped or aggregated, as is done in matching analysis and all molar accounts – a conduct of primary interest to behavior analysts at least since the 1970s. It is important to allow different kinds of behavior analysis – molar, molecular, mathematical orientation or experiments – and to study their strengths and weaknesses. Each has something to offer, keeping the constraints in mind. For instance, it is necessary to study group behavior to interpret convincingly the third level (group behavior – culture) of selection by consequences (genes – individual behavior – culture) (e.g., Glenn, 1988; Skinner, 1984).

Studying individuals is not always achievable or of primary interest. In marketing, individual behavior is important, but for an applied discipline the subject matter is often groups (e.g., segments of consumers), because individuals will not make fast-moving consumer brands successful. Only large numbers of people buying the brand will make it thrive in terms of revenue. Researchers or marketers want to know what functions stimuli have for consumer choices. In consumer behavior analysis this has been done on the basis of observational data (Foxall et al., 2006):

> When dealing with consumer behavior, however, research and managerial interests frequently lie in identifying what functions as reinforcement to large groups of people and, in the large majority of cases, this has to be done on the basis of observational, rather than experimental data. This may increase some already existing ambiguities in defining different types of reinforcement.
>
> *(pp. 105–6)*

The Consumer Behavior Analysis Research Group, based at Cardiff University, has built an essential research methodology to study consumers' choices, both at the individual and group level of analysis (for a review, see Foxall et al., 2007). This research has established the molar law of effect (the matching law) in the realm of consumer behavior with "correlation between output and feedback" (Baum, 1973, p. 141), for instance in the form of the relative amount paid for and the relative amount of a brand received. The correlational methodology is important as in many cases there will be no experimental control available to the consumer behavior analyst. However, in some cases, as here, control will be available in the form of interventions. The consumer researchers will be able to perform macro contingencies, defined as "individual contingencies applied directly to a large number of people" (Branch, 2006, p. 6). This can give the researcher better grounding for functional relationships, which is important when there is an interest in extending the successful use of behavior analysis to the social sciences (like marketing).

Group choice behavior (where individual behavior is also examined) has been studied with matching analysis. Its results show that group behavior by no means mirrors individual choices. Baum and Kraft (1998) state that "results at the level of the flock in no way paralleled behavior at the level of the individual" (p. 227). They present a generalized matching equation for group behavior (Equation 1):

$$\log \frac{N_1}{N_2} = a \log \frac{r_1}{r_2} + \log c \qquad (1)$$

predicting that group choice, number of predators (N), matches obtained resources (r) (Baum & Kraft, 1998). It is possible to transfer this to consumer matching where the number of predators can be seen as analogs to the amount paid, and obtained resources as similar to the number of brands. In a later publication, these authors (Kraft & Baum, 2001) also state that "experiments demonstrate that an IFD analysis [equivalent to matching analysis] of group choice is possible and useful". This strengthens the foundation for matching analysis conducted on choice data from large groups of consumers (see Curry et al., 2010).

Applications: an example

Research in marketing has shown that most consumers want to increase their consumption of so-called healthy food and decrease their unhealthy choices. In line with this, and the fact that most retail purchase decisions are made in the store, prior research has tested in-store applied behavior analysis of both kinds of products (how to increase healthy consumption and decrease unhealthy selections). Research shows that the retail environment is among the diverse barriers to an increased consumption of healthy food products, and it includes factors such as how healthy food products are located within the stores compared with the positioning of unhealthy food products (e.g. sweets), availability, nutrition information and price. It is also common knowledge that in-store shelf placement of sweets and products with high glycemic carbohydrates are most commonly situated in highly visible areas, and sweets are almost always situated at the checkout. Hence, owing to the critical importance of exposure, more emphasis should be placed on maximizing accidental exposure to more healthy food products in the retail environment along with more active promotion of such products. Sigurdsson et al. (2009) conducted an in-store experiment measuring the effects of product placement (highest, middle, lowest shelf and an extra line-up) on consumers' purchases of an international potato chips brand. The results showed that placement of potato chips on the middle shelf was associated with a higher percentage of purchases compared with the lowest and highest shelf. Also, an extra line-up of the potato chips at the store entrance almost doubled its market share. Sigurdsson et al. (2011b) also performed an in-store experiment which consisted of such interventions as placing bananas at the checkout and promotion. An interesting point from a consumer survey that followed the in-store experiment was that consumers had very positive attitudes toward healthy food products (especially bananas) and intended to buy more. In-store interventions, like the one performed, were also deemed to be important and necessary by most consumers in the survey. Despite this, the results from the in-store experiment deviated substantially from the outcome of the survey, such that it was unsuccessful in changing consumers' buying behavior of bananas in the stores. Furthermore, another in-store experiment has shown that those who already buy bananas do so no matter what the price is and therefore lowering the price is not enough to increase the sales of bananas (Sigurdsson et al., 2011a). It seems likely buying (or not buying) a fruit like bananas is very habitual, and that the attitudes are more "favorable" than the ratio of buying suggests.

The inconsistency between consumers' stated intentions and actual buying behavior facilitates better understanding of the marketing problem at hand. It is dangerous for retailers to rely simply on customers' verbal behavior (e.g. complaints, pressure and survey results). The personal account is important but good practice in marketing research encourages the firm to take decisions based on different sources. Finally, Sigurdsson et al. (2014) examined both the immediate and enduring effects of modifying the typical in-store shelf placement of food items at the checkout, with or without an in-store advertisement, on consumer behavior. Instead of unhealthy items (e.g., candy, high glycemic carbohydrate), healthier items were rotated to the checkout lines in different types of stores. The researchers examined the effects of shelf place-ment at the checkout (Place) and in-store advertisement (Promotion) in relation to consumer buying behavior of the healthy products such as dried fish and fruit mix. The effects of these interventions on buying behavior of the moved "unhealthy" products were also assessed. The results demonstrate that placing healthy food items at the checkout (prominent discriminative stimuli) in stores can lead to a substantial impact on sales of these products. The in-store experi-mentation was able to identify healthy food items (e.g., dried fish or nuts) that have the potential to increase their sales about 400–500% if placed at pivotal places within the store. These levels of sales were, however, not maintained during withdrawal conditions or during the follow-up stage (return to baseline). Adding an advertisement at the point of purchase also did not lead to a meaningful generalizable increase in sales beyond the results obtained from stacking these prod-ucts at the checkout. One explanation for the apparent success of dried fish, fruit mix and nuts may be related to the low conservation rate and the small package sizes of the target products selected for the experiment. It is therefore often more sensible to examine the databases (e.g. looking for low conversion rates for healthy food items) rather than consumers (verbal reports).

Summing up

The experimental analysis of consumer choices tends to reveal quite clearly that many marketing interventions that sound sensible will be unsuccessful. It would, however, be a mistake to rely solely on information from experimentation or databases – to dismiss the personal account. Such measures can help identify where the marketing problem lies. The description of consumer behav-ior, as well as prediction and influence, needs the alignment of the personal level of the consumer to contextual behavioral experimentation. The consumer behavior analytical experiments con-ducted have also revealed a surprising inability of pricing to affect sales of all kinds of fast-moving consumer goods (e.g., Sigurdsson et al., 2011a). This finding can be generalized between different types of stores (convenience vs. discount) as for other studies conducted. Pricing is often inefficient in changing sales in different types of stores, and if there is any change it can be that higher pricing generates more sales. For example, in one of the studies conducted at Co-op (our main collabora-tor), the highest sales of cherry tomatoes were when the price in one of the discount stores was 17.46 NOK (the Norwegian currency) compared with 9.56 NOK. This is around 83% higher pricing, giving a gross margin of close to five times higher. Understandably, results like this have significant meaning for the retailer and are also of interest for consumer protection.

References

Alhadeff, D. A. (1982). *Microeconomics and Human Behavior: Toward a New Synthesis of Economics and Psychol-ogy*. Berkeley, CA: University of California Press.

Barker, R. G. (1968). *Ecological Psychology: Concepts and Methods for Studying the Environment of Human Behavior*. Stanford, CA: Stanford University Press.

Baron, A. (1999). Statistical inference in behavior analysis: Friend or Foe? *The Behavior Analyst, 22*(2), 83–85.

Baum, W. M. (1973). The correlation-based law of effec. *Journal of the Experimental Analysis of Behavior, 20*(1), 137–153. doi: 10.1901/jeab.1973.20-137

Baum, W. M. (2002). The Harvard pigeon lab under Herrnstein. *Journal of the Experimental Analysis of Behavior, 77*(3), 347–355.

Baum, W. M. (2005). *Understanding Behaviorism; Behavior, Culture and Evolution* (Second ed.). Malden, MA: Blackwell Publishing.

Baum, W. M., & Kraft, J. R. (1998). Group choice: Competition, travel, and the ideal free distribution. *Journal of the Experimental Analysis of Behavior, 69*(3), 227–245. doi: 10.1901/jeab.1998.69-227

Bowles, S. (2004). *Microeconomics. Behavior, Institutions and Evolution*. Princeton, NJ: Princeton University Press.

Branch, M. N. (2006). Reactions of a laboratory behavioral scientist to a "think tank" on metacontingencies and cultural analysis. *Behavior and Social Issues, 15*, 5–10.

Brehmer, B. (1992). Dynamic decision making: Human control of complex systems. *Acta Psychologica, 81*(3), 211–241. doi: 10.1016/0001-6918(92)90019-A

Brehmer, B., & Dörner, D. (1993). Experiments with computer-simulated microworlds: Escaping both the narrow straits of laboratory and the deep blue sea of the field study. *Computers in Human Behavior, 9*(2–3), 171–184. doi: 10.1016/0747-5632(93)90005-D

Catania, A. C. (2013). *Learning* (5th ed.). Cornwall-on-Hudson, NY: Sloan Publishing.

Curry, B., Foxall, G. R., & Sigurdsson, V. (2010). On the tautology of the matching law in consumer behavior analysis. *Behavioural Processes, 84*(1), 390–399. doi: 10.1016/j.beproc.2010.02.009

Davison, M., & McCarthy, D. (Eds.). (1988). *The Matching Law: A Research Review*. Hillsdale, NJ: Erlbaum.

DiClemente, D. F., & Hantula, D. A. (2003). Applied behavioral economics and consumer choice. *Journal of Economic Psychology, 24*, 589–602. doi: 10.1016/S0167-4870(03)00003-5

DiFonzo, N., Hantula, D. A., & Bordia, P. (1998). Microworlds for experimental research: Having your (control and collection) cake, and realism too. *Behavior Research Methods, Instruments & Computers, 30*(2), 278–286. doi: 10.3758/BF03200656

Fagerstrøm, A., Arntzen, E., & Foxall, G. R. (2011). A study of preferences in a simulated online shopping experiment. *The Service Industries Journal, 31*(15), 2609–2621. doi: 10.1080/02642069.2011.531121

Fagerstrøm, A., & Hantula, D. A. (2013). Buy it now and pay for it later: An experimental study of student credit card use. *The Psychological Record, 63*(2), 323–332. doi: 10.11133/j.tpr.2013.63.2.007

Fisch, G. S. (1998). On methods. *The Behavior Analyst, 21*, 111–123.

Foxall, G. R. (1990/2004). *Consumer psychology in behavioral perspective* (First ed.). New York/Baltimore, MD: Routledge/Beard Books.

Foxall, G. R. (1993). A behaviourist perspective on purchase and consumption. *European Journal of Marketing, 27*(8), 7–16.

Foxall, G. R. (1999). The marketing firm. *Journal of Economic Psychology, 20*(2), 207–234. doi: 10.1016/S0167-4870(99)00005-7

Foxall, G. R. (2001). Foundations of consumer behaviour analysis. *Marketing Theory, 1*(2), 165–199. doi: 10.1177/147059310100100202

Foxall, G. R. (2005). *Understanding Consumer Choice* (First ed.). London: Palgrave Macmillan.

Foxall, G. R. (2007). *Explaining Consumer Choice*. New York: Palgrave Macmillan.

Foxall, G. R. (2010). *Interpreting Consumer Choice*. New York: Routledge.

Foxall, G. R., & James, V. K. (2001). The behavioral basis of consumer choice: A preliminary analysis. *European Journal of Behavior Analysis, 2*, 209–220.

Foxall, G. R., & James, V. K. (2002). Behavior analysis of consumer brand choice: A preliminary analysis. *European Journal of Behavior Analysis, 2*(2), 209–220.

Foxall, G. R., & James, V. K. (2003). The behavioral ecology of brand choice: How and what do consumers maximize? *Psychology and Marketing, 20*(9), 811–836. doi: 10.1002/mar.10098

Foxall, G. R., Oliveira-Castro, J. M., James, V. K., Yani-de-Soriano, M. M., & Sigurdsson, V. (2006). Consumer behavior analysis and social marketing: The case of environmental conservation. *Behavior and Social Issues, 15*, 1–24.

Foxall, G. R., Oliveira-Castro, J. M., & Schrezenmaier, T. C. (2004). The behavioral economics of consumer brand choice: Patterns of reinforcement and utility maximization. *Behavioural Processes, 65*(3), 235–260. doi: 10.1016/j.beproc.2004.03.007

Foxall, G. R., Oliveira-Castro, J. M., James, V. K., & Schrezenmaier, T. C. (2007). *The Behavioral Economics of Brand Choice*. New York: Palgrave Macmillan.

Foxall, G. R., & Schrezenmaier, T. C. (2003). The behavioural economics of consumer brand choice: Establishing a methodology. *Journal of Economic Psychology, 24*(3), 675–695. doi: 10.1016/S0167-4870(03)00008-4

Foxall, G. R., & Sigurdsson, V. (2013). Consumer behaviour analysis: Behavioural economics meets the market place. *The Psychological Record, 63*(2), 231–237.

Glenn, S. S. (1988). Contingencies and metacontingencies: Toward a synthesis of behavior analysis and cultural materialism. *The Behavior Analyst, 11*(2), 161–179.

Green, L., & Myerson, J. (2004). A discounting framework for choice with delay and probabilistic rewards. *Psychological Bulletin, 130*(5), 769–792. doi: 10.1037/0033-2909.130.5.769

Hantula, D. A., Brockman, D., & Smith, C. (2008). Online shopping as foraging: The effects of increasing delays on purchasing and patch residence. *IEEE Transactions on Professional Communication, 51*(2), 147–154. doi: 10.1109/TPC.2008.2000340

Hantula, D. A., & Bryant, K. M. (2005). Delay discounting determines delivery fees in an e-commerce simulation. *Psychology & Marketing, 22*(2), 153–161. doi: 10.1002/mar.20052

Hennig-Thurau, T., & Klee, A. (1997). The impact of customer satisfaction and relationship quality on customer retention: A critical reassessment and model development. *Psychology and Marketing, 14*(8), 737–764. doi: 10.1002/(SICI)1520-6793(199712)14:8<737::AID-MAR2>3.0.CO;2-F

Herrnstein, R. J. (1961). Relative and absolute strength of response as a function of frequency of reinforcement. *Journal of the Experimental Analysis of Behavior, 4,* 267–272.

Herrnstein, R. J. (1970). On the law of effect. *Journal of the Experimental Analysis of Behavior, 13,* 243–266.

Herrnstein, R. J. (1997). *The Matching Law.* New York: Russell Sage Foundation.

Hopkins, B. L., Cole, B. L., & Mason, T. L. (1998). A critique of the usefulness of inferential statistics in applied behavior analysis. *The Behavior Analyst, 21*(1), 125–137.

Jaworski, B. J., & Kohli, A. K. (1993). Market orientation: Antecedents and consequences. *Journal of Marketing, 57,* 53–70.

Johnston, J. M., & Pennypacker, H. S. (1993). *Readings for Strategies and Tactics of Behavioral Research* (Second ed.). Hillsdale, NJ: Erlbaum.

Kerlinger, F. N., & Lee, H. B. (2000). *Foundation of Behavioral Research* (Fourth ed.). Boston, MA: Thomson Learning.

Kohli, A. K., & Jaworski, B. J. (1990). Market orientation: The construct, research propositions, and managerial implications. *Journal of Marketing, 54,* 1–18.

Kraft, J. R., & Baum, W. M. (2001). Group choice: The ideal free distribution of human social behavior. *Journal of the Experimental Analysis of Behavior, 76*(1), 21–42. doi: 10.1901/jeab.2001.76-21

Narver, J. C., & Slater, S. F. (1990). The effect of a market orientation on business profitability. *Journal of Marketing, 54*(4), 20–35.

Oliveira-Castro, J. M., Foxall, G. R., & Schrezenmaier, T. C. (2005). Patterns of consumer response to retail price differentials. *Service Industries Journal, 25,* 309–327.

Omodei, M. M., & Wearing, A. J. (1995). The Fire Chief microworld generating program: An illustration of computer-simulated microworlds as an experimental paradigm for studying complex decision-making behavior. *Behavior Research Methods, Instruments & Computers, 27*(3), 303–316. doi: 10.3758/BF03200423

Perone, M. (1991). Experimental design in the analysis of free-operant behavior. In I. H. Iversen & K. Lattal (Eds.), *Experimental Analysis of Behavior Parts 1 & 2. Techniques in the Behavioral and Neural Sciences* (Vol. 6, pp. 135–171). New York: Elsevier Science.

Pierce, W. D., & Cheney, C. D. (2004). *Behavior Analysis and Learning.* New York: Psychology Press.

Poling, A. D., Methot, L. L., & LeSage, M. G. (1995). *Fundamentals of Behavior Analytic Research.* New York: Plenum Pres.

Rajala, A. K., & Hantula, D. A. (2000). Towards a behavioural ecology of consumption: Delay reduction effects on foraging in a simulated online mall. *Managerial and Decision Economics, 21*(3–4), 145–158. doi: 10.1002/mde.979

Sidman, M. (1960). *Tactics of Scientific Research: Evaluating Experimental Data in Psychology.* New York: Basic Books, Inc.

Sigurdsson, V., Engilbertsson, H., & Foxall, G. R. (2010). The effects of a point-of-purchase display on relative sales: An in-store experimental evaluation. *Journal of Organizational Behavior Management, 30*(3), 222–233. doi: 10.1080/01608061.2010.499028

Sigurdsson, V., Larsen, N. M., & Gunnarsson, D. (2011a). The behavioural economics of neutral and upward sloping demand curves in retailing. *The Service Industries Journal, 31*(15), 2543–2558. doi: 10.1080/02642069.2011.531127

Sigurdsson, V., Larsen, N. M., & Gunnarsson, D. (2011b). An in-store experimental analysis of consumers' selection of fruits and vegetables. *The Service Industries Journal, 31*(15), 2587–2602. doi: 10.1080/02642069.2011.531126

Sigurdsson, V., Larsen, N. M., & Gunnarsson, D. (2014). Healthy food marketing: An in-store experimental analysis. *Journal of Applied Behavior Analysis, 47,* 151–154.

Sigurdsson, V., Menon, V. R. G., Sigurdarson, J. P., Kristjansson, J. S., & Foxall, G. R. (2013). A test of the behavioral perspective model in the context of an e-mail marketing experiment. *The Psychological Record, 63*(2), 295–308.

Sigurdsson, V., Sævarsson, H., & Foxall, G. R. (2009). Brand-placement and consumer choice: An in-store experiment. *Journal of Applied Behavior Analysis, 42*(3), 741–744. doi: 10.1901/jaba.2009.42-741

Skinner, B. F. (1938). *The Behavior of Organisms: An Experimental Analysis.* New York: D. Appleton-Century Company, Inc.

Skinner, B. F. (1974). *About Behaviorism.* New York: Vintage Books.

Skinner, B. F. (1984). The evolution of behavior. *Journal of the Experimental Analysis of Behavior, 41*(2), 217–221. doi: 10.1901/jeab.1984.41-217

Smith, C. L., & Hantula, D. A. (2003). Pricing effects on foraging in a simulated Internet shopping mall. *Journal of Economic Psychology, 24*(5), 653–674. doi: 10.1016/S0167-4870(03)00007-2

Turkle, S. (1984). *The Second Self: Computers and the Human Spirit.* New York: Simon and Schuster.

Behavior analysis of in-store consumer behavior

Valdimar Sigurdsson, Nils Magne Larsen, and Asle Fagerstrøm

> Technical improvements that permit us to bring new behavior into the laboratory, or that permit refined experimental control over behavior, are among the most important contributions that we can make.
>
> *(Sidman, 1960, p. 17)*

Introduction

Behavior analysis is a descriptive science popularized by B. F. Skinner, his students and followers. The aim of this natural science has been the quest for lawful individual behavioral processes studied extensively with within-subject experimental designs. Behavior analysis is particularly concerned with the interplay between behavior and environmental variables. The field is built on extensive experiments with the aim of discovering lawful behavioral processes relevant for consumer research as consumers learn to adapt to their economic environment. In-store consumer behavior, the topic of this chapter, was until rather recently an unexplored territory for behavior analysis. We will here introduce the quest for behavior analysis of in-store consumer behavior, how it deviates from traditional marketing, what has been gained, and problems and possibilities for more refined experimental control over this important economic environmental-behavior relationship for the future of retailing.

Why behavior analysis of in-store consumer behavior is important

For behavior analysis the objective is the discovery of laws and principles governing behavior through experimentation. Skinner (1953, 1976) stressed that behavior is of scientific interest in its own right, not as a sign or symbol of something else. In line with this, several marketing scholars have called for more in-store experiments in retailing. Grewal and Levy (2007) suggest, based on their review of articles published in *Journal of Retailing* over 2002–7, that measurement of "actual behavior" represents a new avenue for further research in consumer behavior. They say, "more work is needed that focus on measuring actual behavior . . . which track and observe actual movement or perhaps determine actual usage and consumption" (Grewal & Levy, 2007, p. 450). Levy et al. (2004) urge researchers to conduct more real-life field experiments to compare for alternative pricing strategies in retailing. In this realm, different concepts and methodologies from behavior analysis should be tested.

Another epistemological focus for behavior analysts has been the avoidance of formal development and testing of theories, or deductive theorizing. Marketing scientists, however, tend to emphasize deductive theory testing. However, one of the cornerstones of marketing is that the marketing mix is made up of elements such as product, price, place and promotion, classes of stimuli that can and often are explicitly used to influence consumer choice. The function of these marketing factors is dependent on consumers' environment and experienced consequences, but this process is not very well understood. The various elements that make up the marketing mix are mainly used as criteria for what is important in marketing strategy. In line with this, Davenport et al. (2011) recommend retailers to think of every offer (in-store offers, coupons etc.) as "a test", and as such to collect and use their customer data in a more sophisticated way to determine the effectiveness of various promotional efforts on consumer choice behavior. Finally, Shankar et al. (2011) claim that *controlled experiments* are needed to test the effectiveness of different aisle placement and shelf positions, as well to understand the usage situation and effectiveness of new technologies and in-store promotional instruments (such as in-store TV, shelf-talkers, and shopping carts). They say, "the model of how shopper marketing works is still a black box. . . . This . . . calls for effective ways to study shoppers in their 'natural habitats' compared to florescent-lit 'lab' environments. That is, more field studies are needed to supplement lab studies and validate the results from the lab studies" (p. 39). Descriptive consumer behavior analytic research and findings can be used to criticize armchair theorizing in marketing; when data deviates from theory or when research becomes too focused on the model instead of the true subject matter, consumer behavior.

The degree of decision-making in the store also suggests there is a considerable upside in doing more in-store experiments. According to POPAI (Point-of-Purchase Advertising International) data, more than 70% of the brand decisions are made after the shopper enters the store (Liljenwall, 2004). Furthermore, many shopping trips take place without a shopping list or any planning from home (Thomas & Garland, 2004). Many consumers therefore use a store's environment and its shelves as cues for what to buy. This suggests that retailers could benefit greatly from an active retailing approach (see Sorensen, 2009) grounded in insight and intelligence derived from behavior analysis of in-store consumer behavior. As retailers continue to invest in their own private labels, shopper behavior insight will also be important to grow these product lines through active retailing.

The importance of in-store applied behavior analysis

Research in behavior analysis has produced many useful applications in terms of methods to predict or control behavior. Applied behavior analysis is now used effectively in many important and diverse areas such as developmental disabilities, problem behavior, education and organizations. On the other hand, the field has "gotten stuck" in developmental disabilities. For example, 60% of data-based articles published in the *Journal of Applied Behavior Analysis*, the field's flagship periodical, from 2001 to 2005 were in this area of research (Woods et al., 2006) and this trend does not seem to be changing. Applied behavior analysis is therefore, unfortunately, not as relevant to society in general as many analysts in the field would like, but the potential is vast. Today, many countries and markets have shown signs of an economic downturn, which has led to more fierce competition among retailers and subsequently a lower turnover and margins. *Overstoring* is thus a challenge in more and more markets (Grewal et al., 2007), which means a disproportional increase in the number of retailers in relation to the growth in the population. With declining growth from new customers entering the store, further growth can only be achieved if existing customers buy more, or start buying more quality brands (growing the *share of wallet* – see e.g. Nitzberg, 2009). That is to use in-store applied behavior analysis to extract more surplus from consumers once they are in the store, for instance boosting sales by more effective aisle and display management strategies (Bezawada et al., 2009). This prompts retailers to focus on in-store merchandising and promotion, which again requires deep understanding of in-store shopping behavior.

In-depth knowledge of in-store consumer behavior is also crucial for brand manufacturers. They have already realized that traditional advertising has lost its traditional effect as consumers are bombarded with marketing messages and tend to zap between TV channels in commercial breaks more than ever before. Fast-moving consumer goods (FMCGs) firms have responded to this development by increasing their sales and trade promotions budgets at the expense of traditional advertising. According to Gomez et al. (2007), trade promotions spending in the US supermarket industry increased eightfold in the period 1996 to 2007, and accounted in 2007 for approximately 70% of a manufacturer's marketing budget. It has become the second-largest manufacturer expense after the cost of goods in the US supermarket industry (Gomez et al., 2007). To maximize return on investment (ROI) from such increased expenses, brand manufacturers need all necessary information on how consumers behave in the store, where they walk and stop, where, when and how they evaluate products as they shop, and how they can most effectively be influenced during their shopping. The increase of trade promotions spending in the US illustrates that reaching customers at the right time and in the right zone of the store is among the cornerstones of modern marketing of FMCGs. Consumer behavior analysis is most appropriate when the behavior-environment relationship is located in the same space and time. This is especially the case if extraneous variables in the retail environment can be controlled, as with in-store experiments. Unlike with mass advertising, there are no or few intermediaries (e.g., changes in budget, advertisements from other manufacturers, or word of mouth) between consumers noticing the interventions in-store and their response.

An introduction to the literature: consumer behavior analysis in stores

Retailers are close to the consumers, have the point-of-sale data on consumer behavior and should thus be in a good position to understand consumer behavior. Despite this, many retailers seem to ignore in-store behaviors (Sorensen, 2009). An explanation found in the literature is that retailers gain more in terms of profits by concentrating on rebates, slotting fees, and other promotional allowances from manufacturers, or even real estate, than the margins derived from sales (see, for instance, Sorensen, 2009). This picture fits well with our own experiences, and may thus partly explain why many retailers do not know a lot about the actual in-store behavior of their customers. These retailers are thus operating their stores based on feelings and common intuition rather than facts and experimentation. However, rules of thumb should be derived from data-driven and fact-based analysis, not convention or lore (Davenport et al., 2011).

Retailers' merchandising practices are also influenced heavily by leading manufacturers through various inducements, such as programs of product placements and payments for shelf space (Gomez et al., 2007; Dulsrud & Jacobsen, 2009). Since some placements and activities are associated with higher costs, manufacturers need to understand their effectiveness. Leading manufacturers thus spend a vast amount of resources to analyze and understand in-store consumer behavior – despite their distance from the behavioral scene, which is controlled by the retailers. Although these efforts have enabled manufacturers to gain a lot of proprietary knowledge, most of this insight is unfortunately unavailable from public sources. A good example is Proctor &

Gamble who built a consumer village in St. Bernard including a convenient-sized store which also stocks non-Proctor & Gamble products (Fasig, 2009). Thousands of shoppers volunteer each year to do in the village what they do at home and in their regular grocery store, but in front of a camera and a two-way mirror. The P&G village conducts as many as 450 studies a year (op.cit).

Rigorous academic experiments on in-store consumer behavior conducted in cooperation with retailers and/or manufacturers in "real" retail stores are much less common than laboratory experiments. The academic in-store experimental literature is limited as most studies are conducted by businesses for their own use (Sigurdsson et al., 2009); therefore, the reliability and validity of these findings are not known. It can be difficult for academics to gain access to stores and there can also be problems of contextual control as salespeople sometimes misunderstand the scientific purpose of the research. However, the amount of published research is increasing (see e.g. Chandon et al., 2009; Gaur & Fisher, 2005; Sigurdsson et al., 2010; Sigurdsson et al., 2010; Sigurdsson et al., 2011a, 2011b; Sigurdsson et al., 2009; Stratton & Werner, 2013). There are also growing opportunities for research with new technologies (e.g. radio-frequency identification (RFID) and digital in-store promotional instruments/vehicles) and improvement of experimental procedures and techniques. Application of new technologies has made it possible to shed light on some types of in-store consumer behaviors that have been difficult to measure earlier. For instance, Larson et al. (2005) collected field data on grocery store shopping paths using RFID tags located on individual customers' shopping carts. The results from their study dispel certain myths about shopper travel behavior that common intuition perpetuates, including behavior related to aisles, end-cap displays, and the "racetrack". Combining data on shopping paths with purchase data has also generated new insight, for instance on how the presence of other consumers in a store zone affects consumers' tendency to visit that zone and shop there (see Hui et al., 2009). The in-store use of wireless eye-tracking equipment in consumer behavior experiments is another example. A recent study sheds new light on consumers' visual attention when searching for a particular product or brand in a grocery store, and examines in particular how package design features are influencing visual attention and how shape and contrast dominate the initial phase of searching (see Clement et al., 2013).

A recent in-store experiment has also provided insight into how retailers can increase sales by several hundred percent for a brand on display. The sales potential offered by displays (under the assumption that the display has a sales-inducing design) is common knowledge in the retail industry, but very little academic work has elaborated on aspects of improving the displays' attention-capturing abilities. Nordfält (2011) observed more than 13,500 customers approaching special displays and found, for instance through design manipulation, that a retailer can increase the sales by as much as 977% by changing from one display design to a design much more effective in directing consumers' observational behavior. Thus, an in-store consumer behavior analysis helps retailers improve the effectiveness of various displays just by observing and analyzing consumers' reactions to different displays' design.

Since in-store experiments are rather costly and time-consuming, some researchers find it more beneficial to use readily available store-level data in their behavioral analyses (which enables ease of analysis). The study by Bezawada et al. (2009) represents an example. They used store-level data from a major retail chain to study the effects of aisle and display placements on cross-category brand sales, while controlling for the effects of marketing-mix activities. They were able to do so since their data (collected from 160 stores) dispelled variations in both aisle and display placements from store to store (spatial distance data). In this study, aisle placements were measured by distance between aisle locations of the two studied categories in the store, while display placement was represented by the distance of a brand's display from the aisles containing the product categories. Since the retail chain provided detailed information on aisle and display placements for the two chosen product categories in each store, as well as the appropriate store-level scanner data, their research objective could be fulfilled by using a combination of store-level spatial distance data and store-level scanner data.

Nevertheless, although a combination of spatial data and scanner data fulfilled the data needed for this particular study, such data are not optimal for all studies concentrating on understanding in-store consumer behavior or testing the effect of various in-store stimuli on the buying behavior of individual shoppers. The research objective will determine what type of data, and hence data collection strategies, are most appropriate in each study.

The lab: on the importance of good collaboration with different retailers

In in-store experimental analysis the store is the main laboratory. To perform an in-store consumer behavior analysis, researchers need permission from the retailer to use its premises as a research setting. Such permission is probably easier to obtain for studies that are built on research designs that do not involve experimental manipulation of one or several of the marketing-mix variables. In such cases, observations and/or interviews of customers in the store might be enough, resulting in a reduced need to coordinate various interventions with the retailer. An example of such a study is Vanhuele and Dreze (2002) who ran an in-store survey that measured consumers' memory for prices immediately after the consumers picked a product from the shelf. Experimental studies involving manipulation of one or several of the marketing-mix elements are more demanding as they require more coordination with the retailer. Also the retailers, in some cases, incur some additional costs and/or lose some incremental revenues because of the experiment. Relevant manipulations include, among others, experimenting with *product placement* (e.g. shelf position, number of facings, and the use of special displays), *retail prices* (coupons, rebates, other types of price promotions), *in-store communication* (shelf-talkers, posters, video etc.), and/or *retail atmospherics* (scent, lighting, music etc.). The retailer might experience a loss of gross margins on sold products as well as sales volumes during such experiments. Sigurdsson et al. (2011b) show for instance that sales of candy (high glycemic carbohydrates – HGC) decreased when the interventions in their study were introduced (involving displaying more healthy products at the cash register and thus moving the candy away from this zone). They also found sales of their HGC remained fairly stable throughout the remainder of the study and that sales of these items were 29% lower during the follow-up period than in the initial baseline period.

Sigurdsson et al. (2014) in a more recent in-store experiment dealt with other types of challenges, outside their control, which ultimately could have reduced the store manager's motivation for participating in their research project. In the middle of their in-store experiment it came as a surprise for both the researchers and the store manager that the store lost money on every sold item of the target product (a can of preserved high-quality fish balls). Hence, the retail chain was selling the target product below its purchase price, and the reason was a national price tactic scheme developed by the chain management aimed at getting a better ranking in the grocery price comparisons performed by the biggest Norwegian newspaper. Since the ultimate behavioral aim of the experiment was to increase the sales of the target product, which was achieved, the financial outcome was an even bigger loss for the retail store. When the store manager realized the situation, she was not as enthusiastic about the experiment as earlier. However, due to a strong and positive relationship developed over a long time between the researchers and the store manager, the experiment continued following the same procedures and research design as outlined initially. What we learn from this example is to scrutinize all aspects that might affect the conduct of the experiment in the planning and research design phase of an in-store experiment – including aspects that might affect the store manager's motivation for supporting the experiment.

The retailer might also experience some frustration among regular customers if changes in the retail environment caused by the experiment make it harder for the individual customer to find a given product. Furthermore, the retailer might lose revenue from its suppliers if the experiment involves using retail space that otherwise could have been sold to manufacturers (a form of alternative costs). Hence, retailers must be willing to accept even a small short-term loss as the price of new insight. This is probably more achievable in periods of economic prosperity than in economic downturns, and more likely to be acceptable for profitable retailers compared to retailers struggling with achieving acceptable profits from their operations. This is what we have experienced in Norway over the last couple of years. The stores belonging to Co-op in Norway that we have collaborated with over a long time span have recently gone from rather large operating profits to considerable operating losses due to a much more competitive retail market characterized by low market growth. The retailer's response has been cost-cutting programs with a particular emphasis on reducing personnel costs through the implementation of best practice routines aimed at increasing efficiency, which eventually will result in a reduction of the number of work hours needed to operate the store. With fewer working hours to operate the store, the risk is that the store managers become *less experiment-friendly*. However, we have managed to run new experiments indicating that acceptance of negative consequences (short-term losses, more work etc.) is more likely if there exists a close bond between the researchers and involved store managers.

Although many barriers can be overcome by developing and nurturing a close relationship with the store managers, in-store experiments might in some cases meet challenges that neither the researcher nor the store manager can control. For example, an intervention representing a higher or lower price on a product during an in-store experiment might sound easy, but can be rather complex in practice, especially if short-term price reductions are planned to take place in some but not all of the retail chain's stores. Nationwide uniform pricing strategies combined with centralized systems and procedures for updating prices might in fact represent too big a challenge for even a good relationship to overcome.

Method triangulation: different types of methodology, data, and philosophy

Many researchers find it useful to combine different methods and data to examine consumer behavior more thoroughly. We also suggest the possibility of using a different philosophy of science in a research program. The in-store experimental research field is no exception as both *method triangulation* and *data triangulation* might enhance the validity of the experiment. Collecting the same type of data from both similar and different contexts using the same methodology (*data triangulation*) offers, for instance, the opportunity to cross-validate the results. One way is to verify or falsify generalizable trends detected in one data set through data triangulation (see Oppermann, 2000). For example, one could conduct a similar experiment in one or more comparable retail stores to check if similar trends can be observed elsewhere and if they are consistent. A researcher could also conduct an identical experiment in other types of retail stores (size, location (mall, rural, or downtown), store types etc.) than the one used as the experimental setting for the initial study to see if similar trends can be observed. In grocery retailing the retailing formats are most often grouped into hard discount stores, soft discount stores, supermarkets and hypermarkets, and customers loyal to one format (e.g. high-quality customers) might show slightly different behaviors than those loyal to other formats (e.g. price sensitivity, time used in the store, fill-in versus stock-up etc.). The only way to verify whether the results derived from experiments conducted in one store format also apply to other formats is to run similar experiments in stores belonging to different retail formats. This has been done in the studies by Sigurdsson et al. (e.g., 2011a, 2014), who have run identical in-store experiments in both convenience stores and discount stores. Researchers are also encouraged to validate trends detected in data sets from one country's markets with results from data sets acquired from other countries' markets using the same method, as well as to validate the results across products. Sigurdsson et al. (2011a, 2011b, 2014) have used the latter approach extensively in their in-store marketing studies. They ran experiments in both Iceland and Norway and experimented with different type of target brands to examine the effect of their manipulations and in-store interventions.

While data triangulation can verify or falsify the results from one experimental setting, method triangulation enables researchers to analyze the research question from multiple perspectives. In fact, information gathered through different methods is in some cases required to obtain a full picture of what goes on at the point of purchase. There are many methods to select from, including observational techniques, transactional data (bar-code scanning data and loyalty card data), and in-store interviews. In addition, technologies such as RFID and eye-tracking equipment offer further insights into shopping behavior that supplement more traditional methods (Uncles, 2010). A relatively new eye-tracking study has for instance added new insight to the extant literature on the effect of more shelf facings and different shelf positions (see Chandon et al., 2009). Apart from confirming the results obtained in earlier studies that increased display size (number of facings a brand gets in a shelf) has a positive effect on sales, their measurement of both consumer brand consideration and choice demonstrated that attention gains from shelf position do not always improve consumers' evaluation of a brand. This difference between attention and evaluation had not been anticipated in the literature. With eye-tracking data they found that vertical shelf position, in particular, directly influenced brand evaluation (after controlling for attention), and shelf position (low, middle, or top shelves) can either strengthen or weaken the positive impact of higher attention. In other words, higher numbers of facings (resulting from increased visual attention) improve consideration and choice, while visual attention gained by positioning the brand on one of the middle shelves does not (Chandon et al., 2009).

Although the eye-tracking data in this study were not gathered in real stores, but by recruiting participants at shopping centers and seating them so that they could look at different planograms (brands displayed on a supermarket shelf), the findings still demonstrate that eye-tracking compared to sales tracking provides different types of insight. Hence, a more fine-grained picture of the effects of in-store marketing at the point of purchase would require a combination of different types of data and thus the use of more than one research method.

Method triangulation has also proven useful to detect anomalies between what consumers *say* (in interviews and questionnaire surveys) and what they *actually do* (real behavior). The experimental study by Sigurdsson et al. (2011b) involving bananas illustrates how consumer intentions do not always transform into actual behavior. Their survey data showed that consumers had very positive attitudes towards fruit and vegetable consumption and intended to buy more, and most of the participants in their consumer survey also agreed, both in closed and open questions, that in-store interventions of the type they conducted were important and necessary. Despite this, the results from their in-store experiment deviated substantially from the outcome of the survey, in that it was unsuccessful in changing consumers' buying behavior of bananas in the stores. Their findings resemble those presented in Achabal et al. (1987) who explored the effects of nutrition point-of-purchase displays on consumer attitudes towards the purchase of fresh products. Customers claimed that the perceived nutrition of the products was of significant importance during the buying decision-making but still the displays had little or no effect on the purchasing behavior of the customers.

As long as triangulation increases our confidence in the empirical results (which it does as long as the results are more or less congruent) or gives us a more fine-grained picture of consumer' behaviors at the point of purchase, we should strive for research designs comprising different methodologies and data sets in behavior analysis of in-store consumer behavior. This has been called for by Shankar et al. (2011) who say that one needs to go beyond behavioral data (such as panel data and loyalty data) to get a 360-degree view of the shopper. Hence, they recommend that other types of data (e.g. survey data) should supplement behavioral data, so that the data collectively offer a better view into shopping patterns. Research in consumer behavior analysis (e.g. Foxall, 2013; Sigurdsson, 2013) has delineated the uses of extensional environmental contingencies and intentional ascriptions (whether verbalized in first, second, or third person) for consumer description, prediction, and control. One important exploration in this direction has been to detect the limits of mainstream behavior analysis (or radical behaviorism as portrayed by Skinner and his followers) when it comes to complex behaviors that are under the influences of many endogenic contingencies in the marketplace. In this regard, Foxall (2013) has created intentional behaviorism; a critical interpretative device that gives the researcher several conceptual layers in dealing with the complexities of consumer choice ranging from the extensional to the intentional. This is important for socially responsible marketing as firms need to focus on the long-term needs and wants of the consumer. In terms of healthy food marketing, if we interpret a particular consumer situation as such that a particular individual wants (*intentional inner behavior*) to eat healthier but does not do so (*behavior*) then the researcher can interpret this as a problem of self-control as the consumer might be better off in behavioral economic terms. Operant behavior is functional and the focus should be on experimental analysis in the environment, but it adds to that explanatory system to have richer data in terms of first-person verbal behavior (e.g. interviews) and third-person observations (e.g. behavioral recording in stores).

The quest for extensive experimentation in stores: large retailers have comprehensive internal databases

Some retailers have considerable quantities of data to draw upon to understand consumer choice. Tesco, Co-op, and Metro, along with other big European retailers, have as part of their loyalty/reward programs built internal databases that are extremely comprehensive and which combine demographics with transactional data. Every time a customer swipes his or her loyalty card at the checkout, information is captured about the basket of goods bought, the frequency of buying, and responsiveness to price and promotions, among others (Uncles, 2010). In fact, loyalty programs generate a ton of data based on shopping patterns at the point of sale. Retailers that gather that information can then act upon the insight it provides as long as they do some data crunching. Such actions include increasing in-store promotions, changing the store layout, adjusting pricing, targeting promotions etc. Since these retailers also have in-store data on the promotion environment at the time when purchases are made (Gedenk et al., 2010), including both in-store and out-of-store promotions, it gives them an opportunity to scrutinize in more detail the effects of various promotions on purchasing behavior, at least when it comes to the household level. Furthermore, the possession of the purchase history of each loyalty card member opens up potential for more one-to-one marketing and targeted promotions. Customers showing no purchasing behavior in a particular category may be stimulated to make a purchase through a targeted coupon with a considerable discount. The British retailer Tesco, for instance, has for a long time focused on increasing sales to regular customers and enhancing loyalty with targeted coupons offers delivered through its Clubcard program. According to Davenport et al. (2011), Tesco's analysis of purchase information belonging to their Clubcard members has provided insight for more sophisticated targeted coupons. As a result, Clubcard members buying diapers for the first time not only get coupons for baby wipes and toys, but also for beer. "Data analysis revealed that new fathers tend to buy more beers, because they are spending less time at the pub" (Davenport et al., 2011, p. 4). Tesco's aim has not only been to expand the range of customer purchases through targeted coupons, but also to target regular customers with deals on products they usually buy. The result of these carefully executed offers has according to Davenport et al. (2011) been that Tesco and its in-house consultant Dunnhumby has achieved redemption rates ranging from 8% to 14% – which they claim is far higher than the 1% or 2% seen elsewhere in the grocery industry. Similarly, the German retailer group Metro has its Payback loyalty program (for more details, see Gedenk et al., 2010, p. 353) and the Norwegian retailer group Co-op has its Co-op Member Program – both with a potential of delivering valuable data for promotion analysis and planning, as well as consumer insight on other areas of interest for the retailers.

Retailers differ in their use of loyalty scheme data to understand behaviors, and the degree to which they experimentally test the effects of various initiatives (e.g. promotions) on consumer purchasing behavior. It is only a few years ago that Co-op in Norway first started to crunch their massive loyalty data for one-to-one communication purposes. To do this Co-op received valuable analytical assistance from Dunnhumby, which clearly illustrates the complexity of making some sense out of huge amounts of consumer purchase data. With help from Dunnhumby, Co-op was able to develop insights based on shopping data gathered from more than 3 million baskets every week (dunnhumby.com/norge). To turn such large batches of data into useful information requires expertise in, for instance, data mining and using appropriate software that looks for patterns.

Dunnhumby also provided assistance when Co-op needed more information when they discovered that a large share of their regular customers stopped visiting one of its hypermarkets due to traffic and parking challenges in 2012. The hypermarket was located in what has become the largest shopping mall in the northern part of Norway, and the data revealed that customers who had left Co-op during the 1.5-year construction phase were mainly those appreciating quality and not those who were price-sensitive. Such information is indeed critical, and helped Co-op find the right tactics to win back their lost customers.

Although loyalty programs generate tons of behavioral data, these data have clear limitations. First, the retailer is only able to capture consumer purchase behavior at the household level and not at the individual level. Second, only transactions made by cardholders are relevant for behavioral analyses. Purchases made by non-members have less value. Furthermore, if the cardholder forgets to swipe his or her card at the checkout, which happens regularly, and if the checkout personnel do not remind the cardholder, the data for this particular shopping trip will be lost. The same is true if the cardholder leaves the loyalty card at home or in the car. Consequently, the purchasing history of this cardholder will not be complete. Loyalty data are also restricted to limited product categories and one retailer (Shankar et al., 2011). In sum, loyalty data captured and stored in the retailers' databases only represent a part of the picture of what goes on at the point of purchase. For those reasons, loyalty and transactional data will not give a full 360-degree view of the shopper (Shankar et al., 2011).

The need for more systematic approaches

The in-store experimental studies reported in the literature have so far to a large extent been ad hoc and context specific. Experimental studies performed in a retail chain's grocery stores in one country (such as the study by Sigurdsson et al., 2011b) may provide useful information for the retail chain and the involved store managers, in particular, but will not tell us whether similar behavioral responses can be expected in other grocery stores in the same country or abroad. To establish some useful industry norms, a more systematic approach has been called for in the literature (see Uncles, 2010). This would require more extensive experimental studies to be conducted, where researchers from several countries collaborate using the same experimental design and procedures.

Another aspect is that society evolves, resulting in changes in a consumer's life, needs, wants and desires, as well as their behavioral choices (Uncles, 2010). Consumer patterns have for instance changed after the economic crisis. As Simon Hay, global CEO of Dunnhumby, puts it:

> There has been a definite shift in consumption pattern post the economic crisis. Retail markets around the world have seen a shift to increasing frequency of shopping and smaller baskets. This is a direct result of people wanting to keep a greater control on their budget and buying food only when they need it.
>
> *(Borpuzari, 2014)*

In such a perspective, there will always be a need for in-store consumer analysis to examine the impact of such changes on existing knowledge of consumers' behavior at the point of purchase. Hence, existing knowledge needs to be challenged and re-tested over time to ensure continued effectiveness (Davenport et al., 2011).

References

Achabal, D. D., McIntyre, S. H., Bell, C. H., & Tucker, N. (1987). The effects of nutrition P-O-P signs on consumer attitudes and behavior, *Journal of Retailing*, 63, 9–24.

Art, T. and Garland, R. (2004). Grocery shopping: List and non-list usage, *Marketing Intelligence & Planning*, 22, 6/7, 623–635.

Bezawada, R., Balachander, S., Kannan, P. K., & Shankar, V. (2009). Cross-category effects of aisle and display placement: A spatial modeling approach and insight, *Journal of Marketing*, 73 (May), 99–117.

Borpuzari, P. (2014). Understanding the customer psyche – An interview with Simon Hay, global CEO of Dunnhumby, Entrepreneur, *entrepreneurindia.in*, 7 January 2014.

Chandon, P., Hutchinson, J. W., Bradlow, E. T., & Young, S. H. (2009). Does in-store marketing work? Effects of the number and position of shelf facings on brand attention and evaluation at the point of purchase, *Journal of Marketing*, 73, 1–17.

Clement, J., Kristensen, T., & Grønhaug, K. (2013). Understanding consumers' in-store visual perception: The influence of package design features on visual attention, *Journal of Retailing and Consumer Services*, 20, 2, 234–239.

Davenport, T. H., Mule, L. D., & J. Lucker. (2011). Know what your customers want before they do, *Harvard Business Review*, December, 84–92.

Fasig, L. B. (2009). At Procter & Gamble's village, a peek into shopper behavior, Cincinnati Business Courier, *bizjournals.com*, published online March 30, 2009.

Dulsrud, A., & Jacobsen, E. (2009). In-store marketing as a Mode of Discipline, *J Consumer Policy*, 32, 203–218.

Dunnhumby.com/norge: *About Dunnhumby Norge* (Accessed 5 February 2014).

Foxall, G. R. (2013). Intentionality, symbol, and situation in the interpretation of consumer choice, *Marketing Theory*, *13*, 105–127.

Gaur, V., & Fisher, M. L. (2005). In-store experiments to determine the impact of price on sales, *Production and Operations Management*, *14*, 377–387.

Gedenk, K., Neslin, S. A., & Ailawadi, K. L. (2010). Sales promotion, in Krafft, M. & Mantrala, M. K. (eds.). *Retailing in the 21st Century – Current and Future Trends*, Heidelberg: Springer Berlin, 345–359.

Gomez, M. I., Rao, V. R., & McLaughlin, E.W. (2007). Empirical analysis of budget and allocation of trade promotions in the U.S. supermarket industry, *Journal of Marketing Research*: August, *44*, 3, 410–424.

Grewal, D., & Levy, M. (2007). Retailing research: Past, present, and future, *Journal of Retailing*, 83, 4, 447–464.

Hui, S. K., Fader, P. S., & Bradlow, E. T. (2009). Testing behavioral hypotheses using an integrated model of grocery store shopping path and purchase behavior, *Journal of Consumer Research*, 36, 478–493.

Larson, J. S., Bradlow, E. T., & and Fader, P. S. (2005). An exploratory look at supermarket shopping paths, *International Journal of Research in Marketing*, 22, 4, 395–414.

Levy, M., Grewal, D., Kopalle, P. K., & Hess, J. D. (2004). Emerging trends in retail pricing practice: Implications for research, *Journal of Retailing*, 80, 3, XIII–XXI.

Liljenwall, R. (ed.) (2004). *The Power of Point-of-Purchase Advertising: Marketing at Retail*. Washington, DC: Point-of-Purchase Advertising International (POPAI).

Nitzberg, M. (2009). Putting the shopper in your shopper marketing strategy, *Shopper Marketing*, June 17 [downloaded at http://www.visualise.ie/wp content/uploads/2011/03/ Dunnhumby-Putting-the-Shopper-in-Your-Shopper-Marketing-Strategy.pdf].

Nordfält, J. (2011). Improving the attention-capturing ability of special displays with the combination effect and the design effect, *Journal of Retailing and Consumer Services*, 18, 3, 169–173.

Oppermann, M. (2000). Triangulation – A methodological discussion, *Int. J. Tourism Res.*, 2, 141–146.

Shankar, V., Inman, J. J., Mantrala, M., Kelley, E., & Rizley, R. (2011). Innovations in shopper marketing: Current insights and future research issues, *Journal of Retailing*, 87S, 1, S29–S42.

Sigurdsson, V. (2013). Commentary on consumer behavior analysis and ascription of intentionality to the explanation of consumer choice, *Marketing Theory*, 13, 133–135.

Sigurdsson, V., Engilbertsson, H., & Foxall, G. (2010). The effects of a point-of-purchase display on relative sales: An in-store experimental evaluation, *Journal of Organizational Behavior Management*, 30, 222–233.

Sigurdsson, V., Foxall, G., & Saevarsson, H. (2010). In-store experimental approach to pricing and consumer behavior, *Journal of Organizational Behavior Management*, 30, 234–246.

Sigurdsson, V., Larsen, N. M., & Gunnarsson, D. (2011a). The behavioral economics of neutral and upward sloping demand curves in retailing, *The Service Industries Journal*, 31, 2543–2558. doi: 10.1080/02642069.2011.531127

Sigurdsson, V., Larsen, N. M., & Gunnarsson, D. (2011b). An in-store experimental analysis of consumers' selection of fruits and vegetables, *The Service Industries Journal*, 31, 2587–2602. doi: 10.1080/02642069.2011.531126

Sigurdsson, V., Larsen, N. M., & Gunnarsson, D. (2014). Healthy food products at the point of purchase: An in-store experimental analysis, *Journal of Applied Behavior Analysis*, 47, 151–154.

Sigurdsson, V., Sævarsson, H., & Foxall, G. (2009). Brand-placement and consumer choice: An in-store experiment, *Journal of Applied Behavior Analysis*, 42, 741–744.

Skinner, B. F. (1953). *Science and Human Behavior*. New York: Macmillan.

Skinner, B. F. (1976). *About Behaviorism*. New York: Vintage Books.

Sorensen, H. (2009). *Inside the Mind of the Shopper*. Upper Saddle River, NJ: Pearson Education.

Stratton, J. P., & Werner, M. J. (2013). Consumer behavior analysis of fair trade coffee: Evidence from field research, *Psychological Record*, 63, 363–374.

Thomas, A., & Garland, R. (2004). Grocery shopping: List and non-list usage, *Marketing Intelligence & Planning*, 22, 6/7, 623–635.

Uncles, M. D. (2010). Understanding retail customers, in Krafft, M. & Mantrala, M. K. (eds.). *Retailing in the 21st Century – Current and Future Trends*. Heidelberg: Springer Berlin, 159–173.

Vanhuele, M., & Dreze, X. (2002). Measuring the price knowledge shoppers bring to the store, *Journal of Marketing*, 66(4), 72–85.

Woods, D. W., Miltenberger, R. G., & Carr, J. E. (2006). Introduction to the special section on clinical behavior analysis, *Journal of Applied Behavior Analysis*, 39(4), 407–411.

4

Behavior analysis of online consumer behavior

Valdimar Sigurdsson, Nils Magne Larsen,
and R. G. Vishnu Menon

Introduction

As online shopping becomes more and more omnipresent, both practitioners and consumer behavior scholars should gain more insight into online consumer behavior. A question of growing interest is how choices made online differ from those made in a traditional brick-and-mortar store (i.e., offline store). Despite in-store consumer behavior analysis in the offline world, researchers have done rather few studies on online consumer behavior from a behavioral perspective. This is unfortunate given the increasing emphasis on decision-making on the Internet and online stores, as well as amplified opportunities for experimentation and data gathering in this respect. There exist enormous opportunities in both lab and online field experimentation in consumer behavior analysis as the web may have the potential to enable behavior analysts and marketing scientists to research important behavioral contingencies related to online purchase behavior faster and with more detail compared with the traditional offline environment. Applied behavior analysis emphasizes behavior-environment relationships of social importance, mostly studied with within-subject experimental designs (Baer et al., 1987). What is most striking, though, is the lack of applied behavior analysis in digital consumer marketing.

Although experimental psychology research in dynamic computer-generated environments has been called for since the early 1990s (e.g., Brehmer and Dörner, 1993; DiFonzo et al., 1998), similar requests were added much later in proposed agendas for e-commerce research (e.g., Parasuraman & Zinkhan, 2002). Nevertheless, the use of experiments has been regarded as a promising approach for research on online consumer behavior and the effectiveness of online retail practices. As Parasuraman and Zinkhan (2002: 292) note, a field experiment "could be used to understand which promotional strategy is most effective on a company's Web site". They also recommend the use of laboratory experiments to "test theories and understand causal relationships" related to e-commerce issues. Due to the profound effect that the Internet has had in reducing the physical constraints on pricing, communication etc., combined with an increase in marketing noise and advertising clutter, firms have also been recommended to test various forms of their marketing or advertising stimuli using experimental design techniques. As Almquist and Wyner (2001) put it, an online retailer can change the prices and promotion of products it offers every minute of the day, as well as change the color of banner ads, the tone of promotional messages and the text in outbound e-mails with relative ease. Since scientific experimentation will allow firms to better communicate with their customers, Almquist and Wyner (2001) are convinced that it is only a matter of time before experimental designs are widely adopted in most industries.

The importance of reinforcement in digital media

The advent of the Internet has resulted in an exponential rise of reinforcement rates. Operant conditioning and environmental control over behavior online is necessary to retain customers. This involves an increase or decrease of behavior, e.g., in terms of frequency or time, depending on the consequences that follow behavioral response. This is represented by the three-term contingency (Skinner, 1953):

$$S^D -> R -> S^{r+/-}$$

where S^D represents the discriminative stimulus for consequences that are contingent on behavior that takes place in its presence, and R is a response that is either reinforced (S^{r+}) or punished (S^{r-}). All stimuli, or events, that follow a particular defined behavior and strengthen it (e.g., frequency or duration) are called reinforcers. All such stimuli that weaken the behavior are named aversive or punishing. Some consequences are classified as neutral, as they do not influence the magnitude of the behavior they follow (e.g., Skinner, 1976). Consumers today have more options to choose from than ever before. The technology today has produced products that can deliver reinforcement at high rates (Daniels, 2001). A positive reinforcement is pivotal in modifying behavior in an online environment. Today, consumers have so many opportunities to engage in activities that produce high rates of positive reinforcements that they move quickly from those that don't provide enough positive reinforcement to those that do. Surfing the Internet is one of the activities that provides high positive reinforcement at a rapid rate. Consumers spend long periods of time surfing the Internet, evaluating different products and eventually purchasing those which give high rates of positive reinforcement.

The most common method of changing the frequency or time of a particular behavior is to use reinforcement or punishment. When behavior is strengthened or weakened in this way, it is presumed that it affects neuronal relationships in the brain that make the activity possible (Carlson, 1998). In most circumstances there are changes in the environment or stimuli that increase the probability of a particular behavior that goes before the change (positive reinforcement). Likewise, avoidance or escape from some stimuli can increase behavior (negative reinforcement). When behavior has been increased with reinforcement (positive or negative) which is then taken away, the behavior should decrease in frequency. This decrease in behavior strength as a function of responses without reinforcement is called extinction. Just as there are stimuli which increase behavioral frequency when present after a particular behavior, there are also stimuli that lower behavior strength when present after the behavior has happened (positive punishment). Likewise, it is possible to lower behavior frequency by removing reinforcement after the target behavior is performed (negative punishment).

The three-term contingency entails molecular-discrete analysis suitable to describe simple environment-behavior relationships (e.g., effects of the price of brand A on it being bought) but does not handle competing environmental influences (the effects of the price of brand Y on the buying of brand X) very well (e.g., Herrnstein, 1997). This is an important limitation, as it is possible to have implicitly the same effect on behavior as direct reinforcement and punishment of the target behavior have by increasing the reinforcement or punishment for other (competing) behavior than the target behavior. This is hard to conceptualize from the standpoint of the three-term contingency alone, but can easily be represented by the matching law (Herrnstein, 1961, 1970), which looks at all behavior as choice:

$$\frac{B_a}{B_a + B_b} = \frac{R_a}{R_a + R_b}, \tag{1}$$

The matching law states that relative behavior (e.g., response rate) matches its relative reinforcement in equilibrium. It is within the framework of relativity of response and matching that behavioral contrast (Reynolds, 1961) can be understood. It is called positive contrast when the frequency of the target behavior, that is not directly influenced, increases as other behavior decreases. A negative contrast is the opposite, when the frequency of the target behavior declines when another response increases. The rapidity of reinforcements is clearly advantageous and a threat to businesses that sell consumer products. Since the rate of changing behavior is associated with the rate of reinforcement, attracting consumers depends on how much reinforcement a product delivers. In the current digital environment where the levels of reinforcement are accelerating, if the purpose is to influence behavior, then it is mandatory to provide higher levels of reinforcement. To provide appropriate reinforcement, it is imperative that we understand the factors that drive consumer behavior. It is possible to use many independent variables for the generalized matching equation (Baum, 1974, 1979; Lander & Irwin, 1968). These can, for example, be variables that research has shown affect behavior such as rate, amount, immediacy and quality of the reinforcers or response effort (for a review see Fisher & Mazur, 1997). To account for this within the framework of the generalized matching equation, it is possible to use the concatenated generalized matching equation (Equation 2):

$$\log \frac{B_a}{B_b} = a_r \log\left(\frac{R_a}{R_b}\right) + a_m \log\left(\frac{M_a}{M_b}\right) + a_q \log\left(\frac{Q_a}{Q_b}\right) + a_d \log\left(\frac{D_b}{D_a}\right) + \log c \tag{2}$$

where R, M, Q and D represent reinforcer frequency, amount, quality and delay. If it is possible to assume that the effects of the independent variables do not interact, then the concatenated generalized matching law can be relevant and useful when researching the effects of two or more independent variables (Landson et al., 2003). Behavior analytical experimentation is the best way to research the effects of R, M, Q and D on consumer behavior online, in one way or another, as our survey of the literature reveals (see Table 4.1).

Online firms following a pragmatic empiricist tradition

Hantula (2005) argues that the Internet has been subject to a series of experimental efforts since retailers and consumers started to appear in this technology-mediated environment. One reason is that the Internet provides an unprecedented opportunity for measuring human online behavior. Online firms and practitioners were as such among the first to conduct experiments online, driven by their search for more effective websites. Following a *pragmatic empiricist tradition* (Hantula, 2005: 103) and using A/B testing, many firms online have adopted a *data-driven culture*. Such firms are running frequent experiments and are using the experimental results as a major input for making operative and/or strategic decisions (Kohavi et al., 2009). This approach gives hard figures behind the suggested changes or improvements. Hence, such firms have understood that a customer's response to different actions and initiatives can be tested rather quickly and at a very low cost online, giving them critical knowledge about the business value of the ideas that such actions are based upon. As Kohavi et al. (2009) note, the culture of experimentation at

Amazon, where data trumps intuition, has allowed Amazon to innovate quickly and effectively. A/B testing at Amazon ten years ago included experimenting with new home page design, moving features around the page, different algorithms for recommendations, changing search relevance rankings etc. (Kohavi & Round, 2004). Newly published research has revealed that firms emphasizing decision-making based on data and business analytics ("data-driven decision-making") show higher performance (see Brynjolfsson et al., 2011).

Online marketing environment: a perfect arena for controlled field experiments

One of the main advantages of online retail field experiments is that it is much easier to assign consumers randomly to different treatment conditions. This is a precondition for an experiment to facilitate causal interpretation since it eliminates potential systematic differences across treatment conditions due to extraneous factors associated with the test subjects (Perdue & Summers, 1986). As long as a randomization algorithm and software using the output of this algorithm are in place (e.g., at the retailer's website), test subjects will randomly be assigned to the different treatment conditions automatically (for more details, see Kohavi et al., 2009). However, it is not very easy to achieve this in physical field experiments in retailing. It is, for example, rather difficult to change the position of a target product on the shelves in a physical experimental retail store from one customer to the next, or to change store layout, in-store promotion or the layout or location of special displays containing the target product, from one customer to another – without having customers standing and queuing. For these reasons, sequential experiments, like those using an alternating-treatments design, are most applicable under such conditions (see, e.g., Sigurdsson et al., 2011, 2014). Instead of randomly assigning test subjects to different treatments, multiple interventions are here evaluated by rapidly interchanging interventions in a random sequence (the order of treatments can be randomized).

Since the online context represents a technology-mediated environment, consumers will be unaware of their participation in an experiment. This is a clear strength since human subjects tend to modify behavior when they are aware of their participation in an experiment (the Hawthorn effect). This is one of the hardest biases to eliminate in a research design involving human subjects, and could at worst lead to skewed results. It would require noticeably less resources (time and money) to acquire large enough sample sizes in an online field experiment compared to a laboratory study or a field experiment involving consumers in a physical retail environment. As Parasuraman and Zinkhan (2002: 292) state, "one advantage of the Internet is that . . . field experiments can be implemented quickly, with relatively little expense". Large samples typically decrease the standard error and bring more representativeness into the sample and also offer greater test sensitivity than smaller samples, and as such improve the statistical power. Another advantage is that results of the experiment are obtained quickly (op. cit.) using clickstream data and transactional data. The online marketing environment is therefore a perfect arena for true controlled experiments.

Hantula (2005) argues that the gap between the laboratory and the field experimental work on e-commerce issues is further narrowed when real websites are used as stimuli and participants access these and complete measures in a laboratory. According to Hantula, this creates a blurring of boundaries between laboratory and real life, which he claims is among the most interesting aspect of experiments in e-commerce from a methodological standpoint. Since the experimental environment and real life "become indistinguishable when both occur on the same type of computer, running the same interfaces to perform the same tasks" (Hantula, 2005: 104), the general concern related to experimental situations might as such be muted. In the same vein, DiFonzo et al. (1998) argue that dynamic computer-generated environments that subjects interact with in the laboratory provide higher experimental realism and thus increasing external validity. However, potential biases attributed to the fact that participants are aware of their participation in a laboratory are not necessarily neutralized. Nevertheless, the electronic environment challenges some of the common assumptions in experimental studies regarding rigor, relevance and artifact (Hantula, 2005).

Gregg and Walczak (2008) argue that online marketplaces, such as eBay, can be exploited as experimental laboratories for testing a variety of hypotheses about purchasing behavior online. They say:

> As researchers attempt to make their research more relevant to practitioners . . . it may be necessary to measure actual purchase behavior. eBay and other online marketplaces provide researchers with platforms that can be used to demonstrate the real-world value in dollars of alternative e-image factors such as website designs, product attributes, and information content to practitioners. The ability to conduct controlled real-world experiments using the large pool of online consumers as subjects could potentially be a great asset to researchers wishing to avoid the potential biases of laboratory or survey research and the limitations of secondary data studies.
>
> *(Gregg and Walczak, 2008: 661–2)*

See Kraut et al. (2004) and Reips (2000) for an in-depth discussion of the advantages and disadvantages of online behavioral research.

Frequently researched digital marketing issues

The literature consists of many experimental studies conducted online that provide relevant findings and implications for firms operating in a digital marketing environment. Although all of these studies use experimental techniques, there is a great diversity among them, and they are not all done in strict behavior analytical fashion, as we want to give a broader picture of possible experimental research.

The following paragraphs represent an attempt to illustrate this diversity, but also to show how the different experimental studies can be structured based on the development of the e-commerce field over the past 20 years or so. Even (if the number of studies referred to are many) with this high number of examples, the list is still not fully comprehensive. The studies are sorted under the following themes (Table 4.1).

Web design issues. Before consumers had access to high-speed broadband, speeding up delivery of online content, *download delays* (delay to reinforcement) was regarded as one of the most irritating aspects of using the Internet. The adoption and use of rich media (quality of reinforcement) technologies (animations, audio, video etc.) on websites created even more challenges, until a growing broadband penetration made download times no longer a critical issue in online retailing for most consumers, at least in the Western world. Research on the role of download time in various issues related to consumers' perceptions and opinions in digital environments appeared in scientific journals around 2000. Rajala and Hantula (2000) performed a laboratory experiment where they tested the effect of delay time related to the search feedback message (whether the store had a particular CD in stock) on the visiting and purchase behavior of participants shopping for CDs in a five-store simulated Internet mall. This study was replicated and extended by DiClemente and Hantula (2003). After the participants had performed their tasks in the simulated Internet mall, they were asked to complete a consumer-satisfaction survey so that

Table 4.1 Experimental studies on digital marketing, 1999–2013

Themes	Author(s)/year(s)
Web design issues	Rajala and Hantula (2000)
	DiClemente and Hantula (2003)
	Hong, Thong and Tam (2004)
	Martin, Sherrard and Wentzel (2005)
	Rose, Meuter and Curran (2005)
	Gregg and Walczak (2008)
	Wu, Cheng and Yen (2008)
Trust, risk and privacy issues	Pires, Stanton and Eckford (2004)
	Yousafzai, Pallister and Foxall (2005)
	Hui, Teo and Lee (2007)
	Tsay, Engelman, Cranor and Scquisti (2011)
	Beresford, Kübler and Preibusch (2012)
Clicking behavior	Murphy (1999)
	Hofacker and Murphy (2009)
Online retail practices	Teo, Oh, Liu and Wei (2003)
	Hantula and Bryant (2005)
	Yang and Lai (2006)
	Fagerstrøm (2010)
	Fagerstrøm and Ghinea (2011)
	Fagerstrøm, Arntzen and Foxall (2011)
	Sigurdsson, Menon, Sigurdarson, Kristjansson and Foxall (2013)
Online advertising issues	Sundar and Kim (2005)
	Moe (2006)
	Catterjee (2008)
	Rosenkrans (2009)
	Goldfarb and Tucker (2011)
	Jung, Min and Kellaris (2011)
Online community issues	Algesheimer, Dholakia and Herrman (2005)
	Algesheimer, Borle, Dholakia and Singh (2010)
Web 2.0 issues and social media marketing issues	Wang, Baker, Wagner and Wakefield (2007)
	Zhu and Tan (2007)
	Aral and Walker (2011)
	Chen, Wang and Xie (2011)
	Bakshy, Rosenn, Marlow and Adamic (2012)
	Bakshy, Eckles, Yan and Rosenn (2012)

the effect of delay times on store preferences could be analyzed. Rose et al. (2005) continued a stream of studies on download delay. Through a laboratory experiment, involving modified real-world retail Web pages, they explored how download times affect the overall evaluation of an e-retailer in terms of attitude towards the page, if the retailer could have designed the website to have it load faster, and how much of the delay was caused by the design of the page. They also measured attitudes towards the delay and perceived waiting time. Hong et al. (2004), on the other hand, performed a laboratory experiment to investigate the fit between informational format (different methods for organizing product information) and shopping task (searching tasks versus browsing tasks), to examine its influence on consumers' shopping performance and perceptions of shopping experience. Research on text versus images is also among the Web design issues where researchers have used experimental methods. Martin et al. (2005) performed a laboratory experiment to explore what could be optimal website designs, in terms of the level of complexity in visual design and level of verbal complexity, for consumers seeking sensations. Wu et al. (2008) studied the effect of atmospheric factors such as music and color on participants' emotional responses and subsequent shopping behavior in an online store setting, using a laboratory experiment. Furthermore, Gregg and Walczak (2008) experimented with two real-world online auction businesses on eBay to examine the effect of creating a more professional online e-image on consumers' willingness to transact with the firm, and the prices they were willing to pay for the firm's goods and services.

Trust, risk and privacy issues. Although trust, risk and privacy issues are still important research themes in e-commerce, they were even more important in earlier phases of the Internet when consumers' transactional behaviors were hampered due to high perceived risk and a lack of privacy and trust. These issues have therefore attracted many researchers in the past, and continue to do so. Yousafzai et al. (2005), for example, examined the effectiveness of potential trust-building strategies for e-banking and their impact on online customers' perceptions of the trustworthiness of the bank. Pires et al. (2004), on the other hand, performed a laboratory experiment to examine whether the perceived risk of online purchasing varies with the participants' online purchasing experiences, level of purchase decision involvement, and the nature of the product to be purchased. Hui et al. (2007) performed a field experiment that assessed the value of privacy assurances on a website. The visitors' behavioral responses towards two types of privacy assurances were observed, and they tested whether the existence of a privacy statement could induce more subjects to disclose their personal information and the effect of a monetary incentive on disclosure. Hui et al. (2007) studied the relationship between the amount of information requested by a firm online and the rate of disclosure, as well as the influence of sensitivity on disclosure. Tsay et al. (2011) designed an experiment to determine whether a more prominent display of privacy information on a website will cause consumers to incorporate privacy considerations into their online purchasing decisions. (They assumed that consumers would tend to buy from online retailers who better protect their privacy.) Beresford et al. (2012) conducted an experiment giving participants the choice to buy a DVD from one of two online stores. By having one store consistently require more sensitive personal data than the other, but at the same time having lower prices, they were able to measure consumers' willingness to pay for privacy.

Clicking behavior. Consumers' clicking behavior has always interested practitioners and users because of the consumer insight that can be derived from clickstream analyses. Murphy (1999) examined website visitors' clicking behavior and ran experiments testing whether the specific location or size of graphics induces more or less clicking on the text links (clickthroughs). Researchers and practitioners were at this point concerned with how a website could be designed so that visitors would stay longer and click on several links. Hofacker and Murphy (2009) ran a field experiment on a live website to find out if visitors are more likely to click on the last link in the navigation menu than middle items. They randomly assigned site visitors, who arrived on the experimental page during the course of their normal web activity, to one of their five treatment conditions. Such knowledge allows firms to improve the efficiency of their website and thus their performance.

Online retail practices. Several experimental studies have explored online retail practices. Hantula and Bryant (2005), for instance, explored delivery issues using a simulated online store where participants ordered music CDs and bargained for delivery time and fees. Their study extends research on the behavioral economics of consumer choice to consider the issue of delivery in the online environment. Yang and Lai (2006), on the other hand, performed a field experiment to examine and compare the performance of three product bundling strategies. The three product bundling strategies tested were based on different types of data collected on online shopping behaviors, which were a strategy based on order data only, a strategy based on browsing data only, and a strategy based on both browsing and shopping cart data. Teo et al. (2003) performed a controlled laboratory experiment to investigate the effects of interactivity level on Web users' attitudes towards commercial websites. The study by Fagerstrøm (2010) introduced the concept of motivating operations (MO) to the field of online consumer behavior and examined the motivating impact of antecedent stimuli on online purchasing. The results indicate that the concept of MO is applicable to the analysis of the motivating impact of antecedent stimuli on consumer purchase behavior. In another study, Fagerstrøm et al. (2011) performed a simulated online shopping experiment to study how environmental contingencies, such as free shipping, can be used in online stores to develop brand loyalty. Fagerstrøm and Ghinea (2011) studied approach/avoidance behavior by examining the motivating impact of price relative to online recommendation at the point of online purchase. Sigurdsson et al. (2013) conducted an e-mail marketing experiment to examine how consumer responses online can be shaped by incorporating informational (social) and utilitarian stimuli with a clear call for action into the firm's outbound e-mail newsletters.

Online advertising issues. Many researchers have investigated issues related to the effectiveness of online ads. Although this still seems to be a highly active research field, some of the research efforts the last few years have been directed towards ads on social networks. Sundar and Kim (2005) performed a laboratory experiment where they examined the effects of structural features of online ads, such as animation, ad shape and level of interactivity, on attitudes towards the ad and product, perceived product knowledge and perceived product involvement. Moe (2006) performed a field experiment to examine online consumers' reaction to pop-up promotions in terms of clickthroughs and website-exit behavior. In this study the experimental design involved manipulation of the timing of pop-up messages (delay time) and time of day. Chatterjee (2008) used a laboratory experiment to examine the enduring effects of banner and pop-up ad exposures on brand memory and attitudes towards the brand. In this study, the experimental design involved manipulation of advertisement size (large versus small) and ad exposure format (intrusive versus voluntary). The participant's unaided recall and recognition were measured after a seven-day delay. Rosenkrans (2009) performed a field experiment on a newspaper's website to determine whether online, interactive, rich media advertising results in more user interactivity (in terms of clickthroughs) than non-interactive, rich media ads. Goldfarb and Tucker (2011) conducted a field experiment to explore what influences the effectiveness of different ad campaigns. Online consumers were randomly exposed to ads on different websites and their preferences towards the advertiser's product and their purchase intent were measured through a survey. Issues that were explored were the link between contextually targeted advertising (product matching the website) and purchase intent, and the link between high-visibility (obtrusive) advertising (e.g., pop-up ads, floating ads) and purchase intent. Jung et al. (2011) used a laboratory experiment to examine how brand attitudes and purchase intentions are affected by online ads' level of entertainment value. The entertainment value of an ad was in this study manipulated using two different online ads that generated different levels of entertaining values (a game ad composed of interactive quizzes versus a banner ad).

Online community issues. Before social websites such as Facebook grew in popularity, many online firms built up customer community facilities on their own websites to achieve higher levels of engagement with the firm's products and brands. In many of these communities customers were motivated to help each other and to actively recruit others to the community (Algesheimer et al., 2005). In this period many firms therefore spent a large share of their online marketing budget on customer community marketing programs. Experimental studies are also found among the research investigating online community issues. Algesheimer et al. (2010) employed data from a field experiment conducted by eBay Germany to investigate the link between customers' participation in a firm's online community and the firm's e-mail-based invitations (with incentives). As experimental manipulation, half of the selected customers were invited to participate in one or more of the communities on eBay through an e-mail message (with an incentive to those posting a message), and the behavior of all selected customers was then tracked for a period of one year after the e-mail invitations.

Web 2.0 issues and social media marketing issues. The phrase Web 2.0 is most often attributed to Tim O'Reilly, who described Web 2.0 as "developments in online technology that enable interactive capabilities in an environment characterized by user control, freedom, and dialogue" (Tuten and Solomon, 2013: 7). Web 2.0 technology allows for user-generated content and user participation on retailers' websites. These advances in technology have given firms an opportunity to facilitate and manage customer social interactions more effectively on their own websites (e.g. by allowing users to post their reviews on products and or experiences). Chen et al. (2011) used a unique natural experimental setting resulting from information policy shifts at Amazon.com to examine the differential impact of word-of-mouth (other consumers' opinions) and observational learning (other consumers' actions) on product sales, as well as to examine the lifetime effects and interaction effects of word-of-mouth and observational learning. Web 2.0 platforms (social media), such as Facebook (launched in 2004) and Twitter (2007), led to major changes in how consumers spent their time online and the amount of time spent on generating, sharing and consuming other users' content online. The potential of reaching thousands or millions of consumers through online word-of-mouth by creating a buzz encouraged many firms to experiment with viral marketing campaigns. In addition, firms gradually became involved in social media marketing (in terms of targeted promotional messages on social media platforms), which has the potential to increase awareness, influence desire, encourage trial, facilitate purchase and cement brand loyalty (Tuten & Solomon, 2013). Experiments have been used as a research method in studies on blog advertising. Zhu and Tan (2007), for instance, used fictitious blogs to investigate the impact of communicator expertise, advertising intent and product involvement on blog advertising effectiveness. Wang et al. (2007) investigated how social cues inherent in avatars influence customers' affect and shopping value. Through a laboratory experiment on a service organization's website they manipulated the sociability of the website by varying the number and type of human-like social cues incorporated into the website. Aral and Walker (2011) conducted a field experiment on Facebook to examine how firms can create word-of mouth peer influence by incorporating viral features into their products and marketing campaigns. In this experiment experimental users were enabled to use passive broadcast and active-personalized viral message capabilities to exchange messages with their friends/network. The treatment groups used different versions of an application, enabling the user to automatically notify their network when a certain action was performed and to send personalized referrals or invitations to their peers to install the application. Bakshy et al. (2012) examined the role of social networks in online information diffusion with a field experiment. Their experiment evaluated the extent to which exposure to a URL on the news feed increases an individual's propensity to share that URL. Tucker (2012) explored the effectiveness of social advertising using data from field experiments of different ads on Facebook. This study estimates the combined effect of social targeting and social cues in ads, and involves ad campaigns targeted to three different groups and the use of various kinds of normative and informational social influence. The effectiveness is measured in terms of click-through rate per ad impression and connection rate (the number of likes). Bakshy et al. (2012) conducted two field experiments on Facebook to identify the effect of social cues on consumer responses to ads (in terms of clicks on the linked content and liking the advertised page). In their first experiment they used sponsored story ad units where the main treatment was the number of peers shown. In their second experiment they examined the effect of having a social cue alongside an ad, and how the effect of social cues in advertising varies with the strength of the relationship between the consumer and affiliated peer.

A multi-method approach

Online behavioral data tell a story about what consumers *do* online, not what they *say*. However, for further insights and understanding of rule-following behavior regarding a particular behavior, both types of data might be needed. Building up knowledge of environmental contingencies attached to shopping cart abandonment (which reduces sales conversion rates) illustrates how behavioral data complement interview data. Consumers' verbal responses have for instance been collected by Forrester Research (see Hult et al., 2010) through interviews. Primary drivers were found to be frustration with the amount of shipping costs, unpreparedness to make a purchase and a desire to comparison-shop for a lower price. Faced with high abandonment rates, a natural step for a firm would traditionally be to improve the checkout process. However, as the Forrester consumer interview data suggest, this is only part of the answer. Another way of studying abandonment is to study the behavior of the visitors abandoning the shopping carts, and in particular the degree to which they are returning to the site to buy the items within a specific time. Such data have given a new perspective on shopping cart abandonment, namely that not all abandonments are bad and that 75 percent of these customers will come back multiple times as they consider the purchase or return to abandon again (Nicholls, 2011).

Measuring online shopping behavior of individual customers over a longer time span therefore allows for the collection of new types of information. As Nicholls (2011) reports, the data suggest that customers are using shopping carts to store items they might buy in the future and that shopping cart abandonment is an important part of the normal buying cycle for many customers. However, he also reports that the first 12 hours after abandonment are critical as the majority of customers that are going to buy do so within a 12-hour time span. By adding an element of experimentation, Nicholls (2011) demonstrates increases in the total return rate through remarketing, and that abandoners spend more on the site when remarketed. In attempts to broaden the literature in this area abandoners could, as experimental units, be subject to more controlled experiments. An example is to test the effect on total return rate, sales and plus sales using utilitarian (functional/economic) stimuli and informational stimuli.

Online behavioral analysis in future research

The current chapter has revealed that online behavioral experiments have a clear, definite advantage in understanding online consumers. As illustrated, these experiments can be enhanced further through a multi-method approach, using in-depth qualitative research, consumer observations and the latest technology. The current chapter has also pointed towards some of the many opportunities of online experimentation in relation to consumer behavior analysis. The Internet has the potential to assist behavior analysts as well as marketers to research important behavioral contingencies faster and possibly with more detail compared with what can be done in a traditional offline environment. Still, despite the advantages, the literature is somewhat scarce when it comes to efforts to study online consumer behavior through more rigorous behavioral experiments. More behavioral researchers are therefore encouraged to use the online arena as an experimental setting for their upcoming experiments. Such a move is crucial in establishing further methodological ground for the application of operant psychology (behavior analysis) to consumer and social marketing.

References

Algesheimer, R., Borle, S., Dholakia, U. M., and Singh, S. S. (2010). The impact of customer community participation on customer behaviors: An empirical investigation. *Marketing Science*, 29(4), 756–769. DOI: 10.1287/mksc.1090.0555

Algesheimer, R., Dholakia, U. M., and Herrman, A. (2005). The social influence of brand community: Evidence from European car clubs. *Journal of Marketing*, 69(3), 19–34. DOI: 10.1509/jmkg.69.3.19.66363

Almquist, E., and Wyner, G. (2001). Boost your marketing ROI with experimental design. *Harvard Business Review*, October, 5–11.

Aral, S., and Walker, D. (2011). Creating social contagion through viral product design: A randomized trial of peer influence in networks. *Management Science*, 57(9), 1623–1639. DOI: 10.1287/mnsc.1110.1421

Baer, D. M., Wolf, M. M., and Risley, T. R. (1987). Some still-current dimensions of applied behavior analysis. *Journal of Applied Behavior Analysis*, 20, 313–327.

Bakshy, E., Rosenn, I., Marlow, C., and Adamic, L. (2012). The role of social networks in information diffusion. *Proceedings of the 21st ACM Conference on the World Wide Web*, 519–528. DOI: 10.1145/2187836.2187907

Bakshy, E., Eckles, D., Yan, R., and Rosenn, I. (2012). Social influence in social advertising: Evidence from field experiments. *Proceedings of the 13th ACM Conference on Electronic Commerce*, ACM, 146–161. DOI: 10.1145/2229012.2229027

Baum, W. M. (1974). On two types of deviation from the matching law: Bias and undermatching. *Journal of the Experimental Analysis of Behavior*, 22, 231–242.

Baum, W. M. (1979). Matching, undermatching, and overmatching in studies on choice. *Journal of the Experimental Analysis of Behavior*, 32, 269–281.

Beresford, A. R., Kübler, D. and Preibusch, S. (2012). Unwillingness to pay for privacy: A field experiment. *Economics Letters*, 117(1), 25–27. DOI: 10.1016/j.econlet.2012.04.077

Brehmer, B., and Dörner, D. (1993). Experiments with computer-simulated microworlds: Escaping both the narrow straits of the laboratory and the deep blue of the field study. *Computers in Human Behavior*, 9, 171–184. DOI: 10.1016/0747-5632(93)90005-D

Brynjolfsson, E., Hitt, L. and Kim, H. (2011). Strength in numbers: How does data-driven decision-making affect firm performance? (December 6, 2011). *ICIS 2011 Proceedings*. Paper 13.

Carlson, A. C. (1998). *Physiology of Behavior* (6th ed.). Boston: Allyn & Bacon.

Chatterjee, P. (2008). Are unclicked ads wasted? Enduring effects of banner and pop-up ad exposures on brand memory and attitudes. *Journal of Electronic Commerce Research*, 9(1), 51–61.

Chen, Y., Wang, Q., and Xie, J. (2011). Online social interactions: A natural experiment on word of mouth versus observational learning. *Journal of Marketing Research*, 48(2), 238–254. DOI: 10.1509/jmkr.48.2.238

Daniels, A. C. (2001). *Other People's Habits: How to Use Positive Reinforcement to Bring Out the Best in People Around You*. New York: McGraw Hill.

DiClemente, D. F., and Hantula, D. A. (2003). Optimal foraging online: Increasing sensitivity to delay. *Psychology & Marketing*, 20(9), 785–809.

DiFonzo, N., Hantula, D. A., and Bordia, P. (1998). Microworlds for experimental research: Having your (control and collection) cake, and realism too. *Behavior Research, Methods, Instruments & Computers*, 30(2), 278–286.

Fagerstrøm, A. (2010). The motivating effect of antecedent stimuli on the web shop: A conjoint analysis of the impact of antecedent stimuli at the point of online purchase. *Journal of Organizational Behavior Management*, 30, 199–220.

Fagerstrøm, A., and Ghinea, G (2011). On the motivating impact of price and online recommendations at the point of online purchase. *International Journal of Information Management*, 31, 103–110.

Fagerstrøm, A., Arntzen, E., and Foxall, G. R. (2011) A study of preferences in a simulated online shopping experiment. *The Service Industry Journal*, 31(15), 2603–2615. DOI: 10.1080/02642069.2011.531121

Fisher, W. W., and Mazur, J. E. (1997). Basic and applied research on choice responding. *Journal of Applied Behavior Analysis*, 30, 387–410.

Foxall, G. R. (1998). Radical behaviorist interpretation: Generating and evaluating an account of consumer behavior. *The Behavior Analyst*, 21, 321–354.

Foxall, G. R. (2001). Foundations of consumer behavior analysis. *Marketing Theory*, 1, 165–199.

Foxall, G. R. (2002). *Consumer Behavior Analysis: Critical Perspectives in Business and Management*. London and New York: Routledge.

Foxall, G. R. (2003). The behavior analysis of consumer choice: An introduction to the special issue. *Journal of Economic Psychology*, 24, 581–588.

Goldfarb, A., and Tucker, C. (2011). Online display advertising: Targeting and obtrusiveness. *Marketing Science*, 30(3), 389–404. DOI: 10.1287/mksc.1100.0583

Gregg, D. G., and Walczak, S. (2008). Dressing your online auction business for success: An experiment comparing two eBay businesses. *MIS Quarterly*, 32(3), 653–670.

Hantula, D. A. (2005). Guest editorial: Experiments in e-commerce. *Psychology & Marketing*, 22(2), 103–107. DOI: 10.1002/mar.20049

Hantula, D. A., and Bryant, K. (2005). Delay discounting determines delivery fees in an e-commerce simulation: A behavioral economic perspective. *Psychology & Marketing*, 22(2), 153–161. DOI: 10.1002/mar.20052

Herrnstein, R. J. (1961). Relative and absolute strength of response as a function of frequency of reinforcement. *Journal of the Experimental Analysis of Behavior*, 4, 267–272.

Herrnstein, R. J. (1970). On the law of effect. *Journal of the Experimental Analysis of Behavior*, 13, 243–266.

Herrnstein, R. J. (1997). *The Matching Law: Papers in Psychology and Economics*. (H. Rachlin and D. Laibson Ed.). New York: Russell Sage Foundation.

Hofacker, C. F., and Murphy, J. (2009). Consumer web page search, clicking behavior and reaction time. *Direct Marketing: An International Journal*, 3(2), 88–96. DOI: 10.1108/17505930910964759

Hong, W., Thong, J., and Tam, K. Y. (2004). The effects of information format and shopping task on consumers' online shopping behavior: A cognitive fit perspective. *Journal of Management Information Systems*, 21(3), 149–184.

Hui, K-L., Teo, H. H., and Lee, S-Y. T. (2007). The value of privacy assurance: An exploratory field experiment. *MIS Quarterly*, 31(1), 19–33. DOI: 10.2307/25148779

Hult, P., Evans, P. F., and McGowan, B. (2010). Understanding shopping cart abandonment, *Forrester Research*, May 20. http://www.forrester.com/Understanding+Shopping+Cart+Abandonment/fulltext/-/E-RES56827?objectid=RES56827. [Accessed 25.06.14]

Jung, J. M., Min, K. S., and Kellaris, J. J. (2011). The games people play: How the entertainment value of online ads helps or harms persuasion. *Psychology & Marketing*, 28(7), 661–681. DOI: 10.1002/mar.20406

Kohavi, R., Longbotham, R., Sommerfield, D., and Henne, R. M. (2009). Controlled experiments on the web: Survey and practical guide. *Data Min Knowl Disc* (2009) 18: 140–181. DOI: 10.1007/s10618-008-0114-1

Kohavi, R., and Round, M. (2004). *Front line internet analytics at Amazon.com*, Emetric Summit 2004. http://ai.stanford.edu/~ronnyk/emetricsAmazon.pdf. [Accessed 24.06.14]

Kraut, R., Olson, J., Banaji, M., Bruckman, A., Cohen, J., and Couper, M. (2004). Psychological research online: Report of board of scientific affairs' advisory group on the conduct of research on the Internet. *American Psychologist*, 59(2), 105–117. DOI: 10.1037/0003-066X.59.2.105

Kunkel, J. H. (1987). The future of JABA: A comment. *Journal of Applied Behavior Analysis*, 20, 329–333.

Landson, J., Davison, M., and Elliffe, D. (2003). Concurrent schedules: Reinforcer magnitude effects. *Journal of the Experimental Analysis of Behavior*, 79, 351–356.

Lander, D. G., and Irwin, R. J. (1968). Multiple schedules: Effects of the distribution of reinforcements between components on the distribution of responses between components. *Journal of the Experimental Analysis of Behavior*, 11, 517–524.

Leahey, T. H. (1997). *A History of Psychology: Main Currents in Psychological Thought*. Upper Saddle River, NJ: Prentice Hall.

Logue, A. W. (2002). The living legacy of the Harvard Pigeon Lab: Quantitative analysis in the wide world. *Journal of the Experimental Analysis of Behavior*, 77, 357–366.

Mace, F. C., and Critchfield, T. S. (2010). Translational research in behavior analysis: historical traditions and imperative for the future. *Journal of the Experimental Analysis of Behavior*, 93, 293–312.

Markin, R. J., and Narayana., C. L. (1976). Behavior control: Are consumers beyond freedom and dignity? *Advances in Consumer Research* (3rd ed.) B. B. Anderson, Ann Arbor, MI: Association for Consumer Research, 222–228.

Martin, B. A., Sherrard, M. E., and Wentzel, D. (2005). The role of sensation seeking and need for cognition on web-site evaluations: A resource-matching perspective. *Psychology & Marketing*, 22(2), 109–126. DOI: 10.1002/mar.20050

Mazur, J. E. (2010). Editorial: Translational research in JEAB. *Journal of the Experimental Analysis of Behavior*, 93, 291–292.

Moe, W. W. (2006). A field experiment to assess the interruption effect of pop-up promotions. *Journal of Interactive Marketing*, 20(1), 34–44. DOI: 10.1002/dir.20054

Murphy, J. (1999). Surfers and searchers: An examination of web-site visitors' clicking behavior. *Cornell Hotel and Restaurant Administration Quarterly*, 40(2), 84–95.

Narver, J. C., and Slater, S. F. (1990). The effect of a market orientation on business profitability. *Journal of Marketing*, 54, 20–35.

Nevin, J. A. (2008). Control, prediction, order, and the joys of research. *Journal of the Experimental Analysis of Behavior*, 89, 119–123.

Nicholls, C. (2011). The science of shopping cart abandonment. *Research Report*, Boston: The Conversion Academy.

Nord, W. R., and Peter, J. P. (1980). A behavior modification perspective on marketing. *Journal of Marketing*, 44, 36–47.

Parasuraman, A., and Zinkhan, G. M. (2002). Marketing to and serving customers through the internet: An overview and research agenda. *Journal of the Academy of Marketing Science*, 30(4), 286–295. DOI: 10.1177/009207002236906

Perdue, B. C., and Summers, J. O. (1986). Checking the success of manipulations in marketing experiments. *Journal of Marketing Research*, 23(4), 317–326. DOI: 10.2307/3151807

Peter, J. P., and Nord, W. R. (1982). A clarification and extension of operant conditioning principles in marketing. *Journal of Marketing*, 46, 102–107.

Peter, J. P., Olson, J. C., and Grunert, K. G. (1999). *Consumer Behavior and Marketing Strategy* (European Edition). London: McGraw Hill.

Pierce, W. D., and Epling, W. F. (1999). *Behavior Analysis and Learning* (2nd ed.). Upper Saddle River, NJ: Prentice Hall.

Pires, G., Stanton, J., and Eckford, A. (2004). Influences on the perceived risk of purchasing online. *Journal of Consumer Behavior*, 4(2), 118–131. DOI: 10.1002/cb.163

Rajala, A. K., and Hantula, D. A. (2000). Toward a behavioral ecology of consumption: Delay-reduction effects on foraging in a simulated internet mall. *Managerial and Decision Economics*, 21, 145–158. DOI: 10.1002/mde.979

Reips, U. D. (2000). The web experiment method: Advantages, disadvantages and solutions. In M. H. Birnbaum (Ed.). *Psychological experiments on the Internet*. San Diego: Academic Press, 89–114.

Reynolds, G. S. (1961). Behavioral contrast. *Journal of the Experimental Analysis of Behavior*, 4, 57–71.

Rose, G., Meuter, M. L., and Curran, J. (2005). On-line waiting: The role of download time and other important predictors on attitude toward e-retailers. *Psychology & Marketing*, 22(2), 127–151. DOI: 10.1002/mar.20051

Rosenkrans, G. (2009). The creativeness and effectiveness of online interactive rich media advertising. *Journal of Interactive Advertising*, 9(2), 18–31. DOI: 10.1080/15252019.2009.10722152

Rothschild, M. L., and Gaidis, W. C. (1981). Behavioral learning theory: Its relevance to marketing and promotions. *Journal of Marketing*, 45, 70–78.

Sigurdsson, V., Menon, R. G., Sigurdarson, J. P., Kristjansson, J. S., and Foxall, G. (2013). A test of the behavioral perspective model in the context of an e-mail marketing experiment. *The Psychological Record*, 63, 295–308. DOI: 10.11133/j.tpr.2013.63.2.005

Sigurdsson, V., Larsen, N. M., and Gunnarsson, D. (2011). An in-store experimental analysis of consumers' selection of fruits and vegetables. *The Services Industry Journal*, 31(15), 2587–2602. DOI: 10.1080/02642069.2011.531126

Sigurdsson, V., Larsen, N. M., and Gunnarsson, D. (2014). Healthy food products at the point of purchase – An in-store experimental analysis. *Journal of Applied Behavior Analysis*, 47(1), 1–4. DOI: 10.1002/jaba.91

Skinner, B. F. (1953). *Science and Human Behavior*. New York: Macmillan.

Skinner, B. F. (1976). *About Behaviorism*. New York: Vintage Books.

Sundar, S. S., and Kim, J. (2005). Interactivity and persuasion: Influencing attitudes with information and involvement. *Journal of Interactive Advertising*, 5(2), 5–18. DOI: 10.1080/15252019.2005.10722097

Teo, H. H., Oh, L. B., Liu, C., and Wei, K. K. (2003). An empirical study of the effects of interactivity on web user attitude. *International Journal of Human-Computer Studies*, 58(3), 283–305. DOI: 10.1016/S1071-5819(03)00008-9

Tsay, J. Y., Engelman, S., Cranor, L., and Scquisti, A. (2011). The effect of online privacy information on purchasing behavior: An experimental study. *Information Systems Research*, 22(2), 254–268. DOI: 10.1287/isre.1090.0260

Tucker, C. (2012). Social advertising. *SSRN eLibrary*. http://ssrn.com/abstract=1975897.

Tuten, T. L., and Solomon, M. R. (2013). *Social Media Marketing*. Upper Saddle River, NJ: Pearson Education.

Yang, T. C., and Lai, H. (2006). Comparison of product bundling strategies on different online shopping behaviors. *Electronic Commerce Research and Applications*, 5(4), 295–304. DOI: 10.1016/j.elerap.2006.04.006

Yousafzai, S. Y., Pallister, J. G., and Foxall, G. (2005). Strategies for building and communicating trust in electronic banking: A field experiment. *Psychology & Marketing*, 22(2), 181–201. DOI: 10.1002/mar.20054

Wang, L. C., Baker, J., Wagner, J. A., and Wakefield, K. (2007). Can a retail web site be social? *Journal of Marketing*, 71(3), 143–157. DOI: 10.1509/jmkg.71.3.143

Woods, D. W., Miltenberger, R. G., and Carr, J. E. (2006). Introduction to the special section on clinical behavior analysis. *Journal of Applied Behavior Analysis*, 39, 407–411.

Wu, C., Cheng, F., and Yen, D. C. (2008). The atmospheric factors of online storefront environment design: An empirical experiment in Taiwan. *Information & Management*, 45(7), 493–498.

Zhu, J. Y., and Tan, B. C. Y. (2007). Effectiveness of blog advertising: Impact of communicator expertise, advertising intent, and product involvement. *ICIS 2007 Proceedings*. Paper 121. http://aisel.aisnet.org/icis2007/121.

Equivalence classes and preferences in consumer choice

Erik Arntzen, Asle Fagerstrøm, and Gordon R. Foxall

Introduction

New product development

Consumers are faced with an increasing number of choices of ever-greater complexity, while, for companies, creating strong brands has become a management imperative. A recurring topic that links both of these considerations is the process by which new brands are introduced into existing product classes. Many of the generalizations about consumer brand choice were established by the work of Andrew Ehrenberg and his colleagues who point out that most consumers are not brand loyal, in the sense of purchasing a single brand 100% of the time; rather, the typical consumer of a product class buys a number of brands over time (sometimes even on the same shopping trip) (Ehrenberg, 1988). Products from this group of tried and tested brands, which is a subset of the brands that comprise the entire product class, are purchased apparently randomly (though in practice often in a structured manner) and are treated as though they were functionally equivalent. That is, the physical properties of each brand in the product class are sufficiently similar that they are closely substitutable. Each consumer's establishment of a particular consideration set of appropriate brands reflects this substitutability based on functional correspondence.

When a new brand is introduced, heavy users of the relevant product class tend to innovate by *trying* it, though whether they continue to purchase it depends on whether it measures up in practice to the demands the consumer makes of members of the product class in question. A brand that does not possess the functional characteristics of other members of the product class is likely to fail in the marketplace since the minimal expectation consumers have of a new brand is that it perform at least as well as existing members. One strength of Ehrenberg's framework of analysis is its reliance on observed patterns of consumer choice rather than speculation about the cognitive processes that might underlie preferences but which are essentially unobservable and untestable. Some of the generalizations on which such observations rest – for example, the idea that brands within the consumer's consideration set are functionally equivalent – have hitherto been untestable too. Moreover, the reasoning on which functional equivalence is attributed to brands comprising a consideration set is circular: we "know" that the brands are functionally equivalent because the consumer buys and uses them apparently interchangeably, while this pattern of behavior is sufficient to suggest that the brands must be functionally substitutable. Another question that arises is how consumers come to perceive the equivalence of existing brands in a product class and a newly introduced brand which a marketer simply claims to be a substitute for the product versions they are already using. In this chapter, we argue that consumer behavior analysis provides a way of thinking about brands that accounts for the inclusion of a new item into the consumer's consideration set.

Brand equity and brand preference

The relative importance of companies' brands has grown significantly in the past 20 years. According to a study by McDonald and Mouncey (2009), companies' brands account for over 80% of the value of organizations in the United Kingdom and United States, and 63% of the value of global organizations. Brands have, for that reason, turned out to be one of the most important assets that today's companies possess, and have become one of the top priorities for most managers. The ability to understand consumer brand choice is crucial to its legitimacy for academic marketing and equally important to marketing practice (Foxall et al., 2007). As a consequence, this has led to a large amount of brand research. According to a review paper (Keller & Lehmann, 2006), five streams of brand research have evolved in the past years: Brand positioning, corporate image and reputation, strategic brand management, brand growth, and brand performance. The focus of this study is the last of these, often referred to as brand equity.

Brand equity has been conceptualized and measured in different ways (Rego et al., 2009). One perspective is to understand and measure brand equity as the marketing effects that are attributable to a brand (Aaker, 1991). From this perspective, brand equity is measured by looking at the different outcomes from a branded product versus an unbranded one. The second perspective is to understand brand equity as the shareholders' value of the brand (Ailawadi et al., 2003). Brand equity is, from this perspective, measured by focusing on how business decisions and actions affect the company's economic value. The third, and most used, perspective is to understand and measure brand equity from a customer viewpoint. From this perspective, brand equity is understood as a result of the customers' perceptions of the marketing activity of the company and their experience over time – often referred to as customer-based brand equity (French & Smith, 2013). Brand equity is usually conceived as an aggregate measure of the strength of a brand for the consumers that make up an entire market. But we can also speak of the relationship between an individual consumer and a brand in terms of that individual's brand equity. This will be reflected in and reflect the pattern of utility maximization the consumer's behavior exhibits.

In customer-based brand equity research there is extensive use of associative model formulation, derived from cognitive psychology (Anderson & Bower, 1973; Wyer & Srull, 1989). There are a number of associative models with different underlying assumptions (e.g., Adaptive Control of Thought, Anderson, 1983; MINERVA 2, A Simulation Model of Human Memory, Hintzman, 1986; Theory of Distributed Associative Memory, Murdock, 1982; Search of Associative Memory, Raaijmakers & Shiffrin, 1981; Diffusion Model, Ratcliff, 1987), but generally they conceptualize associations as a set of nodes and links. In these models, which assume a cognitive perspective, nodes are stored information in the consumer's mind that are connected by links that vary in strength. For example, a node can be a brand (Apple™), a product (mobile phone), or an attribute (design). An association in a consumer's mind is, from this view, represented by links between two or more nodes as, for example, Apple™ – mobile phone – design.

Different research programs within consumer behavior have traditionally been labeled as (1) cognitive program, (2) behaviorist program, (3) economic program, and (4) structuralist program (Anderson, 1986). In the following we will focus on approaches within the behaviorist program. Learning psychologists have shown interest in consumer behavior (for a further discussion see DiClemente & Hantula, 2003). For example, one such program with a high impact is the program in which children and youngsters have been taught to choose healthy food (e.g., Hardman et al., 2011; Horne et al., 2011; Horne et al., 1998; Lowe & Horne, 2009; Pears et al., 2012). In general, one can divide the programs or the models that have used a behavior analytic framework to understand consumer choice into those based on classical conditioning (e.g., Bierley et al., 1985; Gorn, 1982; Janiszewski & Warlop, 1993; McSweeney & Bierley, 1984; Nord & Peter, 1980; Shimp et al., 1991; Zander, 2006) or on operant conditioning (Horne and Lowe and colleagues) or on a mix of techniques (Baker, 1999; Chen & Jiang, 2013). More recently, two different models have evolved within behavior analysis: the Behavioral Perspective Model (Foxall, 1998, 2010) and the Behavioral Ecology of Consumption (e.g., Rajala & Hantula, 2000; Smith & Hantula, 2003) have been put forward to interpret consumer choice.

The prevailing approach has been based on classical conditioning. Some researchers have argued for this in spite of the fact that there are few empirical papers showing that classical conditioning can in fact change or modify behavior within a consumer approach (Bierley et al., 1985). However, two examples of the classical conditioning program are worth mentioning. First, in a study by Shimp et al. (1991), the authors studied the effects of what they labeled as attitudes towards different kinds of brand familiarity (cola brands). They used a selection of unknown, moderately known, and well-known cola brands as conditional stimuli, while the unconditioned stimuli were four attractive water scenes. They found that conditioning of attitudes took place when the participants were aware of the contingency between the conditioned and unconditioned stimulus. Second, studies have shown that pairing a product with some preferred or disliked music can produce an association between the two (Gorn, 1982; Zander, 2006). Furthermore, Bierley et al. (1985) found that participants rated stimuli as preferable if they predicted pleasant music than if the stimuli predicted absence of music.

Another way to study variables influencing preferences in choice situations is through equivalence class formation and transfer of function, which is the approach taken in this chapter. Stimulus equivalence is defined as responding in accordance with the features of reflexivity, symmetry, and transitivity, and concepts are derived from mathematical set theory (e.g., Sidman & Tailby, 1982). Moreover, stimulus equivalence is concerned with stimulus substitutability, where different stimuli, which are not physically similar, may be members of the same class as a result of different types of conditional discrimination training (Green & Saunders, 1998). In contrast to stimulus generalization in which stimuli vary along one dimension, stimulus equivalence is a descriptive model for how arbitrarily related stimuli can become members of the same class and in many cases have the same function. Fields and colleagues used a transfer of function test to assess stimulus relatedness (Fields et al., 1993; Fields et al., 1995).

Research projects within stimulus equivalence research are studying topics such as (1) relations between stimuli that control behavior, (2) how stimuli change functions, and (3) how relations emerge without any programmed consequences. The last issue is related to the emergence of new relations and has been seen as a way behavior analysis can contribute to the study of cognition (e.g., Sidman, 1994). This means that if a certain number of relations are directly trained, a large number of relations will emerge without the arrangement of explicit reinforcement. The relation between the number of trained and emergent relations is illustrated in Figure 5.1. Furthermore, this can be expressed as trained relations = c (m−1) and emergent relations = c (m−1)^2 in which c is the number of classes and m is the number of members (Arntzen, 1999). Therefore, to arrange training and testing in such a format as is argued in this chapter gives enormous potential for getting a number of new relations for free.

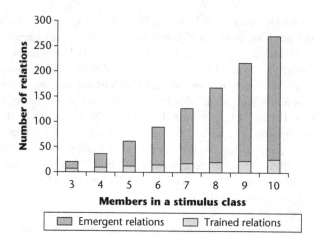

Figure 5.1   The number of trained and emergent relations

A hypothetical example of the relation between pictures of animals and corresponding names in different languages is shown in Table 5.1. The common nomenclature in this research area is that classes are labeled as numbers and members are labeled as letters. It is important to emphasize that in the example used they are already apportioning into different classes. A minimum requirement for training conditional discriminations for testing for stimulus equivalence is three members within two classes. However, it is most common to establish at least three classes as shown in Figure 5.2. In a potential three three-member class (A/B/C), in the presence of A1 (a picture of a cat) the participant is trained to pick B1 (the word cat) and not B2 (dog) or B3 (horse). In the presence of A2 (a picture of a dog), picking B2 (the word dog) is reinforced and not B1 (cat) or B3 (horse). In the presence of A3 (a picture of a horse), picking B3 (the word horse) is reinforced and not B1 (cat) or B2 (dog). Then, in the presence of B1 (the word cat), picking C1 (the word chat) is reinforced and not C2 (chien) or C3 (cheval). In the presence of B2, picking C2 is reinforced and not C1 or C3. In the presence of B3, picking C3 is reinforced and not C1 or C2. When baseline relations are established according to a mastery criterion of 90% or above (for further discussion see Arntzen, 2012), possible derived relations are tested in extinction conditions. Reflexivity is tested as A relations in the presence of A relations, and so forth. Symmetry relations are tested as BA and CB relations, while transitivity relations are tested as AC relations and global equivalence relations are tested as CA relations (e.g., Sidman & Tailby, 1982; Sidman et al., 1986).

The transfer of function can be characterized as a specific psychological function, which is explicitly established for one stimulus that participates in an equivalence relation. The same function may then transfer to the other stimuli participating in the relation without further training (e.g., Barnes-Holmes et al., 2000; Dougher et al., 1994; Roche & Barnes, 1997). Transfer of function refers to "the untrained acquisition or emergence of stimulus functions among members of stimulus classes" (Dougher & Markham, 1996, p. 139). In one study, Barnes-Holmes et al. (2000) trained potentially two three-member classes in a one-to-many (OTM) training structure (AB/AC). The A stimuli were nonsense syllables, VEK and ZID. The B stimuli were the words CANCER and HOLIDAY, and finally the A stimuli were trained to C stimuli, product labels BRAND X and BRAND Y. The participants were tested for equivalence formation following the training of conditional discriminations AB/BC. After finishing the test session, the participants were presented with two samples of cola-based soft drinks labeled BRAND X and

Table 5.1 A hypothetical example of different animal names in six different languages with pictures of the animals

Classes are indicated by numbers and members as letters. A = Pictures, B = English, C = French, D = German, E = Dutch, F = Norwegian, and G = Portuguese

Members	No. of Classes					
	1	2	3	4	5	6
A	Cat	Dog	Horse	Guinea pig	Rabbit	Hen
B	Cat	Dog	Horse	Guinea pig	Rabbit	Hen
C	Chat	Chien	Cheval	Guiné porc	Lapin	Poule
D	Katze	Hund	Pferd	Meerschweinchen	Kaninchen	Huhn
E	Kat	Hond	Hest	Cavia	Konijin	Kip
F	Katt	Hund	Hest	Marsvin	Kanin	Høne
G	Gato	Cão	Cavalo	Cobaia	Coelho	Galinha

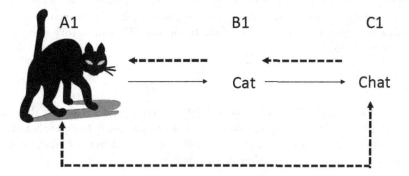

Figure 5.2 How the cat class is trained and tested

The other classes are not shown in the figure. The solid lines indicate the trained relations (AB and BC). The dashed lines indicates the tested relations. BA and CB relations indicate symmetry; AC and CA relations indicate transitivity and equivalence, respectively

BRAND Y. The results showed that when they were asked to rank the pleasantness of the colas there was a significant difference between the participants who passed the equivalence test and those who did not pass the test. They also showed in another experiment that it was possible to reverse participants' preference by reversing the conditional discrimination training.

In the current experiment, we present a stimulus equivalence approach including expansion of equivalence classes by including socially meaningful stimuli to understand consumers' brand choices. Hence, we asked if preference for specific but neutral stimuli is influenced by a test for transfer of function. First, we trained potentially three three-member classes with an OTM training structure (AB/AC). Second, we tested if the participants responded in accordance with stimulus equivalence. Third, social meaning stimuli (D) were trained to the nodal stimulus in the classes (A). Fourth, another test for responding accordance with stimulus equivalence was employed including all 12 stimuli. Finally, a preference test was arranged in which the participants were asked to pick one of three bottles of water labeled with printouts of the B1, B2, and B3 stimuli, respectively.

Method

Participants

Sixteen college students participated in the experiment: three females and 13 males. The average age of the participants was 27 years. They were recruited from the university college of the second author and they were not familiar with stimulus equivalence. The participants were informed that they could withdraw from the experimental session at any time. Each participant then read and signed an informed consent form. Finally, they were debriefed after the experimental session.

Apparatus and setting

The experimental sessions were conducted in a small, quiet room. The participants were seated in booths approximately 3.01 m² (215 × 140 cm), in front of a 45 × 90 cm table. The participants faced a wall or a window with drawn curtains. The booths were situated in two different housing locations affiliated with the laboratory, one approximately 25 m² in size and the other approximately 20 m². An HP computer, Compaq Nc 6320 PC with Windows 7 Professional 32-bit operating system, with custom-made matching-to-sample software, was used to present stimuli and record responses. The screen of the laptop was 15″, with a 16:9 aspect ratio and 1400 × 1050 resolution.

Stimuli

In Figure 5.3, the stimuli used to form potentially three three-member classes are shown, while in Figure 5.4 the stimuli used for expansion of the class size are shown. In Figure 5.3, the letters A, B, and C are the sets and the numbers are the different classes. This means that, for example, A1, B1, and C1 are within one experimenter-defined class.

Three 3-Member Classes

	1	2	3
A	ꃌ	ꆟ	θ
B	ꆌ	ꇓ	ꑤ
C	ꉧ	ꇕ	ꃮ

Figure 5.3 The abstract stimuli when forming three three-member classes

Expansion by D-stimuli

D1   D2   D3

Figure 5.4 The stimuli used as D-stimuli

Procedure

The participants were told that they should not drink anything during the 90 minutes before the start of the experiment. All participants were reminded about this approximately 120 minutes before the experiment. All participants read an information sheet that explained the broad goals of the research conducted at the laboratory, although the purpose of the experiment was not mentioned and stimulus equivalence was neither defined nor explained. Each session lasted approximately 1–2 hours for the participants. The sessions started with instructions as described below.

When seated at the computer the participants were presented with the following instructions on the computer screen:

> In a moment a stimulus will appear in the middle of the screen. Click on this by using the computer mouse. Three stimuli will then appear in three corners of the screen. Choose one of them by clicking on it with the mouse. If you choose the stimulus we have defined as correct, words like "very good," "excellent," and so on will appear on the screen. If you press a wrong stimulus, the word "wrong" will appear on the screen. At the bottom of the screen, the number of correct responses you have made will be counted. During some stages of the experiment, the computer will NOT tell you whether your choices are right or wrong. Please do your best to get everything right. Thank you and good luck!

No further instructions were given before or after the experiment started.

When the participants finished reading the instructions, they pressed a square marked "Begin" on the bottom of the touch screen to start the experiment. A trial started with the presentation of a sample stimulus in the center of the screen. Touching the sample stimulus made it disappear, and three comparison stimuli then appeared simultaneously. The program determined the positioning of the comparison stimuli randomly from trial to trial. The comparison stimuli appeared in a circular layout, 160 mm from the sample stimulus. Choosing one of the comparison stimuli led to a 500-ms programmed consequence in which "good," "excellent," and so forth was displayed, following correct class-consistent responses. Choosing an incorrect comparison stimulus was followed by the display of "wrong." Reaction time was recorded based on the interval between touching the sample stimulus and selecting a comparison stimulus, which was transformed into the inverse reaction time. The intertrial interval (ITI) was set to 1,000 ms in all phases; at the end of the feedback interval, the screen remained black. No consequences resulted from touching the screen during the ITI or presentation of the feedback.

The participants were trained to form three three-member classes with arbitrarily related stimuli in an OTM training structure (AB/AC). An overview of the four steps of the procedure is shown in Figure 5.5. We employed a simultaneous protocol with a concurrent presentation of baseline relations. In the concurrent presentation, a mix of AB and CB trials were presented in a block with 18 trials, three of each trial type. The training trials were as follows: A1/B1B2B3, A2/B1B2B3, A3/B1B2B3, A1/C1C2C3, A2/C1C2C3, and A3/C1C2C3. In all strings, the first code is the sample stimulus and the underlined comparison is the correct stimulus choice. Trials were randomly presented. Following establishment of the conditional discriminations with 100% probability of programmed consequences, the programmed consequences were thinned from 75% to 50% until 0% probability of programmed consequences. The mastery criterion was an accuracy of 90% or more within a block for all phases. Then, a test including baseline trials (AB/AC), symmetry (BA/CA), and equivalence trials (BC/CB) was implemented (Step 1). The trials tested were: A1/B1B2B3, A2B1B2B3, A3B1B2B3, A1C1C2C3, A2C1C2C3,

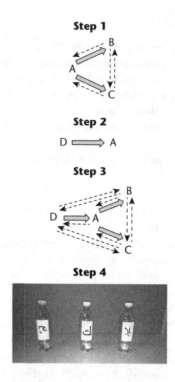

Step 1

Step 2

Step 3

Step 4

Figure 5.5 An overview of the different steps in the procedure

In Step 1, potentially three three-member classes are trained and tested. In Step 2, the D-stimuli are trained to the A-stimuli. In Step 3, all relations are tested. Finally, in Step 4, a preference for bottles of water with B-stimuli as labels is presented

A3C1C2C3 (i.e., directly trained trials), B1A1A2A3, B2A1A2A3, B3A1A2A3, C1A1A2A3, C2A1A2A3, C3A1A2A3 (i.e., symmetry trials), and B1C1C2C3, A2B1B2B3, A3B1B2B3, B1A1A2A3, B2A1A2A3, B3A1A2A3 (i.e., equivalence trials).

The test was done in extinction conditions. If the participants did not respond in accordance with the experimenter-defined classes, they were excluded from the session and thanked for their participation. If the participants responded in accordance with experimenter-defined classes, the test was followed by another training phase in which a picture of a face (smiling (D1), neutral (D2), or sour (D3)) was trained to the nodal stimulus (A1, A2, or A3) (Step 2). The training trials were as follows: D1/A1A2A3, D2/A1A2A3, D3/A1A2A3. Each trial was presented five times, which is a block of 15 trials with a criterion of 90% or above. Another test was implemented to see if the functions were transferred to all the stimuli within the class (Step 3). The trials tested were: A1/B1B2B3, A2/B1B2B3, A3/B1B2B3, A1/C1C2C3, A2/C1C2C3, A3/C1C2C3, D1/A1A2A3, D2/A1A2A3, D3/A1A2A3 (i.e., baseline trials), B1A1A2A3, B2A1A2A3, B3A1A2A3, C1A1A2A3, C2A1A2A3, C3A1A2A3, A1/D1D2D3, A2/D1D2D3, A3/D1D2D3 (i.e., symmetry trials), and B1/C1C2C3, B1/C1C2C3, B3/C1C2C3, C1/B1B2B3, C2/B1B2B3, C3/B1B2B3, D1/B1B2B3, D2/B1B2B3, D3/B1B2B3, B1/D1D2D3, B1/D1D2D3, B3/D1D2D3 (i.e., equivalence trials). The test was done in extinction conditions. After the participants had finished the test in Step 3, they were exposed to a preference test. On a table behind the computer, the experimenter placed three bottles of water, each of which had a different stimulus attached to it from the B set (B1, B2, and B3) (Step 4). The position of the bottles was randomly assigned. The participants were asked to pick a bottle and to give it to the experimenter. The participants were asked "Why did you pick that bottle?"

Results

The number of training trials when establishing the AB/BC relations varied from 150 to 600 trials with an average of 281 (see Table 5.2). The number of training trials for the extension of classes (DA training) varied between 15 and 45 trials. The lowest possible number of trials is 15. Three columns to the left of the "extension" column show the index of correct performance for baseline trials (DT), symmetry (Sym) and equivalence (EQ) in which correct performance is defined as 0.9 or higher. The three seminar columns to the right of the "extension" column show the index of baseline, symmetry, and equivalence trials after the extension training (D→A). The main findings are that the 16 participants formed equivalence classes following the OTM training of six conditional discriminations and, thus, formed three three-member classes. Furthermore, all participants formed three four-member classes following the DA training only. In the preference test after the final testing of equivalence class formation, 13 of the 16 participants picked the bottle of water labeled with the B1 stimulus. In other words, 81% of the participants showed preference for the stimulus in Class 1, the same class as the smiley face (D1).

Discussion

In summary, we used three identical bottles of water to show that it was possible to influence preference by forming equivalence classes followed by training a specific function (smiley,

Table 5.2 The number of training trials (No. of TT), trials during baseline (Bsl), indices of testing for symmetry (Sym) and equivalence (EQ) in Step 1, number of trials in extension with D-stimuli (Ext) in Step 2, indices of testing for symmetry (Sym) and equivalence (EQ), equivalence class formation (ECF) in Step 3, and whether the participants showed transfer of function (TOF) in Step 4

P#	No. of TT	Bsl	Sym	EQ	Ext	Bsl	Sym	EQ	ECF	TOF
13051	600	1.0	1.0	1.0	15	1.0	1.0	1.0	yes	yes
13052	270	1.0	1.0	1.0	30	1.0	1.0	1.0	yes	yes
13053	390	1.0	1.0	1.0	30	1.0	1.0	1.0	yes	yes
13054	330	1.0	1.0	1.0	30	1.0	1.0	1.0	yes	yes
13055	330	1.0	1.0	1.0	15	1.0	0.98	1.0	yes	yes
13056	210	1.0	1.0	0.97	30	1.0	1.0	1.0	yes	yes
13057	180	1.0	1.0	0.97	30	1.0	1.0	0.99	yes	yes
13059	240	1.0	1.0	1.0	30	0.98	0.98	0.99	yes	yes
13061	300	0.97	1.0	1.0	45	1.0	1.0	1.0	yes	yes
13062	210	1.0	1.0	1.0	15	1.0	1.0	1.0	yes	yes
13064	480	0.9	1.0	0.97	30	1.0	1.0	0.93	yes	yes
13067	180	0.9	1.0	0.97	30	1.0	1.0	0.93	yes	yes
13069	240	0.9	1.0	0.97	30	1.0	1.0	0.93	yes	yes
13058	150	1.0	0.93	0.93	15	1.0	1.0	1.0	yes	no
13060	180	1.0	1.0	1.0	30	1.0	1.0	1.0	yes	no
13068	210	0.9	1.0	0.97	30	1.0	1.0	0.93	yes	no

neutral, and sour face) to the nodal stimuli. The results showed that 13 of 16 participants (81%) picked the bottle with the B1-stimulus, indicating that the transfer of function test had influenced the preference. The present experiment replicated the previous findings on the effectiveness of using an OTM training structure in producing equivalence class formation (e.g., Arntzen et al., 2010; Arntzen & Hansen, 2011), the extension of equivalence classes (e.g., Sidman et al., 1985), and transfer of function (e.g., Barnes et al., 1995; Catania et al., 1989; Dougher & Markham, 1994; Ferro & Valero, 2007; Markham & Markham, 2002; Smyth et al., 2006). Furthermore, the results are in accordance with other studies showing that it is possible to influence preference in choice situations (Barnes-Holmes et al., 2000; Bierley et al., 1985; Gorn, 1982).

We know that consumers maximize specific combinations of utilitarian and informational reinforcement (Oliveira-Castro et al., 2015). We suggest that the unique combinations of these sources of reinforcement that consumers actually purchase form the basis of brand equity.

We have in particular established three stages in the process of symbolic learning by consumers which are most relevant to innovation in the sense of the introduction of new brands within established product classes. These three stages are: (1) the establishment of stimulus equivalences among stimuli (brands); (2) the transfer of function to an untrained stimulus (new brand); and (3) the establishment of consumer preference for the untrained stimulus. The first corresponds to consumers' perceptions of the brands that compose their consideration set, all of which exhibit stimulus equivalence. The second corresponds to the introduction of an initially neutral stimulus (untrained, the new brand) which emerges as equivalent to the established stimuli. The third is the extent to which consumers come to prefer the new brand to existing brands, at least to the extent of trying it. Whether they include the new brand in their choice sets will depend on the consequences of purchasing and consuming it. We therefore have (a) initially, a cognitive understanding of how the consumer learns the new stimulus and its equivalence to existing stimuli, and (b) the behavior analytic interpretation of how the new brand becomes accepted as part of the choice set.

We now have an explanation of how new brands come to exhibit functional equivalence to existing brands and can complete Ehrenberg's assertion of such equivalence by pointing to the processes by which functional equivalence is actually established in the marketplace.

Presumably the functional equivalence of the brands that compose a consumer's consideration set is based on the characteristics that define the product class in terms of utilitarian reinforcement while the motivating characteristics of brands reflect differences in informational reinforcement between brands. The establishment of stimulus relations between the utilitarian (functional) characteristic of the produce class and the informational reinforcement that comprises the identities of the brands that make it up is of particular interest.

Further research should include replication of the present experiment with different types of D-stimuli. We have done some pilot studies in the lab using different D-stimuli such as weather charts and monetary symbols. The results so far are quite promising but we need more participants. In addition, further experiments should include a group with neutral stimuli as D1, D2, and D3. The prediction is that the participants will pick B1, B2, and B3 with a probability of 33%. It also seems important to include a more extensive phase of training of D to A, which should be studied to see if this strengthens the relation to functional stimulus.

References

Aaker, D. A. (1991). *Managing brand equity. Capitalizing on the value of brand name.* New York: The Free Press.

Ailawadi, K. L., Lehmann, D. R., & Neslin, S. A. (2003). Revenue premium as an outcome measure of brand equity. *Journal of Marketing, 67*, 1–17.

Anderson, J. R. (1983). *The architecture of cognition.* Cambridge, MA: Harvard University Press.

Anderson, J. R., & Bower, G. H. (1973). *Human associative memory.* Hillsdale, NJ: Erlbaum.

Anderson, P. F. (1986). On method in consumer research: A critical relativist perspective. *Journal of Consumer Research, 13,* 155–173.

Arntzen, E. (1999). *Establishment of stimulus equivalence – effects of training structure and familiarity of stimuli.* Dissertation/Thesis, University of Oslo.

Arntzen, E. (2012). Training and testing parameters in formation of stimulus equivalence: Methodological issues. *European Journal of Behavior Analysis, 13,* 123–135. Retrieved from http://www.ejoba.org/.

Arntzen, E., Grondahl, T., & Eilifsen, C. (2010). The effects of different training structures in the establishment of conditional discriminations and the subsequent performance on the tests for stimulus equivalence. *The Psychological Record, 60,* 437–462. Retrieved from http://thepsychologicalrecord.siuc.edu/index.html.

Arntzen, E., & Hansen, S. (2011). Training structures and the formation of equivalence classes. *European Journal of Behavior Analysis, 12,* 483–503. Retrieved from http://www.ejoba.org/.

Baker, W. E. (1999). When can affective conditioning and mere exposure directly influence brand choice? *Journal of Advertising, XXVIII,* 31–46.

Barnes, D., Browne, M., Smeets, P. M., & Roche, B. (1995). A transfer of functions and a conditional transfer of functions through equivalence relations in three- to six-year-old children. *The Psychological Record, 45,* 405–430.

Barnes-Holmes, D., Keane, J., Barnes-Holmes, Y., & Smeets, P. M. (2000). A derived transfer of emotive functions as a means of establishing differential preferences for soft drinks. *The Psychological Record, 50,* 493–511. Retrieved from http://thepsychologicalrecord.siuc.edu/index.html.

Bierley, C., McSweeney, F. K., & Vannieuwkerk, R. (1985). Classical conditioning of preferences for stimuli. *Journal of Consumer Research, 12,* 316–323.

Catania, A. C., Horne, P. J., & Lowe, C. F. (1989). Transfer of function across members of an equivalence class. *The Analysis of Verbal Behavior, 7,* 99–110.

Chen, Y. F., & Jiang, J. H. (2013, 1–2 April 2013). *Effects of classical and operant conditioning on online consumer purchase and repurchase intention.* Paper presented at the Proceedings of 8th Asian Business Research Conference, Bangkok, Thailand.

DiClemente, D. F., & Hantula, D. A. (2003). Applied behavioral economics and consumer choice. *Journal of Economic Psychology, 24,* 589–602. doi: 10.1016/s0167-4870(03)00003-5.

Dougher, M. J., Auguston, E. M., Markham, M. R., Wulfert, E., & Greenway, D. E. (1994). The transfer of respondent eliciting and extinction functions through stimulus equivalence classes. *Journal of the Experimental Analysis of Behavior, 62,* 331–351. doi: 10.1901/jeab.1994.62-331.

Dougher, M. J., & Markham, M. R. (1994). Stimulus equivalence, functional equivalence and the transfer of function. In S. C. Hayes, L. J. Hayes, M. Sato, & K. Ono (Eds.), *Behavior analysis of language and cognition* (pp. 71–90). Reno, NV: Context Press.

Dougher, M. J., & Markham, M. R. (1996). Stimulus classes and the untrained acquisition of stimulus functions. In T. R. Zentall & P. M. Smeets (Eds.), *Stimulus class formation in humans and animals* (pp. 137–152). Amsterdam, The Netherlands: Elsevier.

Ehrenberg, A. S. C. (1988). *Repeat buying: Facts, theory and applications* (2nd ed.) London: Griffin; New York: Oxford University Press.

Ferro, R., & Valero, L. (2007). Transfer of function of visual stimuli through equivalence relations with verbal stimuli. *European Journal of Behavior Analysis, 7,* 5–14.

Fields, L., Adams, B. J., Brown, J. L., & Verhave, T. (1993). The generalization of emergent relations in equivalence classes: Stimulus substitutability. *The Psychological Record, 43,* 235–254.

Fields, L., Landon-Jimenez, D. V., Buffington, D. M., & Adams, B. J. (1995). Maintained nodal-distance effects in equivalence classes. *Journal of the Experimental Analysis of Behavior, 64,* 129–145. doi: 10.1901/jeab.1995.64-129.

Foxall, G. R. (1998). Radical behaviorist interpretation: Generating and evaluating an account of consumer behavior. *The Behavior Analyst, 21,* 321–354.

Foxall, G. R. (2010). *Interpreting consumer choice. The behavioral perspective model.* New York: Routledge.

Foxall, G. R., Oliveira-Castro, J. M., James, V. K., & Schrezenmaier, T. C. (2007). *The behavioral economics of brand choice.* New York: Palgrave Macmillan.

French, A., & Smith, G. (2013). Measuring brand association strength: A consumer based brand equity approach. *European Journal of Marketing, 47,* 1356–1367.

Gorn, G. J. (1982). The effects of music in advertising on choice behaviour. A classical conditioning approach. *Journal of Marketing, 49,* 94–101.

Green, G., & Saunders, R. R. (1998). Stimulus equivalence. In K. A. Lattal & M. Perone (Eds.), *Handbook of research methods in human operant behavior* (pp. 229–262). New York: Plenum Press.

Hardman, C. A., Horne, P. J., & Fergus Lowe, C. (2011). Effects of rewards, peer-modelling and pedometer targets on children's physical activity: A school-based intervention study. *Psychological Health, 26,* 3–21. doi: 10.1080/08870440903318119.

Hintzman, D. (1986). Schema abstraction in a multiple-trace memory model. *Psychological Review, 93,* 411–428.

Horne, P. J., Greenhalgh, J., Erjavec, M., Lowe, C. F., Viktor, S., & Whitaker, C. J. (2011). Increasing pre-school children's consumption of fruit and vegetables. A modelling and rewards intervention. *Appetite, 56,* 375–385. doi: http://dx.doi.org/10.1016/j.appet.2010.11.146.

Horne, P. J., Lowe, C. F., Bowdery, M., & Egerton, C. (1998). The way to healthy eating for children. *British Food Journal, 100,* 133–140. doi: 10.1108/00070709810207496.

Janiszewski, C., & Warlop, L. (1993). The influence of classical conditioning procedures on subsequent attention to the conditioned brand. *Journal of Consumer Research, 20,* 171–189.

Keller, K. L., & Lehmann, D. (2006). Brands and branding: Research findings and future priorities. *Marketing Science, 25,* 740–759.

Lowe, C. F., & Horne, P. J. (2009). Food dudes: Increasing children's fruit and vegetable consumption. *Cases in Public Health Communication & Marketing, 3,* 161–185. Retrieved from www.casejournal.org/volume3.

Markham, R. G., & Markham, M. R. (2002). On the role of covarying functions in stimulus class formation and transfer of function. *Journal of the Experimental Analysis of Behavior, 78,* 509–525. Retrieved from ISI:000179809700016.

McDonald, M., & Mouncey, P. (2009). *Marketing accountability: How to measure marketing effectiveness.* London: Kogan Page.

McSweeney, F. K., & Bierley, C. (1984). Recent developments in classical conditioning. *Journal of Consumer Research, 11,* 619–631.

Murdock, B. B. (1982). A theory for the storage and retrieval of item and associative information. *Psychological Review, 89,* 609–626.

Nord, W. R., & Peter, J. P. (1980). A behavior modification perspective on marketing. *Journal of Marketing, 44,* 36–47.

Oliveira-Castro, J. M., Cavalcanti, P., & Foxall, G. R. (2015). What consumers maximize: Brand choice as a function of utilitarian and informational reinforcement. *Managerial and Decision Economics*, in press. doi: 10.1002/mde.2722.

Pears, S. L., Jackson, M. C., Bertenshaw, E. J., Horne, P. J., Fergus Lowe, C., & Erjavec, M. (2012). Validation of food diaries as measures of dietary behaviour change. *Appetite, 58,* 1164–1168. doi: http://dx.doi.org/10.1016/j.appet.2012.02.017.

Raaijmakers, J. G. W., & Shiffrin, R. M. (1981). Search of associative memory. *Psychological Review, 88,* 93–134.

Rajala, A. K., & Hantula, D. A. (2000). Towards a behavioral ecology of consumption: Delay-reduction effects on foraging in a simulated internet mall. *Managerial and Decision Economics, 21,* 145–158.

Ratcliff, R. (1987). A theory of memory retrieval. *Psychological Review, 85,* 59–108.

Rego, L. L., Billett, M. T., & Morgan, N. A. (2009). Consumer-based brand equity and firm risk. *Journal of Marketing, 73,* 47–60.

Roche, B., & Barnes, D. (1997). A transformation of respondently conditioned stimulus function in accordance with arbitrarily applicable relations. *Journal of the Experimental Analysis of Behavior, 67,* 275–301. doi: 10.1901/jeab.1997.67-275.

Shimp, T. A., Stuart, E. W., & Engle, R. W. (1991). A program of classical conditioning experiments testing variations in the conditioned stimulus and context. *Journal of Consumer Research, 18,* 1–12.

Sidman, M. (1994). *Equivalence relations and behavior: A research story.* Boston, MA: Authors Cooperative.

Sidman, M., Kirk, B., & Willson-Morris, M. (1985). Six members stimulus classes generated by conditional-discrimination procedures. *Journal of the Experimental Analysis of Behavior, 43,* 21–42. doi: 10.1901/jeab.1985.43-21.

Sidman, M., & Tailby, W. (1982). Conditional discrimination vs. matching to sample: An expansion of the testing paradigm. *Journal of the Experimental Analysis of Behavior, 37,* 5–22. doi: 10.1901/jeab.1982.37-5.

Sidman, M., Willson-Morris, M., & Kirk, B. (1986). Matching-to-sample procedures and the development of equivalence relations: The role of naming. *Analysis and Intervention in Developmental Disabilities, 6,* 1–29. doi: 10.1016/0270-4684(86)90003-0.

Smith, C. L., & Hantula, D. A. (2003). Pricing effects on foraging in a simulated internet shopping mall. *Journal of Economic Psychology, 24*, 653–674. doi: http://dx.doi.org/10.1016/S0167-4870(03)00007-2.

Smyth, S., Barnes-Holmes, D., & Forsyth, J. P. (2006). A derived transfer of simple discrimination and self-reported arousal functions in spider fearful and non-spider-fearful participants. *Journal of the Experimental Analysis of Behavior, 85*, 223–246.

Wyer, R. S., & Srull, T. K. (1989). Person memory and judgement. *Psychological Review*, 58–83. Retrieved from http://www.apa.org/pubs/journals/rev/.

Zander, M. F. (2006). Musical influences in advertising: How music modifies first impressions of product endorsers and brands. *Psychology of Music, 34*, 465–480. doi: 10.1177/0305735606067158.

6

Experimental analyses of choice and matching

From the animal laboratory to the marketplace

Valdimar Sigurdsson and Gordon R. Foxall

Even after we've studied behavior in the laboratory, we can't expect to be able to interpret every instance of behavior outside the laboratory. There are limits to what we can know. . . . In our study of learning, it's important to recognize what remains out of our reach.

(Catania, 1998, pp. 6–7)

Introduction

Marketing needs to have a theoretical and/or empirical foundation to account for the situational influence of the marketing mix on consumer choice. The matching law (Herrnstein, 1961, 1970), or the quantitative law of effect, is a mainstream behavior analysis of choice behavior and has been studied for several decades. The matching law's research history, indeed the history of the whole of behavior analysis, has mainly been conducted in a systematic experimental framework where knowledge is built by constantly putting more factors under experimental control. Most of the research has been done on animal behavior in the behavioral laboratory. The few experimental studies that have been conducted on human behavior have mostly been done in a rather closed setting. This casts doubt on the generalization of the matching law to the more complicated real behavior of humans.

Consumer behavior analysis explores the generalization of the matching law on human behavior in the most open, real setting. This important work has differed in important ways from most other research on the matching equations. The experimental method has not been applied to much extent and the behavior under study is mostly maintained on concurrent ratio schedules (that is pricing, instead of concurrent interval schedules).

The subject matter of consumer behavior analysis is first and foremost the exploration of the possibility of using the concepts and methods of behavior analysis applied in research, on a more simple level, for the study of consumer choice behavior in real settings. As such, it studies the impact of more known important variables on consumer choice in real-life situations. Some of these variables have already been identified from research on matching at a simpler level. To deal with the influences of the marketing mix on consumer choice, behavior analysis needs to find the sole effects of the most important variables to determine its importance in accounting for complex consumer behavior. The experimental method, where the effect of each independent variable is found to keep the others constant, is a necessary step in exploring the ability of behavior analysis to describe, predict and control consumer choice in open settings. This entails behavior analytical evaluations (see, e.g., Johnston & Pennypecker, 1993) and comparisons of the legitimacy of different outcomes from consumer choice and matching analysis of sales data obtained with in-store and/or online consumer experiments.

Behavioral and experimental economics

> We descendants of Bentham can agree about the primacy of pains and pleasures; we can agree even that, as Hirshleifer recently said, there is only one social science. But now, to pursue that social science, and to use it to design social institutions, we need to reconcile the divergent answers provided by empirical approaches, such as that of behavioral psychology, with the formal structures of economic theory.
>
> *(Herrnstein, 1997, p. 264)*

Behavioral economics is a broad term; it can be classified, as was done for psychology in general, as cognitive and behavioral. This classification can be built on the explanatory value in behavioral terms that is given to internal, non-observable variables (cognitive processes). The discussion will begin with the more mainstream behavioral economics, the interplay between cognitive psychology and economics. This is most famously known from the work of such scholars as Simon (e.g., 1955), Kahneman and Tversky (e.g., 1979), Thaler (e.g., anomalies articles in *Journal of Economic Perspectives*), and Rabin (e.g., 2002). This line of research, cognitive psychological experiments on choice and decision making, has bridged the gap between economics and psychology by pointing to the overestimation of human rationality and the relevance of experiments in economics. It has had a major impact on consumer behavior research (Simonson et al., 2001). The discussion will later be limited to research in the tradition of "behavior analytical" behavioral economics, mostly known from former students of B. F. Skinner at Harvard University; such as Herrnstein (e.g., 1997), Rachlin (e.g., 1982), and Baum (e.g., 1979). From these and other behavioral scientists at the Harvard Pigeon lab, and afterwards, came matching analysis with rigorous animal experimental research, and mathematical treatment of behavior. This has stimulated Foxall at Cardiff University, his students and collaborators (the Consumer Behavior Analysis Research Group) to explore to what extent these behavior principles and this methodology are applicable and useful in the realm of consumer behavior. Furthermore, this research has also been connected to, supported and challenged the basic disciplines: behavior analysis and economics (e.g., Foxall, 2001; Oliveira-Castro et al., 2006).

Matching analysis

> Skinner discovered response rate, stimulus control, and schedules. He and his students saw the possibility of a real (natural) science of behavior and set about establishing that science based on those concepts. Herrnstein discovered relative response rate, the matching law, and the psychophysics of choice. He and his students saw that the science could be quantitative and set about making it so.
>
> *(Baum, 2002, p. 355)*

Principles and techniques developed in basic behavior analysis have been transferred from the animal laboratories to the analysis of patterns of consumer choice in open real settings (cf. Foxall, 2007). This has mostly been done within the framework of the matching law, and has dominated research choice in behavior analysis for decades. Theoretically, the matching law has been presented in many forms and played a major part in the mathematical enhancement of behavior analysis, where different parameters have been experimented with and put together. It has been important in the cooperation, or friction, between economics and behavior analysis. It is one of the most successful behavioral laws, discovered with experimentation, in terms of reliability and generalization (Herrnstein, 1997), and has recently been tested in consumer choice research (see literature below).

Schedules

To comprehend matching analysis it is necessary to introduce the topic of schedules. A reinforcement schedule (Ferster & Skinner, 1957) produces behavioral patterns because it is the rule that controls under what conditions reinforcement is delivered. Schedules have been investigated for more than five decades. They determine steady state behavioral patterns and resistance to extinction. In experimental analysis of nonhuman behavior, schedules induce remarkably lawful behavior but their effects on human behavior are more controversial and complex (e.g., Lowe, 1979; Pierce & Epling, 1999).

Continuous reinforcement is the simplest schedule; it requires that every response be reinforced. Intermittent reinforcement, when behavior is reinforced occasionally, is most often the rule in a real environment. This intermittent type can be classified as either ratio schedule or interval schedule. Ratio schedule is response based, meaning that reinforcement follows a number of behaviors or responses. Interval schedule, in contrast, delivers reinforcement only after a particular behavior is performed – when some time has passed since the last reinforcement. Both of these types of schedules are further classified as either fixed or variable. Fixed schedule reinforces after a fixed number of responses or length of time. Variable schedule, however, has changeable reinforcement. It delivers reinforcers after various response requirements or time, and is generally dependent on some average delivery system in the long run.

Relative response rate

The single operant analysis, where behavior is analyzed based on one response class on a single schedule of reinforcement, is important for the discovery of basic laws, principles and applications. It is, though, more natural to study behavior as a choice among alternatives. De Villiers and Herrnstein's (1976, p. 1131) view "that choice is merely behavior in the context of other behavior" is appropriate for consumer marketing, when studying brand substitutability. This is because reinforcement on one schedule can affect the response on another schedule, and vice versa. The concept of relative reinforcement is important in consumer behavior analysis, as different brands compete for consumer choice. It is called "concurrent schedules" when two or more simple schedules are simultaneously available (e.g., concurrent VI VI). These schedules are used in experimental matching analysis, on animals, using a changeover delay (COD); a procedure that penalizes rapid switching by delaying reinforcement for a brief period after each change of a key (Herrnstein, 1961). The COD is necessary to prevent accidental switching, arising from too little latency between changing a key and acquiring a reinforcer, leading to reinforcement of rapid switching behavior that prevents any meaningful choice analysis. The duration of the COD can have an effect on the slope of the relative response function. Research has, however, shown that different delays generally don't have much systematic effect (Davison & McCarthy, 1988). In laboratory experiments on human behavior, factors such as the distance between keys have been used to avoid subjects pressing both keys at the same time (Herrnstein, 1997). Such a procedure is not necessary in the consumer setting as rapid switching or choosing two brands (reinforcers) at approximately the same time is not a problem, but is seen as normal (matching data is found to be dividing behavior with other behavior, not time).

Choice behavior has mainly been studied on concurrent interval schedules (mostly variable), where the schedule on one key is supposed to be independent of the other schedule (e.g., Herrnstein, 1961; Pierce & Epling, 1983). Concurrent variable schedules induce an allocation of behavior between the alternative schedules. This does not, however, happen on concurrent fixed schedules, which make subjects show exclusive choice of the leaner (better) schedule – when in a steady state (Herrnstein, 1997, chapter 4; Pierce & Epling, 1999). According to Herrnstein (1997, chapter 4) concurrent VR VR schedules, or something akin to them, are frequently seen in real environments, including consumer situations (e.g., Foxall et al., 2004).

The strict matching law

The matching law was discovered by Herrnstein (1961, 1970) and was initially developed by him and his students at Harvard, but is now studied nearly worldwide (see Baum, 2002; Logue, 2002). It is a molar law[1] which states that relative response rate (behavior) matches its relative reinforcement (utility: see Herrnstein, 1997), on concurrent interval schedules of reinforcement,[2] in equilibrium (see, e.g., Davison & McCarthy, 1988; Herrnstein, 1997). For example, if 80% of all of the reinforcement in an experimental chamber comes concurrently from one of two possible response sources, then it will be chosen in that exact proportion. The simplest form of the strict matching law for two response possibilities is shown algebraically in Equation 1:

$$\frac{B_a}{B_a + B_b} = \frac{R_a}{R_a + R_b}, \tag{1}$$

where the B term stands for behavior frequency, or specific choice, and R means corresponding reinforcers (e.g., per unit time). The reinforcement alternates between R_a which is contingent on behavior a and R_b is reinforcement derived from behavior b, which can also be defined as all other behavior than a. As long as the behavioral possibilities under study are symmetrical (e.g., pecking discs or two identical lanes to drive on) and the reinforcement is indifferent between the behavioral choices other than reinforcer frequency or any other measurable parameter (e.g., reinforcer amount), then Equation 1 is appropriate. The matching law should therefore, theoretically, be appropriate for accounting for consumer choices between different brands.

The matching law is empirically well established from laboratory experiments (de Villiers, 1977; Herrnstein, 1997). Although the matching law has this empirical foundation, it can be viewed either as an empirical generalization or as a theoretical (tautological) system of equations used to define how environmental consequences control behavior (see, e.g., Killeen, 1972; Rachlin, 1971).[3] It is a simple molar law, which is one of its strengths, but it has univocal explanatory ability and generality. It deals with overall relative frequencies of choice behavior, which has been very useful and significant in behavior analysis because it has forced researchers to take into account the competition of different reinforcers. Herrnstein and colleagues (Herrnstein & Prelec, 1991; Herrnstein & Vaughan, 1980) also developed a theory at the molecular level that they called melioration, to account for how matching occurs in the long run.

Melioration

Melioration predicts that the consumer will always show behavior which has a higher local reinforcement value each time, but will not take the long-run consequences into account (as rational choice theory predicts). It is supposed to predict exactly when the consumer is going to shift from one activity to another.

Unlike melioration that states which behavior is the most likely on each occasion, the matching law predicts the behavioral allocation to different possibilities in the long run, when behavior is steady. It is possible to define behavior in many measurable ways, as for example time spent, frequency of response, magnitude chosen, or money spent on different brands.

In the analysis that follows the concept of melioration, as Vaughan and Herrnstein (1997) defined it, will be used, but the effects of punishment will be added because this is necessary when dealing with consumer behavior. A defining character of consumer behavior like any other economic activity is the reciprocal transfer of rights. It simultaneously presents intended reinforcers and possible punishers (see Alhadeff, 1982; Foxall, 1998). Purchase responses can be reinforced by the acquisition of the commodities, and other benefits, but factors like price and effort can, and will in most cases, make the demand lower than it would otherwise be. The operation of melioration leads to matching in the long run. The reinforcement magnitude will be equal between the brands because of diminishing returns in reinforcement value. If reinforcement (minus punishment) for buying and consuming tomatoes is higher than reinforcement (minus punishment) for buying and consuming chocolate, then melioration predicts that tomatoes will be bought next time and as a consequence the reinforcement value for buying and consuming them will decrease. In most instances this will result in average reinforcement for the different products to be equal in the long run (matching), when everything else is unchanged. Melioration is the behavioral dynamic which is supposed to lie behind matching. The operation of melioration (with punishment) is shown in Equation 2:

$$d\frac{C_a}{C_a + C_b} / dt = f_x(V_a - V_b), \tag{2}$$

where V_a and V_b are functions of reinforcement and punishment per unit time that the consumer spends on a particular brand, which here are two. The terms C_a and C_b represent money spent on a and b, which here can mean tomatoes and chocolate, with a fixed income ($C_a + C_b = 1$). It is assumed that the function f_x is differentiable, strictly monotonically increasing, and $f_x(0) = 0$ (the analysis is built on Vaughan, 1985, with added punishment effects on choice behavior). Equation 2 shows that if reinforcement minus punishment for brand a is more than for brand b then relatively more money will subsequently be spent on brand a. The process that the equation describes comes into equilibrium when:

$$V_a = V_b \tag{3}$$

For consumer behavior the assumption is that the value (V_i) for a particular circumstance is a strictly monotonically increasing function of reinforcement minus punishment in that situation: $V_i = g(R_i - P_i/T_i)$, where R_i represents reinforcement (for example, the magnitude of reinforcers) in situation I, P_i represents punishment (for example, price), and T_i stands for unit of time. By defining melioration with punishment in this way the molar law will be able to account both for the effects of reinforcement and punishment on behavior in the form of the positive and negative law of effect.

The positive and negative law of effect

As there is general agreement in the behavioral and social sciences that behavior is influenced by its benefits and costs,[4] it is important to add punishment to Equation 1. De Villiers (1980) presented Equation 4 to account for how reinforcement and punishment work simultaneously on behavior. From the theoretical point of view of Herrnstein's (1970) matching law:

$$\frac{B_1}{B_2} = \frac{(R_1 - P_1)}{(R_2 - P_2)} .$$ (4)

De Villiers' (1980) equation states that punishers (P) directly decrease the strength of reinforced behavior and shows exactly how reinforcement and punishment jointly control behavior.

The above equations of the strict matching law (1 and 4) describe choice behavior only accurately in symmetrical choice situations. Although it is possible to add parameters to the equations to account for a different quality of reinforcers (Miller, 1976) or other parameters such as reinforcer amount or delay (Herrnstein, 1997), most researchers today choose to use the generalized matching equation when studying matching.

The generalized matching equation

The generalized matching equation (Baum, 1974a, 1979; Lander & Irwin, 1968) was developed so that data that did not conform to strict matching could be portrayed in the same terms as strict matching data. It "is a generalization of the strict matching law in the sense that the strict matching law is a special case of the generalized law" (Davison & McCarthy, 1988, p. 48). It is considered an improvement from the stricter version (McDowell, 2005) and measures how well the strict matching law can account for choice behavior (see Equation 5):

$$\frac{B_a}{B_b} = c \left(\frac{R_a}{R_b} \right)^a .$$ (5)

Here the terms B_a, B_b, R_a, and R_b represent behavior and reinforcers as in the equations above. The parameters c and a are free and found by getting a straight line through data of relative response (choice behavior) and relative reinforcers transformed logarithmically (Equation 6):

$$\log \frac{B_a}{B_b} = a \log \frac{R_a}{R_b} + \log c .$$ (6)

The parameter a accounts for the sensitivity of preference to changes in the independent variable and c is inherently biased. When both a and c are equal to 1 then the data shows strict matching. Then Equation 6 is equivalent to Equation 1, the strict matching law (for a discussion of the generalized matching equation and its parameters see Baum, 1979; Lowe & Horne, 1985).

Different dimensions of matching analysis

Matching analysis can take different forms. Choice can show perfect matching, overmatching, undermatching, antimatching, and bias. The slope a gives a measurement of how much choice behavior changes when the reinforcement ratio is altered. The parameter b represents the intercept or bias, a constant preference for one alternative over another for all points of the independent variable (Davison & McCarthy, 1988).

It is called overmatching (Baum, 1979) if the value of *a* (the slope) is higher than 1 because choices favor the richer reinforcement schedule. This means that the subject chooses this particular possibility (B_a) more often than the proportional reinforcement dimension for the option is [$\log(R_a/R_b)$]. In the laboratory this is considered to be a problem of design if the reinforcers are supposed to be equivalent, indicating that one of the alternatives is qualitatively different, or that switching is being penalized too severely. However, if relative choice behavior is allocated less to the target behavior (B_a) than anticipated from the basis of relative reinforcement, it is called undermatching (Baum, 1974a). This can indicate that either switching between alternatives is accidentally reinforced or that subjects discriminate poorly between the alternatives (Herrnstein, 1997).

In the case of bias there is a systematic preference for an alternative not explainable from the viewpoint of the strict matching law (from the perspective of one dimension of objective reinforce elements, e.g., relative rates of reinforcement alone). Bias indicates differences between response requirements (e.g., different shelf placements for different brands) or reinforcer parameters (e.g., different brand qualities or delivery time). This is represented by the intercept in Baum's generalized matching equation (see Equations 5 and 6). In terms of antimatching, when an increase of choices of one alternative increases the selection of a second option, the reinforcers (products or brands) are gross complements instead of substitutes (e.g., red wine and a steak). This makes the slope parameter *a* less than 0 (Foxall, 2007). In all, the generalized matching equation (sensitivity to reinforcer dimensions, reinforcer parameters, and response requirements), accounting for consumer behavior, should be under the influence of all traditional independent variables known in microeconomic analysis (see Lea, 1978, for a discussion of the analogy between reinforcement analysis and demand analysis).

The concatenated generalized matching equation

It is possible to use many independent variables for the generalized matching equation. These can, for example, be variables that research has shown affect behavior such as rate, amount, immediacy, and quality of the reinforcers or response effort (for a review see Fisher & Mazur, 1997). To account for this within the framework of the generalized matching equation it is possible to use the concatenated generalized matching equation (Equation 7):

$$\log \frac{B_a}{B_b} = a_r \log\left(\frac{R_a}{R_b}\right) + a_m \log\left(\frac{M_a}{M_b}\right) + a_q \log\left(\frac{Q_a}{Q_b}\right) + a_d \log\left(\frac{D_b}{D_a}\right) + \log c, \tag{7}$$

where *R*, *M*, *Q*, and *D* represent reinforcer frequency, amount, quality, and delay, respectively. If it is possible to assume that the effects of the independent variables do not interact, then the concatenated generalized matching law can be relevant and useful when researching the effects of two or more independent variables (Landon et al., 2003).

Critchfield et al. (2003) used the generalized matching equation to test the prediction of Equation 5 on human behavior and compared it to another equation which is in the tradition of two-factor theories of punishment. Their results showed clearly that punishment directly reduces reinforced behavior in the data for six of seven subjects in their research:

$$\log \frac{B_1}{B_2} = a \log\left(\frac{R_1 - P_1}{R_2 - P_2}\right) + \log c. \tag{8}$$

These results are consistent with other research (de Villiers, 1980; Farley, 1980) on nonhuman behavior, which has pointed to the superiority of a direct-suppression punishment model. This increases faith in the generalization of experimental results that have tested the effects of punishment on nonhuman behavior.

Experimental research on the matching law

Research on the matching law has mostly been done with animals as subjects but some has been done on human behavior. Research on human behavior from the framework of the matching law has been increasing. This is how the science of behavior analysis works. It starts on a simple level of analysis, such as experiments on animal behavior, and then moves on to generalization and studies on a more complicated stage. It is possible to classify matching research as that performed on animal/human behavior, and in open–closed settings.

Open–closed settings

In accordance with the summative Behavioral Perspective Model (BPM, Foxall, 1998) of consumer choice and the matching law (more reinforcers in the denominator, *ceteris paribus*, mean less behavioral control from each, and vice versa), we propose a continuum of closed–open behavior settings where the researcher has a different degree of control over the environment. A closed setting can be characterized as a situation where only few reinforcers are available and one has a great effect on behavior. The researcher has control over deprivation and controls the delivery of the reinforcers to behaviors, which are clearly defined, and there are no effective alternative operant consequences (Schwartz & Lacey, 1988). Experimentation on animal behavior in the laboratory can be examples of the most closed settings related to the matching law. Thereafter, on the continuum come experiments on human behavior in the behavioral laboratory, studies on human activity in closed natural settings, and then studies on animal and human behavior in open natural environments. One of the most open settings where the matching law has been used, i.e. on human behavior, is the supermarket (e.g., see Foxall et al., 2004). If analyzed according to the above classification of Schwartz and Lacey (1988), the supermarket has near uncountable numbers of reinforcers, where many can have a strong impact on behavior, and the researcher has no control over deprivation or satiation. The consumer can choose whatever he likes and can afford, he can come hungry, or full, and freely wander around, and walk out when he wants (see Foxall, 1998, for a discussion).

In what follows we will go over research on the matching law from research done in open–closed settings, and looking at animal–human behavior. The discussion will go from closed to open settings; when the setting becomes more open, it is of more interest to the topic of consumer research. For this reason the research carried out in the most closed setting, in which animals were subjects, is not presented here in full detail. This will only be mentioned in terms of experiments conducted to compare the prediction of matching and maximization accounts of choice behavior.

Research on the matching law with animal behavior in open settings

Baum (1974b) published an important quasi-experiment where he studied a flock of free wild pigeons that lived in the attic of his house. Pigeons had access to grain through an experimental apparatus with different concurrent variable-interval schedules. The results showed that the pigeons' choices conformed to the matching law. This experiment showed that matching for animals was not a creation of the laboratory procedure. This is because the pigeons were wild and the apparatus recorded the combined responses of many pigeons. Therefore, the animals could choose from a wide range of different reinforcers, and Baum had no control over deprivation (see also a similar experiment in Graft et al., 1977). Related to this kind of open environment research are studies on the matching law, and the equivalent optimal foraging model of ideal free distribution, done on group choice (for a discussion see Kraft & Baum, 2001). This kind of research has, though, also been done on animal and human behavior in closed settings.

Research on human behavior in closed settings

The matching law has generally been used to predict human behavior with good results. The amount of research on human behavior is thought small compared with research done on animal behavior. It is possible to roughly classify the research done on human behavior from three types of closed settings: experimental setting (e.g., Bradshaw & Szabadi, 1988; Critchfield et al., 2003; Goltz 1999; Hantula & Crowell, 1994; Horne & Lowe, 1993; Lowe & Horne, 1985; Schroeder & Holland, 1969); hospitals and mental institutions (e.g., Martens & Houk, 1989; Oliver et al., 1999); and schools and universities (e.g., Beardsley & McDowell, 1992; Conger & Killeen, 1974; Martens et al., 1992; Mace et al., 1994). In addition to this research it is worth mentioning a study by McDowell (1982/1988) that has similarities to the studies taking place at the hospitals and mental institutions. McDowell reappraised data originally published by himself and Carr (1980). He evaluated the relation between a boy's serious scratching, taking place at his home, and his parents' reprimands that occurred contiguously with the self-injury. Results showed that the matching equation closely predicted the proportion of time the boy spent engaging in self-injury. This correlation was useful for McDowell to experimentally test the hypotheses that the reprimands served as positive social reinforcement for scratching. The functional analysis supported the hypothesis, and behavior modification was used to eliminate the problem behavior.

Overall, the matching law accounted well for the data in the above research (except for a considerable undermatching and bias in the study by Mace et al., and the two studies published by Horne and Lowe). Mace and colleagues pointed to the importance of adjunct procedures (e.g., COD and timers) in matching research. In the studies by Horne and Lowe, some subjects' behavioral data showed approximate matching – but others departed greatly from the prediction of the matching law. Regardless of this, the experiments by Horne and Lowe indicated the importance of matching research by pointing to the possibility that choice behavior is both influenced by the current reinforcement contingencies and the subject's verbal rules. This is an idea that has stimulated other researchers in the field (e.g., Foxall, 1998; see the utilitarian–informational bifurcation in the BPM).

Research on human behavior in open settings

Bold steps have been taken in the direction of studying the predictability of the matching law on human behavior in open natural settings. As stated before, open setting is here defined as any environment which has numerous available reinforcers, where many can have an effect on behavior (inversion of Schwartz & Lacey's, 1988, definition of a closed setting). The open systems can be contrasted with the closed controlled environments of the laboratory, clinical settings, and schools. The matching studies, in open settings, have been undertaken in two different areas of research: sports competitions and consumer marketing. Both types of research have a similar bearing for the external validity of the matching law, and seemingly uniform development, strengths, and weaknesses. It is, however, interesting that the two research streams have not, to date, made any reference to each other.

Research on behavior in sports

In the area of sports behavior Vollmer and Bourret (2000) published an important study for the enhancement of the external validity of matching research. They showed that the relative frequency of two- and three-point shots in a college basketball division matched the relative frequency of the proportional reinforcement rate (scores) produced by each type of shot. The researchers had no control over the behavior but used a version of the concatenated matching equation (9) to describe the allocation of two- and three-point shots:

$$\frac{B_1}{B_1 + B_2} = \frac{R_1(1.5A)}{R_1(1.5A) + R_2(A)}. \tag{9}$$

As three-point shots give more scores than two point shots (3:2 →1.5:1), the concatenated matching equation, applied in the study, used a reinforcement frequency parameter (R), in the form of points acquired, and a reinforcement amount constant (A), representing the difference in reinforcement between the two alternatives.

Reed et al. (2006) followed up on the sports study using the generalized matching equation to describe play-calling data from the American National Football League. The results showed that the matching equation accounted for most of the variance in play calling, although some undermatching and bias was identified. Possibly one of the most interesting contributions of this study to the external validity of the matching law was that the researchers were able to show that estimated matching parameters varied in accordance with important sports conditions such as team success.

Although the sport matching studies are important explorations of the relevance of the matching law in real open environments, they have some limitations that can be classified either as problems of reinforcement schedules, or lack of environmental control. The problem of rein-forcement schedules is that these sport matching analyses differ from other matching studies in a way that both basketball shooting (see discussion in Vollmer & Bourret, 2000) and passing and rushing are best described as being maintained on ratio schedules, but, as previously mentioned, nearly all matching research has been performed on behavior maintained on interval schedules. The reason for the traditional restriction to the interval schedules, most often concurrent VI VI schedules, is that it provides a pure independent variable and behavioral allocation, whereas ratio schedules produce interdependent "independent" variables and monotinical choice pat-terns, not very suitable for the analysis of choice behavior (see, e.g., Pierce & Epling, 1999). As the matching law predicts exclusive choice allocation to the leaner, or better, schedule on concurrent ratio schedules (Foxall & Schrezenmaier, 2003; Herrnstein & Loveland, 1975), there is a serious misunderstanding in stating that the matching law predicts behavioral allocation in the sports research. This holds as long as there is an agreement that the behavior is on ratio schedules, or more accurately, to what extent it is best characterized by ratio schedules. Scoring (reinforcement) is most likely affected not only by frequency of shooting, but also by time, as both two- and three-point shots should be more effective if they are performed unexpectedly, something that should be a function of time (see the tennis riddle in Herrnstein, 1990; and discussion of this point in Vollmer & Bourret, 2000). The sport matching results contradict anticipated choice data from concurrent ratio schedules in being well accounted for by the generalized matching equation (as it should be on interval schedules), as the behavioral allocation quite fairly corresponded to the relative reinforcement produced. However, the meaning and importance of this relationship are questionable because ratio schedules compel matching, as more behavior allocation must mean more reinforcement (at least in most instances). This means that the supposed dependent variable drives, at least in part, the independent variable.

The other problem mentioned in the sports studies, lack of environmental control, is attached to the schedules' problem of interdependency. As these studies have no experimental control, the correlational research is not equipped to deal with the problem of functionality: which variable is controlling which? The problem of reciprocal control is not restricted to studies on behavior maintained on ratio schedules, but it certainly does not make things easier, especially where there is no experimental control. In previously mentioned research by Martens and Houk (1989), using VI VI schedules, they discuss the problem of interdependency in their correlational matching study on the compliance of an 18-year-old developmentally disabled girl, where it is hard to specify whether the teacher's attention ("reinforcement") is controlling the student's behavior or vice versa. This problem with experimental control is, however, more serious when there is little doubt that the "dependent" variable is a source of variation in reinforcement delivery, as is the case for concurrent ratio schedules.

Another publication in the series of sport matching research is a further analysis of the two- and three-point shot allocation, published by Romanowich et al. (2007). It attempts to deal with the lack of experimental control – but does not mention schedules of reinforcement. The research replicates and adds to the original study (Vollmer & Bourret, 2000) by analyzing National Basketball Association (NBA) data from 1991 to 2000. During this time, the distance of the three-point line was decreased in 1994, but was increased again in 1997. This gives data in line with a quasi-experimental ABA reversal design where the reinforcement rate should increase during the time period from 1994, when the three-point line distance was decreased (it should increase the frequency of scores from such shots), until it was increased again. The logic is, if the data conforms to the prediction of the matching law, that is if the proportion of three-point shots increases during the 1994–7 period, and then lowers again, it should show that matching provides a valid description of the behavior, and can be used to predict and control behavior. In fact, the results do support this claim. The difficulty is, however, that this does not support the matching law (on concurrent FR schedules) and it is methodologically flawed because if the rule change is successful in increasing the rate of three-point shots, that will automatically lead to an increase in the score. It is not surprising that more shots (behavior) will increase scoring (reinforcement), leading to a spurious approximation to matching. In fact, Vollmer et al. (St. Peter, Vollmer, Bourret, Borrero, Sloman, & Rapp, 2005) themselves warn against the danger of spurious matching. This could result either from the rate of the behavior under study (the problem behavior in the article) affecting the rate of reinforcement (attention), or if matching occurs by chance, where there is only correlation between the variables but no functional relation. It seems to me that these methodological problems are unfortunately present in the sports matching research. There is no question if there is a functional relationship between scoring and type of shot; however, this relationship is hidden, or overestimated, by the fact that shooting affects the rate of scoring. On top of this, the lack of control over variables, both internal and external, limits the valuation of the matching analyses, and their applications, in the sports settings. This is acknowledged in Vollmer and Bourret (2000) and dealt with cleverly but in a rather methodologically limited way in Romanowich et al. (2007). The next research steps must aim for further experimental control, which amounts to acquiring the autonomous variables controlled by the researcher as well as control of external variables.

Research on consumer behavior

The insufficient amount of research on the matching law in real open settings is surprising for the reason that has been emphasized (e.g., Logue, 2002) and challenged (e.g., Fuqua, 1984) in the literature. The following text taken from Logue (2002) states the need for research testing the relevance of matching on human behavior in real settings:

> Unfortunately, research that speaks directly to the world outside the laboratory has been limited, with the exception of some clinical settings. There are many areas still ripe for investigation. For example, why not examine, within the quantitative framework of the matching law, the tendency to save or spend money given changes in overall level of income and expenses? Another example might be shoppers' trips to one of two aisles of a grocery store as a function of the frequency of free samples of food in those two aisles.
>
> *(p. 363)*

As Logue points out, consumers' settings are an interesting new area for the matching law to be used and tested. In fact, at the time of Logue's publication, this kind of research had already begun under the name of consumer behavior analysis, with similar promises and problems as the sports matching research.

Previous matching research on consumer behavior

At a molar level of analysis the Behavioral Perspective Model comprehends consumer choices, as they are distributed over time, as a function of the rates of both utilitarian and informational reinforcement (Foxall, 1997) and punishment (Foxall, 1999), here put into an algebraic form in Equation 10:

$$\frac{B_1}{B_2} = \frac{((_uQR_1 + _iQR_1) - (_uQP_1 + _iQP_1))}{((_uQR_2 + _iQR_2) - (_uQP_2 + _iQP_2))} . \qquad (10)$$

This is the summative behavioral perspective model's matching equation where the difference from previously shown matching equations (e.g., Equation 9) is that the consequences of behavior are divided into utilitarian[5] ($_uR$) and informational[6] ($_iR$), for the two possibilities. Equation 10 is here shown to characterize the consumer behavior analytical standpoint; this equation has not been empirically quantified. It captures the complexity of consumer behavior as a subject matter for matching research.

Correlational consumer behavior matching

If seen from the point of view of the generalized matching equation, the Consumer Behavior Analysis Research Group (Foxall & James, 2001, 2003; Foxall et al., 2004; Oliveira-Castro et al., 2005; Romero et al., 2006; see research review in Foxall et al., 2007) has studied three different forms of matching relationships in natural consumer settings, with ever-increasing scope. In this panel research households, or participants, have gone from just a few (e.g., Foxall & James, 2001) to thousands, with research taking place for a period of time that extends from several weeks to up to a year. Three different kinds of matching, and matching-related, analyses have been performed: amount matching (classical matching), cost matching (relative demand analysis), and probability matching (maximization analysis). The data analyses have all been done within the framework of the generalized matching equation where matching between different variables in the consumer environment (brand amount, brand price, and reciprocal brand price) and some dimension of consumer behavior have been tested. This research has been performed on the assumption that consumers' buying behavior conforms to concurrent quasi or analogical FR^a or VR^a (a = the number of brand possibilities) schedules. This means that the marketplace analogy to the response requirements in the laboratory, brand price, is known (fixed) on each and every shopping occasion (FR) for fast-moving consumer goods, but can change with time (VR). Consumer behavior is considered to be best represented by being maintained on a quasi schedule because the "independent" (e.g., reinforcement in terms of brand amount) and "dependent" (behavior in terms of spending) variables are reciprocal. For instance, the amount paid (the behavior) seriously affects the amount bought (the reinforcement) and vice versa. As previously mentioned for the sports matching research, this deviates from standard laboratory matching analysis, using variable-interval schedules, which should give a true independent variable because responses do not control this when reinforcers become available. The interval (time period programmed) controls this.

Cost matching

In consumer behavior analysis, price is analyzed using behavioral economics methods of relative demand analysis similar to animal experimental studies done by Kagel et al. (1981). This method is unlike traditional economic demand analysis, as it takes into consideration competition among competing brands in the product category, and uses the x-axis to represent price instead of the y-axis (see a discussion of how psychological and economic demand curves are drawn in different ways in Lea et al., 1987). As for amount matching, cost matching is also studied using ratio analysis. In terms of matching this denotes the connection between relative reinforcers earned, in the form of the quantity of brands (dependent variable) earned, and proportion of punishment in the form of the cost (independent variable) of them:

$$\log \frac{M_1}{M_2} = a \log \frac{P_1}{P_2} + \log c .$$

(11)

Here P stands for average monetary price over the duration of the study. The dependent variable, the relative amount bought, is best represented as being maintained on concurrent ratio schedules, inverse to amount matching; as the price goes down, the amount bought should increase. This relationship is methodologically interesting, as it does not have the problem of interdependency between the independent–dependent variables denoted for sports matching and consumer amount matching analyses. The researcher can control prices (price = aversive stimuli = punishment) which are not a form of behavior (like the amount bought in amount matching), but true environmental stimuli. The results from previous cost matching analyses (e.g., Foxall et al., 2004) reflect this empirical foundation by showing mixed relative demand curves for purchasing data aggregated across purchasers and stores, where the regression lines show either neutral, downward-, or upward-sloping demand curves.

Experimental consumer behavior matching

> Marketing action consists mainly in altering the scope of consumer behavior settings and manipulating the system of rewards which maintain various patterns of consumer choice.
>
> (Foxall, 1996, p. xii)

Consumer behavior analysis has to date indicated the importance of using the matching law in consumer research and takes the important step of making a research program where the matching law is researched in open settings. Johnston and Pennypacker (1993) point out that "[d]oing science is not a matter of following specific rules like recipes in a cookbook. Cookbooks may work quite well when the recipe is well tested, but scientific discovery is more like creating the recipe in the first place" (p. 13). In accordance with this, the Consumer Behavior Analysis Research Group has created methodological recipes (see, e.g., Foxall & Schrezenmaier, 2003) which get increasingly more challenging and extensive. They show behavioral and consumer scientists how it is possible to interpret and perform consumer matching research, something that was previously only speculated about or hoped for (e.g., Logue, 2002; Vaughan & Herrnstein, 1997). This makes the methodological strengths and weaknesses of correlation research, of the particular matching equations used, clearer. But further methodological exploration is needed to assess the capability of the matching law, and the behavioral perspective model in consumer research. The power of further extensive experimental analysis has not yet been explored.

A behavior analysis begins with complex behavior and breaks it down into its components, and functional analysis holds the stimuli and responses of interest constant, while changing their relations (Catania, 1998). This is the ideal methodology that has mainly been used in research on the matching law. The aim of behavioral psychologists and analysts is to describe, predict, and control behavior. Foxall (1998) recognizes this: "given the radical behaviorist provenance of the BPM, the capacity of its analysis to lead to prediction must be demonstrated . . . and to comprehend the control of consumer behavior in its various environments" (pp. 56–7). Acknowledging this, we have a criterion to appraise different ways of doing behavioral science. When comparing different descriptions of behavior it is important to focus on the invented concepts and try to use those which make for economical and comprehensible descriptions of behavior (Baum, 2005). By focusing on control, the effectiveness of different methodologies is assessed by looking at the degree of control over the target behavior that can be produced by each approach (Johnston & Pennypacker, 1993). Foxall (1998, p. 338) asks the important question: "How far can the control of behavior be attributed to the environment when the setting is relatively open?" The sufficient condition for identifying functional relationships is the experimental manipulation of an independent variable (Johnston & Pennypacker, 1993). To answer Foxall's question it is thus necessary to manipulate the retail environment and see how it affects consumer behavior. By not being able to control, or hold constant, important variables of the concatenated generalized matching equation (e.g., reinforcement schedule, effort, and quality), it is hard to find the sole effects of marketing mix variables, like price, shelf placements, and in-store advertisements, on consumer choice. This is because all these variables intervene to produce the results in a purely statistical research.

Consumer behavior analysis, as a sub-discipline of behavioral economics and applied behavior analysis, has the agenda of fully exploring the usefulness of these parent disciplines in real marketing systems. In this respect consumer choice has been researched with panel data, in different forms and with ever-increasing scope in relation to the matching law, with experimental interventions in real market environments such as retailing (Curry et al., 2010) and simulated online consumer environments (Fagerstrøm et al., 2011). However, further examination of the experimental techniques, with their possible ability to control and surrender the situational influences of real marketing mix variables on consumer choice and matching, is necessary to strengthen the generalization of the matching law to the more complicated behavior of humans and consumption.

Summary

The chapter has focused on the importance of consumer behavior analysis which has transferred concepts and data analyses, originally generated in the behavioral laboratory, to consumer choice research in the marketplace. Within the reviewed framework of matching research, this literature review has enforced this conduct by arguing also for the transfer of behavioral analytical research methods and relevant data analysis. How experimental control and relative choice analysis have the possibility to shed further light on methodological opportunities in this area of research, such as those of reinforcement schedules and a lack of environmental control, has been discussed. This was necessary to make possible a judgment of the validity and importance of consumer choice and matching research in terms of generating data which are possible to evaluate in terms of behavior analytical and marketing criteria. As both these fields are applied in orientation, by focusing on the effects of important marketing variables on consumer choice, important new data will hopefully emerge to enhance the ability of this kind of research to accurately and logically describe, predict, and control consumer behavior. This possibility has created the foundation for further research, which reveals the newly generated in-store and online consumer behavior experiments.

Notes

1 Molar accounts of behavior are concerned with large-scale factors that regulate responding over a long period of time (Pierce & Epling, 1999, p. 395).
2 Overall response rate on different FI schedules typically does not fit the matching equation very well (de Villiers & Herrnstein, 1976).
3 Operant behavior (behavior that is under the control of its consequences) will, *ceteris paribus*, match its relative consequences. This is not an empirical question. However, the matching law and its derivatives can enhance empirical research aimed at discovering what enviornmental factors affect behavior in particular circumstances. Is it reinforcer frequency, latency, etc? It is also worth mentioning that although the matching law is logically true, it is not necessarily the best model to account for behaviour. That is an emprical problem.
4 For example, utility/price in economics, and reinforcement/punishment in psychology. These concepts are also used in fields like criminology, political science, and many other social sciences. This comes generally in the form of customer satisfaction/utility, price, and effort in marketing.
5 See Foxall (1998) and Wearden (1988). The shortest definition of utilitarian consequences, in consumer behavior analysis, is those mediated by the product.
6 See Foxall (1998) and Wearden (1988). The shortest definition of informational consequences, in consumer behavior analysis, is those mediated by other persons.

References

Alhadeff, D. A. (1982). *Microeconomics and human behavior*. Berkeley, CA: University of California Press.
Baum, W. M. (1974a). On two types of deviation from the matching law: Bias and undermatching. *Journal of the Experimental Analysis of Behavior, 22*, 231–242.
Baum, W. M. (1974b). Choice in free-ranging wild pigeons. *Science, 185*, 78–79.
Baum, W. M. (1979). Matching, undermatching, and overmatching in studies on choice. *Journal of the Experimental Analysis of Behavior, 32*, 269–281.
Baum, W. M. (2002). The Harvard pigeon lab under Herrnstein. *Journal of the Experimental Analysis of Behavior, 77*, 347–355.
Baum, W. M. (2005). *Understanding behaviorism: Behavior, culture and evolution* (2nd ed.). Oxford: Blackwell Publishing.
Beardsley, S. D. and McDowell, J. J. (1992). Application of Herrnstein's hyperbola to time allocation of naturalistic human behavior maintained by naturalistic social reinforcement. *Journal of the Experimental Analysis of Behavior, 57*, 177–185.
Bradshaw, C. M. and Szabadi, E. (1988). Quantitative analysis of human operant behavior. In G. Davey and C. Cullen (eds.), *Human operant conditioning and behavior modification* (pp. 225–259). New York: Wiley.
Carr, E. G. and McDowell, J. (1980). Social control of self-injurious behavior of organic etiology. *Behavior Therapy, 11*, 402–409.
Catania, A. C. (1998). *Learning* (4th ed.). Upper Saddle River, NJ: Prentice Hall.

Conger, R. and Killeen, P. (1974). Use of concurrent operations in small group research. *Pacific Sociological Review, 17,* 399–416.

Critchfield, T. S., Pallets, E. M., MacAleese, K. R. and Newland, M. C. (2003). Punishment in human choice: Direct or competitive suppression? *Journal of the Experimental Analysis of Behavior, 80,* 1–27.

Curry, B., Foxall, G. R. and Sigurdsson, V. (2010). On the tautology of the matching law in consumer behavior analysis. *Behavioral Processes, 84,* 390–399.

Davison, M. and McCarthy, D. (1988). *The matching law: A research review.* Hillsdale, NJ: Erlbaum.

de Villiers, P. A. (1977). Choice in concurrent schedules and a quantitative formulation of the law of effect. In W. K. Honig and J. E. R. Staddon (eds.), *Handbook of operant behavior* (pp. 233–287). Englewood Cliffs, NJ: Prentice Hall.

de Villiers, P. A. (1980). Toward a quantitative theory of punishment. *Journal of the Experimental Analysis of Behavior, 33,* 15–25.

de Villiers, P. A. and Herrnstein, R. J. (1976). Toward a law of response strength. *Psychological Bulletin, 83,* 1131–1153.

Fagerstrøm, A., Arntzen, E. and Foxall, G. R. (2011). A study of preferences in a simulated online shopping experiment. *The Service Industries Journal, 31*(15), 2609–2621.

Farley, J. (1980). Reinforcement and punishment effects in concurrent schedules: A test of two models. *Journal of the Experimental Analysis of Behavior, 33,* 311–315.

Ferster, C. and Skinner. B. F. (1957). *Schedules of reinforcement.* New York: Appleton-Century.

Fisher, W. W. and Mazur, J. E. (1997). Basic and applied research on choice responding. *Journal of Applied Behavior Analysis, 30,* 387–410.

Foxall, G. R. (1996). *Consumers in context: The BPM research programme.* London and New York: Routledge.

Foxall, G. R. (1997). *Marketing psychology: The paradigms in the wings.* London: Macmillan.

Foxall, G. R. (1998). Radical behaviorist interpretation: generating and evaluating an account of consumer behavior. *The Behavior Analyst, 21,* 321–354.

Foxall, G. R. (1999). Putting consumer behavior in its place: The behavioral perspective model research programme. *International Journal of Management Reviews, 1,* 133–158.

Foxall, G. R. (2001). Foundations of consumer behavior analysis. *Marketing Theory, 1,* 165–199.

Foxall, G. R. (2007). *Explaining consumer choice.* London and New York: Palgrave Macmillan.

Foxall, G. R. and James, V. K. (2001). The behavioral basis of consumer choice: A preliminary analysis. *European Journal of Behavior Analysis, 2,* 209–220.

Foxall, G. R. and James, V. K. (2003). The behavioral economics of brand choice: How and what do consumers maximize? *Psychology and Marketing, 20,* 811–836.

Foxall, G. R. and Schrezenmaier, T. C. (2003). The behavioral economics of consumer brand choice: Establishing a methodology. *Journal of Economic Psychology, 1,* 1–21.

Foxall, G. R., Oliveira-Castro, J., James, V. K. and Schrezenmaier, T. C. (2007). *The behavioral economics of brand choice.* London and New York: Palgrave Macmillan.

Foxall, G. R., Oliveira-Castro, J. M. and Schrezenmaier, T. C. (2004). The behavioral economics of consumer brand choice: Patterns of reinforcement and utility maximization. *Behavioral Processes, 66,* 235–260.

Fuqua, R. W. (1984). Comments on the applied relevance of the matching law. *Journal of Applied Behavior Analysis, 17,* 381–386.

Goltz, S. M. (1999). Can't stop on a dime: The roles of matching and momentum in persistence of commitment. *Journal of Organization Behavior Management, 19,* 37–63.

Graft, D. A., Lea, S. E. G. and Whitworth, T. L. (1977). The matching law in and within groups of rats. *Journal of the Experimental Analysis of Behavior, 27,* 183–194.

Hantula, D. A. and Crowell, C. R. (1994). Behavioral contrast in a two-option analogue task of financial decision making. *Journal of Applied Behavior Analysis, 27,* 607–617.

Herrnstein, R. J. (1961). Relative and absolute strength of response as a function of frequency of reinforcement. *Journal of the Experimental Analysis of Behavior, 4,* 267–272.

Herrnstein, R. J. (1970). On the law of effect. *Journal of the Experimental Analysis of Behavior, 13,* 243–266.

Herrnstein, R. J. (1990). Behavior, reinforcement and utility. *Psychological Science, 1,* 217–224.

Herrnstein, R. J. (1997). *The matching law: Papers in psychology and economics.* (H. Rachlin and D. Laibson Eds.). New York: Russel Sage Foundation.

Herrnstein, R. J. and Loveland, D. H. (1975). Maximizing and matching on concurrent ratio schedules. *Journal of the Experimental Analysis of Behavior, 24,* 107–116.

Herrnstein, R. J. and Prelec, D. (1991). Melioration: A theory of distributed choice. *Journal of Economic Perspectives, 5*, 137–156.

Herrnstein, R. J. and Vaughan, W., Jr. (1980). Melioration and behavioral allocation. In J. E. R. Staddon (ed.), *Limits to action: The allocation of individual behavior*. New York: Academic Press.

Horne, P. J. and Lowe, C. F. (1993). Determinants of human performance on concurrent schedules. *Journal of the Experimental Analysis of Behavior, 59*, 29–60.

Johnston, J. M. and Pennypacker, H. S. (1993). *Strategies and tactics of behavioral research* (2nd ed.). Hillsdale, NJ: Lawrence Erlbaum Associates.

Kagel, J. K., Battalio, R. C., Rachlin, H. and Green, L. (1981). Demand curves for animal consumers. *The Quarterly Journal of Economics, 96*, 1–16.

Kahneman, D. and Tversky, A. (1979). Prospect theory: An analysis of decision under risk. *Econometrica, 47*, 313–327.

Killeen, P. (1972). The matching law. *Journal of the Experimental Analysis of Behavior, 17*, 489–495.

Kraft, J. R. and Baum, W. M. (2001). Group choice: The ideal free distribution of human social behavior. *Journal of the Experimental Analysis of Behavior, 76*, 21–42.

Lander, D. G. and Irwin, R. J. (1968). Multiple schedules: Effects of the distribution of reinforcements between components on the distribution of responses between components. *Journal of the Experimental Analysis of Behavior, 11*, 517–524.

Landon, J., Davison, M. and Elliffe, D. (2003) Concurrent schedules: Reinforcer magnitude effects. *Journal of the Experimental Analysis of Behavior, 79*, 351–356.

Lea, S. E. G. (1978). The psychology and economics of demand. *Psychological Bulletin, 85*, 441–466.

Lea, S. E. G., Tarpy, R. M. and Webley, P. (1987). *The individual in the economy: A survey of economic psychology*. Cambridge: Cambridge University Press.

Logue, A. W. (2002). The living legacy of the Harvard Pigeon Lab: Quantitative analysis in the wide world. *Journal of the Experimental Analysis of Behavior, 77*, 357–366.

Lowe, C. F. (1979). Determinants of human behavior. In M. D. Zeiler and P. Harzem (eds.), *Reinforcement and the organization of behavior (Vol. 1)*. New York: Wiley.

Lowe, C. F. and Horne, P. J. (1985). On the generality of behavioral principles: Human choice and the matching law. In C. F. Lowe, M. Richelle, D. E. Blackman and C. M. Bradshaw (eds.), *Behavior analysis and contemporary psychology* (pp. 97–115). London: Erlbaum.

Mace, F. C., Neef, N. A., Shade, D. and Mauro, B. C. (1994). Limited matching on concurrent-schedule reinforcement of academic behavior. *Journal of Applied Behavior Analysis, 27*, 585–596.

Martens, B. K., Lochner, D. G. and Kelly, S. Q. (1992). The effects of variable-interval reinforcement on academic engagement: A demonstration of matching theory. *Journal of Applied Behavior Analysis, 25*, 143–151.

Martens, B. K. and Houk, J. L. (1989). The application of Herrnstein's law of effect to disruptive and on-task behavior of a retarded adolescent girl. *Journal of the Experimental Analysis of Behavior, 51*, 17–27.

McDowell, J. J. (1982). The importance of Herrnstein's mathematical statement of the law of effect for behavior therapy. *American Psychologist, 37*, 771–779.

McDowell, J. J. (1988). Matching theory in natural human environments. *The Behavior Analyst, 11*, 95–108.

McDowell, J. J. (2005). On the classic and modern theories of matching. *Journal of the Experimental Analysis of Behavior, 84*, 111–127.

Miller, H. L. (1976). Matching-based hedonic scaling in the pigeon. *Journal of the Experimental Analysis of Behavior, 26*, 335–347.

Oliveira-Castro, J. M., Foxall, G. R. and Schrezenmaier, T. C (2005). Patterns of consumer response to retail price differentials. *Service Industries Journal, 25*, 309–335.

Oliveira-Castro, J. M., Foxall, G. R. and Schrezenmaier, T. C. (2006). Consumer brand choice: Individual and group analyses of demand elasticity. *Journal of the Experimental Analysis of Behavior, 85*, 147–166.

Oliver, C., Hall, S. and Nixon, J. (1999). A molecular to molar analysis of communicative and problem behavior. *Research in Developmental Disabilities, 20*, 197–213.

Pierce, W. D. and Epling, W. F. (1983). Choice, matching and human behavior: A review of the literature. *The Behavior Analyst, 6*, 57–76.

Pierce, W. D. and Epling, W. F. (1999). *Behavior analysis and learning* (2nd ed.). Upper Saddle River, NJ: Prentice Hall.

Rabin, M. (2002). A perspective on psychology and economics. *European Economic Review, 46*, 657–685.

Rachlin, H. (1971). On the tautology of the matching law. *Journal of the Experimental Analysis of Behavior, 15*, 249–251.

Rachlin, H. (1982). Economics of the matching law. In M. L. Commons, R. J. Herrnstein and H. Rachlin (eds.), *Quantitative analyses of behavior. Volume II: Matching and maximizing accounts*. Cambridge, MA: Ballinger.

Reed, D. D., Critchfield, T. S. and Martens, B. K. (2006). The generalized matching law in elite sport competition: Football play calling as operant choice. *Journal of Applied Behavior Analysis, 39*, 281–297.

Romanowich, P., Bourret, J. and Vollmer, T. R. (2007). Further analysis of the matching law to describe two- and three-point shot allocation by professional basketball players. *Journal of Applied Behavior Analysis, 40*, 311–315.

Romero, S., Foxall, G., Schrezenmaier, T., Oliveira-Castro, J. and James, V. (2006). Deviations from matching in consumer choice. *European Journal of Behavior Analysis, 7*, 15–39.

Schroeder, S. R. and Holland, J. G. (1969). Reinforcement of eye movement with concurrent schedules. *Journal of the Experimental Analysis of Behavior, 12*, 897–903.

Schwartz, B. and Lacey, H. (1988). What applied studies of human operant conditioning tell us about humans and about operant conditioning. In G. Davey and C. Cullen (eds.), *Human operant conditioning and behavior modification*. Chichester: John Wiley & Sons Ltd.

Simon, H. A. (1955). A behavioral model of rational choice. *Quarterly Journal of Economics, 59*, 99–118.

Simonson, I., Carmon, Z., Dhar, R., Drolet, A. and Nowlis, S. M. (2001). Consumer research: In search of identity. *Annual Review of Psychology, 52*, 249–275.

St. Peter, C. C., Vollmer, T. R., Bourret, J. C., Borrero, C. S. W., Sloman, K. and Rapp, J. (2005). On the role of attention in naturally occurring matching relations. *Journal of Applied Behavior Analysis, 38*, 429–443.

Thaler, R. (2000). From homo economicus to homo sapiens. *Journal of Economic Perspectives, 14*, 133–141.

Vaughan, W. Jr. (1985). Choice: A local analysis. *Journal of the Experimental Analysis of Behavior, 43*, 383–405.

Vaughan, W. Jr. and Herrnstein, R. J. (1997). Stability, melioration, and natural selection. In H. Rachlin and D. I. Laibson (eds.), *The matching law: Papers in psychology and economics* (pp. 194–225). New York: Russell Sage Foundation.

Vollmer, T. R. and Bourret, J. (2000). An application of the matching law to evaluate the allocation of two- and three-point shots by college basketball players. *Journal of Applied Behavior Analysis, 33*, 137–150.

Wearden, J. H. (1988). Some neglected problems in the analysis of human operant behavior. In G. Davey and C. Cullen (eds.), *Human Operant Conditioning and Behavior Modification*. Chichester: John Wiley & Sons Ltd.

Consumer store choice

A matching analysis

Nguyen Bui Huynh and Gordon R. Foxall

Introduction

Consumer decisions are multi-faceted: the buyer must choose whether to buy a product at all, which brand to buy, where to make the purchase, how much to buy, at what price, and so on. Most research in consumer behavior analysis has been concerned with decisions between products and between brands. This chapter fills a gap in current research by examining consumer store choice, a topic that has thus far been given little emphasis. Specifically, it seeks to explain and interpret consumer selection of different types of stores which differ in terms of the scope of the consumer behavior settings they present. An open setting is an environment in which there are relatively many reinforcers available to consumers, who are therefore presented with a multiplicity of different behaviors on each shopping occasion. By contrast, closed settings present one or perhaps a few behavioral alternatives. A large supermarket which carries many lines presents the consumer with the opportunity to buy many different products and brands and is therefore considered an open consumer behavior setting. However, a smaller convenience store which carries fewer lines presents the customer with a limited choice, and is therefore considered a closed consumer behavior setting.

Theoretical framework

The three-term contingency

The three-term contingency shows how the frequency of behavior relates to its previous consequences (Skinner, 1953):

$$S^D \rightarrow R \rightarrow S^{r+/-}$$

where S^D represents the discriminative stimulus, and R is the response that is either reinforced (S^{r+}) or punished S^{r-}. There are two major kinds of consequences: reinforcers, which increase behavior they follow, and punishers, which decrease behavior they follow. Both reinforcement and punishment can be classified as positive and negative. Positive and negative here do not mean good and bad; they mean adding a stimulus and removing a stimulus, respectively. Therefore, positive reinforcement is the presentation of a stimulus after a response so that the response will occur more often. Negative reinforcement is the removal of a stimulus after a response so that the response will occur more often. Similarly, positive punishment is the presentation of a stimulus after a response so that the response will occur less often. Negative punishment is the removal of a stimulus after a response so that the response will occur less often.

Matching analysis

The strict matching law

The matching law expresses a quantitative relationship between the relative rates of response and the relative rates of reinforcement on concurrent schedules of reinforcement (Davison & McCarthy, 1988; Herrnstein, 1961; Herrnstein et al., 1997). If animals such as pigeons and rats in experimental situations are presented with two keys, A and B, and each choice leads to reinforcers like food pellets being delivered according to its particular schedule, they allocate their responses by pecking the keys in proportion to the relative rate of reinforcement. If B_x and B_y are the rate of responses on two schedules that yield obtained rates of reinforcement R_x and R_y, the strict matching law holds that the relative response rate $B_x / (B_x + B_y)$ matches the relative reinforcement rate $R_x/(R_x + R_y)$. That is,

$$\frac{B_x}{B_x + B_y} = \frac{R_x}{R_x + R_y} .$$

The matching law, which is well established empirically (De Villiers, 1977; Herrnstein et al., 1997), is a law at the molar level, which is concerned with overall relative frequencies of choice behavior. Herrnstein and colleagues (Herrnstein & Prelec, 1991; Herrnstein & Vaughan, 1980) also developed a theory of melioration to explain the underlying mechanism of matching.

The generalized matching equation

A generalized form of the matching law which expresses it as a power function between ratios of behavior and ratios of reinforcement rates has been developed (Baum, 1974, 1979; see also Lander & Irwin, 1968) as a means of explaining experimental data that violated the strict version. As a result, the strict matching law can be interpreted as a special case of this generalized law (Davison & McCarthy, 1988, p. 48). The first step in generalization is to express the matching law as the relationship between a behavior ratio and a reinforcement ratio (rather than as it is expressed traditionally in terms of proportions); hence, it becomes:

$$\frac{B_x}{B_y} = \frac{R_x}{R_y} \tag{1}$$

B_x, B_y, R_y and R_y represent behavior and reinforcers as in the equations above. Second, the equation is presented in log-ratio form:

$$log\frac{B_x}{B_y} = s\, log\frac{R_x}{R_y} + logb \cdot \tag{2}$$

If the generalized matching law is in a non-logarithmic form, it becomes the power function:

$$\frac{B_x}{B_y} = b\left(\frac{R_x}{R_y}\right)^s$$

The intercept, b, is interpreted as a measure of bias toward a particular response not accounted for by the reinforcement schedules in place, while the exponent, s, is interpreted as sensitivity to reinforcement, the extent to which unit changes in reinforcer ratios are accompanied by unit changes in response shifting. Only if both b and s equal unity do the data exhibit strict matching. More specifically, bias indicates a systematic preference for one alternative over the other. Choice could, for instance, be biased toward large reinforcers over small reinforcers, immediate reinforcers over delayed reinforcers, easy responses over hard responses, higher-quality reinforcers over lower-quality reinforcers, and reinforcers that occur at unpredictable times (VI) over reinforcers that occur at regular times (FI) (Baum, 1974). In the marketing context, bias may stem from the positioning of alternative brands within the store, the positioning and space allocated to different brands on the shelves for the particular product category, the positioning of substitute and complementary products, and so on (Foxall & Schrezenmaier, 2003; Schrezenmaier, 2005).

Sensitivity (the slope, s, also called the beta) refers to the subject's tendency to "overmatching", "undermatching," "perfect matching", or "antimatching" (Herrnstein et al., 1997). Overmatching occurs when the relative rate of responding on a key is more extreme than predicted by matching, meaning the subject appears to be "more sensitive" to the differences in reinforcement between the alternatives. On the other hand, in undermatching the relative rate of responding on a key is less extreme than predicted by matching. The subject appears to be "less sensitive" to the differences in reinforcement between the two keys than when matching occurs. Matching occurs when the relative rate of responding on a key matches the relative rate of reinforcement. Behavioral economists have also proven that the bias b and sensitivity s achieved from matching analysis links to the degree of substitutability, complementarity, and independence among economic commodities (Green & Freed, 1993; Rachlin et al., 1981). Last but not least, antimatching occurs when the increase of choices of one alternative leads to the selection of the other. In this case, the slope is less than 0. One reason for this is that the reinforcers (products or brands) are gross complements instead of substitutes (e.g., bread and butter) (Foxall et al., 2010).

Matching versus maximization accounts of behavior

According to micro economic theory, an organism behaves by maximizing a set of properties in the environment (Rachlin et al., 1981). The controlled studies assumed that responses (key pecking or bar pressing) are analogous to money; food pellets or other items of reward are analogous to goods; and the ratios of responses to rewards are analogous to price (Wells & Foxall, 2013). As a result, two different schools of thought have developed since: that of behavioral economists, led by Kagel (1995), whose studies provide experimental evidence for maximization, and the other among behavioral psychologists, exemplified by Herrnstein et al. (1997), whose studies arm them with evidence for melioration in which consumers choose the rewarding option without necessarily maximizing their overall returns. Because consumer behavior analysis is a sub-discipline of behavioral economics, it has been concerned with examining maximization theory in the form of the amount of brand returns on the average price. Maximization theory is usually compared with matching theory in terms of predicting behavior so although they are different they are, in some way, related to each other (Herrnstein, 1970; Herrnstein & Loveland, 1975; Herrnstein et al., 1997). One of the biggest differences between the two is that maximization theory is based on rational choice theory, whilst matching law is not. Sigurdsson (2008) believes that this is an advantage of matching law over maximization theory because it enables the predicting of behavior that violates assumptions of rational choice theory such as people's decisions to conform to discounting of delayed outcomes, and preference for rewards that are in the near future. However, it is believed that maximization theory and matching law are not in conflict but support each other in consumer behavior research. According to previous work (Foxall et al., 2004; Herrnstein et al., 1997), the parameters of matching in the marketing contexts lead to a similar pattern of choice in both maximization and matching theories (Wells & Foxall, 2013). Hence, maximization is also called probability matching in consumer behavior analysis.

Substitutability, complementarity, and independence

Substitute goods are similar items that meet largely the same functional need; that is to say, two different goods may be used interchangeably for the same purpose (e.g., two brands of butter). Two goods are complements if they satisfy different parts of a compound need (e.g., bread and butter), and two goods are independent if their consumption or use is not related (e.g., walking sticks and billiard balls) (Henderson & Quandt, 1958; Lattin & McAlister, 1985). Consumers usually seek a substitute when their first-choice product/brand soars dramatically in price. Therefore, it is believed that price is the most powerful reason for consumers' choice of a substitute product/brand over their preferred one. Another factor is individual income. When it decreases, a consumer is forced to spend more wisely. As a result, he/she has to select less expensive substitute products/brands to keep within financial bounds.

Cross-price elasticity of demand, probably the most well known and widely accepted, has been used as a measure of competitive influences of products/brands on one another. It is based on the assumption that demand for a product/brand will change as a response to a change in the price of the other. For instance, if the price of fuel went up 5%, and the demand for new cars decreased by 10%, the cross elasticity of demand would be:

$$\frac{-10\%}{5\%} = -2$$

A positive cross-price elasticity indicates substitutes while a negative cross elasticity denotes two products that are complements (Lattin & McAlister, 1985). The logic for this rule is quite simple. It is assumed that two products, X and Y, are substitutes, meaning that a fall in demand for X stems from a rise in demand for Y. That is to say, if the price of product Y decreases, consumers purchase more Y and less X. As a result, the demand curve for product X shifts to the left, decreasing X's demand and resulting in a positive value for the cross elasticity of demand (both price change of Y and quantity change of X are negative). The exact opposite reasoning holds for complements.

Literature review

Ehrenberg (1972) and his colleagues researched the patterns of multi-brand purchasing, which reveals that there is little loyalty in total for a particular brand and most consumers prefer to try and test brands randomly. The work had limitations, though, as it only described the patterns of brand choice, and failed to answer the question why these patterns exist. Foxall (1999b), inspired by his observation that the pattern of choice revealed by Ehrenberg's research and that which was characteristic of the patterns of choice revealed by matching theorists were broadly similar, argued that patterns of brand choices observed for a buyer during a period of time could be explained in terms of the groups of reinforcements (both rewards and punishments) he/she received and suggested that the relationship between the choices and their reinforcements should be paid more attention. This was the first attempt to bring the matching law – a psychology theory – to the marketplace. It also pioneered the shift of focus from investigating the pattern of choice to interpreting the behavior.

One of the major concerns of consumer behavior analysis is that matching theories are developed through nonhuman experiments whilst consumer behavior occurs in real-life situations. The context makes the behavior more complicated and trickier to understand and explain. Therefore, there is a fundamental need to clarify how researchers transfer methodologically the results of matching analysis into consumer research. Otherwise, the research would be irrelevant and inapplicable. One major step of the transfer is to make adjustments to schedules of reinforcement. Drawing from a general agreement in the literature (Hursh, 1984; Hursh & Bauman, 1987; Myerson & Hale, 1984), Foxall (1999b) claimed that ratio schedules might be more suitable to explain consumption and purchasing activities than the traditional interval schedules that have usually been developed and tested in the laboratory.

Since the idea that matching analysis could play a vital role in explaining and interpreting consumer behavior was developed (Foxall, 1999a; Green & Freed, 1993), a number of studies of consumers' brand and product choices for nondurables within the framework of the generalized matching equation have been conducted based on panel data (Foxall & James, 2001, 2003; Foxall et al., 2004; Oliveira-Castro et al., 2005; Romero et al., 2006). These studies tested the three types of matching in complex and natural consumer contexts with the use of both quantitative and qualitative approaches (though the quantitative one is dominant). The three different forms of matching are: amount matching (classical matching), cost matching (relative demand analysis), and probability matching (maximization analysis). The scope of the research has been broadened both in respect of the sample sizes, increased from just a few to many thousands, and of the data collecting time that has gone from a couple of weeks to a year. First, in amount matching analysis, the researchers have examined the relationship between the proportion of responses in the form of the amount of money spent on a product and the proportion of reinforcers in the form of quantity (Foxall & James, 2001; Foxall et al., 2004; Foxall et al., 2007). The results indicated a strong pattern of matching in the case of brand choice within the same product class and of anti-matching in the case of brand selection between different product classes. Second, for cost matching, consumer behavior analysts have used a method similar to that used in animal experimental studies performed by Battalio et al. (1981). The method puts price on the x-axis instead of the y-axis, in contrast to the traditional economic demand analysis. As in other kinds of matching, cost matching is performed with a ratio in which the amount bought, in the role of response, is the dependent variable and the price, in the role of punishment, is the independent variable. The majority of the demand curves, unsurprisingly, came with downward slopes – as the price goes down, the quantity should increase. Upward-sloping demand curves were found in several cases, though (Wells & Foxall, 2013). Last but not least, probability matching, also called maximization analysis, attempts to test the connection between the reinforcers earned in the form of quantity of brands (the dependent variable) and probability of reinforcement (the independent variable). The probability is calculated "as the reciprocal of the price of brand A (brand 1) over the reciprocal of the mean of the prices of the other brands" (Foxall et al., 2004, p. 241). A tendency toward maximization has been reported from the results of previous research projects into maximization analysis. Also, studies on durable goods like music compact discs bought online in experimental virtual shopping malls (DiClemente & Hantula, 2003; Hantula et al., 2001), research on computer-generated choices (Smith & Hantula, 2003), and in-store field experiments (Sigurdsson et al., 2009) have been carried out. Moreover, various experimental matching studies concerned with online buying behavior have been undertaken such as the examination of the quality of websites, the effect of offers of free shipping, and the combined effects of different marketing activities (Fagerstrøm, 2010).

Although these studies have focused on consumers' product and brand choice rather than store choice, the findings still provide invaluable lessons in terms of applying matching theory to consumer behavior analysis. First, consumers generally do not choose from all of the brands available in a product class but from a small repertoire of brands generated by trial and error (Wells & Foxall, 2013). The repertoire of tried and trusted brands encompasses both functional and symbolic reinforcement. Functional benefit – in the case of a cell phone, for example – is the ability to stay connected with others, and symbolic benefits are prestige and other forms of performance feedback stemming from the latest iPhone or other luxury smart phones. Functional and symbolic benefits (positive reinforcers) have been identified and measured and, more importantly, shown to exert identifiable impacts on buying behavior (Foxall et al., 2004; Oliveira-Castro et al., 2005).

Second, thanks to the idea that the exponent of Baum's generalized matching equation can be used as a measure of the substitutability of the reinforcers (see, e.g., Kagel (1995)), there are a number of studies which show that the results of amount matching analyses can be used to establish the incidence of competing brands within a product class (substitutes), the boundaries between product classes (independent and complementary commodities), and sub-classes of products (Foxall et al., 2010; Romero et al., 2006). The findings of the research had a consensus that the degree to which brands within and between product categories act as substitutes or complements also varies across patterns of reinforcement that incorporate these product/brand features (Foxall et al., 2010). Once again, it can be seen that understanding patterns of reinforcement plays a vital role in interpreting consumer choice.

Methodology

Sample and sampling

This study used data from the ACNielsen Homescan panel compromising 1,500 consumers randomly selected as representatives of the UK population. Panel participants, rewarded with cash-converted points accumulated through each interaction, scanned the barcodes printed on the packages of their purchases into a sophisticated handheld barcode reader after each shopping occasion and the data were transmitted to the company. The information recorded for each such occasion includes brand, price paid, quantity bought (package size), number of units bought (number of packages bought), date of purchase, and name of store from which the product was purchased. Data for four fast-moving consumer product categories purchased during a period of a year (July 17, 2004 to July 15, 2005) were analyzed: fruit juice, baked beans, biscuits, and yellow fats (Figures 7.1–7.4). Table 7.1 shows the data used in this study that include the total number of purchases, the total number of consumers, and the total number of stores for each product class. Only consumers who made at least three purchases in the product category were included in the analyses.

According to Table 7.1, the number of purchases and number of consumers are very high. This increases the reliability of the study. Specifically, each consumer, on average, made 16.50

Table 7.1 Basic information of the sample

	Baked beans	Biscuits	Fruit juice	Yellow fats
Number of purchases	13,729	75,563	21,394	30,906
Number of consumers	832	1,594	895	1,354
Number of stores	50	74	52	58

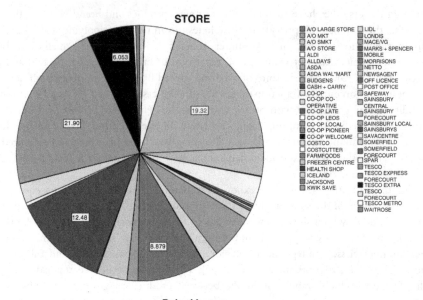

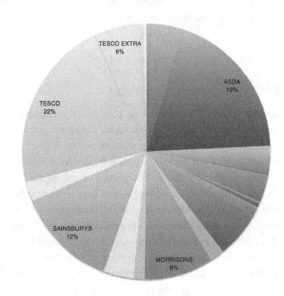

Figure 7.1   Number of purchases of baked beans

purchases of baked beans, 47.40 purchases of biscuits, 23.90 purchases of fruit juice, and 22.83 purchases of yellow fats. Biscuits were available in 74 stores whereas buyers could find baked beans in only 50 locations.

The pie chart compares the number of purchases of baked beans among different stores. As can be seen, Asda (19.3%), Tesco (21.9%), Sainsbury's (12.5%), and Morrisons (8.9%) are the four biggest and most well-known stores in the UK in terms of the number of purchases. Hence, it is reasonable to put these four into the relative open setting class. Intriguingly, the

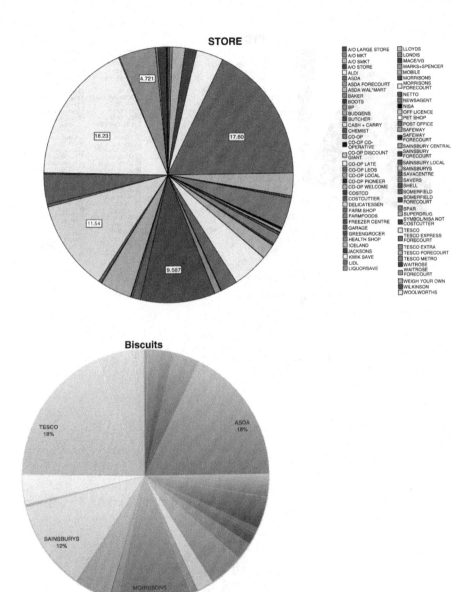

Figure 7.2 Number of purchases of biscuits

number of purchases from Tesco Extra – one of Tesco's convenience stores – is 6.1%, suggesting that Tesco's branding strategy of developing supermarket and convenience store systems at the same time seems to be an effective and successful one.

Tesco had the biggest frequency of buying with 18.23% whilst Asda was the runner-up in terms of number of purchases with only 0.5% lower than Tesco. Sainsbury's (11.54%) and Morrisons (9.6%) ranked third and fourth, respectively. For biscuits, Tesco Extra provided another example of Tesco's success in developing their convenience store chain with a significant percentage of 4.72%.

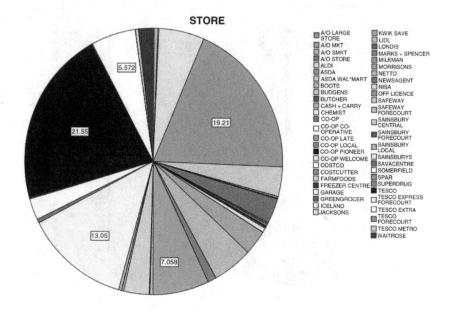

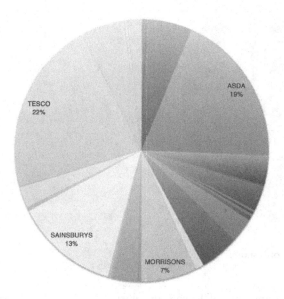

Figure 7.3 Number of purchases of fruit juice

For fruit juice, Tesco, Asda, and Sainsbury's were still favorite places to shop among major consumers. Morrisons' percentage of only 7.06% was very low compared to other names in the "Big Four".

Tesco ranked first in the table of number of purchases with 21.20% while Morrisons, as with fruit juice, had the lowest ranking among the four biggest stores in the UK. Tesco Extra accounted for a large share of purchases among stores in the relatively closed setting group.

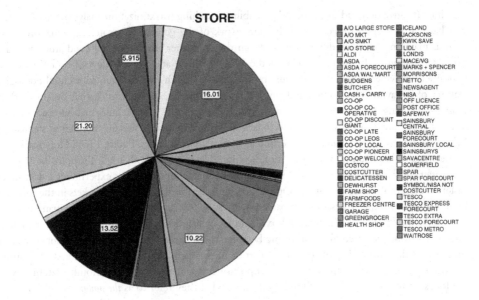

STORE

Yellow fats

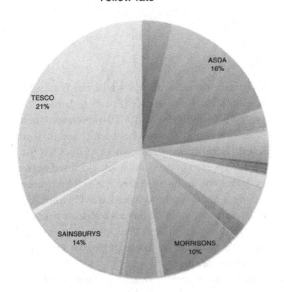

Figure 7.4 Number of purchases of yellow fats

Aggregate level of analysis

The data in this study have been transformed and analyzed using R, which is a free software programming language and software environment for statistical computing and graphics (Figure 7.5–7.6). The detailed data transforming and analyzing are shown in the appendix to this chapter. Three different kinds of matching analysis have been performed: amount matching (classical matching), cost matching (relative demand analysis), and probability matching (maximization analysis). The data analyses have all been performed within the framework of the generalized matching equation where there is matching between different variables in the consumer environment (brand amount, brand price, and reciprocal brand price). The methodology of these analyses was developed and based on consumer behavior analysis demonstrated by Foxall (1999b). The approach includes methodological features of behavioral economics and psychology. Regression analysis was carried out in all three kinds of matching, and the results were demonstrated graphically to make information easier to visualize. The data are also transformed into logarithmic form, which is widely accepted as standard in behavioral psychology and animal experiments in matching (see, e.g., Baum, 1974). The logarithmic transformation has been proven to be more realistic (Slater & Ashcroft, 1990) for both the standard and generalized matching laws as well as to make comparisons to other experimental data much easier. In each of the analyses, Store "Open," covering the four biggest supermarkets in the UK, was used as the base for the analyses in comparison with Store "Closed," representing the remaining stores.

Amount matching (classical matching). Foxall and his colleagues in the Consumer Behavior Analysis Research Group explored the relationship between the relative amount of money spent on a commodity and the proportion of reinforcers earned in the form of quantity of brands. In this study, the researchers employed the following proportional calculations for the amount matching with the focus on the stores instead of the brands; first, what they refer to as *the amount bought ratio*:

$$\frac{Amount\ bought\ in\ Open\ Stores}{Amount\ bought\ in\ Closed\ Stores}$$

and, then, *the amount paid ratio*:

$$\frac{Amount\ paid\ in\ Open\ Stores}{Amount\ paid\ in\ Closed\ Stores}$$

By doing so, the intercept value is considered as a measure of bias whilst the beta value is described as a measure of sensitivity, *s,* to reinforcement schedules (Foxall & James, 2003). Following Baum's ideas (1974, 1979), *s* values between 0.90 and 1.10 represented perfect matching, *s* values over 1.10 stood for overmatching, and *s* values between 0 and 0.90 were described as undermatching. In particular, Kagel (1995) stressed cases where *s* values less than 0 are known as antimatching. These extreme cases, reported in previous work, occurred between brands in different product categories; they were not complementary but fulfilled different needs and wants of consumers. Graphically, perfect matching is presented as a 45° line. Where the slope *s* (the beta) is less than 1, there is undermatching whereas there is overmatching where the slope is more than 1. Amount matching analysis is supposed to give a measurement of the substitutability of the store "open" by the store "closed," or in this example, the giant supermarkets against mid-size supermarkets and convenience stores.

Cost matching (relative demand analysis). Cost matching analysis treats the effects of monetary cost on relative demand. Thus, cost matching analysis is also called relative demand analysis. Like amount matching, cost matching is also studied using ratio analysis. In terms of matching, this denotes the connection between the rate of relative reinforcers earned in the form of the amount bought in behavior settings (dependent variable), and the proportion of punishment in the form of the cost (independent variable) of them:

Amount Bought Ratio:

$$\frac{Amount\ bought\ in\ Open\ Stores}{Amount\ bought\ in\ Closed\ Stores}$$

Average Price Ratio:

$$\frac{Average\ price\ in\ Open\ Stores}{Average\ price\ in\ Closed\ Stores}$$

The data are shown graphically. In accordance with economics, it is supposed that demand curves are usually downward sloping because as the price reduces, generally, the number of purchases increases. In other words, by revealing the store's customers' responses to considerable price reductions, cost matching shows how sensitive consumers' relative choices are to a change in relative prices (Wells & Foxall, 2013). R^2 values also show the role of price in comparison to other factors affecting consumer choice.

Probability matching (maximization analysis). Maximization analysis involves the relationship between relative reinforcers earned in the form of quantity bought in stores (the dependent variable) and probability of reinforcement (the independent variable).

$$\frac{\dfrac{1}{Average}\ Price\ in\ Open\ Stores}{\dfrac{1}{Average}\ Price\ in\ Open\ Stores + \dfrac{1}{Average}\ Price\ in\ Closed\ Stores}$$

The amount bought ratio is calculated in the same way as in amount and cost matching analyses. The price used in the relative probability of reinforcement ratio is the average price in the selected stores. The maximization analysis is demonstrated graphically to determine the extent of maximization behavior and is represented graphically by a step function. If the step function described by the data points falls to the right of the 0.5 line on the abscissa, then buyers are maximizing by selecting the stores considered as open settings; but if it lies on the left of the 0.5 line, closed settings are where buyers maximize (cf. Foxall et al., 2004; Herrnstein & Loveland, 1975). The probability matching analysis will indicate if buyers are maximizing their utility by choosing to shop in stores that provide products relatively cheaper than the others do or in terms of what they gain from the store in informational consequences.

Individual level of analysis

Matching analyses. Among the four biggest supermarkets selected as open behavior settings when analyzing at the aggregate level, Tesco clearly pursues a strategy of developing both supermarket and convenient store chains. Therefore, it is worth examining the company by applying all the matching analysis procedures presented above. The analyses at the individual store level provide a method of testing whether our subjective interpretation of the openness of consumer behavior settings is valid. In other words, they are an attempt to determine the limitations of the research. The details of open stores and closed stores for Tesco are shown in Table 7.2.

Substitutability analysis. In this research, in addition to the discussion on substitutability of stores in the amount matching analyses described earlier (at the aggregate level as well as at Tesco), additional store combinations were analyzed to test their levels of substitutability, independence, and complementarity. Based on the four biggest companies listed as open settings, six combinations of store were analyzed: Asda/Morrisons, Asda/Sainsbury's, Asda/Tesco, Morrisons/Sainsbury's, Morrisons/Tesco, and Sainsbury's/Tesco. The parameters of the

Table 7.2 Information by openness of settings (Tesco)

Name of stores	Baked beans	Biscuits	Fruit juice	Yellow fats
	Number of purchases			
Store "Open"				
TESCO	3007	13772	4611	6552
Store "Closed"				
TESCO EXPRESS FORECOURT	7	112	21	27
TESCO EXTRA	831	3567	1192	1828
TESCO FORECOURT	3	13	3	3
TESCO METRO	41	207	82	56

amount matching's regression have also been adjusted. Instead of store "open" standing for the relatively open setting group and store "closed" standing for the relatively closed setting group, the response ratio becomes:

$$\frac{Amount\ bought\ in\ Store\ 1}{Amount\ bought\ in\ Store\ 2}$$

and the reinforcement ratio becomes:

$$\frac{Amount\ paid\ in\ Store\ 1}{Amount\ paid\ in\ Store\ 2}$$

where the expressions Store 1 and Store 2 represent the stores being compared (e.g., for the first combination, Store 1 refers to Asda and Store 2 refers to Morrisons). The store combinations were designed, as in previous work (Foxall et al., 2010), to represent the nature of consumer choice, in particular natural marketing settings, rather than to cover the entire spectrum of stores available.

Results and discussion

Amount matching

Aggregate level of analysis. This can be seen to be confirmed. At the aggregate level, the general matching equation explains the data very well, all multiple regressions were statistically significant ($p < 0.05$), and R^2 values ranged from 0.985, for fruit juice, to 0.990, for yellow fats. The number of data points (n) used to calculate each regression ranged from 832 for baked beans to 1,594 for biscuits. Values of the intercept were very close to zero and ranged from 0.006 to 0.080, indicating the absence of strong bias when the reinforcing attribute was relatively constant. Values of beta were all significant for all product categories ($p < 0.05$), suggesting that the ratio of amount bought is a true reinforcement. In addition, the betas were all positive, ranging from 0.718 for baked beans to 0.869 for biscuits. This indicates that increases in reinforcement were associated with increases in spending. The betas show undermatching for all four products. The findings can be examined visually as fitted values of regression (the bold line) have a smaller slope than the 45-degree line (the dashed line).

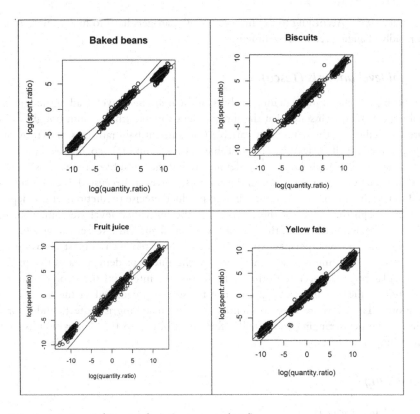

Figure 7.5 Amount matching analysis (aggregate level)

Table 7.3 Parameters calculated for each product (amount matching)

	n	p-value	R-squared	Beta	Intercept
Baked beans	832	0.000	0.987	0.718	0.077
Biscuits	1594	0.000	0.988	0.869	0.006
Fruit juice	895	0.000	0.985	0.753	0.080
Yellow fats	1354	0.000	0.990	0.831	0.049

When the matching law is expressed as a power function, the parameter *s* (the beta) is interpreted as demonstrating the substitutability of the alternative reinforcement. In previous research (Foxall & James, 2001, 2003; Foxall & Schrezenmaier, 2003), perfect matching results in perfect substitutability whilst undermatching is usually found in examples of independent or complementary alternatives. Therefore, it can be concluded that open and closed behavior settings can be either independent of or complementary to each other. Consumers may prefer to shop at supermarkets for regular needs when they have sufficient time and choose to go to convenience stores for "fill-in" items if time for shopping is limited.

Baum mentioned that undermatching happens as a result of indifference (1974, 1979). In this study, the ease with which consumers switch between open and closed settings, that is between supermarkets and convenience stores, implies consumer indifference. This is consistent with the findings of earlier analyses indicating that there is low store loyalty and significant store switching behavior for grocery store purchases (Keng & Ehrenberg, 1984; Popkowski et al., 1997;

Uncles et al., 1995). According to the findings, retail managers have to find a solution to cope with a rapidly changing retail environment.

Individual-level analysis (Tesco)

The results from the amount matching analysis, at the individual level, lead to the rejection of the null hypothesis which states that the independent variable (the amount bought ratio) has absolutely no effect on the dependent variable (the amount paid ratio), as shown by the fact that the p values are all far less than 0.05 (Table 7.4). The multiple coefficient of determination R^2 values are very high (over 90%), demonstrating the good fit of the regression models. These values are not a main indicator in this analysis, however, because the regression models are used to test the matching law rather than to produce precise predictions of the dependent variable. Although the values of the intercept at the individual level are somewhat higher than those at the aggregate level, they are still very small and close to zero in absolute value. From a regression analysis perspective, the value of the intercept is almost always insignificant. However, according to matching theorists, the intercept demonstrates the preference for a particular response over the other. The higher the intercept, the stronger the preference; therefore, there is no strong preference for stores categorized in the relatively open setting group. The betas are used to identify whether matching is perfect, under, or over. Specifically, the betas ranging from 0.691, for baked beans, to 0.844, for biscuits, indicate undermatching in all cases.

Cost matching

Aggregate-level analysis

As Table 7.5 indicates, all multiple regressions were significant (p< 0.05) and R^2 values ranged from 0.601, for baked beans, to 0.655, for yellow fats. Values of beta were significant for all product categories (p< 0.05), suggesting that the ratio of price is a true reinforcer. Besides, the betas were all positive, ranging from 1.604, for biscuits, to 2.044, for baked beans. This indicates that increases in price were associated with increases in amounts bought, meaning that upward-sloping demand curves are observed. The results do not support earlier study results where the expected downward patterns were observed (Foxall & James, 2003), suggesting that downward-sloping demand curves show substitutability among brands; that is to say, consumers buy less of a brand at higher prices because they can switch to other brands. Following the same logic, the results of this study indicate that buyers did not find the stores to be acceptable substitutes for one another and thus were less sensitive to the price changes. Furthermore, open and closed behavior settings seem not to be substitutes but independent or even complementary in terms of the purpose of shopping trips (open settings for main purchases whereas closed settings are used for fill-in requirements).

Table 7.4 Parameters calculated for Tesco (amount matching)

	n	p-value	R-squared	Beta	Intercept
Baked beans	415	0.000	0.983	0.691	−0.035
Biscuits	915	0.000	0.990	0.844	−0.000
Fruit juice	487	0.000	0.983	0.714	0.042
Yellow fats	755	0.000	0.990	0.806	−0.015

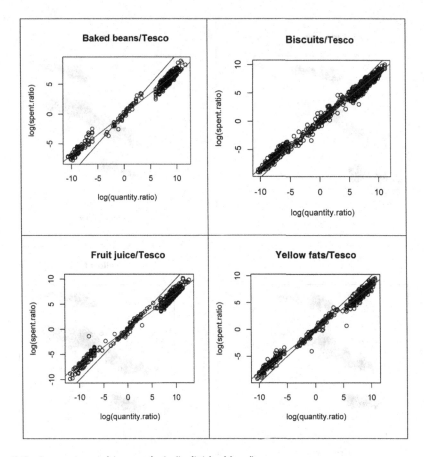

Figure 7.6 Amount matching analysis (individual level)

Table 7.5 Parameters calculated for each product (cost matching)

	n	p-value	R-squared	Beta	Intercept
Baked beans	832	0.000	0.601	2.044	–0.122
Biscuits	1594	0.000	0.625	4.769	–0.115
Fruit juice	895	0.000	0.611	5.720	0.265
Yellow fats	1354	0.000	0.655	6.022	–0.063

Individual-level analysis

Table 7.6 and Figure 7.8 show the results from the cost matching analysis for Tesco. As with the results at the aggregate level, an upward-sloping relative demand curve is observed here, meaning that a reduction in the unit price in "open" stores leads to a decrease in the amount bought ratio of those stores. Besides, the coefficients of determination indicate that the relationship between the relative price in the "open" stores and the relative quantity demanded is strong with all above 90%. This shows that relative prices are an important factor in explaining consumer buying behavior in respect of stores' openness.

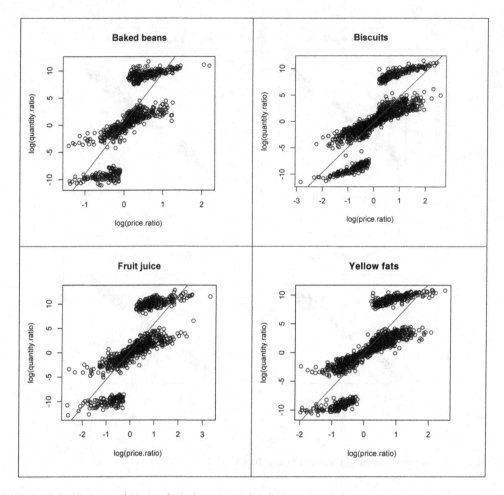

Figure 7.7 Cost matching analysis (aggregate level)

Probability matching

Aggregate-level analysis

As is apparent from Table 7.7, all multiple regressions were significant (p< 0.05). The multiple coefficient of determination R^2 values are all greater than 0.6 and also greater than those of the earlier studies. A step function pattern rather than probability matching is observed in all cases and for all schedules. The betas are all negative and thus the data points graphically fall to the right of

Table 7.6 Parameters calculated for Tesco (cost matching)

	n	p-value	R-squared	Beta	Intercept
Baked beans	415	0.000	0.569	7.761	2.126
Biscuits	915	0.000	0.589	5.964	1.522
Fruit juice	487	0.000	0.567	5.875	1.787
Yellow fats	755	0.000	0.627	6.354	1.412

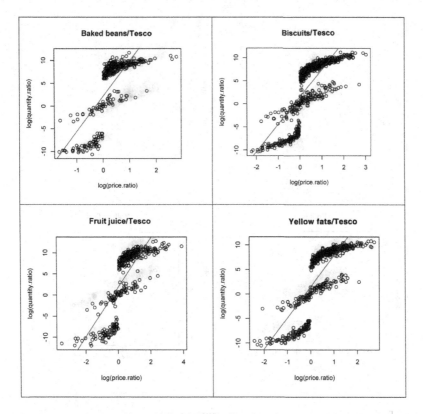

Figure 7.8 Cost matching analysis (individual level)

the 0.5-line on the x-axis. This means that the buyers are maximizing by choosing the open set-ting group of stores Asda, Morrisons, Sainsbury's, and Tesco. In maximization analysis of previous work, there was evidence that consumers tend to maximize their utility by selecting the cheapest brands within a product class. It might be the case here that these giant supermarkets are able and willing to offer good cut-price deals over a long period of time to attract and retain consumers. The intercept values, which indicate the consumers' store preferences, point to the same conclu-sion as their absolute value is a very high number compared to those in amount matching and cost matching. The values show a strong and obvious bias toward the open setting group.

Individual-level analysis

Probability matching at the individual level of analysis gives similar results to those found at the aggregate level. First, the p-values are statistically significant. Second, the R-squared values

Table 7.7 Parameters calculated for each product (probability matching)

	n	p-value	R-squared	Beta	Intercept
Baked beans	832	0.000	0.621	−41.002	20.881
Biscuits	1594	0.000	0.636	−21.910	10.841
Fruit juice	895	0.000	0.642	−27.448	13.924
Yellow fats	1354	0.000	0.672	−27.054	13.439

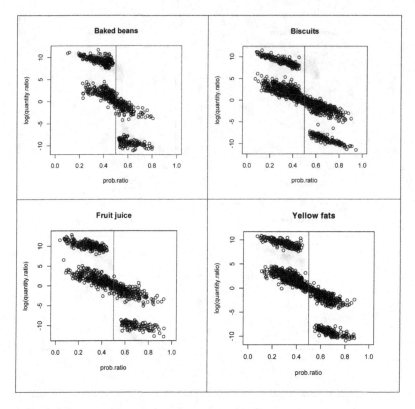

Figure 7.9 Probability matching analysis (aggregate level)

prove that the regression models are a good fit. Next, the betas are negative, meaning the data points fall to the right of the 0.5 line and thus consumers maximize their benefit when selecting a Tesco supermarket rather than Tesco Extra or one of Tesco's other convenience stores. Last, the intercept indicated the consumers' strong preference for Tesco's supermarkets over the company's convenience stores.

Substitutability analysis

Tables 7.9, 7.10, 7.11, and 7.12 summarize the results of the substitutability analysis, showing the slope, intercept, and R squared for each store combination for baked beans, biscuits, fruit juice, and yellow fats. Previous work (Wells & Foxall, 2013) suggested that highly substitutable products followed a near-perfect matching pattern. By contrast, highly complementary products showed undermatching. Products ranked as independents seemed to show undermatching.

Table 7.8 Parameters calculated for Tesco (probability matching)

	n	p-value	R-squared	Beta	Intercept
Baked beans	415	0.000	0.621	−36.982	20.401
Biscuits	915	0.000	0.645	−29.907	16.259
Fruit juice	487	0.000	0.651	−32.175	17.441
Yellow fats	755	0.000	0.678	−31.220	16.792

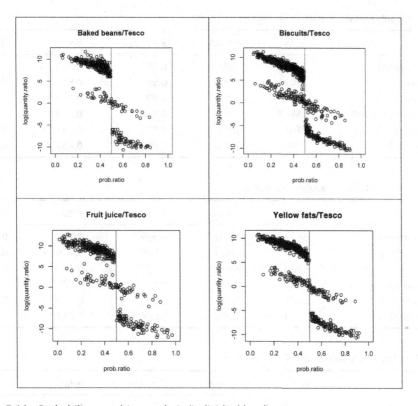

Figure 7.10 Probability matching analysis (individual level)

When designing the combinations of the four supermarkets, the researchers decided to follow these suggestions. Because those four companies are in the same range of number of purchases, they are supposed to be substitute stores rather than independent or complementary ones and thus a near-perfect matching pattern was expected to be observed in all cases. The findings were totally different, however. For baked beans, Table 7.5 indicated that the values of the s parameter varied between 0.685 and 0.695. The findings for biscuits showed a similar pattern with the slope ranging from 0.843, for the combination of Asda and Morrisons, to 0.854, for the combination of Asda and Sainsbury's. Undermatching was also found in the cases of fruit juice and yellow fats. As a result, those stores are independent or complementary ones. This can be explained by a consumer not making detailed comparisons between supermarkets before shopping for fast-moving commodities (e.g. it is unlikely that a buyer chooses to shop at Tesco

Table 7.9 Substitutability analysis for baked beans

	n	p-value	R-squared	Beta	Intercept
Asda/Morrisons	3872	0.000	0.988	0.686	0.028
Asda/Sainsbury's	4366	0.000	0.990	0.693	−0.038
Asda/Tesco	5660	0.000	0.990	0.694	−0.001
Morrisons/Sainsbury's	2932	0.000	0.988	0.685	−0.067
Morrisons/Tesco	4226	0.000	0.986	0.691	−0.020
Sainsbury's/Tesco	4720	0.000	0.987	0.695	0.037

Table 7.10 Substitutability analysis for biscuits

	n	p-value	R-squared	Beta	Intercept
Asda/Morrisons	20544	0.000	0.993	0.843	0.061
Asda/Sainsbury's	22023	0.000	0.994	0.854	0.038
Asda/Tesco	27072	0.000	0.993	0.848	0.017
Morrisons/Sainsbury's	15967	0.000	0.994	0.848	−0.116
Morrisons/Tesco	21016	0.000	0.992	0.845	−0.038
Sainsbury's/Tesco	22495	0.000	0.992	0.852	0.076

Table 7.11 Substitutability analysis for fruit juice

	n	p-value	R-squared	Beta	Intercept
Asda/Morrisons	5619	0.000	0.989	0.715	−0.030
Asda/Sainsbury's	6901	0.000	0.990	0.726	−0.128
Asda/Tesco	8720	0.000	0.989	0.723	−0.028
Morrisons/Sainsbury's	4302	0.000	0.989	0.721	−0.103
Morrisons/Tesco	6121	0.000	0.986	0.720	0.003
Sainsbury's/Tesco	7403	0.000	0.987	0.732	0.104

Table 7.12 Substitutability analysis for yellow fats

	n	p-value	R-squared	Beta	Intercept
Asda/Morrisons	8107	0.000	0.993	0.796	0.003
Asda/Sainsbury's	9126	0.000	0.994	0.805	−0.100
Asda/Tesco	11499	0.000	0.994	0.804	−0.051
Morrisons/Sainsbury's	7339	0.000	0.993	0.802	−0.103
Morrisons/Tesco	9712	0.000	0.992	0.799	−0.062
Sainsbury's/Tesco	10731	0.000	0.992	0.811	0.048

rather than at Sainsbury's simply because the price of a particular cake at Tesco is less than its price at Sainsbury's). Unlike comparing products or brands in-store where differences are easily observed (via list prices, packaging, or color), consumers have to put in a great deal of time and effort when comparing products or brands in different stores and thus the task seems not to be worth considering. As a result, they tend to take for granted the idea that all giant supermarkets are similar. Those stores, in this sense, are independent from, rather than complementary to, one another. The R-squared values were all greater than 0.9, meaning that the regression models fit very well with the data. Besides, all of the intercepts are very close to zero, indicating that there are no strong preferences for a particular store over the others.

Recommendations for future research

Although this chapter has examined several aspects of consumer store choice from a consumer behavior analysis perspective, many more questions remain.

First of all, many factors/reinforcements affecting consumer store choice have not been considered in this study such as the distance between where consumers live and where they buy, or the time needed for other activities in a shopping trip like parking, or checking out (the availability of a large car park or self check-out facilities could be a massive plus for a store). This information can easily be gathered via self-report forms completed by panel participants.

Second, there is a need to refine the characteristics of different groups of behavior settings. For example, the size of stores should be taken into consideration as a criterion when deciding whether a store is a supermarket or a convenience store. Also, it is important to ask consumers about the purpose of their shopping trip. This is a means of identifying the main function of the stores – another crucial criterion of group clarification.

Last but not least, substitutability analysis can produce a better result if the substitutability scale is developed and tested. By doing so, researchers will be able to test whether there is a significant relationship between substitutability and the s parameter. The substitutability scale could be refined and augmented by incorporating qualitative studies that research other issues relating to consumer behavior analysis such as consumers' learning history or informational reinforcement of consumer store choice.

References

Battalio, R. C., Kagel, J. H., Rachlin, H., & Green, L. (1981). Commodity-choice behavior with pigeons as subjects. *The Journal of Political Economy*, 67–91.

Baum, W. M. (1974). On two types of deviation from the matching law: Bias and undermatching. *Journal of the Experimental Analysis of Behavior, 22*(1), 231–242.

Baum, W. M. (1979). Matching, undermatching, and overmatching in studies of choice. *Journal of the Experimental Analysis of Behavior, 32*(2), 269–281.

Davison, M., & McCarthy, D. (1988). *The matching law: A research review*. Hillsdale, NJ: Lawrence Erlbaum Associates, Inc.

De Villiers, P. (1977). Choice in concurrent schedules and a quantitative formulation of the law of effect. *Handbook of Operant Behavior*, 233–287.

DiClemente, D. F., & Hantula, D. A. (2003). Optimal foraging online: Increasing sensitivity to delay. *Psychology & Marketing, 20*(9), 785–809.

Ehrenberg, A. S. C. (1972). *Repeat-buying: Theory and applications*. New York: American Elsevier Publishing Company.

Fagerstrøm, A. (2010). The motivating effect of antecedent stimuli on the web shop: A conjoint analysis of the impact of antecedent stimuli at the point of online purchase. *Journal of Organizational Behavior Management, 30*(2), 199–220.

Foxall, G. R. (1999a). The marketing firm. *Journal of Economic Psychology, 20*(2), 207–234.

Foxall, G. R. (1999b). Putting consumer behaviour in its place: The Behavioural Perspective Model research programme. *International Journal of Management Reviews, 1*(2), 133–158.

Foxall, G. R., & James, V. K. (2001). The behavioral basis of consumer choice: A preliminary analysis. *European Journal of Behavior Analysis, 2*, 209–220.

Foxall, G. R., & James, V. K. (2003). The behavioral ecology of brand choice: How and what do consumers maximize? *Psychology & Marketing, 20*(9), 811–836.

Foxall, G. R., Oliveira-Castro, J. M., & Schrezenmaier, T. C. (2004). The behavioral economics of consumer brand choice: Patterns of reinforcement and utility maximization. *Behavioural Processes, 66*(3), 235–260.

Foxall, G. R., Oliveira-Castro, J. M., Schrezenmaier, T. C., & James, V. K. (2007). *The behavioral economics of brand choice*. Basingstoke: Palgrave Macmillan.

Foxall, G. R., & Schrezenmaier, T. C. (2003). The behavioral economics of consumer brand choice: Establishing a methodology. *Journal of Economic Psychology, 24*(5), 675–695.

Foxall, G. R., Wells, V. K., Chang, S. W., & Oliveira-Castro, J. M. (2010). Substitutability and independence: Matching analyses of brands and products. *Journal of Organizational Behavior Management, 30*(2), 145.

Green, L., & Freed, D. E. (1993). The substitutability of reinforcers. *Journal of the Experimental Analysis of Behavior, 60*(1), 141–158.

Hantula, D. A., DiClemente, D. F., & Rajala, A. K. (2001). Outside the box: The analysis of consumer behavior. *Organizational Change*, 203–223.

Henderson, J. M., & Quandt, R. E. (1958). *Microeconomic theory*. New York: McGraw-Hill.

Herrnstein, R. J. (1961). Relative and absolute strength of response as a function of frequency of reinforcement. *Journal of the Experimental Analysis of Behavior, 4*(3), 267–272.

Herrnstein, R. J. (1970). On the law of effect. *Journal of the Experimental Analysis of Behavior, 13*(2), 243–266.

Herrnstein, R. J., & Loveland, D. H. (1975). Maximizing and matching on concurrent ratio schedules. *Journal of the Experimental Analysis of Behavior, 24*(1), 107–116.

Herrnstein, R. J., & Prelec, D. (1991). Melioration: A theory of distributed choice. *The Journal of Economic Perspectives*, 137–156.

Herrnstein, R. J. (1997). *The matching law: Papers in psychology and economics* (Eds. Rachlin, H., & Laibson, D. I.). Cambridge, MA: Harvard; New York: Russell Sage Foundation.

Herrnstein, R. J., & Vaughan, W. (1980). Melioration and behavioral allocation. *Limits to Action: The Allocation of Individual Behavior*, 143–176.

Hursh, S. R. (1984). Behavioral economics. *Journal of the Experimental Analysis of Behavior, 42*(3), 435–452.

Hursh, S. R., & Bauman, R. A. (1987). The behavioral analysis of demand. *Advances in Behavioral Economics, 1*, 117–165.

Kagel, J. H. (1995). *Economic choice theory: An experimental analysis of animal behavior*. Cambridge: Cambridge University Press.

Keng, K. A., & Ehrenberg, A. S. C. (1984). Patterns of store choice. *Journal of Marketing Research*, 399–409.

Lander, D. G., & Irwin, R. J. (1968). Multiple schedules: Effects of the distribution of reinforcements between components on the distribution of responses between components. *Journal of the Experimental Analysis of Behavior, 11*(5), 517–524.

Lattin, J. M., & McAlister, L. (1985). Using a variety-seeking model to identify substitute and complementary relationships among competing products. *Journal of Marketing Research*, 330–339.

Myerson, J., & Hale, S. (1984). Practical implications of the matching law. *Journal of Applied Behavior Analysis, 17*(3), 367–380.

Oliveira-Castro, J. M., Foxall, G. R., & Schrezenmaier, T. C. (2005). Patterns of consumer response to retail price differentials. *The Service Industries Journal, 25*(3), 309–335.

Popkowski, P., & Timmermans, H. (1997). Store-switching behavior. *Marketing Letters, 8*(2), 193–204.

Rachlin, H., Battalio, R., Kagel, J., & Green, L. (1981). Maximization theory in behavioral psychology. *Behavioral and Brain Sciences, 4*(3), 371–388.

Romero, S., Foxall, G. R., Schrezenmaier, T., Oliveira-Castro, J., & James, V. (2006). Deviations from matching in consumer choice. *European Journal of Behavior Analysis, 7*(1), 15.

Schrezenmaier, T. C. (2005). *A methodological exploration of the relevance of behavioural economics to the study of consumer brand choice*. Cardiff: Cardiff Business School, University of Wales.

Sigurdsson, V. (2008). *Relative sales and matching analysis of consumers' brand choices in open settings*. Unpublished doctoral thesis, Cardiff University.

Sigurdsson, V., Saevarsson, H., & Foxall, G. (2009). Brand placement and consumer choice: An in-store experiment. *Journal of Applied Behavior Analysis, 42*(3), 741–745.

Skinner, B. F. (1953). *Science and Human Behavior*. New York: Simon and Schuster.

Slater, R., & Ashcroft, P. (1990). *Quantitative techniques in a business context*. London: Chapman & Hall.

Smith, C. L., & Hantula, D. A. (2003). Pricing effects on foraging in a simulated Internet shopping mall. *Journal of Economic Psychology, 24*(5), 653–674.

Uncles, M., Ehrenberg, A., & Hammond, K. (1995). Patterns of buyer behavior: Regularities, models, and extensions. *Marketing Science, 14*(3), 71–78.

Wells, V. K., & Foxall, G. R. (2013). Matching, demand, maximization, and consumer choice. *Psychological Record, 63*(2), 239–257.

Appendix

Commands in R used to calculate three types of matching:

```
setwd("/Users/newlife2102000/Google
Drive/Thesis/Biscuits")
library(foreign)
bis<-read.spss("BiscuitsEditedConsumer_Vicky copy.sav",
 to.data.frame=TRUE)
str(bis)
summary(bis$STORE)
library(car)
bis$sto=recode(bis$STORE,"'ASDA
  '='open';'MORRISONS
  '='open';'SAINSBURYS
  '='open';'TESCO
  '='open';else='close'")
attach(bis)

x <- split(bis, f=list(bis$PANELID, bis$sto))

capture.output(for(i in 1:1594){

s=(sum(x[[i+1594]]$TOTALSPENT)+.01)/(sum(x[[i]]$TOTALSPENT
)+.01)
print(s)
   },file="s.txt")

capture.output(for(i in 1:1594){
   q=(sum(x[[i+1594]]$quantity)+1)/(sum(x[[i]]$quantity)+1)
print(q)
   },file="q.txt")

capture.output(for(i in 1:1594){
p=((sum(x[[i+1594]]$PRICE)/1594)+.01)/(sum((x[[i]]$PRICE)/
1594)+.01)
print(p)
   },file="p.txt")

  capture.output(for(i in 1:1594){

p1=((sum(x[[i+1594]]$PRICE)/1594)+.01)
p2=(sum((x[[i]]$PRICE)/1594)+.01)
p=p1/p2
print(p)
   },file="p.txt")
```

```
capture.output(for(i in 1:1594){

pr=(1/((sum(x[[i+1594]]$PRICE)/1594)+.01)))/((1/((sum(x[[i+
1594]]$PRICE)/1594)+.01)+(1/((sum(x[[i]]$PRICE)/1594)+.01)
)))
   print(pr)
      },file="pr.txt")

   capture.output(for(i in 1:1594){
pr1=1/((sum(x[[i+1594]]$PRICE)/1594)+.01)
pr2=1/((sum(x[[i]]$PRICE)/1594)+.01)
pr=pr1/(pr1+pr2)
print(pr)
   },file="pr.txt")

bis=read.table("bis.csv",header=T,sep=",")
attach(bis)
m1=lm(log(spent.ratio)~log(quantity.ratio))
summary(m1)
plot(log(spent.ratio)~log(quantity.ratio),main="Biscuits")
abline(m1,col="darkred")
abline(0,1,col="darkblue")

m2=lm(log(quantity.ratio)~log(price.ratio))
summary(m2)
plot(log(quantity.ratio)~log(price.ratio),main="Biscuits")
abline(m2,col="darkred")

m3=lm(log(quantity.ratio)~(prob.ratio))
summary(m3)
plot(log(quantity.ratio)~(prob.ratio),main="Biscuits",xlim
=c(0,1))
abline(v=0.5,col="darkred")
```

8

Dimensions of demand elasticity

Jorge M. Oliveira-Castro and Gordon R. Foxall

Introduction

Knowing how the quantity consumers buy changes as a function of changes in price is crucial to several marketing activities, including pricing, price promotion and assortment. This is particularly relevant in the case of routinely purchased packaged goods, for which price variations that occur during a year are in most part related to price promotions associated with competing brands. The significant short-term increase in sales related to retail price promotions is very familiar to practitioners and researchers and has been interpreted as an empirical generalization in marketing (cf. Blattberg et al., 1995).

For retailers and manufacturers, it may be fundamental to know the patterns of consumers' choice associated with such increases in sales, for they can be associated to different factors, each one of which requires a different strategic approach. For instance, brand sales may increase during price promotions due to consumers switching across brands without increasing the quantities they buy. Or, they may increase due to increases in quantity, which in turn may be related to increased product consumption or to stockpiling. If increases are mainly related to stockpiling, other things being equal, managers could expect a reduction in the usual sales volume some time after every promotion. However, if they are mainly related to brand switching or increased consumption, they could expect the usual sales volume after promotions. These different predictions would certainly interfere with marketing plans.

In marketing research, price demand elasticity, which relates changes in consumption as a function of changes in price, has been the most commonly adopted measure of consumer responsiveness to changes in price. Mostly based upon this type of measure, several investigations have suggested that the major impact of price promotions is on brand switching, having little influence on the quantity consumers buy which remains almost unchanged (cf. Bell et al., 1999; Gupta, 1988). Even when using other types of measures, some researchers have assumed in their models that the quantity consumers buy of routinely purchased products does not vary across shopping occasions (Ehrenberg, 1972; Uncles et al., 1995). However, more recent investigations, inspired by operant behavioral economics, have shown that choice patterns may be more complex than previously described. When taking into consideration individual demand elasticity measures, inspired by the behavior-analytic tradition of examining individual behavior, and consumer demand for benefits other than quantity, inspired by consumer behavior analysis, these recent studies have revealed the simultaneous occurrence of intra-consumer and inter-consumer elasticity as well as intra-brand and inter-brand elasticity (Oliveira-Castro et al., 2008). The purpose of the present chapter is to give an overview of these different dimensions of demand elasticity.

To do this, the chapter will describe the usual measures of demand elasticity that have been adopted in operant behavioral economics, the kinds of questions involved in such research, and how they have been applied in consumer behavior analysis.

Price elasticity of demand in behavioral economics

A demand curve expresses the relation between the quantity demanded and prices. Typically, as prices increase, the quantity demanded decreases, or, in the other direction, if the quantity demanded decreases, then prices tend to decrease. The usual economic analysis considers that different individuals would have a different reserve price; that is, they differ with respect to the maximum price they are willing to pay for a given good or service. Assuming that everything else is constant, except for prices, there would be fewer individuals willing to buy at higher prices and more individuals willing to buy at lower prices. Therefore, the quantity demanded decreases with increases in price and, in the market, equilibrium will be reached at the price where the quantity demanded approximates the quantity supplied (cf. Varian, 2010). For example, if the price of tomatoes increases, due to seasonality or weather factors, fewer people will buy tomatoes.

These very introductory concepts serve to illustrate the intuitive notion that quantity demanded decreases with increases in prices in the market; that is, when information concerning choices made by many economic agents is aggregated across time. A more detailed analysis of this market phenomenon can be found in the theory of consumer choice in microeconomics. The basic choice model assumes that each agent has preferences across commodity bundles and maximizes utility (i.e., satisfaction) by choosing their most preferred bundle within income restrictions. When choosing between two commodity bundles, A and B, which can function as partial substitutes for one another, there will be an optimum choice point where the individual will have the best combination of quantities of A and B that is obtainable with the available income. Additionally, assuming that income is constant, if the price of bundle A increases, the theory predicts that the individual will reduce the consumption of A and increase the consumption of B. This switch of consumption from A to B is, according to the basic model, what explains the decrease of consumption in a demand function. This can be summarized by stating that a consumer demand function gives the optimum quantities of each of the commodities as a function of prices, given an available income.

This brief and simplified exposition of some concepts from consumer choice theory in economics may serve to illustrate that, although microeconomic models have been tested predominantly with cross-sectional or time-series data from large groups of individuals, as a typical market demand curve illustrates, the theory is based on assumptions concerning individual preferences and choices. Whereas these assumptions have not been explicitly examined in traditional economic research, more than 60 years ago Skinner (1953) had envisioned that this should be one of the goals of operant psychology, when he stated that "an adequate science of behavior should supply a satisfactory account of the individual behavior which is responsible for the data of economics in general" (p. 400).

Such vision has inspired the development of operant behavioral economics, an interdisciplinary field of research that has recognized the bidirectional relevance of economic concepts to behavior analysis and of behavior-analytic conceptual and methodological frameworks to economics (see, for some of the earlier work, Allison et al., 1979; Green & Rachlin, 1975; Kagel & Winkler, 1972; Lea, 1978; Rachlin et al., 1976). A wide and diverse program of research has followed, constituted by systematic investigations of behavior of nonhuman and human individuals in, predominantly, experimental settings, adopting concepts and testing predictions from microeconomics, including areas of preferences and choices between commodity bundles, labor-supply phenomena, choices over uncertain outcomes and intertemporal choices (cf. Bickel et al., 1995; Hackenberg, 2013; Hursh & Roma, 2013; Kagel et al., 1995).

In what concerns demand elasticity, which is the main focus of the present chapter, several experiments with nonhuman subjects have obtained interesting and systematic results in testing economic predictions. Such research has demonstrated that "economics provides a rich area of knowledge and conceptual elegance that offers new independent variables, methods of analysis, and dependent measures" (Bickel et al., 1995, p. 257). In the case of demand analysis, the basic concepts, adopted in behavior economics, are related to the features of a demand curve, which basically constitutes quantity consumed (or purchased) as a function of changes in price. The two main characteristics of the function are intensity of demand, which is the level of consumption at a given price, and elasticity of demand, which gives the amount of change in consumption as price changes. One of the simplest forms of demand function, adopted in operant behavioral economics, is a log-log function that relates quantity of consumption to price (cf. Hursh 1980, 1984; Kagel et al., 1995):

$$Log\ Quantity = a - b\ (Log\ Price) \tag{1}$$

where a and b are empirically obtained parameters that represent the intercept and slope of the function, respectively. The advantage of Equation 1 is that a and b can be interpreted as coefficients that measure the intensity and elasticity of demand, respectively. When the value of the slope is smaller, in absolute value, than one, demand is said to be inelastic, which means that the percentage decrease in consumption is lower than the respective percentage increase in price, and spending increases with increases in price. If the slope is equal to one (i.e., -1.0), elasticity is described as unitary, which implies that the percentage decrease in consumption is equal to the percentage increase in price, and spending remains constant with increases in price. If the slope is larger, in absolute value, than one, demand is described as elastic, which means that the percentage decrease in consumption is larger than the respective percentage increase in price, and spending decreases with increases in price (cf. Hursh, 1980, 1984).

Apart from suggesting new independent and dependent variables and different methods, economic concepts have been useful in explaining results that seemed to contradict operant theory. This was the case, for example, with the prediction that individual response rates should increase with increases in reinforcement rate, which was contradicted with data from experiments conducted under closed economic systems (i.e., a situation where the animal gets all its food and/or water in the "working" chamber), when contrasted with experiments under open economic systems (i.e., the animal receives complementary amounts of food and/or water outside the "working" chamber). In closed systems, animals work more (i.e., show higher response rates) for food when there is less food (i.e., reinforcement). Based upon reinforcement theory alone, one would expect to observe decreases in response rates with decreases in the rate of reinforcement. However, if economic concepts are adopted, these apparently strange phenomena can be easily explained. As predicted from economic theory, demand has been shown to be inelastic (i.e., percentage of consumption decreases less than the percentage increase in price) in closed systems and elastic (i.e., percentage of consumption decreases more than the percentage increase in price) in open systems. (cf. Hursh, 1980, 1984). Therefore, the adoption of this new concept of closed–open systems has clarified these contradictory findings.

In the opposite direction, from behavior analysis to economics, results from several experiments conducted with animal subjects have generated results that are compatible with fundamental predictions derived from economic demand theory (cf. Hursh, 1984). This type of result extends economic demand theory to nonhuman animal behavior, weakening the idea that economic principles are necessarily based on rational evaluations of alternatives (cf. Kagel et al., 1995). Another important feature of these results is that they have been obtained with data for individual subjects. As mentioned above, most studies of consumer demand theory have been based on data from large groups of individuals, despite the fact that the theory is about individual consumer behavior. This inference from individual behavior to large groups is usually based on the idea of a "representative consumer", an assumption that may not resist empirical tests. These experimental results obtained with individual subjects in the laboratory may constitute the first real tests of consumer demand theory (cf. Kagel et al., 1995).

However, considering that laboratory settings differ significantly from typical market settings, the issue raises the question concerning the possibility of generalizing laboratory results to natural open settings. Lea (1978) advanced in the direction of answering this question by comparing demand curves obtained in the laboratory with those stemming from econometric and consumer research. He found that they were similar with respect to important functional aspects and that the observed differences could be explained on the basis of specific characteristics of the existing variables in natural, more open consumer situations that are absent in the laboratory, such as a narrower range of prices, available product alternatives and such like. These differences between laboratory and marketing situations, particularly the use of nonhuman subjects and the closeness of the laboratory setting, may represent an obstacle to the process of generalization of findings across contexts, which indicates the need to develop new ways of bridging this gap (cf. Foxall, 2002).

Individual and group elasticity of demand

As a step in the direction of filling the gap between laboratory and consumer settings, Oliveira-Castro et al. (2006) compared individual and group demand curves for consumers buying routinely purchased food products. The authors used panel data obtained from Taylor Nelson Sofres, a marketing research company that keeps purchase records of 15,000 households (TNS Superpanel), a sample that is representative of the British population, on a range of consumer goods. The data used consisted of information concerning weekly purchases of 80 individual households, randomly selected from the larger Superpanel, concerning nine fast-moving consumer goods categories over 16 weeks. In this panel, after each shopping trip, members of the panel scan their purchased items into a sophisticated handheld barcode reader by passing the scanner across the barcodes, printed on all packaged supermarket products. The information is then automatically sent to the research firm for central processing. The nine product categories selected for the research were: baked beans, biscuits (cookies), breakfast cereals, butter, cheese, fruit juice, instant coffee, margarine, and tea. On each shopping occasion for each consumer, the following information was recorded: brand specification (different versions of the same product category were classified as different brands, e.g., Corn Flakes and Rice Krispies by Kelloggs), package size, name of the supermarket/shop, date, number of units and total amount spent.

Considering the interest of examining individual demand curves, which requires a minimum number of data points for each consumer, data from consumers who bought, within each product category, fewer than four times during the 16-week period were discarded. Following these criteria, the number of consumers in each product category ranged from 19, for coffee, to 59, for biscuits.

Overall price elasticities were calculated for each product, fitting Equation 1 to all data points from all consumers, with the purpose of comparing the results with those obtained with individual data. Quantity bought and prices were interpreted as continuous variables, differing from what has been adopted in other studies where quantity was interpreted as a discrete variable (e.g., Gupta, 1988). To calculate Equation 1 parameters, values of quantity and price were divided by the obtained average for each consumer in each product category. In doing this, parameters from different products, which differ with respect to absolute values and ranges of quantity and price (e.g., average price for baked beans was equal to £0.51 per 100 g, whereas this average for cheese was equal to £2.76 per 100 g), become comparable. Therefore, quantity bought and price paid on each shopping occasion for each consumer, divided by their corresponding average (for each consumer in each category), were entered in the equation.

Results showed all the regression analyses were significant (F statistics, with p ≤ .01) and that values of r^2 varied from .05 to .76, suggesting that there are wide differences across product categories with respect to the influence of variables other than price, which were not investigated here. The values of a, the intercept, were close to zero and ranged from −0.46 to −0.08 across product categories, indicating that at the average price of the category (i.e., *log price* equal to zero) consumers tended to buy a little less than the average quantity for that category. Elasticity coefficient estimates, b in Equation 1, varied from −0.23 to −1.01 across product categories, indicating an inverse relationship between price and quantity demanded, as predicted by consumer demand theory. Elasticity coefficients also indicated that the demand for all the products was inelastic; that is, increases in prices were accompanied by proportionally smaller decreases in quantity demanded.

These *overall demand elasticity* coefficients demonstrate that the quantity demanded decreases with increases in price when all data points from all consumers are included in the equation. Such overall elasticities may result from a combination of intra- and inter-consumer elasticities. *Intra-consumer* elasticity measures the tendency for the same consumers to buy larger quantities when buying products with lower prices, due to price promotions and/or buying cheaper brands. *Inter-consumer* elasticity measures the tendency for consumers who buy smaller quantities, on average, also to buy more expensive brands, on average, than consumers who buy larger quantities.

Figure 8.1 shows, with hypothetical data, a graphical representation that may help the reader to visualize intra- and inter-consumer price elasticities. The straight line represents overall demand elasticity, which would include, in the equation, all data points obtained for all four consumers. *Intra-consumer* elasticity would include, for example, a straight line through the five data points for Consumer 1, which indicates that the quantity demanded for this consumer decreases with increases in prices. A different straight line could be drawn for each one of the consumers through the respective data points. *Inter-consumer* elasticity would include one data point for each consumer; that is, an average for quantity and price would be calculated for each consumer. Then, the five data points obtained from Consumer 1 would become only one average data point. This would be done for the other three consumers. It can be seen in the figure that the average quantity bought by Consumer 1 would be higher than the average quantity bought by Consumer 4, and that the average price paid by Consumer 1 would be lower than that paid by Consumer 4. The straight line for inter-consumer elasticity, in this case, would include four data points, one for each consumer.

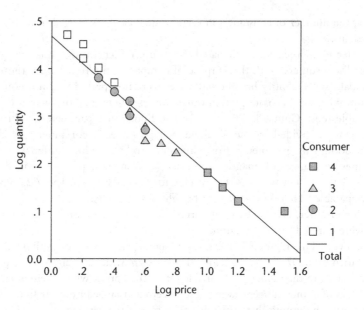

Figure 8.1 Graphical representation of an overall demand elasticity, where it is possible to also see inter-consumer (average for each consumer, i.e., one data point for each) and intra-consumer price elasticities (all data points for a given consumer)

Oliveira-Castro et al. (2006) calculated inter-consumer price elasticity by including in Equation 1 one pair of data points for each consumer for each product category. Each pair of data consisted of the average quantity, across shopping occasions, a given consumer bought for a given category divided by the average quantity purchased by all consumers in that same category. The analogous measure was calculated for price; that is, the average price paid by a given consumer for a given product, divided by the average price paid by all consumers in that same category. In this case, the normalization procedure allows for comparisons across consumers in the same category by indicating whether consumers who buy more or less than the average quantity bought in the category tend to pay prices above or below the average price paid in the category.

The *F statistics* obtained for inter-consumer elasticities showed that seven of the nine regression analyses were significant ($p \leq .05$), and that values of r^2 varied from .09 to .68, suggesting again that there are wide differences across product categories with respect to the influence of variables other than price, which were not investigated here. The values of a, the intercept, ranged from 0.20 to 2.55 across product categories. These values indicate that at the average price of the category (i.e., *log price* equal to zero) consumers tended to buy a little more than the average quantity for that category. Elasticity coefficient (b) varied from -0.31 to -0.91 across products, indicating an inverse relationship between price and quantity demanded, as expected by consumer demand theory. These values also show that the demand for all the products was inelastic; that is, increases in prices were followed by proportionally fewer decreases in quantity demanded (e.g., a 10% increase in price was followed by a less than 10% decrease in quantity). These results demonstrate the occurrence of inter-consumer elasticity in most product categories, showing that, within each product category, consumers who pay higher prices, on average, also tend to buy smaller quantities, on average.

Intra-consumer elasticities were calculated for each consumer across all product categories, using measures of quantity and price observed on each shopping occasion relative to the average quantity and average price obtained for each consumer in each product category. Results showed that elasticity coefficients were negative for 93.4% of consumers and that elasticity coefficients were significantly different from zero for 57 of the 76 consumers; that is, for 75% of consumers. Considering only significant regressions, r^2 ranged from .12 to .95 and elasticity coefficients were negative for all consumers, varying from $-.27$ to -1.23, except for one, whose data showed a positive elasticity coefficient. Overall, these results suggest that the quantity individual consumers buy on each shopping occasion tends to decrease as prices increase, demonstrating that intra-consumer elasticity does occur. Such decreases, however, for the vast majority of consumers, are proportionately smaller than the respective increases in price; that is, most of the consumers show inelastic demand.

Oliveira-Castro et al. (2006) also compared, across products, values of individual elasticity coefficients with overall elasticity coefficients and with inter-consumer coefficients. Results showed similar coefficient values for the three products for which there were enough data points to calculate individual coefficients. The averages of individual values for cheese ($M = -1.07$, $SD = 0.48$) were significantly larger (in absolute value) than for biscuits ($M = -0.47$, $SD = 0.26$), which were similar to overall elasticity (cheese = -1.01 and biscuits = -0.55) and inter-consumer elasticities (cheese = -0.91 and biscuits = -0.55). When comparing cheese with breakfast cereals, average individual coefficients (cheese: $M=-1.05$, $SD=0.53$; cereals: $M = -0.54$, $SD = 0.46$) were also similar to overall elasticities (cheese = -1.01 and cereals = $-.55$) and inter-consumer elasticities (cheese = $-.91$ and cereals = $-.56$). Moreover, a split-sample analysis of individual elasticity for one of the products showed that individual differences in elasticity are reasonably consistent across time.

Taken together, these results indicate that the quantity consumers buy across shopping occasions decreases as prices increase, and that the decrease in quantity is proportionally smaller than the increase in price (inelastic demand). These findings hold for individual consumers; that is, the same consumers across shopping occasions tend to decrease the quantity they buy with increases in price. They also hold for groups of consumers; that is, consumers who buy larger quantities tend to pay lower prices than consumers who buy smaller quantities (inter-consumer elasticity). The results also showed that individual and group analyses of demand elasticity yield similar values for a given product category.

The finding suggesting that individual demand elasticity shows consistency across time has been corroborated by more recent investigation that used a much larger set of panel data. Cavalcanti et al. (2013) examined the consistency of eight different measures of individual differences in buying patterns of fast-moving consumer goods, by calculating the level of correlation of the same measure across three time periods. Individual demand elasticity was one of the measures examined, which showed statistically significant consistency across time and was positively correlated to brand loyalty.

These findings concerning individual and group price elasticities indicate that consumers increase the quantity they buy with decreases in price. This choice pattern can be a consequence of finding a price promotion for a given product or brand, or a consequence of buying a cheaper product or brand. We turn next to research that explored such possibilities.

Elasticity of demand in brand choice

So far we have seen that consumers tend to purchase larger quantities when they pay lower prices. But consumers may pay lower prices in purchasing fast-moving consumer goods when they find a promotion of a given brand (intra-brand elasticity) or when they buy a cheaper

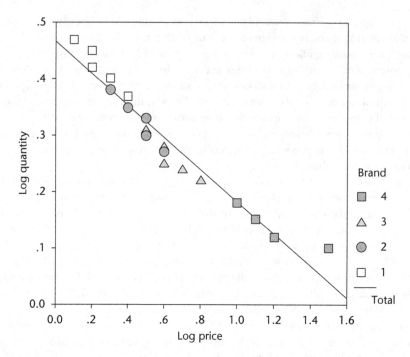

Figure 8.2 Graphical representation of an overall demand elasticity, where it is possible to also see inter-brand (average for each brand, i.e., one data point for each) and intra-brand price elasticities (all data points for a given brand)

brand (inter-brand elasticity). Figure 8.2 above illustrates graphically, with hypothetical data, these two types of elasticities. The straight line shows overall price elasticity, which would be calculated using all data points from all brands. Inter-brand price elasticity would be calculated using only one data point for each brand, which would be the average quantity bought and average price paid for each brand. It is possible to see, for example, that the average data point (mean quantity and mean price) for Brand 1 would yield a larger quantity and lower price than the average data point for Brand 4. The average data points for Brands 2 and 3 would be located somewhat in the middle of the decreasing tendency from Brand 1 to 4. Intra-brand price elasticity would be calculated using all data points for a specific brand. It would be calculated for each brand, for example the five data points for Brand 1 would generate one intra-brand elasticity coefficient, whereas the four data points for Brand 4 would generate another.

Intra-brand price elasticity – that is, decreases in consumption of a given brand when its price increases – is predicted by consumer demand theory and is a common finding in the literature. Although some signs of inter-brand price elasticity appeared in Gupta's (1988) results, the author did not interpret this as a new type of price elasticity, or stress the finding. The phenomenon had not been reported in the literature before Foxall et al. (2004) examined it for groups of consumers, decomposing inter-brand elasticity according to differences among brands.

An important source of difference among brands stems from the distinction between utilitarian and informational benefits offered by different brands, as presented by the Behavioral Perspective Model (BPM) (Foxall, 1990, 1998, 2010). According to this proposal, the behavior of consumers can be explained based upon the events that occur before and after the consumer situation, which influence directly the shaping and maintenance of consumer behavior in specific environments. The consumer situation stands at the intersection between the consumer behavior setting and consumer learning history. The consumer behavior setting includes the stimuli that form consumer environments, in its social, physical and temporal features, for example a supermarket, a bookstore, or a rock concert. As purchase and consumption are followed by different consequences in different settings, the events in the setting become predictive of such consequences, building a learning history that relates elements of the setting to different consequences. According to the model, antecedent events present in the consumer behavior setting signal the possibility of four types of consequences: utilitarian reinforcement, utilitarian punishment, informational reinforcement and informational punishment. One important characteristic of economic behavior is that it involves both aversive and reinforcing consequences, for one needs to give away money or rights (i.e., loss of generalized reinforcers) to get products or services (i.e., reinforcing events).

Utilitarian reinforcement consists in functional benefits derived directly (rather than mediated by other people) from possession and use of a product or service. It is reinforcement mediated by the product or service and refers to consequences associated with increases in the utility (i.e., use value) for the individual obtained from the product or service. The utilitarian, most obvious, consequence of owning a car, for example, is to get door-to-door transportation.

Informational reinforcement is social, mediated by the actions and reactions of other persons, and more closely related to the exchange value of a product or service. It is associated with feedback about consumer performance, indicating the level of adequacy and accuracy of their behavior. Informational reinforcement is derived from the level of social status and prestige that a consumer obtains when purchasing or using certain goods. Then, according to the model, a person who drives a Jaguar© or Bentley© gets, in addition to door-to-door transportation (utilitarian), social status and admiration from friends and acquaintances. These social consequences are usually related to branding or the level of brand differentiation of the product (cf. Foxall, 1999).

To incorporate brand differences into inter-brand elasticity, Foxall et al. (2004) measured the levels of utilitarian and informational reinforcement offered by different brands of nine routinely purchased grocery items (baked beans, cookies, cereals, butter, cheese, fruit juice, instant coffee, margarine and tea). The authors used panel data with approximately 80 households reporting their purchases during 16 weeks. Increases in utilitarian reinforcement level of brands were identified by the addition of (supposedly) desirable attributes. Such attributes usually add value to the product or its consumption, are mentioned on the package or product name, and justify increases in price. Moreover, in most cases, several general brands offer products with and without these attributes. For the product categories in question, utilitarian levels were identified based on additional attributes (e.g., plain baked beans versus baked beans with sausage) and/or differentiated types of products (e.g., plain cookies versus chocolate chip cookies).

Foxall et al. (2004) ranked informational reinforcement levels of brands based on the following general criteria: (1) increases in prices across brands for the same product type (e.g., plain baked beans, plain cookies or plain cornflakes) were considered to be indicative of differences in informational levels; (2) the cheapest store own brands (e.g., Asda Smart Price©, Tesco Value©, Sainsbury Economy©) were considered to represent the lowest informational level (Level 1); (3) store brands that do not mention good value for money or economy (e.g., Asda,

Tesco, Sainsbury's) and the cheapest specialized brands were usually considered to represent the medium informational level (Level 2); and (4) specialized brands (e.g., Heinz©, McVities©, Kelloggs©, Lurpak©), with higher prices, were considered to represent the highest informational level (Level 3).

After finding that most consumers make most of their brand purchases within a set of brands classified at the same level of informational and utilitarian reinforcement, the authors examined if groups of consumers buying at different levels of informational reinforcement would show different price elasticities. Foxall et al. (2004) examined, first, overall price elasticity shown by each consumer group. In a second analysis they investigated intra-brand elasticity and two types of inter-brand elasticities, namely utilitarian inter-brand elasticity and informational inter-brand elasticity. These inter-brand analyses would make it possible to examine if consumers tend to change the quantity they buy with increases in utilitarian and informational level of the brand they purchased. To do that, the authors adopted a log-log elasticity equation including three elasticity coefficients: intra-brand coefficient, utilitarian inter-brand coefficient and informational inter-brand coefficient.

The results showed that consumer groups buying predominantly intermediate levels of utilitarian and informational brands tended to present higher overall price elasticity than the groups that buy low or high levels. This suggests that those consumers buying low levels show little responsiveness to price changes, probably because they buy the cheapest brands. On the other extreme, the results indicate that consumers that buy brands ranked at high levels of utilitarian and informational reinforcement also show little responsiveness to changes in price, probably because they have less rigorous budget restrictions. Decomposed price elasticity results showed that intra-brand coefficients tended to be higher than utilitarian and informational inter-brand coefficients.

Oliveira-Castro et al. (2005) conducted similar analyses, but calculated intra- and inter-brand elasticity coefficients for different product categories rather than for consumer groups. The following equation was adopted:

$$Log\ Q = a - b_1\ (Log\ Price) - b_2\ (Log\ Util) - b_3\ (Log\ Info) \tag{2}$$

where Q represents purchased quantity, Price stands for paid price, and Util and Info represent the utilitarian and the informational level of the brand brought, respectively. Parameters a, b_1, b_2 and b_3 are empirically obtained and represent the intercept, overall intra-brand price elasticity, utilitarian inter-brand elasticity and informational inter-brand elasticity, respectively.

They also used consumer panel data, containing information about the purchase of nine supermarket products by 80 households during 16 weeks. The results indicated statistically significant elasticity coefficients, which corroborate previous findings concerning the occurrence of inter-brand elasticity. Moreover, intra-brand coefficients were, in general, larger than inter-brand utilitarian coefficients, which, in turn, tended to be larger than informational coefficients. Such results suggest that, when buying routinely purchased packaged goods, consumers show at least three choice patterns. First, they tend to buy larger quantities of a brand when its price is below its average price (i.e., intra-brand elasticity). Second, they tend to buy smaller quantities of brands that offer higher utilitarian benefits (i.e., utilitarian inter-brand elasticity). And third, they tend to buy smaller quantities of brands that offer higher informational benefits (i.e., informational inter-brand elasticity). Each of these patterns was observed in eight of nine product categories investigated in the study. Additionally, the results showed that consumers are more responsive to price promotions than to utilitarian benefits, and more responsive to utilitarian benefits than to informational benefits.

Integrating consumer and brand elasticities

The findings described so far suggest some complex relations between the quantity consumers buy of a given product and changes in its price. For instance, inter-consumer elasticity (i.e., consumers who buy larger quantities, on average, tend to pay lower prices, on average) may result from the fact that consumers who buy larger quantities also tend to buy more of promoted, cheaper brands (intra-brand elasticity), or from the fact that they buy more brands that have cheaper regular prices (inter-brand elasticity). The same applies to intra-consumer elasticity, for the same consumer may buy larger quantities of a cheaper brand either because she buys more when the brand is on promotion or because she buys more when choosing a brand with a lower regular price. Therefore, intra- and inter-consumer elasticities can each be subdivided into intra-brand and inter-brand elasticities. Inter-brand elasticity can be further subdivided into the three variables that, according to the BPM, can influence consumer choice; that is, regular price, utilitarian benefits and informational benefits. When varying within brand – that is, intra-brand elasticity – price would be the only differential consequence for buying larger or smaller quantities, because utilitarian and informational benefits are constant. However, changes in prices within brand can be related to changes in intra- and inter-package sizes; that is, price variation may be related to promotional price cuts for a given package or to price reductions related to the choice of a larger package of the brand, which price per unit is usually cheaper than smaller packages.

Considering that the small sample size used in the papers described so far (Foxall et al., 2004; Oliveira-Castro et al., 2005, 2006) prevented the simultaneous analysis of all these choice patterns, Oliveira-Castro et al. (2008) used a larger set of consumer panel data with the purpose of: (1) verifying the robustness and simultaneous occurrence of such choice patterns; (2) examining if such choice patterns differ across product categories; and (3) measuring the relative contribution of each of these patterns to overall consumer quantity elasticity.

Figure 8.3 shows all the components into which overall elasticity was decomposed by Oliveira-Castro et al. (2008). Inter-consumer measures were based on averages, across shopping occasions, obtained for each consumer, whereas intra-consumer measures were based on data from each shopping occasion divided by the average obtained for each consumer for that particular variable. This procedure measures variations in quantity around each consumer average and across consumers, which are complementary in accounting for the disaggregate variance in quantity in the product category. The same intra-brand and inter-brand variables (i.e., price, utilitarian, and informational levels) were calculated for inter- (i.e., average for each consumer) and intra-consumers (i.e., variable divided by each consumer's average). For instance, the inter-consumer measure of level of utilitarian benefit consisted of the average, across shopping occasions, of the utilitarian level of the brands bought by each consumer, whereas the intra-consumer measure of the utilitarian level consisted of the level of utilitarian benefit of the brand bought on each shopping occasion by each consumer, divided by the obtained average for the same consumer. Then, each value of inter-consumer variables for a given consumer was the denominator of intra-consumer variables for the same consumer. So, for example, if the average price paid by Consumer 1 for a given product was equal to £0.75, the intra-consumer measure of price for Consumer 1 on each shopping occasion was equal to the price paid on each occasion divided by 0.75. This same procedure was used for all the variables shown in Figure 8.3, except

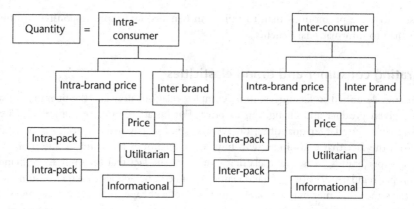

Figure 8.3　Schematic representation of the hypothesized sources of variation in purchased quantity

for quantity, which consisted of the quantity bought by each consumer of each package size of each brand on each shopping occasion.

The following multiple exponential regression equation was used to measure the intra- and inter-consumer and intra- and inter-brand variations presented in Figure 8.3:

$$Ln\,Q_{cpbo} = \beta_1 + \beta_2 Ln\left(\frac{P_{cpbo}/P_{pb}}{\left(P_{cpbo}/P_{pb}\right)_c}\right) + \beta_3 Ln\left(\frac{P_{pb}/P_{pb}}{\left(P_{pb}/P_b\right)_c}\right) + \beta_4 Ln\left(\frac{P_b}{PBC_c}\right) +$$

$$\beta_5 Ln\left(\frac{U_b}{UC_c}\right) + \beta_6 Ln\left(\frac{I_b}{IC_c}\right) + \beta_7 Ln\left(\frac{P_{cpbo}}{P_{pb}}\right)_c + \beta_8 Ln\left(\frac{P_{pb}}{P_b}\right)_c + \qquad (3)$$

$$\beta_9 Ln\left(PBC_c\right) + \beta_{10} Ln\left(UC_c\right) + \beta_{11} Ln\left(IC_c\right)$$

where Q_{cpbo} is the quantity purchased by consumer c of package p of brand b on shopping occasion o; (P_{cpbo}/P_{pb}) is the price paid by consumer c for package p of brand b on shopping occasion o divided by the average price of package p of brand b (this average was calculated across the entire sample); $(P_{cpbo}/P_{pb})_c$ is the average of (P_{cpbo}/P_{pb}) calculated for consumer c, a measure of inter-consumer intra-brand intra-pack elasticity; $\dfrac{P_{cpbo}/P_{pb}}{\left(P_{cpbo}/P_{pb}\right)_c}$ is a measure of intra-consumer intra-brand intra-pack elasticity; (P_{pb}/P_b) is the average price of package p of brand b, calculated across the entire sample, divided by the average price of brand b, calculated across the entire sample; $(P_{pb}/P_b)_c$ is the average of (P_{pb}/P_b) calculated for consumer c, a measure of inter-consumer intra-brand inter-pack elasticity; (P_b/PBC_c) is the average price of brand b divided by the average price of brands purchased by consumer c, a measure of intra-consumer inter-brand price elasticity; (U_b/UC_c) is the utilitarian level of brand b, a rank variable assuming values of 1 or 2, divided by the most frequently utilitarian level purchased by consumer c (assuming values of 1 or 2), a measure of intra-consumer inter-brand utilitarian elasticity; (I_b/IC_c) is the informational level of brand b, a variable ranging from 0 to 3, divided by the average informational level of brands purchased by consumer c, a measure of intra-consumer inter-brand informational elasticity; PBC_c is the average price of brands purchased by consumer c, a measure of inter-consumer inter-brand price elasticity; UC_c is the average utilitarian level of brands purchased by consumer c, a measure of inter-consumer inter-brand utilitarian elasticity; IC_c is the average informational level of brands purchased by consumer c, a measure of inter-consumer inter-brand informational elasticity; and β_1 to β_{11} are empirically estimated parameters.

Oliveira-Castro et al. (2008) used consumer panel data obtained from ACNielsen Homescan™ which, at the period of the research, included data from over 10,000 households in Great Britain who used home barcode scanners. The panel was regionally and demographically balanced to represent the household population. The data set included information about four product categories during 52 weeks from July 2004 to July 2005. The four products were baked beans, biscuits (cookies), fruit juice and yellow fats (including margarine, butter and spreads), for which there were data about the purchases of 1639, 1874, 1542 and 1817 randomly selected households, respectively. To exclude extreme light buyers from the samples, data from consumers who purchased less than seven times in the product category during the 52-week period were excluded. For each purchase, the data included information about the brand, store, item characteristics, package size, total amount spent, number of items and weekly date.

The level of informational benefit offered by each brand was measured with the use of a questionnaire, where respondents were asked to rate brands in each product category. This procedure was adopted to avoid confounding effects of brand prices, which were present in earlier research (e.g., Foxall et al., 2004; Oliveira-Castro et al., 2005). For each brand listed, consumers were asked to answer the following two questions: (1) Is the brand well known? (0 – not known at all, 1 – known a little, 2 – quite well known, and 3 – very well known); and (2) What is the level of quality of the brand? (0 – unknown quality, 1 – low quality, 2 – medium quality, and 3 – high quality). A small sample of consumers who had lived in the UK for most of their lives were selected on a convenience basis and asked to answer one or more questionnaires. Four questionnaires were used, one for each of the products investigated. Each questionnaire included for each product all the brands purchased by the sample of consumers in the panel, after filtering for attributes that are more related to utilitarian benefits than informational benefits. To obtain one informational level score for each brand, the mean score for knowledge and quality was calculated for each respondent and for each brand. The average of these mean values was then calculated for each brand across all respondents and was adopted as the measure of informational level of benefit offered by a given brand. The measure of utilitarian benefit offered by each brand was the same as that adopted in previous research (Foxall et al., 2004; Oliveira-Castro et al., 2005).

Purchase data from the panel were analyzed using Equation 3. The results indicated that intra-brand variables explained more variance in quantity (R^2) than inter-brand variables in all cases examined; that is, this occurred within and across consumer measures for all products. The results also showed that the amount of variance in quantity that was explained by intra-consumer variables depended upon the frequency of purchase of different products. Products that have higher purchase frequency (e.g., biscuits) showed more variance explained by intra-consumer variables, suggesting that the number of individual data points available for analysis influences the level of impact of intra-consumer variables.

Elasticity coefficients were significant and negative for price variables (i.e., β_2, β_3, β_4, β_7, β_8 and β_9), indicating that increases in prices were followed by decreases in purchased quantity, as expected. Informational coefficients (i.e., β_6 and β_{11}) were significant and positive, indicating that increases in informational benefit offered by brands increase the quantity consumers buy. Utilitarian elasticity coefficients were positive for baked beans and biscuits, negative for yellow fats and insignificant for fruit juice. As far as the sizes of coefficients are concerned, intra-brand inter-pack coefficients were the largest ones in both intra-consumer (β_3) and inter-consumer (β_8). This indicates that the changes in the quantity consumers buy are mostly related to the changes in brand price due to switching across package sizes. Inter-brand price coefficients were the second largest coefficients in both intra-consumer (β_4) and inter-consumer (β_9). These results indicate that consumers tend to buy smaller quantities when buying more expensive brands and that consumers who buy, on average, smaller quantities tend to buy, on average, more expensive brands. Intra-brand intra-pack coefficients were the smallest among price coefficients in both intra-consumer (β_2) and inter-consumer (β_7), indicating that consumers tend to buy larger quantities of a given package of a given brand when its price is lower than its average price. Taken together, these results indicate that price coefficients are larger than informational coefficients, and that the size and direction of utilitarian coefficients seem to vary from product to product. Evidence that supports the claim that each product or brand has its own elasticity of demand was reported by Foxall et al. (2013), who also showed that the quantity consumers buy varies as a function of price, utilitarian benefits and informational benefits.

To sum up, the application of demand elasticity measures to brand choice has revealed several complex behavioral patterns concerning how consumers change the quantity they buy across shopping occasions. Such results do not corroborate previous reports that have asserted that the quantity consumers buy across shopping occasions does not vary significantly (cf. Bell et al., 1999; Ehrenberg, 1972; Gupta, 1988; Uncles et al., 1995). This apparent contradiction might be explained, at least in part, by differences in interpretation and methods used to identify different brands. Oliveira-Castro et al. (2008) considered that different package sizes within a brand name should be interpreted as belonging to the same brand, whereas other authors have considered that differently sized packages should be regarded as different brands (e.g., Bell et al., 1999; Gupta, 1988). The present results suggest that research in marketing may have overemphasized the importance of the "what-brand choice" at the expense of the "how-much choice" (cf. Oliveira-Castro et al., 2008).

Demand elasticity and the essential value of brands

An important challenge faced by behavioral scientists is to measure the value that consumers attribute to different commodities. For example, consumer demand theory, in microeconomics, assumes that there are certain regularities concerning consumers' relative preferences for different commodities, in such a way that if a given consumer prefers Commodity A to B and Commodity B to C, there must be a preference for Commodity A when compared to C (transitivity property) (cf. Rubinstein, 2012). However, the theory does not present procedures to measure the value the consumer attributes to Commodities A, B, and C. When products and brands are interpreted as items that offer different types of reinforcers, the problem may be viewed as a question of assessing the strength or value of reinforcers, which has been a long-lasting goal of learning theories.

A promising development in this direction has been the use of demand functions to measure the value of reinforcers, for they favor a conceptual shift of emphasis from feedback functions linking response rates and reinforcement, which is typical in operant learning approaches, to comparison of responding for qualitatively different reinforcers. The idea behind such analysis is that the demand for a product, measured as the price that a consumer is prepared to pay for it, provides an accurate measure of the product's value. Larger demand elasticities would be associated with less valuable products.

However, several factors have posed problems for the adoption of typical demand elasticity procedures to measure the value of commodities. One of them is based on the fact that, in experimental situations, when prices reach extreme values, demand elasticity increases, becoming more elastic (e.g., Hursh, 1991; Hursh & Winger, 1995). This shows that elasticity coefficients are not constant for the same commodity, for they change depending upon the level of prices. Other findings have shown that elasticity coefficients are also influenced by the magnitude of a food reinforcer from one to two pellets (Hursh et al., 1988) or drug dosages (e.g., Winger et al., 1996). Such findings represent important obstacles to the use of linear demand elasticity coefficients in scaling preference across commodities.

Hursh and Silberberg (2008) have advanced an exponential model to measure demand elasticity with the purpose of overcoming the limitations associated with linear approaches. In their proposal, demand elasticity is measured relative to the point at which price is zero, which is the point of free consumption, where consumption reaches its maximum level. Elasticity is measured on the basis of decreases in consumption relative to that maximum quantity, in terms of percentages. This allows for comparisons across products that show different consumption patterns or across different doses or magnitudes of the same commodity. They proposed the following exponential equation:

$$Log\ Q = Log\ Q_0 + K\ (e^{-\alpha Q_0 P} - 1) \tag{4}$$

where Q is the amount consumed, Q_0 is consumption when price is zero, K is a constant that simply specifies the amplitude of the data, α is the rate of decrease in consumption with increase in price, which is a measure of elasticity that is interpreted as the essential value of the reinforcer (smaller α indicating higher value), and P is the price for each reinforcement.

Equation 4 was used in various experiments and has shown a good fit to the data and supplied theoretically consistent results for different reinforcers, different schedules of reinforcement, different reinforcement amounts and magnitudes (Hursh & Silberberg, 2008; Christensen et al., 2008; Foster et al., 2009). Considering that this previous research has either been experimentally based or has involved nonhuman participants, Oliveira-Castro et al. (2011) applied the model to the analysis of changes in the consumption of brands with changes in prices, employing data from actual consumers buying brands of food products in grocery shopping. The authors used consumer panel data containing purchase information of two products (biscuits and baked beans) by more than 1,600 consumers during 52 weeks. Brands bought by consumers in the panel were classified according to the level of informational and utilitarian benefits they offered (cf. Oliveira-Castro et al., 2008).

The model, calculated for different brands, fitted the data only moderately, but its parameters showed good reliability for the same brand across stores. The essential value of brands (i.e., the reverse of α in Equation 4) showed significant increases with increases in the level of informational benefit offered by brands. The results also indicated that the effect of the utilitarian benefit level offered by brands depends upon the specific product that is examined. Informational and utilitarian levels of brand benefits did not show systematic effects upon values of Q_0.

In general, the results showed that the model can be used to measure the essential value of brands and that this value varied systematically with changes in brand attributes that would, theoretically, be expected to influence it. This extension of the model from laboratory environments, where nonhuman subjects were employed, to natural occurring human purchases in supermarkets opens the possibility of using this model to measure the consumer-based value of brands in the market, which has been an enduring goal of marketing research (e.g., Aaker, 1991, 1996; Keller, 1993, 1998). This exponential model has also been used in other applied contexts that can inform public policies related to clinical pharmacology, drug abuse, public transportation and social behavior (cf. Hursh & Roma, 2013).

Conclusion

The contribution of economic concepts to operant psychology has been significant. The use of demand elasticity analysis stands as one of the most important tools that arose from this exchange between the two sciences. Consumer behavior analysis has been one of the fields where demand functions have been used extensively, as the present exposition shows. In the other direction, operant psychology has emphasized the fruitfulness of investigating individual behavior, a tradition that has had a great impact on the use of demand functions in the field of consumer behavior. Several different types of demand elasticity emerged from this research tradition, demonstrating that demand elasticity can be used to describe complex patterns of consumer choice, previously unreported. Combinations of inter-consumer and intra-consumer elasticities with inter-brand and intra-brand elasticities show that a typical overall elasticity measure, which includes all choices made by many consumers, might hide choice patterns that may be crucial to the understanding of consumer preferences and to the planning of managerial strategies.

References

Aaker, D. A. (1991). *Managing Brand Equity*. New York: Free Press.

Aaker, D. A. (1996). Measuring brand equity across products and markets. *California Management Review, 38*, 102–120.

Allison, J., Miller, M. and Wozny, M. (1979). Conservation in behavior. *Journal of Experimental Psychology: General, 108*, 4–34.

Bell, D. R., Chiang, J. and Padmanabhan, V. (1999). The decomposition of promotional response: An empirical generalization. *Marketing Science, 18*(4), 504–526.

Bickel, W. K., Green, L. and Vuchinich, R. E. (1995). Behavioral economics [Editorial]. *Journal of the Experimental Analysis of Behavior, 64*, 257–262.

Blattberg, R. C., Briesch, R. and Fox, E. J. (1995). How promotions work. *Marketing Science, 14*(3), G122–G132.

Cavalcanti, P. R., Oliveira-Castro, J. M. and Foxall, G. R. (2013). Individual differences in consumer buying patterns: A behavioral economic analysis. *The Psychological Record, 63*, 259–276.

Christensen, C. J., Silberberg, A., Hursh, S. R., Huntsberry, M. E. and Riley, A. L. (2008). Essential value of cocaine and food in rats: Tests of the exponential model of demand. *Psychopharmacology, 198*, 221–229.

Christensen, C. J., Silberberg, A., Hursh, S. R., Roma, P. G. and Riley, A. L. (2008). Demand for cocaine and food over time. *Pharmacology, Biochemistry and Behavior, 91*(2), 209–216.

Ehrenberg, A. S. C. (1972). *Repeat Buying: Theory and Applications*. London: North-Holland Publishing.

Foster, T. M., Sumpter, C. E., Temple, W., Flevill, A. and Poling, A. (2009). Demand equations for qualitatively different foods under fixed-ratio schedules: A comparison of three data conversions. *Journal of the Experimental Analysis of Behavior, 92*, 305–326.

Foxall, G. R. (1990). *Consumer Psychology in Behavioral Perspective*. London, New York: Routledge.

Foxall, G. R. (1998). Radical behaviorist interpretation: Generating and evaluating an account of consumer behavior. *Behavior Analyst, 21*, 321–354.

Foxall, G. R. (1999). The substitutability of brands. *Managerial Decision Economics, 20*, 241–258.

Foxall, G. R. (Ed.) (2002). *Consumer Behavior Analysis: Critical Perspectives*. London, New York: Routledge.

Foxall, G. R. (2010). Theoretical and conceptual advances in consumer behavior analysis: Invitation to consumer behavior analysis. *Journal of Organizational Behavior Management, 30*, 92–109.

Foxall, G. R., Oliveira-Castro, J. M. and Schrezenmaier, T. C. (2004). The behavioral economics of consumer brand choice: Patterns of reinforcement and utility maximization. *Behavioral Processes, 66*(3), 235–260.

Foxall, G. R., Yan, J., Oliveira-Castro, J. M. and Wells, V. K. (2013). Brand-related and situational influences on demand elasticity. *Journal of Business Research, 66*, 73–81.

Green, L. and Rachlin, H. (1975). Economic and biological influences on a pigeon's keypeck. *Journal of the Experimental Analysis of Behavior, 23*, 55–62.

Gupta, S. (1988). The impact of sales promotions on when, what, and how much to buy. *Journal of Marketing Research, 25*, 342–355.

Hackenberg, T. D. (2013). From demand curves to public policy: Introduction to the special issue on behavioral economics. *Journal of the Experimental Analysis of Behavior, 99*, 1–2.

Hursh, S. R. (1980). Economic concepts for the analysis of behavior. *Journal of the Experimental Analysis of Behavior, 34*, 219–238.

Hursh, S. R. (1984). Behavioral economics. *Journal of the Experimental Analysis of Behavior, 42*, 435–452.

Hursh, S. R. (1991). Behavioral economics of drug self-administration and drug abuse policy. *Journal of the Experimental Analysis of Behavior, 56*, 377–393.

Hursh, S. R., Raslear, T. G., Shurtleff, D., Bauman, R. and Simmons, L. (1988). A cost-benefit analysis of demand for food. *Journal of the Experimental Analysis of Behavior, 50*, 419–440.

Hursh, S. R. and Roma, P. G. (2013). Behavioral economics and empirical public policy. *Journal of the Experimental Analysis of Behavior, 99*, 98–124.

Hursh, S. R. and Silberberg, A. (2008). Economic demand and essential value. *Psychological Review, 115*, 186–198.

Hursh, S. R. and Winger, G. (1995). Normalized demand for drugs and other reinforcers. *Journal of the Experimental Analysis of Behavior, 64*, 373–384.

Kagel, J. H., Battalio, R. C. and Green, L. (1995). *Economic Choice Theory: An Experimental Analysis of Animal Behavior*. Cambridge: Cambridge University Press.

Kagel, J. H. and Winkler, R. C. (1972). Behavioral economics: Areas of cooperative research between economics and applied behavioral analysis. *Journal of Applied Behavior Analysis, 5*, 335–342.

Keller, K. L. (1993). Conceptualizing, measuring, and managing customer-based brand equity. *Journal of Marketing, 57*, 1–22.

Keller, K. L. (1998). *Strategic Brand Management: Building, Measuring, and Managing Brand Equity*. Upper Saddle River, NJ: Prentice Hall.

Lea, S. E. G. (1978). The psychology and economics of demand. *Psychological Bulletin, 85*, 441–466.

Oliveira-Castro, J. M., Foxall, G. R. and James, V. K. (2008). Individual differences in price responsiveness within and across brands. *Services Industries Journal, 28*(6), 733–753.

Oliveira-Castro, J. M., Foxall, G. R. and Schrezenmaier, T. C. (2005). Patterns of consumer response to retail price differentials. *Service Industries Journal, 25*(3), 309–335.

Oliveira-Castro, J. M., Foxall, G. R. and Schrezenmaier, T. C. (2006). Consumer brand choice: Individual and group analyses of demand elasticity. *Journal of the Experimental Analysis of Behavior, 85*, 147–166.

Oliveira-Castro, J. M., Foxall, G. R., Yan, J. and Wells, V. K. (2011). A behavioral-economic analysis of the essential value of brands. *Behavioral Processes, 87*(1), 106–114.

Rachlin, H., Green, L., Kagel, J. H. and Battalio, R. C. (1976). Economic demand theory and psychological studies of choice. In *The Psychology of Learning and Motivation*, ed. G. Bower. Waltham, MA: Academic Press.

Rubinstein, A. (2012). *Lecture Notes in Microeconomic Theory: The Economic Agent*. (2nd ed). Princeton, NJ: Princeton University Press.

Skinner, B. F. (1953). *Science and Human Behavior*. New York: The Free Press.

Uncles, M., Ehrenberg, A. S. C. and Hammond, K. (1995). Patterns of buyer behavior: Regularities, models, and extensions. *Marketing Science, 14*(3), G71–G78.

Varian, H. R. (2010). *Intermediate Microeconomics: A Modern Approach*. New York: W.W. Norton & Company.

Winger, G., Woods, J. H. and Hursh, S. R. (1996). Behavior maintained by alfentanil or nalbuphine in rhesus monkeys: Fixed-ratio and time-out changes to establish demand curves and relative reinforcing effectiveness. *Experimental and Clinical Psychopharmacology, 4*, 131–140.

9

Essential value in the Behavioral Perspective Model

Ji Yan and Gordon R. Foxall

Introduction

Essential value is a novel measurement of the value of reinforcers, first defined by Hursh and Silberberg (2008) in an exponential model. It measures a fixed rate of behavioral change relative to the change of cost paid to attain a reinforcer. As the given percentage of cost went up, the lower the fixed rate of behavioral change, the higher value of reinforcers, and thus the higher was essential value. This measurement is more advanced than other measurements of the strength of reinforcement, and has been documented empirically by experimental data based on animal food consumption, human drug usage and human economic consumption (Hursh & Silberberg, 2008; Christensen et al., 2008a; Christensen et al., 2008b; Christensen et al., 2009; Yan et al., 2012a, 2012b). Understanding this advanced measurement of the value of reinforcers is important for the Behavioral Perspective Model (BPM) (Foxall, 1990/2004), since essential value not only measures the value of reinforcers but also indicates the demand response sensitivity pattern by comparing the value of reinforcers across different behavioral settings (open vs. closed), different types of reinforcement (utilitarian and informational), and brand groups.

What is essential value?

Essential value and economic demand

Learning theorists have realized the usefulness of microeconomics in scaling reinforcer value (Allison, 1983; Hursh, 1980; Hursh, 1984; Lea, 1978). Demand analysis, which evaluates the strength of reinforcers, has achieved considerable reliability across different essential commodities (Bauman et al., 1996; Foster et al., 2009; Foxall & Greenley, 2000; Foxall et al., 2004; Hursh, 1980; Hursh, 1984; Madden et al., 2007; Tsunematsu, 2000) and inessential commodities (Gunnarsson et al., 2000; Harris et al., 1999; Hursh, 1991; Hursh & Winger, 1995; Jacobs & Bickel, 1999; Johnson & Bickel, 2006; Rowlett, 2000). For example, Hursh (1978) argued that animal subjects working for food and water can demonstrate a behavioral model affected by price and consumption.

Several demand models are examined using experimental laboratory methods and they have successfully been applied to non-human data (primarily rats and pigeons) (Burke et al., 2008; Christensen et al., 2008a; Christensen et al., 2008b; Christensen et al., 2009; Dean et al., 2007;

Foster et al., 2009; Greenwald & Hursh, 2006; Hienz et al., 2008; Hursh & Silberberg, 2008; Madden et al., 2007; Winger et al., 2002; Winger et al., 2006; Winger et al., 2007) and additional studies (i.e., drugs, alcohol) on human beings (Bickel et al., 1990; Bickel et al., 1991; Hursh, 1991; Vuchinich & Tucker, 1988). Recently, the traditional demand curve is also reported to have contributed to the assessment of reinforcer efficacy in human economic consumption data (Foxall et al., 2004; Oliveira-Castro et al., 2006; Oliveira-Castro et al., 2008b).

Demand analysis provides a number of advantages over alternative methods by offering a more straightforward measure (i.e., elasticity of demand) which indicates how sensitive the level of consumption is to changes in price. Demand analysis, like the microeconomic framework to which it belongs, also has the advantage of avoiding referencing hypothetical factors such as deprivation, value, strength or probability (Christensen et al., 2008a; Christensen et al., 2008b; Elsmore et al., 1980; Foster et al., 2009; Hursh, 1991; Jacobs & Bickel, 1999).

Nevertheless, demand analysis differs from the traditional operant methods in language, methods, and predictions. For example, the quantity of consumption of relative reinforcers is required to produce the demand curve. Although in many ways the use of demand analysis is more advantageous than traditional operant analysis, this measure has a significant drawback in that it can sometimes lead to misinterpretation of the data. The linear demand curve confronted several problems to accurately present the curvilinear line that often reflects the base structure of the real data. In this regard, behavioral economists have exploited many alternative functions to scale reinforcer values on the basis of the economics of the demand curve. Their efforts broaden the applicability of demand curve into consumer behavior analysis.

The development journey of essential value

Several attempts have been made to model the demand curve (Hursh & Winger, 1995; Hursh & Silberberg, 2008) to bridge the inter-discipline differences when applying economic demand theory to behavioral analysis. The development of essential value stems from the simplest measure of the elasticity demand curve equation (Equation 1), following the monotonic decreasing law and presenting two essential parameters (i.e., the intensity and elasticity of demand). Price elasticity is measured by fitting the data into log-linear function:

$$LogQ = b_0 + b_1 LogP \tag{1}$$

where Q equals the quantity of commodity/reinforcers consumed in experimental period, P is the price, b_0 is the intercept when price is at a minimum level, and b_1 is a single direct measure of elasticity (called E.C. in Figure 4b in Hursh, 1984).

Equation 1 is the elementary model that behavioral psychologists and behavioral economists have investigated. Based on this equation, numerous influential researchers have found that demand curve analyses can contribute to the assessment of reinforcer efficacy and, subsequently, the validation of preference assessments (e.g. Foxall et al., 2004; Hursh, 1980, 1984; Kagel et al., 1995). It is used to avoid reference to hypothetical factors in experiments, such as deprivation, value, strength, or probability.

Hursh (1984) pointed out that the crucial parameter α (in Figure 4b in Hursh, 1984), elasticity of demand, is determined by: the nature of the commodity, the species of consumer, availability of substitutes, and the degree of openness of the economic context. Foxall et al. (2004) extended the species of consumer from animals to humans and proved that elasticity of demand varies across different consumer groups. It is found that consumers who purchase predominantly intermediate-level brands show higher price responsiveness than those who purchase predominantly the least- and highest-differentiated brands. The traditional demand curve has also been used in analyzing between-group differences in interpreting consumers' brand choice behavior among brand groups differing in functional and symbolic benefits (Foxall et al., 2013).

Hursh (1980) identified four principles as the base for adopting economic measurement in "a more complete science of behavior." First, he believed that a behavioral experiment is an economic system and the contingencies (open/closed economy) can significantly shape the results. A closed economy refers to an optimal state when consumption achieves the equilibrium point of supply and demand. On the contrary, an open economy indicates that one or more experimental arrangements have been added between the consumption and the equilibrium conditions. Hence, animal experiments are analogous to a closed economy, and the subject's consumption is directly determined by the equilibrium of its demand within the environment's supply. Therefore, the economic demand theory is applicable for behavioral analysis.

Second, Hursh (1980) found that elasticity as a functional property is capable of distinguishing reinforcers. In closed economies reinforcers differ in elasticity since presentations of substitutable sources of supply are under control. In an open economy substitutable commodities affect the elasticity of demand, so demand tends to be more elastic for all commodities. Hence, the substitutable effects are applicable to behavioral analysis.

Third, the experimental results support the view that the demand interactions of reinforcers can be complementary or substitutable. Hence, an economic measurement is suitable for behavioral analysis since it is capable of presenting both a complementary and substitutable relationship between commodities.

Fourth, a simple choice rule (such as strict matching) is not able to explain all choice behavior. If interactions of choice behavior are shaped by its local contingencies, Herrnstein's single summed class (Herrnstein, 1970) cannot fulfill the requirement to predict the outcome of a choice among a variety of alternatives.

A considerable amount of experimental evidence supports the idea of applying consumer demand theory to behavioral analysis. The first behavioral-economic demand curve, Equation 2, has been found to be successfully fitted into experimental data to measure reinforcers' value.

Based on Equation 1, two behavioral-economic demand curves (Equations 2 and 3), examining the relationship between consumption and price/income effects, have been investigated for scaling the rate of decline of a demand curve. Hursh et al. (1988) represented the first behavioral-economic model to show elasticity changes as price increases, using a non-linear curve-fitting procedure (SAS Institute Inc., NLIN procedure):

$$LogQ = LogL + bLogP - aP \tag{2}$$

where Q denotes consumption, P refers to price, and L, b and a are fitted parameters. The value of L is the initial level of consumption obtained at the minimal price, the parameter b is the initial slope of the demand curve which is expected to approach zero, a is the rate of change in the slope of the demand curve across price changes, and elasticity is presented as $b - aP$. Several experiments have been based on this equation to measure the strength of a reinforcer or between reinforcers involving nonhumans and humans (Giordano et al., 2001; Hursh, 1991; Hursh & Winger, 1995; Jacobs & Bickel, 1999), showing a satisfactory predictive accuracy.

Although Equation 1 contains two basic parameters to determine a demand curve, the intercept of y-axis (intensity) and the slope of the curve (elasticity), Equation 2 delivers an additional message in that an imperceptibly small increase in price should leave consumption levels unchanged. It empirically fits the experimental data as the consumption levels are inelastic to the price change at the initial level (see Figure 2.3, Hursh et al., 1988; Figure 10.2, Hursh, 1980; Figure 7.2, Jacobs & Bickel, 1999; Figure 3.1, Foster et al., 2009). Hence, it has been verified that Equation 2 produces better predictive accuracy than Equation 1. However, Equation 2 suffers from modeling demand curves by means of two parameters, *a* and *b*, instead of one. To maintain the predictive adequacy and prediction of elasticity by a single parameter, Hursh and Silberberg (2008) tested a range of equations proposed by Allen (1962) and introduced the second behavioral-economic demand equation, Equation 3, which maintains Equation 1's advantage in terms of evaluating the elasticity of the demand curve by one parameter and retains the predictive adequacy of Equation 2:

$$LogQ = LogQ_0 + k(e^{-a_1 P} - 1) \tag{3}$$

where variable Q is consumption, $Q0$ refers to the maximum consumption at zero price, k indicates the range of the dependent variable in logarithmic units, and P denotes the cost of consumption. Minimum consumption is calculated as $LogQ_0 - k$, $-a$ is the rate of change in the exponential function.

A point that has to be addressed here is the normalization of unit price. Although all demand curves confirm the monotonic decreasing trend to present the relationship between price and consumption, behavioral economics does more than simply restate the demand law and it uses elasticity of demand to signify the measure of "hedonic scaling." In human consumer behavior analysis, price is mostly related to the monetary price or time/energy consumed to obtain the commodity.

By contrast, in experimental behavioral analysis, price can be considered to a large extent as being apart from monetary price (i.e., response requirement, delay, changes in the amount of the commodity while holding the price constant). For this reason, in most circumstances of animal experiments, price is the cost paid for making a commodity available. Hence, price, which is used in the behavioral analysis when applied to generating demand curves, requires the process of normalization (Hursh, 1991; Hursh & Winger, 1995, Greenwald & Hursh, 2006; Hursh & Silberberg, 2008).

Accordingly, Equation 3 has been modified into Equation 4 by normalizing demand:

$$LogQ = LogQ_0 + k(e^{-a Q_0 C} - 1) \tag{4}$$

where variable C is the varying cost of the reinforcers. Hursh and Silberberg (2008) show that a is a single parameter that determines the slope of the demand curve. More importantly, a is capable of representing the essential value of a reinforcer. This equation has been tested in a range of closed settings with hens, pigeons, and rats (Christensen et al., 2008a; Christensen et al., 2008b; Christensen et al., 2009; Foster et al., 2009; Hursh & Silberberg, 2008). Foster et al. (2009) examined different behavioral-economic models (all proposed and defined by Hursh and Silberberg, 2008) for what they describe as "qualitatively different" reinforcers, meaning alternative formulations of cereal-based feedstuffs for hens. Hursh and Silberberg (2008) employed data for rats choosing different levels of food and drugs collected by Hursh in 1984 and 1988, and data from Elsmore et al. (1980) for baboons choosing from cocaine and food. Christensen et al. (2008a, 2008b, 2009) investigated food versus cocaine consumption in rats.

Although both behavioral-economic models succeeded in incorporating price effects and, therefore, established a ground for scaling reinforcer value, researchers have not yet absolutely agreed on the success of both equations. Foster et al. (2009) fitted both equations to the experimental data gathered from the same group of hens and found discrepant results. They argued

141

that normalizing consumption and price applied in both equations had been advantageous in terms of concurrent schedule preference, but doubted the internal validity of Equation 4. They pointed out that *a* values vary significantly even within the same product due to selecting different values for *k*.

Furthermore, the less preferred foods were found to have the highest essential value, which is contradictory to the expectation that the less preferred foods have lower essential values. Nevertheless, Foster et al. (2009) defended it because the preferences of hens may change when price (i.e., how hard hens work for food) changes. Therefore, Foster et al. (2009) prefer Equation 2 to Equation 4 in terms of explaining preferences behavior in the laboratory setting. Moreover, Foster et al.'s (2009) contradictory findings inspire us to wonder, apart from price, whether additional attributes of reinforcers interfere with the quantity of consumption, even if differences are small (i.e., wheat, puffed wheat, honey puffed wheat).

Evaluation of demand curves

Given the presence of the traditional demand curve (Equation 1), three behavioral-economic demand curves (Equations 2–4), and alternative demand curves reported in a prior study (Allen, 1935), a natural question is which demand curve fits human economic consumption data best. We conducted an empirical study to compare nine demand models (Table 9.1) based on fast-moving consumer good (FMCG) food consumption data across 52 weeks (Yan et al., 2012a, 2012b).

In particular, we found three main trends in nine demand models (Table 9.1). First, as shown in Table 9.1, the log-linear model (i.e., the traditional demand curve, Equation 1) and Equation 5 do not fit real-world data that is normally presented in a curvilinear form. Second, it is clear that, with the exception of Equation 4, all demand curves suffer from the problem that elasticity of demand changes continuously with changes in price. Although demand analysis provides a promising way to measure reinforcer value (Foxall et al., 2004; Hursh, 1980; Hursh, 1984; Kagel et al., 1995), it has been criticized for its use of direct comparisons of demand elasticity among reinforcers (Hursh, 1984; Killeen, 1995). The rate of change of these demand curves varies among price points (Killeen, 1995), and comparing elasticity of demand across different price points becomes difficult among qualitatively different products. In addition, elasticity of demand for reinforcers is often mixed (inelastic at low prices and elastic at higher prices) when examined across a broad range of prices. The exponential model (Equation 4) is capable of indexing the elasticity of demand by one parameter, which represents considerable progress. Third, according to Table 9.1, not all equations have been applied to non-human and human data. Although Equation 4 seems more advantageous in many ways than Equations 1 and 2, it has not been tested in human economic consumption data. In addition, Equations 1, 2, and 3/4 have not been compared with Allen's Equations 1.5–1.10.

Model comparison results (see Table 9.2) show that Equations 2, 4, and 7 are top performance models. More specifically, *R*-squared in Equation 4 was higher than those in Equations 2 and 7. Furthermore, the Root Mean Square Error (RMSE) in Equation 4 was lower than those in Equations 2 and 7. Moreover, the Akaike Informational Criterion (AIC) and the Bayes informational criterion (BIC) in Equation 4 were lower than those in Equations 2 and 7. Hence, the essential value model (Equation 4) has a higher predictive adequacy and is less biased than other behavioral-economic models in fitting consumer data in a natural setting based on a combined dataset. Hence, essential value has been identified as the best measure among other behavioral-economic measures according to the evaluation of the regression statistics based on a combined dataset.

Table 9.1 Pros and cons for available economic demand curves

Economic demand curves of indexing strength of reinforcers

Equation	Demand Curves	Pros	Cons
1	$LogQ = b_0 + b_1 LogP$	Applicable to both non-human and human data. Elasticity of demand presents the strength of reinforcers.	Elasticity of demand varies constantly with changes of price points. Misinterprets the curvilinear shape of the real data. No application to aggregated human economic consumption data.
2	$LogQ = LogL + bLogP - aP$	Applicable to both non-human and human data. High predictive adequacy. Presents the curvilinear shape of real data.	Elasticity of demand is presented by two parameters. No application to aggregated human economic consumption data.
3/4	$LogQ = LogQ_0 + k(e^{-aQ_0C} - 1)$	Applicable to non-human data. High predictive adequacy. Presents the curvilinear shape of real data. Elasticity of demand is presented by only one parameter.	Applied only for animal data. No application to aggregated human economic consumption data.
5	$Q = b_0 - b_1 P$	All these equations confirm the monotonically decreasing trend. Proposed by Allen (1935) for consumption research. No experimental examination for non-human or human.	
6	$1/Q = b_0 - b_1 P$		
7	$Q = b_0 - b_1 P^2$		
8	$Q = b_0 - b_1 \sqrt{P}$		
9	$Q^2 = b_0 - b_1 P$		
10	$LogQ = b_0 - b_1 P$		

Table 9.2 Rank of predictive adequacy of behavioral economic models using combined dataset

Equation	R^2	RMSE	AIC	BIC
Sort	Descending	Ascending	Ascending	Ascending
4	1st (.3145)	1st (.5201)	1st (213740.9)	1st (213770.4)
2	2nd (.2906)	2nd (.5291)	2nd (218972.1)	2nd (219001.6)
1	3rd (.2709)	3rd (.5364)	3rd (222793.0)	3rd (222812.7)

Why is essential value important for the BPM?

Essential value is seen as the best measure of the value of reinforcers in behavioral demand studies and human economic consumption studies (Christensen et al., 2008a; Christensen et al., 2008b; Christensen et al., 2009; Foster et al., 2009; Hursh & Silberberg, 2008; Yan et al., 2012a, b).

This advanced measure can be applied to and integrated with the BPM to investigate consumers' demand response sensitivity across reinforcement types (utilitarian and informational), brand groups, and even behavioral settings (open vs. closed).

Essential value and type of reinforcement

Two reinforcement types are defined in the BPM as utilitarian and informational reinforcement. Utilitarian reinforcement is mediated by the product itself, deriving from its practical application, and inheres in primary reinforcement and influences the rate of both human and non-human performance. Hence, it represents the functional rewards that a consumer gains directly from the product itself in purchase and consumption (i.e., drinking a bottle of orange juice or eating a can of baked beans). The BPM predicts that the higher the relative utilitarian benefit provided by a brand, the greater the probability that this brand will be bought rather than substitutes. There is, moreover, evidence that this is the case.

For example, Oliveira-Castro et al. (2010) found in a behavioral economics study based on matching analyses that consumers increased the amount they spend to obtain a higher level of utilitarian reinforcement. Behavioral economics research with nonhumans indicates that a reinforcer with greater essential value has a greater probability of being consumed than reinforcers with lower essential value (Christensen et al., 2008a, b). By putting these two findings together it could be predicted that a brand that provides relatively more utilitarian reinforcement than other brands in its product category would exhibit a higher level of essential value than those brands. This prediction has been supported by our empirical findings (Yan et al., 2012a, b). The results support the view that essential value varies across different utilitarian brand groups. A clear pattern has been found which shows that increases of utilitarian benefits in brands are associated with increases of essential value. The results reveal that larger essential values exist in brand groups with higher levels of utilitarian benefits while smaller essential values exist in brand groups with lower levels of utilitarian benefits.

Another reinforcement type defined in the BPM is informational reinforcement, which is conveyed by the symbolic attributes of the product. It is socially mediated and reflects the status and esteem which are accorded by a group to members who display approved patterns of purchase and consumption. Therefore, informational benefits are conveyed by the brand but mediated by other people and, ultimately, by the consumer's self-approval. Increased informational benefit is a characteristic of brands that possess higher perceived quality and/or a more established and prestigious brand name and image.

Essential value is used to measure the value of products that convey attributes to elicit utilitarian and informational reinforcement. The question is whether essential value differs across products with different types of utilitarian and informational benefits. According to the BPM, a brand's sales are directly proportional to the informational benefits it confers on the consumer. It would be expected, therefore, that a brand conferring higher levels of informational reinforcement would have a higher essential value.

Consequently, we decided to examine this proposition. A clear pattern is present which shows that increases of informational benefits are associated with increases of the essential value or with decreases of the price elasticity of demand (Yan et al., 2012a, b). It has also been found that larger essential values exist in brand groups with higher levels of informational benefits while smaller essential values exist in brand groups with lower levels of informational benefits, which is in line with the findings in utilitarian products.

Essential value also varies across products with a combination effect of utilitarian reinforcement (UR) and informational reinforcement (IR). Each brand has its own distinctive characteristics and may have different utilitarian and informational reinforcement from its substitutive brands. Brands differing in the amount of informational and utilitarian benefits were classified into six groups based on the combination of two UR levels and three IR levels: (1) IR1, UR1; (2) IR1, UR2; (3) IR2, UR1; (4) IR2, UR2; (5) IR3, UR1; (6) IR3, UR2. Our results support the view that the distinction among essential values exists in different brand groups. This indicates that utilitarian and informational benefits have combined effects on influencing consumer buying behavior.

Overall, the findings seem to offer authentic support for the expectations from the BPM. Utilitarian and informational benefits have been found to have a combined and individual effect in determining consumer buying behavior. Furthermore, clear patterns have been found across the brand groups differing in utilitarian and informational benefit levels. These patterns show that increases of utilitarian and informational benefit levels in brands are associated with increases in the essential value of these brands. These patterns also corroborate the view that UR and IR are positive reinforcements of consumer buying behavior.

Essential value and consumer behavior settings

The BPM indicates that consumer buying behavior is also determined by consumer settings (Foxall, 2007). Consumer behavior settings are antecedents of buying behavior, defined in terms of discriminative stimuli and motivating operations that set the occasion for consumer behavior. These variables, primed by the consumer's learning history, determine the "scope" of the setting (i.e., the range of potential opportunities for behavior available to the consumer).

Consumer behavior thus conforms to the scope of the setting (Foxall, 2005). More open consumer settings can allow consumers more options for behavior, while more closed settings offer only limited choices. In the case of FMCGs, an important characteristic of the consumer setting is the size of the store. A convenience store, such as a garage forecourt mini-market, is considered a more closed setting because of its limited selection of products and the time available to the consumer to make their selection. In a relatively closed setting, consumers have fewer choices (e.g. a smaller range of brand substitutes). The consumers are more constrained by the choices available to them. A supermarket is a more open setting because it stocks a wider variety of product categories and brand alternatives. In a relatively open setting, consumers have a greater selection of products and more substitutable brands to select.

Hence, the continuum of consumer behavior settings posited by the BPM reveals additional influences on the elasticity of demand for food products, with the possibility that price elasticity varies with the degree of openness of the behavioral situation. The BPM suggests that consumers show less price responsiveness in a relatively closed setting (e.g. a convenience store) and more price responsiveness in a relatively open setting, (e.g. a supermarket). It is important to investigate whether the essential value of products varies across different behavioral settings.

Further analysis was also undertaken using the human economic consumption data points from different consumer settings. We found evidence showing that the essential value of brands presented in more open consumer settings is smaller than the essential value of brands presented in more closed consumer settings. Hence, it is confirmed that consumers in more open settings, like supermarkets, show higher price responsiveness in choice behavior than those in more closed settings, like convenience stores.

In addition, the results also reveal that increases of essential value are positively related to increases of the quantity of consumption. Hence, we may conclude a tentative finding that brands with larger essential values are likely to be purchased in a larger quantity on one shopping occasion, or are purchased more frequently.

Integrating essential value into the BPM

As aforementioned, Foster et al.'s (2009) findings raise the question whether additional attributes of reinforcers have an impact on the quantity of consumption. Moreover, additional attributes would influence a brand's own "value." A brand varying in quality and reputation would impact its "value" as well. The pattern that informational and utilitarian benefits affect consumer buying behavior is mainly focused on the change of quantity of consumption. Hence, it is important to use essential value examining the detailed demand response pattern of utilitarian and informational reinforcement on the quantity of consumption. An exponential model is generated based on the essential value model with additional predictors – UR and IR.

$$LogQ = LogQ_0 + k(e^{-a_1 Q_0 C + a_2 IR + a_3 UR} - 1)$$
(4a)

where Q, Q_0, and k, respectively, denote consumption, the maximum consumption at zero price, and the range of the dependent variable in logarithmic units. C is the standardized price (e.g., 1 penny/gram would have $C = 1$). UR and IR are informational and utilitarian reinforcers, respectively.

Our main purpose is to compare the goodness of fit between Equation 4 and 4a. Based on 10,000+ FMCG consumption data points from 1,600+ consumers, our results support that Equation 4a has higher adjusted R-square and lower RMSE, AIC, and BIC values than Equation 4, which indicates that Equation 4a has a better predictive adequacy than Equation 4.

Incorporating UR and IR into demand curves takes brand-related characteristics and thus managerial marketing into consideration in the prediction of the quantity of consumption. The influence of UR and IR on the quantity of consumption is confirmed by separate analyses of the full dataset and the split-sample datasets. Additionally, the fact that $LogQ_0$ and the a value vary within a small continuum across Equations 4 and 4a and across different time periods indicates the internal reliability of the data set. Hence, increases of IR are associated with increases of the quantity of consumption, while UR does not show this pattern consistently since its influence depends on product category.

Overall, the additional predictors derived from the BPM explain a greater proportion of the variance in the quantity of consumption than does price alone. This finding holds true across different product categories and different time periods. It reveals how essential value can be used to measure different strengths of brands' value when UR and IR are incorporated into the essential value model.

Conclusions

Based on demand analysis, the essential value model indexes the price elasticity of continuously changing demand curves using a single parameter of the exponential equation. Hence, it overcomes the shortcoming of alternative demand curves in which the price elasticity changes continuously with changes in price. Moreover, it maintains high predictive adequacy as well as the linear-elasticity equation. Therefore, the essential value model is evaluated as the most promising equation for its potential contribution to consumer behavior research.

According to the BPM (Foxall, 1990/2004), we apply the essential value model across brand groups differing in utilitarian/informational reinforcement and in closed/open consumption settings. We find that (a) essential value varies across different brand groups within the same products; (b) brands with higher levels of utilitarian reinforcement show larger essential value; (c) brands with higher levels of informational reinforcement show larger essential value; and

(d) the essential value of brands varies inversely with the degree of openness of consumer settings. Furthermore, we generate a new model incorporating utilitarian and informational reinforcement into the essential value model to ascertain the influence of these variables on demand. The new model has greater predictive capacity than the essential value model, suggesting utilitarian and informational reinforcement are influential in consumers' economic consumption.

We have shown that the depiction of the contingencies of reinforcement portrayed by the BPM (i.e., the pattern of utilitarian and informational reinforcement and the scope of the consumer behavior setting) provides a new understanding of the complexities involved in human choice behavior occurring in natural settings for a variety of reinforcers and combinations of reinforcers. Moreover, the settings investigated reflect a variety of competitive market situations, contingencies that cannot be reproduced in animal and human addiction studies; consumer behavior settings also entail controlling factors such as advertising, distribution, and product and brand differentiation which are not present in traditional behavior analytic studies, as these are generally confined to considering price effects and necessarily ignore the remainder of the marketing mix.

References

Allen, R. G. D. (1935/1962). *Mathematical Analysis for Economists*. London: Macmillan.

Allison, J. (1983). *Behavioral Economics*. New York: Macmillan.

Bauman, R. A., Raslear, T. G., Hursh, S. R., Shurtleff, D. and Simmons, L. (1996). Substitution and caloric regulation in a closed economy, *Journal of the Experimental Analysis of Behavior*, 65, 401–422.

Bickel, W. K., Degrandpre, R. J., Higgins, S. T. and Hughes, J. R. (1990). Behavioral economics of drug self-administration. 1. Functional equivalence of response requirement and drug dose, *Life Sciences*, 47, 1501–1510.

Bickel, W. K., Degrandpre, R. J., Hughes, J. R. and Higgins, S. T. (1991). Behavioral economics of drug self-administration. 2. A unit-price analysis of cigarette-smoking, *Journal of the Experimental Analysis of Behavior*, 55, 145–154.

Burke, C. K., Peirce, J. M., Kidorf, M. S., Neubauer, D., Punjabi, N. M., Stoller, K. B., Hursh, S. and Brooner, R. K. (2008). Sleep problems reported by patients entering opioid agonist treatment, *Journal of Substance Abuse Treatment*, 35, 328–333.

Christensen, C. J., Kohut, S. J., Handler, S., Silberberg, A. and Riley, A. L. (2009). Demand for food and cocaine in Fischer and Lewis rats, *Behavioral Neuroscience*, 123, 165–171.

Christensen, C. J., Silberberg, A., Hursh, S. R., Huntsberry, M. E. and Riley, A. L. (2008a). Essential value of cocaine and food in rats: tests of the exponential model of demand, *Psychopharmacology*, 198, 221–229.

Christensen, C. J., Silberberg, A., Hursh, S. R., Roma, P. G. and Riley, A. L. (2008b). Demand for cocaine and food over time, *Pharmacology Biochemistry and Behavior*, 91, 209–216.

Dean, D. A., Flectcher, A., Hursh, S. R. and Klerman, E. B. (2007). Developing mathematical models of neurobehavioral performance for the "real world," *Journal of Biological Rhythms*, 22, 246–258.

Elsmore, T. F., Fletcher, G. V., Conrad, D. G. and Sodetz, F. J. (1980). Reduction of heroin intake in baboons by an economic constraint, *Pharmacology, Biochemistry and Behavior*, 13, 729–731.

Foster, T. M., Sumpter, C. E., Temple, W., Flevill, A. and Poling, A. (2009). Demand equations for qualitatively different foods under fixed-ratio schedules: A comparison of three data conversions, *Journal of the Experimental Analysis of Behavior*, 92, 305–326.

Foxall, G. R. (1990). *Consumer Psychology in Behavioral Perspective*. London and New York: Routledge.

Foxall, G. R. (2005). *Understanding Consumer Choice*. London and New York: Palgrave Macmillan.

Foxall, G. R. (2007). *The Behavioral Economics of Brand Choice*. London and New York: Palgrave Macmillan.

Foxall, G. R. and Greenley, G. E. (2000). Predicting and explaining responses to consumer environments: an empirical test and theoretical extension of the Behavioural Perspective Model, *Service Industries Journal*, 20, 39–63.

Foxall, G. R., Oliveira-Castro, J. and Schrezenmaier, T. C. (2004). The behavioral economics of consumer brand choice: patterns of reinforcement and utility maximization, *Behavioural Processes*, 66, 235–260.

Foxall, G. R., Yan, J., Oliveira-Castro, J. and Wells, V. K. (2013). Brand-related and situational influences on demand elasticity, *Journal of Business Research*, 66, 73–81.

Giordano, L. A., Bickel, W. K., Shahan, T. A. and Badger, G. J. (2001). Behavioral economics of human drug self-administration: progressive ratio versus random sequences of response requirements, *Behavioral Pharmacology*, 12, 343–347.

Greenwald, M. K. and Hursh, S. R. (2006). Behavioral economic analysis of opioid consumption in heroin-dependent individuals: effects of unit price and pre-session drug supply, *Drug and Alcohol Dependence*, 85, 35–48.

Gunnarsson, S., Matthews, L. R., Foster, T. M. and Temple, W. (2000). The demand for straw and feathers as litter substrates by laying hens, *Applied Animal Behavior Science*, 65, 321–330.

Harris, L. D., Briand, E. J., Orth, R. and Galbicka, G. (1999). Assessing the value of television as environmental enrichment for individually housed rhesus monkeys: a behavioral economic approach, *Contemporary Topics in Laboratory Animal Science*, 38, 48–53.

Herrnstein, R. J. (1970). On the law of effect, *Journal of the Experimental Analysis of Behavior*, 13, 243–266.

Hienz, R. D., Brady, J. V., Hursh, S. R., Gasior, E. D., Spence, K. R. and Emurian, H. H. (2008). Effects of incentives on psychosocial performances in simulated space-dwelling groups, *Acta Astronautica*, 63, 800–810.

Hursh, S. R. (1978). Economics of daily consumption controlling food-reinforced and water-reinforced responding, *Journal of the Experimental Analysis of Behavior*, 29, 475–491.

Hursh, S. R. (1980). Economic concepts for the analysis of behavior, *Journal of the Experimental Analysis of Behavior*, 34, 219–238.

Hursh, S. R. (1984). Behavioral economics, *Journal of the Experimental Analysis of Behavior*, 42, 435–452.

Hursh, S. R., Lea, S. E. G. and Fantino, E. (1988). Special issue – Behavior analysis and biological factors, *Journal of the Experimental Analysis of Behavior*, 50, 359–360.

Hursh, S. R. (1991). Behavioral economics of drug self-administration and drug-abuse policy, *Journal of the Experimental Analysis of Behavior*, 56, 377–393.

Hursh, S. R. and Silberberg, A. (2008). Economic demand and essential value, *Psychological Review*, 115, 186–198.

Hursh, S. R. and Winger, G. (1995). Normalized demand for drugs and other reinforcers, *Journal of the Experimental Analysis of Behavior*, 64, 373–384.

Jacobs, E. A. and Bickel, W. K. (1999). Modeling drug consumption in the clinic using simulation procedures: demand for heroin and cigarettes in opioid-dependent outpatients, *Experimental and Clinical Psychopharmacology*, 7, 412–426.

Johnson, M. W. and Bickel, W. K. (2006). Replacing relative reinforcing efficacy with behavioral economic demand curves, *Journal of the Experimental Analysis of Behavior*, 85, 73–93.

Kagel, J. H., Battalio, R. C. and Green, L. (1995). *Economic Choice Theory*. Cambridge: Cambridge University Press.

Killeen, P. R. (1995). Economics, ecologies, and mechanics: the dynamics of responding under conditions of varying motivation, *Journal of the Experimental Analysis of Behavior*, 64, 405–431.

Lea, S. E. G. (1978). Psychology and economics of demand, *Psychological Bulletin*, 85, 441–466.

Madden G. J., Smethells, J. R., Ewan, E. E. and Hursh, S. R. (2007). Tests of behavioral-economic assessments of relative reinforcer efficacy: economic substitutes, *Journal of the Experimental Analysis of Behavior*, 87, 219–240.

Oliveira-Castro, J., Foxall, G. R., James, V. K., Pohl, R., Dias, M. and Chang, S. (2008a). Consumer-based brand equity and brand performance, *The Service Industries Journal*, 28, 445–461.

Oliveira-Castro, J. M., Foxall, G. R. and James, V. K. (2008b). Individual differences in price responsiveness within and across food brands, *Service Industries Journal*, 28, 733–753.

Oliveira-Castro, J. M., Foxall, G. R. and Schrezenmaier, T. C. (2005). Patterns of consumer response to retail price differentials, *Service Industries Journal*, 25, 309–335.

Oliveira-Castro, J. M., Foxall, G. R. and Schrezenmaier, T. C. (2006). Consumer brand choice: individual and group analyses of demand elasticity, *Journal of the Experimental Analysis of Behavior*, 85, 147–166.

Oliveira-Castro, J. M., Foxall, G. R. and James, V. K. (2010) Consumer brand choice: allocation of expenditure as a function of pattern of reinforcement and response cost, *Journal of Organizational Behavior Management*, 30, 161–175.

Rowlett, J. K. (2000). A labor-supply analysis of cocaine self-administration under progressive-ratio schedules: antecedents, methodologies and perspectives, *Psychopharmacology*, 153 (1), 1–16.

Tsunematsu, H. (2000). Effort- and time-cost effects on demand curves for food by pigeons under short session closed economies, *Behavioral Processes*, 53, 47–56.

Vuchinich, R. E. and Tucker, J. D. (1988). Contributions from behavioral theories of choice as a framework to an analysis of alcohol abuse, *Journal of Abnormal Psychology*, 97, 181–195.

Winger, G., Galuska, C. M. and Hursh, S. R. (2007). Modification of ethanol's reinforcing effectiveness in rhesus monkeys by cocaine, flunitrazepam, or gamma-hydroxybutyrate, *Psychopharmacology*, 193, 587–598.

Winger, G., Galuska, C. M., Hursh, S. R. and Woods, J. H. (2006). Relative reinforcing effects of cocaine, remifentanil, and their combination in rhesus monkeys, *Journal of Pharmacology and Experimental Therapeutics*, 318, 223–229.

Winger, G., Hursh, S. R., Casey, K. L. and Woods, J. H. (2002). Relative reinforcing strength of three N-methyl-D-aspartate antagonists with different onsets of action, *Journal of Pharmacology and Experimental Therapeutics*, 301, 690–697.

Yan, J., Foxall, G. R. and Doyle, J. R. (2012a). Patterns of reinforcement and the essential value of brands. I: Incorporation of utilitarian and informational reinforcement into the estimation of demand, *The Psychological Record*, 62, 361–376.

Yan, J., Foxall, G. R. and Doyle, J. R. (2012b). Patterns of reinforcement and the essential value of brands. II: Evaluation of a model of consumer choice, *The Psychological Record*, 62, 377–394.

Triple jeopardy in a behavioral perspective

A Bayesian hierarchical model

Andrew Rogers, Peter Morgan, and Gordon R. Foxall

Introduction

Estimating the volume demand of fast-moving consumer goods (FMCGs) is well established and the evidence of a price elasticity of demand is widely accepted by marketing scholars and practitioners alike (Foxall et al., 2013). The purpose of this chapter is to explore other aspects of marketing and psychological variables which may influence consumer behavior above and beyond that of price elasticity. The "law-like" marketing phenomenon of double jeopardy and psychologically based aspects of the Behavioral Perspective Model are combined with the concept of price elasticity to better understand consumer behavior choices.

Brand equity

A brand is defined as "the name, term, sign, symbol or design or a combination of them intended to identify the goods and services of one seller or group of sellers and to differentiate them from those of competition" (Kotler et al., 1999, p. 571). The brand is an "enduring and profitable asset" to a manufacturer (Dyson et al., 1996, p. 9), its formal recognition coming in 1988 when the wealth of the brand was included on the balance sheet of organizations (Allen, 1990). This occurrence was largely due to the willingness of organizations to pay a premium to influence how consumers associate with the brand both on a tangible and non-tangible basis (Dyson et al., 1996) and it is often seen as offering a bundle of benefits to the consumer (Webster, 1994). Some examples are Nestle paying eight times the market value for Rowntree, Grand Metropolitan paying $800 million for Henblein and Yahoo buying Tumblr for $1.1 billion despite Tumblr revenue for 2012 being just $13 million (Fleury, 2013; Kotler et al., 1999).

Given the importance of a strong brand, marketers have developed a need to measure this brand relevance and strength through what has become widely known as brand equity (Kotler et al., 1999). Equity is defined by the Marketing Science Institute as "the set of associations and behavior on the part of a brand's customers, channel members and parent corporation that permits the brand to earn greater volume or greater margins than it could without the brand name" (Chaudhuri, 1995, p. 27). The *Oxford English Dictionary* defines equity as "the commercial value that derives from consumer perception of the brand name of a particular product or service, rather than from the product or service itself". Aaker (1991, p.15) defines it as "a set of brand assets and liabilities linked to a brand, name and symbol that add or subtract from the value provided by a product or service to a firm and/or to that firm's customers". The relationship of equity to the value and the strength of a brand has been discussed in many ways in the literature. Wood (2000, p. 663) says this determines "brand strength or the degree of brand loyalty", which are antecedents of value. Taylor et al. (2004) show loyalty is a result of equity and value, and Kotler et al. (1999) agree that equity creates brand loyalty. Whereas the benefit of equity and loyalty seems to be clear, there is some disagreement on the order of causality. However, despite this wide acceptance of their importance, the notion was challenged with work uncovering a double jeopardy of marketing effect, based on findings by sociologist William McPhee.

The double jeopardy phenomenon

In 1963, William McPhee observed that comic strips which were read by fewer people were also liked less by those fewer people. Having identified the same pattern among radio presenters, he concluded that smaller brands suffered in two ways: they attracted fewer buyers and were less popular among those fewer buyers. He called this "double jeopardy" or DJ (Ehrenberg et al., 1990). Extensive research shows a similar pattern more widely across behavioral categories and geography including media ratings, newspapers, automobiles, oil companies and many consumer packaged goods (Colombo & Morrison, 1989; Ehrenberg et al., 1990; Ehrenberg & Goodhardt, 2002; Wright & Sharp, 2001).

The reasoning behind double jeopardy

Ehrenberg and Goodhardt (2002) note that the relatively simple logic on which the DJ effect rests means that it can be modeled mathematically. On the basis of the account given by McPhee (1963), these authors explain the logic as follows. Consider a widely known restaurant "W" and a more obscure restaurant "O" which are equal in every way apart from W being better known. When a consumer is asked to name their favorite restaurant, most of the people frequenting W will say restaurant W (as they know not of the more obscure O), whereas of those frequenting O, half will say their favorite is O and half W (as they are equal in every way). Hence O suffers disproportionally: fewer diners and less loyalty among the fewer diners. This is how the DJ phenomenon comes about.

DJ challenges the fundamental importance of brand loyalty, since it implies that penetration is vital to brand growth and that loyalty will follow from this (Ehrenberg et al. 1990). However, Baldinger and Rubinson (1997) argue that brand loyalty and brand volume are highly correlated and loyalty is critical to marketing strategy, while Baldinger et al. (2002, p. 10) state that even though penetration appears to be more important than loyalty, for higher penetration brands, loyalty is "relatively more important than for smaller penetration brands". However, the absence of elasticity coefficients makes it difficult to establish the predictive magnitudes of these relationships. Furthermore, the correlations of loyalty are all less than the correlation of penetration (0.87 vs. 0.81 for small brands and 0.84 vs. 0.62 for smaller brands) which would confirm the importance of penetration over loyalty. Also the correlation of mid-share brands is 0.5, which does not lie between the 0.62 and 0.81 as may be expected given the logic presented.

However, Ehrenberg et al. (1990) do not suggest loyalty is not required, only that larger-share brands have a disproportional effect on loyalty towards those brands. Therefore, increasing share is more efficiently achieved through a focus on penetration which in turn will bring higher loyalty. These authors argue that marketing practitioners need to be aware of the effect of DJ on loyalty measures as they need to expect smaller brands' loyalty measures to be smaller than larger brands and not to overreact when this is the case. Indeed Ehrenberg and Goodhardt (2002, p. 2) state that "marketing people not knowing about [DJ] on customer loyalty is like rocket scientists not knowing that the earth is round". Furthermore, there is research evidence that new product launches attain a level of loyalty almost instantly, after which changes in loyalty are almost wholly accounted for by the DJ effect (Ehrenberg & Goodhardt 2000; Wright & Sharp, 2001). The implication is that brands are not strong or weak in equity: they are simply large or small in size (Ehrenberg & Goodhardt, 2000; Wright & Sharp, 2001).

The NBD-Dirichlet model has been extensively used to describe how FMCGs are purchased, including the DJ phenomenon (Goodhardt et al., 1984; Sharp et al., 2012). However, the NBD-Dirichlet does not incorporate marketing mix variables, since it assumes that the marketplace is essentially stationary (showing a small trend in sales in the medium term) and, on this basis, these variables can be assumed to have been taken into consideration (Bassi, 2011). This is because the marketing mix by and large determines the size of the brand and differences in loyalty are systematic (Ehrenberg et al., 1990). The model does not, however, assume the marketing mix variables are absent, but proposes that, within a stationary market, brand volume is unaffected by changes in the marketing mix (Ehrenberg, 1972). However, consumers are still making choices, usually among a repertoire of brands, and certain factors will influence which brand they choose at any one time. The NBD-Dirichlet states that these, on average, will form the predictive nature of the stationary market rather than on individual purchases of the consumer within that marketplace. Hence, the NBD-Dirichlet describes the pattern of purchase rather than the reason for the individual purchase, i.e. "why one person (or household) generally consumes more toothpaste or soup than others, or somewhat prefers brand j to k or vice versa, is not accounted for by the model and is in fact at this stage still largely unknown" (Goodhardt et al., 1984, p. 638). Research aimed at understanding this consumer behavior has been increasing over recent decades, spanning cross-disciplinary fields (Jobber, 2004; Kotler et al., 1999; Miller, 1995).

One model which incorporates different factors in explaining consumer choice is the Behavioral Perspective Model (BPM).

The Behavioral Perspective Model

The BPM has been used as a theoretical and methodological behavioral framework to explain consumer choice (Foxall & James, 2003; Foxall & Schrezenmaier, 2003; Foxall et al., 2004; Foxall et al., 2006; Oliveira-Castro et al., 2005; Romero et al., 2006). The model (Figure 10.1), an extension of the Skinnerian three-term contingency, proposes that behavior can be viewed as a function of a consumer's learning history within a specific temporal setting together with the benefits (or disbenefits) to be gained from the action (Foxall, 1990; Foxall, 2004).

The BPM states that consumption behavior is followed by a combination of utilitarian and informational reinforcement, and that this *pattern of reinforcement* influences the rate of subsequent behavior of a similar kind (Foxall, 2005). Consumer behavior settings range from relatively open (e.g. browsing supermarket shelves where a variety of alternative behaviors are available) to relatively closed (e.g. standing in line in an airport security queue, where a rather inflexible sequence of behaviors is enjoined upon the consumer). Hence, the freedom (in the sense of the number of behavioral options available) the consumer enjoys varies along this open–closed continuum (Foxall et al., 2013). The consumer behavior setting includes physical surroundings, including temporal constraints, and social surroundings, which include verbal rules (Foxall, 2007). Discriminative stimuli, that comprise the consumer behavior setting, include marketing mix variables. Hence, brand and product characteristics are discriminative stimuli that set

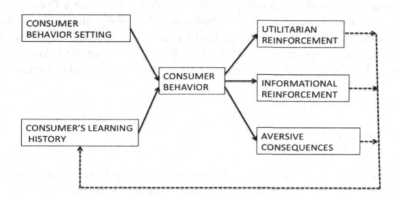

Figure 10.1   The Behavioral Perspective Model

Source: After Foxall (2010)

the occasion for reinforcement conditional on the consumer's enacting specific purchase and consumption responses (Foxall, 1987). The BPM also embraces the principles of behavioral economics within the purchase decision (Foxall, 2001). Choice is not assumed to be an internal psychological process but a consequence of reinforcements within a situational setting (Foxall, 1986a; Foxall 1986b).

Triple jeopardy

There is evidence of further effects beyond that of DJ on consumer choice. Bhat and Fox (1996) note that, compared to larger stores, smaller stores have fewer customers who visit less regularly (i.e. DJ) *and also* spend less money during their visits, a phenomenon to which they refer as "triple jeopardy" (TJ). However, presumably this would be due to the distribution of items rather than a systematic TJ effect. Recalling McPhee's explanation of DJ among restaurants "O" and "W", one might be led to agree with Sharp and Riebe (2005) that we should not expect the smaller-share restaurant "O" to also suffer further by people eating/spending less per visit than in restaurant "W". Presumably a nationwide fast food outlet enjoys higher penetration and more regular visits than say a Michelin star restaurant, though doesn't benefit further by higher average revenue per visit. In fact research into the TJ claim at the level of the retail chain (accounting somewhat for distribution limits) is dismissive of this notion of TJ (Sharp & Riebe, 2005).

At the level of the individual consumer, however, there has emerged some evidence that a further effect may indeed be present. Bandyopadhyay et al. (2005) observe that lower-volume brands from smaller consumer repertoires systematically score better on attitudinal measures than lower-volume brands in large consumer repertoires (albeit both less than larger brands as would be expected under DJ). This may suggest a further effect above and beyond that of DJ. Fader and Schmittle (1993) add weight to this argument via their finding instances when the NBD-Dirichlet model could not explain the market share of excessively high or low-volume brands, a strong indicator that there are other factors in play. Furthermore, research by Chaudhuri (1995) indicates that brand loyalty is a mediating variable in the creation of brand equity which supports both the equity and the DJ concepts.

We must conclude at this point, however, that there is no clear evidence on whether a TJ may exist, though some research seems to signal the possibility at the consumer level.

The research we describe in this chapter seeks to understand whether a TJ effect may exist on a psychological level which can be described within the variables that comprise the BPM. To establish the existence of this TJ, the model needs to account for the well-established elasticity of demand (Foxall et al., 2013). This can be obtained using the following equation (Equation 1). These coefficients are compatible with economic theory and consistent over time (Oliveira-Castro et al., 2006).

Equation 1. Elasticity of demand:

$$Log Q_i = \alpha + \beta Log \text{Price}_i + \varepsilon_i \tag{1}$$

The DJ phenomenon is also extensive in the literature and hence these will be included in the model to account for its existence. A suitable model structure is required.

Models for evaluating the DJ effect

The NBD-Dirichlet model is widely acknowledged to explain the DJ effect and, as we have said, the marketing mix variables are assumed within this model to be accounted for by the nature of the marketplace. However, the model also assumes the market is not segmented (Goodhardt et al., 1984). Within this study, the data are segmented by biscuit type and by supermarket store, which imply a segmented market. The specific aim is to understand the effects of the utilitarian and informational measures rather than the overall structure of the marketplace and hence the Dirichlet model is less relevant to the purpose of this study.

These informational and utilitarian elements of the BPM were not available at the time of development of the Dirichlet and a predictive model is, therefore, required to test these while also taking into account established factors affecting the size of a brand. Evaluating loyalty within the literature is not restricted to the Dirichlet model, for example Labeaga et al. (2007) build a discrete choice model where positive and significant coefficients for the loyalty measures demonstrate smaller brands suffer from less loyalty, hence showing the DJ effect. Chaudhuri and Holbrook (2001) use the LISREL structural equation model to assess the role of loyalty while Bandyopadhyay et al. (2005) also use a structural equation modeling approach. The implication is that other models outside of the Dirichlet have successfully been developed which incorporate or demonstrate the DJ effect and a relevant model is required in this case. Before discussing model selection, a discussion of the available data and a preliminary analysis is conducted.

Preliminary analysis of the data

The data relate to a panel sample of 1,594 households and 75,563 purchases of the UK biscuit (sweet and savory) market from the week ending 17 July 2004 to 9 July 2005. The data are assembled at stock keeping unit (SKU) level, whereby each descriptor contains a string relating to the brand and the number of items within the pack. The SKU element is not structured in any systematic way, hence to extract information about the SKU, the 2,783 SKUs are individually analyzed and the relevant information is consistently extracted and coded. This information relates to the brand name, the weight and the number of items per pack.

Some records appear to have an extremely low price per SKU (as low as 1 pence per item) and a decision is required as to how these observations are treated. The lowest-value biscuit ranges are classed as supermarket own label or value brands. There seems to be a minimum price of 20p per pack. Hence a minimum price of 20p is used as a minimum acceptable price for a

Table 10.1 Biscuit categories

	Count	% Count	Volume	% Volume
Blsc choc countlines	17,293	28.3%	5,089,771	28.3%
Blsc choc fully coated	1,715	2.8%	468,712	2.6%
Blsc choc semi ctd/latticed	7,033	11.5%	2,736,751	15.2%
Blsc coconut	397	0.6%	119,320	0.7%
Blsc cream/jam filled inc sandwich	3,381	5.5%	986,035	5.5%
Blsc digestives exc choc	526	0.9%	176,500	1.0%
Blsc fruit filled	1,910	3.1%	552,825	3.1%
Blsc ginger	1,124	1.8%	362,650	2.0%
Blsc marshmallow fully choc ctd	821	1.3%	191,293	1.1%
Blsc marshmlls choc semi/uncoated	76	0.1%	17,484	0.1%
Blsc sav crispbrd/rice cakes	5,332	8.7%	913,185	5.1%
Blsc sav extruded crckrs/waterbiscs	2,723	4.5%	775,180	4.3%
Blsc sav remaining	6,650	10.9%	1,543,272	8.6%
Blsc shortbread	1,295	2.1%	443,455	2.5%
Blsc shortcakes	1,295	2.1%	381,622	2.1%
Blsc sweet rem types	6,197	10.1%	2,001,843	11.1%
Blsc sweet/semi sweet assortmnt	913	1.5%	601,675	3.3%
Blsc tea & coffee	1,062	1.7%	324,066	1.8%
Blsc wafers	1,344	2.2%	285,418	1.6%

packet of biscuits. In the same manner, there are very low price per 100g values. Likewise, an analysis of the supermarket value range suggests a cut-off point of 15p per 100g is appropriate and hence this is used as a cut-off for all brands. This leaves a base sample of 61,087 records to analyze (80.8% of the original sample). As well as the SKU name, there is a product description field. Table 10.1 shows the distribution of data within this.

Some categories have low counts and hence are not suitable for modeling. A method is required to group the data. Chang (2007, p. 107) suggests a five-band classification yielding the groups shown in Table 10.2.

From the SKU field, it is possible to identify the number of items per pack. For each SKU, the number of items per pack is extracted manually. The number ranges from as few as one biscuit per pack to 48. There are also other larger formats such as drums, bags and barrels which do not contain the actual number of items but all imply larger packs. A sensible structure for modeling purposes is required. Hence the biscuit pack sizes are grouped as per Table 10.2 based on both the distribution of records within groups and logical groupings. Note that for packets of biscuits which contain many standard biscuits (such as digestive), the figure relates to the number of packets within the SKU; in this case, one. Where biscuits are individually wrapped, biscuits tend to be single-serve portions rather than multiple serve. For example, a single packet of six Kit-Kat biscuits will be classed as "6".

Initial analysis of utilitarian and informational reinforcement

Before a model is built, the analysis seeks to explore the potential relationship between the size of brands and the informational and/or utilitarian variables. Within the data, the informational score is obtained by averaging two scales and hence a score can be obtained for each brand. The

Table 10.2 Redefined biscuit categories

Subcategory	Definition
Chocolate countlines	Individually wrapped chocolate-covered biscuit bars which can be sold in multipacks, including Penguin, Club, Breakaway, Classic, Kit-Kat, Twix etc., which are marketed and packaged both as confectionary and biscuits.
Plain sweet biscuits	Plain sweet biscuits are uncoated, untopped or unfilled but can be flavored, for example coconut or chocolate, including chocolate chips, digestives, sweet assortment, shortbread, shortcakes, wafers, coconut, tea/coffee biscuits and ginger.
Chocolate-coated biscuits	Plain sweet biscuits coated partially, topped or completely with chocolate.
Filled biscuits	Sweet cookies which can either be filled, topped or sandwiched between plain biscuits.
Non-sweet biscuits	Plain savory biscuits, savory crackers and bread-like savory biscuits. Often flavored or topped with salt, cheese or other savory products.

	Count	% Count	Volume	% Volume
Countlines	17,293	15.2%	5,089,771	14.9%
Plain sweet	14,153	12.4%	4,696,549	13.7%
Chocolate coat	9,645	8.5%	3,414,240	10.0%
Filled	5,921	4.6%	1,538,860	4.5%
Non sweet	14,705	12.9%	3,231,637	9.4%

utilitarian scores are two categories and it will be more difficult for the data to show patterns which may correlate with the size of the brand. However, category 2 is seen to be a higher level of utilitarian benefit than group 1, therefore the utilitarian element is used as an ordinal/categorical variable and analysis techniques will reflect this.

With regards to the informational variable, the correlation with brand volume can be assessed. A Pearson's correlation test is considered. The informational variable is robustly normally distributed and hence no transformation is undertaken (see Figure 10.2).

The biscuit volume data are not normally distributed and hence a natural logarithmic transformation is undertaken with the resulting data being robustly normally distributed (recognizing longer tails). See Figures 10.3 and 10.4 respectively.

Table 10.3 Biscuit pack size distribution

	Count	% Count	Volume	% Volume
1	33743	55.2%	9,354,867	52.1%
2–5	3922	6.4%	1,195,547	6.7%
6–7	6880	11.3%	1,665,044	9.3%
8–11	7349	12.0%	2,056,553	11.4%
12+	6771	11.1%	2,597,211	14.5%
pack	2422	4.0%	1,101,835	6.1%

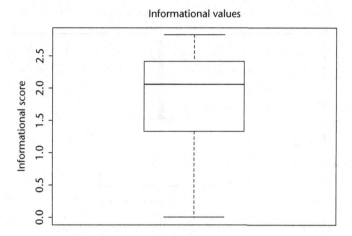

Figure 10.2 Boxplot of informational reinforcement

For DJ to be tested, the volume of each brand needs to be summed across the database. If DJ exists this will be correlated to the average informational score attributed to that brand. The correlation is set up by assuming the null hypothesis of no correlation between the informational and (naturally logged) volume. The two-tailed Pearson's correlation coefficient is .17, which is statistically significant and hence this null hypothesis is rejected, suggesting a positive correlation between the levels of informational scores and the volume size of each brand. Hence it seems the DJ phenomenon is present as larger brands have a statistically significant higher level of perceived informational benefit than smaller brands.

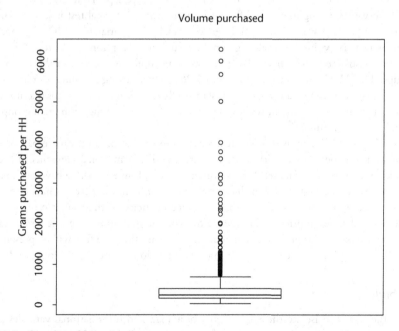

Figure 10.3 Boxplot of biscuit volume

LN volume purchased

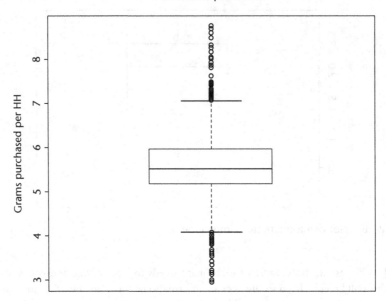

Figure 10.4 Boxplot of logged biscuit volume

Next, the analysis seeks to understand whether the higher utilitarian group has a higher average volume than the lower group. This would again inform the presence of DJ within the utilitarian element of the BPM (at least for the category in question). The mean LN (volume) values of the lower and upper utilitarian groups are 5.39 and 5.57 with 95% confidence intervals of (5.38, 5.40) and (5.57, 5.58) respectively. The lack of overlap of the confidence intervals suggests these values are significantly different to each other. A formal test is set up. The utilitarian variable is treated as categorical and hence an analysis of variance (ANOVA) approach is employed on the LN (volume) variable, given the Gaussian assumptions of the test. A two-tailed ANOVA is constructed with the null hypothesis of no difference between the means of the two groups. The ANOVA yields an F-ratio of 1,262, hence strong evidence to reject the null hypothesis and suggest the mean difference is statistically significant. This means that it is evident that the DJ phenomenon is present within the utilitarian group as higher utilitarian group brands have a higher mean volume.

Let us reflect on the analysis thus far. It has been shown that on a univariate basis the DJ of marketing seems to be present within the utilitarian and informational elements of the BPM when looking at the biscuit data set. It is important to note, however, these have been based on univariate analysis. Past studies within this category have shown other factors have implications for market share. Chang (2007) shows that the price elasticity of the biscuit category is circa −0.5 and hence changes in price will influence the volume of brands. The UK biscuit category is a stationary market and therefore Sharp et al. (2002) claim the DJ effect will be present in this category. Therefore it is wise to take these into consideration before conclusions are drawn.

Model build

As stated, the aim is to isolate the effect of the utilitarian and informational variables and test whether the DJ effect is present above and beyond those variables which would naturally be expected to predict the volume of the biscuit category. Hence a discussion as to the variables to be included in the model is presented.

Price. Recent studies have indicated the biscuit category data have a negative elasticity of demand and this value is close to −0.5 (Chang, 2007; Oliveira-Castro et al., 2006) and in general food products tend to be inelastic (Driel et al., 1997). To gain comparability across brand size, the price per 100g is used. The natural logarithm of this variable ensures the data are robustly normally distributed and the coefficient can be interpreted as the elasticity given a log-log model.

Supermarket own brand price. An offset relating to the prevalence of a supermarket own brand is included to account for systematic differences in supermarket elasticity.

Behavioral DJ effects. Traditional DJ studies show that larger brands have more purchasers and more loyalty among them. To account for the first of these measures, a variable is constructed that indicates how many unique purchasers (i.e. households) have purchased the product over the 52-week period. This is referred to as "*Penetration*". To represent these purchasers' loyalty, a variable is constructed to represent the share of how many times each brand was purchased within each individual's purchase history. This matches the share of category requirements (Goodhardt et al., 1984). This is called "*Loyalty*" and is the brand's share of each household's purchases. The larger this share, the larger the loyalty towards that brand. The combination of these two variables will allow for the identification of DJ within the purchases of a category, i.e. do smaller brands suffer twice by having a smaller set of purchasers (*penetration*) and less loyalty among this smaller set (*loyalty*)? If both these constructed variables have a statistically significant and positive coefficient then the DJ effect is evident.

Effects of utilitarian and informational reinforcement. The informational variable is included as scalar and utilitarian as dichotomous. The base value will relate to the lower utilitarian group of brands and the offset will allow the calculation of the higher utilitarian group. If the coefficient of the offset is positive and significant then this will indicate the presence of DJ within the utilitarian variables.

Including brand attributes as independent variables

Foxall et al. (2013) suggest that the characteristics of the brand may contribute to the purchase quantity of that brand. From a model perspective, the data being analyzed span many SKUs. Modeling all SKUs separately is demanding in terms of the degrees of freedom required (Fader & Hardie, 1996). Conversely, modeling all SKUs in a pooled functional form can ignore differences between SKU sizes and effects. An alternative structure proposed by Fader and Hardie (1996) sets to use the brand attributes as variables in themselves, arguing that consumers rarely choose brands but select an item based on their attributes. Singh et al. (2005, p. 196) and Webster (1994) agree and say consumers perceive a product as a "bundle of benefits" based on these attributes. Also Foxall (1987) says these characteristics are discriminative stimuli with regards to purchase response. The utilitarian variables from the earlier analysis seemed to have a positive effect on biscuit purchase volume, though product characteristics may be the cause of this and so they are included (Foxall et al., 2013).

Therefore, before firm conclusions can be made, the analysis proceeds by incorporating these terms into a multivariate model to test whether the utilitarian and informational DJ characteristics are present when simultaneously accounting for these other known factors. Equation 2 represents this model.

$$LN(Volume_j) = \beta_0$$
$$+ \beta_1 LN(Price_j)$$
$$+ \beta_2 Utilitarian_1 \star Informational_j + \beta_3 Utilitarian_2 \star Informational_j$$
$$+ \beta_4 Supermarket \star LN(Price_j)$$
$$+ \beta_5 Penetration_j$$
$$+ \beta_6 Loyalty_j$$
$$+ \sum_{i=1}^{5} \beta_{i+6} Biscuit\, type_i$$
$$+ \sum_{i=1}^{6} \beta_{i+11} Pack\, type_i$$
$$+ \varepsilon_j$$

Equation 2: Non-hierarchical model:

where $\varepsilon_j \sim N(0, \sigma^2)$ $\qquad\qquad j = 1,2,\ldots,n$ $\qquad\qquad$ (2)

Fixed and random effects

The Homescan panel data are constructed of multiple purchases within households. It is likely that purchases within households are less likely to be independent and a model to accommodate this is desired. This data structure lends itself to a hierarchical framework, simultaneously allowing different households to take different values at each level (Duncan et al., 1996). This is an advantage over conventional regression models which ignore any hierarchy in the data (Coker et al., 2013; Merino & Vargas, 2013) and can be subject to generalizing relationships, and hence "explain everything in general and nothing in particular". Multilevel models allow relationships to be calculated both across levels and also at specific levels (Duncan et al., 1996, p. 819). The multilevel model allows the cross-level estimation of the parameters, which may partially explain the variable that it is nested within (Merino & Vargas, 2013). Hence the assumption of data independence is relaxed (Field et al., 2012). Not accounting for the hierarchical structure may result in underestimated regression standard errors which may produce causal relationships when in fact the occurrence is through chance (Browne & Rabat, 2004).

Within multilevel models, variables can be modeled as fixed or random effects. A fixed effect is one where all possible variations of the population are contained in the variable. If the variable contains only a sample of the wider population values, it is deemed a random effect (Field et al., 2012). Within the Homescan database, the product attributes represent the available products within the population of the stores (or at least of the stores within the study). It is suggested these are treated as fixed effects. However, since the Homescan database is a representative sample of the UK population, it is logical these households are included as a random effect within the model.

Hence a random element is added to the current fixed effects model above. The random part of the model represents the purchaser and *panel id* is used to represent this. The functional form of the model is updated and shown in Equation 3.

$$LN(Volume_j) = \beta_{0j}Purchaser_{ij}$$
$$\beta_{0j} = \beta_0 + v_{0j}$$
$$+ \beta_1 LN(Price_j)$$
$$+ \beta_2 Utilitarian_1 \mid Informational_j + \beta_3 Utilitarian_2 \mid Informational_j$$
$$+ \beta_4 Supermarket \mid LN(Price_j)$$
$$+ \beta_5 Penetration_j$$
$$+ \beta_6 Loyalty_j$$
$$+ \sum_{i=1}^{5} \beta_{i+6}Biscuit\ type_i$$
$$+ \sum_{i=1}^{6} \beta_{i+11}Biscuit\ type_i$$
$$+ \varepsilon_j$$

Equation 3: Hierarchical model:

$$where\ \varepsilon_j \sim N(0, \sigma^2) \qquad v_{0j} \sim N(0, \sigma_{v0}^2) \qquad j = 1,2,\ldots,n \qquad (3)$$

Bayesian estimation of the parameters

Traditionally, statistics has been dominated by what is known as a frequentist approach (Poirier, 2006), so-called as probability is defined as the long-run frequency of an event (Koop et al., 2007). A statistical paradigm, which has come to be known as Bayesian statistics, was first published posthumously in 1763 in a work by the Reverend John Bayes titled "An essay towards solving a problem in the doctrine of chances".

Despite the Bayesian theorem being prevalent throughout statistics literature, applying the paradigm in the building of predictive models has been limited until relatively recently. The main reason is that the nature of the model requires integration of the posterior function, which for non-trivial functional forms is extremely complicated (Lunn et al., 2000). However, the development of a Markov Chain Monte Carlo (MCMC) algorithm in 1995 has led to strong growth within the Bayesian discipline (Poirier, 2006). This MCMC allows the posterior to be constructed by generation of a Monte Carlo style method which bypasses the need for integration of the function (Lunn et al., 2000). Instead, the posterior distribution is derived through a large number of iterations. This, paired with increased computational power during the same period (which directly facilitates this MCMC methodology), has led to Bayesian models being applied to a broad range of disciplines (Lunn et al., 2000). So much so that the Bayesian framework is now seen as a "well established alternative to classical inference" (O'Hagan, 1994, p. 1).

The Bayes theorem states the conditional probability of a parameter (θ) given the observed data (X_i) is proportional to the probability of the data given the parameter, multiplied by the probability of the parameter (Congdon, 2003). Or mathematically,

$$P(\theta \mid X_i) \propto P(X_i \mid \theta)P(\theta)$$

The left-hand part of the equation is known as the posterior probability. The right-hand side terms are known as the likelihood and prior, respectively. A major difference of Bayesian statistics over frequentist statistics is the embracing of the prior knowledge about an event or parameter. This prior is the initial belief of a parameter or event before any (new) data are considered. It can come from past studies, expert opinion or what may be considered as common sense (Hansen et al., 2004; O'Hagan, 1994). The likelihood is the addition of new data to be evaluated. The posterior probability is the blend of the prior and the likelihood, and the result is seen as the updated view of the estimate of the parameter (or event). Bernardo (1999) argues this concept closely matches what is seen in everyday life and Bernardo and Smith (2000, p. 4) say it illustrates how beliefs "fit together in the light of changing evidence".

However, risk assessment work by Viscusi (1985) states that a person's prior knowledge can be systematically biased and, although not criticizing Bayesian learning, points out the challenges by citing work by Lichtenstein (1978). This work demonstrates individuals over-assessing small risks and under-assessing larger risks. Indeed the frequentist perspective argues any knowledge should be free from any interpretation bias; however, Leamer (1992) says that in practice the researcher must have some prior incline and would reject any absurd parameters anyway. Koop (2006) argues that more information is better than less and allows for uncertainty to be embraced and quantified, not ignored in the decision-making process (Aspinall, 2010), while O'Hagan (1998, p. 21) says developing realistic prior estimates is preferable to relying on "ignorance".

Another difference in the paradigms relates to the parameter distribution itself. The frequentist views a parameter of a model as unknown but fixed (Abelard, 2013). This means the parameter has a definite value and the analysis is the probability of observing the data given the estimated parameter value (Abelard, 2013), i.e. $P(X_i | \theta)$. The Bayes theorem turns this on its head and calculates the probability of the parameter, given the data, i.e. $P(\theta | X)$. While no criticism of the frequentist methodology is offered by the author, it seems clear why O'Hagan (1994) says the Bayesian interpretation is more intuitive to management and allows more transparent means of embracing the uncertainty of a parameter. The debate of the Bayesian vs. frequentist approach has been prevalent in statistical literature and this text is not intended to input into this discussion. The author acknowledges the benefit of Bayesian methodology has been favored in this short text, though his wider philosophical view is very much in line with Efron (2005), who states that the 21st century will involve problems being resolved using a combination of different analytical tools and approaches from both paradigms. The purpose of this study is not to evaluate the paradigms, but to use their benefits and contextualize the results within a management decision framework. Hansen et al. (2004) make use of relevant frequentist diagnostics when evaluating the relevance of the Bayesian model and parameter estimates.

WinBUGS

To calculate these Bayesian functions, specialized software is required. The BUGS Bayesian software stands for Bayesian inference Using Gibbs Sampler (Lunn et al., 2000). WinBUGS is the Windows version of the software. Both use the MCMC method to analyze Bayesian full probability models (Lunn et al., 2000). The Gibbs sampler samples from the full conditional probability of each parameter in turn, keeping the others constant, and convergence is monitored and achieved after a number of iterations (Spiegelhalter et al., 2003).

An overview only of the WinBUGS process is offered here. The model is specified within the WinBUGS environment. The software first checks the syntax of the model. Next the data are loaded and WinBUGS checks they are of the correct format. The model is compiled, which creates the data structure for the Gibbs sampler. Finally, initial values are loaded or generated from the prior distributions of each parameter (Spiegelhalter et al., 2002). The parameters need to be monitored to ensure convergence and also to obtain the posterior statistics when convergence is achieved (Spiegelhalter et al., 2002).

Prior discussion of informative model

The Bayesian model requires the inclusion of prior estimates of the parameter. Congdon (2003) says it may be difficult to do and sometimes better to resort to non-informative priors. Therefore a model is initially constructed where the prior information is considered non-informative or vague and is defined as normally distributed with mean zero and small precision (0.0001). The term precision is used when referring to the prior distribution within a Bayesian modeling framework and is the inverse of the variance (Congdon, 2003). This model will be known as model "vague".

A second mixed-effect model is constructed where the move is to informed priors, embracing knowledge available from past studies or from common sense. Refer to this as model "informative". Informed priors are now discussed.

Price. It is natural to assume that price elasticity will be negative given the non-luxury nature of the category. Also, as discussed earlier, other studies of the same data suggest this measure is of small magnitude. However, given the different model structure, the author does not wish to impose too rigid a prior distribution and hence a truncated normal distribution is applied where the upper boundary is controlled to be a maximum of 0. The small precision allows the model to produce any estimate on the negative real number line $\mathfrak{R}^-$.

DJ variables. The traditional DJ variables would both be positive given the prevalence of the phenomenon, but the author poses no more influence other than this, as these values have not been run in similar studies and hence the data should have a greater influence over and above this truncation. Hence a lower limit of 0 is offered. The small precision allows the data to take any range within the positive real numbers $\mathfrak{R}^+$.

The informational and utilitarian variables would both be positive if DJ exists and hence a lower boundary of zero and small precision will infer a coefficient estimate within $\mathfrak{R}^+$. Other coefficients offer no prior logic of scale or sign and hence these are retained with vague prior distributions.

Model diagnostics

The coefficients of the three models are shown in Table 10.4. The R-squared (adjusted) values for the hierarchical models are far larger than the non-hierarchical model, suggesting that allowing for within-household effects is positively contributing to the fit of the model. Table 10.4 below shows the mean estimate of the parameter and their standard error.

As well as the higher R-squared (adj) value, the deviance information criteria (DIC) measurement for the hierarchical model is less than the non-hierarchical (45,543 vs. 71,677, respectively), suggesting the inclusion of the random element better predicts a replicated data set of the same structure (Spiegelhalter et al., 2002). DIC is preferred in this case to the Bayesian information criteria (BIC) as the random effects are of interest (Spiegelhalter et al., 2002). Furthermore the non-hierarchical model will assume all observations are independent; however, the percentage of the random variance component versus the total model residual is:

$$\frac{\sigma_0^2}{\sigma_0^2 + \sigma^2} = 32.7\%$$

demonstrating the importance of the household random effect in estimating the model. The parameters are visualized graphically in Figure 10.5, demonstrating the differences between the hierarchical and non-hierarchical estimates.

Table 10.4 Model results

	Vague		Informative		Non-hierarchical	
	Beta (st err)		Beta (st err)		Beta (st err)	
Log price	−0.5537	(0.0036)	−0.5482	(0.00631)	−0.6778	(0.00387)
Informational	0.0206	(0.00271)	0.0207	(0.00301)	0.0165	(0.0032)
Informational (Util 2)	0.0305	(0.00329)	0.0302	(0.00331)	0.0541	(0.00379)
Log price (Sprmkt)	0.0838	(0.00322)	0.0818	(0.00373)	0.1351	(0.00373)
Penetration	0.0007	(0.00008)	0.0006	(0.00011)	0.0025	(0.00008)
Loyalty	0.1575	(0.00094)	0.1617	(0.00442)	0.0727	(0.00074)
Coatline	base		base		base	
Chocolate	0.1028	(0.00534)	0.1022	(0.00547)	0.1204	(0.00633)
Plain sweet	0.1100	(0.00744)	0.1097	(0.00738)	0.1581	(0.0087)
Filled	0.0045	(0.00663)	0.0055	(0.00702)	−0.0135	(0.00776)
Non sweet	0.0048	(0.0086)	0.0067	(0.00856)	0.0140	(0.00958)
Number 1	base		base		base	
Number 5	0.1500	(0.00627)	0.1482	(0.00649)	0.1930	(0.00758)
Number 7	0.0971	(0.00562)	0.0964	(0.00556)	0.1030	(0.00644)
Number 11	0.1749	(0.00604)	0.1733	(0.00657)	0.2119	(0.00733)
Number 12	0.2512	(0.00566)	0.2486	(0.00623)	0.3348	(0.0066)
Number pack	0.3653	(0.0079)	0.3584	(0.01033)	0.5030	(0.00909)
R-squared *(adj)*	71.0%		71.1%		53.2%	

The similarity (almost exact) of the vague and informative hierarchical models is due to the high level of agreement between the prior distribution and the likelihood. The informative prior distributions are relatively weak in terms of magnitude but tight in terms of signs and the likelihood is reinforcing this prior belief. From the coefficients, it can be seen that assuming independence between all observations and hence ignoring the within-household hierarchy leads to possible overestimation of the price elasticity, supermarket own brand effect on price elasticity, informational benefits in the higher utilitarian group and penetration, while underestimating the effect of informational impact and loyalty.

Given the similarity of the two hierarchical models, one can be discarded. The vague mixed model is used as the basis for the mixed effects model as the prior belief is not impacting the coefficients. The actual and predicted fit of the hierarchical model is shown in Figure 10.6, showing the relationship between the data and the included variables.

The residual plot is shown in Figure 10.7 and demonstrates a spread of residuals, with a few exceptions. While interesting to understand which characteristics may be driving these outliers, given the charted fits and the R-squared (adjusted) values, the discussion assumes a good model diagnostics and a discussion of the parameter values now follows.

Discussion

Price elasticity

Given the log-log model, the coefficient is the price elasticity. The non-hierarchical model shows a higher coefficient (slightly) than the mixed model, suggesting the ignorance of the

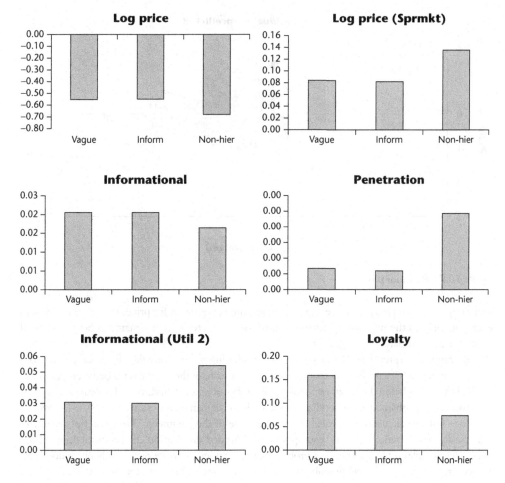

Figure 10.5   Plot of model coefficients

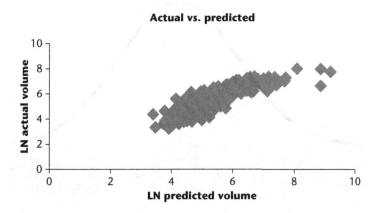

Figure 10.6   Actual vs. predicted

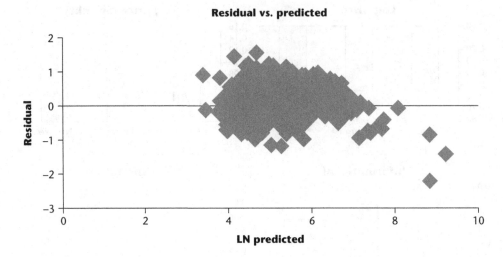

Figure 10.7   Residual plot

hierarchy of the data may produce a greater magnitude coefficient for price. Recall, the Bayesian estimation allows the probability distribution of the parameter to be estimated. The mixed-level model result is displayed in Figure 10.8.

This can be interpreted by saying that given the prior information and the likelihood gained from the data, there is a 95% probability that the posterior estimate of the parameter is between −.560 and −.546, with −.554 being the mean estimate. Whereas frequentist methods would construct a hypothesis around the probability of observing the data, given the parameter estimate of −0.554, Bayesian inference instead calculates the probability of the value of the parameter. This posterior parameter is normally distributed, given the assumptions of the prior distribution. If the distribution of the parameter straddles zero then there is a probability the parameter may be zero (and hence redundant). However, there is a very small probability that the parameter is in fact greater than −0.543.

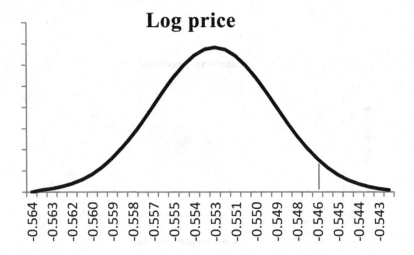

Figure 10.8   Price coefficient

Figure 10.9   Supermarket own price offset coefficient

Supermarket own brand price elasticity offset

For both hierarchical and non-hierarchical models, the offset for supermarket own brands is positive and significant with values of .08 and .14, respectively. This means supermarket own brands are less responsive to average price changes. This may be due to the promotional nature of the category where branded names tend to benefit from price reductions over supermarket own brands. The hierarchical model's distribution of the posterior of this parameter is shown in Figure 10.9. Again, there is no reason to believe this parameter is redundant as there is very little probability that the distribution contains the value 0.

Traditional DJ variables

The penetration (or number of households purchasing) variable is linear and hence, given the dependent variable is naturally logged, the coefficient is raised to the exponential to interpret the value.

$$\text{linear coef} = e^{\beta} - 1$$

The linear coefficient is therefore 0.246% and 0.068% for the non-hierarchical and hierarchical models, respectively, so there is a factor of 10 difference between them. Figure 10.10 shows the hierarchical posterior distribution of the penetration parameter. The numbers are small but still there is just a very small chance that the parameter value is zero and hence redundant in the model.

What does this mean? There are 1592 unique households purchasing the category. If one extra household decides to purchase, then this is an increase of $1/1592 = 0.063\%$ increase in the number of households buying. This is compared to a change of 0.068% change in the volume for the hierarchical model. Equating these gives a $0.068\%/0.063\% = 1.09$. Hence every 1% increase in the number of households purchasing a biscuit brand will increase the volume by 1.09% on average. The equivalent number for the non-hierarchical model is 3.9%. This would

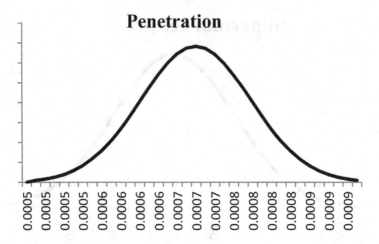

Figure 10.10 Penetration coefficient

imply that increasing the households by 1% increases volume by 3.9%. Logic would suggest that increasing the amount of households purchasing by 1% would increase the volume by a like 1% which is remarkably close to what the hierarchical coefficient suggests.

The loyalty measure is already in percentage terms (i.e. values fluctuate between a possible 0 and 100%). Hence the measures, when modeled against the logged volume, closely reflect the percentage change in the variable and therefore can be read as elasticity measures. Figure 10.11 shows the hierarchical model's posterior distribution for loyalty.

The elasticity measure for the hierarchical model is 0.16% and 0.07% for the non-hierarchical model so again there is some difference between the two.

We have noted that Ehrenberg et al. (1990) state that DJ commands smaller brands have fewer consumers and less loyalty among the smaller set of consumers. The same effect is evident here with the positive and statistically significant coefficient signifying the same observation.

Figure 10.11 Loyalty coefficient

Ehrenberg et al. (1990) state that penetration is more important than loyalty and this pattern is observed in this data. Hence the DJ effect is apparent within the data, above and beyond the effect of price.

Utilitarian and informational reinforcement variables

The informational variable is the base value and the informational variable for utilitarian group 2 (the higher group) is an offset, hence the base informational coefficient can be interpreted as the value for utilitarian group 1 (the lower utilitarian group). Adding the offset will give the value for utilitarian group 2.

The coefficients are transformed to linearity in the same way as the DJ variables:

linear coef $= e^\beta - 1$

Figure 10.12 shows the hierarchical posterior distribution estimates of the informational variable.

The values for the lower utilitarian groups are 0.021 and 0.017 for the hierarchical and non-hierarchical models, respectively, showing more similarity between the two models, though the hierarchical model in general is preferred for the reasons discussed. From Figure 10.12, again we see very little evidence to suggest this parameter is zero. Therefore we see that the nature of the positive coefficient suggests that larger (volume) brands within the lower utilitarian group are being perceived to have a higher informational benefit than smaller brands, over and above what can be accounted for by behavioral economic and traditional DJ effects.

Figure 10.13 shows the hierarchical posterior distribution for the offset informational variable for utilitarian group 2.

The offset values are positive and there is no evidence to suggest that the value of the parameter is non-positive given the distribution of the parameter in Figure 10.13. This suggests the higher utilitarian group is enjoying a higher perceived level of informational benefit over the lower utilitarian group. Combining the results of the two informational variables, it can be seen that, within the BPM structure, having taken account of known behavioral economic variables and traditional DJ effects, there seems to be a TJ effect, in that larger brands are being perceived

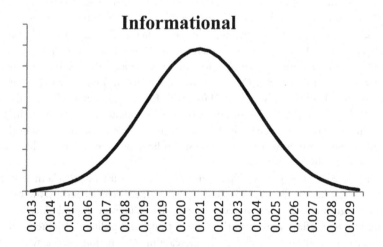

Figure 10.12 Informational coefficient

169

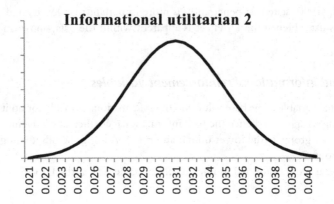

Informational utilitarian 2

0.021 0.022 0.023 0.025 0.026 0.027 0.028 0.029 0.030 0.031 0.032 0.034 0.035 0.036 0.037 0.038 0.039 0.040

Figure 10.13   Informational coefficient offset for utilitarian group 2

to have a higher level of informational benefits. Furthermore, this effect is greater for brands which are perceived to have a greater utilitarian benefit. At least, this effect seems present within the UK biscuit category.

Conclusion

Within the biscuit category in the UK, a model has been built to describe consumer behavior. The model demonstrates that the volume of the brands within the category can be explained by a combination of elements from behavioral economics, marketing theory and psychological factors. Combining these complements the level of consumer behavior understanding which can be gained from this particular data set.

Price elasticity of demand in the UK biscuit category is negative and inelastic, in line with past studies (Chang, 2007; Driel et al., 1997; Oliveira-Castro et al., 2006) with a coefficient of Regular 0.554 (which decreases in magnitude to −0.47 for supermarket own brands). This change in magnitude can be explained through the promoted nature of the category where supermarket own label brands are not responding as well to promotional reductions as branded products.

The two constructed DJ variables are positive and hence show that smaller brands are suffering twice: less penetration and less loyalty among the smaller set of buyers. This is in line with marketing theory discussed mainly through the DJ studies of Ehrenberg. The elasticity of the penetration variable of 1.09% suggests an increase of 1% in the number of households would yield a 1.09% increase in volume, which is logical. Furthermore, the loyalty elasticity of 0.16% is much lower, again in line with DJ theory discussed earlier. This shows the importance of penetration in stimulating brands' growth. However, Ehrenberg et al. (1990) say that for DJ to be present, the brands need to be indistinguishable in a blind taste test. However, the DJ effect is apparent within this taste- and shape-diversified category which questions whether this assumption is required. Similarly, how a blind taste test can be applied to, for example, aviation fuel, comics or radio stations is questionable.

While the DJ effect is apparent, Ehrenberg and Goodhardt's (2002) claim that brands are not strong or weak in equity, simply large or small in size, is challenged by the existence of a further psychological effect demonstrated in the model. While much credibility is given to the claim, there is also an effect seen from the informational and utilitarian elements of the BPM. For the lower utilitarian group, a one-point increase in informational score would produce a 2.1% increase in volume (and a 3.1% increase in the higher utilitarian group). Therefore the perception of informational and utilitarian values is also exhibiting a DJ-type effect above and beyond what can be described by price elasticity or the (traditional) DJ variables. This TJ effect could start to explain the importance of psychological reinforcements to consumers, which may be construed as a form of equity. This may potentially start to explain why manufacturers are willing to pay a premium for brands eliciting stronger equity. By no means is the author stating this in any way replaces or supersedes the "law-like" DJ effect, but it is additional to it. Note the scale of the informational variable is a three-point scale. Hence the level of incremental volume which could be realized *purely* through the BPM informational and utilitarian reinforcements[1] would be a maximum of 6.2% (moving from level 1 to level 3 in the higher utilitarian group). Compare this to the DJ effect, where, according to this model, a 6% increase in penetration would render a $(6 \times 1.09 = 6.54\%)$ increase in volume and also a $(6 \times 0.165 = 0.96\%)$ further increase in volume through loyalty (so a total of 7.5%). Though this study is currently just for one category in one market, it does have implications for management.

Prior to this study, the recommended way in which to grow a brand would be through price changes/discounting and/or through increasing penetration (which would also increase loyalty a little). Focusing for the moment on the marketing theory and assuming constant pricing, increasing penetration for smaller or medium-sized brands clearly shows the benefit of the DJ theory in increasing volume. However, brands with high penetration may be reaching saturation point and hence the TJ effect presents a further opportunity to management to consider increasing brand size.

The study also offers contributions to the topic in the way the model is technically built. The hierarchical model structure better represents the data with a higher R-squared (adjusted) value than the non-hierarchical model and the random effects variance component accounts for 32.7% of the total variability of the model. The removal of the assumption of independence of purchases within households is arguably more logical than assuming purchases are independent. This allows the model to better understand purchase levels of brands given a specific household and hence allows the parameters to better represent the behavior. In some instances the difference between the hierarchical and non-hierarchical model is small (e.g. log price) and some are much higher (e.g. penetration coefficient is over twice the magnitude). The implications to management in ignoring the hierarchical structure of the data could lead to over or underestimation of the anticipated effect of marketing levers on consumer behavior. The random effects here are limited to the household intercept as these are a random sample of the population, whereas the other factors in the model are representative of the population (Field et al., 2012).

Bayesian estimation has been used in this instance to estimate the parameters. Bayesian estimation allows for prior information to be mathematically incorporated into the model. The informative model has produced estimates almost exactly in line with the non-informative model and hence the prior information is in strong agreement with the likelihood, resulting in aligned posterior estimates. The Bayesian estimation process also allows the direct observation of the posterior distribution of the parameters, given the data, and hence a confidence interval of the mean of the estimate can be directly observed. For each parameter, the posterior distribution does not straddle zero, indicating a high probability that each parameter is contributing to the model predictiveness.

Further research

The current research is restricted to one category within one market and hence further research is required to verify results and offer any general hypothesis. The coefficients of the DJ seem sensible, but further studies could confirm or contradict these findings. The price elasticity is very much in line with other studies and hence a higher degree of confidence is maintained. The "triple jeopardy" effects are new to this study and again need to be tested further in different studies. However, this model provides a good representation of the data; the assumptions and structure it offers make logical sense and the interpretation seems a sensible offering for management decisions.

Note

1 This is purely the informational and utilitarian effects of the model, not accounting for situational or learning history effects.

References

Aaker, D. (1991). *Managing brand equity*. New York: The Free Press.

Abelard (2013). *Cause, chance and Bayesian statistics*. Available at http://www.abelard.org/briefings/bayes.htm.

Allen, D. (1990). Creating value – The financial management of brands. *CIMA*. Available at http://hdl. handle.net/10068/507293.

Aspinall, W. (2010). A route to more tractable expert advice. *Nature* 463(21), 294–295.

Baldinger, A. L. and Rubinson, J. (1997). The jeopardy in Double Jeopardy. *Journal of Advertising Research* November, 37–49.

Baldinger, A. L., Blair, E. and Echambadi, R. (2002). Why brands grow. *Journal of Advertising Research*, 7–14.

Bandyopadhyay, S., Gupta, K. and Dube, L. (2005). Does brand loyalty influence double jeopardy? A theoretical and empirical study. *Journal of Product and Brand Management* 14, 414–423.

Bassi, F. (2011). The Dirichlet model: analysis of a market and comparison of estimation procedures. *Marketing Bulleting* 22, Technical Note 1.

Bernardo, J. M. (1999). Bayesian methods in the sciences. *Special Issue of Rev. Acad. Cien Madrid* 93. Available at http://www.uv.es/~bernardo/academia.html.

Bernardo, J. M. and Smith, A. F. M. (2000). *Bayesian theory*. Chichester: Wiley.

Bhat, S. and Fox, R. (1996). An investigation of jeopardy effects in store choice. *Journal of Retailing and Consumer Services* 3(3), 129–133.

Browne, W. and Rabat, J. (2004). *New developments in modeling, multilevel modeling*. In M. Hardy and A. Bryman eds. *Handbook of data analysis*. London: Sage.

Chang, S. W. (2007). *Behavioral economics: an empirical investigation of consumer buying behavior and price responsiveness in the British biscuit market*. PhD: Cardiff.

Chaudhuri, A. (1995). Brand equity or double jeopardy? *Journal of Product and Brand Management* 4, 26–32.

Chaudhuri, A. (1999). Does brand loyalty mediate brand equity outcomes? *Journal of Marketing Theory and Practice* 7, 136–146.

Chaudhuri, A. and Holbrook, M. B. (2001). The chain of effects from brand trust and brand affect to brand performance: the role of brand loyalty. *Journal of Marketing* 65(2), 81–93.

Coker, C., Altobello, S. A. and Balasubramanian, S. K. (2013). Message exposure with friends: the role of social context on attitudes toward prominently placed brands. *Journal of Consumer Behaviour* 12, 102–111.

Colombo, R. A. and Morrison, D. G. (1989). A brand switching model with implications for marketing strategies. *Marketing Science* 8, 89–99.

Congdon, P. (2003). *Applied Bayesian modeling*. London: Wiley.

Driel H. V., Nadall, V. and Zeelenberg, K. (1997). The demand for food in the United States and the Netherlands: a systems approach with the CBS model. *Journal of Applied Economics* 12, 509–532.

Duncan, C., Jones, K. and Moon, G. (1996). Health related behavior in context: a multilevel approach. *Social Science and Medicine* 42, 817–830.

Dyson, P., Farr, A. and Hollis, N. S. (1996). Understanding, measuring and using brand equity. *Journal of Advertising Research* November/December, 9–21.

Efron, B. (2005). Bayesians, frequentisits and scientists. *Journal of the American Statistical Association* 100, 1–5.

Ehrenberg, A. S. C. (1972). *Repeat-buying: theory and applications*. New York: North-Holland.

Ehrenberg, A. S. C. and Goodhardt, G. (2000). New brands: near-instant loyalty. *Journal of Marketing Management* 16, 607–617.

Ehrenberg, A. S. C. and Goodhardt, G. (2002). Double Jeopardy revisited again. *Marketing Learnings* 7, The Southbank University, 1–2.

Ehrenberg, A. S. C., Goodhardt, G and Barwise, P. T. (1990). Double Jeopardy revisited. *Journal of Marketing* 54, 82–91.

Fader, P. S. and Schmittle, D. C. (1993). Excess behavioral loyalty for high-share brands: deviations from the Dirichlet model for repeat purchasing. *Journal of Marketing Research* 30, 478–493.

Fader, P. S. and Hardie, B. G. S. (1996). Modeling consumer choice among SKUs. *Journal of Marketing Research* 33 (November), 442–452.

Field, A., Miles, J. and Field, Z. (2012). *Discovering statistics using R*. London: Sage.

Fleury, M. (2013). *Yahoo to buy Tumblr for $1.1bn*. Available at http://www.bbc.co.uk/news/business-22591026.

Foxall, G. R. (1986a). Consumer theory: some contributions of a behavioral analysis of choice. *Management Bibliographic and Reviews* 12, 27–51.

Foxall, G. R. (1986b). The role of radical behaviorism in the explanation of consumer choice. *Advances in Consumer Research* 13, 187–191.

Foxall, G. R. (1987). Radical behaviorism and consumer research. *International Journal of Research in Marketing* 4, 111–129.

Foxall, G. R. (1990/2004). *Consumer psychology in behavioral perspective*. London and New York: Routledge. (Reprinted 2004 by Beard Books, Frederick, MD.)

Foxall, G. R. (2001). Foundations of consumer behavior analysis. *Marketing Theory* 1, 165–199.

Foxall, G. R. (2004). *Context and cognition: interpreting complex behavior*. Reno, NV: Context Press.

Foxall, G. R. (2005). *Understanding consumer choice*. New York: Palgrave Macmillan.

Foxall, G. R. (2007). Explaining consumer choice: coming to terms with intentionality. *Behavioural Processes* 75, 129–145.

Foxall, G. R. (2010). *Interpreting consumer choice: the behavioral perspective model*. New York: Routledge.

Foxall, G. R., Yan, J., Oliveira-Castro, J. M. and Wells, V. K. (2013). Brand-related and situational influences on demand elasticity. *Journal of Business Research*, 66, 73–81.

Foxall, G. R. and James, V. K. (2003). The behavioral ecology of brand choice: how and what do consumers maximize? *Psychology and Marketing* 20, 811–836.

Foxall, G. R., Oliveira-Castro, J. M. and Schrezenmaier, T. C. (2004). The behavioral economics of consumer brand choice: patterns of reinforcement and utility maximization. *Behavioural Processes* 66, 235–260.

Foxall, G. R., Oliveira-Castro, J. M., James, V. K., Yani-de-Soriano, M. and Sigurdsson, V. (2006). Consumer behavior analysis and social marketing: the case of environmental conservation. *Behavior and Social Issues* 15, 101–124.

Foxall, G. R. and Schrezenmaier, T. C. (2003). The behavioral economics of brand choice: establishing a methodology. *Journal of Economic Psychology* 25, 675–695.

Foxall, G. R., Yan, J., Oliveira-Castro, J. M. and Wells, V. K. (2013). Brand-related and situational influences on demand elasticity. *Journal of Business Research* 66, 73–81.

Goodhardt, G. J., Ehrenberg, A. S. C. and Chatfield, C. (1984). The Dirichlet: a comprehensive model of buying behavior. *Journal of the Royal Statistical Society* A 147, 621–655.

Hansen, M. H., Perry, L. T. and Reese, C. S. (2004). A Bayesian operationalization of the resource-based view. *Strategic Management Journal* 26, 1279–1295.

Jobber, D. (2004). *Principles and practice of marketing* (4th ed.). London: McGraw-Hill.

Jones, G. and Morgan, N. J. (1994). *Adding value brands and marketing in food and drink*. London: Routledge.

Koop, G. (2006). *Bayesian econometrics*. Chichester: Wiley.

Koop, G., Poirier, D. J. and Tobias, J. L. (2007). *Bayesian econometric methods*. Cambridge: Cambridge University Press.

Kotler, P., Armstrong, G., Saunders, J. and Wong, V. (1999). *Principles of marketing*. 2nd European edition. Upper Saddle River, NJ: Prentice Hall.

Labeaga, J. M., Lado, N. and Mercedes, M. (2007). Testing the double jeopardy loyalty effect using discrete choice models. *Documento De Trabajo* 21, 1–22.

Leamer, E. E. (1992). Bayesian elicitation diagnostics. *Econometrica* 60, 919–942.

Lichtenstein, S. (1978). Judged frequency of lethal events. *Journal of Experimental Psychology* 4, 557–578.

Lunn, D. J., Thomas, A., Best, N. and Spiegelhalter, D. (2000). WinBUGS – A Bayesian modeling framework: concepts, structure and extensibility. *Statistics and Computing* 10, 325–337.

McPhee, W. N. (1963). *Formal theories of mass behavior*. New York: The Free Press.

Merino, M. and Vargas, D. (2013). How consumers perceive globalization: a multilevel approach. *Journal of Business Research* 66, 431–438.

Miller, D. (1995). Consumption and commodities. *Annual Review of Anthropology* 24, 141–161.

O'Hagan, A. (1994). *Kendall's advanced theory of statistics, volume 2b: Bayesian inference.* Cambridge: Cambridge University Press.

O'Hagan, A. (1998). Eliciting expert beliefs in substantial practical applications. *Journal of the Royal Statistical Society Series D* 47, 21–35.

Oliveira-Castro, J. M., Foxall, G. R. and Schrezenmaier, T. C. (2005). Patterns of consumer response to retail price differentials. *Service Industries Journal* 25, 309–335.

Oliveira-Castro, J. M., Foxall, G. R. and Schrezenmaier, T. C. (2006). Consumer brand choice: individual and group analysis of demand elasticity. *Journal of the Experimental Analysis of Behavior* 85, 147–166.

Oliveira-Castro , J. M., Foxall, G. R., James, V. K. B., Pohl, R. H. B. F., Dias, M. B. and Chang, S. W. (2008). Consumer-based brand equity and brand performance. *The Service Industries Journal* 28, 445–461.

Poirier, D. J. (2006). The growth of Bayesian methods in statistics and economics since 1970. *Bayesian Analysis* 1, 969–980.

Romero, S., Foxall, G. R., Schrezenmaier, T. C., Oliveira-Castro, J. M. and James, V. (2006). Deviations from matching in consumer choice. *European Journal of Bevavior Analysis* 7, 15–39.

Sharp, B. and Riebe, E. (2005). *Does Triple Jeopardy exist for retail chains?* Adelaide: Marketing Science Centre University of South Australia, School of Marketing.

Sharp, B., Riebe, E. and Dawes, J. (2002). A marketing economy of scale – big brands lose less of their customer base than small brands. *Marketing Bulletin* 13, 1–8.

Sharp, B., Wright, M., Dawes, J., Driesener, C., Meyer-Waarden, L., Stocchi, L. and Stern, P. (2012). It's a Dirichlet world. Modeling individuals' loyalties reveals how brands compete, grow, and decline. *Journal of Advertising Research*, 203–213.

Singh, V. P., Hansen, K. T. and Gupta, S. (2005). Modeling preferences for common attributes in multi-category brand choice. *Journal of Marketing Research* 42, 195–209.

Spiegelhalter, D. J., Best, N. G., Carlin, B. P. and van der Linde, A. (2002). Bayesian measures of model complexity and fit. *Journal of the Royal Statistical Society B* 64, 583–639.

Taylor, S. A., Celuch, K. and Goodwin, S. (2004). The importance of brand equity to customer loyalty. *Journal of Product and Brand Management* 13, 217–227.

Viscusi, W. K. (1985). Are individuals Bayesian decision makers? *The American Economic Review, Papers and Proceedings of the Ninety-Seventh Annual Meeting of the American Economic Association* 75, 381–385.

Webster, F. E. Jr. (1994). *Market-driven management.* New York: Wiley.

Wood, L. (2000). Brands and brand equity: definition and management. *Management Decision* 38, 662–668.

Wright, M. and Sharp, B. (2001). The effect of a new brand entrant on a market. *Journal of Empirical Generalizations in Marketing Science* 6, 15–29.

11

Consumer purchase and brand performance

The basis of brand market structure

Rafael Barreiros Porto and Jorge M. Oliveira-Castro

Introduction

As an aggregated indicator of brand performance, market share lacks an explanation of why it occurs and how it is built in everyday sales. In a broad outlook, some brands have a high market share while others do not (Ehrenberg et al., 2004; Habel & Lockshin, 2013; Uncles et al., 1995). However, in a day-by-day analysis, the behavior of market share is far more dynamic.

Retail stores usually sell and stimulate many brands of the same product, but not all of them have major efforts all of the time. This can lead to different daily sales per brand. Consequently, even smaller brands can have a high market share depending on what occurs in everyday sales in the store. The daily market share predictors are still unknown, but have a lot in common with consumer purchases (Baumgartner, 2013), predictors of consumer purchase (Foxall, 2005; Gabaix et al., 2006; Rao, 1973), brand equity (Agarwal & Rao, 1996; Netemeyer et al., 2004; Washburn & Plank, 2002) and marketing strategies (Ataman et al., 2010) to stimulate brand sales. Testing in what circumstances this phenomenon can be estimated, taking a behavioral economic approach to explain the relations, is the main objective of this chapter.

Consumers usually buy brands that offer greater utilitarian and informational reinforcements (Foxall & James, 2003; Foxall et al., 2010). This can lead to different levels of consequences: (1) consumers may meliorate or maximize their own purchase performance, gaining benefits attached to "richer" brands and (2) brands, which attract more consumers, are the best market performers – most sold (Ehrenberg et al., 2004). These consequences allow for the supposition that there are some antecedents in common between the consumer level of analysis and the brand level of analysis.

Study 1 empirically tested the first level of analysis; that is, what kinds of manageable and unmanageable antecedents of purchase are predictors of consumer purchase, taking into consideration the utilitarian and informational consequences attached to brands. Study 2 tested the second level of analysis and proposed to determine if brand past attractiveness (aggregated data of consumers' learning history) and brand manageability (aggregated data of marketing activities) predict the daily market share of brands at classes of reinforcements magnitudes. These classes are dimensions of brand market structure, a term originated in economics to represent the concentration of markets on a firm or industrial level (Shaked & Sutton, 1990) and adjusted to a brand level of analysis in this chapter.

In general, Study 1 and 2 examined: (1) how a behavioral model can explain the consequences of brand purchases; (2) how these consequences may be used to describe (or analyze) brand market structure; and (3) what are the forecasters of daily market share for brands that offer a similar magnitude of reinforcements. By doing this, an empirical model able to bridge individual levels of analysis (consumer purchase) and brand-level analysis (brand performance) could explain the influence of brand attractiveness (Barnett, 1976; Bell et al., 1975) and marketing activities (Stewart, 2009; Hanssens & Dekimpe, 2012) in market structures (Shaked & Sutton, 1990; Urban et al., 1984).

The fundamental basis of market share: consumer brand purchases

Modeling market share has been a traditional area of research in marketing (Bell et al., 1975; Buzzell, 1964; Naert & Bultez, 1973; Weiss, 1968). This has been studied on an industry level (Sutton, 2007) and product/service level (Ehrenberg et al., 2004) and has implications about brand performance (Keller & Lehmann, 2006). As one of the indicators of marketing efforts (Cooper & Nakanishi, 1988; Fok et al., 2014), market share ignites the debate about whether it can be linearly normalized (Barnett, 1976), empirically tested (Chatfield, 1976), if it has a long-term effect (Golder, 2000), and if a disaggregate approach can be used to estimate segment response (DeSarbo et al., 2002). Specifically, segment responses depend on defining the correct competitive structure within which a brand competes (Urban et al., 1984). This means that brands may compete with those that are close competitors, but defining these competitors has been difficult. One possible way to answer this question is to have a comprehensive empirical model able to bridge the level of purchase antecedents/consequences and, at the same time, take these variables to a higher level (competitive structure of brands).

A major problem in aggregate-level models is that sample heterogeneity masks the real effect of marketing efforts (DeSarbo et al., 2002). For example, in one segment, price is a sign of quality, which increases its market share; in another segment, it is the lower price that increases market share. This appears to be partially disentangled when this market is broken down into sub-markets (e.g., attributes, use-situations or user characteristics) and different price strategies are investigated (e.g., promotional price, premium price and so on). However, this method does not consider how purchasers are benefiting from buying that particular brand (Foxall, 2005); that is to say, it does not take into consideration the real dimensions of brand market structure that are based on consumer brand response and its consequences programmed to be delivered by brands.

Identifying increases in market share for smaller brands is another subject of concern in the marketing literature and a somewhat difficult issue, since there are few brands of the same product that have a high market share (Ehrenberg et al., 2004). One way to work with this is by discovering the origins of market share (Ivanova, 2007), at a consumer level. Marketing activities (and other consumer variables) should greatly influence the purchase of some brands (though less so for others) in a store. This purchase can concomitantly lead to a rise in daily brand share. If this occurs, even small brands can have a high market share on a certain day, because their forecasters may have been stronger and attract more consumers while those of the leading brand have been weaker, keeping away potential buyers. Then, the first step should be to uncover consumer purchases.

Brand reinforcements as consequences of purchases

The learning literature suggests that purchases in a store can be explained from a behavioral perspective (Nord & Peter, 1980). The Behavioral Perspective Model (BPM) (Foxall, 2004, 2005)

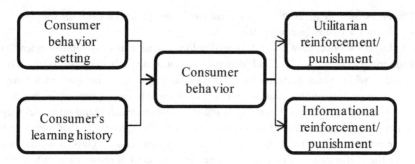

Figure 11.1 Behavioral Perspective Model (Foxall, 2004)

has been supported by empirical evidence (Foxall & Greenley, 2000; Oliveira-Castro et al., 2005; Oliveira-Castro et al., 2006; Oliveira-Castro et al., 2008) and is a good way of explaining the consequences of brand choices (Foxall et al., 2007; Cavalcanti et al., 2013). According to the BPM (Figure 11.1), consumer purchase has antecedents (consumers' learning histories and consumer behavior settings) and consequences (utilitarian and informational reinforcements/ punishments).

The consumer's learning history is the experience a consumer has before encountering the current behavior setting (Foxall, 2004). These experiences enable consumers to predict the likely consequences of a person's behavior in a certain situation. Consumer behavior setting is the social, temporal, regulatory and physical environments in which the consumer is exposed, signaling a choice situation (Foxall, 2004). In the case of brand choice, the consumer setting signals which brand has the greatest probability of delivering certain combinations of consequences at each moment of choice.

Brand utilitarian reinforcement refers to the direct and functional benefits that the purchase or consumption of a product (or service) delivers (Foxall et al., 2007). These are benefits mediated by a product or service. In brand choices, these reinforcers are contingencies programmed by the manufacturer, such as the main functions of a given brand attribute (e.g., cleaning white clothes). They have been measured by an enforced ranking system (Foxall et al., 2004), which takes into account added attributes in the formulation of a product (e.g., baked beans with or without sausage) or a more sophisticated formulation of a product (e.g., plain sweet cookies *vs.* chocolate-chip cookies) (see the method section in Study 1).

Brand informational reinforcements are symbolic benefits offered by products and services, such as social status, exclusivity, and self-esteem. These consequences are mediated by other people and function as feedback for the consumer, showing how well he or she is performing (Oliveira-Castro et al., 2008). It can be measured in multiple ways, but Oliveira-Castro et al. (2008) used a questionnaire, with brand ratings for every category of product. This contains a listing of all the brands found in the supermarkets investigated during the period of the research. For each brand listed, consumers were asked the following two questions: (1) is the brand well known? (0 – not known at all; 1 – known very little; 2 – quite well known; 3 – very well known); and (2) what is the quality magnitude of the brand? (1 – low quality; 2 – medium quality; 3 – high quality). To obtain a score for each brand, the authors calculated the mean score for knowledge and quality (MKQ) for each brand.

Brand utilitarian punishments are aversive functional consequences, such as spending time and money. Brand informational punishment occurs when third parties do not approve or are critical of what the consumer has purchased, which can function as negative feedback (Foxall,

2005; Oliveira-Castro et al., 2008). As these last two consequences are not the focus of the present research, they are only briefly explained.

All products or services vary in the degree of utilitarian/informational reinforcement/punishment from one product to another and from one situation to another (Foxall, 2004). According to the model, whenever a consumer buys a specific brand, it delivers a certain magnitude of utilitarian and informational reinforcements. Therefore, if several consumers buy a specific brand, this will deliver the same benefits to each one of them. Such brand purchases may bring together persons from very diverse backgrounds, who are all responsive to that particular brand's stimuli, irrespective of its characteristics or where it was purchased. Thus, it seems reasonable to compare the performance of brands that offer the same kind of reinforcement to consumers, which are associated with increases in their purchases.

Taking the antecedents and the consequences of brand purchases to a higher level

Measuring brand reinforcements makes it possible to rise from one level (consumer brand purchase) to another (brand performance). A brand may reinforce a behavior, delivering a social and a functional benefit, and, at the same time, all brands offering similar magnitude of consequences are competitors. Thus, a brand market structure can be empirically tested by examining, at the individual level, whether consumers purchase brands that have similar/different reinforcements and, at the brand level, whether these brands compete to generate more sales. This is operationalized by revealing if what influences brand purchase (Baumgartner, 2013) also influences brand performance – brand market share (Cooper & Nakanishi, 1988). If this is so, the antecedents of consumer purchases should be similar to the ones of brand market share.

Unfortunately, this relation is not yet well established. At the individual level, some studies serve as the building blocks. Generic purchase tendencies such as the product purchase frequency, time elapsed since last purchase occasion, and making a shopping list have been used as independent variables in some studies to predict subsequent purchase (Ehrenberg & Goodhardt, 1970; Ehrenberg et al., 2004; Kim & Rossi, 1994; Rao, 1973; Thomas & Garlant, 2004; Vilcassim & Jain, 1991). Other studies have investigated aspects of consumers' history with certain brands, such as the tendency to buy the same brand constantly (habit), and consumers' prior experiences with a brand (Bridges et al., 2006; Foxall, 2005; Neal et al., 2006). Moreover, intention and last brand purchased are also topics very well documented in the literature as predictors of subsequent brand purchase (Kahn & Louie, 1990; Morwitz et al., 2007; Warshaw, 1980).

All these predictors might be classified as being traditional because there are many studies in consumer behavior that have already tested their impact on consumer purchase. If these are good predictors of purchase, it means that consumer buying behavior may be related to the store situation (brand marketing activities prepared by the retailer), to generic tendencies of buying behavior (product purchase frequency, time elapsed since last purchase occasion, and doing a shopping list of products), and to their personal history with the brand (habit of buying the same brand, being a first-time buyer, having an intention to buy a specific brand and so on).

However, such antecedents have been studied without considering previous reinforcements of buying a brand (Foxall et al., 2010), which have usually been omitted in the equations of brand purchase. This has blocked the knowledge coming from behavioral consequences in empirical models and precluded highlighting possible causes derived from them. Study 1 of the present chapter overcomes these problems, showing the impact of manageable predictors (brand marketing activities) and unmanageable predictors (generic purchase tendencies, consumer brand history, and behavioral tendencies towards brands with different magnitude of reinforcements) on the purchase of brands which lead to different utilitarian and informational reinforcements.

If consumers benefit from purchasing brands, at the brand performance level of analysis, those that offer the same types of reinforcements are close substitutes. The same reinforcers have the common function of reinforcing the brand purchase of a class to which the brand pertains (Foxall et al., 2010). Cuvo (2000) argues that the concept of "consequence class" provides a means to integrate data and theory from behavioral economics, discussing functional similarities and dissimilarities among products. Products are substitutes if they share common consequences to consumers. Two of the main dimensions that affect the number of substitutes a good has and its demand elasticity are the degree of specificity of the definition of goods, such as beverages (functionally equivalent members) or juices (subclass of functionally equivalent members), and the degree to which a good is a necessity (primary reinforcer) or a luxury (secondary reinforcer).

The first dimension is concerned with a general/restricted set of properties and the transfer functions among the members of a class (Cuvo, 2000). All beverages could quench thirst (general consequence property) and only specific types of beverage (restricted consequences properties) are the best to hydrate (e.g., plain drinkable water). By contrast, the transfer of functions occurs when the consequences spread to other members of the same class that are not recipients of the purchase operations. Thus, perfect substitutes, such as two brands of drinkable water, have many transfers of functions while imperfect substitutes, such as one brand of sparkling water and another of orange juice, have fewer. The specificity of a good generally is concerned with the utilitarian reinforcements, but can plausibly be applied to informational reinforcements. Nevertheless, it is more difficult to transfer socially mediated consequences for they deal with feedback performance to the consumer, which is usually less controllable by managers and manufacturers.

The second dimension regards the effectiveness of the relations between purchase/reinforcement and the dependency of the reinforcers (Cuvo, 2000). When this effectiveness is independent of another reinforcer, such as drinking water, which is a reinforcer to everyone as it meets biological needs, it is a primary reinforcer. When the effectiveness depends on another reinforcer, besides the primary reinforcer, such as drinking bottled water, which has branding attributes (Foxall, 2004; Alhadeff, 1982), it is a secondary reinforcer. Therefore, the specificity of the goods and their degree of primary or secondary reinforcers could disentangle the problems of classifying the brands and pave the way to uncover the brand market structure.

Beneath the same consequence class, the predictors affect brands' shares. These could be from two types, one manageable (stimulus control – Vella & Foxall, 2011) and the other unmanageable (consumer's learning history – Foxall, 2004). Since market share indicators deal with aggregate data of quantity purchased (Nair et al., 2005), the aggregated purchases predictors should also be derived from the brand-level performance to explain why some brands, occasionally, achieve more market share than others on a daily basis. The aggregation from consumer level means that these individual variables must be transformed to represent brand level. Usually, they are aggregated by averaging or summing up the original variable (Bolger et al., 2003). Thus, the aggregation reduces individual differences, but disentangles problems of a confounding level of analysis (Lincoln & Zeitz, 1980).

As this technique mischaracterizes the original variables, they should be named differently. For instance, what managers do about brands (stimulus control) could be named brand manageability, since brands are managed in ways that could be effective or not in generating purchases (Foxall, 1999). What consumers have experienced or have tendencies to do in relation to brands could be named brand past attractiveness, considering that brands that have histories with consumers have attracted them someday and somehow (Foxall, 1999).

Taking a standpoint of economic business (Villas-Boas, 2007), brands belong to manufacturers and are retailed to consumers. In a product category, usually, one is a pioneer in the market (Lieberman & Montgomery, 2012), some are first followers and others are later followers (Shankar & Carpenter, 2012). Therefore, the success of what managers do to a brand depends on investments and activities that modify consumer purchases over time (Stewart, 2009). For example, some brands are not able to have "everyday lowest price" or "everyday advertising" or even "everyday highest exposure" because they require, simultaneously, high resource investment and profitability. However, other brands have these abilities for long periods. So, brand manageability is expanded by some organizational conditions (Ambrosini & Bowman, 2009; Zollo & Winter, 2002) which encourage managers to implement dynamic marketing activities (Hanssens & Dekimpe, 2012) by learning mechanisms. A challenge facing firms is how to configure their offerings to deliver superior brand performance output (Cui et al., 2014). Revealing how brand manageability is a driver of brand performance may help identify the basis of brand market structure.

Brand past attractiveness may stem from inclination, tendency, inducement or seduction that a brand has already achieved through time. A brand may appear very attractive if there are many consumers frequently buying it. The attraction of many consumers (Chatterjee et al., 2011; Spiteri & Johnson, 2011) may turn out to be a strong social sign that some people are getting something (informational reinforcement – Foxall, 2004) in buying/having the products. It could generate, under some circumstances, general behaviors like "I want it too" at the individual level of analysis or "herd behavior" at the aggregate level of analysis (Hanson & Putler, 1996; Rook, 2006). However, because it has the propensity to generate "crowds", this could also be aversive in some sense (Foxall, 2004), inhibiting or restraining future attractiveness. Study 2 focuses on brand-level analysis and shows how brand manageability and brand past attractiveness influence market share, using a behavioral economic approach by grouping brands that offer a similar magnitude of reinforcements, which is a way of describing market structure (Urban et al., 1984).

Overall, the current state of the research suggests that links can be made across measures belonging to different levels of analysis, examining consumer purchase and brand performance simultaneously by testing possible forecasters of purchase and daily market shares. To do this, an in-store experiment was conducted, in which all these variables were measured, with the perspective of searching for antecedent-behavior-consequence relations.

Study 1: Effect of manageable and unmanageable antecedents on consumer purchase that lead to a different magnitude of brand reinforcements

Study 1 (Figure 11.2) aims to investigate the impact of manageable (consumer behavior setting) and unmanageable (consumer's learning history) antecedents on purchases that lead to different magnitude of brand reinforcements. Foxall (2005) suggests that the consumer's learning history (past exposure to contingencies of reinforcements) could mean any variable that shows the consumer's behavioral tendencies in subsequent situations. If they are good predictors of purchase, it means that consumers are responsive to long and/or recent learning histories provided by the brand and category. If, alternatively, manageable activities are good predictors, this means that the management of the consumer setting is central to generate brand purchases.

Since consumers could purchase any brand within a given product category, these were classified according to the magnitude of their programmed reinforcements. Thus, consumers that buy brands with a different magnitude of reinforcements have different behavioral patterns.

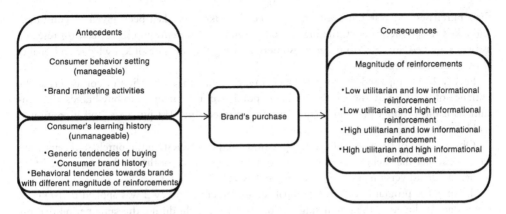

Figure 11.2 Empirical model of antecedents and consequences of brand purchase

Foxall (2010) shows these patterns are operant classes of consumer behavior such as: accomplishment (high utilitarian and high informational reinforcements), hedonism (high utilitarian and low informational reinforcements), accumulation (low utilitarian and high informational reinforcements) and maintenance (low utilitarian and low informational reinforcements). Following the same reasoning, consumers who buy at the same magnitude of reinforcement have a similar pattern. This study tries to test these possibilities when consumers purchase brands.

As the samples of this research are made up of cosmetics and treats, those with higher levels of programmed reinforcement are better suited to delivering a variety of aesthetic pleasure, delicious taste, body enhancement and sensations of wellbeing (utilitarian reinforcements). They also allow the sharing of the purchases with friends and family, with a strong possibility of receiving compliments for the brand acquired (informational reinforcements).

Method

This study was designed experimentally and used a mixed method of retail auditing, survey and purchase observation over a nine-week period in a large discount store in Brazil. This store was chosen because of its very high number of consumers and because it changes the brand's marketing activities almost daily.

Retail auditing allowed us to map the marketing activities for each brand as elaborated by the retailer, which included the day-to-day prices for all brands within a range of four products (hair dyes, body moisturizers, cereal bars, and boxes of chocolate); the presence (or absence) of brand advertising in a fortnightly promotional leaflet; shelf space for each brand and the location of each shelf; the use of promotional gifts associated with each brand and each brand's attributes – used to classify the programmed utilitarian reinforcements, according to the method used by Foxall et al. (2004). Brands were classified into two programmed utilitarian reinforcement magnitudes: (1) low utilitarian benefit magnitude, which are basic versions of the products, without differentials or with few attributes; and (2) high utilitarian benefit magnitude, which are more sophisticated versions of the products – those with differentials or with several attributes.

The following procedure was used to collect consumer data: (1) research assistants approached the consumers at the entrance of the store; (2) they applied Survey 1 appraising consumer learning history; (3) consumers were given a token code after completing the questionnaire so that the researchers could later observe their purchases; (4) the consumers entered the store and made their purchases; (5) research assistants collected the token that had been given to consumers and asked to see the product, the brand, and the number of items purchased; and (6) research assistants applied Survey 2 to other consumers assessing the measure of knowledge and quality (MKQ) of each brand purchased.

Survey 1 encompassed the four products investigated and was applied to consumers at the entrance of the store. It assessed the last brand purchased, the intention to buy brands, the consumer's habit, product purchase frequency, time elapsed since last purchase, and if consumers had brought a shopping list.

Observations of the purchases were operationalized by requesting the purchase receipt from each consumer that held a token code. Researchers took note of the product type, the brand name, the brand version and the quantity purchased.

To map the programmed informational reinforcements, Survey 2 was applied to 100 consumers not included in the purchasing section of the research, during the same period that the consumer data occurred. This was based on a four-point scale appraisal of the magnitude of brand familiarity as well as a further three-point scale used to appraise the perceived magnitude of brand quality, a procedure adapted from Oliveira-Castro et al. (2008). A statistical test was conducted to verify the brand ratings at two informational magnitudes: (1) low informational benefit magnitude, with lesser-known brands and those perceived as being of low quality, and (2) a high informational benefit magnitude, with well-known brands and those perceived as being of high quality. An analysis of variance (brands as the independent variable and MKQ as the dependent variable) showed a significant effect ($p < .01$), demonstrating that the two brand groups were perceived to be different from one another in each product category.

To avoid possible spurious results, another simultaneous experiment was conducted to investigate whether the application of the questionnaire (Survey 1) could have influenced the purchase of brands at different reinforcement magnitudes. The tests were two vs. four factorials, with 102 in the experimental and 102 in the control group. The contingency coefficient based on chi square showed that there was no effect ($CC = .16$; $p > .05$). Thus, the relation between the variables is probably due to chance. That is, full implementation of the questionnaire did not influence the consumer to change his or her brand choice.

The sampling of 364 consumers made it possible to achieve a total power of 98.9% (with an error probability equal to 5%) using the logistic regression test. In addition, we alternated the order of products researched in Survey 1, representing a random sampling. Thus, the internal and external validity of the experiment could be attained with reasonable certainty.

The authors used a hierarchical multinomial logit regression in Study 1, with the dependent variable representing purchases leading to four programmed reinforcement categories: low informational and low utilitarian consequence, high informational and low utilitarian consequence, low informational and high utilitarian consequence and high informational and high utilitarian consequence. All metrics of the variables, their means and standard deviation or percentages are shown in Table 11.1. Variables one to five represent the brand marketing activities, variables six to eight represent the generic tendencies of buying, variables nine to ten represent the consumer brand history, variables eleven to fourteen represent the behavioral tendencies towards brands with different magnitudes of reinforcement, and variables fifteen to sixteen represent the dependent variables.

As a whole, the brands purchased were priced at a slightly lower level, had a premium price, occupied more shelf space, had slight advertising exposure and had an associated gift offer. Most purchasers stated that they usually buy the product only once a month, go into the store every four weeks, rarely bring a shopping list, are usually in the habit of buying a brand and they had already tried the purchased brand. The consumer usually intends to buy brands that offer high

Table 11.1 Descriptive data of brand purchase with different brand reinforcements and its antecedents

N.	Variables	Metric	Mean	S.D.	%
1	Promotional price	Daily price of the brand bought relative to its average price during all days	0.97	0.30	
2	Premium price	Average price of the brand bought relative to the average price of the product during all days	1.09	0.45	
3	Shelf space	Daily shelf space of the brand bought relative to its average shelf space during all days	1.64	1.64	
4	Advertising	Presence – or absence – of advertising in fortnightly promotional leaflets for brand purchased			18.2
5	Promotional gift	Presence – or absence – of promotional gifts associated with the brand purchased			21.7
6	Product purchase frequency	How many times the consumer bought the product per month	1.06	1.64	
7	Time elapsed since last purchase	Time elapsed in weeks since last purchase occasion in the store	4.04	6.05	
8	Shopping list	Whether a consumer brings a shopping list to the store			2.9
9	Consumer's habit	If the consumer is in the habit – or otherwise – of buying the same brand before entering the store			81.5
10	First-time purchaser	First-time (versus experienced) brand purchaser			10.2
11	Intention to buy brands with high infor. reinfor.	Intention to buy the brand which offers different magnitude (high vs. low) of informational reinforcements			62.9
12	Intention to buy brands with high utilit. reinfor.	Intention to buy the brand which offers different magnitude (high vs. low) of utilitarian reinforcements			57.6
13	Last brand purchased with high infor. reinfor.	Last brand purchased which offers a different magnitude (high vs. low) of informational reinforcements			61.5
14	Last brand purchased with high utilit. reinfor.	Last brand purchased which offers a different magnitude (high vs. low) of utilitarian reinforcements			54.9
15	Purchase that leads to high infor. reinfor.	Purchasing the brand which offers different magnitude (high vs. low) of informational reinforcements			59.4
16	Purchase that leads to high utilit. reinfor.	Purchasing the brand which offers different magnitude (high vs. low) of utilitarian reinforcements			57.3

informational and utilitarian reinforcements and had previously bought brands that also offered high informational and utilitarian reinforcements. In this research, he or she usually bought brands that led to high informational and utilitarian reinforcements.

A Kruskal-Wallis test (Figure 11.3) shows that there were differences in the amount purchased among the combinations of utilitarian and informational reinforcements ($\chi^2 = 19.5$; $p \leq 0.01$). More purchases led to low utilitarian and high informational reinforcers and to high utilitarian and high informational reinforcers than to the other consequences.

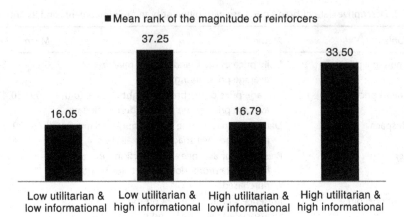

Figure 11.3 Purchases that lead to different magnitude of consequences

Results

The analysis (Table 11.2) shows that the statistic model had a good fit (-2 log likelihood = 225.31; $p < .01$) and a high R^2 Nagelkerke of 89.9%.

Compared to purchases that led to low informational and low utilitarian reinforcements, brand marketing activities and behavioral tendencies towards brands with different magnitudes of reinforcements were good predictors of purchases that led to higher magnitudes of informational reinforcements or utilitarian reinforcements or both. Applying a partial formula of the logistic probability [Probability of purchase = $1/1 + e^{-(\Sigma \beta X)}$], brand marketing activities comprising advertisement, extra gift, average shelf space, average promotional price, and an

Table 11.2 Predictors of purchases that lead to different magnitudes of reinforcements

Magnitude of consequences	Type of antecedents	Predictors	Estimates	Std. Error
High Info. and Low Util.[a]	Brand marketing activities	Intercept	-2.52	1.81
		Promotional price	.21	1.71
		Premium price	-1.37	1.52
		Advertising	2.56**	1.64
		Promotional gift	1.03	1.39
		Shelf space	-.29***	.16
	Generic tendencies of buying	Shopping list	18.35***	2.76
		Product purchase frequency	.14	.20
		Time elapsed since last purchase	.15	.13
	Consumer brand history	First-time purchaser	-1.08*	1.68
		Consumer's habit	.76	.79
	Behavioral tendencies towards brands with different magnitudes of reinfor.	Intention to buy brands with high info. reinfor.	3.79***	.84
		Intention to buy brands with high util. reinfor.	-2.28*	1.36
		Last brand purchased with high info. reinfor.	1.07	.73
		Last brand purchased with high util. reinfor.	-1.07	1.16

		Intercept	−34.12	2.22
	Brand marketing	Promotional price	−1.88	1.43
	activities	Premium price	.66	1.09
		Advertising	1.64***	1.37
		Promotional gift	.43*	1.59
		Shelf space	−.58***	.31
Low Info. and	Generic tendencies of	Shopping list	16.6***	1.38
High Util.ᵃ	buying	Product purchase frequency	−.13	.30
		Time elapsed since last purchase	.27	.24
	Consumer brand	First-time purchaser	−2.75**	1.30
	history	Consumer's habit	1.15**	.97
	Behavioral tendencies	Intention to buy brands with high info.	.75	1.20
	towards brands	reinfor.		
	with different	Intention to buy brands with high util. reinfor.	3.44***	1.36
	magnitudes of	Last brand purchased with high info. reinfor.	−3.41***	1.25
	reinf.	Last brand purchased with high util. reinfor.	2.93***	1.17
High Info. and		Intercept	−1.93	1.56
High Util.ᵃ	Brand marketing	Promotional price	−4.01***	1.34
	activities	Premium price	2.36***	.79
		Advertising	2.41**	1.31
		Promotional gift	1.00***	1.52
		Shelf space	−.34	.23
	Generic tendencies of	Shopping list	.43	1.65
	buying	Product purchase frequency	.10	.25
		Time elapsed since last purchase	.36	.25
	Consumer brand	First-time purchaser	−1.77	1.10
	history	Consumer's habit	1.33	.86
	Behavioral tendencies	Intention to buy brands with high info.	2.43***	.99
	towards brands	reinfor.		
	with different	Intention to buy brands with high util. reinfor.	4.70***	1.26
	magnitudes of	Last brand purchased with high info. reinfor.	−.36	.98
	reinfor.	Last brand purchased with high util. reinfor.	1.43	1.11
R² Nagelkerke			89.9%	
Total % corrected predicted			85.0%	
−2 Log likelihood %			225.3**	

ᵃ The reference category is: Low informational and utilitarian magnitude level (Low Info and Low Util)

*p < .1, **p < .05, ***p < .01

average premium price raised the probability to nearly 90.60% of buying brands with a high magnitude of informational reinforcements associated with a low magnitude of utilitarian reinforcement.

Nevertheless, if a consumer arrived at the store with the intention of buying brands with high informational reinforcements and low utilitarian reinforcements, it raised the probability to nearly 95.00% of their buying brands with these programmed benefits. If he or she arrived intending to buy brands that led to high utilitarian reinforcements and had previously bought brands with high utilitarian and informational reinforcements, it raised the chances of buying brands of high utilitarian reinforcements and low informational reinforcements to about 99.74%. If he or she arrived intending to buy brands which led to high utilitarian and informational reinforcements, it raised the chances of buying brands with these consequences to 99.99%.

Generic tendencies of buying and consumer brand history were also good predictors of purchasing brands but only the ones that led to either high informational reinforcements or high utilitarian reinforcements – not for both. If a consumer brought a shopping list to the store, it raised the likelihood of buying brands that led to high informational reinforcements or high utilitarian reinforcements to 99.99%. Nevertheless, if a consumer purchased the brand for the very first time, the probability of buying brands which led to high informational and low utilitarian reinforcements was 25.35%. Otherwise, if he or she had experience with the brand and was in the habit of buying it, it raised the chance of buying brands that led to high utilitarian and low informational reinforcements to 75.98%.

Discussion

Overall, the results of Study 1 show that consumers' learning history and consumer behavior setting (Foxall, 2004) can greatly alter the probability of purchasing a brand that leads to a different magnitude of programmed reinforcements. That is, by planning events that may stimulate purchases of consumers through marketing activities and considering their experiences, a manager would be able to predict the likelihood of choosing brands in real retail situations.

The results show in general that there are antecedents that stimulate the purchasing of brands associated with higher reinforcement levels, such as advertising, promotional gifts, bringing a shopping list to the store, promotional price, premium price, consumers' habit, experience with brands in the category, intention to buy a brand or having previously bought a brand. But all of these depend upon the contingencies related to the specific choice, especially those concerning brand reinforcement levels.

Thus, consumers face complex chains of programmed reinforcements and new stimuli contexts, but usually obtain higher magnitudes of brand reinforcements (the more rewarding ones – Foxall et al., 2010). This is no coincidence. Retail managers usually create a favorable scenario for some brands but not for others (some brands may even acquire some aversive functions). Besides, the experiences of consumers are not similar among brands (Bridges et al., 2006; Neal et al., 2006). They usually have positive experiences with the ones that offer higher reinforcements, which are the top-selling brands and are widespread (Ehrenberg et al., 2004). In this research, brands with higher reinforcements were better able to deliver a variety of aesthetic pleasures, delicious tastes, body enhancement and sensations of wellbeing, in addition to the possibility of social compliments derived from brand choice. Therefore, there is a context of supply and demand (Vella & Foxall, 2011) favorable for some brands (with higher reinforcements) and unfavorable for others (with lower reinforcements).

The allocation of different magnitudes of reinforcers is a consequence of brand managerial tactics of each firm, who have different resources to build brands and use different brand equity strategies (Agarwal & Rao, 1996; Netemeyer et al., 2004; Washburn & Plank, 2002). Some brands are managed in a business environment that gives all the support needed to modify or add differentials or even enhance the favorable perceptions of consumers by introducing better materials and images and meeting new demands. Others are managed in small businesses and are not so well supported (Berthon et al., 2008). So, reinforcers' programs by brands are not and could not be equal among brands in real situations. This suggests that some brands are better built than others due to managers' efforts from each firm, directly, by offering the higher benefits and, indirectly, through consumer experiences.

This condition explains the purchase patterns of consumers (Cavalcanti et al., 2013) showing the sources of those patterns. The stability of the purchase patterns seems to be due both to individual consumers' experiences and to marketing activities, varying according to the combination of the magnitude of reinforcements. For instance, the results indicated that bringing a shopping list to the store is the most powerful predictor of purchasing a brand with a higher utilitarian benefit or a brand with a higher informational benefit. Similarly, the behavioral tendencies towards brands with different magnitudes of reinforcements are predictors of purchasing a brand whether it leads to higher utilitarian benefit, higher informational benefit or both.

Analysis of brand marketing activities shows that they are also predictors that depend upon the combination of reinforcement levels, especially when the brand that leads to higher informational and utilitarian reinforcements is purchased. It seems that there is an interacting web of influence, which complements findings from Cavalcanti et al. (2013): consumers have some purchase tendencies due to their previous consumptions, on the basis of which they have learned what and how to buy, a finding from that previous research. However, when they arrive at the store, and encounter brand marketing stimuli, these reinforce their tendencies towards certain brands (which are usually the ones that they have already learned how to buy) and at the same time signal the most advantageous one at the purchase occasion. For example, a consumer that has tendencies to buy a specific brand with higher reinforcement arrives at the store, which has planned marketing activities for that particular brand. Together, the experience and marketing activities of that brand strengthen its purchase probability. Thus, there is a context favoring the purchase of some brands and discouraging the purchase of others.

Study 1 highlighted that models of brand purchase (Foxall, 2005) should include brand marketing activities, generic buying tendencies, consumers' brand history and the behavioral tendencies towards brands with different magnitudes of reinforcements. The predictive power gains strength by adding some of the variables in each of these antecedents and allows for checking of consumer performance among brand choice on each purchase occasion.

Study 2: Substitutability in the brand market structure

The relation between purchase and market share is obvious, for the latter is the aggregated data (per brand) of the first (Cooper & Nakanishi, 1988). As the predictors of buying behavior vary from time to time and sometimes they are modified inconsistently, purchases are dynamic by nature. If these predictors are also antecedents of daily market share, they bring an instability to it. This means that the supply of, and the demand for, brands will vary a great deal, signaling that the drivers of brand performance (Ehrenberg et al., 2004) may have changed.

However, all these changes take place in a market context. Sometimes they encourage the fluctuation of market share between close substitute brands in a category and sometimes they discourage these fluctuations (Shaked & Sutton, 1990; Urban et al., 1984). In a dynamic perspective, even if brands do not modify their consequences to consumers, their shares vary considerably among them. For example, it is very difficult to detect how low-equity brands (or those with basic attributes) can take shares from high-equity brands (or those with sophisticated attributes) and vice-versa. Nevertheless, it is very common to see a high-equity brand (or ones that have sophisticated attributes) taking shares from an equally high-equity brand (or the sophisticated ones). This situation calls for an analysis of the brand market structure, which has not yet been explained.

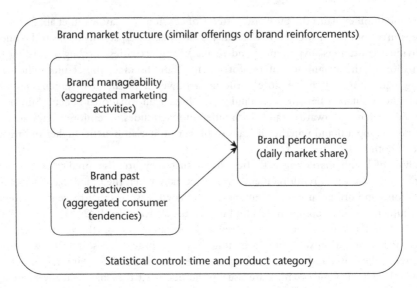

Figure 11.4 Empirical model of variables in brand market structure

One possible way to clarify the role of the market context in brand substitutability is by testing the fluctuations in market share among brands when they offer the same magnitude of reinforcements. Study 2 sheds light on this phenomenon, by analyzing which predictors of purchase can be used to forecast daily market share for groups of brands that offer similar levels of reinforcement.

In Figure 11.4, an empirical model suggests the relations among the variables involved. All the antecedents of Study 1 were aggregated by brand and day, but here we propose that the brands have abilities and have attracted consumers. The brand performance metric is operationalized through the daily market share and all the variables are under the same brand market structure, after controlling for the effects of time and product categories.

Method

The daily market share of the four products analyzed in Study 1 were calculated by aggregating the amount purchased per brand relative to the total amount purchased in the category in each day. To compare increases or decreases in daily market share of a given brand, market share was divided by the average daily product share. Therefore, if it equals one, it means that the market share of a particular brand is at the average of its category in that day. A value smaller than one indicates that the market share was below the average of its category in that particular day. This was the dependent variable for Study 2.

The descriptive data of daily market share are shown in Table 11.3. Some brands have a high average daily market share, even though their overall market share is low. Some brands also have a high standard deviation, while others do not. This shows that daily market share varies depending on some daily factors.

For 26 days of brand sales, data and all the antecedents contained in Study 1 were recorded. These were aggregated in Study 2. Daily records of all the quantitative variables contained in Study 1 were kept and all the qualitative variables were counted by brand and by day. Table 11.4 shows the metric of each one and the descriptive statistics. All together, these variables represent the attractiveness and the manageability of a brand to induce more sales.

Table 11.3 Descriptive data of market share and reinforcements classifications

Brand's name (1)	Overall market share %	Average of daily market share	Std. deviation of daily market share	Informational reinforcer	Utilitarian reinforcer
Body moisturizer					
Paixão	3.5	.30	.34	Low	High
Elle Ella	1.0	.23	.14	Low	High
Phytoderm	0.8	.26	.01	Low	High
Hidramais	10.1	.37	.12	Low	Low
Nutritive	8.8	.30	.06	Low	High
Corpo a Corpo	1.5	.15	.07	Low	High
Leite de Aveia	0.9	.09	.03	Low	Low
Vasenol	3.0	.16	.05	Low	High
Monange	8.1	.19	.13	Low	High
Nivea	26.7	.34	.18	High	High
Dove	2.5	.27	.17	High	High
Johnson & Johnson	33.3	.30	.14	High	High
Hair dye					
Aney	0.2	.20	.01	Low	Low
Beauty Color	1.9	.20	.08	Low	High
Preference	.9	.50	.01	Low	High
Wellaton	1.5	.13	.01	Low	High
Surya	1.9	.33	.01	Low	Low
Natucor	0.7	.12	.05	Low	Low
Nutrisse	2.6	.61	.35	Low	High
SoftColor	4.0	.25	.17	Low	High
Cor e Ton	9.6	.36	.32	Low	High
L'Óreal Casting	2.5	.42	.35	Low	High
Maxton	18.3	.42	.28	Low	High
Biocolor	7.9	.25	.20	High	High
Koleston	23.6	.31	.24	High	High
L'Óreal Imedia	24.4	.36	.18	High	High
Box of chocolates					
Garoto Sortidos	33.0	.37	.18	High	Low
Garoto Mix	9.7	.18	.08	Low	Low
MonteVergine	0.5	.05	.01	Low	High
Nestlé Especialidades	30.0	.32	.20	High	Low
Lacta Grandes Sucessos	24.3	.19	.09	High	Low
Ferrero Rocher	2.7	.08	.06	High	High
Cereal bars					
Corpo e Sabor	13.9	.26	.18	Low	Low
Forma e Sabor	3.4	.23	.14	Low	Low
Troop	1.3	.15	.08	Low	Low
Sollys	0.6	.17	.11	Low	Low
Ritter	15.7	.21	.12	Low	High
Supino	5.1	.24	.19	Low	Low
Hershey's	1.5	.14	.13	Low	High
Quaker	1.0	.40	.09	Low	Low
Neston	1.8	.22	.25	High	Low
Nutry	24.5	.26	.22	High	High
Trio	31.2	.34	.20	High	High

Table 11.4 Metric, mean and standard deviation of the independent variables in Study 2

Types of antecedents	Index	Metric	Mean	Std. deviation
Brand manageability	Promotional price	Price of each offered brand in day X divided by its average price during all days	1.00	0.23
	Shelf space	Shelf space in cm of each offered brand in day X divided by its average shelf space during all days	1.00	0.94
	Premium price	Average of the price of the brand offered divided by the average of the price of the product	1.00	0.48
	Proportional promotional gift	Sum of the quantity of gifts by brand on each day divided by the total volume of gift in product on each day	0.06	0.13
	Proportional promotional advertising	Sum of the quantity of advertisement on the fortnightly leaflet by brand divided by the total volume of advertisement in product at the same period	0.07	0.17
Brand past attractiveness	Rate of time since last purchase	Average rate of time elapsed since last purchase for each brand	3.30	3.59
	Rate of product purchase	Average monthly rate of product frequency purchase for each brand	1.09	1.45
	Rate of appearance on shopping lists	Average daily rate of bringing a shopping list to the store for each brand	0.01	0.04
	Relative number of habitual buyers	Daily quantity of consumers who buy the same brand divided by the daily average of consumers of the product	1.00	0.90
	Relative number of first-time buyers	Daily sum of consumers who buy the brand for the very first time divided by the daily average of consumers of the product	1.00	2.88
	Relative number of previous time brand purchasers	Daily sum of consumers who bought one particular brand with a reinforcement on the last occasion divided by the daily average of consumers of the product	1.00	0.63
	Relative number of planned brand purchasers	Daily sum of consumers who intend to buy one particular brand with a reinforcement at the store entrance divided by the daily average of consumers of the product	1.00	0.66

Based on the combination of the magnitude of utilitarian and informational reinforcers in Study 1 (differentiation, familiarity and quality perception), brand market structure was built. Each combination of brands' reinforcements (Low Informational and Low Utilitarian group – LILU, Low Informational and High Utilitarian group – LIHU, High Informational and Low Utilitarian group – HILU and High Informational and High Utilitarian group – HIHU) represents this structure.

For instance, in LILU, brands have no differentiation and are almost unbranded, shown by the low level of consumers' perception towards them. These brands act like commodities with homogeneous brand features. They have a name and the basic characteristics to be commercialized (Gordon et al., 1999). Brands belonging to small businesses or local brands usually start in this dimension of the market structure and achieve the basic requirements to perform in the category (Berthon et al., 2008).

In LIHU, brands have technical differentiations, but they are not perceived as outstanding or very famous by consumers. This competitive dimension embraces "to the masses" image brands (Danziger, 2005), the ones with a generic image (Park et al., 1986) or a niche image brand (Parrish et al., 2006). These images are visual or verbal signs (Zaichkowsky, 2010) of utilitarian or informational reinforcements obtained if the brand is bought. Their manufacturers promote them loosely or promote them to a specific small segment, but do not concentrate on promoting them widely. Thereby, they lack a strong brand leader or premium image appeal.

In HILU, brands are famous and sometimes global (Johansson, 2011; Sullivan, 1992), but they lack an innovation appeal in the category. This is a market structure dimension for prestigious brands; they are usually followers in technology of a pioneering brand (Lieberman & Montgomery, 2012) in a category but sometimes sale leaders (Johansson, 2011). They belong to big enterprises that use brand extension strategies (Sullivan, 1992) or are imitative of successful strategies. The brands in this dimension rely strongly on their names. Therefore, managers build a brand with a leader image and disseminate it anywhere possible including around the pioneering brand.

Finally, in HIHU, brands are outstanding and/or innovative (Ambler, 1997). Consumers recognize the premium image of these brands and production efforts are constantly deployed (Beverland et al., 2010). This is a market structure for large, specialized and rich brands; large because they are in every possible commercial place for the category in any time, specialized because they deploy extra attributes pushing the limits of functionality, and rich because although they demand a high enterprise structure to justify the high costs of the innovations, they usually exceed the boundary of profitability. Some of them are pioneering in the category and use images of exclusivity, stylishness or refinement.

Based on the dimensions of the brand market structure, a daily panel equation was built. The dependent variable, relative daily market share and the independent variables, brand past attractiveness and brand manageability, are represented in Equation 1. Temporal and product categories dummies, as control variables, were added to show the intercept for each day and product:

$$Y_{igd} = \beta_1 X_{1igd} + \beta_2 X_{2igd} + \beta_d D_{dummy} + \beta_d P_{dummy} + \text{\euro}_{igd}, \tag{1}$$

where Y_{gd} refers to relative daily market share for brand i in group g at day d, X_{1igd} represents each variable related to brand past attractiveness for brand i in group g at day d, X_{2igd} refers to each variable related to brand manageability for brand i in group g at day d, D_{dummy} stands for the day of the data registry, taking the last day of registry as the reference, P_{dummy} represents the product data registry, taking another product as the reference, $\beta_{1,2,d}$ are regression coefficients, and $\text{\euro}_{igd}$ is the error terms for brand i in group g at day d.

Generalized Estimating Equations proved to be suitable for this analysis. The multicollinearity test presented no problem ($VIF < 2$) and the data showed no heteroscedasticity (White test $p > 0.05$), but the dependent variable had a positive asymmetry and the Durbin-Watson showed a serial autocorrelation. Therefore, the daily market share was transformed by a gamma log link and an interchangeable work correlation matrix proved to be a reasonable way to overcome the serial autocorrelation.

Results

The statistic model fitted the data reasonably well. The corrected quasi-likelihood under independence model criterion – QICC – for the whole model was equal to 55.87 against QICC = 112.36 for the null model. In other words, the full model with the predictors decreased 61% of the information lost and simultaneously reduced the complexity of the model. The overall linear prediction was high (R^2 = 83.4%). Table 11.5 shows the significant forecasters of the daily market share in brand market structure. The controlled variables (time in days and categories) are not shown as they are not part of the main result.

For the LILU group, all types of aggregated purchase antecedents (brand marketing activities, generic tendencies of buying, consumer brand history, and the behavioral tendencies towards brands with different magnitude of reinforcements), but not all variables, were significantly related to daily market share. Past attractiveness of these brands raised brand performance in this market structure, especially by increasing the rate of appearance on shopping lists. Increases in

Table 11.5 Predictors of daily market share under the brand market structure

Brand market structure	Daily predictors	Estimates	Std. error
LILU group	Promotional price	−0.80*	0.09
	Proportional promotional advertising	−1.77*	0.06
	Relative number of planned brand purchasers	0.25*	0.09
	Relative number of previous time brand purchasers	0.32*	0.05
	Rate of appearance on shopping lists	17.03*	4.62
	Relative number of habitual buyers	0.31*	0.10
HILU group	Shelf space	0.93*	0.03
	Premium price	3.45*	0.04
	Promotional price	−0.61*	0.13
	Proportional promotional advertising	12.08*	0.86
	Proportional promotional gift	1.90*	0.84
	Relative number of planned brand purchasers	0.70*	0.03
	Relative number of previous time brand purchasers	0.93*	0.02
	Rate of appearance on shopping lists	41.19*	3.44
	Rate of time since last purchase	0.15*	0.04
	Rate of product purchase	0.52**	0.26
	Relative number of first-time buyers	−0.13*	0.00
	Relative number of habitual buyers	0.45*	0.13
LIHU group	Shelf space	−0.63*	0.07
	Premium price	3.22*	0.33
	Promotional price	−1.09*	0.30
	Relative number of planned brand purchasers	−0.30*	0.03
	Relative number of previous time brand purchasers	−0.36*	0.03
HIHU group	Proportional promotional advertising	2.16*	0.84
	Relative number of planned brand purchasers	0.11*	0.04
	Relative number of previous time brand purchasers	0.14*	0.03
	Rate of appearance on shopping lists	14.25*	3.43
	Rate of product purchase	−0.62*	0.12
	Relative number of habitual buyers	0.18*	0.06

*$p \leq 0.01$; **$p \leq 0.05$

three other variables were also noticeable: the relative number of previous time brand purchasers of low informational and utilitarian reinforcements, the relative number of habitual buyers, and the relative number of planned brand purchasers of low informational and utilitarian reinforcements.

For the HILU group, all variables and aggregated purchase antecedents (brand marketing activities, generic tendencies of buying, consumer brand history and the behavioral tendencies towards brands with different magnitude of reinforcements) were significantly related to daily market share. Past attractiveness of these brands raised brand performance in this market structure, especially the rate of appearance on shopping lists. Increases in five other variables were also noticeable: the relative number of previous time brand purchasers of exclusively high informational reinforcements, the relative number of planned brand purchasers of exclusively high informational reinforcements, the rate of product purchase, the relative number of habitual buyers and the rate of time since last purchase. The relative number of first-time buyers decreased the daily market share.

For the LIHU group, only some brand marketing activities and the behavioral tendencies towards brands with different magnitude of reinforcements were forecasters of daily market share. Past attractiveness of these brands raised brand performance in this market structure, especially by decreasing the relative number of previous time brand purchasers of exclusively high informational reinforcements and by decreasing the relative number of planned brand purchasers of exclusively high informational reinforcements.

For the HIHU group, all types of purchase antecedents (brand marketing activities, generic tendencies of buying, consumer brand history and the behavioral tendencies towards brands with different magnitude of reinforcements) were related to the daily market share, but not all variables. Past attractiveness of these brands raised brand performance in this market structure, especially by increasing the rate of appearance on shopping lists. Increases in four other variables were also noticeable: the relative number of habitual buyers, the relative number of previous time brand purchasers of high informational and utilitarian reinforcements, and the relative number of planned brand purchasers of high informational and utilitarian reinforcements.

Figure 11.5 shows all the regression lines with the standardized predicted values of the set of the antecedent variables for the four dimensions of the market structures. They demonstrate that the variables were good forecasters of daily market share (R^2 varied from 78.5% to 95.5%). Overall, Study 2 corroborates that brand past attractiveness and brand manageability forecast brand performance in brand market structure. When aggregated, predictors of consumer choice also predict brand performance, but some variables are better in each dimension of the market structure based on the magnitude of the estimates shown in Table 11.5. Therefore, the reinforcements offered to consumers may be used to interpret brand market structure.

Discussion

In the present chapter, brand market structure was interpreted on the basis of programmed reinforcement level offered by groups of brands. Low and high levels of utilitarian and informational reinforcement, offered by brands, were used to describe a two-by-two market structure. The results showed that the proposed antecedent variables, included in the model, predict brand performance at each level of brand market structure with good reliability. The aggregated variables of consumer purchase also predict the daily market share. Moreover, the consequences consumers achieve by purchasing each group of brands form the brand competition setting, since the brands in each group offer similar levels of utilitarian and informational reinforcement and are, consequently, highly substitutable within each group.

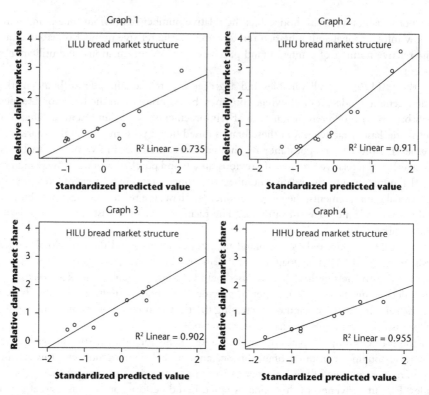

Figure 11.5 Linear influence of the set of antecedents on the brand performance in brand market structure

All the variables represented by the brand past attractiveness (Bridges et al., 2006; Chatterjee et al., 2011; Kahn & Louie, 1990; Kim & Rossi, 1994; Morwitz et al., 2007; Neal et al., 2006; Thomas & Garlant, 2004; Vilcassim & Jain, 1991; Warshaw, 1980) and brand manageability (Ambrosini & Bowman, 2009; Cui et al., 2014; Stewart, 2009; Zollo & Winter, 2002) predicted the daily market share, but some of them only in some dimensions of the brand market structure. Others vary in strength among the dimensions.

For instance, in LILU, the brands in this dimension could successfully use promotional price (decreasing it) to leverage daily market share. However, they could not successfully use increases in shelf space as it did not have any significant impact and their advertisements generated reductions in market share, highlighting their weak images. In HILU, the brands in this dimension could successfully use proportional promotional advertising, premium price, proportional promotional gifts, exposure on shelf space and promotional price (decreasing it) to leverage daily market share. In LIHU, the brands in this dimension could successfully use premium price and promotional price (decreasing it) as they leveraged the brand performance. Nevertheless, managers should expose them in an exclusive shelf space to increase the daily market share. Finally, in HIHU, the rate of product purchase decreased daily market share. The brands in this dimension could successfully use proportional promotional advertising, as it increased the daily market share.

Increases in price reductions generate better brand performance when brands have technical differentiations, but are not outstanding (LIHU group). Famous global brands (Johansson, 2011;

Sullivan, 1992) and the unbranded ones (Berthon et al., 2008) could also use this strategy, but it might not be as effective as it would be for brands in the LIHU group (Danziger, 2005; Park et al., 1986; Parrish et al., 2006). Therefore, brands that will most benefit from promotional prices are those that embrace a mass appeal image, those with a niche image or those with a generic image. Increase in price reduction is a discriminative stimulus (Foxall, 1987) that signals that consumers could retain more money. On the other hand, increases in premium price (Foxall et al., 2007) have a good effect for prestigious brands and for niche ones (HILU and LIHU groups, respectively). This kind of strategy signals superior quality or tailored brands that can be reasonably overpriced.

Increases in proportional promotional advertising (Blattberg et al., 1995) generate better brand performance when brands are already famous, even if they lack an innovation appeal in the category (HILU group). These advertisements are informational statements (suggestions, prompts, promises) in favor of the owner (Foxall, 1987) and they signal the availability of reinforcement if a brand is purchased. The outstanding brands – HIHU group – (Beverland et al., 2010; Danziger, 2005) could also use this strategy effectively, but managers should not expect greater influence as in the HILU group. The unbranded options (Berthon et al., 2008) should not use this strategy for it signals low reinforcements to consumers and reduces market share.

Increases in proportional promotional gift (Liao et al., 2009) and shelf space (Eisend, 2013) are only good strategies when brands compete in a HILU market structure. That means that these strategies are worth using when a brand is already well known. They are, respectively, extrinsic reinforcers (Scott Jr. et al., 1988) and arrangement of stimuli (Foxall, 2004) that the manager controls. It is likely the brands in the LIHU group do not offer many opportunities for reinforcement to managers (Vella & Foxall, 2011), which could perhaps explain why there was a negative relation between shelf space and daily market share.

Increases in the rate of product purchase (Ehrenberg & Goodhardt, 1970; Rao, 1973), the rate of time since last purchase (Vilcassim & Jain, 1991), the relative number of habitual buyers (Ehrenberg et al., 2004) and the relative number of experienced buyers (Ehrenberg et al., 2004) are tendencies that stimulate brand performance in the HILU context. In other words, the options that previously have attracted consumers with a huge repertoire of brands in the category (experienced) are resistant to change (habitual ones), have a high response rate in the category (product purchase), and the ones who are in higher product deprivation (establishing operations – Fagerstrøm et al., 2010) will perform better in this brand market structure of higher informational reinforcement. This is why these brands are sometimes also sale leaders. They have already established how good consumers are at buying these brands and generate "herd behavior" (Hanson & Putler, 1996; Rook, 2006), but have the propensity to generate crowding if managers do not control the speed of supply in response to demand.

The higher the rate of appearance on a shopping list (Thomas & Garlant, 2004), the higher will be the brand market performance, especially in HILU, LILU and HIHU groups. Although its incidence is low, when the rate increases, it seems to be the best variable to forecast brand performance in these competitive contexts. Usually a shopping list covering brands indicates specific brands rather than just any one, which may signal a small subset in the category that had already reinforced consumer purchases (Foxall et al., 2007). It is also a personal brand choice pattern, which deliberately avoids the influence of retailers' strategies. When aggregated, the rate indicates that these consumers that use a shopping list want the same reinforcers or the same magnitude of reinforcement and should not buy any other. It seems to be a very robust personal strategy to become impervious to subsequent contingencies programmed by the retailer.

Increasing the relative number of planned brand purchasers forecasts daily market share in every competitive context. This situation strengthens the claim that what consumers intend to buy (Morwitz et al., 2007; Warshaw, 1980) predicts well, at the aggregate level, the subsequent brand purchase when brand reinforcement levels are taken into account (Porto et al., 2011). The more purchase planners a brand has, the more managers can expect to sell in each market structure.

However, increasing the relative number of previous time brand purchasers is more relevant in all brand groups. When they plan to buy brands, they do not consider point-of-sale contingencies and the brands already bought take precedence in subsequent choices under uncertain reinforcement conditions. If this is so, the main information that is relevant to consumers in subsequent purchases is the level of reinforcers delivered by each brand (the last purchased brand – Kahn & Louie, 1990). This may increase insensitivity to current contingencies programmed by the retailer (Foxall, 2004).

General discussion

The analysis of consumer brand choice needs to consider the level of informational and utilitarian reinforcement programmed by different brands. The higher the magnitude of utilitarian and/or informational reinforcements (Foxall et al., 2007), the higher the probability of that particular brand being chosen. Study 1 analyzed this phenomenon by showing systematic relations among antecedents, purchase behavior, and the magnitude of reinforcements. The antecedents cover consumer behavior setting (manageable variables) and consumers' learning history (unmanageable variables). Together, they increase the probability of choosing a brand with higher levels of reinforcement, which shows that there are programmed reinforcement contingencies that influence consumers in the direction of obtaining higher benefits attached to brands.

This occurrence is consistent with those studies that showed maximization of reinforcement in consumer brand choice (Foxall et al., 2004; Foxall et al., 2010). Thus, if the brand bought can provide more reinforcements (more aesthetic and sensory satisfaction, body enhancement, a feeling of wellbeing or the satisfaction of sharing with friends and family), the consumer will be more inclined to buy it again. Therefore, the brand previously chosen that led to a higher level of reinforcement increases the tendency of buying similar brands, which might explain the small brand repertoire (Ehrenberg et al., 2004). Nevertheless, occasionally, consumers buy another brand offering a different magnitude of reinforcement, possibly due to variations in consumer settings (Foxall, 2005) – marketing stimuli. This broadens their experiences and may change the previous subset of low brand reinforcement to another subset of brands, usually choosing the ones that bring higher reinforcement or lower levels of punishment (e.g., spending less money and time). This means that consumers occasionally change their repertoire of brands to the ones of higher reinforcements and then maintain their purchase behavior with some "famous" or "outstanding" brands. If no other brand is launched in the market, this pattern may bring stability to the market share for all brands during an extended period of time (Golder, 2000).

This phenomenon helps explain brand performance at the level of market structure (Shaked & Sutton, 1990), which was examined in Study 2. The brands that have more purchases are the best market performers (highest market share) on a daily basis. However, some sales peaks are observed occasionally in a non-overall leader brand. This is because the brand attracted more purchases on that day, due to past attraction and its manageability implemented by the retailer on that particular day. As these manageable brand features depend upon the marketing efforts of manufacturers, some brands are better able to offer competitive strategies (enhance substitutability).

However, brand managers need not program the best strategy in the category, but should rather emphasize the brand strategy towards its close substitutes (Foxall et al., 2010). The ones that bring the same class of consequences to consumers are the closest substitutes. They provide them with similar levels of utilitarian and informational magnitude of reinforcement. Even if they have similar consequences, sometimes one will have a higher market share than others. This may be due to the brand manageability and past brand attractiveness on a day-by-day basis.

Within a category, brands are part of a market structure (Shaked & Sutton, 1990). First, there are unbranded goods, offered by small or local enterprises (low magnitude of utilitarian and informational reinforcement). Second, there are those directed towards a niche, or to the mass market or with a generic image, usually offered by medium enterprises (combination of high utilitarian and low informational). Third, there are well-known and superior image brands offered by big enterprises not innovative in the category (combination of low utilitarian and high informational). Finally, there are outstanding or premium ones (combination of high utilitarian and high informational), offered by specialized or innovative big enterprises.

Each dimension of this structure is a context of brand performance that shows which are the closest substitute brands. If brands are in the same category, they already have a general set of properties (Cuvo, 2000), offering primary reinforcers (e.g., aesthetic pleasure, body enhancement, and such like), some have the same specific attributes, so they also share a restricted set of properties (e.g., body moisturizer with sun block). However, as the brands also offer secondary reinforcers (Alhadeff, 1982), these dimensions of the market structure highlight their many transferable functions (e.g., stylishness, refinement and so on), for they share the same magnitude of utilitarian and informational consequences for consumers.

Conclusion

Researchers have not emphasized the relations of everyday purchases and daily market share. The present work proposes to build the necessary bridge to interpret and explain such phenomena. Based upon a behavioral economic explanation, the model adopted here dynamically links brand performances to consumer brand choice that takes place in-store. On an individual level, the model encompasses the influence of both the consumer behavior setting (manageable stimuli) and the consumer's learning history (unmanageable stimuli) influencing each purchase. At the brand level, it encompasses the influence of brand past attractiveness and brand manageability, resulting in reasonable predictions of daily market share.

The combinations of the consequences of brand purchases constitute the basic dimensions of the brand market structure. They provide the contexts of the substitutability of brands. The members of the same brand market structure deliver similar consequences and the antecedents – brand past attractiveness/brand manageability – form the mechanisms that give rise to market share. More research is expected to be done to verify if the dimensions found here are stable and applicable to other non-routine markets.

As this was a natural experiment, the results should be replicable in similar in-store situations involving the purchase of routine products. Nevertheless, the present research was carried out only in one store and research in other types of retail environment might well reveal other predictors and verify if both consumer and brand levels of analysis are sustainable. Furthermore, tests could clarify if other brand metric performances (e.g., profit margin) would be better forecast when brand utilitarian and informational reinforcement levels are considered in characterizing brand market structure. Another way of generalizing these results is to check the same antecedent-behavior-consequence relations with different brands, which have irregular purchasing frequency. They could provide other sets of properties and transferable functions among brands.

References

Agarwal, M. K. and Rao, V. R. (1996). An empirical comparison of consumer-based measures of brand equity, *Marketing Letters*, 7, 237–247. doi: 10.1007/BF00435740

Alhadeff, D. A. (1982). *Microeconomics and Human Behavior: Towards a New Synthesis of Economics and Psychology*. Los Angeles, CA: University of California Press.

Ambler, T. (1997). Do brands benefit consumers? *International Journal of Advertising*, 16, 167–198. doi: 10.1111/j.0265-0487.1997.00053.x

Ambrosini, V. and Bowman, C. (2009). What are dynamic capabilities and are they a useful construct in strategic management? *International Journal of Management Reviews*, 11, 29–49. doi: 10.1111/j.1468-2370.2008.00251.x

Ataman, M. B., Van Heerde, H. J. and Mela, C. F. (2010). The long-term effect of marketing strategy on brand sales, *Journal of Marketing Research*, 47, 866–882. doi: 10.1509/jmkr.47.5.866

Barnett, A. I. (1976). More on a market share theorem, *Journal of Marketing Research*, 13, 104–109.

Baumgartner, H. (2013). Repetitive purchase behavior. In: A. Diamantopoulos, W. Fritz and L. Hildebrandt (Eds.), *Quantitative Marketing and Marketing Management: Marketing Models and Methods in Theory and Practice* (pp. 269–286). Wiesbaden: Springer DE.

Bell, D. E., Kenney, R. L. and Little, J. D. C. (1975). A market share theorem, *Journal of Marketing Research*, 12, 136–141.

Berthon, P., Ewing, M. T. and Napoli, J. (2008). Brand management in small to medium-sized enterprises, *Journal of Small Business Management*, 46, 27–45. doi: 10.1111/j.1540-627X.2007.00229.x

Beverland, M. B., Napoli, J. and Farrelly, F. (2010). Can all brands innovate in the same way? A typology of brand position and innovation effort, *Journal of Product Innovation Management*, 27, 33–48. doi: 10.1111/j.1540-5885.2009.00698.x

Blattberg, R. C., Briesch, R. and Fox, E. J. (1995). How promotions work, *Marketing Science*, 14 (Supplement), G122–G132. doi: 10.1287/mksc.14.3.G122

Bolger, N., Davis, A. and Rafaeli, E. (2003). Diary methods: capturing life as it is lived, *Annual Review of Psychology*, 54, 579–616. doi: 10.1146/annurev.psych.54.101601.145030

Bridges, E., Briesch, R. A. and Yim, C. K. B. (2006). Effects of prior brand usage and promotion on consumer promotional response, *Journal of Retailing*, 82, 295–307. doi: 10.1016/j.jretai.2006.08.003

Buzzell, R. D. (1964). Predicting short-term changes in market share as a function of advertising strategy, *Journal of Marketing Research*, 1, 27–31.

Cavalcanti, P. R., Oliveira-Castro, J. M. and Foxall, G. R. (2013). Individual differences in consumer buying patterns: a behavioral economic analysis, *Psychological Record*, 63, 259–276. doi: 10.11133/j.tpr.2013.63.2.003

Chatfield, C. (1976). A comment on a market share theorem, *Journal of Marketing Research*, 13, 309–311.

Chatterjee, S., Roy, R. and Malshe, A. V. (2011). The role of regulatory fit on the attraction effect, *Journal of Consumer Psychology*, 21, 473–481. doi: 10.1016/j.jcps.2010.05.001

Cooper, L. G. and Nakanishi, M. (1988). *Market-Share Analysis: Evaluating Competitive Marketing Effectiveness* (Vol. 1). Norwell: Springer.

Cui, A. P., Hu, M. Y. and Griffith, D. A. (2014). What makes a brand manager effective? *Journal of Business Research*, 67, 144–150.

Cuvo, A. J. (2000). Development and function of consequence classes in operant behavior, *The Behavior Analyst*, 23, 57.

Danziger, P. (2005). *Let Them Eat Cake: Marketing Luxury to the Masses as Well as the Classes*. Chicago, IL: Dearborn Trade Publishing.

DeSarbo, W. S., Degeratu, A. M., Ahearne, M. J. and Saxton, M. K. (2002). Disaggregate market share response models, *International Journal of Research in Marketing*, 19, 253–266. doi: 10.1016/S0167-8116(02)00078-2

Ehrenberg, A. S. and Goodhardt, G. J. (1970). Pack-size rates of buying, *Applied Economics*, 2, 15–26. doi: 10.1080/00036847000000013

Ehrenberg, A. S., Uncles, M. D. and Goodhardt, G. J. (2004). Understanding brand performance measures: using Dirichlet benchmarks, *Journal of Business Research*, 57, 1307–1325. doi: 10.1016/j.jbusres.2002.11.001

Eisend, M. (2013). Shelf space elasticity: a meta-analysis, *Journal of Retailing*, 90, doi: 10.1016/j.jretai.2013.03.003

Fagerstrøm, A., Foxall, G. R. and Arntzen, E. (2010). Implications of motivating operations for the functional analysis of consumer choice, *Journal of Organizational Behavior Management*, 30, 110–126. doi: 10.1080/01608061003756331

Fok, D., Paap, R. and Franses, P. H. (2014). Incorporating responsiveness to marketing efforts in brand choice modeling, *Econometrics*, 2, 20–44. doi: 10.3390/econometrics2010020

Foxall, G. R. (1987). Radical behaviorism and consumer research theoretical promise and empirical problems, *International Journal of Research in Marketing*, 4, 111–127. doi: 10.1016/0167-8116(87)90003-6

Foxall, G. R. (1999). The marketing firm, *Journal of Economic Psychology*, 20, 207–234. doi: 10.1016/S0167-4870(99)00005-7

Foxall, G. R. (2004). *Consumer Psychology in Behavioural Perspective*. London and New York: Routledge. (Reprinted by Beard Books, Frederick, MD.)

Foxall, G. R. (2005). *Understanding Consumer Choice*. New York: Palgrave Macmillan.

Foxall, G. R. (2010). Invitation to consumer behavior analysis, *Journal of Organizational Behavior Management*, 30, 92–109.doi: 10.1080/01608061003756307

Foxall, G. R. and Greenley, G. E. (2000). Predicting and explaining responses to consumer environments: an empirical test and theoretical extension of the behavioural perspective model, *The Service Industries Journal*, 20, 39–63. doi: 10.1080/02642060000000019

Foxall, G. R. and James, V. K. (2003). The behavioral ecology of brand choice: how and what do consumers maximize, *Psychology and Marketing*, 20, 811–836. doi: 10.1002/mar.10098

Foxall, G. R., Oliveira-Castro, J. M. and Schrezenmaier, T. C. (2004). The behavioural economics of consumer brand choice: patterns of reinforcement and utility maximization, *Behavioural Processes*, 66, 235–260. doi: 10.1016/j.beproc.2004.03.007

Foxall, G. R., Oliveira-Castro, J. M., Schrezenmaier, T. C. and James, V. K. (2007). *The Behavioural Economics of Brand Choice*. London: Palgrave Macmillan.

Foxall, G. R., Wells, V. K., Chang, S. W. and Oliveira-Castro, J. M. (2010). Substitutability and independence: matching analyses of brand and products, *Journal of Organizational Behavior Management*, 30, 145–160. doi: 10.1080/01608061003756414

Gabaix, X., Laibson, D., Moloche, G. and Weinberg, S. (2006). Costly information acquisition: experimental analysis of a boundedly rational model, *American Economic Review*, 96, 1043–1068. doi: 10.1257/aer.96.4.1043

Golder, P. N. (2000). Historical method in marketing research with new evidence on long-term market share stability, *Journal of Marketing Research*, 37, 156–172. doi: 10.1509/jmkr.37.2.156.18732

Gordon, D. V., Hannesson, R. and Kerr, W. A. (1999). What is a commodity? An empirical definition using time series econometrics, *Journal of International Food & Agribusiness Marketing*, 10, 1–29. doi: 10.1300/J047v10n02_01

Habel, C. and Lockshin, L. (2013). Realizing the value of extensive replication: a theoretically robust portrayal of double jeopardy, *Journal of Business Research*, 66, 1448–1456. doi: 10.1016/j.jbusres.2012.05.012

Hanson, W. A. and Putler, D. S. (1996). Hits and misses: herd behavior and online product popularity. *Marketing Letters*, 7, 297–305. doi: 10.1007/BF00435537

Hanssens, D. M. and Dekimpe, M. G. (2012). Short-term and long-term effects of marketing strategy. In: V. Shankar and G. Carpenter (Eds.), *Handbook of Marketing Strategy* (pp. 457–469). Northampton: Edward Elgar Publishing Inc.

Ivanova, M. (2007). Genesis and evolution of market share predictive models, *Economic Studies Journal*, 27, 117–148.

Johansson, J. K. (2011). The promises of global brands: market shares in major countries 2000–2009. In: S. C. Jain and D. A. Griffith (Eds.), *Handbook of Research in International Marketing* (pp. 20–47). Northampton: Edward Elgar Publishing Inc.

Kahn, B. E. and Louie, T. A. (1990). Effects of retraction of price promotions on brand choice behavior for variety-seeking and last-purchase-loyal consumers, *Journal of Marketing Research*, 27, 279–289. doi: 10.2307/3172586

Keller, K. L. and Lehmann, D. R. (2006). Brands and branding: research findings and future priorities, *Marketing Science*, 25, 740–759. doi: 10.1287/mksc.1050.0153

Kim, B. and Rossi, P. E. (1994). Purchase frequency, sample selection and price sensitivity: the heavy-user bias, *Marketing Letters*, 5, 57–67. doi: 10.1007/BF00993958

Liao, S. L., Shen, Y. C. and Chu, C. H. (2009). The effects of sales promotion strategy, product appeal and consumer traits on reminder impulse buying behaviour, *International Journal of Consumer Studies*, 33, 274–284. doi: 10.1111/j.1470-6431.2009.00770.x

Lieberman, M. B. and Montgomery, D. B. (2012). First-mover/pioneer strategies. In: V. Shankar and G. Carpenter (Eds.), *Handbook of Marketing Strategy* (pp. 339–361). Northampton: Edward Elgar Publishing Inc.

Lincoln, J. R. and Zeitz, G. (1980). Organizational properties from aggregate data: separating individual and structural effects, *American Sociological Review*, 45, 391–408.

Morwitz, V. G., Steckel, J. H. and Gupta, A. (2007). When purchase intentions predict sales, *International Journal of Forecasting*, 23, 347–364. doi: 10.1016/j.ijforecast.2007.05.015

Naert, P. A. and Bultez, A. (1973). Logically consistent market share models, *Journal of Marketing Research*, 10, 334–340.

Nair, H., Dubé, J. P. and Chintagunta, P. (2005). Accounting for primary and secondary demand effects with aggregate data, *Marketing Science*, 24, 444–460. doi: 10.2139/ssrn.945416

Neal, D. T., Wood, W. and Quinn, J. M. (2006). Habits – a repeat performance, *Current Directions in Psychological Science*, 15, 198–202. doi: 10.1111/j.1467-8721.2006.00435.x

Netemeyer, R. G., Krishnan, B., Pullig, C., Wang, G., Yagci, M., Dean, D., Ricks, J. and Wirth, F. (2004). Developing and validating measures of facets of customer-based brand equity, *Journal of Business Research*, 57, 209–224. doi: 10.1016/S0148-2963(01)00303-4

Nord, W. R. and Peter, J. P. (1980). A behavior modification perspective on marketing, *Journal of Marketing*, 44, 36–47. doi: 10.2307/1249975

Oliveira-Castro, J. M., Ferreira, D. C. S., Foxall, G. R. and Schrezenmaier, T. C. (2005). Dynamics of repeat buying for packaged food products, *Journal of Marketing Management*, 21, 37–61. doi: 10.1362/0267257053166730

Oliveira-Castro, J. M., Foxall, G. R., James, V. K., Pohl, R. H., Dias, M. B. and Chang, S. W. (2008). Consumer-based brand equity and brand performance, *The Service Industries Journal*, 28, 445–461. doi: 10.1080/02642060801917554

Oliveira-Castro, J. M., Foxall, G. R. and Schrezenmaier, T. (2006). Consumer brand choice: individual and group analyses of demand elasticity, *Journal of the Experimental Analysis of Behavior*, 85, 147–166. doi: 10.1901/jeab.2006.51-04

Park, C. W., Jaworski, B. J. and MacInnis, D. J. (1986). Strategic brand concept-image management, *Journal of Marketing*, 50, 135–145. doi: 10.2307/1251291

Parrish, E. D., Cassill, N. L. and Oxenham, W. (2006). Niche market strategy for a mature marketplace, *Marketing Intelligence & Planning*, 24, 694–707. doi: 10.1108/02634500610711860

Porto, R. B., Oliveira-Castro, J. M. D. and Seco-Ferreira, D. C. (2011). What consumers say and do: planned and actual amounts bought in relation to brand benefits, *The Service Industries Journal*, 31, 2559–2570. doi: 10.1080/02642069.2011.529607

Rao, T. R. (1973). Is brand loyalty a criterion for market segmentation: discriminant analysis, *Decision Sciences*, 4, 395–404. doi: 10.1111/j.1540-5915.1973.tb00564.x

Rook, L. (2006). An economic psychological approach to herd behaviour, *Journal of Economic Issues*, 40, 75–95.

Scott Jr., W. E., Farh, J. L. and Podsakoff, P. M. (1988). The effects of "intrinsic" and "extrinsic" reinforcement contingencies on task behaviour, *Organizational Behavior and Human Decision Processes*, 41, 405–425. doi: 10.1016/0749-5978(88)90037-4

Shaked, A. and Sutton, J. (1990). Multiproduct firms and market structure, *The RAND Journal of Economics*, 21, 45–62.

Shankar, V. and Carpenter, G. S. (2012). Late-mover strategies. In: V. Shankar and G. Carpenter (Eds.), *Handbook of Marketing Strategy* (pp. 362–375). Northampton: Edward Elgar Publishing Inc.

Spiteri, J. M. and Johnson, W. C. (2011). A new attraction model for evaluating the effectiveness of selling effort, *International Business & Economics Research Journal*, 2, 1–16.

Stewart, D. W. (2009). Marketing accountability: linking marketing actions to financial results, *Journal of Business Research*, 62, 636–643. doi: 10.1016/j.jbusres.2008.02.005

Sullivan, M. W. (1992). Brand extensions: when to use them, *Management Science*, 38, 793–806. doi: 10.1287/mnsc.38.6.793

Sutton, J. (2007). Market share dynamics and the persistence of leadership debate, *The American Economic Review*, 97, 222–241. doi: 10.1257/000282807780323613

Thomas, A. and Garlant, R. (2004). Grocery shopping: list and non-list usage, *Marketing Intelligence & Planning*, 22, 623–635. doi: 10.1108/02634500410559015

Uncles, M. D., Ehrenberg, A. S. C. and Hammond, K. (1995). Patterns of buyer behavior: regularities, models and extensions, *Marketing Science*, 14, G71–G78. doi: 10.1287/mksc.14.3.G71

Urban, G. L., Johnson, P. L. and Hauser, J. R. (1984). Testing competitive market structures, *Marketing Science*, 3, 83–112. doi: 10.1287/mksc.3.2.83

Vella, K. J. and Foxall, G. R. (2011). *The Marketing Firm: Economic Psychology of Corporate Behaviour*. Northampton, MA: Edward Elgar Publishing.

Vilcassim, N. and Jain, D. C. (1991). Modeling purchase-timing and brand-switching behavior incorporating explanatory variables and unobserved heterogeneity, *Journal of Marketing Research*, 28, 29–41. doi: 10.2307/3172724

Villas-Boas, S. B. (2007). Vertical relationships between manufacturers and retailers: inference with limited data, *The Review of Economic Studies*, 74, 625–652. doi: 10.1111/j.1467-937X.2007.00433.x

Warshaw, P. R. (1980). Predicting purchase and other behaviors from general and contextually specific intentions, *Journal of Marketing Research*, 17, 26–33. doi: 10.2307/3151113

Washburn, J. H. and Plank, R. E. (2002). Measuring brand equity: an evaluation of a consumer-based brand equity scale, *Journal of Marketing Theory and Practice*, 10, 46–61.

Weiss, D. L. (1968). Determinants of market share, *Journal of Marketing Research*, 5, 290–295. doi: 10.2307/3150346

Zaichkowsky, J. L. (2010). Strategies for distinctive brands, *Journal of Brand Management*, 17, 548–560. doi: 10.1057/bm.2010.12

Zollo, M. and Winter, S. G. (2002). Deliberate learning and the evolution of dynamic capabilities, *Organization Science*, 13, 339–351. doi: 10.1287/orsc.13.3.339.2780

12

What do consumers maximize?

The analysis of utility functions in light of the Behavioral Perspective Model

*Jorge M. Oliveira-Castro, Paulo R. Cavalcanti,
and Gordon R. Foxall*

Introduction

What do consumers maximize when choosing among products, services, or brands? A common assumption in marketing and economic sciences is that consumers have individual preferences and that their choices reflect such preferences. According to this view, consumers' maximizing behavior would derive from their obtaining the goods or services they prefer at the lowest possible prices. Taking this approach, one might be able to predict consumers' choices, as long as information concerning their preferences was available. For instance, knowing that someone prefers margarine over butter, one can predict that, if prices are the same, the person would maximize utility by choosing margarine over butter.

Although useful in some contexts, this approach has theoretical limitations. When one considers the logic of the usage of the term "preference" (cf. Ryle, 1949), this type of prediction is not really surprising and may, in some situations, even be seen as trivial. To describe someone as preferring margarine to butter is a way of saying that, if offered the opportunity to choose between the two, then the person will choose margarine. Sometimes one does not get to know what the person usually consumes but only what the person says she would choose if given the opportunity. That is to say, in many situations one only knows consumers' stated preferences, which are not necessarily their actual preferences. However, if what the person says about her preferences does not coincide with the choices she makes, we tend to accept what she does rather than what she says (cf. Peters, 1958). For example, questions will be raised if someone who states that she prefers margarine is seen repeatedly choosing butter. Either the person has not been sincere or there are other unknown factors that influence her choices.

Independently of knowing consumers' past choices or their stated preferences, this approach tends, theoretically, to an extreme form of subjective analysis of consumers' preferences in the sense of not pointing to anything that consumers, in general, prefer. Each consumer would have his or her own preferences that remain unknown before we gather information about them. It is a relativistic, *post-hoc* manner of theorizing, which suggests that preferences are totally subjective and cannot be predicted in any way. Preferences can be used to predict choices, but they are not predictable in themselves. This kind of theory does not say anything about why consumers have the preferences they have.

The subjective relativism that permeates this approach limits utility maximization proposals, since the factors that influence preferences and, consequently, utility remain unknown. In the present chapter, we demonstrate how the Behavioral Perspective Model (BPM) can avoid this subjectivism by pointing to variables in the environment that influence the formation of consumers' preferences and, consequently, how utility is maximized. The BPM, by emphasizing the role of situational variables, can be used to locate consumer behavior in space and time, in contrast to the emphasis that has been given to intra-individual variables in current approaches of consumer behavior, which predominantly have adopted social-cognitive frameworks. The proposed conception of utility is much closer to Samuelson's (1965) *revealed preference* but emphasizes not simply observed patterns of behavior but the patterns of reinforcement that shape and maintain them.

The Behavioral Perspective Model

The BPM offers a framework to interpret consumer behavior, largely based on principles derived from behavior analysis, behavioral economics, and marketing (Foxall, 1990/2004, 2002, 2010). According to this perspective, consumer behavior occurs at the intersection of the consumer's learning history and the current consumer behavior setting, producing environmental consequences (reinforcement and punishment). These consequences alter the probability of recurrence of the behavior in similar settings on future occasions. Consumer behavior typically involves both reinforcing and punishing consequences, because the acquisition of goods and services is accompanied by some punishers, such as monetary costs or time investment (Foxall, 2010).

The BPM proposes that consumer behavior is predominantly influenced by two types of consequence: utilitarian and informational reinforcement (and punishment). Utilitarian consequences are directly related to the use or consumption of a given product or service, whose physical characteristics and practical benefits strengthen (reinforcers) or weaken (punishers) the probability of acquiring the product or service. They are mediated by the product or service. For instance, the major utilitarian reinforcement associated with owning a car is to have door-to-door transportation. Informational consequences are mediated by other persons and are similar to what Skinner (1992) identified as social and verbal consequences. Specifically, in the BPM, these consequences are related to symbolic elements of the consumer context, which can be defined as *status* or *social feedback* (either positive or negative) that are associated with a particular purchase (Foxall, 2010). For example, in the case of owning a car, programmed social reinforcement, in the form of social *status*, is usually higher if the car is a Bentley or a Mercedes rather than a Renault, given similar car models. In either case, the consumer would get door-to-door transportation (i.e., the basic utilitarian reinforcement), but owning a prestigious car make is likely to increase social admiration and approval.

Consumer responses, such as searching, purchasing, and consuming, are followed by utilitarian and informational consequences, which may increase or decrease the probability of similar responses occurring in similar situations in the future. Features and dimensions of such situations that become associated with utilitarian and informational reinforcement (or punishment) become discriminative stimuli in the behavior setting whose presence increases (or decreases) the probability of a consumer response. Associations between elements of the setting and the respective consequences constitute the learning history of each consumer.

In the case of utilitarian and informational reinforcement, generally the more the consumer obtains of them, the better. The model predicts that consumers prefer products, services, and brands that offer higher levels of utilitarian and informational reinforcement to those that offer lower levels. From this, one can consider that the model predicts that consumers maximize utility via increases in utilitarian and informational reinforcement obtained from products and services, and decreases in utilitarian and informational punishment associated with products and services.

Before presenting a utility function based upon the BPM, it seems appropriate to explore some features of utility maximization models in general, introducing some basic concepts used in microeconomics.

Utility maximization

In consumer demand theory in microeconomics, consumers' preferences are usually represented as choices between different quantities of commodities.[1] Assuming that consumers have limited income, the amount spent on each commodity may influence directly the amount that can be spent on the others. Indifference curves, such as those shown in Figure 12.1, represent graphically possible commodity bundles; that is, combinations of quantities of two commodities that are equivalent to the consumer. The figure shows commodity bundles that combine quantities of products (or services or brands) X and Y and three indifference curves.

Each indifference curve (i.e., I_1, I_2, and I_3) contains commodity bundles that would give the consumer the same level of utility (i.e., "satisfaction", "happiness", "reinforcing value"). So, for instance, points L, N, and J, which are all located on I_1, give the same level of utility. Suppose that J represents a bundle formed of six units of Y and two units of X, whereas L represents a bundle formed of two units of Y and four units of X, but they are on the same indifference curve, I_1. The consumer would be indifferent to whether they obtained bundle J or L. Typically utility increases as the curve is farther from the origin; that is, the level of utility represented by bundles on I_3 is higher than the utility on I_2, which, in turn, is higher than on I_1. So, utility is higher in M than in K, which is higher than in J, N, and L. Based upon the assumption that more is better, the best alternative to the consumer would then be to consume bundles on the highest indifference curve (i.e., I_3).

However, this is not a possible alternative due to budget restrictions. The straight line xy represents the budget line; that is, how much the consumer can spend on commodities X and Y. If it is assumed, for example, that the consumer has a budget of US\$10 and that each unit of X and Y costs US\$2 and US\$1, respectively, all possible combinations of quantities of X and Y are on the budget line, ranging from spending all on X (i.e., nothing on Y) to spending all on Y (i.e., nothing on X), which are the extreme points of the budget line (x and y). With this budget, the consumer cannot afford any bundles on I_3.

Another relevant characteristic of typical indifference curves (i.e., those for commodities that are partially substitutable) is that the more the consumer has of commodity X, the more the consumer is likely to give up units of X to obtain units of Y; and vice versa, the more the consumer has of Y, the higher the propensity to give up units of Y to obtain units of X. This is why indifference curves are curved and convex to the origin. This propensity to substitute one commodity for the other gives the *marginal rate of substitution* and can be measured by the slope of the indifference curve

According to this approach, the optimum consumer choice would be to consume bundles on the highest possible indifference curve that can be reached with the available budget. In the example given, this occurs at point K, where the budget line is tangent to the highest indifference curve it can reach, which is I_2, and where the slope of the budget line equals the slope of the indifference curve.

An advantage of adopting this economic framework is that it offers a set of integrated assumptions, concepts, and equations to interpret choice phenomena. For example, adopting a

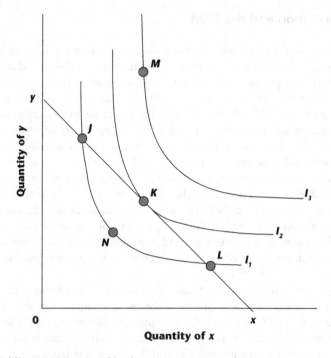

Figure 12.1 Indifference curves and budget constraint

Cobb-Douglas function, which is commonly employed in microeconomics, the utility function would be:

$$U_{(x,y)} = x^a y^b \tag{1}$$

where U represents utility, x is the quantity of commodity X, y is the quantity of commodity Y, and a and b are empirically obtained parameters. The two parameters could be reduced to one, by adopting a monotonic transformation of the Cobb-Douglas function, which has the same values of parameters (i.e., a and b; consequently, indifference curves would be the same), taking a and b to the $1/a+b$ power (Varian, 2010). The exponents would become $a/a+b$ and $b/a+b$, which would be equivalent to:

$$a = 1 - b \tag{2}$$

The budget line for the function is:

$$m = p_x x + p_y y \tag{3}$$

where p_x and p_y stand for the price of X and Y, respectively, and m is income.

Maximization of the function will occur when the marginal rate of substitution (slope of the indifference curve) is equal to the slope of the budget line; that is, when:

$$\frac{a}{b}\frac{y}{x} = \frac{p_x}{p_y} \tag{4}$$

This set of concepts and equations enables the calculation of the values of parameters a and b, which give the solution to the utility function (Equation 1).

Utility maximization and the BPM

In typical applications of demand theory, commodities X and Y are products, such as hamburgers and ice cream, or potatoes and beef steaks. Commodities bundles would be, for example, various combinations of quantities of hamburgers and ice cream. The curvature of indifference curves is easily understood with concrete examples, such as choice between hamburgers and ice cream: the more units of hamburger one has, the higher the propensity of trading units of hamburger for units of ice cream; that is, the higher the marginal rate of substitution.

We have noted that, according to the BPM, consumers' choices are influenced by the utilitarian and informational consequences that a given behavior produces in similar occasions, and that utility would, on this assumption, be a function of the quantity of obtained utilitarian and informational reinforcement. Rather than choosing among different quantities of products (or services or brands), consumers would be choosing among different quantities of utilitarian and informational reinforcement offered by different products (or services or brands). In the utility maximization framework presented in Figure 12.1, commodities X and Y would be utilitarian and informational reinforcement obtained by purchasing or consuming products, services, or brands.

This change in interpretation suggests that, for example, when looking for a car to buy, a consumer might actually be searching for a means of transportation that is comfortable, speedy, and safe, which are typical utilitarian consequences of owning a car. The person might also be looking for social recognition and status, because owning a car, in some social circles, might also generate social admiration and approval. However, if public transportation can offer comfortable, speedy, and safe means to move around, a consumer may choose this type of transportation instead of buying a car. Here the consumer is obtaining similar quantities of utilitarian reinforcement and, most likely, spending less money. Depending upon the consumer's social environment, using public transportation might also produce more social approval than owning a car, particularly in groups that value environmentally friendly acts. But even if owning a car is valued in one's social group, the consumer may decide to trade informational reinforcement for utilitarian reinforcement, considering, among other things, that using public transportation is cheaper (i.e., budget restrictions).

The same type of analysis would apply to simpler daily choices, such as choosing between eating, as a snack, chocolate cookies or fruit. The utilitarian reinforcement of having the cookie, derived from its sweet taste, may be greater than that obtained by eating an apple. However, informational reinforcement, in the form of social approval concerning health and looks, may be higher for eating the apple than the cookie. The consumer would choose a bundle that maximizes the combination of quantities of utilitarian and informational reinforcement.

This also applies to brand choice. When deciding between two different brands of baked beans, for example, a famous, high-quality, well-known brand would offer a high level of informational reinforcement, whereas a supermarket own brand, positioned as being cheap, gives little social reinforcement. Different formulations of the brand would offer different levels of utilitarian reinforcement, such as baked beans with or without sausages. Within budget restrictions, the consumer would choose certain combinations of quantities of utilitarian and informational reinforcement offered by the available brands.

Considering that utilitarian and informational reinforcement are part of the environment, this interpretation reduces the subjectivism of current utility maximization analyses. Attributes of products and services that function as utilitarian reinforcement are objectively identified and usually the theme of advertisements. So, for example, if a given model of car has air-conditioning and a more modern engine that consumes less fuel and is more powerful than its rivals, this would be known to the manufacturer and therefore widely publicized to consumers. These features would, most probably, also justify the establishment of a higher price for that type of vehicle.

The same is true of other factors associated with products and services that have utilitarian reinforcing properties. Packaged food items that have additional features added to their basic versions include baked beans with sausages, juice made from organic fruits, diet or lite versions of chocolate, cookies or yogurt, and double chocolate layers for cookies. Hotel services may offer additional utilitarian benefits, such as parking, breakfast, or airport transportation. One important characteristic of utilitarian reinforcement is its specificity relative to each product or service category. Due to its association with functional benefits, each product or service category has its own possible sources of utilitarian features. The features that can be added to cookies are of a different kind than those that can increase the utilitarian level of soups or butters. Attributes of cars are different from those that can be added to flats or to bicycles or to hotels. Each category presents its own possible utilitarian sources of reinforcement. Moreover, the reinforcing or punishing functions of utilitarian features will depend upon certain circumstantial variables surrounding consumers, such as regional preferences, cultural eating habits, and regional weather. Despite the programmed utilitarian contingencies offered by the market, different consumers may be differently influenced by such programmed contingencies.

The level of utilitarian reinforcement offered by different products has been measured using a dichotomous variable to indicate a lower or higher level of utilitarian reinforcement (Foxall et al., 2004; Oliveira-Castro et al., 2008; Cavalcanti et al., 2013). The level of programmed reinforcement was defined by analyzing the marketable features of each product category, which are usually apparent on the package and item description. They were then classified into two levels, offering higher or lower utilitarian reinforcement. The kind of scale to be used is relative to the main research interest. A measure with multiple levels could be adopted if it is possible and convenient to develop a scale with more points. If one were to classify car models, for instance, motor engines and bundles of accessories could be the base for scaling utilitarian features in several levels.

In the case of informational reinforcement, the main source of consequence is the social environment. This type of consequence is derived from feedback to consumer responses. Purchasing a product of a well-known, high-quality brand is likely to be followed by social manifestations of approval and admiration, functioning as social reinforcement. Similarly, buying an unknown brand of questionable quality might be accompanied by negative and doubtful comments concerning the deal, which will function as social punishment. These social contingencies can be measured in different ways. For example, previous research has measured the level of informational reinforcement programmed by different brands by examining the positioning of the brands in terms of their market amplitude (i.e., multinational, national, or regional) and pricing (i.e., premium, medium, or own brand) (Foxall et al., 2004). Another measurement of informational reinforcement adopted a simple questionnaire which asked respondents to rate the quality level and familiarity of brands (Oliveira-Castro et al., 2008; Pohl & Oliveira-Castro, 2008). The application of a questionnaire functions as a probe to investigate existing social contingencies, in the sense that brands that consumers consider to be well known and having high quality are those whose purchases are more likely to be followed by social approval.

In general, informational reinforcement may be similar across different products and services, considering that in all of them such reinforcement would be associated with social approval or *status*. Despite such a general characteristic, specific types of informational reinforcement are programmed by specific groups of people. An environmentalist group would, for instance, approve the use of bicycles and condemn the use of large SUVs, whereas among many other groups of people a large expensive car would confer high social *status*. Therefore, depending on group characteristics, different types or variations of products and services will bring social approval and *status*.

Maximizing utilitarian and informational reinforcement

Oliveira-Castro et al. (2015) tested the adequacy of this utility maximization framework in the context of brand choice. The authors used consumer panel data containing information from more than 1,000 consumers purchasing four products during 52 weeks. The data were divided into three periods of 17 or 18 weeks each, with the purpose of testing the reliability of parameters and individual differences. All brands purchased in the panel had their level of utilitarian reinforcement defined as higher or lower, according to additional attributes or a more sophisticated formulation they offered (cf. Foxall et al., 2004). So, less sophisticated formulations of a product, for example rich tea biscuits, were ranked as offering a lower utilitarian level of reinforcement (equal to 1), whereas more sophisticated formulations, such as chocolate chip biscuits, were ranked as offering a higher level of utilitarian reinforcement (equal to 2).

Informational reinforcement programmed by each brand was measured using a questionnaire, which asked respondents to state, on a four-point scale, the level of familiarity (e.g., this brand is "not known at all" to "very well known") and quality (e.g., this brand has "unknown quality" to "high quality") of each brand (Oliveira-Castro et al., 2008). These respondents were not part of the consumer panel and formed a convenience sample of persons that had lived most of their lives in the United Kingdom. Four questionnaires were used; one for each of the products investigated. Each questionnaire included, for each product, all the brands purchased by the sample of consumers in the panel, after filtering for attributes that are more related to utilitarian reinforcers than informational reinforcers. Then, variations of pack sizes and product formulations (e.g., plain baked beans vs. baked beans with sausage; rich tea cookies vs. chocolate chip cookies; plain baked beans vs. organic) by a given brand name were all classified as the same brand. Brand names that belonged to a more general brand but differed with respect to their positioning were classified as different brands (e.g., Asda vs. Asda Smart Price; Tesco vs. Tesco Value). The same group of respondents answered the questionnaires about baked beans (23 respondents), fruit juice (22 respondents), and yellow fats (22 respondents), whereas another group (33 respondents) answered the questionnaire about cookies. The main reason for this separation was the number of brands in each category. The questionnaire for cookies included 315 brands, whereas for baked beans, fruit juice, and yellow fats, the numbers of brands were 45, 99, and 89, respectively.

To obtain one informational level score for each brand, the mean score for knowledge and quality was calculated for each respondent and for each brand. The averages of these mean values were then calculated for each brand across all respondents, referred to as *MKQ* hereafter. A reliability analysis of MKQ was conducted by randomly assigning questionnaire respondents into two or three groups of approximately equal sizes, whose average MKQ given to each brand was correlated (Pearson) across all brands (*N* ranged from 45 for baked beans to 315 for cookies). Correlation coefficients between scores obtained by pairs of groups, three pairs for cookies and one for each of the other products, ranged from .872 to .984, showing acceptable reliability. According to this procedure, a value of MKQ was attributed to each brand purchased on each shopping occasion by each consumer in the panel data. For instance, Heinz™ baked beans was given a value of MKQ equal to 2.957, whereas Asda Smartprice™ baked beans received an MKQ equal to 1.065.

Having defined the levels of utilitarian and informational reinforcement offered by each brand, the next step was to estimate the prices of utilitarian and informational reinforcement. This is required to calculate parameters of the utility function (Equation 1), since maximization is dependent upon consumers' budgets, which is defined in terms of the quantity bought and price paid of each commodity (i.e., utilitarian and informational reinforcement), as shown in

Equations 3 and 4. Considering that the prices of products and services are not explicitly defined in terms of utilitarian and informational reinforcement, these prices were estimated based upon the changes in prices associated with changes in the levels of utilitarian and informational reinforcement. This was accomplished using the following linear regression:

$$PU_{ci} = m\ UTI_{ci} + n\ INF_{ci} \tag{5}$$

where PU refers to the price per unit of measure (e.g., 100 g), UTI and INF stand for the level of utilitarian and informational reinforcement of the brand bought, m and n are empirical obtained parameters, and subscripts c and i refer to each consumer and each shopping occasion, respectively. Parameters m and n can be used to estimate how product prices change with changes in utilitarian and informational reinforcement, and the ratio m/n can be interpreted as an estimate of the proportion of utilitarian and informational prices in the market, as follows:

$$\frac{p_{1c}}{p_{2c}} = \frac{m}{n} \tag{6}$$

where p_{1c} and p_{2c} refer, respectively, to the average prices of utilitarian and informational units paid by each consumer, calculated across all shopping occasions during each 17-week period. Combining Equation 6 with the following adaption of Equation 3, it was possible to calculate p_{1c} and p_{2c}:

$$I_C = p_{1c}x_{1c} + p_{2c}x_{2c} \tag{7}$$

where I_c refers to the total amount spent by a given consumer across all shopping occasions of a given period, a *proxy* of *income*, and x_{1c} and x_{2c} stand for the average quantity bought of utilitarian and informational reinforcement by each consumer during a given 17-week period. The values of x_{1c} were obtained with the following formula:

$$x_{1c} = \frac{\sum_{i=1}^{n}\left(q_{ci}UTI_{ci}\right)}{\sum_{i=1}^{n}q_{ci}} \tag{8}$$

where q_{ci} refers to the quantity of product bought (e.g., grams or milliliters) by each consumer on each shopping occasion. The variable UTI and the subscripts c and i are as previously defined. Then, Equation 8 was calculated across all shopping occasions of a given consumer, for each period and for each product. The values of x_{2c}, i.e. the average quantity bought of informational reinforcement, were calculated analogously:

$$x_{2c} = \frac{\sum_{i=1}^{n}\left(q_{ci}INF_{ci}\right)}{\sum_{i=1}^{n}q_{ci}} \tag{9}$$

Therefore, after calculating the values of I_c, x_{1c} and x_{2c}, and assuming that p_{1c} is equal to $(p_{2c}.m/n)$, from Equation 6, it was possible to calculate p_{2c} using Equation 7 and p_{1c} from Equation 6. These were calculated for each period of each consumer buying each product category.

These values of x_{1c}, x_{2c}, p_{1c}, and p_{2c} were then used to calculate the parameters of the utility function from Equation 4. This was done using a linear regression through the origin, calculated across consumers within a given period, whose slope was equal to b/a. By combining this value of the slope with Equation 2 (i.e., $a = 1 - b$), it was possible to obtain the values of a and b, Equation 1, for each period of each product category.

The results indicate that Equation 4 fitted the data very well, with all values of r^2 above .74. The values of parameters a and b obtained for Equation 1 were specific for each product category and consistent for the same product across time periods, showing a always larger or always smaller than b, with the exception of one out of 12 cases, probably due to effects of market price increases.

The analyses based upon this model enable the calculation of the level of utility obtained by each consumer buying each product during each time period. With such information it is possible to examine whether individual differences in utility level for each product are stable across time. To do this, Pearson correlation coefficients were calculated, relating the level of utility obtained by each consumer, on each product category, in the first and second, second and third, and third and first periods. The results indicated that all correlation coefficients were all significant and higher than .80, except for biscuits, whose coefficients were all significant and higher than .60. These results demonstrate that individuals differ with respect to the level of utility they obtain by buying each product and that such differences are stable and consistent across time. It is reasonable to suppose that such differences may be related to income level, considering that consumers with higher income can obtain higher levels of utility, since products and brands offering higher levels of utilitarian and informational reinforcement are typically more expensive.

The temporally consistent values of parameters a and b demonstrate the reliability of the proposed measures and suggest that these values can be used to estimate the importance or weight of utilitarian and informational reinforcement in generating utility for consumers when purchasing each product category. This finding has several managerial implications, such as information concerning the type of marketing strategy that is more promising to each product category; for example, it could help managers in deciding if they should invest more in innovation concerning product attributes (utilitarian reinforcement) or in brand differentiation (informational reinforcement).

Conclusions

This adaption of a standard utility maximization model for the analysis of consumers' brand choices made it possible to measure the average level of utility, calculated across consumers, obtained in buying each product category. The results indicate that consumers obtain, on average, significantly different levels of utility when buying specific products, in the following order: biscuits higher than baked beans, baked beans higher than yellow fats, and yellow fats higher than fruit juice. Such results might be very useful in the analyses of inter-category choices and money allocation. When consumers decide how much to spend in each product category, their choices might be influenced by the level of utility they can obtain from purchasing each product. Given an equal amount of money to spend between two products, it is reasonable to suppose, *ceteris paribus*, that consumers will allocate resources to the product that generates higher utility. In the same vein, it would be interesting to investigate possible relations between utility levels across products and elasticity of demand. More inelastic demand would be expected for consumption of products that bring higher levels of utility, *ceteris paribus*.

The application of this utility maximization model to brand choice produced encouraging results in showing that the BPM may constitute a theoretical framework to explain consumer utility functions. The possibility of identifying and measuring programmed utilitarian and informational reinforcement can reduce the level of subjectivity inherent in current consumer behavior interpretations. Although individual differences in consumption will not be totally eliminated, considering that programmed contingencies may influence different consumers differently, preferences will not be interpreted as subjective and unexplainable. Questions about what makes some features reinforcing to some individuals and not others still need to be answered, and the model suggests that those answers will be found in consumers' past experiences with different attributes and products. But, according to the analysis proposed here, given certain programmed utilitarian and informational contingencies, much can be predicted about consumers' preferences. Attributes that function as utilitarian and informational reinforcements usually do so for the majority of consumers, although not necessarily for all of them.

This can be conceived as an intermediate level of explanation, filling the gap between total subjectivism (i.e., each consumer has preferences whose sources are unknown) and total objectivity (i.e., given such contingencies will all behave in such a way). Much of what marketing managers do is related to identifying what is considered to be important or desirable for different segments of consumers. The BPM provides a framework that is useful in executing such a task by pointing to different types of consequences that influence consumers' choices, namely consequences derived from consumers' social environment and consequences generated using products and services.

Note

1 Introductions to utility functions are readily available in foundational economics texts such as Samuelson and Nordhaus (2009). Very accessible intermediate treatments can be found in Estrin et al. (2012) and Varian (2010). A key advanced treatment is that of Rubinstein (2012). For an informative discussion in terms of the development of economic theory and cognitive science, see Ross (2005). Staddon (2001) provides an illuminating account in the context of behavior theory, and Glimcher (2011) in that of neuroeconomics.

References

Cavalcanti, P. R., Oliveira-Castro, J. M., & Foxall, G. R. (2013). Individual differences in consumer buying patterns: A behavioral economic analysis. *The Psychological Record, 63*, 259–276. doi:10.11133/j.tpr.2013.63.2.003

Estrin, S., Laidler, D., & Dietrich, M. (2012). *Microeconomics*. London: Pearson.

Foxall, G. R. (2002). *Consumer behavior analysis: Critical perspectives in business and management*. New York: Routledge.

Foxall, G. R. (2004). *Consumer psychology in behavioral perspective*. Washington, DC: Beard Books.

Foxall, G. R. (2010). Theoretical and conceptual advances in consumer behavior analysis: Invitation to consumer behavior analysis. *Journal of Organizational Behavior Management, 30*, 92–109. doi:10.1080/01608061003756307

Foxall, G. R., Oliveira-Castro, J. M., & Schrezenmaier, T. C. (2004). The behavioral economics of consumer brand choice: Patterns of reinforcement and utility maximization. *Behavioural Processes, 66*(3), 235–260. doi:10.1016/j.beproc.2004.03.007

Glimcher, P. (2011). *Foundations of neuroeconomic analysis*. New York: Oxford University Press.

Oliveira-Castro, J. M., Foxall, G. R., & James, V. K. (2008). Individual differences in price responsiveness within and across brands. *Services Industries Journal, 28*(6), 733–753. doi:10.80/02642060801988605

Oliveira-Castro, J. M., Cavalcanti, P. R., & Foxall, G. R. (2015). What consumers maximize: Brand choice as a function of utilitarian and informational reinforcement. *Managerial and Decision Economics*, in press. doi:10.1002/mde.2722

Peters, R. S. (1958). *The concept of motivation*. London: Routledge & Kegan Paul.

Pohl, R. H. B. F. & Oliveira-Castro, J. M. (2008). Effects of the informational benefit level of brands on the duration of search behavior. *RAC-Eletrônica, 2*(3), 449–469. Retrieved from: http://anpad.org.br/periodicos/content/frame_base.php?revista=3

Ross, D. (2005). *Economic theory and cognitive science: Microexplanation*. Cambridge, MA: MIT Press.

Rubinstein, A. (2012). *Lecture notes in microeconomic theory: The economic agent*. 2nd edition. Princeton, NJ: Princeton University Press.

Ryle, G. (1949). *The concept of mind*. London: Hutchinson.
Samuelson, P. (1965). *Foundations of economic analysis*. Cambridge, MA: Harvard University Press.
Samuelson, P. & Nordhaus, W. D. (2009). *Economics*. 19th edition. New York: McGraw-Hill.
Skinner, B. F. (1992). *Verbal behavior*. Acton, MA: Copley Publishing Group.
Staddon, J. E. R. (2001). *Adaptive dynamics*. Cambridge, MA: MIT Press.
Varian, H. R. (2010). *Microeconomics: A modern approach*. 8th edition. New York and London: W. W. Norton & Company.

13

The Behavioral Perspective Model in the Latin-American context

Empirical and conceptual contributions

Marithza Sandoval-Escobar and Iván Felipe Medina

Introduction

The Behavioral Perspective Model (BPM) represents an approach to integrate the principles of behavior analysis to consumer research (Foxall, 1990, 1997), where the operant contingency model is used to explain the determinants of purchase and consumption (Sandoval et al., 2010). The BPM suggests that consumer behavior is a function of the interaction of the individual and the context of purchase and consumption; the latter is determined by the history of individual learning in each of these purchase contexts, in connection with a product category, and the consequences that this behavior produces in the current context (Foxall, 2007).

Many phenomena related to purchase and consumption can be addressed through the approach provided by BPM, including brand loyalty, purchasing patterns in the contexts of developing economies and the peculiarities of market scenarios in these economies and cultures. Other phenomena can also be investigated, such as inhibition or replacement of purchase, i.e. the circumstances that promote saving money, protecting natural resources with the purchase of green brands, or the involvement of consumers in behaviors such as donations, activism and other pro-ecological behaviors (Foxall, 1995).

These phenomena have been traditionally addressed by consumer psychology from a pre-eminently cognitivist view of the decision process, where intention is assumed to be a fundamental determinant of the observed behavior – either purchase or consumption, social interaction or environmental conservation. From this perspective, individuals construct sets of brands which are accepted, neutral or rejected, from a set of decision rules that define the type of attributes and combinations taken into account when choosing one or several of them. Said sets and their attributes are the result of exposure to the media and other sources of influence controlled by marketing firms, but once they are constituted, they determine the purchase of products and services on their own.

Under the central assumption of a rational decision, consumers choose different purchase options based on their preferences and what each brand represents. Knowing purchase intent from this perspective is equivalent to predicting the occurrence of the actual behavior, but as Foxall (2001, 2007) states, evidence shows a low correlation between the verbal expression of purchase intent and the actual transaction in commercial venues. Both applications of BPM analysis of purchasing patterns and their extensions for the study of various phenomena of consumption have been derived from a line of multi-year research developed in countries with different economic structures to Latin America and characterized by greater distribution of wealth, more extended middle classes and decreasing poverty indicators (Ehrenberg et al., 1990; Foxall, 1999, 2004, 2007; Oliveira-Castro et al., 2005, 2006; Uncles et al., 1995; Foxall et al., 2007).

In the case of pro-environmental behavior, attitudinal models are predominant in the field in Latin America. Medina and Páramo (2014) state in their review of perspectives and interventions in environmental education that more than half of the empirical work in the field of promoting pro-environmental behavior is oriented from the attitudinal perspective. In this regard, Gifford (2014) notes that the overall study of attitudes has been the central construct of environmental psychology, although its potency as a predictor continues to be in discussion. The BPM is a robust alternative that can be more effective as an approach to pro-environmental behavior in context interventions.

Latin America overview

The economic structure in the Latin-American region is characterized by increased poverty, extended lower classes and greater concentrations of wealth, which cause the distribution of products and services to have significant differences with regard to developed countries. Studies show that the percentage of people who shop in large supermarkets (hypermarkets) is lower and this pattern of supermarket use occurs mainly in middle and upper socioeconomic strata. According to the company Kantar Worldpanel (2013), consumer panels in Latin America and particularly in Colombia show that people distribute their shopping in the modern channel (hypermarkets, supermarkets and warehouses with a percentage between 47% and 60% of sales in Latin America), in the traditional channel (shops and corner stores with 42% of households buying in this channel throughout Latin America), in catalog purchases and other alternative channels such as drug stores, butcher shops and specialty stores depending on the product category or service. The lower strata buy products needed in smaller quantities and more frequently, concentrating their purchases in the so-called "traditional channel" in small shops near the residence of the consumer and where they can find basic household goods (food products, grooming products, products for washing clothes, sweets, etc.). Big brands have focused their marketing strategies on this channel in Latin America since about 42% of households keep shopping in the traditional channel despite completing transactions in the other channels as well (Nielsen Homescan, 2014). This percentage is even higher in Colombia, since 53% of households go to the neighborhood store two to three times a week (Kantar Worldpanel, 2013). The pattern of purchasing supplies daily is even more pronounced in the lower strata (about 40% of the population of Latin America), since family income can be produced by the informal day-based wages and trade. The traditional small channel has available small, unit and personal sizes of many foods and toiletries, but also offers the possibility of direct credit from the grocer. Prestigious international brands also distribute their products through that channel and expend a lot of effort to maintain good relations with the grocer, to the extent that it is he who determines the choice set consumers have.

Both academic and professional research groups of consumer behavior in the region have taken a close look at consumer psychology and models derived from the traditional economy to do research on purchases (see examples in Deloitte, 2013; García-Landa & Montero, 2013;

Rangel et al., 2013; Sergueyevna, 2013). In the particular case of brand substitution, studies have been carried out from an economic and marketing perspective using large aggregates from which conclusions can be drawn with regard to preferences and consumer trends (e.g. sectorial and macroeconomic studies conducted by CEPAL, 2014).

In the case of individual patterns, the model which underlies these studies is associated with significant changes which have taken place in the neoclassical economic vision, especially with regard to the extension in time of choice behavior and the relationship between the latter and demand, but with an undeniable closeness to internal constructs which cause consumer behavior. This standard model is a theory of rational choice in which individuals collect information on alternatives, using the rules of probability to transform this information into perceived attributes and then develop a cognitive process that can be represented as an array of attribute levels levied at a rate of one-dimensional steady income which is then maximized. Psychological factors which are introduced into decision-making concepts include processes of perception, preference and process (Sandoval et al., 2006).

For this reason, most studies exclusively use surveys and interviews in which the consumer responds to questions about their behavior pattern and its determinants. However, many questions may have false or inaccurate answers, because they refer to aspects which are ignored by consumers; for instance, loyalty to brands, reasons for the purchase, consistency of their intention to purchase, or their attitude towards certain products, pro-ecological behaviors or environmental issues.

Given the conflicting evidence regarding the cognitivist decision model and the need to answer questions related to the explanation of the behavior of Latin-American consumers, the priority is to change the methodological and conceptual approach. The BPM and working with consumer panels and simulations of purchase contexts are appropriate to achieve this goal. For example, the panel methodology allows longitudinal analysis of buying patterns and analysis of the processes of brand choice with regard to changes in prices in the same product category over time, which can empirically demonstrate elasticity in purchasing behavior (Crouch & Housden, 2003; Foxall, 2007; Oliveira-Castro et al., 2006). However, as Sandoval et al. (2006) claim, it is not enough to prove the existence of buying patterns or other consumer phenomena; the analysis of the psychological processes related to the observed pattern, beyond the simple description of the stages of decision or purchase intent, is also required. The behavior analytic view assumes that consumer behavior includes the activities of buyers before, during and after purchase and consumption (Foxall, 1998, 2001), and the design of scenarios and consequences of alternative responses to make alternative consumption responses likelier for the promotion of eco-friendly shopping (Foxall, 1995; Foxall et al., 2006).

Although it has been established that every country in Latin America has trends which vary hand in hand with social, political and cultural conditions, few studies actually aim at identifying patterns of purchasing behavior and the specific variables that determine these patterns. The explanations for this lack of information are related to the fact that in Latin America most research on buying patterns has been developed by different market research agencies for multinational brands, and to the low number of university researchers in the consumer behavior field, and the even fewer groups which link consumer psychology work with eco-friendly consumption.

Behavioral Perspective Model: studies in Latin America

Five different studies based on the BPM have been conducted in Brazil; this demonstrates the applicability of the model for understanding patterns of behavior in cultural contexts different from those that created them. These studies include Oliveira-Castro et al. (2005), who investigated the dynamics of buying patterns in 80 consumers for 16 weeks in eight product categories. Also, the study carried out by Phol and Oliveira-Castro (2008) with a panel of 1,477 consumers shows that there is a relationship between the informational benefit of brands and the duration of the search during the purchasing process, thus allowing the development of the concept of brand force from the measured duration of the search. Likewise, the study by Veiga Neto and Melo (2013) with children aged 10 to 12 shows the importance of utilitarian benefits (organoleptic properties) of food for children in determining their choice, as opposed to informational-type factors. In addition to the above, studies by Oliveira-Castro et al. (2008) demonstrate the applicability of BPM to analyze brand equity of brands, from the balance the utilitarian and informational consequences have within the product category. From a behavioral perspective, brand equity is conceptualized from brand awareness and quality, thereby emphasizing the role of situational variables to generate MKQ (Market, Knowledge, Quality).

Only more recently did Barreiros et al. (2011) compare the vision of consumer choice with the study of effective choice. The authors investigated whether consumers buy the amount they had planned, and whether those purchases depend on levels of utilitarian and informational benefits of brands, using a questionnaire survey of 1,010 consumers in a supermarket. When these shoppers verified their purchases upon leaving the mart, they were found to have purchased more units of brands with low benefits, when they planned to buy quantities above the average of other consumers. Also, Conque Seco and Oliveira-Castro (2011) have determined the effects of the purchase environment on consumer behavior from the perspective of scenarios. For this, the background music of two stores was manipulated and better effects were found on purchasing and customer satisfaction in the condition of better quality, thus demonstrating the motivational influence of the behavior setting and its characteristics.

In addition to the small number of research projects based on BPM that have taken place in the region, different points need further comparison and analysis for the context of Latin America. First, BPM has been applied to the description and explanation of purchasing patterns of consumer panels in countries where the purchases occur mainly in supermarkets in large areas and not in the traditional channels of purchase of the Latin-American region which are characterized by highly closed settings resulting in narrower choice sets, and by a majority of consumers belonging in the lower strata and minimum-income variables. Moreover, it is important to determine whether the predictions of intra- and inter-elasticity are met in those scenarios where the choice set is determined by the shopkeeper who negotiates with distributors the brands which bring greater profitability for their business, but which completely limit the choice of consumers.

To answer these questions, Sandoval et al. (2010) investigated the relationship between changes in levels of both utilitarian and informational reinforcement and measures of elasticity of intra- and inter-brand demand in seven categories of consumer products in 41 families from the lower strata of the city of Bogotá (Colombia). To avoid defining the level of informational reinforcement from the sales of brands, a new component was included to allow for a more complete approach regarding factors related to possible changes in the levels of mainly informational reinforcement, including a report of the participants with regard to the changes perceived in brand communication that could change their symbolic value.

Moreover, logs were kept of purchase venues, purchase frequency, brands purchased, purchase price and the conditions thereof (regular price or promotion), inter alia. Finally, the analysis of data from the household panel aimed to identify the levels of utility and informational reinforcement for brands within the categories studied. The data to define consumer choice sets available were derived from 120 retail establishments, broken down as follows: 40 supermarkets (hypermarkets), 40 convenience stores and 40 neighborhood stores in 13 geographic areas of the city. The shops were chosen considering their proximity to the participating families, and their purchase frequency. One hundred and twenty points of sale were visited to obtain data corresponding to brands available. Twelve views were carried out on the same number of points of sale every 2 weeks, over a total of 5 months (20 weeks). At each visit to each household, stock in cupboards was verified and a questionnaire was applied which aimed to monitor promotions, advertising and other marketing efforts made by points of sale and those reported by consumers.

The study results are consistent with the findings of the panels in developed countries. In particular, there was evidence of the effect identified by Ehrenberg et al. (2004) called double jeopardy – which consists of a progressive and strong decline in the share and penetration for the leading brand "A" in contrast to brand "H". Similarly, the indicator of brand loyalty is similar to that reported by other authors, thereby finding a multibrand pattern for six product categories studied, and the likelihood that the percentage of loyal customers exceeds 20% of its consumer base is very low.

Analysis of price elasticity in all product categories demonstrates the existence of a covariation between the quantities purchased and the unit price in each of the categories studied (see Figure 13.1). It was found that demand is price inelastic, e.g. the quantities purchased decrease in a less than proportionate fashion compared to the increase in prices, as previously reported by Oliveira-Castro et al. (2006). Regarding inter-consumer price elasticity of demand, the slopes of the functions demonstrate the existence of inter-consumer demand in each of the categories studied, with the exception of soap. The analysis of inter-consumer elasticity in the households section of the study shows that it was negative in every home, and therefore there is elasticity of inter-consumer price.

With regard to the level of utilitarian and informational reinforcement, factor analysis showed that there are two factors within the analyzed matrix which account for 53.4% of the variance explained. The items that show a high load on Factor 1 correspond to brand assessment behaviors (e.g. "It's a good quality product"). In Factor 2, items correspond to the elements of situational assessment (e.g. "Someone recommended it to me"). Inter-elasticity of the brand assessment behavior and inter-elasticity of the elements of situational assessment were analyzed using the equation developed by Oliveira-Castro et al. (2005). Intra-elasticity coefficients were significant and negative for all categories; in addition, greater situational assessment (albeit negative) intra-brand elasticity was found in four of the nine categories (detergent, dish detergent, hand soap and fabric softener). Moreover, intra-brand elasticity was higher than elasticities of brand assessment and situational assessment in three of the nine product categories (coffee, floor cleaners and chocolate).

Multiple regression analysis was also applied, wherein the criterion variable was the amount of product purchased, including predicting variables of unit price, socioeconomic status, monthly household income and the choice set considered to establish possible relationships with the amount acquired in each product category. The coefficients for the unit price were all significant and negative and ranged from −0.56 to −1.15. The coefficients for the choice set were all significant and positive and ranged from 0.51 to 2.26.

Furthermore, an analysis of simple linear regression was conducted to determine the level of maximum explanation for each predicting variable regarding the quantities purchased. It was found that as the number of brands available increases, the quantities purchased also increase. It was also found that with increasing socioeconomic status, the quantities purchased by consumers increase. Finally, each of the variables analyzed individually significantly contributes to explaining the quantities purchased, by highlighting in particular the contribution generated by the choice set within the estimated model. It is important to clarify that price elasticity of demand

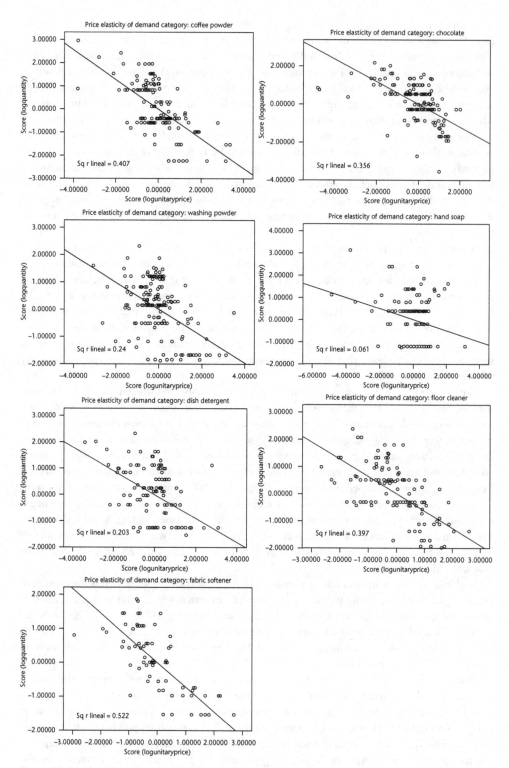

Figure 13.1 Elasticity of price of global demand (taken from Sandoval et al., 2010)

was found, with a decreasing linear function as unit prices of the brands increase; however, demand tends to be more resilient to the most expensive products in the basket, including fabric softener, floor cleaners and instant coffee. This effect was seen in almost every home for the seven categories of study.

The notion that consumers collectively reduce the quantities purchased as prices increase could be interpreted in a better way by including in the analysis other socio-demographic variables such as income level or social class, which might indicate the type of consumer (e.g., low, middle or upper class) more sensitive to increases in commodity prices (Sandoval et al., 2010).

Factor analysis reflected the existence of two factors from the verbal response of participants to items designed for evaluation of the brand, or to account for the elements of situational assessment. The first factor was very directly associated with more tangible and functional consequences arising from the use of the brand acquired. It was found that the second factor grouped items as "it was on sale", "someone recommended it to me" and "I was looking for variety". What these statements have in common is the fact that they refer to conditions or situations where the background environment plays an important role in consumer choice behavior, like seeking variety, which would be manifested in the behavior of exploration and comparison of brands at the point of sale by the customer. This allows researchers to identify this factor as "elements of situational assessment", which are covered by BPM as social and linguistic elements affecting consumer behavior. Functional analysis was conducted to establish the functional relationship which could exist between these two factors, together with unit price and intra- and inter-brand elasticity. The results show that the two factors proposed, e.g. brand assessment and situational assessment, had coefficients with significant elasticity in four and five product categories, respectively.

The study designed specific measures to assess the size of the choice set and its variations, which sought to reflect as closely as possible the number of brands available at the point of sale at the time in which the consumer performed the purchase. It is assumed that a smaller number of brands available is associated with a more closed scenario, and a scenario where the number of brands is higher would be regarded as an open scenario. The results show that consumers reduce the amount purchased when the price of brands increases. The most interesting finding is related to the coefficients obtained for the choice set. All results were found to be significant and positive, which leads to the conclusion that as the number of brands available at point of sale increases, the quantity of the product purchased also increases. When testing the level of predictability of the choice set individually, a range of explanation of variance was found ranging from .05 to .34 of the quantities purchased, thus representing a significant contribution to the interpretation of the purchase patterns observed.

These results together indicate that consumers would probably acquire more quantities of product in environments in which they find a larger number of brands available (open economy), since it is likely that in the latter one or more brands appear at that time and provide an acceptable level of reinforcement at a suitable price. In an environment where the number of brands is reduced (closed economy), the probability of finding one or more brands with more attractive prices should also be reduced. In these cases the consumer may be forced to buy a brand that, although perhaps not the most advantageous in terms of price-ratio reinforcement received, is the only one available at the time or the one with the most acceptable price compared to the few alternatives available.

Behavioral Perspective Model and environmental behavior

Other panel studies that have taken place in Colombia have focused on the study of so-called pro-environmental or pro-ecological consumption (Agudelo & Barreto, 2014; Barreto &

Sandoval, 2013; Garzón et al., 2014). Eco-friendly consumption in particular, and pro-environmental behavior in general, are increasingly important in the global social and economic agenda (Sandoval, 2012), and pose a challenge to the design of behavioral modification strategies given the information about the consequences of inaction on the environment and the number of actors involved in its promotion, maintenance, dissemination and regulation (Sandoval, 2012).

In the case of the Behavioral Perspective Model, its extension to pro-environmental behavior focuses primarily on the analysis of environmental factors to which non-ecological consumer behavior relates, and secondly in environmental conditions that are critical for maintaining pro-environmental behavior (Foxall, 1995; Foxall et al., 2006).The consequences that maintain ecological behavior cannot be differentiated in terms of sources, those arising from the use/consumption of goods and services and those derived from the social groups to which individuals belong. Therefore, an analysis of any non-ecological behavior undertaken to modify the behavior to a more ecological one must first analyze the consequences of which behavior is a function and promote changes accordingly. Thus, behaviors such as using private transport are maintained both for utilitarian aspects (comfort, door-to-door travel) and social aspects (prestige in social groups). Given this scenario, promoting the use of public transportation should emphasize utilitarian aspects (comfortable, agile and fast services) and social aspects (exemplary contingencies on the use of public transport services) (Foxall et al., 2006).

The behavior of consumption and overconsumption inevitably results in reducing the resources required for their production, thus jeopardizing the sustainability of the commercial practice in the future, since consumption of resources can take place faster than the ability of the planetary system to recover them. Two aspects stand out in theory with regard to the comprehension of non-environmental behavior: the immediacy of the consequences and the individual–consequence relationship. Foxall (1995) highlights how the consequences that reinforce purchasing behavior and consumption are usually immediate, as opposed to those consumer patterns aimed at lower consumption of resources, whose consequences take more time to become apparent.

Moreover, the activities that affect the environment are not generated by the behavior of a single consumer acting alone, but occur as a result of the aggregate behavior of millions of consumers, in such a way that the experienced consequences occur as a result of the individual's own behavior but changing the behavior of that, or any other, single individual will not affect the resulting state of things. This change will only occur as aggregate, and with long delays related to the recovery characteristics of the planetary system, thus implying changes in other human systems like the regulation of production, inter alia (for a review, see Sandoval, 2012).

This type of analysis places non-ecological behavior as a behavior of local or immediate maximization of available consequences (utilitarian and informational reinforcers). In this context, long-term aversive consequences as well as reinforcing consequences of greater magnitude – also available in the long term – affect behavior, and thus descriptively affect individuals' choice for non-ecological behavior alternatives; this is considered an impulsive response (Logue, 1995).

Also, Logue (1995) stresses that the label "impulsive" does not imply a pejorative reference to the consumer's behavior; actually, sensitivity to the immediacy of the reinforcing consequences is critical to ensure the survival of the species. Along the above-mentioned lines of thought, the case of the human species would not be exceptional.

Foxall (1995) and a subsequent paper by Foxall et al. (2006) suggest that an analysis of the non-ecological behavior should then consider: (a) the specific contextual conditions that maintain no ecological behavior, such as the behavioral configuration of a scenario, the discriminant function of the same when it comes to identifying the reinforcing consequences – whether informational or utilitarian; (b) the pattern of delivery of the consequences, to allow the

Table 13.1 Factorial design of the research conducted by Barreto and Sandoval (2013)

Socioeconomic strata (NSE)	Environmental program			
	Control group	Informational design	Informational design with environmental design	Total
NSE 2	10*	10	10	30
NSE 3	10	10	10	30
NSE 4	10	10	10	30
NSE 5	10	10	10	30
Total	40	40	40	120

*The unit corresponds to the number of families per condition

Source: Agudelo and Barreto (2014)

implementation of forms of consequences that compete with the patterns of consequences of not delivering environmental performance; (c) focusing on the role of non-utilitarian reinforcers of environmental behavior – since their role is more critical than the informational reinforcers, and therefore an environmental intervention based solely on information aspects would be less effective; (d) successful interventions in favor of pro-ecological behavior involve modifications of behavioral aspects in the scenario, for example the amplitude of the stage; and (e) the relationship between antecedent stimuli and consequences of behavior works best in the presence of specific rules that indicate the relationship between the two.

According to these principles, Agudelo and Barreto (2014) evaluated the effectiveness of two types of intervention programs on the consumption of green brands for the categories of personal care and pantry food; strategies focused on providing information to consumers and fostering the consumption of green brands, feedback behavior and environmental design that promote pro-environmental behavior. For this purpose, they selected the data in the macro study conducted by Barreto and Sandoval (2013); the latter studied, by means of a panel with 120 families of socioeconomic strata 2, 3, 4 and 5 over 32 weeks, the effect of two programs for promoting pro-environmental behavior, with three levels (control, informational design and informational design with environmental design). A design with consumer panel was used, and 3×4 factorial arrangement was operated as shown in Table 13.1.

The results selected by Agudelo and Barreto (2014) reveal that the environmental design strategy was more effective than the informational design strategy in the categories of personal care and pantry food; the socioeconomic stratus that was most sensitive to the intervention was 2, and in this socioeconomic stratus there was an increase in the average consumption of green brands after treatment. Although there was an increase in the consumption of green brands on the two interventions (information only and informational design with environmental design), the use of environmental design proved to be more effective. These findings support the tenets of BPM with regard to the promotion of pro-ecological behavior thus: (1) the importance of modifying the behavioral scenario for making the desired environmental behavior likelier, and (2) the specific relationship established by the rules between context or antecedent stimuli, and the timely reinforcing responses, thus making known the consequences of behavior that are present in the short term and which were given to the panel through feedback on the purchasing behavior.

In an analysis of other categories of consumption by the above-mentioned study panel, Garzón et al. (2014) evaluated the behavior of the intention stated by the participants to consume or not to consume transgenic foods or green food brands and the actual consumption of these products in the period of the study. This category is critical in terms of previous findings in panel studies, where the highest sensitivity for switching between the different alternatives by consumers is related to, first, the price at the time of purchase as stated by Foxall et al. (2006), second, with utilitarian reinforcers, and, third, with informational reinforcers. The category of consumption of green brands in the case of food is particularly difficult to promote as a functional class, as these are purchasing alternatives with double jeopardy, they have a low market share, they are poorly bought, they have a high price, and dissemination of their consequences is less than dissemination of the consequences for their contenders.

The findings of this category of consumption are consistent with the available evidence; chiefly price sensitivity on the part of consumers, and therefore the weakness of interventions based primarily on the delivery of information – whether in the form of rules linking the context with the consequences or behavioral feedback (Foxall, 1995; Foxall et al., 2006). Moreover, the weakness of the theoretical construct of intent to purchase in predicting the actual purchasing behavior is also noteworthy.

To summarize, the findings of the studies reviewed, where consumption was analyzed in traditional channels for low socioeconomic strata, and pro-ecological consumption at all socioeconomic strata, allow us to draw the following conclusions:

1. The findings of BPM are consistent with data from other countries in the analysis of intra-consumer elasticity, inter-consumer elasticity, intra-brand elasticity and inter-brand elasticity.
2. Assessment of consumer reports indicates two major sources of explanation of consumption aspects; aspects related to the situation of choice and aspects related to attributes of brands. These reports are consistent with informational aspects and aspects of situations of consumption covered by BPM.
3. The environmental design with direct feedback on consumption practices is effective for changing consumption practices towards green brands on two categories of consumption.
4. Environmental design with feedback and information strategies is not enough to foster changes in consumption patterns in consumption categories where price is the most critical factor.
5. The behavior intention report in the case of change in consumption towards eco-friendly consumption alternatives turns out to be a measure of little predictive power in adopting this pattern of behavior.

Reflections on BPM from the regional research standpoint

The BPM is no stranger to the epistemological discussions which characterize psychology as a discipline and behavior analysis as a particular way of approaching the scientific practice of behavioral science. In this regard, the monographic volume of the *Behavior and Philosophy Journal* about the role of intentionality in explaining the behavior and the article about intentionality and BPM are examples of this.

Machado et al. (2000) argue that scientific knowledge is advanced by three kinds of research. To illustrate their interaction they use the metaphor of a triangle called the *epistemic triangle*. The epistemic triangle consists of three vertices which are the types of research/actions undertaken by scientists.

In one vertex lies research about facts, such as cumulative records of the time of consumption of products in a particular business category within a group of families, or a consumer's choice behavior. Another vertex contains theoretical investigations, the attempt of theorizing an explanation of the factual findings of research, such as the attempts of explanation of variability in the consumption of products under observation. Finally, the third vertex includes conceptual research; i.e. research on theories, their scope, their intelligibility and sensitive domains (Machado et al., 2000).

Theoretical systems are not purely empirical statements; while the findings of the panel studies are quintessential to show the usefulness of the BPM, the latter as a theoretical system is in turn composed of conceptual statements which not only point out specific aspects in the field of events, but also allow researchers to perform conceptual classification and organization of the phenomena recorded (Harzem & Miles, 1978).

Based on this context, the work of Medina Arboleda and Sandoval-Escobar (2011) aimed at a conceptual review of the BPM. To do so, the aforementioned authors identified the conceptual categories and changes in these conceptual categories over time. They then conducted a review of the categories identified in the theoretical review, and finally suggested several changes in the conceptual categories of the BPM. The changes are intended to contribute to the consolidation of a model to analyze economic exchange from a set of assumptions and forecasts consistent with behavioral economics on the one hand, and behavior analysis on the other.

To foster unity of the names and categories of the BPM, a review was conducted of articles written from 1974 to 2011 in which conceptual categories of BPM are presented as well as the different definitions presented in each item thereof. The body of theoretical analysis was composed of 10 articles; Table 13.2 presents said summary of categories and the frequency of occurrence thereof in said articles.

As expected in a model which includes references for over 20 years, the BPM has changed the conceptual categories it presents, as well as their definition; Table 13.3 presents the changes identified in this model.

The work of conceptual revision allows several suggestions to be made with regard to the conceptual management model when it comes to the academic tradition it belongs to, as well as a series of recommendations for researchers who want to carry out their research under this perspective (Medina & Sandoval, 2011).

When it comes to purchasing behavior, the suggestion is for researchers to limit the behaviors analyzed under the perspective of consumer psychology to those in which an economic exchange occurs. This observation takes place in terms of the initial scope of the model; albeit

Table 13.2 Conceptual categories most frequently addressed in BPM articles

Conceptual categories	Frequency
Purchasing behavior	9/10
Behavioral context or scenario	9/10
Informational reinforcement	9/10
Utilitarian reinforcement	8/10
Aversive consequences	3/10
Hedonic reinforcement	1/10
Informational consequences	1/10
Utilitarian consequences	1/10
History of reinforcement	1/10
Aversive consequences	3/10

Source: Medina and Sandoval (2011)

Table 13.3 Conceptual variations in the BPM model (1992–2007)

Source	Categories presented	Variations
Foxall (1992)	Purchasing behavior	
	Behavioral context	
	Informational reinforcement	
	Hedonic reinforcement	
Foxall (1997)	Purchasing behavior	Elimination of the hedonic reinforcement category
	Context behavior	
	Utilitarian reinforcement	
	Informational reinforcement	
Foxall (1998)	Purchasing behavior	Utilitarian reinforcement as use value
	Behavioral context	Inclusion of aversive consequences such as transaction costs
	Informational reinforcement	
	Utilitarian reinforcement	
	Aversive consequences	
Greenley and Foxall (2000)	Purchasing behavior	The category of aversive consequences is maintained
	Context behavior	The term "reinforcement" is tied to profits
	Informational reinforcement	
	Utilitarian reinforcement	
	Aversive consequences	
Foxall et al. (2004)	Purchasing behavior	Elimination of the category of aversive consequences
	Context behavior	
	Informational reinforcement	
	Utilitarian reinforcement	
Foxall et al. (2005)	Purchasing behavior	Elimination of the category of aversive consequences
	Context behavior	Informational reinforcement as feedback on utilitarian benefits
	Informational reinforcement	
	Utilitarian reinforcement	
Foxall, et al. (2006)	Context behavior	Inclusion of the category of consequences
	Informational consequences	Elimination of informational reinforcement and utility
	Utilitarian consequences	
Yani-de-Soriano and Foxall (2006)	Purchasing behavior	Consequences categories eliminated
	Informational reinforcement	Aversive consequences category eliminated
	Utilitarian reinforcement	
Foxall et al. (2007a)	Purchasing behavior	Reincorporation of the categories of utilitarian and informational reinforcement
	Context behavior	
	Learning history	Aversive consequences such as transaction costs
	Informational reinforcement	

	Utilitarian reinforcement	Categories of informational punishment and utilitarian punishment are presented in the graph, not the article
	Aversive consequences	
Foxall (2007a)	Scenario behavior	Elimination of informational punishment from the graph
	Learning history	
	Informational reinforcement	Presentation of aversive consequences in the graph, but lack of definition in the article
	Utilitarian reinforcement	

Source: Medina and Sandoval (2011)

as a model of choice it can be applied to different contexts, it is crucial to emphasize that operant behavior implies BPM analysis as a necessary condition – at least for Western economic systems – the acquisition of goods or payment of a stipulated price for the same service. It is also important to point this out as panel studies and exercises to achieve comparability between the matching laws from laboratory studies on the analysis of demand take price as a counterpart to the response (Foxall, 2007).

As regards the consequences, albeit the article by Foxall et al. (2006) uses the denomination of consequences as a noun (reinforcers and punishers) so that in both cases a difference is made between informational consequences and utilitarian consequences, this description is not predominant in the model. Indeed, recent publications by Foxall (2011) use the terms "reinforcement" and "punishment". These names are used in the tradition of learning psychology, usually with an objective description of the process (reinforcing behavior), i.e. on the outcome of the application of consequences, not like the consequences per se. To make this analytical distinction, Medina and Sandoval (2011) propose maintaining the denomination by consequences – typical of a synchronic analysis – and using the denominations reinforcement and punishment whenever the object of analysis is diachronic in nature.

It is also important to note that the notion of learning history as a factor in graphical presentations of the model is related to consumer behavior, but not the situation of consumption. This type of presentation when training researchers in the field promotes learning history as being linked to the memory of the purchasing process by the consumer. In this regard, it is worth thinking about a review that places learning history as an update of psychological functions of the context (excitatory and inhibitory psychological functions fostered by experience with the situation), rather than a factor that is conceptually and graphically differentiated from the situation (Medina and Sandoval, 2011).

With the suggestions above, the model is expected to gain accuracy (specific operant behavior), differentiating it from the type of behavior analysis according to time, allowing us to identify when the study is a synchronic interaction or a process which is diachronic in nature, and finally to avoid confusion regarding the ontological status of learning history, thus causing it to be analyzed as a present psychological function and not as an internal construct for the retrieval of information.

Finally, and from the evidence presented, the BPM has strong support, at least in the case of Colombia. This adds validity to its methodological and conceptual framework as an alternative analysis for consumer behavior in economic and social conditions which are dissimilar to those where it was developed, allowing researchers to approach the phenomena of purchase, saving and eco-friendly consumption from a monistic perspective, focusing on behavior, and with ample empirical support.

References

Agudelo, M. and Barreto, I. (2014). *Influencia de un Programa de Educación Ambiental Sobre el Consumo de Marcas Verdes en Hogares de Nivel Socio Económico 2, 3, 4 y 5 de la Ciudad de Bogotá. Tesis de Maestría en Psicología del consumidor.* Bogotá, Colombia: Fundación Universitaria Konrad Lorenz.

Barreiros, R., Oliveira-Castro, J. and Conque Seco, D. (2011). What consumers say and do: planned and actual amounts bought in relation to brand benefits. *The Service Industries Journal, 31*, 2559–2570.

Barreto, I. and Sandoval, M. (2013). *Análisis longitudinal de los factores determinantes de la efectividad de un programa de comportamiento sustentable (CS) en el desarrollo de patrones de compra, uso y disposición de bienes de consumo y servicios públicos en hogares bogotanos.* Bogotá, Colombia: Proyecto financiado por COLCIENCAS.

Conque Seco, D. and Oliveira-Castro, J. (2011). Effects of background music on consumer behaviour: behavioural account of the consumer setting, *The Service Industries Journal, 31*(15), 2571–2585.

Crouch, S. and Housden, M. (2003). *Marketing Research for Managers* (3rd ed.). Oxford: Butterworth-Heinemann.

Deloitte Touche Tohmatsu (2013). Estudio anual Navidad 2013: Percepciones sobre los hábitos de consumo de los latinoamericanos. http://webserver2.deloitte.com.co/industrias/Encuesta%20Consumo%20en%20Navidad%202013%20-%20Latinoam%C3%A9rica.pdf

Desarrollo Económico de la Comisión Económica para América Latina y el Caribe (CEPAL) (2014). La elaboración de la edición de 2014 estuvo encabezada por Jürgen Weller, Oficial a Cargo de la División. http://repositorio.cepal.org/bitstream/handle/11362/36891/S1420037_es.pdf?sequence=1

Ehrenberg, A., Goodhardt, G. and Barwise, P. (1990). Double Jeopardy revisited. *Journal of Marketing, 54*, 82–91.

Ehrenberg, A., Uncles, M. and Goodhardt, G. (2004). Understanding brand performance measures: using Dirichlet benchmarks. *Journal of Business Research, 57*, 1307–1325.

Foxall, G. R. (1990). *Consumer Psychology in Behavioural Perspective.* London/New York: Routledge.

Foxall, G. R. (1992). The Behavioral Perspective Model of purchase and consumption: from consumer theory to marketing practice. *Journal of the Academy of Marketing Science, 20*, 189–198. doi: 10.1177/0092070392202009

Foxall, G. R. (1995). Environment-impacting consumer behavior: an operant analysis. *Advances in Consumer Research, 22*, 262–268.

Foxall, G. R. (1997). *Marketing Psychology: The Paradigm in the Wings.* London: Macmillan.

Foxall, G. R. (1998). Radical behaviorist interpretation: generating and evaluating an account of consumer behavior. *The Behaviour Analyst, 21*, 321–354.

Foxall, G. R. (1999). The substitutability of brands. *Managerial and Decision Economics, 20*, 241–257.

Foxall, G. R. (2001). Foundations of consumer behaviour analysis. *Marketing Theory, 1*, 165–169.

Foxall, G. R. (2004). *Consumer Psychology in Behavioral Perspective.* Frederick, MD: Beard Books (1st ed. 1990). London and New York: Routledge.

Foxall, G. R. (2007). Explaining consumer choice: coming to terms with intentionality. *Behavioural Processes, 75*, 129–145.

Foxall, G. R. (2011). Brain, emotion and contingency in the explanation of consumer behaviour. *International Review of Industrial and Organizational Psychology, 26*, 47–92.

Foxall, G. R. and Greenley, G. (2000). Predicting and explaining responses to consumer environments: an empirical test and theoretical extension of the behavioural perspective model. *The Service Industries Journal, 20*, 39–63.

Foxall, G. R., Oliveira-Castro, J. and Schrezenmaier, T. (2004). The behavioral economics of consumer brand choice: patterns of reinforcement and utility maximization. *Behavioural Processes, 66*, 235–260.

Foxall, G., Oliveira-Castro, J., James, V. and Schrezenmaier, T. (2007). Consumer Behaviour Analysis and the Behavioural Perspective Model. *Management Online Review*, European School of Management, www.morexpertise.com.

Foxall, G. R., Oliveira-Castro, J. O., James, V. K., Yani-de-Soriano, M. M. and Sigurdsson, V. (2006). Consumer behavior analysis and social marketing: the case of environmental conservation. *Behavior and Social Issues, 15*(1), 101–124.

Foxall, G. R. and Yani-de-Soriano, M. (2005). Situational influences on consumers' attitudes and behavior. *Journal of Business Research*, *58*, 518–525.

García-Landa, C. and Montero, M. (2013). Propuesta de medición para toma de decisiones sobre el consumo de energía eléctrica. *Revista Latinoamericana de Psicología*, *45*, 375–388.

Garzón, C., Barreto, I. and Sandoval, M. (2014). *Efectividad de un programa de comportamiento sustentable en la compra y el consumo de alimentos transgénicos y marcas verdes. Tesis de Maestría en Psicología del Consumidor.* Bogotá, Colombia: Fundación Universitaria Konrad Lorenz.

Gifford, R. (2014). Environmental psychology matters. *Annual Review of Psychology*, *65*, 541.

Harzem, P. and Miles, T. R. (1978). *Conceptual Issues in Operant Psychology.* London: John Wiley & Sons.

Kantar Worldpanel (2013). Situación de los canales en Latinoamérica. http://www.kantarworldpanel.com/co/Noticias/Situacin-de-los-canales-en-Latinoamrica

Logue, A. W. (1995). *Self-Control: Waiting Until Tomorrow For What You Want Today.* Englewood Cliffs, NJ: Prentice Hall.

Nielsen Homescan (2014). Consumo de saludables se sigue afianzando en las compras de los consumidores latinoamericanos. http://www.nielsen.com/co/es/insights/news/2014/saludables.html

Machado, A., Lourenço, O. and Silva, J. (2000). Facts, concepts, and theories: the shape of psychology's epistemic triangle. *Behavior and Philosophy*, *28*, 1–40.

Medina Arboleda, I. F. M. and Sandoval-Escobar, M. (2011). Modelo de la perspectiva conductual: análisis y revisión conceptual. *Revista Latinoamericana de Psicología*, *43*, 429–442.

Medina Arboleda, I. and Páramo, P. (2014). La investigación en educación ambiental en América Latina: un análisis bibliométrico. *Revista Colombiana De Educación*, *66*, 55–72. http://revistas.pedagogica.edu.co/index.php/RCE/article/view/2586

Oliveira-Castro, J. M., Conque Seco, D., Foxall, G. R. and Schrezenmaier, T. (2005). Dynamics of repeat buying for packaged food products. *Journal of Marketing Management*, *21*, 37–61.

Oliveira-Castro, J. M., Foxall, G. R., James, V. K., Roberta, H. B. F., Pohl, M. B., Dias, B. and Chang, S. W. (2008). Consumer-based brand equity and brand performance. *Service Industries Journal*, *28*, 445–461.

Oliveira-Castro, J. M., Foxall, G. R. and Schrezenmaier, T. (2005). Patterns of consumer response to retail price differentials. *Service Industries Journal*, *25*, 1–27.

Oliveira-Castro, J. M., Foxall, G. R. and Schrezenmaier, T. C. (2006). Consumer brand choice: individual and group analyses of demand elasticity. *Journal of the Experimental Analysis of Behavior*, *85*, 147–166.

Phol, R. and Oliveira-Castro, J. (2008). Efeitos do Nível Efeitos do Nível de Benefício Informativo das Marcas sobre a Duração do Comportamento de Procura. *RAC-Eletrônica Curitiba*, *2*, 449–469.

Rangel, E., Cevallos, T. and Ruiz, E. (2013). Variables determinantes de la lealtad a la marca: una aproximación empírica. Contribuciones a la Economía, Noviembre 2013. www.eumed.net/ce/2013/lealtad-marca.html

Sandoval, M. (2012). Comportamiento sustentable y educación ambiental: una visión desde las prácticas culturales. *Revista Latinoamericana de Psicología*, *44*, 181–196.

Sandoval, M., Díaz, G., Cortés, O., Rincón, J., Ramírez, N., Piñeros, Torres, M. and Vargas, C. (2006). La influencia de la experiencia de compra, el ingreso y la información sobre los procesos de decisión en un procedimiento de elección discreta. *Suma Administrativa*, *1*, 9–60.

Sandoval, M., Robayo, O., Rincón, J. C. and Cortés, O. F. (2010). Patrones de elección de marca en función de los cambios en los niveles de refuerzo utilitario e informacional en categorías de productos de consumo masivo. *Revista Latinoamericana de Psicología*, *41*, 497–517.

Sergueyevna, N. (2013) Demographic, cultural and psychographic consumer characteristics of Central America. *Revista Negotium*, *9*, 21–36.

Uncles, M., Ehrenberg, A. and Hammond, K. (1995). Patterns of buyer behavior: regularities, models and extensions. *Marketing Science*, *14*, 71–87.

Veiga Neto, A. and Melo, L. (2013). Factors influencing children's food purchasing behaviour. *Saude e Sociedade*, *22*, 441–455.

Yani-de-Soriano, M. and Foxall, G. R. (2006). The emotional power of place: the fall and rise of dominance in retail research. *Journal of Retailing and Consumer Services*, *13*, 403–416.

Part III
Behavioral interpretation of consumer choice

Gambling behavior

Mark R. Dixon and Jordan Belisle

Introduction

Every day is the same for Evan. Evan wakes up around the same time each day, which isn't hard to do because he rarely leaves the house. When he does leave the house, it is for one of two reasons: to get food or to gamble. Evan gambles twice a day, every day, at the exact same time each day. He walks into the casino – so many options and nothing but time. He sniffs around searching for the perfect game. Perhaps the next press of a lever will be the one that produces the contents of his dreams. He chooses the high-risk machine – he always chooses the high-risk machine. High risk, high reward. He has been losing a lot recently, so a win must be just around the corner. He presses the lever, this is it. He feels so close to winning that he can taste it. Just another second. Nothing, try again. Evan has not won in a very long time. Occasionally he wins something, but he used to win much more often. He used to play more conservatively and at this particular casino, playing conservatively is the optimal strategy. Evan moved on from "playing the odds" to adopting a more high-risk strategy when scientists began injecting Evan with a serotonergic receptor agonist (8-OH-DPAT) that has been shown to contribute to disordered gambling (Grant & Potenza, 2007; Marazziti et al., 2008). Evan is a rat, and may have been one of 32 male Long-Evans rats that were subjects in a study examining the interaction between reinforcement, punishment, and neurochemical manipulations on choice behavior in a "rat gambling task" (Zeeb et al., 2009). In this experiment at the University of British Columbia, rats were placed in an apparatus with four concurrently available machines that dispensed sugar pellets. The machines were different in that they delivered smaller or larger amounts of pellets at varying probabilities and resulted in a punishing time-out period when wins did not occur. The reinforcement and punishment schedules were arranged such that optimal decision making necessitated choosing the smaller and more probabilistic choice to have the most pellets at the end of a 30-minute interval. The rats, like most people in similar gambling tasks, made the choices that optimized their reward (i.e., smaller, more probable). It wasn't until they were administered drugs that stimulated neurochemical changes similar to the neurochemical differences observed in disordered gamblers that the rats behaved less optimally.

Of course, the neurochemical makeup of disordered gamblers and their habitual gambling behaviors are not the product of drug injections by scientists in lab coats. The source of their addiction cannot be found exclusively inside their brains as they deviate from others. Many of the neurological mechanisms underlying disordered gambling are also present where there are symptomatically different addictions. If all addictions were directly caused by events within the skin, then why aren't all disordered gamblers also addicted to heroin? We know that their brains are different and that their gambling behavior is suboptimal, but how did they become that way? Two percent of adults have a gambling addiction, and this percentage has been rising since the 1980s (Williams et al., 2012). Gambling is an enterprise that generates more revenue than "movies, spectator sports, theme parks, cruise ships and recorded music combined" (Frontline, 1996). For many people gambling is a recreational activity that is only a small part of their lives, but for a portion of the population gambling is ruining their lives one bet at a time. A considerable amount of research has been conducted to better understand the sources of gambling addictions and treatments for them, and several models exist across many levels of analysis that provide more or less comprehensive accounts of disordered gambling.

The environment–behavior interaction

Watson (1913) spearheaded a movement in psychology that laid the foundation for the emergence of behaviorism in the early 1900s when he proposed that behavior, rather than the subjective consciousness, ought to be the datum of interest. From then on the field was not so concerned with what people experienced internally, but rather what they did after a stimulating condition. B. F. Skinner (1966) refocused the analysis by adding significant discussion regarding the effects of consequences, and not just the preceding stimuli of Watson. Thirty years later, Johnston and Pennypacker (1993) put forth a definition of behavior whereby it "is characterized by detectable displacement in space through time of some part of the organism and that results in measurable change in at least one aspect of the environment" (p. 363). This definition is important for several reasons. It specifies that behavior is detectable movement, meaning that it must be directly measurable. A scientific analysis requires a quantifiable unit, and detectable displacement allows for quantification that does not require a reference to something occurring at some other place at some other time. The second criterion specified in the definition suggests that behavior must interact with the environment in an equally measurable way. As we seek to understand what is in the "mind" of the gambler, the solution is counterintuitive, for we need to examine what is outside of the gambler. The environment is where we shall find our answers. It is the gambling environment itself that produces the gambling event. Interestingly, non-gambling environments may also participate in the eventual gamble as well.

The environment as it pertains to gambling can be thought of as occurring in two contexts: within the gambling context and outside of it. Within the gambling context are environmental variables that are immediately present in the setting in which gambling occurs. Stimuli within the gambling environment include things like a casino layout, the reels of a slot machine, and momentary wins and losses. They are the things that affect the gambler in the moment, and are most in line with a molecular analysis of gambling behavior. Contextual events outside of the environment include environmental variables that exist more broadly and are often not present in the immediate gambling setting. These variables include things like a less than pleasurable job, a dysfunctional home life, or the accumulation of debt. These contextual events are most in line with a molar analysis of gambling behavior. They are the aggregate outcomes of many responses and behaviors over the course of an individual's learning history. Disordered gambling does not occur in a vacuum, and analyses at both of these levels are important for understanding its development.

Casino environments have many similarities to experimental operant chambers typically used with rats, pigeons, and other nonhuman organisms. A gambler enters the chamber, expends tokens and effort to pull a lever or press a button, and is subject to a conditioned reinforcing visual array in the form of spinning wheels and flashing lights and may receive monetary reinforcement on some programmed schedule. Skinner (1974) suggested that "all gambling systems are based on variable-ratio schedules, although their effects are usually attributed to thoughts and feelings" (p. 67). Skinner's analysis of gambling as a product of variable-ratio schedules highlights an intuitive explanation of why people gamble from a behavioral perspective. Within this conceptualization, gamblers are reinforced around an average number of spins with a monetary reward of some amount. Researchers have generally moved on from this conceptualization, suggesting that it is not variable-ratio schedules that maintain problem gambling, but rather random-ratio schedules (Knapp, 1976; Schwartz, 1992). A random-ratio schedule is distinct from a variable-ratio schedule in that the results of previous spins do not modify the probability of a win on subsequent spins. On a variable-ratio schedule, the probability of reinforcement increases the further the response count gets from the schedule requirement. As an example, imagine that you are on your ninety-ninth unreinforced response on a variable-ratio 3 schedule; you would be correct in saying that the hundredth response is likely to be reinforced. On a random-ratio schedule, this is not the case. Each response must be viewed independently, with the same probability of reinforcement associated with each individual response. Armour and Bizo (2014) provide a mathematical model of gambling behavior under a random-ratio reinforcement schedule, suggesting that the response rate of gamblers fits a bitonic response gradient, which matches similar results obtained with humans in non-gambling tasks under random-ratio requirements (e.g., Bizo et al., 2002). The mistaken belief that variable-ratio schedules are in operation instead of random-ratio schedules may be the reason that gamblers think that a win is hiding just around the corner, but the reality of the random-ratio schedule is that the chance of a win this time is never greater than it was the last time.

The reinforcement schedules that maintain disordered gambling were originally discovered in laboratory settings with more basic animals, like rats and pigeons. Humans, however, have developed a capacity for language that complicates the analysis further. Humans think. They ruminate on the past, worry about the future, and make predictions. They think that they can "beat the odds" if they play at the right time or that their "luck" will somehow change if they just keep spinning the reels. They develop irrational strategies that have been superstitiously reinforced (Lund, 2011) in ways that confer no true advantage. Skinner (1966) offered rule-governed behavior as an explanatory model for why overt and covert verbal behavior mediate the probability of other behaviors. Rule-governed behavior is a verbal behavior that occurs either in the environment or at the covert level that specifies a contingency. Dixon et al. (2000) demonstrated that rules, whether accurate or inaccurate, can have an effect on both the riskiness of participants' gambling decisions and their length of play. In this experiment, the authors recruited 45 undergraduate students to play a computerized version of roulette. Following a baseline condition, the participants were divided into three groups where they either received no rules, accurate rules, or inaccurate rules. All of the participants then completed a mandatory set of spins followed by the option to continue playing for 25 more spins. The study revealed that participants who were given inaccurate rules made riskier decisions than participants who received either accurate rules or no rules at all. In addition, participants who were given either accurate or inaccurate rules played for longer than participants who were not given any rules. The results of the experiment are important because rules may serve as augments (Hayes et al., 1987) that increase risk-taking behavior in a gambling context. In a casino, gamblers are bombarded with rules from fellow gamblers or advertisements posted in and around the casino. They are shown images of a jackpot winner surrounded by attractive people, holding money that he has just won, standing in front of the car that he will most certainly buy. These instructions specify the contingencies of continued play, but in a gambling context these instructions are incomplete and misleading. Narayanan and Manchanda (2012) suggest that individuals with gambling addictions are also the most affected by these marketing strategies, which highlights the potentially large contribution of rule governance in their gambling behavior.

Research from Relational Frame Theory (Hayes et al., 2001) has further highlighted the role of verbal behavior on the development of disordered gambling (Dymond & Roche, 2010). Relational frame theory provides a behavior analytic model of how verbal behavior may both interact with, and potentially overcome, the random-ratio contingencies of casino games. There are two aspects of Relational Frame Theory that have especial utility in a study of gambling behavior – derived relational responding and the transformation of stimulus functions. Derived relational responding is the process through which verbally sophisticated people learn inter-connected networks, or relations, that are not all directly trained and are formally dissimilar (arbitrarily related). To illustrate, if you are taught that a Stimulus A is related to a Stimulus B, and that a Stimulus B is related to a Stimulus C, you will likely derive that Stimulus A is also related to Stimulus C. For example, if you are taught that "Ben" is a dog (A-B) and that dogs have tails (B-C), you also know that Ben has a tail (B-C). An analysis of gambling from a Relational Frame Theory perspective becomes especially relevant when transformations of stimulus function are included in the analysis. A transformation of stimulus function occurs when the psychological functions of class members transform the function of other members. To continue with the example, if you are deathly afraid of dogs, you are likely to be deathly afraid of Ben as well, despite never having met Ben. The name Ben may even be enough to elicit a physiological fear response where previously "Ben" was a neutral stimulus.

In the context of gambling, Zlomke and Dixon (2006) demonstrated that a gambler's prefer-ence for one slot machine over another can be conditionally trained using the relations "greater than" and "less than". Participants completed a simulated computerized gambling task that pre-sented two concurrently available slot machines, where one was blue and the other was yellow. The participants gambled on the slot machines before and after a relational training task. In the relational training task, the participants were taught to select the "greater" of two stimuli when presented with a yellow contextual cue, and the "lesser" of two stimuli when presented with a blue contextual cue. When the participants returned to the gambling task, eight of the nine participants showed a preference for the yellow machine. The results of this study have been replicated with various relational training strategies (e.g., Hoon et al., 2008), contingency reversals (Nastally & Dixon, 2010), and disordered and non-disordered gamblers (Hoon & Dymond, 2013). The rules generated in these tasks are not directly stated, but rather are derived by the gamblers themselves under pre-arranged environmental contingencies. These within-context environmental variables are largely believed to be the things that maintain gambling behavior once people have crossed through the doors of a casino. Research pertaining to within-context environmental variables, however, does not speak to why gamblers actually go to the casino in the first place.

Gambling is not the problem; it is the outcome of a bigger problem. The notion that gam-bling is not really a gambler's problem seems puzzling. Yet consider that many persons with addictive disorders who undergo treatment find themselves simply swapping one addiction for another (Blaszczynski et al., 2008). Instead of examining the maladaptive behavior as the cause, we should consider a behavior such as disordered gambling as the outcome of something deeper. When we stick to exploring the behavior in isolation, we ignore the key factors of the Behavioral Perspective Model (BPM). A key factor of the BPM is a focus on a functional clas-sification of behavior rather than a syndromal classification of behavior, which is commonplace in addiction treatment and research. Syndromal classifications are concerned with what a behav-ior looks like. Behavior function, conversely, is concerned with the environmental conditions that maintain single or multiple topographies of behavior. Personality psychologists suggest that there exists an "addictive personality" type, but this phenomenon may simply be the product of a variety of "addictive" behavior topographies that are under the control of the same function. Function is concerned with "why" people do things. If we stop asking "what", we may begin to answer "why".

The Gambling Functional Assessment (GFA; Dixon & Johnson, 2007) and the Gambling Functional Assessment – Revised (GFA-R; Weatherly et al., 2011) are psychometric tools that were developed to categorize gambling behavior based on function. The original GFA was designed to measure four functions of gambling behavior, including tangible, social, sensory, and escape. A great deal of the existing literature has focused on the role of tangible reinforcers in the form of money or credits in the maintenance of gambling behavior, but tangible reinforcers can also take the form of all of the free things, like drinks and hotel accommodations, that casinos hand out to entice gamblers. Moreover, functions other than tangible reinforcers also play a significant role, if not an even greater role, in the maintenance of disordered gambling. Some people gamble to escape. They gamble to escape temporarily from a less than pleasurable home life. They may even gamble to escape thoughts that they have about gambling. They may also seek sensory reinforcement when their lives lack excitement. Winning not only produces flashing lights and colorful sounds, but it also produces increases in heart rate and neurochemical changes in the brain (Potenza, 2013). The social rewards of gambling also cannot be ignored. People congratulate others when they achieve a big win, and some games like craps even have an embedded social component. It is likely that disordered gamblers also get attention from others who feel bad for them when they gamble. They beg for forgiveness and promise to do better, propagating a cycle that is analogous to that found in abusive relationships. The GFA-R simplifies the functional assessment of the GFA by suggesting only two functions of gambling behavior, positive reinforcement and escape. This simplification was made to account for psychometric deficits in the GFA, which increased the construct validity of the assessment tool (Weatherly et al., 2012). The modifications made to the GFA-R also allowed Weatherly and Terrell (2014) to discover a very interesting distinction between the function of gambling for disordered gamblers relative to non-disordered gamblers. The distinction was that the gambling behavior of non-disordered gamblers was largely maintained by positive reinforcement; however, the gambling behavior of disordered gamblers was significantly more escape maintained. However, Dixon and Wilson (in review) have developed the GFA-2, which has been reported to eliminate even more critical shortcomings of the GFA-R, and maintain the construct validity of a four-factor model (attention, sensory, escape, and tangible) which keeps in line with the functional assessment literature more broadly described.

The notion of gambling being maintained by the removal of aversive states of the gambler instead of acquiring monetary reinforcement does seem in line with Hayes et al. (1996), who suggest that the escape-maintained nature of behavior is grounded in the functional dimension of experiential avoidance. Within this conceptualization, the various topographies of addictive behaviors are largely viewed as unhealthy attempts to avoid or escape aversive events in the present moment. Aversive events can be things that are happening in the environment, or private events occurring beneath the skin. Whatever they are, engaging in behaviors such as gambling can momentarily provide an escape from the aversive thoughts and feelings occurring here-and-now. In fact, a study conducted by Wilson et al. (2014) suggests that many people would rather administer electric shocks to themselves than spend 6–15 minutes in a room alone with nothing to do but think. Hayes suggests that experiential avoidance is ubiquitous in part because we discount future punishment for immediate escape, and this merely serves to exacerbate the underlying problem. Disordered gamblers frequently report that they gamble to regulate the occurrence of unwanted private events (Wood & Griffiths, 2007), and Riley (2014) provided evidence suggesting that disordered gamblers also exhibited high rates of experiential avoidance and thought suppression. We already know where gamblers are running to, but we need to ask where gamblers are running from. If we can answer this question then we may be able to solve the gambling epidemic, and the lives of those affected by the contingencies that gambling provides.

The advance of gambling technologies and contemporary issues

Take a walk through any modern casino, or many local restaurants, and you will see that the landscape of gambling has changed considerably over the past two decades. Gone are the days of three-reel slot machines with manual reels and a lever; they have been replaced with computerized alternatives that display an interface that is more like watching a movie than playing a simple game of chance. The advance of technology has led to contemporary issues that must be considered in an analysis of disordered gambling. The game has changed since Skinner's 1974 discussion of variable-ratio schedules. Not only are the games more complex, but they are also everywhere. Opportunities to gamble can be found in bars, restaurants, and even online. If we hope to solve the gambling problem, our research and clinical technologies will have to evolve alongside gambling technology.

In 1989, the computer algorithms used by one slot-machine manufacturer were brought before the Nevada Gaming Commission (Nevada Gaming Commission, 1989). It was revealed that the manufacturers had embedded near-misses into the algorithm at a rate of five near-misses for every total loss (Harrigan, 2007). The Nevada Gaming Commission ruled that the technique used by the manufacturing company was "unacceptable", and it has been a common understanding that the intentional programming of excessive near-misses is a banned practice in casinos. A near-miss occurs when a gambler "almost" wins. In the case of a three-reel slot machine, a near-miss occurs when two of the same symbol appear on the line. It seems intuitive that a near-miss is somehow closer to a win than a total loss; however, neither a near-miss nor a total loss ever result in monetary gain. Following near-misses, gamblers report that they feel closer to a win (Dixon & Schreiber, 2004) and research suggests that there is an increased likelihood that gamblers will continue to play even when wins stop occurring if there are frequent near-misses (MacLin et al., 2007). Neurological data have also shown that near-misses produce chemical changes in the brain similar to those produced by wins, and that these changes are especially apparent in disordered gamblers (Habib & Dixon, 2010). Despite the ruling of the Nevada Gambling Commission in 1989, near-misses still occur in casinos more frequently than would be expected by chance alone (Harrigan, 2009). They occur because virtual reel mapping of near-misses above and below the payout line is still acceptable on contemporary slot machines.

Virtual reel mapping has also made possible a specific type of near-miss – losses disguised as wins (LDWs). Now it is standard to present gamblers with anywhere from one to 20 "bet lines" that increase the probability of receiving a payout on any given turn. Although betting on multiple lines means that there are more ways to win, it also means that there are more ways to lose. LDWs rely on the momentary reluctance of a gambler to do math. Simply put, betting on multiple lines costs more money than betting on a single line. An LDW occurs when the payout from a win does not equal or exceed the total amount bet. When this happens, it appears as though the gambler has won money as the lights flash and credits are added to the game, but the gambler is no further ahead than they were before they spun. Gamblers often misinterpret LDWs as real wins (Jensen et al., 2013), and experimental research has shown that gamblers are more likely to play machines that offer multiple bet lines and will over-estimate the number of times that they actually win during a fixed number of trials (Dixon et al., 2014). The computerization of the user interface presented to gamblers has brought near-misses back to life, and highlights the fact that the images displayed on the screen are just a distraction from the real contingencies at play.

Technology has grown considerably within the casino, but a great deal of gambling does not even take place inside a casino at all. Opportunities to gamble are everywhere, from neighborhood bars to donut shops. The state of Illinois passed a bill in 2009 allowing for video gambling inside any institution with a liquor license, and video gambling has been fully operational since late 2012 (Gilroy, 2013). Since then, the prevalence of small gambling parlors has been on the rise in the state (Caufield & Stella, 2014), offering gamblers a place to gamble that is conveniently located and easy to access. Many similar deregulations have occurred globally in the past decade. Even more convenient, however, is internet gambling. Internet gambling has made it so convenient that gamblers do not even have to leave the comfort of their own home, where they are provided with constant access to unlimited gambling with no consumer protection. Online gambling refers to any form of gambling that takes place on the internet, including wagering and betting on "skill games". The ability to take part in online gambling on personal computers, tablets, and cell phones means that gambling options are always at your fingertips. Several studies have demonstrated that disordered gambling is far more common among internet gamblers (e.g., Brunelle et al., 2012), and internet gambling now accounts for 8 percent of all gambling revenue (Global Betting and Gaming Consultants, 2011). Internet gambling has also led to a rise in gambling in younger populations. Young gamblers are more likely to gamble online and to experience problems with gambling because of it (Gainsbury et al., 2013). They are more accustomed to the internet, and the internet provides a degree of anonymity that makes illegal gambling easier for gamblers who are underage. Global Betting and Gaming Consultants (2011) estimated that online gambling would generate US$43 billion in total revenue by 2015. Gambling is evolving and it is everywhere. We are only just now discovering the mechanisms that slot-machine manufacturers have recently added to encourage people to keep gambling when they should walk away: features such as multi-player games, movie and character-based games, and small denomination games with 100-plus payoff lines. Now more than ever, opportunities to gamble are everywhere and the within-gambling context is increasingly becoming blurred with life's context itself. If we hope to eliminate disordered gambling, we must continue to advance our understanding of these technologies and develop functional treatments to combat them.

Implications for gambling treatment and future research

In traditional behavioral fashion, research has preceded treatment approaches, thus leaving clinicians with few resources by which to optimally treat disordered gamblers. The challenge is to translate basic laboratory research into treatment protocols. Unfortunately, basic research on the sources of gambling addiction has not produced a great deal of translational research telling us exactly how to treat the problem (Dymond & Roche, 2010). This failure to translate may be because gambling is seen as the fault of the gambler. It is different than alcohol or illicit substance addictions because gamblers are not consuming a substance that is in itself addictive. In a sense, they "choose" to go to the casino and bet money that they do not have. Research at the neurological level has repeatedly shown, however, that the neurochemical changes that disordered gamblers undergo are identical to those of individuals with substance-based addictions. As well, this chapter has highlighted many of the ways that disordered gambling is the product of a behavior–environment interaction, and not just some dysfunction of the gambler. Regardless of the public's philosophies on autonomy and responsibility, disordered gambling is a socially relevant issue that needs to be addressed. Disordered gambling not only affects the life of the gambler, but can have a marked impact on family members and society (Walker, 2008).

For gambling treatment to be successful, it needs to focus on things that are not just about gambling. The BPM suggests that we need to explore how the context influences our choices. If we reserve our analysis to factors within the gambling context, then our efforts to treat problem gamblers are not likely to be fruitful. Researchers have provided suggestions for how casinos and businesses can detect problem gamblers (Pike, 2002) and deter their pathological play. This is unlikely, however, when doing so competes directly with a financial bottom line. Even if they were to make changes to the gambling context to deter disordered gambling, it may not be enough for two reasons. The first is that gambling is everywhere. Many casinos offer gamblers the ability to "ban themselves" from the casino and other casinos in the state. Having said that, it is easy to drive to another state or region to gamble, and it is even easier to open an online account and gamble from your own home. The second reason is that disordered gambling is not the problem; it is the outcome of a bigger problem. The context that produces disordered gambling is not just the context that gambling takes place in; it is the entire life of the gambler. It is for this reason that persons with addictions simply swap one addiction for another. It is not the symptoms of gambling, but rather its function that must be the focus of gambling treatments.

The events that gamblers are running from or to, either private or public, are bound to be idiosyncratic and largely unknown. Acceptance and Commitment Therapy (ACT) may provide a clinical tool that can deal with the underlying problems associated with disordered gambling. ACT is effective across an array of disorders because it does not treat the symptoms of the problem; it treats the function of the problem. The therapy was developed using a combination of acceptance and mindfulness techniques coupled with empirically supported behavior change strategies. The goal of ACT is not to decrease symptomology, but rather to increase psychological flexibility. Psychological flexibility is the ability for a person to contact the present moment and behave in a way that is congruent with their chosen values. ACT emerged from a growing body of literature in Relational Frame Theory, and uses metaphor, paradox, and experiential exercises to help clients see the incongruence between their actions and their values, and to commit to change. The major difference between ACT and other cognitive-behavior therapies is that ACT teaches people to accept their thoughts rather than suppress them. In the case of gambling, disordered gamblers are already trying to suppress their thoughts, so providing them with another way to do this may not be optimal.

Whiting and Dixon (2012) conducted a study on the effect of mental imagery on gambling persistence. In this study, undergraduate students were divided into two groups. The first group was required to imagine that they were gambling at a slot machine for 30 trials. They were instructed to imagine that they were pulling the lever and seeing the reels spin. The other group was required to imagine that they were putting coins into a laundry machine for the same number of trials. Both groups were then brought into a laboratory casino with real slot machines and asked to gamble, and were told that they could leave whenever they liked. The results of the study showed that the gambling imagery group actually stopped gambling significantly sooner. This study suggests that sitting with the potentially aversive thoughts of gambling – accepting thoughts as they come – may be effective at reducing the actual losses experienced in the casino setting. In fact, being willing to sit with the thoughts may be enough to keep people from going to the casino in the first place. Although preliminary, there is evidence supporting the potential effectiveness of ACT with disordered gamblers. Nastally and Dixon (2010) demonstrated that a single session of ACT delivered on the computer was sufficient to reduce participants' subjective ratings of the closeness of near-misses to total wins. The subjects were never informed of the near-miss effect, and changes in their subjective ratings were only observed after the ACT session. As the near-miss effect seems to be grounded in language (Dixon et al., 2009), the results suggest that ACT may be able to defuse some of the verbal behavior that contributes to phenomena like the near-miss effect. Mindfulness-based techniques have also been shown to increase the effectiveness of existing cognitive-behavioral therapies when used with disordered gamblers (e.g., Toneatto et al., 2014).

A considerable amount of research has been conducted in the area of disordered gambling, which is a good sign since a truly integrated model of gambling wasn't put forward until 2007 (Weatherly & Dixon, 2007; Weatherly & Flannery, 2008). Future research must pit the components of the BPM against each other to determine why people gamble, and how we can help them to reduce their gambling once it has become addictive. We must continue to explore aspects of the gambling setting itself. We know that gamblers win on a random-ratio schedule and that near-misses can also act as reinforcers, but what else is there? A recently developed slot machine actually allows multiple gamblers to play together, and community jackpots are embedded into the machine's programming. Contrivances like this most certainly play on the social function of gambling, and there may be utility in better understanding this function among others. Another avenue that researchers may explore is how information that gamblers are aware of affects their behavior in the gambling setting. Research has shown that instructions presented as rules affect gambling behavior, but we do not know how a gambler's knowledge of the probabilistic nature of gambling will affect their susceptibility to a gambling disorder. The greatest value, though, may be in understanding how the complex and ubiquitous nature of a person's life affects their gambling behavior. How does the perceived reinforcement from gambling compare to the reinforcement available in the rest of their life? Disordered gamblers are choosing to gamble, but they are also choosing not to do other things. What are those other things, and how can we make them more reinforcing? As we move forward, we must use what we know to affect the lives of people with gambling disorders, and those that are affected by their gambling behavior. The BPM provides a method for describing and predicting complex human behavior, and we must use this information to influence and improve the lives of people with addictions.

References

Armour, R. A., & Bizo, L. A. (2014). Modeling gambling: an application of the mathematical principles of reinforcement. *Analysis Of Gambling Behavior, 8*(1), 23–37.

Bizo, L. A., Remington, B., D'Souza, L. S., Heighway, S. K., & Baston, C. (2002). Human variable ratio performance. *Learning and Motivation, 33*, 411–432.

Blaszczynski, A., Walker, M., Sharpe, L., & Nower, L. (2008). Withdrawal and tolerance phenomenon in problem gambling. *International Gambling Studies, 8*, 181–194. doi: 10.1080/14459790802140007.

Brunelle, N., Leclerc, D., Cousineau, M., Dufour, M., Gendron, A., & Martin, I. (2012). Internet gambling, substance use, and delinquent behavior: an adolescent deviant behavior involvement pattern. *Psychology of Addictive Behaviors.* doi: 10.1037/a0027079.

Caufield, K., & Stella, R. (2014). Area video gaming parlors in jeopardy? NewsTribune. Retrieved from: http://newstrib.com/main.asp?SectionID=2&SubSectionID=232&ArticleID=38035.

Clark, L., Liu, R., McKavanagh, R., Garrett, A., Dunn, B. D., & Aitken, M. F. (2013). Learning and affect following near-miss outcomes in simulated gambling. *Journal of Behavioral Decision Making, 26*(5), 442–450. doi: 10.1002/bdm.1774.

Dixon, M. J., Graydon, C., Harrigan, K. A., Wojtowicz, L., Siu, V., & Fugelsang, J. A. (2014). The allure of multi-line games in modern slot machines. *Addiction, 109*(11), 1920–1928.

Dixon, M. R., Hayes, L. J., & Aban, I. B. (2000). Examining the roles of rule following, reinforcement, and preexperimental histories on risk-taking behavior. *Psychological Record, 50*(4), 687–704.

Dixon, M. R., & Johnson, T. E. (2007). The Gambling Functional Assessment (GFA): an assessment device for identification of the maintaining variables of pathological gambling. *Analysis of Gambling Behavior, 1*, 44–49.

Dixon, M. R., MacLin, O. H., & Daugherty, D. (2006). An evaluation of response allocations to concurrently available slot machine simulations. *Behavior Research Methods, 38*, 232–236.

Dixon, M. R., Nastally, B. L., Jackson, J. E., & Habib, R. (2009). Altering the near-miss effect in slot-machine gamblers. *Journal of Applied Behavior Analysis, 42,* 913–918.

Dixon, M. R., & Schreiber, J. E. (2004). Near-miss effects on response latencies and win estimations of slot machine players. *The Psychological Record, 45,* 335–348.

Dixon, M. R., Wilson, A. N., & Whiting, S. W. (2012). A preliminary investigation of relational network influence on horse-track betting. *Analysis of Gambling Behavior, 6*(1), 23–36.

Dymond, S., & Roche, B. (2010). The impact of derived relational responding on gambling behavior. *Analysis of Gambling Behavior, 4,* 38–53.

Frontline (1996). Statistics: Gambling facts and stats. Retrieved from: http://www.pbs.org/wgbh/pages/frontline/shows/gamble/etc/facts.html.

Fiorito, B. S. (2006). Calling a lemon a lemon: regulating electronic gambling machines to contain pathological gambling. *Northwestern University Law Review, 100,* 1325.

Foxall, G. R. (2010). *Interpreting Consumer Choice: The Behavioral Perspective Model.* New York: Routledge.

Gainsbury, S. M., Russell, A., Hing, N., Wood, R., & Blaszczynski, A. (2013). The impact of internet gambling on gambling problems: a comparison of moderate-risk and problem Internet and non-Internet gamblers. *Psychology of Addictive Behaviors, 27*(4), 1092–1101. doi: 10.1037/a0031475.

Gilroy, K. (2013). Video gambling: bad bet for Illinois communities. *The Regional News.* Retrieved from http://www.theregionalnews.com/index.php/opinion/columns/431-video-gambling-bad-bet-for-illinois-communities.

Global Betting and Gaming Consultants (2011). *Global Gaming Report* (6th ed.). Castletown, Isle of Man: GBGC.

Grant, J. E., & Potenza, M. N. (2007). Treatments for pathological gambling and other impulse control disorders. In: Nathan, P. & Gorman, J. (eds) *A Guide to Treatments That Work.* Oxford: Oxford University Press.

Habib, R., & Dixon, M. R. (2010). Neurobehavioral evidence for the "near-miss" effect in pathological gamblers. *Journal of the Experimental Analysis of Behavior, 93,* 313–328.

Harrigan, K. A. (2007). Slot machine structural characteristics: creating near misses using high award symbol ratios. *International Journal of Mental Health and Addiction, 6*(3), 353–368.

Harrigan, K. A. (2009). Slot machines: pursuing responsible gaming practices for virtual reels and near misses. *International Journal Of Mental Health & Addiction, 7*(1), 68–83. doi: 10.1007/s11469-007-9139-8.

Hayes, S. C., Wilson, K. G., Gifford, E. V., Follette, V. M., & Strosahl, K. (1996). Experiential avoidance and behavioral disorders: a functional dimensional approach to diagnosis and treatment. *Journal of Consulting and Clinical Psychology, 64*(6), 1152–1168.

Hayes, S. C., Zettle, R. D., & Rosenfarb, I. (1987). Rule-following. In: Hayes, S. C. (ed.) *Rule-Governed Behavior: Cognition, Contingencies, and Instructional Control.* New York: Plenum Press.

Hayes, S. C., Barnes-Holmes, D., & Roche, B. (2001). *Relational Frame Theory: A Post-Skinnerian Account of Human Language and Cognition.* New York: Kluwer Academic/Plenum Publishers.

Hoon, A., Dymond, S., Jackson, J. W., & Dixon, M. R. (2008). Contextual control of slot-machine gambling: replication and extension. *Journal of Applied Behavior Analysis, 41*(3), 467–470.

Hoon, A. E., & Dymond, S. (2013). Altering preferences for concurrently available simulated slot machines: nonarbitrary contextual control over gambling choice. *Analysis of Gambling Behavior, 7*(2), 35–52.

Jensen, C., Dixon, M. J., Harrigan, K. A., Sheepy, E., Fugelsang, J. A., & Jarick, M. (2013). Misinterpreting 'winning' in multi-line slot machine games. *International Journal of Gambling Studies, 13,* 112–126.

Johnston, J. M., & Pennypacker, H. S. (1993). *Strategies and tactics of behavioral research.* Hillside, NJ: Lawrence Erlbaum Associates, Inc.

Kassinove, J. I., & Schare, M. L. (2001). Effects of the 'near miss' and the 'big win' on persistence at slot machine gambling. *Psychology of Addictive Behaviors, 15*(2), 155–158. doi: 10.1037/0893-164X.15.2.155.

Knapp, T. J. (1976). A functional analysis of gambling behavior. *Gambling and Society,* 276–294.

Lund, I. (2011). Irrational beliefs revisited: exploring the role of gambling preferences in the development of misconceptions in gamblers. *Addiction Research & Theory, 19*(1), 40–46. doi: 10.3109/16066359.2010.493979.

MacLin, O., Dixon, M. R., Daugherty, D., & Small, S. L. (2007). Using a computer simulation of three slot machines to investigate a gambler's preference among varying densities of near-miss alternatives. *Behavior Research Methods, 39*(2), 237–241. doi: 10.3758/BF03193153.

Marazziti, D., Golia, F., Picchetti, M., Pioli, E., Mannari, P., Lenzi, F., & Dell'Osso, L. (2008). Decreased density of the platelet serotonin transporter in pathological gamblers. *Neuropsychobiology, 57*(1–2), 38–43. doi: 10.1159/000129665.

Narayanan, S., & Manchanda, P. (2012). An empirical analysis of individual level casino gambling behavior. *Quantitative Marketing and Economics, 10*(1), 27–62.

Nastally, B. L., & Dixon, M. R. (2010). The effect of relational training on the near-miss effect in slot machine players. *Analysis Of Gambling Behavior, 4*(1), 16–26.

Nevada Gaming Commission (1989). *Hearing to consider further action required pursuant to the declaratory ruling issued on December 1, 1988, by the Nevada Gaming Commission, as described therein, and in the Stipulation and Order approved by the Nevada Gaming Commission on September 22, 1988, in the matter of Universal Company, Ltd. and Universal Distributing of Nevada, Inc.*, Case No. 88–4. January 26, Las Vegas, Nevada. Sierra Nevada Reporters. pp. 212–308.

Petry, N. M., Wienstock, J., Ledgerwood, D., & Morasco, B. (2008). A randomized trial of brief interventions for problem and pathological gamblers. *Journal of Consulting and Clinical Psychology, 76,* 318–328.

Pike, C. (2002). Measuring video gambling: instrument development and validation. *Research on Social Work Practice, 12*(3), 389–407.

Potenza, M. N. (2013). Neurobiology of gambling behaviors. *Current Opinion in Neurobiology, 23*(23/4 Addiction), 660–667. doi: 10.1016/j.conb.2013.03.004.

Riley, B. (2014). Experiential avoidance mediates the association between thought suppression and mindfulness with problem gambling. *Journal of Gambling Studies, 30*(1), 163–171.

Schwartz, B. (1992). *Psychology of Learning and Behavior.* New York: Norton.

Skinner B. F. (1966). An operant analysis of problem solving. In: Kleinmuntz, B. (ed.) *Problem Solving: Research, Method and Theory* (pp. 133–171). New York: John Wiley & Sons.

Skinner, B. F. (1974). *About Behaviorism.* New York: Vintage Books.

Toneatto, T., Pillai, S., & Courtice, E. L. (2014). Mindfulness-enhanced cognitive behavior therapy for problem gambling: a controlled pilot study. *International Journal of Mental Health and Addiction, 12*(2), 197–205. doi: 10.1007/s11469-014-9481-6.

Walker, D. M. (2008). Classification of the social costs of gambling. *Journal of Public Budgeting, Accounting, & Financial Management, 20*(2), 141–152.

Watson, J. (1913). Psychology as the behaviorist views it. *Psychological Review, 20*(2), 158–177.

Weatherly, J. N., & Dixon, M. R. (2007). Toward an integrative behavioral model of gambling. *Analysis of Gambling Behavior, 1,* 4–18.

Weatherly, J. N., & Flannery, K. A. (2008). Facing the challenge: the behavior analysis of gambling. *The Behavior Analyst Today, 9*(2), 130–142. doi: 10.1037/h0100652.

Weatherly, J. N., Miller, J. C., Montes, K. S., & Rost, C. (2012). Assessing the reliability of the Gambling Functional Assessment – Revised. *Journal of Gambling Studies, 28,* 217–223. doi: 10.1007/s10899-0119275-8.

Weatherly, J. N., Miller, J. C., & Terrell, H. K. (2011). Testing the construct validity of the Gambling Functional Assessment – Revised. *Behavior Modification, 35,* 553–569. doi: 10.1177/0145445511416635.

Weatherly, J. N., & Terrell, H. K. (2014). Magnitude effects in delay and probability discounting when monetary and medical treatment outcomes are discounted. *The Psychological Record, 64*(3), 433–440.

Whiting, S. W., & Dixon, M. R. (2012). Effects of mental imagery on gambling behavior. *Journal of Gambling Studies, 29*(3), 525–534.

Williams, R. J., Volberg, R. A., & Stevens, R. M. G. (2012). *The Population Prevalence of Problem Gambling: Methodological Influences, Standardized Rates, Jurisdictional Differences, and Worldwide Trends.* Report prepared for the Ontario Problem Gambling Research Centre and the Ontario Ministry of Health and Long Term Care. May 2012. http://hdl.handle.net/10133/3068.

Wilson, T. D., Reinhard, D. A., Westgate, E. C., Gilbert, D. T., Ellerbeck, N., Hahn, C., & Shaked, A. (2014). Just think: the challenges of the disengaged mind. *Science, 345*(6192), 75–77.

Wood, R., & Griffiths, M. (2007). A qualitative investigation of problem gambling as an escape-based coping strategy. *Psychology and Psychotherapy: Theory, Research and Practice, 80*(1), 107–125.

Zeeb, F. D., Robbins, T. W., & Winstanley, C. A. (2009). Serotonergic and dopaminergic modulation of gambling behavior as assessed using a novel rat gambling task. *Neuropsychopharmacology, 34*(10), 2329–2343. doi: 10.1038/npp.2009.62.

Zlomke, K. R., & Dixon, M. R. (2006). Modification of slot-machine preferences through the use of a conditional discrimination paradigm. *Journal of Applied Behavior Analysis, 39*(3), 351–361.

15

When loss rewards

The near-miss effect in slot-machine gambling

Gordon R. Foxall and Valdimar Sigurdsson

Introduction

It is well established that slot-machine gamblers whose scores closely resemble a winning combination (but which objectively are losses) often seem encouraged thereby to continue playing (Côté et al., 2003; Griffiths, 1994; Reid, 1986; Skinner, 1953). Attempts to explain this "near-miss effect" often implicate neural functioning (e.g., Qi et al., 2011). After all, the same brain regions are recruited in the case of near-misses as are apparent for wins (notably the reward circuits of the midbrain dopaminergic system and the orbitofrontal cortex of the forebrain which they innervate), while losing activates separate neural areas (Chase & Clark, 2010; Habib & Dixon, 2010). This is consistent with a corpus of research findings indicating that pathological gambling (PG) recruits similar neuronal systems as substance addiction.

Another explanation invokes "cognitive distortion" to account for gamblers' apparently judging near-misses as indications that the probability of winning has been increased (Griffiths, 1994). This cognitive approach involves the attribution to gamblers of beliefs about the nature of the game, how it operates, and their own progress as players. Such a judgment might be relevant to the learning of a skill, but is unjustified in the context of games that have probabilistic outcomes. But this "gambler's fallacy" is actually widespread, as is supported by the finding that regular gamblers perceive a greater degree of skill to be involved in slot-machine gambling than do non-regular gamblers and that gamblers' perceived control is related to their gambling persistence (Clark et al., 2009, 2012; Chase & Clark, 2010). An implication is that the treatment of problem gamblers ought to concentrate on the (re-)learning of cognitive judgments by means, inter alia, of cognitive-behavior therapy.

A third explanation attributes gamblers' persistence to environmental factors that would be expected to influence the rate of behavioral performance if it were conceptualized as operant (e.g., Hoon et al., 2008). These include the primary and secondary schedules of reinforcement in effect when slot machines permit near-miss outcomes, and the temporal and spatial positioning of symbols indicating performance outcomes (e.g., prevalence of near-misses). This approach elucidates not only the influence that direct physical situational factors, such as reinforcement schedule(s) and the design configuration of the gambling machine, exert on playing, but also that of gamblers' verbalizations in the course of play that may guide their behavior.

Research on these "self-rules," verbalizations of the apparent contingencies, may inform the search for cognitive distortions that influence gamblers' choices.

None of these approaches, taken alone, provides a comprehensive account of the near-miss phenomenon. To synthesize the disparate results on the near-miss effect, this paper argues that the near-miss phenomenon can be understood if gambling is placed within the context of consumer choice. It conceptualizes gambling as a mode of consumer behavior within a model of economic choice that embraces both routine, everyday buying and the extreme consumption involved in addiction. The empirical research generated by this behaviorist model of consumption indicates that reinforcement includes both the functional or utilitarian benefits of consumer behavior and the symbolic or informational sources of benefit that are recognized in social status and self-esteem. This model, the Behavioral Perspective Model of purchase and consumption (BPM; Foxall, 1990), integrates the neurophysiological, verbal, and contextual elements identified in research on the near-miss phenomenon, showing that the construct of informational or symbolic reinforcement, allied to arousal, provides a key to understanding this otherwise anomalous phenomenon.

Neurophysiology of the near-miss

Classifying PG as an addiction requires more than the observation that it is irrational or compulsive at the behavioral level. It requires a convincing degree of continuity of such gambling with substance addiction. Ross et al. (2008) argue that this is the case and that PG should be considered a genuine addiction on biophysical grounds, indeed the paradigm case. This has been supported by some correlational research that has revealed a relationship between PG and a deficiency of the mesolimbic dopaminergic reward system. Reuter et al. (2005) found a lower activation of the right ventral striatum in PG compared with a control group and a regression analysis revealed a negative correlation between signal changes in the ventral striatum and the severity of gambling behavior as revealed in a questionnaire. Notwithstanding this, more arguments regarding gambling as addiction are needed, especially as the neurophysiological studies tend to deal with correlational issues instead of experimental analysis. Hence, patterns of behavior which may become addictive if reinforced might be identifiable through early identification of their neurophysiological correlates. The widespread assumption that increasingly persistent gambling in the face of near-misses constitutes such a precursor of addiction would be supported if a neurophysiological basis were established for it.

Griffiths: psychobiology of the near-miss

In early contributions, Griffiths (1990a, b, c) drew attention to the biological import of research on near-misses, mentioning specifically investigations of a potential neurophysiological substrate in PGs, the role of arousal in gambling, and the role of endorphins. Among the literature he reviewed at that time, Griffiths (1991) mentioned Carlton and Manowitz's (1987) use of electroencephalogram (EEG) measures to determine whether hemispheric dysregulation is related to impulse-control failure. PGs (compared with controls) showed hemispheric activation deficits on verbal and nonverbal tasks similar to those found in some kinds of Attention Deficit/ Hyperactivity Disorder involving inattention and impulsivity. In addition, PGs tend to be deficient in serotonin, a neurotransmitter which inhibits control of inattention and impulsivity. In the context of a possible substrate for excessive gambling, Griffiths (1991) also mentioned the work of Roy et al. (1988), who found PGs had "a significantly higher centrally produced fraction of cerebrospinal fluid level of 3-methoxy-4 hydroxyphenolglycol" which is believed to stimulate impulsive behavior and sensation seeking (Griffiths, 1990a, p. 349).

The role of arousal is sufficiently established in excessive gambling for the comment that excitement is the "gambler's drug" to have become a cliché (Brown, 1986, 1987). A prevalent neurophysiological measure is heart rate (HR), which is shown to increase during gambling. Also important from the point of view of relating neurophysiological and cognitive/social research is the finding that physiological measures of arousal correlate well with verbal reports of arousal as a subjective reaction (Mehrabian, 1980). Finally, there was emerging evidence in 1991 that endorphins (endogenous morphine) mimic the effect of opiates and mediate PG. Despite the emerging evidence for a biological basis for PG, however, Griffiths (1990b) con-cluded emphatically from his own research, based on questionnaire and interview methods, that both neurophysiological and cognitive factors play a part in excessive slot-machine gambling. In particular, persistent gambling entails cognitive bias: illusions of control, biased evaluations, and near-miss as a reinforcer rather than a punisher (see also Reid, 1986). His respondents' sole recreation was fruit (slot) machine playing since nothing else stimulated them in the same way. They played especially when they reported being "depressed" or "feeling down," since the slot-machine gambling changed their mood to a "high" (during gambling), though this was followed by a "low" and, eventually, anger. They mentioned excitement, which was immediate albeit short-lived, as the predominant reinforcer, but winning money was also important. Importantly, PGs differed from non-PGs in experiencing statistically significantly higher levels of excitement during gambling. These results support the findings of others with respect to arousal and endor-phins (though the research was not specifically intended to elucidate any biological substrate). Griffiths speculated that arousal, confirmed by his investigation as a major reinforcer, may pro-duce endorphins leading to tolerance which leads to more gambling. Moreover, he suggested that gamblers' representing their near-misses to themselves as near-wins might expand their arousal, which might reinforce play. This is noteworthy as an early indication that cognitive distortion may have a neurophysiological basis.

In recent years, considerable sophistication in the investigation of the neurophysiological basis of the near-miss is apparent in two major research programs: by Clark and colleagues at Cambridge University, and by Dixon and colleagues at Southern Illinois University. Both programs are characterized by a strong interdisciplinary methodology which allows the neuro-physiological and cognitive distortion views of the phenomenon to be compared and contrasted. In addition, Dixon's program has made explicit the role of contingencies of reinforcement and behavioral rules in the shaping and maintenance of near-miss effects.

Clark: neurophysiology and cognition

Employing a laboratory simulation of slot-machine gambling,[1] Clark et al. (2009) reported that both outright monetary wins and near-misses activated identical striatal and insular circuitry. Moreover, near-misses were associated with a greater blood oxygenation level-dependent (BOLD) signal in the ventral striatum and anterior insula, something also achieved by outright wins, and near-misses produced additional responses in the meso-limbic reward system (rostral anterior cingulate cortex, midbrain, thalamus) in a similar manner to that found in reinforcer processing. They implicated the tendency of near-misses to recruit the reward circuitry that is the neurophysiological basis of reinforcement as a factor that invigorates gambling propensity despite the objective lack of reward.

Clark et al. (2009) also contribute to the issue of biological versus cognitive/behavioral cau-sation, reporting that activity in the rostral anterior cingulate cortex varies with personal control.

Those gamblers given the opportunity to exercise personal control over arranging the gamble reported near-misses as less pleasant than full-misses but the former nevertheless increased those gamblers' desire to play. Moreover, insular activity for near-misses correlated with both a self-reported and a questionnaire measure of gambling propensity. Clark et al. (2009) also recorded *subjective verbal responses to near-misses* which for gamblers with personal control were less pleasant than full-misses but nevertheless increased the desire to play. This interaction between near-miss and personal control could be detected in fMRI data: "In the rostral portion of the ACC [anterior cingulate cortex], anterior to the genus of the corpus callosum, participant-selected near-misses were associated with a greater BOLD signal than personally-chosen full misses" (Clark et al., 2009, p. 485). The opposite was observed for computer-chosen trials but the result was not statistically significant. Both monetary wins and near-misses recruited the anterior insula. The BOLD signal in this area was associated with two aspects of what Clark et al. call "psychological variables": a positive correlation between insula activity and scores on the Gambling Related Cognitions Scale (GRCS), a measure of susceptibility to cognitive biases (Raylu & Oei, 2004) and a negative correlation between insula activity to near-misses and scores on "How much do you want to continue to play the game?" Only the insula, within the win-related circuit, was predictably associated with these verbal behaviors. By assuming a combined biological/cognitive paradigm, Clark et al. (2009) were able to demonstrate that neural responses associated with near-misses are related to both subjective experience of these events recorded during scanning and a trait-based index of gambling propensity on which problem gamblers exhibit significantly elevated scores.

Chase and Clark (2010) confirm that near-misses recruit neuro-circuitry associated with the acquisition of behavioral rewards and define PG by reference to its neurobiological commonalities with substance addiction; from the point of view of potential treatment, their work raises the possibility that dopamine- (DA-)induced responses to gambling may be regulated by the impediment of this neurotransmitter.

fMRI scan data were used to compute four contrasts: (1) Between monetary wins minus non-wins; (2) Near-misses minus full-misses; (3) Near-misses minus full-misses depending on computer versus participant selection of left-hand icon; and (4) Win activity for participant-selected versus computer-selected icons. The contrast of all winning with all non-winning outcomes (1) revealed signal change in areas usually associated with reinforcement learning, notably the ventral striatum. The contrast of near-miss with full-miss outcomes (2) indicated that both recruited the same striatal regions, despite the non-win status of both types of outcome. However, neither the contrast of wins for participant-selected minus computer-selected icons (3) nor the interaction contrast for near-miss activity as a function of personal control (4) revealed significant neural recruitment within the chosen ROI mask.

The study combined data from two sources by computing fMRI responses to gambling outcomes by scores on the South Oaks Gambling Screen (SOGS), a verbal test of gambling propensity which enquires of borrowing money, lying, etc. (Lesieur & Blume, 1987). While SOGS scores did not reveal neural correlates of increases or decreases in winning, they were related positively to midbrain responses and negatively to caudate responses to near-miss outcomes. Disordered gamblers showed a more pronounced midbrain response to near-misses than did others, a finding that contradicts previous research.

Clark et al. (2012) present a further study in this series, the aim of which was to trace the capacity of win, near-miss, and full-miss outcomes to generate physiological arousal in laboratory-based gambling simulations. They employed two physiological measures, HR and electrodermal activity (EDA). Both were found to vary with gambling outcomes. Near-misses elicited a greater increase in EDA than full-misses, especially on player-selected icon trials.

Near-misses also evoked a higher level of HR acceleration than alternative outcomes. Overall the results for the neuro-physiological measures indicated that "[n]ear-miss outcomes are capable of eliciting phasic changes in physiological arousal consistent with a state of subjective excitement, despite their objective non-win status" (Clark et al., 2012, p. 123).

The authors also manipulated perceived personal control by means of player (as opposed to computer) icon selection. As in earlier research, near-misses were experienced as less pleasant than outright losses but, in the case of personal icon choice, were followed by a greater verbally reported willingness to continue playing. Against the assertion that laboratory studies of gambling do not produce similar levels of arousal to those encountered in real-time gambling (e.g. Dixon et al., 2010) is evidence that the kinds of result found by Clark et al. (2012) are representative of play on actual video slot machines. Dixon et al. (2010) arranged the contingencies of gambling so that players whose probability of winning was enhanced by increasing the number of gambles made for each spin failed nevertheless to recoup the amounts they had staked. Such "losses disguised as wins" were associated with similar EDA and HR increases to those engendered by wins compared to full-losses.

Dixon: neurophysiology and contingency

Habib and Dixon (2010) were the first researchers to investigate neurophysiological and behavioral differences between pathological and non-pathological gamblers in the context of slot-machine near-misses. Their overriding hypothesis was that pathological gamblers would view near-misses as closely allied to wins while non-pathological gamblers would see them as more akin to the losses which, objectively, they are. This expectation was not borne out at the behavioral level: both types of gambler rated near-misses as close to wins. At the neurophysiological level, however, they identified greater overlap between the win-like elements of near-misses and the win network for pathological gamblers. Moreover, the loss-like aspects of the near-miss and the network activated for full-losses exhibited greater overlap in the case of the non-pathological gamblers.

The authors sought to identify brain regions common to pathological and non-pathological gamblers and those exclusive to each of these groups as they experienced the various gambling outcomes: these were termed the win, near-miss, and loss networks. The *win networks* were entirely discrete for the two groups. However, non-pathological gamblers displayed an activation of the right superior temporal gyrus that was peculiar to that group in the case of wins, while for pathological gamblers separate activations in the uncus and posterior cingulated gyrus constituted the win network: Habib and Dixon (2010) note that both of these regions identified for pathological gamblers are located in the extended medial temporal lobe system. It was also possible to define a *loss* network: for losses, activations common to pathological and non-pathological gamblers were apparent in bilateral medial parietal region (precuneus), bilateral middle/superior occipital gyrus, and bilateral superior frontal gyri. A notable difference was observed between the pathological and non-pathological gamblers groups' unique loss networks, however. Non-pathological gamblers demonstrated peculiar activations in a broad network including the medial and bilateral lateral parietal cortices and the medial, bilateral middle frontal, and left inferior frontal gyri. Pathological gamblers evinced a much smaller loss network consisting only of the right lateral parietal cortex. While the authors recorded no more than minimal common activation in the case of near-misses, the results were intriguing for the identification of the neurophysiology of gambling experience. Non-pathological gamblers recruited similar neurology in the case of near-misses to that found for losses: more precisely, they evinced activation in part of the left inferior parietal lobule close to a region that was activated for their loss-win contrasts. The pattern of association among the networks that might be expected on a priori grounds was substantiated in the case of pathological gamblers: *their* near-miss activations had more in common with their wins (win-loss contrasts) located in the uncus in the right anterior medial temporal lobe as well as the right inferior occipital gyrus. These results indicate that non-pathological gamblers are more realistic in judging the status of near-misses, seeing them as losses. Pathological gamblers, by contrast, are disposed to view near-misses as more closely related to wins.

Habib and Dixon (2010) stress not only the greater extent of the win network in pathological gamblers but that in this group this network comprised "emotional regions of the brain" and elements of the midbrain that constitute the reward system. This is especially interesting in that all players taking part received similar monetary rewards for their participation in the experiment but did not receive further compensation for winning. They suggest in interpretation that wins were more pleasant, positive, or rewarding for pathological gamblers, irrespective of monetary gain.

Winstanley et al. (2011) identify more specifically the neurophysiological activity involved in the near-miss by investigating the role of DA during slot-machine gambling, albeit simulated in rats. The construction of research framework in which rats' behavior simulates near-miss activity (Zeeb et al., 2009) facilitated experimental refinement in the further investigation of near-misses' associations with DA-ergic activity in disordered gamblers. For instance, Schultz (2002) had implicated the midbrain DA-ergic system in generating reward prediction errors (RPEs), and Schott et al. (2008) demonstrated that monetary rewards produce BOLD reactions and related striatal DA transmission. More specifically, Chase and Clark (2010) argued that positive RPEs occur as gamblers foresee a win when the right-hand reel slows, negative RPEs when its stopping reveals a no-win. Positive RPEs are especially associated with BOLD signals, suggesting a neural basis for the gamblers' overconfident beliefs. These effects are difficult to demonstrate for in situ human gamblers for technical and ethical reasons. Winstanley et al. (2011) arranged contingencies so that rats' responses determined whether flashing lights were lit/unlit: three illuminated lights constituted a win. Each trial concluded with the opportunity for the rat to select the collection of rewards for wins, also incurring a time penalty for losses, or a new trial. The rats preferred the collect option even if two lights were lit, suggesting an analogy with near-misses in human gambling. "Near-misses" apparently engender a reward expectancy similar to that characteristic of a win.

Qi et al. (2011) measured event-related potentials (ERPs) in an examination of the neural and cognitive correlates of the near-miss effect. As in other research, gamblers rated near-misses less pleasant than full-misses but found them more motivating. P300 amplitude increased from the full-miss condition to that of the near-miss. Further analysis indicated that the initiators of the P300, located in the putamen and orbitofrontal cortex, may be involved, respectively, in motivational evaluation and regret. The authors argue that the near-miss phenomenon may have dual origins in higher motivational level and the incidence of regret resulting from counterfactual thinking.

Summing-up: neurophysiology

Wins activate neural systems related to reward and DA release while no-wins fail to do so. Near-successful behavior is likely to be reinforced during the acquisition of skills, enhancing further improvement. But a gambling near-miss does not affect the probability of a subsequent win. The consequent intellectual challenge is to account for the influence of non-winning gamblers' cognitive responses to near-misses (i.e., their apparently illogical persistence in playing). Further research suggested by the authors may corroborate these findings by investigating, first, whether problem gamblers' generalizations of reward-predictive stimuli (e.g., contextual stimuli present prior to or simultaneously with gambling) correlate with midbrain activity; and second, whether midbrain neurons code adaptively to anticipated reward levels (Chase & Clark, 2010).

One line of critical review of the neurophysiological approach to explaining near-misses involves minutely analyzing the methods employed and proffering advice on improvement. Judging from the commonalities revealed by results from several highly reputable international laboratories and the contrasting methodological positions of the researchers, such recommendations would be incremental at best. An alternative critique contextualizes neurophysiological research by highlighting alternative insights into the near-miss phenomenon and links with the neurophysiological approach. This perspective is more likely to engender the interdisciplinary synthesis that understanding near-misses requires.

Cognitive distortion

A near-miss is not an outcome that *actually* "comes close to being successful" as in Reid's (1986, p. 32) definition: it is an outright failure that *may be interpreted* by the gambler as approximating a win. Explanation of the subsequent patterns of playing in terms of cognitive distortion take as its key variable not the objectively observable similarity of the pattern of symbols achieved to those that denote a win but the interpretation put upon this by the gambler. Its interpretation in terms of "closeness" is an independent variable for those researchers who seek to explain losing gamblers' persistence by invoking it; it is also necessary to view it as a dependent variable, enquiring of its causal origins.

Several of the studies reviewed here investigated cognitive distortion in addition to the neurophysiological basis of the near-miss. The tendency for slot-machine gamblers to be motivated by near-misses to continue gambling has been shown to depend on the illusion that their selecting the target icon increases their personal control over the outcome of the gamble (Dixon et al., 2007). A feeling of personal control also results from the belief that playing slot machines successfully is a matter of skill and that apparently coming close to winning signals its acquisition. Some tasks are perfected by the acquisition of skill through practice but in the cases of sports performance and accuracy in electronic information processing, for instance, there is a genuine probability that continued performance will enhance expertise. This is not so in gambling where the probability of winning is reset on each trial (Langer, 1975). Slot-machine design nevertheless takes advantage of the illusion of control through skill by affording players the opportunity of "nudging" or "holding" their icons seemingly to influence the generation of a winning line. Moreover, the self-perception of skillfulness is higher among pathological than other gamblers (Griffiths, 1990c). Griffiths (1994) reported that irrational statements about win-propensities are more frequent among more regular than other gamblers, though the incidence of irrational verbalizations was lower in his study of arcade gamblers than earlier research (e.g. Ladouceur et al., 1988) encountered. Griffiths (1994) interpreted his own research, nonetheless, as confirming the general trend of work on cognitive bias. Importantly, he found that regular gamblers were more likely than others to comprehend their behavior in terms of the acquisition of a skill.

Ariyabuddhiphongs and Phengphol (2008) sought to establish the relative importance of near-miss, gambler's fallacy, and entrapment on gambling persistence; entrapment is a variation of the sunk-cost effect in which, having invested so much time and money in a pursuit, the individual feels the costs of quitting are insuperable, hence persists. A model measuring the independent effects of the independent variables on the dependent shows that near-miss alone has a strong and significant effect on behavior; the other two independent variables are weak and non-significant. However, a model that examines the effects of gambler's fallacy and entrapment, mediated by near-miss, on gambling behavior fits the data as closely as the initial model. The overall conclusion is that the strong effect of near-miss on gambling motivation is strengthened by the other two variables.

Wohl and Enzle (2003) revealed that more important in gambling motivation than the incidence or magnitude of a gain or loss is the extent to which the gambler feels lucky. The subjective experience of luck is, in turn, influenced by whether a modest win ($10) is presented as the near-miss of a JACKPOT (delivering $70) or of BANKRUPT. These outcomes are hypothesized as involving upward or downward counterfactual thinking, respectively. As predicted, gamblers who have escaped a near big loss feel luckier than those avoiding a near big gain and are indeed more likely to continue gambling, perhaps as a result of the arousal felt as a result of being lucky. Self-perception of luck in an individual who has narrowly avoided a big loss is greater and this eventuates in continued play. Self-perception of luck is reduced in the player who narrowly misses a large payout and may thereafter doubt their ability to gain the jackpot. Daugherty and MacLin (2007) conducted a follow-up research related to Wohl and Enzle (2003) and found that only participants who experienced near-win situations at a high rate (45% levels) persisted in their gambling behaviors more than the participants in other conditions. Furthermore, Dixon and Schreiber (2004) question the capacity of cognitive distortion to explain the near-miss phenomenon characterizing such bias, from a behavior analytic perspective, as "a hypothetical construct within or characteristic of the individual responsible for an illogical calculation of the reality that explains gambling behavior" (p. 336). They also reject Reid's (1986) conjecture that near-misses constitute reinforcers because they generate arousal in a similar fashion to wins. They broadly endorse Griffiths' (1994) suggestion that near-misses are a sort of feedback that encourages further play, though they are skeptical of his idea that near-misses constitute a reward in themselves. These are all ideas that need to be taken seriously in formulating a general model of near-miss response.

In their own work, Dixon and Schreiber (2004) recorded response latency between plays (trials or spins), and the type of outcome (win, near-miss, or loss). All participants (12 undergraduates knowledgeable of slot-machine use) reported that their near-misses more closely approximated a win than a loss. Moreover, all but one participant estimated higher estimations of a near-miss when the similar symbols on the payout line were adjacent. Dixon and Schreiber (2004) propose tentatively that two adjacent symbols are visually closer to the three required for a win than the separated symbols. Response latencies for eight participants were longer in the case of winning; the four exceptions showed much greater response latency following a near-miss than a full-miss. These results corroborate earlier work by the authors (Dixon & Schreiber, 2004; Schreiber & Dixon, 2001) who suggest that the losing trial is an aversive stimulus from which the gambler seeks to escape quickly (negative reinforcement). This "negative reinforcement and avoidance paradigm" is supported by the longer response latencies shown by three-quarters of the participants after near-misses as opposed to full-misses, raising the possibility that near-misses do reinforce in some way. Schreiber and Dixon (2004) raise the possibility that a near-miss is a verbal event, that gambling is reinforced by the player's saying to him/herself "Wow! Nearly made it!" or similar.

Dixon et al. (2007) showed that participants in video poker games prefer to gamble on the basis of cards they have chosen personally rather than those that have been selected by computer. A similar effect is apparent in roulette where players prefer self-selected numbers over those chosen by the experimenter (Dixon et al., 1998). However, Weatherly and Flannery-Woehl (2009) counter the view that cognitive fallacies predict slot-machine gambling based on an empirical investigation of the value of such biases in the prediction of gambling behavior.

Fallacious beliefs, assessed by questionnaire, were used to predict financial gambling on video poker and slot machines. Erroneous beliefs were poor predictors of actual gambling; in the single instance in which they predicted gambling behavior, they were associated with less rather than more.

Summing-up: cognitive distortion

Any suggestion that cognitive distortion is the principal influence on gambling persistence requires qualification. First, it is difficult to establish that such beliefs influence behavior since, like other cognitive ascriptions, they are not directly amenable to experimental investigation. They are at best an inference that raises the philosophical question of how cognitive factors produce neurological effects. Second, near-misses are associated with neural changes that are known to be influential in motivating behavior through an established reward mechanism. Although cognitive distortion may be a by-product of the near-miss which, when verbally expressed, predicts further gambling, it is difficult to accord it causal preference over the meso-limbic reward system. Cognitive distortion may well be a result of the arousal engendered by the activation of this system by near-misses, in which case it is itself an effect of past behavior rather than a cause of future play. Hence, any attempt to treat PG by acting directly on biased beliefs is unlikely to succeed. Third, an alternative perspective which considers contextual influences on gambling persistence in the face of near-misses, including those inherent in rule-governed behavior, suggests a means of integrating neurophysiological and behavioral research.

Contingencies of reinforcement

The near-miss phenomenon is puzzling for behaviorists who interpret monetary gains as reinforcers (consequential stimuli that increase the rate of responding) and their absence as punishers (that reduce it). While there are few such behaviorists and even Skinner (1953) interpreted near-misses as reinforcing behavior, knowledge of the effects of reinforcement contingencies on gambling is valuable for three reasons. First, they permit further critical analysis of the neurophysiological approach to explaining near-misses. Second, they suggest theoretical enhancement of the behavior analysis of gambling. Third, they suggest ways in which treatment programs might benefit.

Haw (2009) investigated two aspects of reinforcement contingencies in an experiment in which students were allowed to select one of two machines on which to play. These were the frequency of payouts (wins) and payback rate. Both predicted when individuals changed machines but not overall machine choice. Those participants who did change machines, however, revealed a preference for the machine programmed with the larger payback rate (though not for that providing the greater frequency of wins), indicating a relationship between learning history (prior reinforcement) and machine selection. Haw (2008) reported that the effectiveness of variable ratio and random ratio schedules derives not from the average frequency of wins they engender, as is widely believed, but from the number of early wins and unreinforced trials.

The density of programmed near-misses may be more important in sustaining play than big wins. Kassinove and Schare (2001) used machines programmed to produce near-misses at different rates (15%, 30%, and 45%). Wins of $10 ("big" for the undergraduate participants) were also programmed to occur. Gambling persistence was assessed as the number of trials undertaken during extinction (i.e., when the near-miss and big-win outcomes were no longer available). Near-miss rate was significantly related to persistence (the 30% near-miss contingency produced the greatest persistence) but the big-win contingency was not. A further experiment indicated that when a 0% near-miss outcome was included, the highest level of persistence was produced by the (coincidentally?) greatest density of near-misses (45%).

Ghezzi et al. (2006) examined the effects of win magnitude and near-miss frequency on persistence in a series of three experiments in which near-miss effects took a variety of forms. In Experiment 1, the number of trials played in normal, rewarded, play was maximized when near-misses constituted 66% of outcomes (alternatives were 0%, 33%, and 100%). The second experiment revealed that maximum persistence accompanies medium-sized wins and 0% near-misses. The third showed that a 33% rate of near-misses indicated by adjacent symbols to the right of the payout window secured the most endurance. The experiment conducted by MacLin et al. (2007) required a group of students who gambled recreationally to play slot machines programmed to produce wins on a VR5 schedule. The machines differed, however, in the rate at which they generated near-misses: 15%, 30%, and 45%. In a pre-extinction phase, the 45% contingency generated the greatest level of play. Weatherly et al. (2009) report that female non-pathological gamblers gambling on commercial slot machines which paid out at different rates did not invariably prefer the machine with the highest payout. The authors conclude that neither the programmed nor the obtained reinforcement rate controlled gambling behavior, and argue that behavior analysts should seek to comprehend gambling in terms other than those of "direct, contingency-driven" outcomes. Nastally et al. (2010) report a study of contextual control of slot-machine gamblers' behavior based on different-colored machines (see also Zlomke & Dixon, 2006). Hoon et al. (2008, p. 467) also found that "participants allocated most of their responses to the slot machine that shared formal properties of color with the contextual cue for more than."

Summing-up: contingencies of reinforcement

The efficacy of contextual factors including reinforcement contingencies derives from their capacity to evoke arousal in gamblers. Arousal may result from a surprise gambling outcome due to changing schedules of reward or symbolic features such as flashing lights and loud noises that accompany not only a large win but a narrow win or even a loss masquerading as a "near-miss." Such symbolic reinforcement undoubtedly has neural correlates (though these have not been investigated in research seeking causes of the near-miss phenomenon) and counterparts in gamblers' verbal behavior that may indicate cognitive distortion. More sophisticated behavior analytic research that takes into consideration gamblers' verbalizations of the contingencies they perceive to be in operation (e.g. Dixon & Delaney, 2006; Nastally, 2010; Wood & Clapham 2006), which is beyond the scope of this review, promises to enhance this avenue of investigation and link it more closely with that concerning cognitive distortion.

Addictive gambling as consumer behavior

A recurring theme in all three research perspectives reviewed is the role of arousal as a consequence of near-misses which resembles that felt during a win and impacts subsequent behavior similarly. A second theme is discussion of the role of slot-machine symbols and audio effects as reinforcers of some kind, a conclusion that has been tentatively accepted, though sometimes without strong conviction, by behaviorists and cognitivists alike. While monetary rewards perhaps remain the primary source of behavioral reinforcement, symbols are a secondary influence on behavioral continuity. This is consonant with a theory of consumer choice which embraces compulsive and addictive behaviors such as problem and pathological gambling (Foxall & Sigurdsson, 2012).

The theory posits that consumer motivation is the outcome of two sources of reinforcement, utilitarian or functional (this would include monetary rewards in gambling) and informational or symbolic (such as the signs of near-misses displayed on slot machines). There is considerable evidence, first, for the role of symbolic reinforcement in maintaining non-compulsive consumer behavior and, second, for the capacity of symbolic reinforcement to engender arousal. Both symbolic reinforcement and arousal are closely related to verbal behavior and rule-governance, both of which assume importance in the explanation of the near-miss effect in terms of contingencies of reinforcement.

According to the BPM, the emotional states are a direct outcome of the reinforcement contingencies (Foxall, 2011; Foxall & Yani-de-Soriano, 2011; Rolls, 2014). During the Primrose Path gambling is governed by informational (mostly social) more than utilitarian (monetary) results, and is often motivated through social drinking and organized gambling in public places. As reinforcing social approval is overtaken by the addictive consequences of monetary and symbolic consequences, the contexts become progressively more closed. Symbolic reinforcement occurs as a consequence of the pathological gambler's conditioning history.

The critical aspect of this history involves a correspondence between the colors, lights, and sound generated by gambling machines in response to so-called near-misses. These effects not only arbitrarily signal a reduction in time to reinforcement (Fantino & Logan, 1979), but are also correlated with aroused happiness to this performance feedback. This can be defined in terms of the facial expression or vocalization sometimes shown by pathological gamblers when "winning" (Dixon et al., 2010; Green & Reid, 1996), or with the use of subjective rating scales (e.g., Foxall & Yani-de-Soriano, 2011; Foxall et al., in press), to provide a means of relating emotional responses to contingencies of reinforcement. With the pathological gambler's sources of motivation to gamble tied to utilitarian as well as to symbolic sources, the situation gets closer to an errorless discrimination contingency as the system does not give as many chances of "mistakes" as one would think. If and how the symbolic feedback increases its reinforcement value and capabilities to arouse positive feelings as gambling progresses needs to be studied more carefully. As the symbolic reinforcement seems to diminish the aversive effects from the normal extinction generated from losses, similar to what happens with errorless discrimination training, it is of value to measure the intensity of aversive emotions generally detected during extinction.

It is well established (Azrin et al., 1966) that animals and humans often show aggressive responses during extinction and as such the arousal, the intensity of the emotion, should be part of the functional analysis. Furthermore, there is evidence that suggests that PG may be maintained by negative reinforcement or an escape function (Miller et al., 2010; Weatherly et al., 2010). This needs to be studied with laboratory methods as well as with field studies, if boredom – a low arousal state – is to be systematically related to gambling behavior. Dixon et al. (2010) showed, for example, that a simulated gambling activity that did not involve monetary outcomes increased happiness levels in elderly individuals. This begs the question how different combinations of utilitarian and informational reinforcement work on operant gambling behavior and classically conditioned emotional responses in normal populations compared to pathological gamblers and how the effectiveness and emotions change during different stages of gambling. The further investigation of PG and other forms of addiction in terms of a broad continuum of consumer choice seems indicated by the foregoing critical review. Equally, an approach to treatment based on changing symbolic reinforcement and verbal behavior is more likely to produce effective results than one that emphasizes cognitive dysfunction and seeks to change beliefs and desires that are not empirically available.

Conceptualizing gambling and addiction as consumer behavior emphasizes the continuity between routine purchasing decisions (e.g., food brand choices) which exhibit a stochastic selection of alternatives (Ehrenberg, 1988) and extreme modes of consumption marked by compulsion. The analysis of factors influencing the more amenable modes of consumption, the routine choices, suggests how more extreme behaviors may be defined and studied. The routine and extreme consumer behaviors just mentioned are polar extremes on a continuum that also includes credit buying, environmental despoliation, and compulsive purchasing. All of these are influenced by a similar array of genetic, neurobiological, economic, contextual, and cultural factors (Foxall, 2010; Heyman, 2009), though these differ in salience according to the nature of the behavior in question. The location of a particular consumer behavior on the continuum is a measure of the impulsivity/self-control shown by the consumer. Although addiction has been shown to follow the matching law (Herrnstein, 1997), it is only recently that routine consumer behaviors have been shown to exhibit this process (e.g., Foxall et al., 2007) which underlies temporal discounting. Indeed, consumer behaviors are marked by temporal discounting regardless of their positioning on the continuum, albeit to differing extents. Findings generated by a model of consumer behavior for the more routine behaviors may therefore generate understanding of more impulsive forms of choice.

For instance, research inspired by BPM identifies two sources of reinforcement that are germane to the shaping and maintenance of economic behaviors: utilitarian (functional) and informational (symbolic/social), which act in tandem to affect consumer choices that reflect different underlying patterns of consumer valuations of the products chosen, measured in terms of differing elasticities of demand and levels of essential value (Foxall et al., in press; Yan et al., 2012a, b). The relevance of this to the present discussion lies in the verbal nature of informational reinforcement which reflects social norms of performance (in terms, for example, of social status and esteem). Symbolic reinforcement of this kind has been reliably related to emotional feelings of arousal in eight studies of consumer response to a wide range of consumption environments (Foxall et al., in press), a finding that is highly relevant to the results for near-miss gambling discussed in this chapter.

The import of interpreting these results in terms of informational reinforcement is that the outcomes of near-misses are in themselves as reinforcing as monetary gains; moreover, the efficacy of these symbolic reinforcers is enhanced by the arrangement of the paraphernalia of gambling, namely the ways in which slot machines respond to play-outcomes that are actually losses in a similar fashion to those that are outright wins. We can now understand why the sights and sounds generated by gambling machines in response to so-called near-misses are as effective in promoting further gambling as the financial gains that follow unmistakable successes. It is perfectly comprehensible why the cognitive mediation of these rewards by gamblers results in their reporting that they are feeling lucky and want to continue playing. It is not a matter of loss being rewarding: a near-miss is as much a successful outcome in view of the symbolic meaning it has acquired in the course of a gambling history as it would be if every near-miss were marked by the receipt of money. The application of the consumer behavior model to gambling confirms what has been suspected: that the potency of slot-machine gambling as a potential contributor to personal and social disruption is not as likely to be meliorated by the manipulation of schedules of reinforcement that govern the payout rate to gamblers as by the control of the symbolic reinforcers that influence arousal and thereby promote continued playing.

Conclusions

The assiduity with which casino managers and machine manufacturers seek to incorporate features that reward failure as well as success provides eloquent testimony to their practical value. The scale of gambling problems encourages critical reviewers to move beyond the minutiae of proliferating findings to the synthesis of salient results into applicable models for research and treatment. This is a time for bold conclusions rather than prescriptions for further penetration of well-worn paths. The consumer behavior framework outlined here is capable of integrating the biological, economic, social, and situational influences on gambling behavior that are known to be closely connected with the incidence of the near-miss effect.

Further research

Additional evidence is required of the role of experience in determining structural differences between pathological and non-pathological gamblers. There is certainly plenty of evidence that experience changes brain structures in laboratory enrichment studies, and in the study of London taxi cab drivers, so why not gamblers?

Various addictions, both drug-dependent and non-drug problematic behaviors, such as PG seem to share similar neurobiological foundations (Martin & Petry, 2005). With increased experience, the vulnerable individual develops increased sensitization, or inverse tolerance, a neuroadaptive response that is to a large degree dependent on context and learning (Berridge & Robinson, 2003). This alters neuronal circuitry involved in the normal processes of motivational operations and reinforcement. PG is characterized by changed reinforcement contingencies, the incapacity to experience or be motivated by reinforcers usually working in the local environment. This is due to reduced sensitivity to endogenous brain dopamine, and a striking responsiveness to cues that are associated with gambling, both inside the skin (e.g. anxiety or depressive symptoms) and in the environment. What is missing, though, in the literature are longitudinal studies looking at the long-term effects of gambling on brain chemistry.

Note

1 "The Slot Machine Task." One of six icons having been selected on the left-hand reel (by the participant or by computer), spinning the right-hand reel reveals one or other of the icons. If left- and right-hand icons match, the participant receives a small cash prize. A mismatch between the icons of one vertical position is a "near-miss"; other mismatches, "full-misses." Following initial icon selection, participants rate their chances of winning by responding to the question "How do you rate your chances of winning?" Following the outcome, participants state how much they want to continue to play on the question "How much do you want to continue to play the game?"

References

American Psychiatric Association (2000). *DSM-IV*. Washington, DC: American Psychiatric Association.
Amsel, A. (1958). The role of frustrative nonreward in noncontinuous reward situations. *Psychological Bulletin, 55*, 102–119.
Ariyabuddhiphongs, V., & Phengphol, V. (2008). Near miss, gambler's fallacy and entrapment: their influence on lottery gamblers in Thailand. *Journal of Gambling Studies, 24*, 295–305.
Azrin, N. H., Hutchinson, R. R., & Hake, D. F. (1966). Extinction-induced aggression. *Journal of the Experimental Analysis of Behavior, 9*, 191–204.
Berridge, K. C., & Robinson, T. E. (2003). Parsing reward. *Trends in Neurosciences, 26*, 507–513.
Brown, R. I. F. (1986). Arousal and sensation-seeking components in the general explanation of gambling and gambling addictions. *Substance Use & Misuse, 21*(9–10), 1001–1016.
Brown, R. I. F. (1987). Classical and operant paradigms in the management of gambling addictions. *Behavioural Psychotherapy, 15*(02), 111–122.
Carlton, P. L., & Manowitz, P. (1987). Physiological factors in determinants of pathological gambling. *Journal of Gambling Behavior, 3*, 274–285.
Chase, H. W., & Clark, L. (2010). Gambling severity predicts midbrain response to near-miss outcomes. *Journal of Neuroscience, 30*, 6180–6187.

Clark, L. (2010). Decision making during gambling: an integration of cognitive and psychobiological approaches. *Philosophical Transactions of the Royal Society B, 365*, 319–330.

Clark, L., Lawrence, A. J., Astley-Jones, F., & Gray, N. (2009). Gambling near-misses enhance motivation to gamble and recruit win-related brain circuitry. *Neuron, 61*, 481–490.

Clark, L., Crooks, B., Clarke, R., Aitken, M. R., & Dunn, B. D. (2012). Physiological responses to near-miss outcomes and personal control during simulated gambling. *Journal of Gambling Studies, 28*, 123–137.

Côté, D., Caron, A., Aubert, J., Desrochers, V., & Ladouceur, R. (2003). New wins prolong gambling on a video lottery terminal. *Journal of Gambling Studies, 18*, 433–438.

Daugherty, D., & MacLin, O. H. (2007). Perceptions of luck: near wins and near loss experiences. *Analysis of Gambling Behavior, 1*, 123–132.

Dixon, M. R., Hayes, L. J., Binder, L. M., Manthey, S., Sigman, C., & Zdanowski, D. M. (1998). Using a self-control training procedure to increase appropriate behavior. *Journal of Applied Behavior Analysis, 31*(2), 203–210.

Dixon, M. J., Harrigan, K. A., Sandhu, R., Collins, K., & Fufelsang, J. A. (2010). Losses disguised as wins in modern multi-line video slot machines. *Addiction, 105*, 1819–1824.

Dixon, M. R. (2000). Manipulating the illusion of control: variations in risk-taking as a function of perceived control over chance outcomes. *The Psychological Record, 50*, 705–720.

Dixon, M. R., & Delaney, J. (2006). The impact of verbal behavior on gambling behaviour. In Ghezzi, P. M., Lyons, C. A., Dixon, M. R., & Wilson, G. R. (Eds.) *Gambling: Behavior Theory, Research and Application* (pp. 171–189). Reno, NV: Context Press.

Dixon, M. R., Nastally, B. L., & Waterman, A. (2010). The effect of gambling activities on happiness levels of nursing home residents. *Journal of Applied Behavior Analysis, 43*, 531–535.

Dixon, M. R., & Schreiber, J. B. (2004). Near-miss effects on response latencies and win estimations of slot machine players. *The Psychological Record, 54*, 335–348.

Dixon, M. R., Jackson, J. W., Delaney, J., Holton, B., & Crothers, M. C. (2007). Assessing and manipulating the illusion of control of video poker players. *Analysis of Gambling Behavior, 1*, 90–108.

Dixon, M. R., Nastally, B. L., Jackson, J. W., & Habib, R. (2009). Altering the "near-miss" effect in slot machine gamblers. *Journal of Applied Behavior Analysis, 42*, 913–918.

Dixon, M. R., Nastally, B. L., Haha, A. D., Horner-King, M., & Jackson, J. W. (2009). Blackjack players demonstrate the near miss effect. *Analysis of Gambling Behavior, 3*, 56–61.

Ehrenberg, A. S. C. (1988). *Repeat Buying Facts, Theory and Applications*. New York: Oxford University Press.

Fantino, E., & Logan, C. A. (1979). *The Experimental Analysis of Behavior: A Biological Perspective*. San Francisco, CA: W. H. Freeman.

Foxall, G. (1990). *Consumer Psychology in Behavioral Perspective*. London and New York: Routledge.

Foxall, G. R. (2010). Accounting for consumer choice: Inter-temporal decision-making in behavioral perspective. *Marketing Theory, 10*, 315–345.

Foxall, G. R. (2011). Brain, emotion and contingency in the explanation of consumer behaviour. *International Review of Industrial and Organizational Psychology, 26*, 47–92.

Foxall, G. R., & Sigurdsson, V. (2012). Drug use as consumer behavior. *Behavioral and Brain Sciences, 34*, 313–314.

Foxall, G. R., Oliveira-Castro, J. M., James, V. K., & Schrezenmaier, T. C. M. (2007). *The Behavioral Economics of Brand Choice*. London and New York: Palgrave Macmillan.

Foxall, G. R., Yan, J., Oliveira-Castro, J. M., & Wells, V. K. (in press). Brand-related and situational influences on demand elasticity. *Journal of Business Research*.

Foxall, G. R., & Yani-de-Soriano, M. (2011). Influence of reinforcement contingencies and cognitive styles on affective responses: An examination of Rolls' theory of emotion in the context of consumer choice. *Journal of Applied Social Psychology, 41*, 2508–2537.

Foxall, G. R., Yani-de-Soriano, M., Yousafzai, S., & Javed, U. (in press). The role of neurophysiology, emotion and contingency in the explanation of consumer choice. In Wells, V. K. & Foxall, G. R. (Eds.) *Handbook of Developments in Consumer Behaviour*. Cheltenham, UK and Northampton, MA: Edward Elgar.

Ghezzi, P. M., Wilson, G. R., & Porter, J. C. K. (2006). The near-miss effect in simulated slot machine play. In Ghezzi, P. M., Lyons, C. A., Dixon, M. R., & Wilson, G. R. (Eds.) *Gambling: Behavior Theory, Research and Application* (pp. 155–170). Reno, NV: Context Press.

Green, C. W., & Reid, D. H. (1996). Defining, validating, and increasing indices of happiness among people with profound multiple disabilities. *Journal of Applied Behavior Analysis, 29*, 67–78.

Griffiths, M. (1990a). The cognitive psychology of gambling. *Journal of Gambling Studies, 6,* 31–42.

Griffiths, M. (1990b). Addiction to fruit machines: a preliminary study among males. *Journal of Gambling Studies, 6,* 113–126.

Griffiths, M. (1990c). The acquisition, development and maintenance of fruit machine gambling in adolescents. *Journal of Gambling Studies, 6,* 193–204.

Griffiths, M. (1991). Psychobiology of the near-miss in fruit machine gambling. *The Journal of Psychology, 125,* 347–357.

Griffiths, M. (1994). The role of cognitive bias and skill in fruit machine gambling. *British Journal of Psychology, 85,* 351–369.

Habib, R., & Dixon, M. R. (2010). Neurobehavioral evidence for the "Near-Miss" effect in pathological gamblers. *Journal of the Experimental Analysis of Behavior, 93,* 313–328.

Haw, J. (2008). The relationship between reinforcement and gambling machine choice. *Journal of Gambling Studies, 24,* 55–61.

Haw, J. (2009). The multiplier potential of slot machines predict (*sic*) bet size. *Analysis of Gambling Behavior, 3,* 1–6.

Herrnstein, R. J. (1997). *The Matching Law: Papers in Economics and Psychology* (Ed. by H. Rachlin & D. I. Laibson). New York: Russell Sage Foundation/Cambridge, MA: Harvard University Press.

Heyman, G. (2009). *Addiction: A Disorder of Choice.* Cambridge, MA: MIT Press.

Hoon, A., Dymond, S., Jackson, J. W., & Dixon, M. R. (2008). Contextual control of slot-machine gambling: replication and extension, *Journal of Applied Behavior Analysis, 41,* 467–470.

Jessup, R. K., & O'Doherty, J. P. (2011). Human dorsal striatal activity during choice discriminates reinforcement learning behavior from the Gambler's Fallacy. *Journal of Neuroscience, 31,* 6296–6304.

Kassinove, J. I., & Schare, M. L. (2001). Effects of the "near miss" and the "big win" on persistence at slot machine gambling. *Psychology of Addictive Behaviors, 15,* 155–158.

Ladouceur, R., Gaboury, A., Dumont, M., & Rochette, P. (1988). Gambling: relationship between the frequency of wins and irrational thinking. *The Journal of Psychology, 122,* 409–414.

Langer, E. J. (1975). The illusion of control. *Journal of Personality and Social Psychology, 32,* 311–328.

Lesieur, H. R., & Blume, S. B. (1987). The South Oaks Gambling Screen (SOGS): a new instrument for the identification of pathological gamblers. *American Journal of Psychiatry, 144,* 184–188.

MacLin, O. H., Dixon, M. R., Daugherty, D., & Small, S. L. (2007). Using a computer simulation of three slot machines to investigate a gambler's preference among varying densities of near-miss alternatives. *Behavior Research Methods, 39,* 237–241.

Martin, Peter, R., & Petry, N. M. (2005). Are non-substance-related addictions really addictions? *The American Journal on Addictions, 14,* 1–7.

Mehrabian, A. (1980). *Basic Dimensions for a General Psychological Theory.* Cambridge, MA: Oelgeschlager, Gunn and Hain.

Miller, J. C., Dixon, M. R., Parker, A., Kulland, A. M., & Weatherly, J. N. (2010). Concurrent validity of the gambling function assessment (GFA): correlations with the South Oaks Gambling Screen (SOGS) and indicators of diagnostic efficiency. *Analysis of Gambling Behavior, 4,* 61–75.

Nastally, B. L. (2010). *Functional Investigation of and Treatment Strategies for the Near Miss Effect in Gambling.* PhD Dissertation. Southern Illinois University.

Nastally, B. L., Dixon, M. R., & Jackson, J. W. (2010). Manipulating slot machine preference in problem gambling through contextual control. *Journal of Applied Behavior Analysis, 43,* 125–129.

Qi, S., Ding, C., Song, Y., & Yang. D. (2011). Neural correlates of near-misses effect in gambling. *Neuroscience Letters, 493,* 80–85.

Petry, N. M. (2005). *Pathological Gambling: Etiology, Comorbidity, and Treatment.* Washington, DC: American Psychological Association.

Raylu, N., & Oei, T. P. (2004). The Gambling Related Cognitions Scale (GRCS): development, confirmatory factor validation and psychometric properties. *Addiction, 99,* 757–769.

Reid, R. L. (1986). The psychology of the near miss. *Journal of Gambling Behavior, 2*(1), 32–39.

Reuter, J., Raedler, T., Rose, M., Hand, I., Gläscher, J., & Büchel, C. (2005). Pathological gambling is linked to reduced activation of the mesolimbic reward system. *Nature Neuroscience, 8,* 147–148.

Rolls, E. T. (2014). *Emotion and Decision-Making Explained.* Oxford: Oxford University Press.

Ross, D., Kincaid, H., Spurrett, D., & Collins, P. (2010). (Eds.) *What is Addiction?* Cambridge, MA: MIT Press.

Ross, D., Sharp, C., Vuchinich, R. E., & Spurrett, D. (2008). *Midbrain Mutiny. The Picoeconomics and Neuroeconomics of Disordered Gambling.* Cambridge, MA: MIT Press.

Roy, A., Adinoff, B., Roerich, L., Custer, R., Lorenz, V., Barbaccia, M., Guidotti, A., Costa, E., & Linnoila, M. (1988). Pathological gambling: a psychobiological study. *Archives of General Psychiatry, 45,* 369–373.

Schott, B. H., Minuzzi, L., Krebs, R. M., Elmenhurst, D., Lang, M., Winz, O. H., Seidenbecher, C., Hoenen, H. H., Heinze, H. J., Ziles, K., Durzel, E., & Bauer, A. (2008). Mesolimbic functional magnetic resonance image activations during reward-related ventral striatal dopamine release. *Journal of Neuroscience, 28,* 14311–14319.

Schreiber, J., & Dixon, M. R. (2001). Temporal characteristics of slot machine play in recreational gamblers. *Psychological Reports, 89,* 67–72.

Schüll, N. D. (2012). *Addiction by Design.* Princeton, NJ: Princeton University Press.

Schultz, W. (2002). Getting formal with dopamine and reward. *Neuron, 36,* 241–263.

Skinner, B. F. (1953). *Science and Human Behavior.* New York: Macmillan.

Weatherly, J. N., & Flannery-Woehl, K. A. (2009). Do cognitive fallacies predict behavior when nonpathological gamblers play slot machines and video poker? *Analysis of Gambling Behavior, 3,* 7–14.

Weatherly, J. N., Thompson, B. J., Hodny, M., & Meier, E. (2009). Choice behavior of nonpathological women playing concurrently available slot machines: effect of changes in payback percentages. *Journal of Applied Behavior Analysis, 42,* 895–900.

Weatherly, J. N., Montes, K. S., & Christopher, D. M. (2010). Investigating the relationship between escape and gambling behavior. *Analysis of Gambling Behavior, 4,* 79–87.

Winstanley, C. A., Cocker, P. J., & Rogers, R. D. (2011). Dopamine modulates reward expectancy during performance of a slot machine task in rats: evidence for a "near-miss" effect. *Neuropsychopharmacology, 36,* 913–925.

Wohl, M. J. A., & Enzle, M. E. (2003). The effects of near wins and near losses on self-perceived personal luck and subsequent gambling behaviour. *Journal of Experimental Social Psychology, 39,* 184–191.

Wood, W. S., & Clapham, M. M. (2006). Rules gamblers play by – and shouldn't. In Ghezzi, P. M., Lyons, C. A., Dixon, M. R., & Wilson, G. R. (Eds.) *Gambling: Behavior Theory, Research and Application* (pp. 191–205). Reno, NV: Context Press.

Yan, J., Foxall, G. R., & Doyle, J. R. (2012a). Patterns of reinforcement and the essential value of brands: II. Evaluation of a model of consumer choice. *The Psychological Record, 62,* 361–376.

Yan, J., Foxall, G. R., & Doyle, J. R. (2012b). Patterns of reinforcement and the essential value of brands: I. Incorporation of utilitarian and informational reinforcement into the estimation of demand. *The Psychological Record, 62,* 377–394.

Zeeb, F. D., Robbins, T. W., & Winstanley, C. A. (2009). Serotonergic and dopaminergic modulation of gambling behaviour as assessed using a novel rat gambling task. *Neuropsychopharmacology, 34,* 2329–2343.

Zlomke, K. R., & Dixon, M. R. (2006). Modification of slot-machine preferences through use of a conditioned discrimination paradigm. *Journal of Applied Behavior Analysis, 39,* 351–361.

A functional analysis of corruption from a behavioral-economic perspective

Patrícia Luque Carreiro and Jorge M. Oliveira-Castro

Corruption

Corruption is a global phenomenon. Transnational surveys, such as the Corruption Perception Index, conducted yearly by Transparency International, show that corruption is widespread throughout the world. Unfortunately, there is no country completely free from the tentacles of corruption. However, it may differ in level or frequency among nations. In some of them, it seems that corruption has reached minimum levels. It is a challenge for more corrupt countries to learn how they made this possible.

Corruption can take many forms. It can be petty, in bureaucratic contexts, or grand, when political leaders are involved (Tanzi, 1998). It exists both in private firms and the public sector, even though in private firms, owners and boards are responsible for watching closely what is being done with their own resources and assets. In the public sector, corruption shows its harshest effects: public money changes hands and does not reach the neediest beneficiaries (Lambsdorff, 2005).

Among the many definitions of corruption that can be found in the literature, the most accepted is "the abuse of entrusted powers for private gains" (e.g., Aidt, 2003; Lambsdorff, 2005; Tanzi, 1998; TI, 2014). It happens when private wealth and public power intersect; when decision-making is influenced by money outside legal controls (Rose-Ackerman, 2006, 2008). Considering its prevalence in the public sector, corruption can also be defined as "the misuse of public office for private gain" (Svensson, 2005). In this situation, corruption involves not only bribery, but also kickbacks in public procurement, racketeering in public companies, embezzlement of government funds, administrative misconduct, and influence peddling.

There are two important aspects to defining corruption. First, there is the idea of rule-breaking constantly present (Banerjee et al., 2012; Sheiffer & Vishny, 1993). Corruption is always illicit and clandestine. It may be morally and ethically questionable when a mayor employs his wife as a secretary, but as long as there is no rule to forbid it, it cannot be considered a corrupt act. That demonstrates differences in legal frameworks, and, therefore, in anti-corruption measures among countries. Identical acts may or may not be considered corrupt, according to the legislation of the country in which they are committed, and moral considerations do not play a role in identifying corrupt acts. Frequently, corruption may be the second or third illicit act in a sequence, to cover up a behavior that occurred first. For example, when a traffic officer stops a speeding driver, speeding is the first illicit act. To avoid worse consequences, such as a heavy fine, the driver offers a bribe to the officer, making corruption the second illegal act. Furthermore, as the driver offers the bribe, he risks being charged with two offences, speeding and bribery, instead of one, if the officer behaves honestly. Depending on the law of the country, a dishonest officer may also be guilty of one or more offences.

The second important aspect is the concept of gain. It does not apply only to monetary and financial rewards. Bribery can be much more than just money. It can cover any other form of advantage, benefit, profit, or privilege, including intangible gains, such as prestige, employment, compliments, vengeance, favors, or even time, when a public servant does not show up for work, but keeps receiving wages. Corruption and low rates of growth seem to go hand in hand but the causal relation between the two is not yet clear. Most probably, both belong to the same vicious circle (Lambsdorff, 2005; Rose-Ackerman, 2006; Treisman, 2007). Nevertheless, there are exceptions. Some very corrupt countries, low-positioned in corruption rankings, have experienced strong economic growth periods (Svensson, 2005; Rose-Ackerman, 2006, 2008). Perhaps, in these countries, corruption has developed into a less harmful form, a "grease-the-wheels" kind, where it is possible for moderate government inefficiency to co-exist with durable expansion (Aidt, 2003; Jain, 2001).

The incidence of corruption heavily influences a nation's institutions. Many studies (e.g., Lambsdorff, 2005; Svensson, 2005; Banerjee et al., 2012) emphasize the impact corruption might have on firms and governments, by focusing on bribery and its effects on the economy. But, as a broad phenomenon, corruption plays a role in judicial systems, in political relations, and in the structure of government, as well as in the ordinary life of society. In certain circumstances and countries, corruption can be considered contagious and may reach epidemic levels. It may become widespread throughout government and society. High levels of corruption in the upper ranks of government probably encourage corruption at lower levels. Incentives and impunity create patterns of vassalage, protection, clientelism, and distorted relationships based on bribery and blackmail (Cadot, 1987). Officials may be offered such large incentives to behave corruptly that the inducements threaten to overcome honest inclinations especially when honest action is frustrated by the behavior of the corrupt.

The purpose of this chapter is to offer an analysis of corruption phenomena in the light of the Behavioral Perspective Model (BPM). It is organized as follows. The next sections propose, first, a model of crime and corruption as developed by important economic theorists, and then a proposition for a model of corruption, suggesting typical cases in which corruption can often be seen. Following this, corruption is described according to the BPM approach with multiple consequences for behavior. Contingencies will be analyzed as behavioral classes, including the setting and history as antecedents and the informational and utilitarian consequences of the crime, in a systemic model. Finally, concluding remarks and further suggestions for analysis are presented.

Economics of crime and corruption

Becker (1968) inaugurated an economic model of crime, according to which the decision to commit a crime would be a result of a cost–benefit analysis. Crime would not be a matter of internal issues, of personality or inner motivation, as determinants of behavior. Citizens become criminals when they find a larger utility in crime than in work or legal activities. Illegal activities obey a supply–demand curve, complying with laws similar to those in effect in the market. As the probability of punishment or conviction increases, the number of crimes will probably fall. Therefore, a combination of surveillance and punishment could effectively control criminal behavior (Becker, 1968), including acts of corruption. Becker's perspective, however, has its critics. Lambsdorff (2012) argues that, if such economic thinking often prevailed, with an individual opting for a criminal act if the expected benefit of the action exceeds the estimated sanction multiplied by the probability of punishment, corruption would be much more frequent. Sanctions are usually mild across the world and the probability of a criminal being detected, prosecuted, and convicted is tiny.

It is a fact that only a small part of any population becomes criminal. Honest citizens are still in the majority. Some individuals commit crimes when others do not, even though circumstances may be identical. As heterogeneous agents, people differ in their earning abilities and have different incentives to participate in both legal and illegal activities (Fender, 1999). As a result, the decision to become a criminal, or be corrupt, is rational, based on a comparison of the benefits and costs of crime and work for each person, according to history and present settings. Fighting illegal activities depends on the allocation of public resources. In a purely economic analysis, resource allocation to prevent crimes should be prioritized. It could be more advantageous than spending money on punishment, such as imprisonment, after the crime is committed, because punishment adds to the costs to society. Furthermore, a combination of variables should be considered, such as probability of punishment or monitoring and the type and size of the penalty to be applied to the convicted.

Costs related to increasing the probability of punishment, such as improving surveillance and monitoring, creating new jobs in law enforcement for prosecutors and judges and raising the salaries of law enforcement officials, appear higher than simply increasing the magnitude of punishment, which needs only changes in the law. That is the main reason why the strategy of increasing the size of the penalty is usually preferred in fighting corruption (Alencar & Gico, 2011). According to Lambsdorff (2010), however, increasing penalties and the likelihood of detection is not always advisable. Stiffer penalties can have the effect of encouraging corrupt agents to create stronger relationships to protect each other. Frank and Schulze (2000) argue that monitoring may even increase corruption levels, should it reduce trust among agents. As corruption by its nature cannot be protected judicially, there would be no reason to honor corrupt pacts. In pure economic thinking, it might be more cost-effective for the public agent to act opportunistically, keeping the bribe and not reciprocating. Although some corruption cases are built upon the reputation of corrupt agents, there would be no punishment of any kind for those who change their minds (Lambsdorff, 2012). Instead of a "zero-tolerance" policy, Lambsdorff (2009, 2010) suggests mild penalties for those who act opportunistically and do not reciprocate favors, as well as leniency for those who report their actions. That would break the cycle of corruption careers.

Although it seems reasonable to believe that the effort applied in law enforcement may determine the probability of punishment, that is not necessarily true. The probability of punishment may be influenced by the level of crime, more than by the allocation of resources (Fender, 1999). Suppose, for example, that in a highly corrupt country, there are 10,000 criminals. A task force is organized and endeavors to catch 1% of them, resulting in 100 fewer criminals on the streets. In another less corrupt country with a similar population size, however, there is an estimated 100 corrupt individuals. If effort is applied with the same rate of success, it will result in only one criminal being arrested, which does not have a significant impact on society. The higher the number of existing criminals, the easier it will be to find and detect at least some of them, no matter how much effort is put into it.

Anti-corruption policies include monitoring and defining fines (Mishra, 2006). From Becker's rational economic point of view (1968), fines are punishments that restore the *status quo*, by compensating victims for the criminals' behavior. They seem to be useful in cases of monetary crime, as the offence is easy to measure in financial terms. However, when the institution responsible for implementing anti-corruption policies is also in charge of punishing corrupt agents and collecting fines, as non-judicial entities, there might be a conflict of interest. After all, if the monitoring and prevention strategies go well, corruption may be reduced, and consequently fines will fall, as long as there is integrity in the system and it is not prone to more bribery and corruption. The conflict may have an impact on the institution's revenue, causing ambivalence with regard to future actions: whether to pursue anti-corruption efforts or keep a good income from fines.

Because corruption is always illegal, it is also inherently as risky (Abbink et al., 2002) as any other crime. The individual's assessment of whether to engage in a criminal act should include the risk and nature of the penalties associated with corrupt acts. In this sense, corruption can be seen as a gamble (Cadot, 1987), as a result of the uncertain probabilities of gains and losses involved. There is the probability of being caught, and once caught, being punished (Jain, 2001). For the public official, risk involves an uncertain probability of losing both the revenue from the bribery and the public job, in addition to conviction and prison. Risk is dynamic, and involves a substitution effect. When incomes and bribes are highly substitutable, which makes the indifference curve relatively flat, an increase in the risk of the public official losing the job could be responsible for more corruption, or higher bribes, once there is a perceived time constraint on the opportunity to accumulate money (Cadot, 1987).

If the bribe is offered by a criminal there are other risks for public agents such as being given counterfeit money or fake antiques, as has happened in India and China (Lambsdorff, 2010). On the other hand, the briber faces short-term risks, such as whistleblowing by the official, or not having the offer reciprocated and losing bribery money because the official fails to act as agreed, as well as medium- and long-term risks of prosecution and conviction. If the briber is detected, there might be an opportunity to bribe law enforcement agents, to drop charges or hide evidence. In this case, the cycle starts over. Therefore, both agents are gambling with high stakes on a risky activity, and they both may lose everything. From a behavioral perspective, gambling can be interpreted in the light of schedules of reinforcement, producing high rates of responses and stronger resistance for the periods with no reinforcement available (Knapp, 1997). Gambling can also be understood as a series of choices or events in time with a fixed outcome, and not as a simple one-shot event. The lost bets are added up only after a win, and then the system starts over. It means that the string of responses is influenced mainly by gains and not very much by losses before the winning bet (Rachlin, 1990).

It has been demonstrated that winning and losing have different values, even when the amount of money involved is the same. Kahneman and Tversky (1984) showed that losing can be more aversive than winning is attractive,[1] and individuals would be more reluctant to indulge in risky behavior when there are equal chances to win or lose. However, sometimes, the gains and losses do not immediately follow behavior. There could be delays in outcomes, characterized in terms of the degree of temporal discounting (Rachlin, 1990). Choice is made between alternatives of different temporal offers: "now" vs. "later", in a self-control paradigm (Rachlin, 1974, 2010). Is it better to wait for a larger reward in the future or get a smaller reward in the present?

The basic study in self-control presents to the subject two options: a Choice A with an immediate, small reward, whose selection is often regarded as impulsive behavior, and a Choice B, with a delayed, larger reward, interpreted as self-controlled selection, and therefore usually a behavior to be pursued. Choice A may be preferred because it has a greater subjective value than the larger reward, due to the long delay that precedes it. Studies have shown that present rewards are more valuable than delayed ones. It is preferable to get, for instance, $100 now than wait five years to get $300 (Green et al., 1994). Future rewards are discounted more steeply because of the possible risk involved in waiting for them (Green et al., 1994; Myerson & Green, 1995). After all, so many things can happen in five years that it may be better to take advantage of less money, right now. The same results apply to probabilistic rewards as well, when the choice is between receiving $100 for sure and $120 with a 20% chance. Subjects have discounted probabilistic rewards the same way, preferring smaller, certain ones (Green & Myerson, 2004).

Discounting is very helpful in understanding some of the moral dilemmas people face in everyday life. Some choices present certain gains but may bring some substantial losses, within a given probability. That goes for opening a business, following a weight-loss diet, and also perpetrating criminal activities. The public official may have to face the choice between the guaranteed wages or a higher reward, with some possibility of losing everything, including job and freedom. At some point, a loss at a given probability may be discounted, which might explain why a public official may decide to engage in a corrupt act.

A typical corrupt act

To develop a model of corruption from a BPM perspective, it is useful to outline a typical act of corruption, including the main players, interactions, and existing rules.

First of all, typically, corruption occurs in the public sector. It is where corruption causes more damage, in terms of negative externality and consequent loss to society (Abbink et al., 2002). From this sector comes the first player: the official. The official can be any public servant or agent: a procurement bureaucrat, a diplomat, a national health system worker, a traffic officer, a tax collector, or any other government representative or employee, who can, due to her[2] occupation, legally issue a benefit to the citizenry (e.g., a business license), or not deliver any benefit at all (e.g., privileged information) (Treisman, 2007). The second actor in the corruption scenario is the briber. It is usually a private citizen who needs something from the government. It could be an entrepreneur or a businessperson who wants to pay less tax, to get a building contract or a public service concession, or an individual who has committed traffic offences or other minor crimes and wants to get away with it. It could occasionally be another public servant, behaving as a briber to gain some advantage. It may even be a politician who offers money, fuel, or meals to get votes in an election.[3] Or, it could involve any civilian who wants some benefit from the government.

The concept of "benefit" can be broadly understood. A benefit can refer, for example, to an enrolment in a public school or a registration for a new business. In these cases, the benefit is legal and reachable, once normal procedure is followed. There are legal opportunities for a citizen to get the benefit for free or by paying a fixed fee, universally defined for everyone in the same condition. However, either the briber is not personally entitled to the benefit, or the bribery represents a short-cut, making the acquisition of the benefit faster and easier. More seriously, the benefit may be something such as a tax discount or cancelation of a traffic fine. It could be some advantage in a specific public procurement process, such as being placed on a list of preferred contractors, or gaining privileged information, say, where the government is planning to build a bridge or when the next procurement session will be held. It could also refer to employment or internship, obtained when the briber is able to bypass the public selection process. In these cases, the briber is not entitled to the benefit, even through great effort; otherwise he could have taken it legally, without payment or other inducement.

On his side, the briber holds advantages that the official may lack. The concept of advantage should also be taken broadly. It usually refers to money, which seems to be involved in most corruption cases, since it is a powerful generalized incentive that gives access to many other rewards, but it is not restricted to it. It could as well be advances in career, new positions and promotions, invitations to important ceremonies, or demonstrating power and prestige, which could also lead to money, more indirectly. It could be a promise of a future favor in return, which enlarges the possibilities even more. In situations of endemic corruption, career advancement or even keeping the current post is reserved to those who play by the same corrupt rules as their superiors.

Figure 16.1 illustrates the basic elements of a typical corruption case. At first sight, it seems like a perfect exchange paradigm: the seller has a product, the buyer has the money, they exchange goods. The official has a legal power to award a benefit desired by the briber. The briber, on the other hand, has something to offer the official in exchange. The reciprocity involved in corrupt acts seems to be a key element in understanding corruption (Lambsdorff, 2012). But there are other elements in the middle of this relationship: illegality and, consequently, risk.

Illegality is at the center of any corruption case. Corruption always implies rule-breaking (Banerjee et al., 2012), stressing the possibility that the act is subject to the law. Because the benefit pursued and the advantage traded are both illicit, participants face the risk of being detected, prosecuted, and convicted. There are different probabilities at each stage of the judicial process and as the risks accumulate, it may be difficult for the players to estimate the total probability of an adverse outcome. Assessing risk depends on numerous variables that are completely out of the players' control or even knowledge. These variables include law enforcement initiatives, political interest, pressure from international watchdogs, ongoing police operations, available surveillance tools, monitoring efforts which, in turn, take into account the magnitude of kickbacks, whistleblowing, the number of red flags in the procedure, and the social position of both the briber and the official, among others.

Besides the risk of criminal charges, both characters face other hazards. Usually, the players believe that the chances of being caught can be minimized as a result of their careful behavior. Actions, such as deleting files, not keeping receipts, dealing only in cash, assigning nicknames for institutions and people, and other hiding behaviors, create the feeling that the characters are in control of the situation. However, many corrupt deals are uncovered as a result of these important pieces of evidence coming to light through carelessness or spite, when they have been kept by one or both offenders as insurance against blackmail, extortion, or failure to deliver on

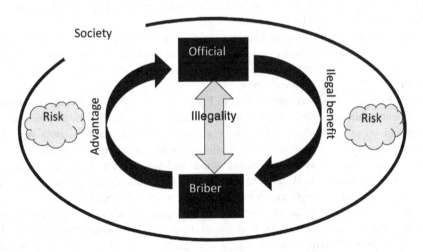

Figure 16.1   Basic elements of a typical corruption case

promises. Note also that when several people are involved in a network of corruption, however discreet and careful individuals may be, they are at the mercy of their co-conspirators' actions, whether accidental or deliberate, and any precautions may prove useless.

Choosing between a legal or an illegal way to behave is like choosing between certain or uncertain rewards, with some probability of being punished. By behaving in a legal way, the official gets certain but smaller amounts of money, as monthly wages. The briber, on his turn, may get larger and long-term rewards, as many attempts may be necessary to get a public procurement contract. It resembles the choice made in the self-control paradigm, for a larger, delayed alternative. On the other hand, for both players, behaving illegally will lead to possibly larger, yet uncertain amounts of money, with an indefinite chance of punishment by losing both rewards. Nevertheless, the larger, uncertain reward is preferred to the smaller option.

A Behavioral Perspective Model of corruption

Because the BPM simultaneously considers gains and losses, as reinforcers and punishers, it seems a suitable model to investigate corruption. Foxall (e.g., 1998, 2010) proposed the BPM, inspired by learning theories and the three-term contingency, which integrates antecedent and consequent events with the initial aim of analyzing consumer behavior.

In the case of corruption, the setting can be divided into two categories of elements. One category concerns macro-elements, or important characteristics that highly corrupt countries share. Cross-section studies (e.g., Lambsdorff, 2005, 2014; Svensson, 2005; Treisman, 2007; Olken & Pande, 2012) found positive correlations between several features and the indexes, notably the Corruption Perception Index, organized by Transparency International, and the Control of Corruption, by World Bank, which, in a certain way, give some measure of corruption in each country (for a complete explanation of the indexes' methods and differences, refer to Treisman, 2007).

These descriptions are not to be taken as causal effects. It is not clear whether economic development reduces corruption or corruption slows economic development, or if they are both caused by some third factor (Rose-Ackerman, 2006; Treisman, 2007). Nevertheless, the correlations undeniably show that the poorest countries in the world are also the highest ranked in perceived corruption indexes. In general, all of the top-ranked corrupt countries are developing or transition countries, which are or have recently been ruled by socialist governments, with low per capita income levels, and most of them are closed economies (Svensson, 2005). These are just some of the various tendencies highly corrupt countries reveal. They also include, for instance, more restricted markets and competition, accompanied by bad regulation. Again, it may be difficult to find out whether a restricted regulatory mechanism comes before or after corruption. The truth is that they co-exist.

The main characteristics are summarized in Figure 16.2. It seems reasonable to assume that these elements which are often seen in corrupt countries may influence the institutional environment and act as discriminative stimuli or as motivating operations for both bribers and officials, signaling that corrupt acts may be reinforced or have a lower punishment risk.

The second category involves elements which make a situation more favorable to the occurrence of a corrupt act. Rather than looking at the country's wider background, these micro-elements focus on single conditions that any briber and official may encounter. In a micro-analysis, some features are connected with the operation of the institution. One of the elements in the setting of a corrupt deal involves unclear or non-standardized procedures. Officials may have different approaches to similar problems, resulting in different solutions, and this, coupled with the unlimited discretion granted to officials, allows bribers to choose

Government Investments and Expenditure	Political Institutions
• Large size of government (overall size of budget relative to GDP) • Small shares of subnational expenditure in total public spending • Higher military spending and arms procurement • Lower government spending on education • Inefficient government services • Low quality of public health care (given by child mortality and percent of low-birth-weight babies in total births) and education (given by dropout rates)	• Short tradition of democracy • Low electoral participation • Presidential system, especially when combined with closed-list proportional representation • No re-election possible • Parliamentary party lists • Small voting districts • Federalism
Regulatory Quality	**Economic Background**
• Reduced competition (e.g. short number of years open to trade, market dominance, absence of anti-trust laws) • Bad regulation (e.g. public procurement not open to foreign bidders, non-equal fiscal treatment to all enterprises) • Large number of procedures required to start new business, in addition to long time and large official costs • Broad government involvement in private markets • Diversified trade tariffs	• Low GDP per capita • Inflation or recent experience with hyperinflation • Low ratio of investment to GDP • Low rate of foreign direct investments • Low international credit rating (e.g. Moody's) • Weak bank supervision • High income inequality • High proportion of labor force employed in primary production
Judiciary System	**Administration and Public Sector**
• High de jure independence (given by e.g., life tenure, promotion as result of appointment by politicians) • Low de facto independence (resulting in forced retirement, frequent changes in legal foundations, decreasing income and budget for prosecutors)	• Low public sector salaries • Low number of public servant convictions • Low level of rotation of staff in functions • Reduced complaints mechanisms • Low number of automatic processes in public sector • Low level of separation of functions
Geography and Environment	**Press**
• Abundance of natural resources, especially for extractive industries • High levels of air and water pollution, representing inefficiency of environmental regulation • Reducing total coverage of forest • Corrupt neighbors, who share cultural affinities and norms, performing regional exchange • Larger distance to world's major trading centers, including limitations on transport to those centers	• Limited freedom of press, accounted for by the existence of laws and regulations that influence or control media content, political and/or economic influence over media content and repressive actions against journalists • State ownership of news agencies and high concentration in ownership of news agencies • Low newspaper circulation per person

(continued)

(continued)

Population	Gender Issues
• Large total population size • Lower levels of human capital stock, proxied by years of schooling • More college enrolment in law and business (instead of productive activities) • Low level of trust among its people • High percentage of members of hierarchical religions (Catholics, Eastern Catholics, Orthodox, Muslims, tribal religions) • Material success domination over quality of life • High power distance (the extent to which the less powerful members of institutions expect that power is distributed unequally)	• Low proportion of seats held by women in parliament • Low share of women employed in the non-agricultural sector

Figure 16.2 Highly corrupt countries' characteristics, given by cross-section study findings (Lambsdorff, 2005, 2014; Svensson, 2005; Treisman, 2007)

an official who seems likely to offer the most beneficial outcome. In an operational context, there might be complex legal requirements to be complied with to obtain any given benefit. Applications that are susceptible to bribery frequently demand a comprehensive list of documents, with certified signatures, in numerous stages, each taking a frustratingly long time to achieve. These complex, long drawn-out processes show the less desirable face of bureaucracy.

Finally, in most cases, there is a low level of technological intervention, and the interactions are carried out personally between briber and official. This face-to-face approach may be an important element of the setting, as it is not possible to offer bribes to systems, although a human official may have the final word in the case. The use of technological systems would also increase the traceability of the corrupt act, with a possible deterrent effect. In these micro-elements, corruption can be understood as a "grease-the-wheel" procedure, which in a certain way compensates for the state's inefficiency. Another micro-element is the mildness of sanctions applied to previous cases of corruption. Both the briber and the official may feel that no real punishment will occur, or those convicted will be back on the streets soon enough. Moreover, the implementation of sentences may take too long. Corruption can also be seen as "part of the game", a notion that nothing can be done without collusion. In what is known as "the paradox of corruption" (Gico, 2010), press publicity aimed at demonstrating police efficiency in catching corrupt individuals may simply suggest to the public that there is an increase in corruption rather than an increase in detection rates. This perceived, rather than real, increase in corruption leads people to doubt the effectiveness of the authorities so that the crimes are no longer reported (Treisman, 2007).

The other element of BPM that works as an antecedent for behavior is the learning history of the official and the briber. Although some elements may be shared by them, such as moral standards, accounted-for pro-social behaviors, or the general knowledge of corrupt acts, given by the number of pieces of news recently read about corruption schemes, some are specific to each one's role. The official's learning history may include the incidence of punishment or commendation in her career. The absence of commendations in the official's file may increase the chances of engaging in a corrupt action. The barriers to obtaining the job, represented by the level of difficulty in public selection examinations and the number of competitors per vacancy, makes the job more or less valuable, and therefore, in a highly rated post, the official may be less tempted to risk its loss through criminal activity. The monthly wages and other financial aids (e.g. a health care plan, pre-schooling care for children), as well as intangible benefits, such as the length of the working week, and the number of vacation days, also figure in the official's learning history. The better these conditions are, the less likely the official is to perform a corrupt act. Outside work, family pressures such as the number and ages of children and her spouse's job may result in occasional debts being incurred, making extra income desirable. Having more prosperous friends may tempt her to close the financial gap by taking bribes.

Finally, in countries where corruption is widespread, there might be strong pressure on the official to take part in illegal schemes from her own peers and co-workers. If every official becomes corrupt, it is less likely that one of them will expose the system. As all the officials are running the same risk, the group gains mutual trust and protection and can exert control over each participant's behavior, ensuring that none of them will be careless, endangering the scheme.

Moving to the briber's learning history, the importance of the benefit or the urgency in obtaining it strongly increases the chance of resorting to bribery when ordinary, legal procedures are long and drawn-out. Where commercial issues are involved, pressure on the briber may come from his superiors, from stakeholders, suppliers and competitors. As in the case of the official, a social network in which all members are corrupt probably encourages further corrupt acts, as a form of inter-group protection. Furthermore, the briber's learning history may depend on the resources available to him, or how much he can afford to bribe. Different wealth levels may impact corruption. Studies showed that lower-class drivers were asked higher bribes by traffic officers than upper-class drivers (Fried et al., 2010), since an upper-class individual can probably afford higher bribes, but may be more disposed to press charges against a corrupt official.

Another general factor is the history of tax and fee payment. Whenever the potential briber pays the correct taxes on time, he may be more reluctant to pay bribes, considering his commitment to carrying out his civil obligations. On the other hand, a tax evader probably cares less about the state budget and might be more disposed to accept or offer a bribe proposal. At the core of the BPM analysis, there is the corrupt act. The behavior may be different, but the function is always the same: trading an advantage for a benefit, both of them illegal or illegitimate. Examples would go on forever and can be seen worldwide in a sample collection of news items:

- illegal goods, such as weapons and drugs, being allowed into a country as a result of bribery paid to port officials;[4]
- a national health system doctor who charges extra fees to perform surgery;[5]
- a journalist who pays bribes to a police officer to get details of investigations;[6]
- companies who agree to make donations to political parties' funds before winning billion-dollar contracts;[7]
- building contractors who offer housing benefits to a high-ranking public servant in exchange for favorable government decisions;[8]
- a telecommunications giant who pays huge bribes to gain entry to another country's mobile market.[9]

All these possible topographies show how the corrupt act can vary. However, they all come with the same drawback: risk, meaning that, given specific circumstances, there is a higher probability of punishment than of reinforcement. Obviously, there are different consequences for each individual corrupt act in real life. Nevertheless, it is reasonable to assume some potential utilitarian and informational consequences for each of the players involved in the corrupt act, as it will be shown for the official, the briber and the society, as a third party affected by corruption.

From the official's perspective, the main utilitarian reinforcer to the corrupt behavior is the advantage per se, whenever it refers to money, a higher pay-grade, promotion, a larger office, or any other tangible asset. The informational reinforcers from a corrupt act are more extensive and could include feelings of self-esteem, for example being bold and audacious, or feelings of counter-control against a possibly unfair government or institution, or simply for challenging the system and breaking the law. It could also refer to family support, especially if there was initially pressure for extra money. Regarding the corrupt group, the informational reinforcer could increase prestige and status, represented by compliments and a good reputation for brokering future deals, as well as feelings of group belonging.

On the negative consequences, utilitarian punishers may include feelings of anxiety caused by the probability of punishment, leading the official to have to conceal evidence, and take extra care with the content and timing of phone calls, emails, and letters, as well as having some unconditioned fear responses. Other concerns include whistleblowing against her or not receiving her share of the deal, such as being paid with counterfeit money, fake assets, or being given less money than agreed. The possible utilitarian punishers which might follow detection include dismissal, reimbursement of losses to the government, fines, or imprisonment. It might be necessary for the official to spend money on lawyers and appear in court. As part of the informational punishers, the official may face criticism and hostility from family and honest peers, regardless of being detected. If detected, the official may see her name published by news media, acquire a criminal record, lose prestige and power, have to deal with social shame and loneliness in prison. From the briber's perspective, the utilitarian reinforcers are larger. The benefit could be a short-cut, meaning less work or less time spent in dealing with bureaucracy, but it usually implies money saved or to be earned in the near future. For having helped the company, the briber can get promotion and a better pay-grade. With regard to informational reinforcers, the corrupt act can bring the briber power and prestige, including compliments from the corrupt boss or institution he works for, admiration from peers, a good reputation for being the right man to make future deals, and feelings of group belonging. If promoted, the briber can gain support from his family and social group, as a result of a better salary.

When it comes to the utilitarian punishment, the briber risks losing money and time in negotiation, if the official does not reciprocate, as he would have to restart the bribery process with another official. He also may fear whistleblowers and being betrayed by his group. The briber and the official may share fears of similar consequences arising from detection and the fear of detection.

As for the informational punishers, the briber may meet the same kind of criticism from family and friends, and experience the same shaming social consequences. Society also suffers several consequences through corrupt acts, as a third party. Whenever corrupt deals are made, individuals living in that society will experience the externalities of the transactions between the briber and the official. There may be some positive consequences, though. Perhaps more jobs are created in law enforcement. Also, as money changes hands, there might be some increased money flow, encouraging the official to consume more goods in the market. These goods may, therefore, generate revenue and jobs for society. Some other institutions, such as accountability and governance companies, exist just to assure stakeholders that a deal is legitimate, to maintain a good image of a company. They may profit indirectly from bribery, just because corruption exists elsewhere.

In the public sector less revenue is available for government spending, due to tax fraud; contracts not being awarded to the right bidders, which could lead to greater expense or worse service; and more money being spent in law enforcement, instead of health and education. Individuals would have less opportunity to go to good schools, receive quality medical treatment, and get better jobs. The success of small acts of corruption leads to more frequent and complex activities which, in turn, present a danger of corruption becoming endemic to the society. A bad position in international anti-corruption indexes such as the CPI is undesirable, as is criticism from international watchdog institutions, such as Transparency International, the Organization for Economic Cooperation and Development (OECD), the World Bank, and others. A country's reputation for corruption may prejudice opinions against its citizens when they travel abroad.

Every model is a simplified representation of reality and it is not possible to include all the possible ramifications and consequences of corruption in the public sector, but it is possible to have a broad perspective of the main outcomes for those involved in a corrupt act, which will lead to its repetition in the future. If a corrupt act produces money and other positive consequences for the official and for the briber, more illegal acts can be expected in the future, in a sequential career in crime (Becker, 1963/2009). In this model of multiple consequences, corruption can be interpreted as an event in which the official accepts an inducement to favor a briber with a benefit. By behaving in a corrupt way, the official and the briber are reinforced by a possibility of a larger magnitude of rewards, compared to the rewards available from legal behavior, combined with an unclear probability of severe punishment.

Even though individuals are more sensitive to losses than to gains, punishment is hard to estimate, in terms of the probability of occurrence and magnitude, and it is delayed in time. Therefore, players discount the value of the probabilistic losses, and choose the more immediate gains related to crime. If this is the pattern, the system may restart continuously, leading to an endemically corrupt society.

Conclusion

The BPM is a powerful conceptual and theoretical tool. Its capacity to elucidate human behavior goes beyond its first objective, that of understanding and explaining consumer behavior, extending to the interpretation of several other types of behavior in different contexts, which have positive and negative results simultaneously.

Corruption is one type of behavior that the BPM can help to explain. It seems to fit well into the BPM outline, especially for demonstrating the social consequences of the crime. Individuals are not only driven by their own self-regarding motives, but the social payoffs should also be considered (Lambsdorff, 2012). Furthermore, as the BPM shows, punishment and rewards have different values, making one more attractive than the other, depending on their magnitude and occurrence probability. The model might even provide a basis for calculating the elasticity of crime: what is the size of the punishment that a criminal is willing to risk as a function of the amount of benefits that can be obtained? That could help law-enforcers to adopt a better anti-corruption approach, since it would be based upon behavioral-economic predictions.

It is not yet clear, though, what makes any of the players refrain from engaging in a corrupt response. It may be the likelihood of detection or the magnitude of the penalty. It is also unclear whether the official would refrain from corruption if her rewards for legal behavior were larger. Furthermore, it is not yet known if and how the punishment of one player influences peer behavior; that is, not much is known about the potential deterrent effect of punishment. These questions remain to be addressed by experimental procedures.

In any case, there seems to be a tipping point: the moment when an increase in either risk or reward is perceived. Then there is a shift in preference, as seen in discount studies. When the official can potentially both gain and lose from her action, there is a point where the value of the penalties and losses associated with the corrupt behavior is larger than the value of the money that can be made illegally. Learning when that shift in preference occurs is a key factor to understanding and fighting corruption.

Notes

1 Experimental studies corroborated the asymmetry between the value of reinforcers and punishers (e.g., Rasmussen & Newland, 2008).
2 To make reading easier, the official will always be referred to as "she", and the briber as "he", in this chapter.
3 Although this case does not occur in the public sector and with a public agent, the model seems to fit in this particular situation of electoral corruption.
4 Forbes, 9 Dec 2013, "Stuck In A Bottleneck, Latin American Ports Breed Corruption". Available at: http://www.forbes.com/sites/riskmap/2013/12/09/stuck-in-a-bottleneck-latin-american-ports-breed-corruption
5 G1, 31 Jan 2014, "Pacientes afirmam que médico cobra por serviços do SUS, no Paraná". Available at: http://g1.globo.com/pr/campos-gerais-sul/noticia/2014/01/pacientes-afirmam-que-medico-cobra-por-servicos-do-sus-no-parana.html
6 BBC, 16 Jan 2015, "Police commander sacked over 'sensitive leak'". Available at: http://www.bbc.co.uk/news/uk-30858871
7 Business Insider, 3 Jan 2015, "Corruption In Brazil". Available at: http://uk.businessinsider.com/corruption-in-brazil-the-big-oily-2015-1
8 CNN International, 22 Dec 2014, "Hong Kong tycoon and ex-official found guilty in city's biggest corruption trial". Available at: http://edition.cnn.com/2014/12/19/world/asia/hong-kong-kwok-brothers-verdict/index.html
9 Sveriges Radio, 14 Jan 2015, "Telenor till svars för korruptionshärva". Available at: http://sverigesradio.se/sida/artikel.aspx?programid=83&artikel=6067800

References

Abbink, K., Irlenbusch, B., & Renner, E. (2002). An experimental bribery game, *Journal of Law, Economics, and Organization*, 18, 428–454.
Aidt, T. S. (2003). Economic analysis of corruption: a survey, *The Economic Journal*, 113, F632–F652.
Alencar, C. H. and Gico Jr., I. T. (2011). Corrupção e judiciário: a (in)eficácia do sistema judicial no combate à corrupção, *Revista Direito GV*, 7, 75–98.
Becker, G. S. (1968). Crime and punishment: an economic approach, *The Journal of Political Economy*, 76, 169–217.
Banerjee, A., Mullainathan, S. and Hanna, R. (2012). Corruption, *National Bureau of Economic Research*, Working Paper Series RWP12-023.
Becker, H. S. (1963/2009). *Outsiders: estudos de sociologia do desvio*. Rio de Janeiro: Zahar.
Cadot, O. (1987). Corruption as a gamble, *Journal of Public Economics*, 33, 223–244.
Fender, J. (1999). A general equilibrium model of crime and punishment, *Journal of Economic Behavior & Organization*, 39, 437–453.
Frank, B. and Schulze, G. G. (2000). Does economics make citizens corrupt?, *Journal of Economic Behavior & Organization*, 43, 101–113.
Fried, B. J., Lagunes, P. and Venkataramani, A. (2010). Corruption and inequality at the crossroad: a multimethod study of bribery and discrimination in Latin America, *Latin American Research Review*, 45, 76–97.
Foxall, G. R. (1998). Radical behaviorist interpretation: generating and evaluating an account of consumer behavior, *The Behavior Analyst*, 21, 321–354.
Foxall, G. R. (2010). Invitation to consumer behavior analysis, *Journal of Organizational Behavior Management*, 30, 92–109.
Gico Jr., I. T. (2010). Metodologia e epistemologia da análise econômica do direito, *Economic Analysis of Law Review*, 1, 7–33.

Green, L. and Myerson, J. (2004). A discounting framework for choice with delayed and probabilistic rewards, *Psychological Bulletin*, 130, 769–792.

Green, L., Fry, A. F. and Myerson, J. (1994). Discounting of delayed rewards: a life-span comparison, *Psychological Science*, 5, 33–36.

Kahneman, D. and Tversky, A. (1984). Choices, values, and frames, *American Psychologist*, 39, 341–350.

Knapp, T. J. (1997). Behaviorism and public policy: BF Skinner's views on gambling, *Behavior and Social Issues*, 7, 129–139.

Jain, A. K. (2001). Corruption: a review, *Journal of Economic Surveys*, 15, 71–121.

Lambsdorff, J. G. (2005). Consequences and causes of corruption: what do we know from a cross-section of countries?, *Passauer Diskussionspapiere: Volkswirtschaftliche Reihe*, 34, 1–34.

Lambsdorff, J. G. (2009). The organization of anti-corruption getting incentives right. In Rotberg, R. I. (Ed.). *Corruption, global security, and world order*. Washington: Brookings Institution Press, 389–415.

Lambsdorff, J. G. (2010). Deterrence and constrained enforcement: alternative regimes to deal with bribery. *Passauer Diskussionspapiere: Volkswirtschaftliche Reihe*, 60, 1–39.

Lambsdorff, J. G. (2012). Behavioral and experimental economics as a guidance to anticorruption, *Research in Experimental Economics*, 15, 279–300.

Lambsdorff, J. G. (2014). *The economics of corruption 2014: seeking the nudges for reform.* [PowerPoint slides]. Universität Passau.

Mishra, A. (2006). Corruption, hierarchies and bureaucratic structure. In Rose-Ackerman, S. (Ed.). *International handbook on the economics of corruption*. Cheltenham: Edward Elgar Publishing, 189–216.

Myerson, J. and Green, L. (1995). Discounting of delayed rewards: models of individual choice, *Journal of the Experimental Analysis of Behavior*, 64, 263–276.

Olken, B. A. and Pande, R. (2012). Corruption in developing countries, *Annual Review of Economics*, 4, 479–509.

Rachlin, H. (1974). Self-control, *Behaviorism*, 2, 94–107.

Rachlin, H. (1990). Why do people gamble and keep gambling despite heavy losses?, *Psychological Science*, 1, 294–297.

Rachlin, H. (2010). How should we behave? A review of reasons and persons by Derek Pabfit, *Journal of the Experimental Analysis of Behavior*, 94, 95–111.

Rasmussen, E. B. and Newland, M. C. (2008). Asymmetry of reinforcement and punishment in human choice, *Journal of the Experimental Analysis of Behavior*, 89, 157–167.

Rose-Ackerman, S. (2006). *International handbook on the economics of corruption*. Cheltenham: Edward Elgar Publishing.

Rose-Ackerman, S. (2008). Corruption and government, *International Peacekeeping*, 15, 328–343.

Sheiffer, A. and Vishny, R. (1993). Corruption, *Quarterly Journal of Economics*, 108, 599–617.

Svensson, J. (2005). Eight questions about corruption, *The Journal of Economic Perspectives*, 19, 19–42.

Tanzi, V. (1998). Corruption around the world: causes, consequences, scope, and cures, *International Monetary Fund Staff Papers*, 45, 559–594.

TI (2014). Transparency International Website. Retrieved from http://www.transparency.org/whatwedo, 25 June 2014.

Treisman, D. (2007). What have we learned about the causes of corruption from ten years of cross-national empirical research? *Annual Review of Political Science*, 10, 211–244.

From consumer response to corporate response

The Behavioral Perspective Model of marketing practices

Kevin J. Vella[1]

Introduction

The Behavioral Perspective Model (BPM) is a parsimonious selectionist framework constructed upon a critical evaluation of the potential that an experimental analysis of behavior (EAB) may provide in interpreting the situational influences on human economic choice behavior in natural settings. The BPM draws extensively from the study of human operant behavior (Foxall, 1990, 1993c) and from critical appreciations of cognitive theories from a behaviorist perspective (Foxall, 1996b, 1997a, 2005, 2010a). In twenty-five years of progressive theorizing and research, the BPM now also rests strongly on a varied and extensive base of empirical research (e.g., Foxall, 1997b; Foxall, 2005; Foxall et al., 2007; Foxall, 2010b; Vella and Foxall, 2011; Yan et al., 2012b, a; Foxall and Sigurdsson, 2013; Yani-de-Soriano et al., 2013; Foxall, forthcoming).

In "The marketing firm", Foxall (1999b) extends the BPM in application to corporate practices permitting the functional analysis of marketing and consumer behavior to proceed using a common terminological, theoretical, and philosophical foundation. Importantly, Foxall provides the means to interpret the mutually reinforcing interlocked behavioral exchanges (termed as *bilateral contingencies of reinforcement*) of the two more important participants to affluent and dynamic markets: customers and marketers (Foxall, 1999b).

In extending the BPM to corporate practices, Foxall (1999b) provides a very broad sketch of the possible topography of individual BPM components. However, he neglects to consider whether and how the individual components correspond in interpretation to the firm. For example, how is the phrase "the firm is in a state of deprivation" operationalized? What firm-related phenomena should we be looking at when we refer to the "genetic endowment" of an organization?

In qualitative case study research, Vella and Foxall (2011) demonstrate the usefulness of the BPM as an interpretive device and provide important operational definitions of the BPM variables. However, the authors focus primarily on the more pressing methodological issues and on showing the dynamics within the bilateral contingencies. Vella and Foxall (2011) miss the opportunity to provide an empirically based description of the variables of BPM as these relate to corporate practices. As a result, the definitions remain as tentative and broad characterizations and, in some respects, ambiguous. This impairs structured, focused, and consistent application of the BPM in research related to the firm.

Presently, qualitative case study research is being undertaken to assess the applicability of Skinner's core evolutionary analogy as it relates to the *process of selective retention and elimination for and against cultural practices* to the firm (Vella, 2015). The core dimension of Skinner's evolutionary analogy that is of interest to this research is the statement that operant conditioning processes characterize the dynamics involved in socio-cultural selection (Skinner, 1953, 1961, 1969, 1971, 1973, 1974, 1978, 1981, 1984c, d, b). Thus, the key propositions being qualitatively examined are as follows: (a) cultural practices are acquired, maintained, weakened, and extinguished via the individual's interaction with physical and social environmental contingencies; and (b) the processes by which physical and social environmental contingencies select cultural practices are characterized by positive and negative reinforcement and punishment (Vella, 2015).[2] Thus, the need for greater precision in specifying the components of the BPM in relation to corporate practices becomes more pressing.

The purpose of this chapter is to address this failure and thus reinterpret the BPM in application to corporate behavior to provide a deeper specification of its various components while drawing from earlier research (Vella and Foxall, 2011, sections 2 to 4). The chapter also proposes how qualitative descriptions of behavior-environment interactions may be interpreted to provide a valid and reliable operant account of selective retention and elimination of marketing practices through reinforcement and punishment.

The Behavioral Perspective Model

Consumer Behavior Analysis (CBA) (Foxall, 2001) has emerged to critically apply radical behaviorist philosophy and operant principles to produce an alternative explanation to purchase and consumption behavior, on the one hand, and to marketing, on the other. Cognitive understanding of both spheres of application dominates in the literature, and radical behaviorism occupies an underappreciated niche. In parallel, the EAB presents problems with respect to the extent to which the principles uncovered in an experimental science may be extended to the real world (Foxall, 1990, 1994, 1995a, 2010a).

In applying operant principles outside the confines of the experimental space, extrapolation is rampant. Conventional operant interpretations are considered as conceptual or retrospective narratives and do not entail "empirical scientific work" (Leigland, 2010, p. 207). Conducting such interpretations simply entails drawing inferences directly from principles established in the EAB and applying them to the current situation, assuming continuity of principle (Leigland, 2010; Moore, 2010) without regarding the methodological implications associated with such an approach. The argument is made in favor of developing a systematic and rigorous methodology that incorporated a valid and reliable framework through which to conduct these interpretations (Foxall, 1990, 1994, 1995a, 2010a) to remain within the framework of behavior analysis while avoiding invalid (Foxall, 1998a; Staddon, 2001; Foxall, 2010a; Mace and Critchfield, 2010) or unreliable accounts (Foxall, 1998a, 2010a; Neuringer, 2011) and ad hoc assumptions (Dennett, 1975). The BPM is the central and unifying framework of the CBA (Foxall, 1996b, 2005, 2010a; Foxall and Sigurdsson, 2013; Vella and Foxall, 2013) that has been proposed to achieve this purpose.

The bulk of the theoretical, interpretative, and empirical work undertaken so far using the BPM focuses on purchase and consumption within affluent societies where marketing is an inherent dimension of the context of behavior (Foxall, 1990, 1996b, 1997a, 2005, 2007; Foxall et al., 2007; Foxall, 2010a; Foxall and Sigurdsson, 2013). The psychology and philosophy underlying the BPM are particularly suited to the study of environmental influences on behavior (e.g., Foxall, 1990).

The origins of the marketing firm (Foxall, 1999b) lie in the early and recurring contention that using a common conceptual framework (the BPM and its underlying philosophy and principles) provides a strong basis for investigating and understanding the nature of the interrelationship between purchase and consumption behaviors and marketing (Foxall, 1990, 1994, 1997b, 1999b, 2001; Vella and Foxall, 2011). Simply put, within affluent societies marketing is one of the more important situational influences of purchase and consumption and vice versa. The marketing firm provides an operant interpretation of the behavior of the firm to complement the one developed on purchase and consumption behaviors (Foxall, 1990, 1997a, 2001, 2005, 2007; Vella and Foxall, 2011, 2013).

Accounting for real-world human behavior

The BPM is an elaboration of the three-term contingency and provides a theoretical device to interpret behavior that is not amenable to an EAB. The framework is specifically constructed to account for what Foxall (1990, 1996b, 1997a, 1999a, 2010a) classes as the fundamental weaknesses of the EAB.[3]

First, non-human animal experiments provide very limited insights into the situational influences on the behavior of humans (e.g., Foxall, 1990, 1993c, 1994, 2001). Given the human susceptibility to operant conditioning and that verbal behavior is uniquely human, surely some reinforcers and punishers may be particular only to humans (Wearden, 1988). This point has implications for the nature of reinforcement in humans and gives rise to conceptualizing the influence of utilitarian and informational sources of rewards and punishment on human behavior within the BPM (e.g., Foxall, 1990, 1993c, a, 1996b, 1997a, 1998b, 2005, 2010a; cf. Kollins et al., 1997).

Utilitarian reinforcement and punishment relates to the positive and negative consequences of behavior mediated by the direct usable, economic, and technical benefits of a product and its cost (generally associated with contingency-shaped behavior) (Foxall, 1997a, 2005, 2010a; Vella and Foxall, 2011; Yan et al., 2012a, p. 363; Vella and Foxall, 2013). This form of reinforcement is operationally defined in terms of processes wherein the rate of future emissions is altered through incentives, practical outcomes, functional or instrumental benefits, and costs (positive and negative utilitarian reinforcers and punishers). Behavior also generates informational consequences or outcomes relating to verbal feedback on performance and on accomplishment and is usually mediated by the behavior of others. Informational reinforcement and punishment is operationally defined in terms of processes wherein the rate of future emissions is altered through positive and negative feedback on performance, on level of achievement, and on the accuracy of such performance respectively (generally associated with rule-governed behavior) (Foxall, 1996b, 1997a, 2005, 2010a; Vella and Foxall, 2011, 2013). Therefore, informational reinforcement contributes to resolving the problems posed by the prevailing nexus of contingencies more effectively by providing individuals with the necessary feedback on the appropriateness and accuracy of their performance. The feedback is expressed in terms of the appropriateness of behavior with respect to the generation of utilitarian outcomes of purchase and consumption and in terms of such social outcomes as status and prestige (Foxall, 1997a, 2010a). Utilitarian reinforcement is considered of similar character to "value in use" or functional properties of the product class, and the brand and informational reinforcement is considered of similar character to "exchange value" as feedback on the performance and accomplishments of the individual's behavior as a consumer (Foxall, 1997a, 2005, 2010a; Yan et al., 2012b).

The BPM portrays reinforcement in terms of combinations or *patterns* that exert relatively low to relatively high levels of control over behavior.

The bifurcation of reinforcement is a fundamental contention of BPM as utilitarian reinforcers and punishers are strong environmental consequences that act independently, simultaneously, and interactively within a situation to generate consumer behavior (Foxall, 1990, 1992b, 1993c, 1995a, 1997a, 1998b, 2005, 2010a; Vella and Foxall, 2011; Yan et al., 2012a; Yani-de-Soriano et al., 2013).

Moreover, even when experiments are carried out on humans, laboratory settings are significantly more restrictive than natural ones (e.g., Foxall, 1990, 1994, 1996b, 2005, 2010a). This point becomes salient when a contrast is made between the contrived setting for behavior engineered within an experimental space where antecedent and consequential stimuli are few (or even one) and are controlled by a single researcher and the less contrived setting characterized by a supermarket where antecedent and consequential stimuli are many and in the control of several marketers (e.g., Foxall, 1990, 1997a, 2010a). These situational influences include different ranges of products, differentiated brands, atmospherics, and so on (Vella and Foxall, 2011).[4]

The BPM characterizes as the *setting scope* the range and extent of differences in behavior settings through a set of antecedent stimuli. In the EAB, the scope reflects the extent to which behavior may be brought under the contingency control by the experimental researcher. On the other hand, in operant interpretations, the scope reflects the extent to which the environmental (i.e., extra-personal variables) control of behavior may be established through an accurate and objective specification of the contingencies (Foxall, 1990, 1996b, 2010a). In other words, the distinction between the relative scope strictures of behavior settings may be explained in terms of (a) the relative extent to which the environment, as the "behavior modifier" (Schwartz and Lacey, 1988) or behavior modification agent, gains contingency control over an individual's behavior, and (b) the extent to which the individual's rate of responding may be related to extra-personal (i.e., environmental) variables (Foxall, 1993c, p. 218). The BPM assumes that all consumer behavior may be interpreted in terms of extra-personal influences but recognizes the methodological limitations in reliably, objectively, and accurately relating the rate of responding to its actual situational determinants (Foxall, 1990, 1993c, 1996b, 2010a). Generally, the more closed the behavior setting, the less unambiguous and the more easily identifiable are the extra-personal influences. Conversely, the more open the behavior setting, the greater the ambiguity and difficulty in relating behavior to its situational determinants (Foxall, 1992b, 1993c). In operationalization, the scope of the setting reflects the extent to which individuals are compelled by situational influences to behave in particular ways and, therefore, behavior settings are said to vary in the range of emissions available to individuals (Foxall, 1999a, 2005, 2010a; Vella and Foxall, 2011, 2013).

It should also be noted that the greater the degree of control over consumer contingencies, the more predictable consumer behavior will be (Foxall, 1997a, 2005). Thus, purchase and consumption behavior follows a more stable, regular, and routinized pattern. From a marketing perspective, this stability reduces environmental uncertainty (Vella and Foxall, 2013) and enhances predictability for better planning and more stable revenue and profit streams. Conversely, the more open the behavior setting, the greater the ambiguity and difficulty in relating behavior to its situational determinants (Foxall, 1992b, 1993c). This implies greater variability and fluctuation in consumer behavior patterns and related revenue/profit streams as environmental uncertainty increases.

The scope runs along a continuum from relatively closed to relatively open settings. Figure 17.1 depicts the portion of the continuum wherein consumer and marketer behavior settings reside to denote the situational influences of consumers and marketers respectively. These settings are significantly different from experimental spaces.

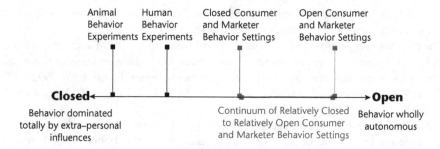

Figure 17.1 The theoretical continuum of behavior settings conceptualized by Foxall

Source: Adapted from Foxall (1992b, p. 386) and Foxall (1993c, pp. 215–19)

The BPM considers a third departure from behaviorist orthodoxy: the possibility that in certain purchase and consumption situations, consumers may privately specify rules (summaries of contingencies) which function as discriminative stimuli and may provide a proximal or immediate explanation of behavior. Ultimately, however, these verbal stimuli are under external environmental control (Foxall, 1990, 1993a, c, 1994). Although consumer behavior may be characterized as rule-governed (e.g., following the specifications by marketers of the reinforcement patterns contingent upon purchasing a specific brand over others), ultimately such behavior is shaped by direct exposure to the contingencies (Foxall, 1990, 1993a, c, 1997a, 2010a). This is because whereas contingency-shaped behavior comes under the control of discriminative stimuli and is maintained by its consequences, rule-governed behavior comes under verbal stimulus control and is only indirectly maintained by consequences (Skinner, 1966a, 1969, 1984a).

Although the BPM does assume continuity of operant principles, the primary emphasis is on these three departures: first, to account for those situations where the generalization of the results obtained in EAB to real-world behavior may fall short; and, second, to continually attempt to refute the extent of such generalization through valid and reliable systematic interpretation or empirical research.

Instead of rejecting the EAB outright or simply assuming complete continuity, the BPM offers a mode for interpreting behavior systematically and rigorously within a radical behaviorist philosophy via the principles of operant psychology.

Purchase and consumption in terms of the BPM

The BPM characterizes real-world purchase and consumption behaviors from a molar approach to encompass an entire patterned sequence of pre-purchase, purchase, and post-purchase activities (Foxall, 1990, 1996b) (Figure 17.2).

Antecedent spatial or physical (a brand, point-of-purchase displays), temporal (opening hours), regulatory (brand information), and social (a salesperson) events comprise the consumer environment, and thus define the *behavior setting*. These events may be classed as consequential marketing stimuli that may occasion reinforcement and punishment contingent upon the emission of certain repertoires over others (Foxall, 1990, 1997a, 2010a). The BPM also provides for stimulus events that may achieve motivating function (Fagerstrøm et al., 2010).

As stated, behavior settings are also characterized as varying in scope along a continuum of relatively closed to relatively open settings (Figure 17.3).

In relatively closed settings, for example, a retail outlet at a train station that exclusively sells ice cream brands from a given manufacturer reflects the degree of control marketers have on the ice cream purchase and consumption contingencies of travelers and commuters. Customers wanting an ice cream have little choice – they either purchase the brands on sale, go elsewhere

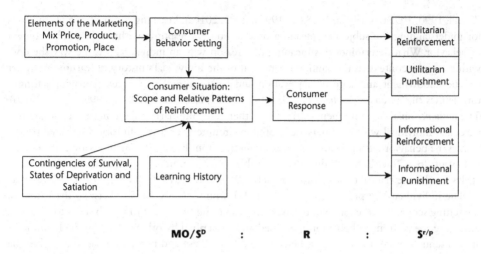

Figure 17.2 The Behavioral Perspective Model explains pre-purchase, purchase, and post-purchase consumer behavior in natural settings

Source: Foxall (1997a, 2010a)

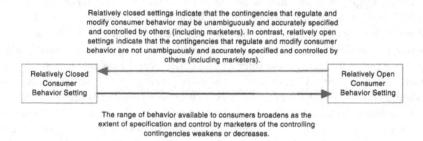

Figure 17.3 Behavior Setting Scope

Source: Adapted from Foxall (1990, 1996b, 1997a, 1999a, 2010a)

if ice cream is available at other locations within the station, or do without. Alternatively, consumers may emit escape–avoidance behaviors. The range of behaviors available to consumers widens if the same retail outlet stocks rival brands. Buyers are then able to emit a broader range of choice behaviors among available brands. In relatively closed situations, consumers are found following the patterns of behavior prescribed (and proscribed) by marketers: the more closed the behavior setting, the greater the extent to which an individual will be found following closely the patterns of behavior prescribed by others (Foxall, 1997a; Vella and Foxall, 2013).

As such, any of the various stimuli programmed and implemented by marketers (i.e., the elements of the marketing mix) may function either as consequential or scope stimuli (Foxall, 1990, 1997a; Vella and Foxall, 2011).

Antecedent and consequential stimulus events are presumed neutral and may acquire stimulus function in the presence of the individual's learning history, her genetic endowment (i.e., contingencies of survival), and the current state of deprivation and satiation (Foxall, 1990, 1992b, 1997a, 2001, 2010a).

Learning history, on the one hand (as the central personal variable, i.e., the temporal dimension), and the behavior setting, on the other (as an environmental or extra-personal variable, i.e., the spatial dimension), are the essential components in constructing behaviorist explanations

(Foxall, 1990, 1995a, b, 1997a, 1998a, b, 1999a, 2005, 2010a). Learning history provides the basis for understanding the subjective meaning of a consumer's response within a particular context of behavior. What determines this meaning (the reason why an individual acts the way she does within a given context) is the unique interaction of the individual's history of learning (plus her genetic endowment and state of deprivation and satiation) and the current behavior setting – this defines the *consumer situation* (Foxall, 1992b, 1995a, b, 1997a, 1998b, a, 1999a, 2005, 2010a). The *consumer situation* component of the BPM, therefore, summarizes the unique interaction of a particular individual with an otherwise neutral environment. Learning history is activated by and primes the behavior setting to form the consumer situation (Foxall, 1997a): this is a specific empirical event (Jo at Tesco's) that is directly observable and, therefore, constitutes the deepest level of analysis and is the critical explanatory core of the BPM (Foxall, 1996b, 1997a, 1998b, 2005, 2010a).

The individual interprets the setting through learning history and predicts: (a) the extent of the setting scope, i.e., the range of behaviors available and the extent to which she is to be found following the patterns of behavior prescribed and proscribed by others; (b) most likely immediate consequences contingent upon behavioral pre-purchase and purchase emissions within the setting; and (c) the most likely subsequent consequences contingent upon consumption and other post-purchase behavior. Thus, the consumer situation regulates the rate of purchase and consumption behavior (e.g., Foxall, 1996b; 1997a, 2005, 2010a).

In the absence of learning history (e.g., a new product on the market), the BPM considers consumers as engaging in deliberative or private or public verbal behavior. Foxall (1997a, 1998a, 1999a, 2005, 2007) characterizes such behavior as being primarily rule-following behavior contingent upon a history of following rules *and* following the instructions provided by *marketers* and by others. For example, before trying out a new brand for the first time, consumers would heed adverts, search for information on the Internet, and talk to peers or opinion leaders. In addition, consumers construct their own rules from a history of purchase and consumption in unrelated settings and/or from observations of the choices made by shoppers already present in the specific setting. These behaviors gradually help construct learning history in relation to the new product in question and may also function as heuristics in future similar or unrelated settings (Foxall, 2007).

Consumer behavior is simultaneously reinforced and punished by its utilitarian and informational consequences: the acquisition of reinforcers (a particular brand of product, praise on purchasing an item of prestige) entails relinquishing money (the surrender of reinforcers, therefore a punishing act) *and* these rewards and costs are likely to increase/decrease the probability of future purchase and consumption behaviors (e.g., Alhadeff, 1982; Foxall, 1990, 1992a, 1996b, 1997a, 1999b, 2010a; Vella and Foxall, 2011).

Patterns of consumer behavior may be conveniently conceptualized in terms of *strengths* (i.e., magnitude and frequency on a given occasion) in the rate of *approach* and *escape–avoidance* (Alhadeff, 1982; Foxall, 1990, 1997a, 2010a). Given the respective learning history of individual consumers, patterns of consumer behavior either *approach* the net positively reinforcing patterns represented by a particular brand on sale or *escape-avoid* its punishing consequences. Window-shopping, browsing brands on a supermarket shelf, product trials, and purchasing a particular brand are all examples of approach. Shopping elsewhere, requiring non-stocked brands, and exiting a store are examples of escape–avoidance (Vella and Foxall, 2011).[5]

The likelihood that a particular brand will be purchased may be represented as the intersection of the two opposing approach and escape tendencies or functions (Alhadeff, 1982; Foxall, 1990, 1992a, 1996b, 1997a, 2010a; Vella and Foxall, 2011) (Figure 17.4).

Within the BPM the allocation of consumer purchase and consumption behaviors to one brand over other brands is a function of the net relative strength of patterns of utilitarian and informational reinforcers of buying and using the one brand vis-à-vis the relative patterns offered

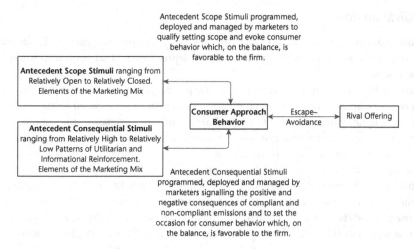

Figure 17.4 Approach and escape–avoidance of marketer programmed stimuli

Source: Adapted from Vella and Foxall (2011)

by the functional substitutes in a brand repertoire (Foxall et al., 2007). The *net relative strength of patterns of utilitarian and informational reinforcement* refers to the net positive and negative utilitarian and informational consequences generated in buying and consuming a particular brand.

Utilitarian reinforcement and punishment, informational reinforcement and punishment, and antecedent setting scope stimuli are considered as orthogonal extra-personal variables acting independently and in interaction within a particular situation to generate purchase and consumption behavior (Foxall, 1990, 1998b, 2010a; Vella and Foxall, 2011; Yani-de-Soriano et al., 2013).

Marketing practices in terms of the BPM

The BPM for marketing practices is summarized diagrammatically in Figure 17.5.

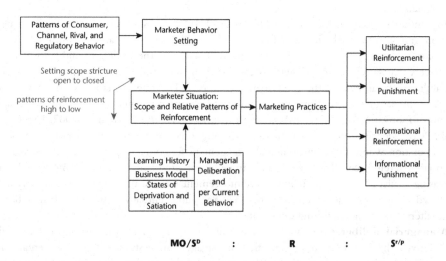

Figure 17.5 The Behavioral Perspective Model for marketing practices

Source: Vella (2015)

The individual firm

The individual firm is represented in the BPM by the contingencies specified by its learning history and by its business model, and the state of deprivation and satiation in relation to the business model.

Learning history: Any individual firm is unique by virtue of its learning history. Foxall (1997a) defines learning history as the cumulative "sum total of . . . emitted behaviors and their consequences under particular conditions . . . learning history summarizes the cumulative contingencies of reinforcement and punishment under which the individual . . . has previously behaved" (p. 58). Learning history represents "habit" or the potential for the continuity of behavior within sufficiently similar behavior settings (Foxall, 1993b, 1997a, 2010a). Repeated interaction with the environment modifies the learning history of the individual, altering the probability of similar emissions being repeated in future (e.g., Foxall, 1992a, 2010a).

Business models: Each profit-making organization has an explicit or implicit business model that describes the particular way in which organizations are designed or structured to create and deliver value to customers and through which to generate revenue and make profit (Teece, 2012). The case study of Vella and Foxall (2011) showed the importance of business models: manufacturers, distributors, and retailers need to satisfy certain conditions, e.g., economies of scale in production (manufacturers), distribution economies, and location with volume consumer traffic (retailers) that are particular to the type of business they operate. As such, therefore, satisfying the business model would appear to be a useful analogy to satisfying the contingencies of survival particular to different types of profit-making organizations.[6] The formulation should not be taken to imply that all firms within a particular category have identical business models or that there is an optimal route towards survival and growth. Indeed, business models are not static but may be changed (Teece, 2012).

State variables: Within the BPM, state variables are not properly defined. The more recurring description, however, emphasizes the consumer levels of deprivation/satiation and the ability of the consumer to pay due to budgetary constraints and the availability of credit (Foxall, 1996b, 2010a), i.e., spending power (Vella and Foxall, 2011). Further, deprivation and satiation are tied to the effectiveness of reinforcers and punishers (e.g., Foxall, 1990, 1997a, 2010a; Vella and Foxall, 2011).

In contrast to Vella and Foxall (2011), Vella (2015) limits state variables to levels of deprivation and satiation, which are defined as follows: *Deprivation* is an operation where the environmental arrangement functions to withhold access to the utilitarian and informational reinforcers that satisfy the contingencies expressed in the business model either by reducing availability or by increasing the reinforcement interval. The reinforcers involved are working and investment capital, cash flow, profits, and production/marketing capacity. Given the definitions of motivating operations (MOs) (e.g., Laraway et al., 2003; Michael, 2007; Fagerstrøm et al., 2010), deprivation may have a value-altering effect in establishing operations. *Satiation* is an operation where the environmental arrangement functions to present the utilitarian and informational reinforcers that satisfy the contingencies expressed in the business model either by increasing availability or by reducing the reinforcement interval until emissions that originally produced such environmental consequences weaken and eventually stop. Satiation may have a value-altering effect in abolishing operations.

Managerial deliberation: Vella and Foxall (2011) also draw the analogy between the deliberative behavior of consumers and that of managers, suggesting that environmental stimuli acquire meaning in the presence of the process of deliberation. This notion is analogous to managerial decision-making. *Managerial deliberation* (and precurrent behavior) may thus be characterized as observable in explicit self-rules such as production and marketing objectives and plans, and in the rules of others such as the profit, market share, and related goals imposed by a mother company (Vella and Foxall, 2011).

Given the behavioral interpretation of problem-solving (Skinner, 1966a, 1969, 1984a), managerial deliberation also serves to extract rules with respect to prevailing (e.g., observations on the behavior of rivals) and past contingencies. Within this research, deliberation is also understood to encapsulate explicit (e.g., coded within business intelligence databases) or tacit, formal or informal, firm-specific instruction sets for retaining and replicating those dimensions of the marketing mixes that were functionally effective in generating acceptable levels of profitable exchange (and, therefore, survival value). Managerial deliberation is primarily rule-following behavior contingent upon a history of following rules (Foxall, 1999a; Vella and Foxall, 2011).

The four elements (managerial deliberation, learning history, the business model, and the state of deprivation/satiation) are analogous to what Foxall (e.g., 1996b) calls consumer "personal variables". In conjunction, these elements prime the *marketer behavior setting* and, in turn, are activated by the setting. Not all (or any) of the prevailing events achieve discriminative or motivating function. Some events function as reinforcers while others act as punishers and some other stimuli remain neutral. The components are also understood as functioning to determine the extent of setting scope stricture.

The dependent variable: marketing practices

Within the marketing firm, the marketing mix is a proxy for corporate marketing practices. The mix is defined in terms of the four Ps: price, product, promotion, and place (Vella and Foxall, 2011), which are categories of the different elements of a firm's marketing program aimed at and designed for delivering value to target business and consumer markets (Kotler et al., 2013). Value is interpreted in terms of the positive and negative utilitarian and informational outcomes of purchase and consumption (e.g., Foxall, 1993c, 1996b; Foxall, 1997a, 1999a, 2010a; Vella and Foxall, 2011). It is important to distinguish between the actual effects of the marketing mix and the programmed effects for which mixes are designed (Foxall, 2010a; Vella and Foxall, 2011).

Product elements revolve around all variables related to delivering physical or service offerings that satisfy functional and symbolic customer needs. The category covers packaging, branding, product features, warranties, labeling, product development, and so on. The *Price* category involves elements related to how much a firm will charge for its product offering and includes such aspects as distribution and retail discounts, credit terms, rebates etc. The *Promotional* category involves personal selling, advertising, sales promotions (special incentive schemes, additional discounts and bonus payments, prizes), and public relations efforts. The *Place* category relates to atmospherics, distribution, and retail strategies, merchandising (space allocation, point-of-sale materials, special displays, freezer cabinets), retail outlet type, locational convenience, cold chain delivery, channel coverage, warehousing, and so on (Vella and Foxall, 2011; Kotler et al., 2013). These and other elements of the marketing mix are interpreted as possible physical, temporal, social, and regulatory utilitarian and informational reinforcers and punishers.

Two types of marketing mixes are to be identified: one that is geared for consumer markets and another geared for channel markets. Both forms of mixes are assumed to work in tandem – advertising by the manufacturer that targets consumers helps generate and pull demand at retail and at distribution channels. Volume targets and channel performance bonuses operate in conjunction with outlet exclusivity push demand downstream.

The definition of marketing mixes also includes exploratory and search behavior such as conducting regular market research to facilitate sales and production planning, new brand and product launches, gathering and processing data on the physical surroundings (e.g., weather forecasts) and maintaining a market intelligence information system.

The strategic options open to the firm

According to the marketing firm, ultimately, firms emerge and exist to market while economizing on the costs of market transactions (Foxall, 1999b; Vella and Foxall, 2011, 2013).

The underlying theory does not predict the topography of the mixes that firms deploy. Instead it focuses on hypothesizing the manner in which price, products, brands, promotion, and logistical variables operate on the environment (a) to shape and maintain customer and consumer approach behavior and increase the probability that such behavior terminates in literal exchange, and (b) to weaken and terminate escape–avoidance and reduce the likelihood that such behavior terminates in literal exchange with rivals (Foxall, 1990, 1997a, 1999b; Vella and Foxall, 2011, 2013). Vella and Foxall (2011) establish comprehensive and extensive non-generalizable evidence supporting the claim by Foxall (1990, 1997a, 1999b) that the various strategic options of the firm may be interpreted, via the BPM, to function as attempts to gain control of customer contingencies of utilitarian and informational reinforcement to generate profitable literal exchange in either or in both of the following ways: First, by regulating and modifying the various elements of the marketing mix to manage the stricture of the scope of the behavior setting by controlling the range of behavioral alternatives available to customers and consumers and compelling them to act in favorable ways. Second, by regulating and modifying the various elements of the marketing mix to manage the customer and consumer patterns of utilitarian and informational reinforcement to compel customers and consumers to act in particular ways (Foxall, 1990, 1992a, 1997a, 1999b; Vella and Foxall, 2011, 2013).

Vella and Foxall (2011) describe the manner in which the marketing mix of Wall's at distribution functioned in terms of these two functional interpretations. For example, in 1998 Wall's was found managing a set of exclusivity contracts with a number of distributors. These channel members were precluded from trading in any ice cream brands other than those of Wall's. In return, Wall's offered generous patterns of utilitarian and informational reinforcement including passing about 60% of its total traded volumes through this handful of distributors. Other arrangements that varied in the relative setting stricture also varied in the richness of patterns of reinforcement. Relatively more open behavior settings resulted in poorer patterns of reinforcement (see Figure 17.6).

Thus, marketing practices are said to shape, strengthen, maintain channel and customer approach behavior, and weaken escape–avoidance to increase the likelihood of profitable literal exchange through qualifying the setting scope and/or regulating consumer and channel patterns of reinforcement. In so doing, marketing behavior also thwarts competitive encroachment (Foxall, 1990, 1999b; Vella and Foxall, 2011, 2013) (see Figure 17.7). Marketing practices facilitate the interaction between the firm and its market environment and, ultimately, serve to generate profitable literal exchange.

The greater the degree of control over consumer contingencies, the more predictable consumer behavior will be (Foxall, 1997a, 2005). Thus, purchase and consumption behavior would follow a more stable, more regular, and habitual or routinized pattern. Stability reduces environmental uncertainty (Vella and Foxall, 2013) to enhance predictability for better planning and more stable revenue and profit streams.

The marketing firm (Foxall, 1999b; Vella and Foxall, 2011, 2013) claims that the firm does not simply supersede the market by organizing market relations that reduce the cost of transacting in the open market via the price mechanism (that is, by offering a significantly lower price) as suggested by Coase (1937, 1960, 1988). Rather it *circumscribes* exchange via all the elements

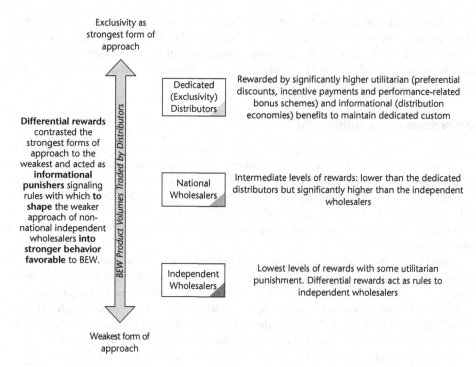

Figure 17.6 Differential reward scheme of Wall's: the interaction of scope qualification and reinforcer management

Source: Vella (2010, p. 65)

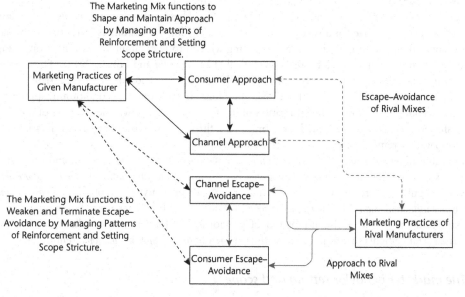

Figure 17.7 Managing patterns of reinforcement and setting scope stricture: effects on approach and escape–avoidance

Source: Vella (2015)

of a marketing mix that functions to control existing contingencies by regulating and modifying setting stricture and patterns of reinforcement (Foxall, 1999b; Vella and Foxall, 2011, 2013). Vella and Foxall (2011), for example, demonstrate the power of the setting scope as a situational independent variable influencing purchasing and consumption patterns and prescribing distributor and retailer approach while proscribing their escape–avoidance.

Reinforcement and punishment

The marketing firm contemplates the bifurcation of reinforcement contingent upon the firm's marketing emissions: the consequences of marketing practices lie primarily in the positive and negative utilitarian and informational outcomes of its behavior within the market expressed in terms of consumer and channel approach, escape–avoidance, profitable literal exchange, and rival action (Foxall, 1999b; Vella and Foxall, 2011, 2013). The definitions of such outcomes are presented in Table 17.1 and are based on the operational definitions and empirical findings of Vella and Foxall (2011).

It should be noted that marketer and consumer behavior are characterized as a chain of interlocked sequences of events extending over space and time that eventually either terminate in literal exchange or in escape–avoidance behaviors (Foxall, 1990). Literal exchange constitutes a transaction between two parties involving the mutual surrender of property rights (Foxall, 1999b; Vella and Foxall, 2011, 2013) and therefore is best conceptualized as the intersection of two terminal responses. Exchange behavior is simultaneously reinforced and punished.

From the point of view of the firm, consumer and channel approach and escape–avoidance behaviors are informational reinforcers and punishers because these behaviors signal some relatively high to low likelihood of terminating in literal exchange and, eventually, profit.

Conceivably, the only source of net utilitarian reinforcement for the firm is literal exchange less the costs of transacting. Within the marketing firm (Foxall, 1999b; Vella and Foxall, 2011), these costs are those which Coase originally called "marketing costs" (Coase, 1937, p. 392) or the "cost of market transactions" (Coase, 1960, p. 15). These *market transaction costs* involve any of the expenses incurred and investments made in searching for customers, gathering information about them, communicating and negotiating with customers, administering and monitoring contracts, and so on (Coase, 1960, 1988; Foxall, 1999b; Vella and Foxall, 2011). These latter costs are examples of utilitarian punishers (Foxall, 1999b; Vella and Foxall, 2011, 2013).

From the point of view of the BPM, therefore, tracing operant conditioning processes requires taking into account the bifurcation of reinforcement as follows: the practices of the firm are shaped, maintained, weakened, or extinguished through positive and negative utilitarian and informational reinforcement and punishment. Shaping involves practices which are acquired through differential *positive and negative utilitarian and informational* reinforcement and successive approximation. Maintenance involves *positive and negative utilitarian and informational reinforcement* which regulate the recurrence of past emissions. Weakening involves a process of *positive and negative utilitarian and informational punishment* to reduce the rate of emissions of such repertoires. Extinction involves the discontinuation of previously reinforced practices through environmental arrangements that function to withhold such *utilitarian and informational* reinforcement.

The marketer behavior setting and scope

Vella and Foxall (2011) treat any feature of the antecedent environment as a possible stimulus event. The presence or absence of a retail trade, the number of retailers, the structure of the retail trade, the geographical location of a given retailer, the issue of whether a retail business

Table 17.1 Utilitarian and informational reinforcers and punishers, definitions and empirical generalizations

	Operational definition	*Empirical examples*
Utilitarian reinforcers	Incentives, functional or instrumental benefits, or payoffs arising directly from literal exchange.	The presence or increase or strengthening of sales revenues and volumes, positive cash flow and profits. The absence, decreases, or weakening of the costs involved in the acquisition and retention of consumers and customers.
Utilitarian punishers	Disincentives, functional or instrumental costs.	The absence, decreases, or weakening of sales revenues and volumes, positive cash flow and profits. The presence or increase or strengthening in the costs involved in the acquisition and retention of consumers and customers.
Informational reinforcers	Positive feedback on performance with respect to the generation of utilitarian outcomes, on level of achievement, on the accuracy of such performance, and on the extent to which behavior contributes to resolving the problems posed by the prevailing nexus of contingencies more effectively.	The presence or increase or strengthening of consumer and customer approach, market share, rival escape–avoidance, profitability, working and investment capital, positive alignment of performance with respect to the achievement of organizational plans, goals (including problem resolution), and targets, and positive capacity utilization. The absence, decreases, or weakening of consumer and customer escape–avoidance, rival approach, losses, working and investment capital, negative (mis)alignment of performance with respect to the achievement of organizational plans, goals (including problem resolution), and targets, and negative capacity utilization. Relative increases or strengthening in utilitarian and informational reinforcers and relative decreases or weakening in utilitarian and informational punishers. Increases in the quality and a reduction in reinforcement delay also appear to have reinforcing effects. The absence, decreases, or weakening of regulatory intervention that adversely affects business. For example, deregulation of telecommunications. The presence or increase or strengthening of regulatory intervention that positively affects business. For example, the removal of trade barriers.
Informational punishers	Negative feedback on performance with respect to the generation of utilitarian outcomes, on level of achievement, on the accuracy of such performance, and on the extent to which behavior contributes to resolving the problems posed by the prevailing nexus of contingencies more effectively.	The presence or increase in consumer and customer escape–avoidance, rival approach, negative cash flows, losses, working and investment capital, negative (mis)alignment of performance with respect to the achievement of organizational plans, goals (including problem resolution), and targets, and negative capacity utilization. The absence, decrease, or weakening of consumer and customer approach, market share, rival escape–avoidance, profitability, working and investment capital, positive alignment of performance with respect to the achievement of organizational plans, goals (including problem resolution), and targets, and positive capacity utilization. Relative decreases or weakening of utilitarian and informational reinforcers and relative increases or strengthening in utilitarian and informational punishers. Decreases in the quality of and an increase in reinforcement delay also appear to have punishing effects. The absence, decreases, or weakening of regulatory intervention that positively affects business. The presence or increase or strengthening of regulatory intervention that adversely affects business.

Source: Elaborated and adapted from Vella and Foxall (2011)

has one location or several, and the actual and potential volume of business that a retailer generates due to its location (within the M25, the London Orbital Motorway that circumscribes the most heavily populated areas in the UK) and due to its target consumer segment (supermarket, petrol forecourt) (Vella and Foxall, 2011). These and other elements are interpreted as possible physical, temporal, social, and regulatory utilitarian and informational reinforcers and punishers.

Given learning history, these events have two main stimulus effects, thereby formulating two different types of stimulus classes: (a) as antecedent scope stimuli they may compel particular behaviors depending upon the degree of setting scope stricture, and/or (b) signal the availability of reinforcement within the current setting (as S^D) or signal the degree to which a consequence is reinforcing or punishing within a particular situation (as MOs). Vella and Foxall (2011) find interaction of events within each class of events and interaction of both classes of events bringing to bear on the behavior of the firm. An exclusivity contract is an example of an antecedent scope stimulus event. Consumer demand and the size of a distributor's refrigerated fleet are examples of consequential stimuli. Regulatory intervention acquired motivating function with respect to Wall's (Vella and Foxall, 2011, 2013).

Stimulus events may be either internal or external to the firm: the *managerial behavior setting* characterizes the physical, social, temporal, and regulatory events that define the context for managerial deliberation, and, thus, in conjunction with learning history and the business model, mediates the interpretation of the marketer behavior setting to determine (a) the extent of the setting scope and whether events acquire discriminative or motivating function, and (b) the appropriate emissions (cf. Vella and Foxall, 2013).

The *marketer behavior setting* characterizes the context of behavior and the situational influences on firm behavior external to the firm. These influences are delineated by the aggregate regulatory, social, temporal, and physical dimensions of the behavior of all other individual stakeholders as stimulus events external to the firm (Foxall, 1999b; Vella and Foxall, 2011).

The external environment may be characterized in research as follows: (1) any special characteristics of the physical behavior setting. Vella and Foxall (2011) found that the ice cream sales and consumption in the UK were relatively susceptible to fluctuations in weather during any given year and from one year to the next. The authors also mention the impact of the need to have a cold chain delivery system. These, therefore, correspond to physical contingencies. (2) The aggregate behavior of individual consumers, channel customers, rivals, and the regulator composing the stakeholder environment as follows: (a) Consumer behavior: aggregate patterns of consumer approach and escape–avoidance to the net relative richness (quality and quantity) utilitarian and informational reinforcers and punishers signaled by the respective marketing mix of manufacturers and retailers given consumer personal variables and other prevailing contingencies. (b) Channel behavior: aggregate patterns of retailer and distributor approach and escape–avoidance to the net utilitarian and informational reinforcers and punishers signaled by the respective marketing mix of manufacturers given channel personal variables and other prevailing contingencies. (c) Rival behavior: aggregate patterns of firm approach and escape–avoidance to the net utilitarian and informational reinforcers and punishers associated with a particular consumer and customer segment given rival personal variables and other prevailing contingencies. (d) Regulatory intervention: aggregate patterns of government behavior that function to modify and control the competitive behavior of firms for proper operation of a market to the benefit of consumers, firms, and the economy.

Figure 17.8 represents the main elements of the marketer behavior setting as the selective system.

A given marketing mix configuration generates some strength of approach and escape–avoidance among channel members and customers. Customer and channel approach is characterized here as holding a relatively high probability of terminating in literal exchange, whereas escape-avoidance is characterized as having a relatively low probability of terminating in literal exchange with the given firm. Rival behavior functions to either increase or decrease the probability of consumer and channel behavior in terminating in literal exchange with any single firm. Rival offerings that offer richer patterns of reinforcement appear/are assumed to increase the rate of escape–avoidance as more channel customers and consumers defect to rival brands. Conversely, poorer patterns of reinforcement offered by rivals reduce defection rates. Rivals gaining control of contingencies through setting scope stricture produce similar effects on consumer and channel approach and escape-avoidance (Vella and Foxall, 2011; Vella, 2012; Vella and Foxall, 2013).

Consumer and channel approach and escape–avoidance is operationalized by assessing: (a) qualitative evidence that indicates channel and consumer choice towards the brands owned by a particular manufacturer (for example, if the demand for Wall's products is reported as increasing, it indicates an increase in the relative strength of approach and a decrease in the strength of escape–avoidance); (b) the reported sales made by the various manufacturers (actual sales volumes and revenues associated with any given brand indicate the extent to which approach net of escape–avoidance behaviors terminate in literal exchange); and (c) the related performance metrics (e.g., profitability, rate of brand sales, brand and market share, and so on). Rival approach and escape–avoidance is measured through comparisons of these values (Vella and Foxall, 2011).

The marketer behavior setting also varies in relative scope stricture along a continuum from relatively closed to relatively open settings. The *marketer behavior setting scope* reflects the extent to which the current behavior setting compels a particular pattern of marketing practices and indicates how far physical characteristics, consumers, channel customers, rivals, the regulator, and other stakeholders (e.g., banks, investors, shareholders) other than the firm control the settings in which marketing occurs.

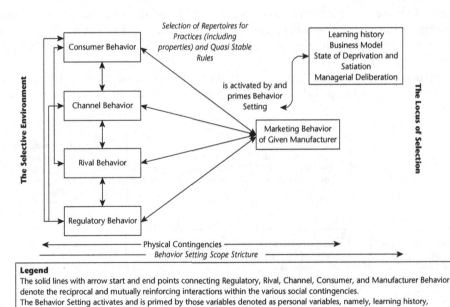

Figure 17.8 The main elements of the marketer behavior setting as the selective environment

Source: Vella (2015)

The marketer situation

A construct analogous to the consumer situation, the *marketer situation*, is proposed as an empirically available summary of the interaction of the firm (i.e., its unique learning history including business model, state of deprivation and satiation, managerial deliberation dimension) and elements within the marketer behavior setting.

Environmental interaction: bilateral contingencies of reinforcement

Behavior-environment interactions lie at the heart of behaviorist explanations. The main protagonists of environmental interactions within the marketing firm are marketers and their existing and prospective channel customers and consumers as situated within a broader physical and social context. The marketing firm introduces the concept of the *bilateral contingency of reinforcement* to analyze mutually contingent patterns of interaction between the firm and any or all of its stakeholders. The analysis emphasizes the reciprocal nature of this relationship *and* makes the distinction between reinforcement and punishment arising from social exchange and from literal exchange (Foxall, 1999b).

Foxall (1990, 1999b) draws from social exchange theory to emphasize social exchange and to cast marketer and consumer behavioral interactions as reciprocal mutually reinforcing and mutually contingent. These social exchange interactions may be understood in terms of "a complex lattice arrangement of interrelated S^D:$R\rightarrow S^{r/p}$" (Kunkel, 1977, p. 452; Foxall, 1990) or patterns of mutually contingent interactions (Foxall, 1990) or *bilateral contingencies of reinforcement* (Foxall, 1999b) where the behavior of one agent may set the occasion for the behavior of another. Any change in the antecedent and/or consequential variables within these relationships may alter the likelihood of behavior being *repeated* across similar situations (Kunkel, 1977, p. 446).

Figure 17.9 uses the three-term contingency to demonstrate mutually contingent and interlocking social interactions among marketers and consumers. The figure, drawn from Foxall (1999b), represents the lattice arrangement of three-term contingencies by Kunkel (1977).

Bilateral contingencies are, therefore, a second interpretive device useful in analyzing the various relationships held by the firm (Vella and Foxall, 2011, 2013) and which

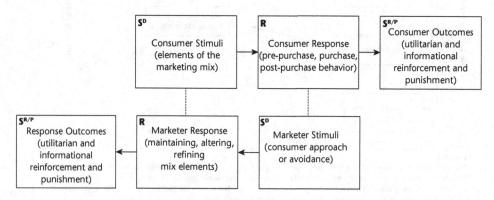

Figure 17.9 Bilateral contingency of reinforcement or patterns of mutually contingent interactions

Source: Adapted from Foxall (1999b, pp. 221–2)

reflect the meaning of relationships as envisaged within economics, i.e., "associated bilateral expectations and behavior between parties" (Hart, 1989; Brousseau, 2008; Vella and Foxall, 2011, p. 33).

The operation of the environment within bilateral contingencies

The research of Vella and Foxall (2011) aimed at showing how marketing behavior, as a significant extra-personal situational variable in real-world markets, operated to shape, maintain, weaken, and eliminate various channel customer and consumer behaviors. As stated earlier, the strategic options open to the firm are described in functional terms as the qualification of setting scope and the management of reinforcers.

As a direct corollary of these arguments, therefore, Vella (2015) proposes that the aggregate behaviors of the individuals composing the stakeholder environment of the firm function as the selective agent. The selective agent operates on the marketing practices of the firm, as the locus of selection, by qualifying the scope of the setting in which marketing practices are emitted and/or by posing arrangements of patterns of reinforcement.

Therefore, Vella (2015) centers his research around the following research propositions to hypothesize the mode in which reinforcement and punishment processes characterize the real-world behavior of market participants within respective bilateral contingencies.

Independently and in aggregate, consumer, customer, rival, and regulator patterns of behavior function as antecedent scope, discriminative or motivational stimulus events within the marketer behavior setting and, historically, have come to regulate and modify the marketing practices of the firm at retail: (a) Consumer, customer, rival, and regulator patterns of behavior function as antecedent utilitarian and informational scope stimulus events by virtue of the learning history of the firm to selectively restrict or encourage patterns of marketing practices, thereby regulating and modifying particular practices over others. (b) Consumer, customer, rival, and regulator patterns of behavior function as utilitarian and informational consequential stimulus events by virtue of the learning history of the firm to selectively restrict or encourage patterns of marketing practices, thereby regulating and modifying particular practices over others.

These propositions account for the real-world differences between experimental spaces and the market as a behavioral environment that need to be invoked when interpreting behavior from an operant perspective.

Since operant interpretation of real-world events cannot achieve the precision of the EAB, Vella (2015) adapts two measures derived from Foxall (1990, 1992a, 1997a, 2010a) to qualitatively demonstrate these propositions (Tables 17.2 and 17.3).

Conclusions

The BPM was originally proposed as a framework within which to systematically and rigorously interpret purchase and consumption behaviors in natural settings from the perspective of operant psychology and radical behaviorism. Its application to understanding the situational influences on real-world marketing practices has generated a budding research program referred to as the marketing firm perspective. The chapter suggests definitions and operational measures for the structured, focused, and consistent application of the BPM in research relating to the firm. The chapter also proposes how qualitative descriptions of behavior-environment interactions may be interpreted to provide a valid and reliable operant account of selective retention and elimination of marketing practices through reinforcement and punishment.

Table 17.2 Measuring environmental qualification of the behavior setting scope

(1) Environmental conditions function to regulate access or routes to and availability of reinforcement and punishment. This is determined by establishing:

    (a) The quantity and prominence of reinforcers (response-strengthening events) and punishers (response-weakening events) available.

    (b) The number of ways in which these reinforcers may be obtained/increased and punishers removed/weakened.

    (c) The extent to which it is necessary to perform specific and prescribed tasks *and/or* the extent to which other specific tasks are proscribed to generate reinforcement. Three additional parameters help ascertain the relative setting stricture on this dimension:

        (i) The extent to which the necessary tasks that are to be performed are clearly and precisely specified and defined. Usually, the necessary tasks are expressed through explicit rules and instructions imposed by others.

        (ii) Necessary tasks are typically reinforced.

        (iii) Different tasks are interchangeable for ones that are reinforced.

(2) The degree of external control of the contingencies within a given situation is determined by:

    (a) Whether externals (environmental agents) control access to reinforcers which involves:

        (i) Establishing the nature, number, and quality of those who control access to reinforcers.

        (ii) The degree to which externals control access to reinforcement by means of regulating states of deprivation and satiation (for example, by withholding or delaying reinforcement).

    (b) The extent to which there is ready access to being in alternative (and substitute) situations which is determined by:

        (i) The number and quality of possible alternative situations.

        (ii) Whether non-compliant behavior (avoidance) is clearly punished to reduce or eliminate the incidence of such responses. Behavior that functions to approach alternatives is punished.

        (iii) Whether compliant behavior is negatively reinforced within the particular situation to dilute reinforcement contingent upon defecting to alternative situations.

    (c) The number of externals who appear to be arranging and controlling the contingencies of reinforcement and punishment (not just access to reinforcement).

    (d) The nature of the externally imposed contingencies and the cost to the individual of escaping from or avoiding the imposed contingencies.

    (e) The extent to which those in control of the contingencies are themselves subject to such contingencies.

Source: Vella (2015)

Table 17.3 Measuring environmental regulation of patterns of reinforcement (the APR measure)

Environmental conditions, independently and in combination, operate on the marketer behavior setting to pose different arrangements of patterns of reinforcement as follows:

(1) Environmental conditions are arranged in a manner that increases or decreases the effectiveness of reinforcers and/or punishers where the effectiveness of such reinforcers or punishers is a function of (a) stimuli being stated explicitly as rules (e.g., the provisions within a contract), (b) the level of deprivation and satiation (Foxall, 1990, 1997a; Vella and Foxall, 2011), (c) the business model of the firm, and (d) its learning history.

(2) Environmental conditions are arranged in a manner that regulates *the quantity and quality of reinforcers and punishers*.

    (a) The *quantity* of reinforcers and punishers

        Environmental conditions are arranged in a manner that increases or decreases the quantity of reinforcers and/or punishers: Increasing or decreasing quantity refers to environmental events that function to increase (addition) or decrease (removal) the number of reinforcers and punishers, thereby strengthening the rate of emission of some marketing practices or weakening others.

        (i)   Environmental conditions quantitatively strengthen certain marketing practices by "adding to or increasing the number of utilitarian and informational benefits and/or decreasing from or removing the number utilitarian and informational aversive consequences" (Vella and Foxall, 2011, pp. 61–2).

        (ii)   Environmental conditions quantitatively weaken certain marketing practices by "decreasing or removing the number of utilitarian and informational benefits and/or adding to or increasing the number utilitarian and informational aversive consequences" (Vella and Foxall, 2011, pp. 61–2).

    (b) The *quality* of reinforcers and punishers

        Environmental conditions are arranged in a manner that increases or decreases the quality of reinforcers and/or punishers: Increasing or decreasing quality refers to environmental events that function to augment, improve, or weaken the effect of present reinforcers and punishers, thereby strengthening the rate of emission of some marketing practices or weakening others.

        (i)   Environmental conditions qualitatively strengthen certain marketing practices by "increasing the [salience] of present utilitarian and informational benefits or decreasing or making less prominent the effect of present utilitarian and informational aversive consequences" (Vella and Foxall, 2011, pp. 61–2).

        (ii)   Environmental conditions qualitatively weaken certain marketing practices through quality by "increasing the [salience] of present utilitarian and informational aversive consequences or decreasing or making less prominent the effect of present utilitarian and informational benefits" (Vella and Foxall, 2011, pp. 61–2).

(3) Environmental contingencies are arranged in a manner analogous to schedules of reinforcement specifying the relative frequency with which behavioral emissions are followed by reinforcers or punishers (Foxall, 1990, 2005; Cooper et al., 2007; Vella and Foxall, 2011, p. 62), thereby strengthening or weakening certain practices.

    (a) Environmental conditions strengthen certain marketing practices in a manner that is analogous to improving ratio and interval schedules of reinforcement:

        (i)   Improving the ratio schedule by reducing the number of responses to be performed to generate reinforcement or by increasing the number of responses to be performed before punishment is generated.

        (ii)   Improving the interval schedule by decreasing reinforcement delay or by increasing punishment delay.

    (b) Environmental conditions weaken certain marketing practices in a manner that is analogous to worsening the ratio and interval schedules of reinforcement.

        (i)   Worsening the ratio schedule by increasing the number of responses to be performed to generate reinforcement or by reducing the number of responses to be performed before punishment is generated.

        (ii)   Worsening the interval schedule by increasing reinforcement delay or decreasing punishment delay.

Source: Vella (2015)

Notes

1 The analysis contained herein is part of my doctoral thesis to be submitted to Cardiff Business School as a member of the Consumer Behaviour Analysis Research Group. I wish to thank Gordon Foxall for his invaluable supervision, useful suggestions, and good-humoured patience.

2 According to Skinner (1966b, 1981, 1984d, 1984b, 1986, 1989), behavior is acquired through shaping, observation, imitation, and modeling processes. Given the nature of the qualitative evidence, Vella (2015) disregards imitation and modeling to focus on shaping.

3 For a complete account of the theoretical development of the BPM and the role of interpretation see (Foxall, 1990, 1992a, 1992b, 1993c, 1993a, 1994, 1995a, 1997a, 1998b), (Fagerstrøm et al., 2010), and (Foxall, 2010a). Foxall (1996a) provides an overview of the initial years of theoretical and conceptual development.

4 Contrast this criticism with Skinner's strict parallel drawn between a cultural environment and the experimental space to claim "designing a culture is like designing an experiment" (Skinner, 1971, p. 150) since "the difference between contrived and natural conditions is *not a serious one*" (Skinner, 1971, p. 156, emphasis added). While admittedly the analogy is useful to conceptualize strategic marketing behavior in terms of the strategies used by experimental researchers to identify consequential and signaling operations, Skinner's claim is not plausible because it is not qualified in any way and thus trivializes the complexity of real-world settings.

5 In contrast to the definitions of the terms *approach* and *escape–avoidance* adopted by Vella and Foxall (2011, 2013), Vella (2015) suggests retaining the definitions of the terms as used in the EAB. Non-reinforced responses made in the presence of a positive or reinforcing stimulus event are called *approach* responses (Alhadeff, 1982; Pierce and Cheney, 2008, p. 86). Approach is shaped and maintained by positive reinforcement contingencies. Both avoidance and escape are responses to aversive stimulus events and as the intensity of these events increases, so does the likelihood of escape–avoidance behaviour (Cooper et al., 2007, p. 337). Emissions that terminate or remove existing or ongoing stimulus events are termed *escape* behavior. On the other hand, emissions that prevent or postpone the presentation of aversive stimuli are termed *avoidance* (Alhadeff, 1982; Cooper et al., 2007; Pierce and Cheney, 2008).

6 The representation differs significantly to the manner in which Vella and Foxall (2011) draw on their analogy of genetic endowment in application to the firm, which, in retrospect, does not seem very useful and appears confused.

References

Alhadeff, David. A (1982). *Microeconomics and Human Behavior: Toward a New Synthesis of Economics and Psychology*. Berkeley and Los Angeles, CA: University of California Press.

Brousseau, Eric (2008). Contracts: From bilateral sets of incentives to the multi-level governance of relations. In: Brousseau, Eric and Glachant, Jean-Michel (eds). *New Institutional Economics*. Cambridge, UK: Cambridge University Press, pp. 37–66.

Coase, Ronald H. (1937). "The nature of the firm." *Economica* 4(16), pp. 386–405.

Coase, Ronald H. (1960). "The problem of social costs." *Journal of Law and Economics* 3(October), pp. 1–60.

Coase, Ronald H. (1988). *The Firm, the Market, and the Law*. Chicago, IL: The University of Chicago Press.

Cooper, John O., Heron, Timothy E. and Heward, William L., Eds. (2007). *Applied Behaviour Analysis*. Upper Saddle River, NJ:, Pearson Education Inc.

Dennett, Daniel C. (1975). "Why the law of effect will not go away." *Journal for the Theory of Social Behaviour* 5(2), pp. 169–188.

Fagerstrøm, Asle, Foxall, Gordon Robert and Arntzen, Erik (2010). "Implications of motivating operations for the functional analysis of consumer behavior." *Journal of Organizational Behaviour Management – Special Issue: Consumer Behaviour Analysis* 30(2), pp. 110–126.

Foxall, Gordon Robert (1990). *Consumer Psychology in Behavioural Perspective*. Washington DC: Beard Books.

Foxall, Gordon Robert (1992a). "The behavioral perspective model of purchase and consumption: From consumer theory to marketing practice." *Journal of the Academy of Marketing Science* 20(2), pp. 189–198.

Foxall, Gordon Robert (1992b). "The consumer situation: An integrative model for research in marketing." *Journal of Marketing Management* 8(4), pp. 383–404.

Foxall, Gordon Robert (1993a). "A behaviourist perspective on purchase and consumption." *European Journal of Marketing* 27(8), pp. 7–16.

Foxall, Gordon Robert (1993b). "Consumer behaviour as an evolutionary process." *European Journal of Marketing* 27(8), p. 46.

Foxall, Gordon Robert (1993c). Situated consumer behavior: A behavioral interpretation of purchase and consumption. In: Costa, Janeen Arnold and Belk, Russell W. (eds). *Research in Consumer Behaviour.* Greenwich, CT: JAI Press, 6, pp. 113–152.

Foxall, Gordon Robert (1994). "Behavior analysis and consumer psychology." *Journal of Economic Psychology* 15(1), pp. 5–91.

Foxall, Gordon Robert (1995a). "Science and interpretation in consumer research: A radical behaviourist perspective." *European Journal of Marketing* 29(9), pp. 2–95.

Foxall, Gordon Robert (1995b). The consumer situation as an interpretive device. In: Hansen, Flemming (ed). *European Advances in Consumer Research.* Provo, UT: Association for Consumer Research, 2, pp. 104–108.

Foxall, Gordon Robert (1996a). An approach to consumer psychology. In: Foxall, Gordon Robert (ed). *Consumers in Context: The BPM Research Program.* London: Routledge, pp. 3–29.

Foxall, Gordon Robert, Ed. (1996b). *Consumers in Context: The BPM Research Program.* London: Routledge.

Foxall, Gordon Robert (1997a). *Marketing Psychology: The Paradigm in the Wings.* Basingstoke: Macmillan Press Ltd.

Foxall, Gordon Robert (1997b). The explanation of consumer behaviour: From social cognition to environmental control. In: Cooper, Cary L. and Robertson, Ivan (eds). *The International Review of Industrial and Organizational Psychology.* Chichester: Wiley, 12, pp. 229–287.

Foxall, Gordon Robert (1998a). "Intention versus context in consumer psychology." *Journal of Marketing Management* 14(1/3), pp. 29–62.

Foxall, Gordon Robert (1998b). "Radical behaviourist interpretation: Generating and evaluating an account of consumer behaviour." *The Behaviour Analyst* 21(2), pp. 321–354.

Foxall, Gordon Robert (1999a). "Putting consumer behaviour in its place: The behavioural perspective model research programme." *International Journal of Management Reviews* 1(2), pp. 133–157.

Foxall, Gordon Robert (1999b). "The marketing firm." *Journal of Economic Psychology* 20(2), pp. 207–234.

Foxall, Gordon Robert (2001). "Foundations of consumer behaviour analysis." *Marketing Theory* 1(2), pp. 165–199.

Foxall, Gordon Robert (2005). *Understanding Consumer Choice.* New York: Palgrave Macmillan.

Foxall, Gordon Robert (2007). *Explaining Consumer Choice.* New York: Palgrave Macmillan.

Foxall, Gordon Robert (2010a). *Interpreting Consumer Choice: The Behavioral Perspective Model.* New York: Routledge.

Foxall, Gordon Robert (2010b). "Theoretical and conceptual advances in consumer behavior analysis: Invitation to consumer behavior analysis." *Journal of Organizational Behavior Management* – *Special Issue: Consumer Behaviour Analysis* 30(2), pp. 92–109.

Foxall, Gordon Robert, Ed. (forthcoming). *Routledge Companion to Consumer Behaviour Analysis.* Oxford: Routledge.

Foxall, Gordon Robert, Oliveira-Castro, Jorge M., Schrezenmaier, Teresa and James, Victoria, K., (eds.) (2007). *The Behavioral Economics of Brand Choice.* Basingstoke: Palgrave Macmillan.

Foxall, Gordon Robert and Sigurdsson, Valdimar (2013). "Consumer behavior analysis: Behavioral economics meets the marketplace." *Psychological Record* 63(2), pp. 231–237.

Hart, Oliver (1989). "An economist's perspective on the theory of the firm." *Columbia Law Review* 89(7), pp. 1757–1774.

Kollins, Scott H., Newland, M. Christoper and Critchfield, Thomas S. (1997). "Human sensitivity to reinforcement in operant choice: How much do consequences matter?" *Psychonomic Bulletin and Review* 4(2), pp. 208–220.

Kotler, Philip, Armstrong, Gary, Harris, Lloyd C. and Piercy, Nigel (2013). *Principles of Marketing.* Harlow: Pearson Education Limited.

Kunkel, John Howard (1977). The behavioural perspective of social dynamics. In: Hamblin, R.L. and Kunkel, John Howard (eds). *Behaviour Theory in Sociology: Essays in Honour of George Homans.* New Brunswick, NJ: Transaction Books, p. 433.

Laraway, Sean, Snycerski, Susan, Michael, Jack and Poling, Alan (2003). "Motivating operations and terms to describe them: Some further refinements." *Journal of Applied Behavior Analysis* 36(3), pp. 407–414.

Leigland, Sam (2010). "Functions of research in radical behaviorism for the further development of behavior analysis." *The Behavior Analyst* 33(2), pp. 207–222.

Mace, F. Charles and Critchfield, Thomas S. (2010). "Translational research in behavior analysis: Historical traditions and imperative for the future." *Journal of the Experimental Analysis of Behavior* 93(3), pp. 293–312.

Michael, Jack (2007). Motivating operations. In: Cooper, John O., Heron, Timothy E. and Heward, William L. (eds). (2nd). *Applied Behaviour Analysis*. Upper Saddle River, NJ: Pearson Education Inc, pp. 374–391.

Moore, Jay (2010). "Behaviorism and the stages of scientific activity." *The Behavior Analyst* 33(1), pp. 47–63.

Neuringer, Allen (2011). "Reach out." *The Behavior Analyst* 34(1), pp. 27–29.

Pierce, W. David and Cheney, Carl D. (2008). *Behaviour Analysis and Learning*. New York: Psychology Press.

Schwartz, Barry and Lacey, Hugh M. (1988). What applied studies of human operant conditioning tell us about humans and about operant conditioning. In: Davey, Graham C. L. and Cullen, Chris (eds). *Human Operant Conditioning and Behaviour Modification*. New York: John Wiley & Sons, pp. 27–42.

Skinner, B. F. (1953). *Science and Human Behaviour*. New York: The Free Press.

Skinner, B. F. (1961). "The design of cultures." *Daedalus* 90(3: Evolution and Man's Progress, Summer), pp. 534–546.

Skinner, B. F. (1966a). An operant analysis of problem-solving. In: Kleinmuntz, B. (ed). *Problem-Solving: Research, Methods and Theory*. New York: John Wiley & Sons, pp. 225–257.

Skinner, B. F. (1966b). "The phylogeny and ontogeny of behavior." *Science* 153, pp. 1205–1213.

Skinner, B. F. (1969). *Contingencies of Reinforcement: A Theoretical Analysis*. New York: Appleton-Century-Crofts Inc.

Skinner, B. F. (1971). *Beyond Freedom and Dignity*. Harmondsworth: Penguin Books.

Skinner, B. F. (1973). "Are we to have a future?" *Impact* 3, pp. 6–12.

Skinner, B. F. (1974). *About Behaviorism*. London: Jonathan Cape Limited.

Skinner, B. F. (1978). *Reflections on Behaviourism and Society*. Upper Saddle River, NJ: Prentice-Hall Inc.

Skinner, B. F. (1981). "Selection by consequences." *Science* 213(4507), pp. 501–504.

Skinner, B. F. (1984a). "An operant analysis of problem-solving." *The Behavioral and Brain Sciences* 7(4), pp. 583–591.

Skinner, B. F. (1984b). "Problems of selection and phytogeny, terms and methods of behaviorism: Reply to catania." *The Behavioral and Brain Sciences* 7(04), pp. 718–719.

Skinner, B. F. (1984c). "Some consequences of selection: Reply to commentaries on 'selection by consequences'." *The Behavioral and Brain Sciences* 7(04), pp. 502–510.

Skinner, B. F. (1984d). "The evolution of behaviour." *Journal of the Experimental Analysis of Behaviour* 41(2), pp. 217–221.

Skinner, B. F. (1986). "The evolution of verbal behaviour." *Journal of the Experimental Analysis of Behaviour* 45(1), pp. 115–122.

Skinner, B. F. (1989). *Recent Issues in the Analysis of Behavior*. Columbus, OH: Merrill.

Staddon, J. E. R. (2001). *The New Behaviorism: Mind, Mechanism and Society*. Philadelphia, PA: Psychology Press.

Teece, David J. (2012). "Business models, business srategy and innovation." *Long Range Planning* 43, pp. 172–194.

Vella, Kevin James (2010). *Towards a Theory of the Marketing Firm*. MSc. Thesis in Social Science Research Methods, Cardiff University.

Vella, Kevin James (2012). *Towards an Evolutionary Theory of the Marketing Firm*. British Academy of Management Conference: Management Research Revisited: Prospects for Theory and Practice. Symposium on Consumer Behaviour Analysis and the Marketing Firm. Cardiff.

Vella, Kevin James (2015). *Selection by Consequences and the Marketing Firm*. PhD Thesis, Cardiff University.

Vella, Kevin James and Foxall, Gordon Robert (2011). *The Marketing Firm: Economic Psychology of Corporate Behaviour*. Cheltenham: Elgar Publishing.

Vella, Kevin James and Foxall, Gordon Robert (2013). "The marketing firm: Operant interpretation of corporate behaviour." *The Psychological Record* 63 (Special Issue: Consumer Behavior Analysis: Behavioral Economics Meets the Market Place), pp. 375–402.

Wearden, J. H. (1988). Some neglected problems in the analysis of human operant behavior. In: Davey, Graham C. L. and Cullen, Chris (eds). *Human Operant Conditioning and Behaviour Modification*. New York: John Wiley & Sons, pp. 197–224.

Yan, Ji, Foxall, Gordon Robert and Doyle, John R. (2012a). "Patterns of reinforcement and the essential value of brands: (i) incorporation of utilitarian and informational reinforcement into the estimation of demand." *The Psychological Record* 62(3), pp. 361–376.

Yan, Ji, Foxall, Gordon Robert and Doyle, John R. (2012b). "Patterns of reinforcement and the essential value of brands: (ii) evaluation of a model of consumer choice." *The Psychological Record* 62(3), pp. 377–393.

Yani-de-Soriano, M. Mirella, Foxall, Gordon Robert and Newman, Andrew J. (2013). "The impact of the interaction of utilitarian and informational reinforcement and behaviour setting scope on consumer response." *Psychology and Marketing* 30, pp. 148–159.

Motivating operations and consumer choice

Asle Fagerstrøm and Erik Arntzen

Introduction

In consumer research, motivation is most often understood as a means of goal attainment (see Bagozzi & Dholakia, 1999). The assumption is that consumers make choices to produce or yield one or more end-state goals. Goals in a consumer choice situation can be achieved by buying a bicycle for the purpose of transport, joining a fitness club for the purpose of getting fit, or searching out and buying laundry detergent that is both effective and gentle on clothes. This approach to consumer motivation focuses on goals, which are specific outcomes that purchase and consumption can produce. According to Pervin (1989, p. 474), goals can be understood as a "mental image or other end point representation associated with affect toward which action may be directed." Moreover, understanding the process of consumer motivation from this perspective lies in the meaning of, and the relationship between, goal setting and goal attainment/failure (Bagozzi & Dholakia, 1999). Goal setting is related to the goal that is pursued and the reason the consumer wants to pursue it, while goal attainment/failure is concerned with the consumer's degree of success or failure in achieving the goals.

Behavior analysts, who emphasize that environmental analysis of choice behavior is scientifically and practically necessary (see Olson et al., 2001), see the cognitive information processing conception of motivation as not quite comprehensive. First, how can we understand the process of consumer motivation by starting with a mental image of goal setting? What about environmental conditions that generate the specific mental image of goal setting, such as the consumption of a salty food that probably has a motivating function toward buying and consuming water? According to Olson et al. (2001), excluding environmental conditions results in an incomplete understanding of motivation. Second, if motivation starts with a mental image of goal setting and ends with an environmental output (goal attainment/failure), marketing practitioners can only influence consumers' motivation by altering the environmental output. Including antecedent environmental conditions doubles the marketing practitioners' potential to influence the consumer's motivation to purchase and consume (see Olson et al., 2001).

The motivating operations concept is described as (Laraway et al., 2003): an environmental event that (a) establishes (or abolishes) the reinforcing or punishing effect of another event (the value-altering effect) and (b) evokes (or abates) behaviors related to that event (the behavior-altering effect). To put it in non-behavioral terms, motivating operations change how much a consumer "wants" something and how hard he will "work" to get it. The motivating operations concept has made a significant contribution to both conceptual and applied behavior analysis, inspiring new research and leading to innovative intervention strategies (Laraway et al., 2014). The concept has also been shown to be a comprehensive framework for studying consumer behavior in general (Fagerstrøm et al., 2010) and, especially, for studying consumer purchasing behavior online (Fagerstrøm, 2010; Fagerstrøm & Ghinea, 2011). This chapter gives an update on the work that has been done based on the motivating operations concept and its potential to understand motivation in a consumer choice situation.

Consumer choice

The dependent variable in behavior analysis is the rate of response. However, behavior analysts do not talk about behavior as if it was composed of discrete responses. They consider behavior as a performance that follows a specific stimulus and/or results in a particular consequence. When a response is strengthened or weakened by the events or stimuli that follow the response, it is called operant behavior (Catania, 2013). As "operate" means to perform a function and produce an effect, operants are emitted responses that increase or decrease depending on the consequences they produce. Pierce and Cheney (2004) clarify the distinction between emitted behavior and operants by comparing the action word "walking" with the phrase "walking to the store." According to Pierce and Cheney (2004, p. 29), "Walking is emitted behavior, but it has no specified function. In contrast, walking to the store is an operant that is defined by getting food at the store." In an operant, like walking to the store, the performance changes from one occasion to the next. The consumer can take different routes, walk slowly or jog. Careful observation of this everyday behavior will reveal an almost infinite variety of responses. The important point is that each variation of response has the common effect of getting food at the store. All types of performance that have a similar function (to get some food) are denoted response class, or just operant.

Behavior analysts use the term "environment" to refer to events and stimuli that change behavior (Skinner, 1969). All events and stimuli, whether private or external, may acquire the capacity to affect behavior. It is important to note, when a stimulus is used functionally, it is not a stimulus unless it exerts control over behavior (Catania, 2013). Any stimulus (or event) that follows a response and increases the probability of a similar response has a reinforcement function. Contrarily, any stimulus (or event) that follows a response and decreases the probability of a similar response has a punishing function. In addition, a procedure of withholding reinforcement for a previously reinforced response is called extinction (Catania, 2013). Extinction is, therefore, also a behavioral process and refers to a decline in the rate of response caused by withdrawal of reinforcement. Either extinction or punishment can cause a decrease in the probability of the response. Moreover, both of these processes work in the opposite direction from reinforcement.

When a consumer's behavior is reinforced (or punished), those events that reliably precede responses come to have a discriminative function (Catania, 2013). These events are said to set the occasion for behavior and are called discriminative stimuli. Discriminative stimuli are antecedents that acquire this function because they predict reinforcement (or punishment). Another kind of antecedent stimulus is an extinction stimulus which is denoted s-delta (Catania, 2013). An s-delta is a stimulus that sets the occasion for extinction of a response. Discriminative stimuli and s-delta correspond to what is commonly denoted as signals or cues in consumer research. However, they do not elicit a response, which is the case of reflexes. Rather, they set the occasion on which responses have consequences and are said to occasion responses (Catania,

2013). Those antecedent events or stimuli that are effective in producing responses are said to have stimulus control over the responses (Skinner, 1969). Stimulus control refers to a change in behavior that occurs when either a discriminative stimulus or s-delta is presented. In a situation when a discriminative stimulus is presented, the probability of a response increases (or decreases if it predicts punishment). In a situation when s-delta is presented, the probability of a response decreases.

The motivating operations concept

Behavior analysis has focused its attention on motivational concepts since the field was established. Skinner (1938, 1953, 1957) spoke of motivational variables in terms of deprivation, satiation and painful (aversive) stimulation. He also uses the term "predisposition" that includes the so-called emotional operations in this collection. The more general term establishing operation was introduced by Keller and Schoenfeld (1950) to describe (the) motivating events, and later expanded upon by Millenson (1967). However, it was in Michael's (1982, 1988, 1993, 2000) papers that establishing operation was established in the behavior analysis community. Michael has since suggested that the term "establishing operation" should be replaced with the omnibus term "motivating operation" (see Laraway et al., 2003). This is why some authors use the term "establishing operation" while authors of recent publications use the term "motivating operation." To avoid confusion, the omnibus term "motivating operation" is used through this chapter.

In describing the motivating operations concept, Michael (1982) proposed a more functional description of the concept, and attempted to distinguish between discriminative and motivational functions of stimuli. The discriminative stimulus evokes behavior as a result of a history of being correlated with an increased availability of a particular reinforcer. Hence, a gas station sign may act as a discriminative stimulus for fuel since in the past its presence has been correlated with the availability of fuel. A motivating operation is correlated with the differential effectiveness of a reinforcer (or punisher); that is, the extent to which the consequence is "reinforcing" (or "punishing") in that situation. Thus, a fuel gauge that indicates a low level of fuel (a motivating operation) increases the value of fuel; a gas station sign (the discriminative stimulus) does not. To put it in non-behavioral terms, a motivating operation determines how much the consumer wants something, while a discriminative stimulus signals its availability.

Motivating operations are defined as stimuli, events or conditions that (Laraway et al., 2003, p. 412) "alter (a) the effectiveness of reinforcers or punishers (the value-altering effect) and (b) the frequency of operant response classes related to those consequences (the behavioral-altering effect)." From this definition we can see that motivating operations have two main effects: first, they establish or abolish the reinforcing (or aversive) effect of another event (the value-altering effect) and second, they evoke (or abate) behaviors associated with that event (the behavior-altering effect). The motivating event might (see Table 18.1), for example, involve a person who is fluid deprived. Fluid deprivation establishes the effectiveness of something to drink (water, soft drink, etc.). Simultaneously, fluid deprivation evokes the immediate activity of looking for something to drink, walking to a soft drink machine, choosing a drink, paying for it, etc. Satiation can also be an event that serves as a motivating operation where a person has encountered/engaged with a large amount of a reinforcer (e.g. has drunk a lot of water). Fluid satiation abolishes the reinforcing effectiveness of getting something to drink, and simultaneously abates the immediacy of looking for something to drink.

Table 18.1 Example of the value-altering effect and the behavior-altering effect of the motivating operations

The value-altering effect	The behavior-altering effect
Establishing operations: Fluid deprivation	Evocative effect: Evokes behaviors maintained by access to something to drink
Abolishing operations: Drinking a lot of water	Abative effect: Abates behaviors maintained by access to something to drink

Unconditioned motivating operations

Unconditioned motivating operations are unlearned (Michael, 1993); for example, people are born with the propensity to be more reinforced by food when they are hungry than when they are full. In other words, food deprivation (motivating event) increases the reinforcing effectiveness of food, without learning taking place. Unconditioned motivating operations can help understanding of motivating events, operations or stimulus conditions in regard to a variety of consumer responses such as buying and consuming water and food as already explained, but also consumer choice related to sleep, temperature and stimuli related to sexual reinforcement. Unconditioned motivating operations may be: sleep deprivation (establishing the reinforcing effect of sleep), being too cold (establishing the reinforcing effect of warming up), being too warm (establishing the reinforcing effect of cooling down) and sexual deprivation (establishing the reinforcing effect of sexual stimulation). These unconditioned motivating operations can also have an abolishing effect as the consumer becomes satiated; the act of sleeping abolishes sleep as a reinforcer, being warm abolishes heat as a reinforcer, becoming cold abolishes cooling off as a reinforcer and sexual activity abolishes sexual stimulation as a reinforcer.

Conditioned motivating operations

Conditioned motivating operations function in the same way as unconditioned motivating operations: they alter the efficacy of events, operations or stimulus conditions to function as reinforcers (or aversives) and they evoke (or abate) behaviors associated with that event. The difference between unconditioned motivating operations and conditioned motivating operations lies in the fact that the latter is acquired as a result of the consumer's learning history. In other words, they are events, operations or stimulus conditions that were originally neutral in relation to a particular reinforcer (or aversive), but have acquired motivating functions as a result of their association with either unconditioned motivating operations or previously established conditioned motivating operations. As with the unconditioned motivating operations, they also alter the immediate frequency of the type of behavior that has been reinforcing (or aversive) in response to those other events.

Michael (1993) describes three types of conditioned motivating operations: (1) Surrogate conditioned motivating operations, (2) Reflexive conditioned motivating operations and (3) Transitive conditioned motivating operations. These conditioned motivating operations will now be described, and their relevance to consumer choice will be deduced.

Surrogate conditioned motivating operations

Surrogate conditioned motivating operations develop when previously neutral stimuli, objects or events are temporally paired with an unconditioned motivating operation or another conditioned motivating operation (Michael, 1993). A study by Calvin et al. (1953) suggested that it may be possible to establish surrogate conditioned motivating operations for food in rats. In their experiment they placed rats in a distinctively striped box for 30 minutes a day over a period of 24 days. The first group of rats was placed in the box after 22 hours of food deprivation and the second group was placed in the box after just 1 hour of food deprivation. Following the 24-day training period both groups of rats were allowed free access to food in the striped box after 11.5 hours of food deprivation. The rats with a history of being in the box after a 22-hour deprivation period ate significantly more than those with a history of being in the box after a 1-hour deprivation period. Thus by being reliably paired with food deprivation, the striped box may have come to function as a surrogate conditioned motivating operation for food among the first group of rats. It must be noted that replications of this study have not yielded very consistent findings (see Cravens & Renner, 1970). A human example of surrogate conditioned motivating operations is the case of a person driving up a mountain who starts to encounter snow and ice. The presence of snow and ice tends to be correlated with a decrease in body temperature and may therefore function as a surrogate conditioned motivating operation for action to increase body temperature. This may result in the driver turning up the heating in the car, even though the temperature inside the car may not have changed.

A surrogate conditioned motivating operation related to consumer choice might be a person who on the way to work calls at the local Starbucks™ for a cup of coffee when he is caffeine deprived. The Starbucks™ coffee may become a surrogate conditioned motivating operation for coffee because it has been consistently paired with caffeine deprivation. A visit to the local Starbucks™ coffee shop (or maybe any Starbucks™ coffee shop), even when not caffeine deprived, may occasion feelings of "longing for coffee", resulting in the purchase and drinking of a cup of coffee. Support for this comes in a study by Durlach et al. (2002) where they demonstrated that specific drinks that were repeatedly paired with thirst appeared to become surrogate conditioned motivating operations for fluid consumption.

After leaving Johns Hopkins University, John B. Watson went into the advertising business where he wanted to use his scientific theories of behaviorism. Watson claimed that advertisements depended not upon an appeal to reason but upon emotional conditioning and stimulation of emotions of fear, rage and love (e.g., DiClemente & Hantula, 2000; Hantula et al., 2001). Sundberg (1993) states that the surrogate conditioned motivating operations concept is relevant to analyses of emotional behavior. The concept of surrogate conditioned motivating operations offers, therefore, a plausible explanation of Watson's idea of how neutral stimuli acquire their motivating effect as a result of being paired with another motivating operation, and produce effects that are identical to the original motivating operation. However, further clarification and examination of this topic are necessary.

Reflexive conditioned motivating operations

A reflexive conditioned motivating operation invokes a process where previously neutral stimuli, objects or events whose termination comes to be reinforcing (or aversive) through systematically preceding "worsening" (or "improvement") when not terminated (Michael, 1993). Where correlated with worsening, they establish their own termination as a reinforcer and evoke behaviors associated with their termination. Where correlated with improvement, they establish their own termination as an aversive and suppress behaviors associated with their termination. Michael (1993) termed these operations "Threat or Promise." For example, if a rat learns that a particular tone is always followed by an electric shock (threat), it will also learn to perform behaviors that terminate the tone. In this case the tone, as well as being a conditioned aversive event, is also a reflexive conditioned motivating operation that establishes its own termination as a reinforcer. Conversely, if a rat learns that a particular tone is always followed by food (promise), it will also learn to suppress behaviors associated with the termination of the tone. Here the tone, as well as being a conditioned reinforcer, is a reflexive conditioned motivating operation that establishes its own termination as aversive.

Consumer choices often involve entering into a transaction which, in general, has two consequences (Alhadeff, 1982): the acquisition of the product and the loss of money surrendered in payment. The price that the consumer has to pay for the product signals loss of conditioned reinforcers and/or increased work effort. From the concept of reflexive conditioned motivating operations, price can be interpreted as a "worsening" that establishes its own termination as a reinforcer and evokes responses related to escape. However, when the price is low and/or temporary (e.g., "Get a 35% discount when you buy any mobile phone this week") it may abolish its own termination as a reinforcer and abate behaviors related to escape.

A study by Fagerstrøm (2010) aimed to test the applicability of the reflexive conditioned motivating operation concept for online consumer research. A conjoint analysis was designed to investigate prediction and control of online purchase behavior. Five different reflexive conditioned motivating operations were used in an online scenario where participants were asked to purchase an item on a simulated web shop. The result (n = 90) indicates prediction and control of point-of-online-purchase behavior from four reflexive conditioned stimuli (in-stock status, price, other customers' reviews and donation to charity), and partial prediction and control from one reflexive conditioned stimulus (order confirmation procedures) (Fagerstrøm, 2010). Thus, findings from this interpretive study show that the concept of motivating operations is adequate for analysis of point-of-online-purchase behavior. The study demonstrated that the reflexive conditioned motivating concept offers a comprehensive analysis of antecedent stimuli that have a motivating impact at the point of online purchase.

Another interpretive study by Fagerstrøm and Ghinea (2011) tested the motivating function from price and online recommendations at the point of online purchase. The study was anchored in consumer behavior analysis (see Foxall, 1990/2004, 2007), focusing on prediction and control in an online shopping context. Two reflexive conditioned motivating operations were used in an online scenario where participants were asked to purchase an mp3 player from a simulated web shop. Results (n=268) from a conjoint analysis indicate prediction and control of online purchase behavior from manipulation of price and other customers' reviews. The result shows that (Fagerstrøm & Ghinea, 2011), in general, price, rather than online recommendations, is the most influential stimulus in the purchase situation, as price is the stimulus that has the greatest impact (both positive and negative) on the likelihood of online purchase. When price and customer reviews were analyzed relative to shopping frequencies (light, medium and heavy shoppers), results showed an increase in the relative impact of price when shopping frequencies increase.

Transitive conditioned motivating operations

Michael (1993) describes a transitive conditioned motivating operation as a stimulus condition temporally paired with another stimulus condition that precedes a worsening or improving condition. He uses an example that the sight of a slotted screw evokes a worker's request to his assistant for the appropriate screwdriver. The screwdriver is just as available with or without the presence of a slotted screw, but it is more reinforcing in the presence of the screw (the relation is motivative). Tapper (2005) gives an example that in England licensing laws mean that many bars and public houses stop serving alcohol at 11 pm, with "last orders" called at the bar a few minutes beforehand. In this case, the call for last orders may function as a transitive conditioned motivating operation that establishes a half-empty glass as a punisher, since on previous occasions when "last orders" has been called, a half-empty glass is likely to have been correlated with having nothing to drink later on. Thus the call for last orders evokes behaviors that avoid having a half-empty glass, such as buying another drink.

In a consumer choice situation, a conditioned transitive motivating operation may occur when a purchasing behavior is blocked or interrupted. One example is a fluid-deprived person who wants to buy a drink from a vending machine. Unfortunately, the ongoing response chain is blocked because he does not have the correct change. In this situation, the sight of the vending machine functions as a transitive conditioned motivating operation. It establishes the value of correct change for the machine, and simultaneously evokes behaviors stimulated by the need for correct change such as asking someone to exchange coins. Another example is someone buying a cell phone online. When he or she advances to the checkout phase, there is a presentation of supplementary items for that particular cell phone, such as a memory card. In this situation, the cell phone functions as a transitive conditioned motivating operation that establishes the value of a memory card for the particular cell phone, and may evoke behaviors maintained by access to supplementary items such as adding the memory card to the shopping list before checkout and confirming the online order.

Motivating operations and verbal behavior

Skinner (1969, p. 160) describes rule-governed behavior as behavior evoked by "rules derived from the contingencies in the form of injunctions and descriptions which specify occasions, responses and consequences." In a consumer behavior context, a rule can be statements, instructions or advice(s) that signal the relationship between choice (the behavior) and its consequences (reinforcers and punishers). For example, the advertised offer "Two for the price of one" indicates that the consequence of purchasing the product, in addition to ownership and consumption, is less loss of the money surrendered in payment. Another advertisement may announce "This car comes with free insurance in the first year," indicating that the consequence of purchase, in addition to ownership, is free insurance the first year.

There are in general three types of rule-governed behavior, characterized by different kinds of reinforcement history (Hayes et al., 2001) – pliance, tracking and augmenting. Pliance is rule-governed behavior primarily under the control of apparent speaker-mediated consequences for a correspondence between the rule and the relevant behavior (Hayes et al., 2001). An example of pliance can be a customer that brings his old cell phone to the store to get 25% off when buying a new cell phone, assuming that this is done under the control of the apparent speaker-mediated consequences specified in the rule. The rule is termed a ply.

Tracking is rule-governed behavior under the control of a history of correspondence between the rule and "natural" social or non-social contingencies (Hayes et al., 2001). Natural contingencies are those produced entirely by the exact form of the behavior in a particular setting. An example of tracking would be the behavior of a person walking in a particular direction after seeing the "McDonalds 300 meters" signs, assuming that this is done under the control of the apparent correspondence between the rule (the sign) and the actual location of the McDonalds restaurant. The rule is termed a track.

Augmenting is particularly relevant for understanding motivating functions in relation to consumer choice. Augmenting is defined by Hayes et al. (2001, p. 109) as "rule-governed behavior due to relational networks that alter the degree to which events function as reinforcers or punishers." The rule is termed augmental. There are two types of augmenting: formative augmenting and motivative augmenting. Formative augmenting is "behavior due to relational networks that establish given consequences as reinforcers or punishers" (Hayes et al., 2001, p. 110). An example of a formal augmental is a message that says "booking flights on the Internet earns double frequent flyer points this month." If booking a flight on the Internet had not previously functioned as a reinforcer for the actual behavior, the statement "earns double frequent flyer points" would be an example of a formative augmental if it increased online bookings. Motivational augmenting is defined as rule-governed behavior controlled by "rational networks that temporarily alter the degree to which previously established consequences function as reinforcers or punishers" (Hayes et al., 2001, p. 109). A consumer choice example given by Hayes et al. (2001) is the question "Wouldn't an ice-cold Pepsi be good right now?" If this advertisement results in consumers buying a Pepsi, then it is probably functioning as a type of verbal establishing stimulus. It would not be defined as a discriminative stimulus, because Pepsis are probably available whether or not the rule is presented (see Michael, 1982).

According to Schlinger and Blakely (1987), the primary function of rules, which they perceive as verbal stimuli that specify relations among other stimuli and responses ("contingencies"), is to alter the behavioral function of those stimuli. The authors call rules "function-altering contingency-specifying stimuli" (cf. Hayes, 1989). Schlinger and Blakely (1987) argue that if rules alter the effectiveness of other stimuli as reinforcers or punishers (and also alter the likelihood of the occurrence of behaviors that historically have produced those stimuli), then it appears proper to consider them motivating operations.

Conclusions

The major motivation theory in consumer research is the goal-setting theory (Bagozzi & Dholakia, 1999). This theory assumes that consumer motivation and consumption are functions of goal accomplishment. Consumers set goals on the basis of their values, and they select means that they believe will help them achieve their desired goals (Pervin, 1989). Motivation is, from this perspective, believed to be highest when the goals set are difficult. However, goal-setting theory is limited to the cognitive component focusing on information processing.

The presentation of motivating operations in relation to consumer choice demonstrates that this concept has several conceptual advantages compared with the goal-setting theory. The motivating operations concept helps to distinguish between discriminative and motivational functions of antecedent stimuli in the consumer behavior setting. The motivating operations concept does not draw a distinction between cognitive and non-cognitive variables; all variables are accounted for by the same processes (Tapper, 2005). This shows the motivating operations concept to be just as applicable when understanding the motivating impact of promotion and advertising (conditioned motivating operations/rule-governed behavior) as it is to understanding the motivating effect of food deprivation (unconditioned motivating operations). Some types of rules (e.g., augmentals) could be motivating operations, too. Including the motivating operations concept as part of our understanding of what "motivates" consumer choices leads to a more comprehensive analysis and, as a result, expands our understanding of the complex world of contingencies operating within consumer situations.

Consumer behavioral analysis is a field that focuses on the application of the principles, methods and procedures of behavior analysis. The behavior analytic approach to "motivation" has several advantages in its application, as demonstrated in this chapter. The motivating operations concept is designed specifically to facilitate intervention as it is formulated in terms of environmental variables that can be manipulated directly (Tapper, 2005). Thus, findings from motivation operation-based treatments can be more immediately applied to behavior change.

This issue would seem to be important in marketing where so much of the research is applied. Moreover, if a theoretical understanding of motivation begins with an internal state (e.g., belief, attitude or intention) and ends with a behavioral outcome, a company can only directly alter the outcomes of behavior (consequences). Including antecedent environmental variables in the analysis of consumer motivation at least doubles the number of potentially manipulable motivational variables in the environment (see Olson et al., 2001), which should be an attractive strategy for marketers. However, the concept of motivating operations does not change completely the way we market to consumers. It rather increases our precision when explaining consumer behavior. However, our marketing activities can be made more effective by knowing the value-altering effects and the behavior-altering effects from companies' marketing events.

References

Alhadeff, D. A. (1982). *Microeconomics and Human Behavior: Toward a New Synthesis of Economics and Psychology*. Berkeley, CA: University of California Press.

Bagozzi, R. P., & Dholakia, U. (1999). Goal setting and goal striving in consumer behaviour. *Journal of Marketing, 63*, 19–32.

Calvin, J. S., Bicknell, E. A., & Sperling, D. S. (1953). Establishment of a conditioned drive based on the hunger drive. *Journal of Comparative and Physiological Psychology, 46*, 173–175.

Catania, A. C. (2013). *Learning* (5th ed.). Cornwall-on-Hudson, NY: Sloan Publishing.

Cravens, R., & Renner, K. E. (1970). Conditioned appetitive drive states: Empirical evidence, and theoretical status. *The Psychological Bulletin, 73*(3), 212–220. doi: 10.1037/h0028685

DiClemente, D. F., & Hantula, D. A. (2000). John Broadus Watson: I/O psychologist. *The Industrial/Organizational Psychologist, 37*, 47–55.

Durlach, P. J., Elliman, N. A., & Rogers, P. J. (2002). Drinking while thirsty can lead to conditioned increases in consumption. *Appetite, 39*, 119–125.

Fagerstrøm, A. (2010). The motivating effect of antecedent stimuli on the web shop: A conjoint analysis of the impact of antecedent stimuli at the point of online purchase. *Journal of Organizational Behavior Management, 30*, 199–220.

Fagerstrøm, A., Foxall, G. R., & Arntzen, E. (2010). Implications of motivating operations for the functional analysis of consumer choice. *Journal of Organizational Behavior Management, 30*(2), 110–126. doi: 10.1080/01608061003756331

Fagerstrøm, A., & Ghinea, G. (2011). On the motivating impact of price and online recommendations at the point of online purchase. *International Journal of Information Management, 31*(2), 103–110. doi: 10.1016/j.ijinfomgt.2010.10.013

Foxall, G. R. (1990/2004). *Consumer Psychology in Behavioral Perspective*. New York: Routledge. (Reprinted 2004: Maryland, MD: Beard Books.)

Foxall, G. R. (2007). *Explaining Consumer Choice*. New York: Palgrave Macmillan.

Hantula, D. A., DiClemente, D. F., & Rajala, A. K. (2001). Outside the box: The analysis of consumer behavior. In L. Hayes, J. Austin, R. Houmanfar, & M. Clayton (Eds.), *Organizational Change* (pp. 203–223). Reno, NV: Context Press.

Hayes, S. C. (Ed.). (1989). *Rule-Governed Behavior: Cognition, Contingencies, and Instructional Control*. New York: Plenum.

Hayes, S. C., Barnes-Holmes, D., & Roche, B. (Eds.). (2001). *Relational Frame Theory: A Post-Skinnerian Account of Human Language and Cognition*. New York: Kluwer Academic/Plenum Publishers.

Keller, F. S., & Schoenfeld, W. N. (1950). *Principles of Psychology*. New York: Appleton-Century-Crofts.

Laraway, S., Snycerski, S., Michael, J., & Poling, A. (2003). Motivating operations and terms to describe them: Some further refinements. *Journal of Applied Behavior Analysis, 36*(6), 407–414. doi: 10.1901/jaba.2003.36-407

Laraway, S., Snycerski, S., Olson, R., Becker, B., & Poling, A. (2014). The motivating operations concept: Current status and critical responses. *The Psychological Record, 64*, 601–623.

Michael, J. L. (1982). Distinguishing between discriminative and motivational functions of stimuli. *Journal of the Experimental Analysis of Behavior, 37*, 149–155.

Michael, J. L. (1988). Establishing operations and the mand. *The Analysis of Verbal Behavior, 6*, 3–9.

Michael, J. L. (1993). Establishing operations. *The Behavior Analyst, 16*, 191–206.

Michael, J. L. (2000). Implications and refinements of the establishing operation concept. *Journal of Applied Behavior Analysis, 33*, 401–410.

Millenson, J. R. (1967). *Principles of Behavioral Analysis*. New York: Macmillan.

Olson, R., Laraway, S., & Austin, J. (2001). Unconditioned and conditioned establishing operations in organizational behavior management. *Journal of Organizational Behavior Management, 21*(2), 7–35. doi: 10.1300/J075v21n02_03

Pervin, L. A. (1989). Goal concepts: Themes, issues, and questions. In L. A. Pervin (Ed.), *Goal concepts in personality and social psychology* (pp. 473–479). Hillsdale, NJ: Lawrence Erlbaum Associates.

Pierce, W. D., & Cheney, C. D. (2004). *Behavior Analysis and Learning*. New York: Psychology Press.

Schlinger, H. D., & Blakely, E. (1987). Function-altering effects of contingency-specifying stimuli. *The Behavior Analyst, 10*(1), 41–45.

Skinner, B. F. (1938). *The Behavior of Organisms: An Experimental Analysis*. New York: D. Appleton-Century Company, Inc.

Skinner, B. F. (1953). *Science and Human Behavior*. New York: Macmillan.

Skinner, B. F. (1957). *Verbal Behavior*. New York: Appleton-Century-Crofts.

Skinner, B. F. (1969). *Contingencies of Reinforcement: A Theoretical Analysis*. New York: Appleton-Century-Crofts.

Sundberg, M. L. (1993). The application of establishing operations. *The Behavior Analyst, 16*(2), 211–214.

Tapper, K. (2005). Motivating operations in appetite research. *Appetite, 45*(2), 95–107. doi: 10.1016/j.appet.2005.05.002

19

Consumers as inforagers

Wooyang Kim and Donald A. Hantula

Introduction

Most accounts of consumer behavior proceed either explicitly or implicitly from an economic rational choice perspective, depicting consumers as *Homo economicus*. This view of consumer choice has been challenged by different models. Perhaps one of the best-known challenges is "bounded rationality" (Simon, 1955, 1956, 1957), which has also been applied in a variety of other fields, including anthropology, biology, ecology, economics, marketing, psychology, and sociology (for further review, see Conlisk, 1996). Among economists and psychologists, bounded rationality provokes arguments regarding the traditional axioms of economics (e.g., violations of independence and preference intransitivity) (Capra & Rubin, 2011; Einhorn & Hogarth, 1986; Foxall et al., 2010; Herrnstein, 1990; Herrnstein & Prelec, 1991; Kahneman & Tversky, 1979; Thaler, 1980; Tversky & Thaler, 1990). Although the paradigm of bounded rational choice has a relatively long history, numerous behavioral studies have shown that it too has difficulty explaining human behavior (Herrnstein, 1990; Mayr, 1983), possibly due to its mechanistic nature. For example, Mayr (1983) argued that the logic of evolutionary biology is very different from physical sciences with evolutionary biology explanations derived from a Darwinian Theory of natural selection. Moreover, Mayr's argument implies that human behavioral research is likely to fit an explanation of human decision-making processes according to Darwinism rather than Newtonism.

To a certain degree, bounded rationality implies this important aspect: understanding biological limitations of human responses to the immediate environment that require an evolutionary view of humans and interactions with their environment. Nonetheless, the field of marketing has broadly overlooked this view (Griskevicius & Kenrick, 2013; Hantula, 2012; Saad, 2008, 2011, 2013). For example, according to Saad and colleagues (Saad, 2008, 2011; Saad & Gill, 2001; Stenstrom et al., 2008), biological limitations do not mean *ideological drivers* but indicate *sexual or social limitations* due to different biological norms in particular environments (Saad, 2007, 2011). These biological limitations imply that the proper basis for human rationality is an *ecological rationality*, based on evolutionary theories (Gigerenzer et al., 1999; Goldstein & Gigerenzer, 2002; Saad, 2007; Todd & Gigerenzer, 2007). According to Gigerenzer and Todd (1999), ecological rationality is the "rationality that is defined by its fit with reality" (p. 5), implying issues of survival and reproduction in particular environments to explain decision-making (Todd & Gigerenzer, 2007, p. 167). This interactive perspective suggests a rethinking of bounded rationality in the context of a purchaser's biological, social, and learning history and immediate environments in real-life decisions and/or choices, as explained by Foxall's Behavioral Perspective Model (Foxall, 2001, 2010b).

Normative rationality indicates that humans might maximize choices through a universal optimality according to their bounded abilities and capabilities, despite some cases requiring absoluteness (such as machine systems). This indicates that normative rationality may be necessary in some computational situations involving mathematical calculation; but not for ordinary situations and decisions such as choosing a meal (Herrnstein, 1990; Winterhalder & Kennett, 2006). If all ordinary choices are normative (arguably, a valid proposition), explaining humans' seemingly sub-maximizing behavior in choices rather than one unified maximization principle becomes problematic from the perspective of *Homo economicus*. If human behavior deviates from normative criteria, then a question of consumer foolishness or irrationality arises. For example, consider a common choice, such as one among electronic gadgets (e.g., Apple iPhone 6 vs. Samsung Galaxy S5). In this choice, no such universal optimal statement exists; instead, a particular immediate environment or consumer situation (Foxall, 2001) provides the structure of an individual's information set (e.g., service providers or countries). This normative perspective seems to overlook science's positive view of human nature, which is an important consideration for consumer behavior research (Gigerenzer, 1996; see also Hunt, 2002). Similarly, Shelby D. Hunt, a pioneering marketing theorist, argued that many marketing theories have a normative basis (e.g., rational or systematic choices) rather than a positive basis (e.g., empirical or predictable choices); however, *good normative theories are based on good positive theory* (e.g., empirically *law-like* generalizations) to provide better understanding through explaining and predicting mundane phenomena (Hunt, 2002, pp. 236–9). A normative theory that does not have a solid basis in positive theory will yield prescriptions for "optimal" choice that, ironically, will prove to be less optimal than if the prescriptions were not heeded.

A common explanation invokes humans' limited cognitive abilities or subjective utilities. However, another argument in ordinary choices is that humans cannot pursue a globally optimal choice, not due to any inherent limitations, but due to biological and environmental constraints. Humans seek a "good enough" or "rule of thumb" choice (i.e., *satisficing*). The perspective of satisficing necessarily implies ecological rationales as a prerequisite for a framework of human behavior, such as an ecological cost-benefit framework that accounts for *survival* – e.g., benefits compared to certain amounts of cost to adapt immediately to confront environments (Todd & Gigerenzer, 2000; Todd et al., 2005; Winterhalder & Kennett, 2006). Therefore, this perspective suggests that, at least, ordinary human behavior does not sufficiently function according to normative bases for examining information, and subsequent decisions and choices (Herrnstein, 1990; Mayr, 1983; Schwartz, 2000; Todd et al., 2005). Consider again, for example, an individual who wants to buy a cell phone. Calculations for this decision do not include all attributes at normative optimality but rather *satisfice* the decision at an acceptable level beyond the individual's satisfied criteria to fit an individual's surroundings. In other words, the context of purchasing an item includes selective information processing with some preferred or considered features (e.g., recognition heuristics and tunnel visioning), not a fully normative information processing with all available attributes (e.g., mathematical calculation) (Gigerenzer & Goldstein, 2011; Goldstein & Gigerenzer, 2002; Posavac et al., 2010; Sanbonmatsu et al., 2011). This example implies that when consumers render a purchase decision, the basis for their processing behavior tends toward an ecological rationale rather than a normative rationale, due to selective concern for attributes. Thus, they do not consider all accessible or available attributes. The result is intentional ignorance as a mirror of immediate environment derived from the human biological limitation for acquiring information (e.g., information in a foreign language, albeit good information) (Todd et al., 2005). That is, consumers are prone to decisions that interplay emotional cost-benefit values and nominal cost-benefit values of products or services, not exclusively either.

Assuming that decisions and choices occur at the "good enough" level, fundamental questions of information acquisition arise: What kinds of acquisition processes result in obtaining good-enough information? When does the acquisition of information cease? What sources help confirm choices? What are the indicators of feelings of satisfaction or dissatisfaction, or regret? Consumers' choices occur when the information satisfactorily meets an individual's emotions in an adaptive way that repeatedly encounters the target product/service in immediate environments (e.g., Tooby & Cosmides, 2005). For example, Häubl and Trifts (2000) investigated pre-purchase information searches on the formation of consideration sets' size and quality, and purchase decision quality. Häubl and Trifts found that both product comparison among selected alternatives and recommendations in the immediate environment online simultaneously influence consumers' decisions and the formation of consideration sets. Particularly the recommending agent – frequently containing agents' emotional statements, such as repetition of attributes like relative price as a feature – plays a role in increasing purchase decision quality while decreasing the size of consideration sets. This result implies a substantial effect of an interaction between people and immediate environments to stimulate an individual's achieving a satisfactory emotional level (cf. website environment in consumer decision-making: Chen et al., 2011; Fagerstrøm et al., 2010; Kock, 2009, 2010; Stenstrom et al., 2008; Stevenson et al., 2000; Yang et al., 2003).

From a series of debates on the rationality of human choices, an evolutionary paradigm has currently emerged to apply *Darwinism*, the cornerstone of ecological rationality. This paradigm argues that normative mechanisms are innately limited in describing the nature of human behavior (Herrnstein, 1990). Hence, researchers who espouse *Darwinism* postulate "ecological rationality" to explain humans' choices (i.e., the adaptation of decision-making processes) (Capra & Rubin, 2011; Gigerenzer et al., 1999; Hantula, 2012; Todd & Gigerenzer, 2000, 2007). This implication arises, perhaps, from Darwin's emphasis on *natural selection* within a given environment, and ultimately explains human behavior (Cosmides & Tooby, 1987, 1996; Kock et al., 2008; Mayr, 1983; Saad, 2006, 2008; Stenstrom et al., 2008; Symons, 1992). Saad (2008) stipulated "most scientists agree that evolutionary theory is one of the three most important intellectual breakthroughs in the history of human thought" (p. 425) – i.e., Newton (Newtonian theory), Einstein (Theory of Relativity), and Darwin (Darwinian Theory) (cf. Hagen, 2005; Saad, 2007: Chapter 1). Then, Saad (2008) emphasized that *Darwinism* only has theoretical application to any discipline without hindrance. Furthermore, Saad criticized marketing's failure to consider Darwinian origins of *Homo Consumericus* (p. 426). Notably, *Homo Consumericus* emanates from *Homo sapiens*, not *Homo economicus* (see also Saad, 2007, Chapters 2 and 7). Although this interaction between human and environment in natural selection is an important premise, numerous researchers among many disciplines have overlooked this critical relationship. Based on this review, two dominant rationalities divide to constitute three perspectives for consumer decisions and choices: rational choice, heuristics and biases, and ecological choice, as shown in Table 19.1.

The demarcation in Table 19.1 forms the bases for different assumptions about human rationality in terms of how each school describes humans and environments and considers humans' processing to accomplish ultimate decisional optimization. A primary difference between normative and ecological rationalities, perhaps, has bases in the different philosophical perspectives of whether physical law (e.g., humans as machines) or biological evolution (e.g., humans as

Table 19.1 Consumer decision making: major perspectives of rationality

	Rational choice	Heuristics and biases	Ecological choice
Theory	Newtonian theory	Newtonian theory	Darwinian theory
Discipline	Economics	Cognitive psychology	Evolutionary theory
Focus	Prescriptive	Descriptive	Descriptive
Reasoning	Deductive	Deductive	Inductive
Rationality	Normative	Normative	Ecological
Role of emotion	Emotion ignored	Emotion is error	Emotion is information
Application of heuristics	Heuristics overlooked	Heuristics are applicable to low cognition	Heuristics are ways to achieve decisional efficiencies
Research program	Develop rules for universally optimal choice	Compare choice to normatively rational model and catalog errors	Analyze choice as adaptation
View of humanity	People are irrational	People are foolish	People are ameliorators
Behavior of consumers	Consumers are passive	Consumers are responsive	Consumers are proactive
Focal component	Commodities' demand and supply	Human's ability	Human minds and immediate environments

Note: The table is a modification of Hantula (2012, p. 552). In addition, we adopt the Goldstein and Gigerenzer (2002) conceptual definition of heuristics from the standpoint of an ecological rationale rather than the Tversky and Kahneman (1974) conceptual definition

organisms) is the appropriate foundation for understanding human behavior. That is, normative rationality seeks a global optimality, while ecological rationality pursues sub-optimizations that permit consumers' behavioral deviations, providing a basis for consumers' freedom of choice in natural environments.

An ecological rationality perspective provides insights into such disciplines as agriculture (Winterhalder & Kennett, 2006), anthropology (Winterhalder & Kennett, 2009), consumer behavior (Hantula et al., 2008; Hantula & Wells, 2010), ecology (Bolhuis et al., 2011), economics (Kanazawa, 2006; Levine & Kurzban, 2006), human behavioral ecology (Cronk, 1991; Nettle et al., 2013), organizational studies (Saad & Vongas, 2009; Wine et al., 2012), politics (McDermott et al., 2008), and psychology (Goldstein & Gigerenzer, 2002; Haselton & Nettle, 2006; Todd & Gigerenzer, 2007). Despite this attention to an ecological rationality, an application of Darwinian-based perspective remains a relatively unexplored research area in marketing (Hantula, 2012; Wells, 2012).

Information acquisition activity in an ecological perspective

Foraging theory

Foraging represents a descriptive and inductive framework that follows an ecological rationality for *biobasic* behavior (Hantula, 2010). The concept of foraging derives from the foundations of behavioral ecology to explain predators' strategic prey-searching and prey-exploiting behavior in response to the immediate environment (e.g., optimal foraging strategies, Charnov, 1976; Nettle et al., 2013). Hantula (2012) argued that the best conceptualization of foraging is an "economic theory" to determine the how and why of decisions by "looking not inside the organism but outside in the environment," and considering foraging behavior as involving acquisition and exchange, not simply and exclusively searching or feeding. That is, foraging is beyond a *metaphor*, which indicates management of naturally selected surroundings and which allows variation in behavioral strategies that humans employ to maximize their inclusive fitness (i.e., adaptedness) in the specific environment (e.g., phenotypic variation) (Cronk, 1991; Rosenzweig, 2007). This conceptualization suggests that foraging follows elaborate *organismic* decision rules to acquire targets and organismic behavior to explain humans' acquisition activities (Goldstein, 1939; Hantula, 2012).

Early studies of foraging focused on modeling non-humans' adaptive behaviors based on consumption patterns, such as time allocation (Charnov, 1976; Stephens & Charnov, 1982). This approach to optimization assumes that the relationship between foraging strategy and obtaining optimal prey indicates the best trade-off decision within a particular environment. For example, classical foraging studies concentrate on optimal strategies in terms of an organism's foraging for prey according to the patch model, the *marginal value theorem* (e.g., Abarca & Fantino, 1982; Charnov, 1976; Iwasa et al., 1981; McNamara, 1982; Stephens & Charnov, 1982), and on matching relationships between relative rates of responses and relative rates of reinforcement, the *matching law* (e.g., Fantino, 1969; Herrnstein, 1961, 1970; Lea, 1979; Taylor et al., 1978). These classic studies attempt to explicate the inclusive fitness of an organism within its immediate environment. The foraging model, based primarily on *patch–prey* relationships, accounts for a relationship of optimal patch-exploitation associated with time duration and energy consumption (Giraldeau & Caraco, 2000; Stephens & Krebs, 1986). The term *patch* denotes "any bounded spatial or temporal co-location of prey items" (Hantula, 2012). The patch includes two types of areas: *within-patch* and *between-patch*. "Within-patch" involves searching activities to find prey (e.g., searching for target information within a source) while "between-patch" entails browsing activities to scan for a variety of sources. The foraging model is applicable not only to non-human species in predator–prey relationships, but also humans in hunter–food or cost–benefit relationships (Hantula, 2012; Winterhalder & Kennett, 2006). For example, Winterhalder and Kennett (2009) described a socioeconomic change in agriculture through a farmer-domestication relationship, arguing that this socioeconomic change entails a societal transition from primitive foraging to modern cultivation, which is called *hunter–gatherer* relationships. This example is a clear explanation of humans' abilities to adapt from reflections of the past to behavior in the present. Analogously, the patch concept equivalently portrays simultaneous browsing and searching activities of consumers' information processing, such as online and offline shopping that entails iterations of behavior, which switches between browsing among stores – between-patches, and searching for items within a targeted store – within-patch.

This concept is formalized as *foraging theory*, based on economic models (Stephens & Krebs, 1986). Foraging theory has two critical assumptions: 1) *currency* assumption, that is spending time and energy on acquiring an item, and 2) *constraint* assumption, which represents foraging activities occurring within a forager's physical abilities and habitats. The assumptions imply two important analogies for application to consumers' processing behavior. First, investment of time and energy to forage for value (currency assumption) is ubiquitous in consumer behavior as a form of the cost-benefit relationship (e.g., Saad, 2007). Second, consumers' processing capabilities and surroundings (constraint assumption) interactively affect foraging behavior to accomplish subjectively optimized outcomes (e.g., Todd & Gigerenzer, 2007).

A series of studies of online shopping introduced *foraging theory* into business disciplines to establish a foundation for ecological rationality (DiClemente & Hantula, 2003a, 2003b; Hantula, 2012; Hantula et al., 2008; Hantula & Bryant, 2005; Rajala & Hantula, 2000; Smith & Hantula, 2003, 2008). Hantula and co-authors primarily argued that consumers' consumption behavior in everyday life shows similar patterns to foraging behavior exhibited by non-human animals. Current research argues that animal studies are helpful in explaining human decision-making in biology, neuroscience, and economics, from an ethological perspective (Biernaskie et al., 2009; Kalenscher & van Wingerden, 2011; Rosati et al., 2007; Saad, 2008; Santos & Chen, 2009). For example, Saad (2008) emphasized the ability of Darwinism to explain a singular process of the evolution between mosquito, lion, and humanity. Furthermore, Bruce Winterhalder, an anthropologist, applied foraging theory to human behavior, like the *hunter–gatherer* relationship, in investigating the relationship between primitive agricultural and industrial eras, and has argued that foraging theory can successfully explain humans' adaptive behavior (e.g., domestication) within the context of a given environmental change (Winterhalder & Kennett, 2006, 2009). These studies suggest that the foraging concept provides a holistic approach to integrate various perspectives or theories. Existing studies that apply foraging theory cover various research fields to explain human behavior regarding choice, and those studies include the *matching law* (Herrnstein, 1990; Herrnstein et al., 1993; Herrnstein & Prelec, 1991), risk-sensitive adaptive selection in the hunter–gatherer relationship (Winterhalder & Kennett, 2009; Winterhalder et al., 1999), human foraging in patch models (Hutchinson et al., 2008; Wilke et al., 2004; Wilke et al., 2009), and information foraging theory (Pirolli, 2005, 2007; Pirolli & Card, 1999).

Currently, studying *human behavior ecology* (HBE) has advanced social and life sciences, suggesting that HBE can not only help link natural and social sciences but also integrate interdisciplinary approaches (Nettle et al., 2013). Nevertheless, Wells (2012) pointed out a scarcity of applications of the foraging concept in marketing. This current review of research suggests the presence of ample niches for applying foraging theory in the study of consumer behavior although Wells (2012) argued that its application might be limited to the environment of online marketing.

Consumers as inforagers: infusing an ecological perspective into marketing

Integration of evolutionary theory with non-evolutionary theory may explain consumer behavior for acquiring information as a unified theoretical form. This theoretical integration concentrates on the online environment that has become ubiquitous to consumer information processing for transactions involving products and services. The offline environment remains relevant, and therefore no restriction applies to consideration of human foraging behavior.

Foraging theory in everyday behavior

Foraging is about organisms' decision-making rules. The potential benefit from using the foraging concept is transferable among organisms, as suggested by Saad (2008) and Hantula (2012) who addressed the usefulness of Darwinian-based theories for understanding consumer behavior. Moreover, previous literature suggested the existence of reasonable analogical inferences between human behavior and animal behavior (Biernaskie et al., 2009; Kalenscher & van Wingerden, 2011; McKerchar et al., 2009; Rosenzweig, 2007; Santos & Chen, 2009). A series of recent studies applying foraging theory have received attention for exploring processes, including artificial intelligence, consumer studies, information science, library science, organization studies, and psychology, for human decision-making (Duggan & Payne, 2009; Flavián et al., 2012; Fu & Pirolli, 2007; Hantula et al., 2008; Hantula & Wells, 2010; Hutchinson et al., 2008; Kock et al., 2008; Payne et al., 2007; Pirolli, 2005; Puvathingal & Hantula, 2012; Rode et al., 1999; Sandstrom, 1994, 1999; Weber et al., 2004; Wilke et al., 2004; Wilke et al., 2009; Wine et al., 2012; Winterhalder et al., 1999). These studies applied the foraging concept to explain a variety of human behavior, such as decisions and choices, communication, consumption, risk sensitivity, and information processing. The empirical results from existing studies plausibly support theoretical propositions of the foraging theory, originating from behavioral ecology, to examine inclusive fitness of organisms. Two research avenues on foraging theory are currently dominant for application to consumer behavior: the behavioral ecology of consumption and information foraging (Hantula, 2010; Pirolli & Card, 1999). These focus on the online environment, rather than offline circumstances (as noted by Wells, 2012).

The behavioral ecology of consumption mainly deals with foragers' consumption within uncertain environments through implementing temporal discounting and intertemporal preferences for choices (Critchfield & Atteberry, 2003; Foxall, 2010a; McKerchar et al., 2009), thereby following the matching law (DiClemente & Hantula, 2003b; Hantula et al., 2008; Hantula & Bryant, 2005; Rajala & Hantula, 2000; Smith & Hantula, 2008; Wine et al., 2012). Consumption research describes foragers as time-sensitive and profit-seeking financiers, and portrays the investment-profit relationship pursed with temporal constraints (Hantula, 2010, 2012). For example, in a theory-based foraging study, Rajala and Hantula (2000) concluded that consumers' purchasing rates are hyperbolically sensitive and negatively related to time delays to in-stock feedback. In further studies of consumption, Hantula and colleagues empirically extended and confirmed the finding of consumers' time sensitivity for delayed outcomes (DiClemente & Hantula, 2003a, 2003b; Hantula & Bryant, 2005).

Information foraging considers the predator-prey relationship as an "informavores" relationship, regarding the acquisition of information (Pirolli, 2007; Pirolli & Card, 1999). According to information foraging theory, humans (informavores) seek and acquire necessary information through simultaneously browsing and searching patches of information and then selecting the final information through efforts to determine trade-offs (time and energy) against the information's value (a rate of return on information). The foraging concept delineates the same ecological cost–benefit relationship (Hantula, 2012). That is, consumers forage for information at the level that deliberation cost (time and energy) does not exceed the information value, because consumers are competent *financiers*, and thus are not likely to invest time and energy beyond the value received (Hantula, 2010). This can also apply to consumer behavior in that consumers find information for choosing goods and services (prey) in stores (patches). In other words, the relationship of foragers-prey-consumption, among patches, plausibly represents that of consumers-information-decision. A study by Reed et al. (2014) provides an example. According to foraging theory, scarcity of a prey item motivates search for that item or a substitute. For informavores, scarcity of a prey item would also be expected to motivate search for information about substitutes. Reed et al. found that when ultra-violet indoor tanning bans for minors were enacted in the UK, internet searches for information about spray tanning (a logical substitute) increased.

Information foraging theory (Pirolli & Card, 1999) accounts for the functional similarity of foragers and people seeking information online. According to Pirolli and Card, information foraging theory is an approach to understanding "how strategies and technologies for information seeking, gathering, and consumption are adapted to the flux of information in the environment" (p. 643). For humans, as *informavores*, longing for increased information (Dennett, 1991, p. 181), the theory includes three models to enhance foraging and exploiting information with maximum rates of return for information gained in an adaptive manner (i.e., ecological cost–benefit relationship). Pirolli and Card proposed three models for achieving ecological optimization in information foraging processes: *information patch model*, *information scent model*, and *information diet model* (see also Pirolli, 2007). First, the patch is a source for any information for an item (e.g., websites that contain information). Second, the scent is a proximal cue that interacts with surroundings of provided information (e.g., textual information with vivid pictures). Third, the diet is stream-lined informative data aiding repetitive foraging via browsing and searching (e.g., summarized informative data from abundant sources). These models reciprocally interact during processing of information according to time allocation both within and between patches, during deliberations of cost for selection, gathering relevant information using proximal cues in patches, and optimizing rate of return for information's relevance from information scents. Notably, this optimized foraging is distinguishable from the normative optimality model, because the optimization model focuses on adaptive, *corrective tendencies*, for efficiency of foraging for information, not pursuing a *global optimal state* (e.g., an existence of inevitable ignorance of information) (Pirolli & Card, 1999, p. 6). For example, Pirolli and Card (1999) suggested that people do not need every piece of information; instead, they tend to ignore most information, regardless of relevance, and capture necessary information selectively during a certain time, as animals do in the wild (for the Darwinian-based psychology examples, see Todd et al., 2005).

Integration of foraging and information processing theories into consumer behavior of information acquisition

The theoretical integration of evolutionary and non-evolutionary theories covers the four mandatory preconditions suggested by Kock (2010): 1) Theories should refer to the same general type of task. 2) Theories should refer to the same general type of technology. 3) Theories should comprise similar theoretical constructs. 4) Theories should complement each other. In other words, the theoretical integration between foraging theory and information processing theory satisfies those four mandatory preconditions according to: 1) processing behavior for acquiring information; 2) similar technological environments for consumers; 3) similar measuring constructs for consumption and acquisition of information, and 4) reciprocal perspectives for acquiring information in terms of philosophical and theoretical frameworks for explaining the ontological issues of the information overload.

Both theories appear to be very similar in terms of information acquisition, so integration enhances understanding of consumer behavior for acquiring information through complementarily reconciling each theory's shortcomings. In accordance with information processing theory (Bettman, 1979), foraging theory has similar assumptions: First, both theories assume that humans, in general, attempt to gather information using a variety of sources, not one source (e.g., informavores), and include browsing and searching as a continuum in a decision-making process. Second, constraints for consumer information processing occur in immediate environments in association with individuals' processing capabilities as synchronized, bilateral communications (e.g., ecological rationality). Third, when acquiring information, consumers use adaptive decision-making processes, which indicate repeated, circular modification and correction of received information, during updates (e.g., ameliorators). Fourth, humans implement various heuristics to acquire targeted information until attaining a level of "good enough" in association with some constructive processing (e.g., *homo heuristicus*). Last, a certain degree of information ignorance (i.e., incompleteness of information) exists in the information acquisition process when reaching a quality decision (e.g., satisficer). These similarities among assumptions represent what Kock (2010) clearly emphasized as important requirements for evolutionary and non-evolutionary theories, and arise from Kock's research to integrate two theories of information richness theory and information naturalness theory. Moreover, one of the primary purposes of theoretical integration is to provide a better explanation of an unsolved phenomenon in descriptive data (see also Fantino, 1985; Flavián et al., 2012; Yadav, 2010).

From this perspective, in conjunction with the information processing framework, foraging has several advantages for comprehending consumer behavior during the acquisition of information. First, the foraging concept can help explain the browsing and searching continuum through using the patch framework, which Xia and Monroe (2005) claimed overemphasized search behavior during information acquisition. The patch framework provides a different perspective for information structure in terms of the amount of data as a combination of within-patch and between-patch, thereby covering the issue of the browse-search continuum to explain issues of amount for information overload (e.g., Detlor et al., 2003). Second, the patch concept considers inevitable informational ignorance during information acquisition to achieve informational optimization through reducing overload. Third, human emotion clarifies the behavior of information processing linked with cognition, such as ignoring information, which consumers confront, and kinds of information structures in association with quantities of data. Fourth, immediate environments provide insight into new reasons for information overload by considering outside environments, instead of within organisms, during consumer information acquisition. In a broad sense, this integrative perspective provides some pivotal answers for adaptive techniques to survive in an information-rich environment. Table 19.2 summarizes the juxtaposed, capsulated theories.

Explaining this process in detail requires assuming several points suggested by both foraging and information processing frameworks. The perspective identifies consumers as *inforagers* – information foragers – seeking to acquire necessary information in the informational ecosystem

Table 19.2 Two dominant theories of consumer information acquisition

	Information processing	Foraging
Theory base	Rational choice	Foraging theory
Origin of discipline	Marketing/cognitive psychology	Behavioral ecology
Focus	Descriptive	Descriptive
Reasoning	Deductive	Inductive
Rationality	Normative	Ecological
Role of learning	Learning is mandatory	Learning is not necessarily mandatory
Inevitability of ignorance	Not assumed	Assumed as mandatory
View of environment	Independent structure of information as a situational condition	Interactive structure of information as a prerequisite condition
View of heuristics	Shortcomings to achieve an optimal decision in the information processing	Advantage to achieve an optimized decision in the information processing
Driver of heuristics	Heuristics from memory	Heuristics from experience and surroundings
Research program	Analyze information as hierarchical adaptation	Analyze information as naturally selected adaptation
View of human	Processor of information	Biobasic informavore
Behavior of human	Goal-driven processor as a cognitive machine	Goal-driven informavore as a biological organism
Focal component	Human processing capacity	Interaction of behavior and surroundings
Search and browse	Emphasis of search behavior	Emphasis of both search and browse behavior

Note: The bases for comparison are perspectives of Bettman (1979) and Pirolli (2007)

through achieving ecological cost–benefit efficiency within individuals' emotional states for decisional accuracy. First, based on an ecological cost–benefit relationship, inforagers always favor saving time and effort for decisional efficiency. Second, inforagers attempt to acquire essential information using information scents (i.e., proximal cues in response to surroundings) in a scatter-gather processes that is terminated upon reaching the criteria for sufficiency (e.g., good enough). Notably, information cues and scents differ in terms not only of the level of abstraction (i.e., information cues have a higher level of abstraction than information scents), but also a reciprocal interaction with surroundings (i.e., cues focus more on memory while scents interweave with informational surroundings). Third, inforagers conduct a scatter-gather process to acquire necessary information. This process is recursive and selective, based on information scents, and includes both browsing and searching activities (i.e., browsing information between patches and searching for particular information within patches, based on the intensity of information scents). However, if a forager has one particular item in mind, skipping the scatter-gather process is possible due to completion of this process during an early period or due to strong retention of characteristics of the particular item. Fourth, searching for information is likely to occur within a particular patch while browsing for information likely occurs between patches (i.e., searching activities require more deliberative foraging than browsing activities). This contrast arises from searching behavior's tendency to be more elaborate than browsing behavior, like hunting animals as an example (e.g., browsing an abundant prey patch and then searching a target prey). Fifth, information diet is a funneling process, which completes the foraging process after terminating the scatter-gather processes, and the eventual acquisition of necessary information occurs at the last pre-decisional phase. The information after the diet process forms the selection of useful information to affect inforagers' decision-making, such as a choice, consideration sets, choice deferral, or no choice (yes, choosing to not choose is in fact a choice, a fact that is overlooked by rational and semi-rational choice models). In other words, inforagers' decisions are not always *one* choice, caused by immediate environmental conditions such as informational equivocality, somatic and/or mental fatigue, and financial restriction within a certain period.

For instance, in the online context, an inforager initially retrieves various keywords for a given task (schema-like cue), navigates search engines to gather targeted information (browsing for a patch's existing higher level of information scents; proximal cue-like heuristics), and accesses a particular information patch (searching for informative data within a patch). An inforager attempts to integrate and streamline the selected informational sets into a whole (information diet), then acquires the necessary information and completes the foraging process. This information gathering repeats in some information patches until the "good enough" criterion requires no more information (end of scatter-gather process with using rule-of-thumb). This stop rule's basis is an inforager's time and energy consumption, which cannot exceed negative somatic and mental states. Finally, an inforager confronts a decision phase and determines one of the three courses (choose one, form consideration sets, defer a choice, or choose nothing), depending upon the degree of satisfaction with the information acquired. If an inforager does not make "a choice" as a final decision, the information foraging repeats, partly, or begins again adaptively during a certain time. Notably, new information plays a crucial role in reconstituting the renewed foraging structure with an *only-if* condition (e.g., a new product launched today or selected products on sale now). If an inforager's final decision is "no choice," this final decision is regarded as a completed decision, caused either by positive or negative consequences. As a result, no choice differs from choice deferral and a new process of information foraging will begin *only* if motivation newly stimulates consumers' interest.

Consequences of information structure on information foraging

A recent meta-analytic study argued that information structures in the information overload paradigm extensively focus on the amount of information and showed that the effect size among studies is nearly zero (Scheibehenne et al., 2010). This result suggests that researchers should consider other possibilities for determining the reasons for the issues of information overload, because information is bilateral communication with a variety of structures in the immediate environment associated with minds, not solely with numeric processing (e.g., informational quantity) of cognitive consequences (e.g., the degree of computing mistakes as that of dysfunctionality). In this respect, this result implies that consequences, previously considered controversial, are attributable not only to the quantity of information but also to the quality of information and the environmental information, as components of information structure. Moreover, the ecological perspective emphasizes environmental factors that affect consumer decision-making as prerequisite conditions (e.g., currency and constraint assumption in foraging theory) (Hantula, 2010, 2012; Hantula & Wells, 2010). To some degree, Scheibehenne et al. (2010) supported this notion and suggested an assortment structure (information structure) and satisfaction (emotional consequence). We define *information structure* as the holistic structure of information, including quantity and quality of information, and environmental information, encompassing a particular item (product or service) that influences evaluation and judgment of the item (cf. Chen et al., 2002; Furnas, 1997; Lurie, 2004; Meyer et al., 1999). This definition's bases are two assumptions of foraging theory (currency and constraint assumptions). Particularly, consumers usually confront these three components forming an information structure in online contexts when foraging for information, yet the components extend into offline contexts.

Decision-related alternatives and decision-related responses in marketing

Ecological information foraging competes with information processing in much the same fashion as consumer decision-making after gathering sufficient information. Notably, numerous studies of consumer decision-making imposed a must-choose context, although decisions do not mean that consumers must make a choice, which is inconsistent with most cases in real life (e.g., Dhar, 1997). Marketing literature corroborates the evidence that three different types of decision-making occur in the final phase after information foraging, including *a choice, choice deferral* through forming consideration sets (Hauser et al., 2010; Hauser & Wernerfelt, 1990; Punj & Moore, 2009; Ratchford, 1982), and *no choice* (Dhar, 1997; Dhar & Nowlis, 1999, 2004; Parker & Schrift, 2011). Determination of the type of decision is basically according to the degree of perceived risks that indicate decisional difficulty in a goal-oriented condition (e.g., informational equivocality) (Daft & Macintosh, 1981). For example, while consumers tend toward one choice if clear criteria (e.g., preferred brand) for the satisfactory decision for choosing a specific item exist, consumers are unlikely to choose without the clear criteria due to competing or ambiguous information with the item, or to no satisfied item (Dhar, 1997). This example indicates that the provided information affects the decision-related alternatives and responses, based on the degree of perceived risks.

Previous studies of decision-making suggested these different types of decision-making influence ultimate consequences; that is, decision-related responses as forms of emotional states like satisfaction, dissatisfaction, or regret (or disappointment) in the post-purchase phase (Inman et al., 1997; Inman & Zeelenberg, 2002; Loomes & Sugden, 1982; Lynch & Zauberman, 2007; Mick et al., 2004; Reutskaja & Hogarth, 2009; Su et al., 2009; Thaler, 1980; Thompson et al., 2005;

Tsiros, 1998; Tsiros & Mittal, 2000; Zeelenberg et al., 2000). Those studies primarily viewed emotional states as ultimate decisional consequences after completing a decision and emphasized "choice experience," which provides a causal relationship from choices (decision-related alternatives) to emotional states (decision-related responses) in the decision process (i.e., measuring post-purchase emotional state). Although many studies examined choosing on decision-related responses at the post-purchase phase after choosing decision-related alternatives, arguably the effect on decision-related responses and alternatives also appears as "foraging experience" after information foraging phases (e.g., processing experience; Creyer & Ross, 1999). In other words, the foraging is an individual's experience from the process of acquiring information, and thus this foraging experience affects evaluation or judgment for acquired information. In this case, the causal relationship has an inverse relationship from choices to emotional state. That is, the experience from information foraging determines an individual's emotional state as a decisional accuracy that forms satisfaction, dissatisfaction, or regret (decision-related responses from the foraging experience). Then, the determined emotional state accounts for the final decision related to the options of choices such as a choice, choice deferral or no choice (decision-related alternatives from the level of emotional accuracy).

Quantity of information and consequences

Associated with the amount of information, some researchers suggested increasing amounts of information cause consumers to incur greater uncertainty, resulting in negative decision-related responses (Garner & Hake, 1951). For the negative perspective of increasing amounts of information, previous studies argued that consumers tend toward dissatisfaction or regret as assortments of choice increase (Iyengar & Lepper, 2000; Mogilner et al., 2008; Schwartz, 2000). Moreover, the emotional states through the information acquisition process are likely to affect the decision-making phase, resulting in different decision-related alternatives: one choice, shaping consideration sets, decisional deferral, or forgoing the decision altogether. For example, consumers are likely to make no choice or choose deferral when products include highly ambiguous information and a large assortment of products among sources, because confidence in a correct choice declines (Wang & Shukla, 2013). The consequence implies that unfavorable decision-related responses lead to greater demotivation for choosing in response to an increase for undesirable self-responsibility (Diehl & Poynor, 2010; Iyengar & Lepper, 2000; Klein et al., 2005; Russo et al., 1998). In the contexts of high uncertainty, consumers have a tendency to invest relatively more time and effort in searching, resulting in consumers' propensity to perceive an unfairness from the demands, and consequently reducing satisfaction in the post-purchase phase (Thirkell & Vredenburg, 1982; van Dijk et al., 1999).

From a positive perspective, an increase in information from a wide range of brands is likely to provide greater satisfaction if consumers have prior preferences or recognize those brands (Chernev, 2003a, 2003b; Mogilner et al., 2008). In early studies of this issue, Russo (1974), replicating Jacoby et al. (1974), argued that more information is better to improve choice accuracy in terms of informational completeness. For example, related to the number of a product's attributes, consumers tend to ascribe more weight to many attributes when considering an initial choice of a product (Thompson et al., 2005). Furthermore, larger sizes of assortments can be preferable when organized and/or categorized well, resulting in greater recognition; otherwise, the larger assortments may produce the opposite effect (Diehl, 2005; Diehl et al., 2003). Similarly, in the study of consideration sets, consumers tend to compose larger consideration sets from a wide range of available brands to prevent an incorrect decision or minimize an inadvertent exclusion of the best choices encountering greater uncertainty, characterized by lower recognition (Lapersonne et al.; Ratchford, 1982). A series of studies implied that the effect of more-is-better is likely to be affirmative when consumers recognize particular brands or believe more information helps reduce decisional risk and uncertainty. With a large amount of information, the logic of recognition-based decision-making as a useful heuristics helps make quality decisions, particularly in the context of great ambiguities but not in all situations (Gigerenzer & Goldstein, 2011).

The controversial consequences regarding the amount of information imply that consumers' decision-related responses rely on the perception of information structures associated with particular decision-making contexts (Scheibehenne et al., 2010), such as idiosyncratic information structures (e.g., the degree of equivocality and uncertainty from given information sets and the perception of the quality of information from heterogeneous sources) (Pierro et al., 2012). In other words, from the issue of numbers of attributes within a patch and/or alternatives between patches, consumers are prone to express negative decision-related responses as a form of dissatisfaction or regret when processing information exceeds perceptional criteria; otherwise, consumers are likely to maintain positive decision-related responses. Accordingly, this controversy may suggest that the amount of information clearly leads to decision-related alternatives after completion of foraging, although no apparent normative terminal point exists to determine a universal standard for more or less information. Therefore, when consumers implement information foraging, as exchanges between information providers and receivers, consumers, as the receivers, are likely to accept information proactively and to interpret information based on prior beliefs or knowledge (Kettinger & Li, 2010; Miranda & Saunders, 2003). The perspective of information exchange implies that information simultaneously provides objective and subjective meanings (e.g., fact and belief) when consumers interpret, at the subjective level of self-satisfaction, information for justification or determination (Cardozo, 1965; Schwartz, 2000). In this regard, highly recognizable items contain clear-cut information on attributes less likely to exist in ordinary situations; the amount of information, as a risk factor, has a negative relationship with decision-related alternatives (i.e., increasing choice sizes) and decision-related responses (i.e., inclining to dissatisfaction or regret). As a result, an increase in the quantity of information causes a stimulation of negative emotional states, resulting in increasingly greater degrees of choice deferral or engendering no choice.

Quality of information and consequences

Scheibehenne et al. (2010) found that the effect of quantity in information overload is nearly zero, and suggested another information structure such as arrangement of information as qualitative information. The suggestion regarding arranged informational structure implies that the quality of information may be more important than the quantity of information although both are crucial to the effects of information overload. Some early studies also noted that both quantity and quality of information consist of information structures whose factors have an effect on information overload (Keller & Staelin, 1987; Lurie, 2004). Moreover, Keller and Staelin (1987) argued that the quality of information has positive characteristics for improving decisional effectiveness but that the quantity of information has negative characteristics for promoting effectiveness. Furthermore, Lurie (2004) argued that simple accounting of the amounts of information is inappropriate for explaining information overload in the online context; instead, a structural approach for measuring information, that includes levels of attributes and distribution of those levels among attributes in alternative sets, provides more effective explication of information overload. This result implies that by holding the amount of information as constant, a well-arranged structure of information (i.e., quality) provides a better understanding of information overload. In addition, consumers may interpret the presented information from various angles during foraging, which indicates communicational exchanges perceived through quality of information, when consumers, based on the degree of ambiguity of attributes or alternatives, evaluate products (Hoch, 2002). The existing studies with the quality of information suggested that a perceptual subjectivity is a critical factor when consumers evaluate that quality of information from the perspective of information exchange (Kettinger & Li, 2010). This evidence implies that information quality affects information equivocality, resulting in decision-related responses and alternatives according to the degree of equivocality. In other words, as the information equivocality increases, consumers are likely to increase the size of consideration sets or defer a choice, which derives from negative decision-related responses (dissatisfaction, or regret or disappointment). For example, imagine a situation of two information foraging contexts between categories of computers and daily foods. Consumers may expect complex information foraging for purchasing a computer more than for daily food because the information structure for computers seems to be complicated in terms of the quantity of competitive information among attributes, resulting perhaps in great conflict (i.e., high equivocality). However, the structures for those two categories of products can lead to an opposite equivocality level in some cases when considering nutritional information of foods, in terms of the quality of information, compared to computers (e.g., multivitamins). This reversal is due to the informational uncertainty from nutritional terminologies, resulting in great ambiguity (i.e., high equivocality). In many cases, the information for purchasing foods contains unknown (or unreadable) data regarding nutrition in terms of the quality of information, such as calories, ingredients and fats. In turn, the effort of analyzing this information would be greater than that of comparing a computer's information for a choice, although a smaller amount of information is included. To determine the degree of equivocality, not only the number of attributes or alternatives, but also the quality of information, which influences the decision-related responses and alternatives after foraging for information, should be considered.

Accordingly, the quality of an information structure consists of two components: the degree of targeted information easily recognized (Cain et al., 2012; Pirolli, 2007) and the degree of arrangement for ease of comparison (Mogilner et al., 2008; Scheibehenne et al., 2010). Those two components of information quality are more likely to determine the information structure from a within-patch perspective, because the information is about a particular product or service. Whichever leads to less searching effort to obtain targeted information, consumers likely perceive the information structure to be less equivocal, resulting in ecological optimization. For example, some visual studies emphasized frequency of appearance of targeted data to reflect the quality of information in an optimal foraging model. The higher frequency of the appearance of visual targets in within-patch (i.e., higher quality), the lower the rates for overlooking foraging targets (i.e., better performance). To the contrary, higher rates for overlooking targets result when a patch contains lower visual frequency of targets along with numerous ambiguous targets (e.g., blur or similar targets) (Cain et al., 2012; Fleck et al., 2010). The results imply that if consumers easily and frequently recognize the targeted information (e.g., clearly differentiated features), decision-making incurs lower deliberation costs for foraged targets (e.g., time and/or effort). In other words, the high quality of targeted information based on the frequency is likely to help consumers reduce the degree of informational ambiguity, which results in reducing perceived uncertainties (Flavián et al., 2012), and thereby engenders a positive feeling and a clear final choice. This implication proffers evidence that if consumers frequently find recognizable information, they are likely to obtain necessary information with higher rates of return on foraging investment through adapting cumulative experiences with the link of the information from past to current sources (Fu & Pirolli, 2007; Pirolli & Card, 1999).

Similarly, the literature considering brand assortments in a retail context suggests that consumers prefer the presence of many recognizable brands (e.g., targeted brands) and result in an experiential satisfaction, conjecturing lower equivocality regarded as a high quality of information (Chernev, 2003a, 2003b; Mogilner et al., 2008). The implication is that better decision-making requires higher-quality information, regardless perhaps of the mere quantity of information. That is, the easily recognizable information indicates high-quality information and thus tends to lead to reduced information overload. Along with rates of appearance of targeted information, Chakravarti and Janiszewski (2003) examined the effect of information arrangement (i.e., well-organized attributes or alternatives, or not) in the formation of consideration sets. The results provided evidence that consumers favor forming consideration sets from well-organized product information, which provides ease of comparison of attributes (Mogilner et al., 2008). This result implies that well-organized information structure is more likely to reduce equivocality, resulting in smaller sizes of consideration sets that help increase the likelihood of making a choice. In this respect, consumers prefer a well-organized information structure to an ill-organized information structure, regardless of the mere quantity of information (Chakravarti & Janiszewski, 2003; Mogilner et al., 2008). Therefore, when consumers perceive the immediate structure of information as high quality (i.e., the information structure with highly recognizable and well-arranged information), the resultant consequences (i.e., decision-related responses and alternatives) are likely to be affirmative.

Environmental information and consequences

Foraging aims to find processes and reasons for decision-making through investigating outside of organisms in the immediate environments (Hantula, 2012), and ecological rationality pursues an interaction between human minds and surroundings to find reasoning for decision-making (Todd & Gigerenzer, 2007). As a prerequisite, the environmental information includes both quantity and quality dimensions in composing the information structure. Nonetheless, environmental information as another dimension composing the information structure has been overlooked in the information overload paradigm, such as collateral information associated with information sources (e.g., policies of retailers and reviews). For example, when consumers forage for the necessary information, they consider not only item-specific attributes that directly relate to an item's attributes but also immediate environments that are involved in the information sources of the item (e.g., delivery cost or customers' reviews) (Hantula & Bryant, 2005; Häubl & Trifts, 2000; Stenstrom et al., 2008). In naturalistic contexts of informational acquisition (e.g., everyday decisions for purchasing items), the information structure consists not only of item-specific attributes (e.g., item's features) but also other environmental attributes (e.g., seller's policy). For example, based on foraging theory, Hantula and Bryant (2005) examined the effect of delay discounting in consumers' online consumption, and suggested that the delivery cost depending on time-delay hyperbolically influences online buyers' preference when making a purchase decision. Moreover, a recent study suggested that well-designed websites tend to help consumers understand information from well-considered organization of information (Chen et al., 2011), leading to an implied decrease in time and energy costs and tending to increase positive decision-related responses in terms of the cost–benefit relationship. In a study of online hunting and gathering, Stenstrom et al. (2008) argued that website design recommendations affect consumers' navigation paths. In line with web design, in a study of online advertisements, formation of positive attitudes for a website relies on the types of webpage backgrounds, and results showed that simpler web-page backgrounds are more effective than complex ones (Stevenson et al., 2000). Furthermore, in the decision process, the prior literature emphasized the role of reviews as environmental information and suggested that the review is an integral factor in the process of information acquisition, resulting in different shapes of decision-related responses and alternatives. For example, Häubl and Trifts (2000) argued that consumers' informational acquisition includes the process of an interaction between direct, item-related factors through comparison of alternatives and indirect, item-related factors such as a review or recommendation (e.g., Mudambi & Schuff, 2010; Park & Park, 2013). Therefore, information structures should include environmental information as a prerequisite dimension in conjunction with the other dimensions (the quantity and quality of information), so that we may be able to determine more precisely the degree of information overload during information foraging.

Conclusions

Consumers acquire not only goods, but also information. Consumers are "inforagers" who interact with their immediate environments as suggested by a Darwinian perspective of ecological rationality perspective, especially as derived from foraging theory in collaboration with the non-Darwinian theory. The emphasis is a reciprocal relationship between the ecological perspective and the normative perspective. This theoretical integration demonstrated how an ecological rationality perspective can address shortcomings in an information processing model (derived from rational choice models) of consumer information acquisition. Information is a communication between minds and immediate environments from an organismic perspective. The integrative perspective between evolutionary and non-evolutionary frameworks suggests a holistic information structure and provides some evidence that this theoretical integration helps identify the phenomena of information overload through information foraging. As complementary rather than alternatives, each philosophical, theoretical viewpoint is useful for delineating consumer foraging behavior and very new theories are unnecessary to clarify this behavior. Revised understanding of the implications of existing, older theories is necessary. The implication is an adaptive ability of instincts gained from ancestral, historical precedents.

References

Abarca, N., & Fantino, E. (1982). Choice and foraging. *Journal of the Experimental Analysis of Behavior, 38*(2), 117–123.

Bettman, J. R. (1979). *An information processing theory of consumer choice.* Reading, MA: Addison-Wesley.

Biernaskie, J. M., Walker, S. C., & Gegear, R. J. (2009). Bumblebees learn to forage like Bayesians. *American Naturalist, 174*(3), 413–423.

Bolhuis, J. J., Brown, G. R., Richardson, R. C., & Laland, K. N. (2011). Darwin in mind: new opportunities for evolutionary psychology. *PLoS Biol, 9*(7), e1001109.

Cain, M. S., Vul, E., Clark, K., & Mitroff, S. R. (2012). A Bayesian optimal foraging model of human visual search. *Psychological Science, 23*(9), 1047–1054.

Capra, C. M., & Rubin, P. H. (2011). Rationality and utility: economics and evolutionary psychology. In G. Saad (Ed.), *Evolutionary Psychology in the Business Sciences* (pp. 319–338). London: Springer.

Cardozo, R. N. (1965). An experimental study of customer effort, expectation, and satisfaction. *Journal of Marketing Research, 2*(3), 244–249.

Chakravarti, A., & Janiszewski, C. (2003). The Influence of macro-level motives on consideration set composition in novel purchase situations. *Journal of Consumer Research, 30*(2), 244–258.

Charnov, E. L. (1976). Optimal foraging, the marginal value theorem. *Theoretical Population Biology, 9*(2), 129–136.

Chen, C., Cribbin, T., Kuljis, J., & Macredie, R. (2002). Footprints of information foragers: behaviour semantics of visual exploration. *International Journal of Human-Computer Studies, 57*(2), 139–163.

Chen, J. V., Lin, C., Yen, D. C., & Linn, K.-P. (2011). The interaction effects of familiarity, breadth and media usage on web browsing experience. *Computers in Human Behavior, 27*(6), 2141–2152.

Chernev, A. (2003a). Product assortment and individual decision processes. *Journal of Personality and Social Psychology, 85*(1), 151–162.

Chernev, A. (2003b). When more is less and less is more: the role of ideal point availability and assortment in consumer choice. *Journal of Consumer Research, 30*(2), 170–183.

Conlisk, J. (1996). Why bounded rationality? *Journal of Economic Literature, 34*(2), 669–700.

Cosmides, L., & Tooby, J. (1987). From evolution to behavior: evolutionary psychology as the missing link. In J. Dupr (Ed.), *The Latest on the Best Essays on Evolution and Optimality* (pp. 277–306). Cambridge, MA: MIT Press.

Cosmides, L., & Tooby, J. (1996). Are humans good intuitive statisticians after all? Rethinking some conclusions from the literature on judgment under uncertainty. *Cognition, 58*(1), 1–73.

Creyer, E. H., & Ross, W. T. (1999). The development and use of a regret experience measure to examine the effects of outcome feedback on regret and subsequent choice. *Marketing Letters, 10*(4), 373–386.

Critchfield, T. S., & Atteberry, T. (2003). Temporal discounting predicts individual competitive success in a human analogue of group foraging. *Behavioural Processes, 64*(3), 315–331.

Cronk, L. (1991). Human behavioral ecology. *Annual Review of Anthropology, 20*, 25–53.

Daft, R. L., & Macintosh, N. B. (1981). A tentative exploration into the amount and equivocality of information processing in organizational work units. *Administrative Science Quarterly, 26*(2), 207–224.

Dennett, D. C. (1991). *Consciousness Explained*. Boston, MA: Back Bay Books.

Detlor, B., Sproule, S., & Gupta, C. (2003). Pre-purchase online information seeking: search versus browse. *Journal of Electronic Commerce Research, 4*(2), 72–84.

Dhar, R. (1997). Consumer preference for a no-choice option. *Journal of Consumer Research, 24*(2), 215–231.

Dhar, R., & Nowlis, S. M. (1999). The effect of time pressure on consumer choice deferral. *Journal of Consumer Research, 25*(4), 369–384.

Dhar, R., & Nowlis, S. M. (2004). To buy or not to buy: response mode effects on consumer choice. *Journal of Marketing Research, 41*(4), 423–432.

DiClemente, D. F., & Hantula, D. A. (2003a). Applied behavioral economics and consumer choice. *Journal of Economic Psychology, 24*(5), 589–602.

DiClemente, D. F., & Hantula, D. A. (2003b). Optimal foraging online: increasing sensitivity to delay. *Psychology & Marketing, 20*(9), 785–809.

Diehl, K. (2005). When two rights make a wrong: searching too much in ordered environments. *Journal of Marketing Research, 42*(3), 313–322.

Diehl, K., Kornish, L. J., & Lynch, J. G. (2003). Smart agents: when lower search costs for quality information increase price sensitivity. *Journal of Consumer Research, 30*(1), 56–71.

Diehl, K., & Poynor, C. (2010). Great expectations?! Assortment size, expectations, and satisfaction. *Journal of Marketing Research, 47*(2), 312–322.

Duggan, G. B., & Payne, S. J. (2009). Text skimming: the process and effectiveness of foraging through text under time pressure. *Journal of Experimental Psychology: Applied, 15*(3), 228–242.

Einhorn, H. J., & Hogarth, R. M. (1986). Decision making under ambiguity. *Journal of Business, 59*(4), S225–S250.

Fagerstrøm, A., Foxall, G. R., & Arntzen, E. (2010). Implications of motivating operations for the functional analysis of consumer choice. *Journal of Organizational Behavior Management, 30*(2), 110–126.

Fantino, E. (1969). Choice and rate of reinforcement. *Journal of the Experimental Analysis of Behavior, 12*(5), 723–730.

Fantino, E. (1985). Behavior analysis and behavioral ecology: a synergistic coupling. *Behavior Analyst, 8*(2), 151–157.

Flavián, C., Gurrea, R., & Orús, C. (2012). An integrative perspective of online foraging behavior with search engines. *Psychology & Marketing, 29*(11), 836–849.

Fleck, M. S., Samei, E., & Mitroff, S. R. (2010). Generalized "satisfaction of search": adverse influences on dual-target search accuracy. *Journal of Experimental Psychology: Applied, 16*(1), 60–71.

Foxall, G. R. (2001). Foundations of consumer behaviour analysis. *Marketing Theory, 1*(2), 165–199.

Foxall, G. R. (2010a). Accounting for consumer choice: inter-temporal decision making in behavioural perspective. *Marketing Theory, 10*(4), 315–345.

Foxall, G. R. (2010b). Invitation to consumer behavior analysis. *Journal of Organizational Behavior Management, 30*(2), 92–109.

Foxall, G. R., Wells, V. K., Chang, S. W., & Oliveira-Castro, J. M. (2010). Substitutability and independence: matching analyses of brands and products. *Journal of Organizational Behavior Management, 30*(2), 145–160.

Fu, W.-T., & Pirolli, P. (2007). SNIF-ACT: a cognitive model of user navigation on the world wide web. *Human-Computer Interaction, 22*(4), 355–412.

Furnas, G. W. (1997). *Effective view navigation.* Paper presented at the Proceedings of the SIGCHI conference on Human Factors in Computing Systems.

Garner, W. R., & Hake, H. W. (1951). The amount of information in absolute judgments. *Psychological Review, 58*(6), 446–459.

Gigerenzer, G. (1996). On narrow norms and vague heuristics: a reply to Kahneman and Tversky. *Psychological Review, 103*(3), 592–596.

Gigerenzer, G. (2008). Why heuristics work. *Perspectives on Psychological Science, 3*(1), 20–29.

Gigerenzer, G., & Brighton, H. (2009). Homo heuristicus: why biased minds make better inferences. *Topics in Cognitive Science, 1*(1), 107–143.

Gigerenzer, G., & Gaissmaier, W. (2011). Heuristic decision making. *Annual Review of Psychology, 62*(1), 451–482.

Gigerenzer, G., & Goldstein, D. G. (2011). The recognition heuristic: a decade of research. *Judgment and Decision Making, 6*(1), 100–121.

Gigerenzer, G., Hoffrage, U., & Goldstein, D. G. (2008). Fast and frugal heuristics are plausible models of cognition: reply to Dougherty, Franco-Watkins, and Thomas (2008). *Psychological Review, 115*(1), 230–237.

Gigerenzer, G., & Todd, P. M. (1999). Fast and frugal heuristics: the adaptive toolbox. In G. Gigerenzer, P. M. Todd & T. A. R. Group (Eds.), *Simple Heuristics That Make Us Smart* (pp. 1–34). New York: Oxford University Press.

Gigerenzer, G., Todd, P. M., & Group, T. A. R. (1999). *Simple Heuristics That Make Us Smart.* New York: Oxford University Press.

Giraldeau, L.-A., & Caraco, T. (2000). *Social Foraging Theory.* Princeton, NJ: Princeton University Press.

Goldstein, D. G., & Gigerenzer, G. (2002). Models of ecological rationality: the recognition heuristic. *Psychological Review, 109*(1), 75–90.

Goldstein, K. (1939). *The Organism: A Holistic Approach to Biology Derived from Pathological Data in Man.* New York: American Book Company.

Griskevicius, V., & Kenrick, D. T. (2013). Fundamental motives: how evolutionary needs influence consumer behavior. *Journal of Consumer Psychology, 23*(3), 372–386.

Hagen, E. H. (2005). Controversial issues in evolutionary psychology. In D. M. Buss (Ed.), *The Handbook of Evolutionary Psychology* (pp. 145–173). Hoboken, NJ: John Wiley & Sons.

Hantula, D. A. (2010). The behavioral ecology of human foraging in an online environment: of omnivores, informavores, and hunter-gatherers. In N. Kock (Ed.), *Evolutionary Psychology and Information Systems Research: A New Approach to Studying the Effects of Modern Technologies on Human Behavior* (pp. 85–99). New York: Springer.

Hantula, D. A. (2012). Consumers are foragers, not rational actors: towards a behavioral ecology of consumer choice. In V. Wells & G. R. Foxall (Eds.), *Handbook of Developments in Consumer Behaviour* (pp. 549–577). Cheltenham: Edward Elgar.

Hantula, D. A., Brockman, D. D., & Smith, C. L. (2008). Online shopping as foraging: the effects of increasing delays on purchasing and patch residence. *IEEE Transactions on Professional Communication 51*(2), 147–154.

Hantula, D. A., & Bryant, K. (2005). Delay discounting determines delivery fees in an e-commerce simulation: a behavioral economic perspective. *Psychology & Marketing, 22*(2), 153–161.

Hantula, D. A., & Wells, V. K. (2010). Outside the organization: the analysis of consumer behavior. *Journal of Organizational Behavior Management, 30*(2), 87–91.

Haselton, M. G., & Nettle, D. (2006). The paranoid optimist: an integrative evolutionary model of cognitive biases. *Personality and Social Psychology Review, 10*(1), 47–66.

Häubl, G., & Trifts, V. (2000). Consumer decision making in online shopping environments: the effects of interactive decision aids. *Marketing Science, 19*(1), 4–21.

Hauser, J. R., Toubia, O., Evgeniou, T., Befurt, R., & Dzyabura, D. (2010). Disjunctions of conjunctions, cognitive simplicity, and consideration sets. *Journal of Marketing Research, 47*(3), 485–496.

Hauser, J. R., & Wernerfelt, B. (1990). An evaluation cost model of consideration sets. *Journal of Consumer Research, 16*(4), 393–408.

Herrnstein, R. J. (1961). Relative and absolute strength of response as a function of frequency of reinforcement. *Journal of the Experimental Analysis of Behavior, 4*(3), 267–272.

Herrnstein, R. J. (1970). On the law of effect. *Journal of the Experimental Analysis of Behavior, 13*(2), 243–266.

Herrnstein, R. J. (1990). Rational choice theory: necessary but not sufficient. *American Psychologist, 45*(3), 356–367.

Herrnstein, R. J., Loewenstein, G. F., Prelec, D., & Vaughan, W. (1993). Utility maximization and melioration: internalities in individual choice. *Journal of Behavioral Decision Making, 6*(3), 149–185.

Herrnstein, R. J., & Prelec, D. (1991). Melioration: a theory of distributed choice. *Journal of Economic Perspectives, 5*(3), 137–156.

Hoch, S. J. (2002). Product experience is seductive. *Journal of Consumer Research, 29*(3), 448–454.

Hunt, S. D. (2002). *Foundations of marketing theory: toward a general theory of marketing.* Armonk, NY: M. E. Sharpe.

Hutchinson, J. M. C., Wilke, A., & Todd, P. M. (2008). Patch leaving in humans: can a generalist adapt its rules to dispersal of items across patches? *Animal Behaviour, 75*(4), 1331–1349.

Inman, J. J., Dyer, J. S., & Jia, J. (1997). A generalized utility model of disappointment and regret effects on post-choice valuation. *Marketing Science, 16*(2), 97–111.

Inman, J. J., & Zeelenberg, M. (2002). Regret in repeat purchase versus switching decisions: the attenuating role of decision justifiability. *Journal of Consumer Research, 29*(1), 116–128.

Iwasa, Y., Higashi, M., & Yamamura, N. (1981). Prey distribution as a factor determining the choice of optimal foraging strategy. *American Naturalist, 117*(5), 710–723.

Iyengar, S. S., & Lepper, M. R. (2000). When choice is demotivating: can one desire too much of a good thing? *Journal of Personality and Social Psychology, 79*(6), 995–1006.

Jacoby, J., Speller, D. E., & Kohn, C. A. (1974). Brand choice behavior as a function of information load. *Journal of Marketing Research, 11*(1), 63–69.

Jansen, B. J., Booth, D. L., & Spink, A. (2008). Determining the informational, navigational, and transactional intent of Web queries. *Information Processing & Management, 44*(3), 1251–1266.

Jansen, B. J., & Spink, A. (2006). How are we searching the World Wide Web? A comparison of nine search engine transaction logs. *Information Processing & Management, 42*(1), 248–263.

Kahneman, D., & Tversky, A. (1979). Prospect theory: an analysis of decision under risk. *Econometrica, 47*(2), 263–291.

Kalenscher, T., & van Wingerden, M. (2011). Why we should use animals to study economic decision making – a perspective. *Frontiers in Neuroscience, 5*, Article 82.

Kanazawa, S. (2006). "First, kill all the economists . . . ": the insufficiency of microeconomics and the need for evolutionary psychology in the study of management: introduction to the Special Issue. *Managerial and Decision Economics, 27*(2/3), 95–101.

Keller, K. L., & Staelin, R. (1987). Effects of quality and quantity of information on decision effectiveness. *Journal of Consumer Research, 14*(2), 200–213.

Kettinger, W. J., & Li, Y. (2010). Infological equation extended: towards conceptual clarity in the relation between data, infomation and knowledge. *European Journal of Information Systems, 19*(4), 409–421.

Klein, E., Bhatt, R., & Zentall, T. (2005). Contrast and the justification of effort. *Psychonomic Bulletin & Review, 12*(2), 335–339.

Kock, N. (2009). Information systems theorizing based on evolutionary psychology: an interdisciplinary review and theory integration framework. *MIS Quarterly, 33*(2), 395–418.

Kock, N. (2010). Evolutionary psychology and information systems theorizing. In N. Kock (Ed.), *Evolutionary Psychology and Information Systems Research: A New Approach to Studying the Effects of Modern Technologies on Human Behavior* (pp. 3–37). New York: Springer.

Kock, N., Hantula, D. A., Hayne, S. C., Saad, G., Todd, P. M., & Watson, R. T. (2008). Introduction to Darwinian perspectives on electronic communication. *IEEE Transactions on Professional Communication, 51*(2), 133–146.

Lapersonne, E., Laurent, G., & Le Goff, J.-J. (1995). Consideration sets of size one: an empirical investigation of automobile purchases. *International Journal of Research in Marketing, 12*(1), 55–66.

Lea, S. E. G. (1979). Foraging and reinforcement schedules in the pigeon: optimal and non-optimal aspects of choice. *Animal Behaviour, 27, Part 3*, 875–886.

Levine, S. S., & Kurzban, R. (2006). Explaining clustering in social networks: towards an evolutionary theory of cascading benefits. *Managerial and Decision Economics, 27*(2/3), 173–187.

Loomes, G., & Sugden, R. (1982). Regret theory: an alternative theory of rational choice under uncertainty. *Economic Journal, 92*(368), 805–824.

Lurie, N. H. (2004). Decision making in information-rich environments: the role of information structure. *Journal of Consumer Research, 30*(4), 473–486.

Lynch, J. G., & Zauberman, G. (2007). Construing consumer decision making. *Journal of Consumer Psychology, 17*(2), 107–112.

Mayr, E. (1983). How to carry out the adaptationist program? *American Naturalist, 121*(3), 324–334.

McDermott, R., Fowler, J. H., & Smirnov, O. (2008). On the evolutionary origin of prospect theory preferences. *Journal of Politics, 70*(2), 335–350.

McKerchar, T. L., Green, L., Myerson, J., Pickford, T. S., Hill, J. C., & Stout, S. C. (2009). A comparison of four models of delay discounting in humans. *Behavioural Processes, 81*(2), 256–259.

McNamara, J. M. (1982). Optimal patch use in a stochastic environment. *Theoretical Population Biology, 21*(2), 269–288.

Meyer, J., Shamo, M. K., & Gopher, D. (1999). Information structure and the relative efficacy of tables and graphs. *Human Factors, 41*(4), 570–587.

Mick, D. G., Broniarczyk, S. M., & Haidt, J. (2004). Choose, choose, choose, choose, choose, choose, choose: emerging and prospective research on the deleterious effects of living in consumer hyper-choice. *Journal of Business Ethics, 52*(2), 207–211.

Miranda, S. M., & Saunders, C. S. (2003). The social construction of meaning: an alternative perspective on information sharing. *Information Systems Research, 14*(1), 87–106.

Mogilner, C., Rudnick, T., & Iyengar, S. S. (2008). The mere categorization effect: how the presence of categories increases choosers' perceptions of assortment variety and outcome satisfaction. *Journal of Consumer Research, 35*(2), 202–215.

Mudambi, S. M., & Schuff, D. (2010). What makes a helpful online review? A study of customer reviews on Amazon.com. *MIS Quarterly, 34*(1), 185–200.

Nettle, D., Gibson, M. A., Lawson, D. W., & Sear, R. (2013). Human behavioral ecology: current research and future prospects. *Behavioral Ecology, 24*, 1031–1040.

Park, S.-B., & Park, D.-H. (2013). The effect of low- versus high-variance in product reviews on product evaluation. *Psychology & Marketing, 30*(7), 543–554.

Parker, J. R., & Schrift, R. Y. (2011). Rejectable choice sets: how seemingly irrelevant no-choice options affect consumer decision processes. *Journal of Marketing Research, 48*(5), 840–854.

Payne, S. J., Duggan, G. B., & Neth, H. (2007). Discretionary task interleaving: heuristics for time allocation in cognitive foraging. *Journal of Experimental Psychology: General, 136*(3), 370–388.

Pierro, A., Mannetti, L., Kruglanski, A. W., Klein, K., & Orehek, E. (2012). Persistence of attitude change and attitude–behavior correspondence based on extensive processing of source information. *European Journal of Social Psychology, 42*(1), 103–111.

Pirolli, P. (2005). Rational analyses of information foraging on the web. *Cognitive Science, 29*(3), 343–373.

Pirolli, P. (2007). *Information Foraging Theory: Adaptive Interaction with Information.* New York: Oxford University Press.

Pirolli, P., & Card, S. K. (1999). Information foraging. *Psychological Review, 106*(4), 643–675.

Posavac, S. S., Kardes, F. R., & Brakus, J. J. (2010). Focus induced tunnel vision in managerial judgment and decision making: the peril and the antidote. *Organizational Behavior and Human Decision Processes, 113*(2), 102–111.

Punj, G., & Moore, R. (2009). Information search and consideration set formation in a web-based store environment. *Journal of Business Research, 62*(6), 644–650.

Puvathingal, B. J., & Hantula, D. A. (2012). Revisiting the psychology of intelligence analysis: from rational actors to adaptive thinkers. *American Psychologist, 67*(3), 199–210.

Rajala, A. K., & Hantula, D. A. (2000). Towards a behavioral ecology of consumption: delay-reduction effects on foraging in a simulated internet mall. *Managerial and Decision Economics, 21*(3/4), 145–158.

Ratchford, B. T. (1982). Cost-benefit models for explaining consumer choice and information seeking behavior. *Management Science, 28*(2), 197–212.

Reed, D. D., Yanagita, B. T., Becirevic, A., & Kaplan, B. A. (2014). Consumer foraging for safer tanning alternatives: a naturally occurring experiment on informational reinforcement in the UK. *European Journal of Behavior Analysis, 15*, (2), 241–248.

Reutskaja, E., & Hogarth, R. M. (2009). Satisfaction in choice as a function of the number of alternatives: when "goods satiate". *Psychology & Marketing, 26*(3), 197–203.

Rode, C., Cosmides, L., Hell, W., & Tooby, J. (1999). When and why do people avoid unknown probabilities in decisions under uncertainty? Testing some predictions from optimal foraging theory. *Cognition, 72*(3), 269–304.

Rosati, A. G., Stevens, J. R., Hare, B., & Hauser, M. D. (2007). The Evolutionary origins of human patience: temporal preferences in chimpanzees, bonobos, and human adults. *Current Biology, 17*(19), 1663–1668.

Rosenzweig, M. L. (2007). On foraging theory, humans and the conservation of diversity: a prospectus. In D. W. Stephens, J. S. Brown, & R. C. Ydenberg (Eds.), *Foraging: Behavior and Ecology* (pp. 483–501). Chicago, IL: University of Chicago Press.

Russo, J. E. (1974). More information is better: a reevaluation of Jacoby, Speller and Kohn. *Journal of Consumer Research, 1*(3), 68–72.

Russo, J. E., Meloy, M. G., & Medvec, V. H. (1998). Predecisional distortion of product information. *Journal of Marketing Research, 35*(4), 438–452.

Saad, G. (2006). Applying evolutionary psychology in understanding the Darwinian roots of consumption phenomena. *Managerial and Decision Economics, 27*(2/3), 189–201.

Saad, G. (2007). *The Evolutionary Bases of Consumption* (1st ed.). New York: Psychology Press.

Saad, G. (2008). The collective amnesia of marketing scholars regarding consumers' biological and evolutionary roots. *Marketing Theory, 8*(4), 425–448.

Saad, G. (2011). The missing link: the biological roots of the business sciences. In G. Saad (Ed.), *Evolutionary Psychology in the Business Sciences* (pp. 1–16). London: Springer.

Saad, G. (2013). Evolutionary consumption. *Journal of Consumer Psychology, 23*(3), 351–371.

Saad, G., & Gill, T. (2001). Sex differences in the ultimatum game: an evolutionary psychology perspective. *Journal of Bioeconomics, 3*(2), 171–193.

Saad, G., & Vongas, J. G. (2009). The effect of conspicuous consumption on men's testosterone levels. *Organizational Behavior and Human Decision Processes, 110*(2), 80–92.

Sanbonmatsu, D. M., Vanous, S., Hook, C., Posavac, S. S., & Kardes, F. R. (2011). Whither the alternatives: determinants and consequences of selective versus comparative judgemental processing. *Thinking & Reasoning, 17*(4), 367–386.

Sandstrom, P. E. (1994). An optimal foraging approach to information seeking and use. *Library Quarterly, 64*(4), 414–449.

Sandstrom, P. E. (1999). Scholars as subsistence foragers. *Bulletin of the American Society for Information Science and Technology, 25*(3), 17–20.

Santos, L. R., & Chen, M. K. (2009). The evolution of rational and irrational economic behavior: evidence and insight from a non-human primate species. In P. W. Glimcher, C. F. Camerer, E. Fehr, & R. A. Poldrack (Eds.), *Neuroeconomics: Decision Making and the Brain* (pp. 81–93). London: Academic Press.

Scheibehenne, B., Greifeneder, R., & Todd, P. M. (2010). Can there ever be too many options? A meta analytic review of choice overload. *Journal of Consumer Research, 37*(3), 409–425.

Schwartz, B. (2000). Self-determination: the tyranny of freedom. *American Psychologist, 55*(1), 79–88.

Simon, H. A. (1955). A behavioral model of rational choice. *Quarterly Journal of Economics, 69*(1), 99–118.

Simon, H. A. (1956). Rational choice and the structure of the environment. *Psychological Review, 63*(2), 129–138.

Simon, H. A. (1957). *Models of Man: Social and Rational.* Oxford: Wiley.

Smith, C. L., & Hantula, D. A. (2003). Pricing effects on foraging in a simulated Internet shopping mall. *Journal of Economic Psychology, 24*(5), 653–674.

Smith, C. L., & Hantula, D. A. (2008). Methodological considerations in the study of delay discounting in intertemporal choice: a comparison of tasks and modes. *Behavior Research Methods, 40*(4), 940–953.

Stenstrom, E., Stenstrom, P., Saad, G., & Cheikhrouhou, S. (2008). Online hunting and gathering: an evolutionary perspective on sex differences in website preferences and navigation. *IEEE Transactions on Professional Communication, 51*(2), 155–168.

Stephens, D. W., & Charnov, E. L. (1982). Optimal foraging: some simple stochastic models. *Behavioral Ecology and Sociobiology, 10*(4), 251–263.

Stephens, D. W., & Krebs, J. R. (1986). *Foraging Theory.* Princeton, NJ: Princeton University Press.

Stevenson, J. S., Bruner, G. C., & Kumar, A. (2000). Webpage background and viewer attitudes. *Journal of Advertising Research, 40*(1/2), 29–34.

Su, S., Chen, R., & Zhao, P. (2009). Do the size of consideration set and the source of the better competing option influence post-choice regret? *Motivation and Emotion, 33*(3), 219–228.

Symons, D. (1992). On the use and misuse of Darwinism in the study of human bahavior. In J. H. Barkow, L. Cosmides, & J. Tooby (Eds.), *The Adapted Mind: Evolutionary Psychology and the Generation of Culture* (pp. 137–159). New York: Oxford University Press.

Taylor, L. R., Woiwod, I. P., & Perry, J. N. (1978). The density-dependence of spatial behaviour and the rarity of randomness. *Journal of Animal Ecology, 47*(2), 383–406.

Thaler, R. H. (1980). Toward a positive theory of consumer choice. *Journal of Economic Behavior & Organization, 1*(1), 39–60.

Thirkell, P., & Vredenburg, H. (1982). *Prepurchase Information Search and Post Purchase Satisfaction: An Empirical Examination of Alternative Theories.* Paper presented at the An Assessment of Marketing Thought & Practice – 1982 Educators' Conference Proceedings, Chicago.

Thompson, D. V., Hamilton, R. W., & Rust, R. T. (2005). Feature fatigue: when product capabilities become too much of a good thing. *Journal of Marketing Research, 42*(4), 431–442.

Todd, P. M., & Gigerenzer, G. (2000). Précis of simple heuristics that make us smart. *Behavioral and Brain Sciences, 23*(05), 727–741.

Todd, P. M., & Gigerenzer, G. (2007). Environments that make us smart: ecological rationality. *Current Directions in Psychological Science, 16*(3), 167–171.

Todd, P. M., Hertwig, R., & Hoffrage, U. (2005). Controversial issues in evolutionary psychology. In D. M. Buss (Ed.), *The Handbook of Evolutionary Psychology* (pp. 776–827). Hoboken, NJ: John Wiley & Sons.

Tooby, J., & Cosmides, L. (2005). Conceptual foundations of evolutionary psychology. In D. M. Buss (Ed.), *The Handbook of Evolutionary Psychology* (pp. 5–67). Hoboken, NJ: John Wiley & Sons.

Tsiros, M. (1998). Effect of regret on post-choice valuation: the case of more than two alternatives. *Organizational Behavior and Human Decision Processes, 76*(1), 48–69.

Tsiros, M., & Mittal, V. (2000). Regret: a model of its antecedents and consequences in consumer decision making. *Journal of Consumer Research, 26*(4), 401–417.

Tversky, A., & Kahneman, D. (1974). Judgment under uncertainty: heuristics and biases. *Science, 185*(4157), 1124–1131.

Tversky, A., & Kahneman, D. (1991). Loss aversion in riskless choice: a reference-dependent model. *Quarterly Journal of Economics, 106*(4), 1039–1061.

Tversky, A., & Thaler, R. H. (1990). Anomalies: preference reversals. *Journal of Economic Perspectives, 4*(2), 201–211.

van Dijk, W. W., van der Pligt, J., & Zeelenberg, M. (1999). Effort invested in vain: the impact of effort on the intensity of disappointment and regret. *Motivation and Emotion, 23*(3), 203–220.

Wang, Q., & Shukla, P. (2013). Linking sources of consumer confusion to decision satisfaction: the role of choice goals. *Psychology & Marketing, 30*(4), 295–304.

Weber, E. U., Shafir, S., & Blais, A.-R. (2004). Predicting risk sensitivity in humans and lower animals: risk as variance or coefficient of variation. *Psychological Review, 111*(2), 430–445.

Wells, V. K. (2012). Foraging: an ecology model of consumer behaviour? *Marketing Theory, 12*(2), 117–136.

Wilke, A., Hutchinson, J. M. C., & Todd, P. M. (2004). *Testing Simple Rules for Human Foraging in Patchy Environments.* Paper presented at the Proceedings of the Twenty-Sixth Annual Conference of the Cognitive Science Society, Mahwah, NJ.

Wilke, A., Hutchinson, J. M. C., Todd, P. M., & Czienskowski, U. (2009). Fishing for the right words: decision rules for human foraging behavior in internal search tasks. *Cognitive Science, 33*(3), 497–529.

Wine, B., Gilroy, S., & Hantula, D. A. (2012). Temporal (in)stability of employee preferences for rewards. *Journal of Organizational Behavior Management, 32*(1), 58–64.

Winterhalder, B., & Kennett, D. J. (2006). Behavioral ecology and the transition from hunting and gathering to agriculture. In D. J. Kennett & B. Winterhalder (Eds.), *Behavioral Ecology and the Transition from Hunting and Gathering to Agriculture* (pp. 1–21). Berkeley, CA: University of California Press.

Winterhalder, B., & Kennett, D. J. (2009). Four neglected concepts with a role to play in explaining the origins of agriculture. *Current Anthropology, 50*(5), 645–648.

Winterhalder, B., Lu, F., & Tucker, B. (1999). Risk-senstive adaptive tactics: models and evidence from subsistence studies in biology and anthropology. *Journal of Archaeological Research, 7*(4), 301–348.

Winterhalder, B., & Smith, E. A. (2000). Analyzing adaptive strategies: human behavioral ecology at twenty-five. *Evolutionary Anthropology: Issues, News, and Reviews, 9*(2), 51–72.

Xia, L., & Monroe, K. B. (2005). Consumer information acquisition: a review and an extension. In N. K. Malhotra (Ed.), *Review of Marketing Research* (Vol. 1, pp. 101–152). Armonk, NY: M.E. Sharpe.

Yadav, M. S. (2010). The decline of conceptual articles and implications for knowledge development. *Journal of Marketing, 74*(1), 1–19.

Yang, C. C., Chen, H., & Hong, K. (2003). Visualization of large category map for Internet browsing. *Decision Support Systems, 35*(1), 89–102.

Zeelenberg, M., van Dijk, W. W., Manstead, A. S. R., & van der Pligt, J. (2000). On bad decisions and disconfirmed expectancies: the psychology of regret and disappointment. *Cognition & Emotion, 14*(4), 521–541.

Decision-"making" or how decisions emerge in a cyclic automatic process, parsimoniously modulated by reason

José Paulo Marques dos Santos and Luiz Moutinho

Approach

Sometimes we ask our students whether they would prefer a difficult question or an easy one. The first time that happens, the answers are unanimous: an easy one. The easy question is: given three brand categories, let's say favorite, indifferent, and unknown, why do decisions about which is preferred take significantly different times? This was an easy question to put, but the paradox is usually that easy questions have long and complex answers, if they have answers at all.

The tentative theory described in this chapter was sparked by a collateral observation in a consumer neuroscience experiment. We realized that favorite brands were statistically and significantly faster rated than indifferent or unknown brands (Santos et al., 2011). Furthermore, indifferent and unknown brands statistically and significantly belong to the same distribution. The graph in Figure 20.1 depicts these observations.

The study encompassed fictitious logos that were designed specifically for the experiment, therefore do not exist in reality, and hence were unknown to the subjects at the time of the experiment. The distinction between favorite and indifferent brands was made by means of the Pleasure–Arousal dimensions of the Pleasure, Arousal, Dominance (PAD) scale (Russell & Mehrabian, 1977).

Problems arise when we try to get an explanation for the phenomenon. The given view is that decision-making is a straightforward process, a transforming device that is fed with stimuli and which yields outputs (actions) in the end. This model largely overlaps with the computer metaphor which is the pinnacle of reason. We wonder if such a model is not a reflection of the (reasoning) method established in scientific research, i.e. are scientists contaminating their analyses with the process that they use in their studies and which precludes other possible alternatives?

In this chapter, first, we will describe the given view and how the construct decision-making contains a bias which inherently calls for the participation of reasoning. After that, we will introduce a model that does not include reliance on systematic reasoning, although it still may yield purposeful decisions and actions. This model inheres in the S–R (stimulus–response) paradigm, although it encompasses the regulatory intervention of reason, rendering it in an S–R × S–O–R hybrid. There follows an explanation of the experimental data which will be presented,

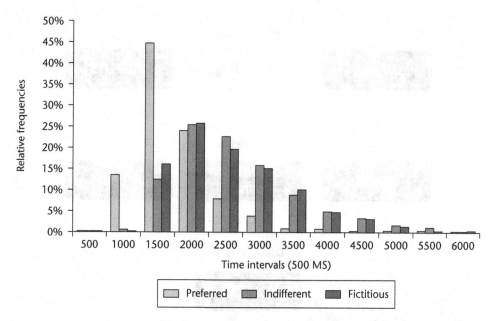

Figure 20.1 Relative frequency of response times when subjects were asked to assess assorted brand logos as preferred, indifferent, and unknown

highlighting the role of shortcuts within the decision process. Finally, we merge this model with the Behavioral Perspective Model (BPM) (Foxall, 1990/2004) and will conclude that they largely share elements and connections. Throughout this chapter, neuroscience will be a regular presence. We just do not believe in psychology apart from biology.

The given view: abridged behavioral models

Behaviorism, cognitivism, and the dual-process system

We begin by noting that most theories in psychology and in consumption studies were not constrained by physiological factors in their construction. In this respect, everything was possible then. Biological functions were not considered to have an active influence in behaviorally pertinent decisions. Rather, it seems that neurons, dendrites, axons, astrocytes, glia, etc. have a passive role where psychological processes are concerned. In economy and management, a theory or a model of international trading which did not consider the influence of the ease or difficulty of use of communication channels for commodities and services would not be accepted. How would a French wine company trade their bottles worldwide without considering the available communication structure: roads, air and maritime routes, and, nowadays, the digital highway? Recent technical improvements have enabled the study of the functioning human brain non-invasively and with sufficient spatial definition, using, for example, positron emission tomography (PET) or functional magnetic resonance imaging (fMRI). In the last five years more than 150,000 articles have been published using these techniques (source: PubMed.gov). Hence, the way opens to construct physiologically inspired models that illuminate psychological processes.

This does not mean, however, that theorists were blind to this aspect, but the fact is that, because of ethical concerns and limited availability of techniques, traditionally the brain has been

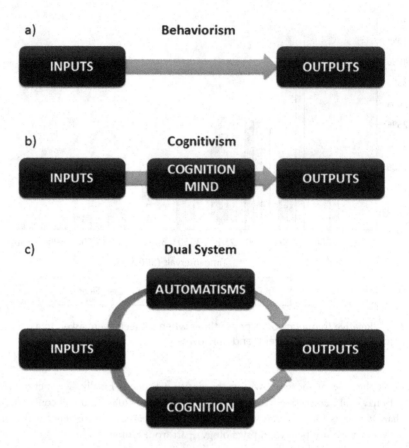

Figure 20.2 Parsimonious models of psychological processes: a) in behaviorism there are direct connections between inputs and outputs; b) in cognitivism the mediation of cognition (or a mind) is introduced between inputs and outputs; c) the dual-process system is the sum of the two previous systems with automatisms and cognition competing for the output

considered a black box, placed between inputs and outputs. In summary, three abridged models have been considered, which are depicted in Figure 20.2.

Mainly derived from animal studies, some admit simple and direct connections between inputs and outputs, as behaviorists do. In this case, the brain is metaphorically a set of relays which establish temporary linkages between incoming stimuli and behavioral responses, i.e. when a certain input takes place the respective output is automatically prompted (see panel (a)) in Figure 20.2). There are stimuli (S), responses (R), and their associations, which are known as S–R models. The linkages may be acquired by heritage (e.g. genetic), or learning. For example, this is the approach taken in classical conditioning, where a behavioral response is paired with a new stimulus and is automatically performed thereafter. The critical point here is the formation of the association (linkage). This is also the case in operant conditioning (or instrumental learning), where the result of an experience may reinforce or extinguish the behavior. An important advantage of the S–R model is its simplicity, which allows its implementation in parsimonious systems, for instance in the rudimentary neural system of jellyfish, which are animals lacking cephalization (they just have a nerve net).

Others, like cognitivists, deny direct linkages and introduce the participation of some sort of intelligence, the "organism", between stimulus and response, allowing processes like reasoning (see panel (b)) in Figure 20.2). This model is ultimately founded on Plato and Cartesian dualism and the traditional separation between body and mind, or spirit, or soul, or whatever non-bio-logical entity it is that non-automatically transforms inputs into outputs (an extensive and deep neuro-based argument against dualism can be found in Damásio, 1994). Robert S. Woodworth created the expression S–O–R, where O represents the organism. The organism is an entity that has its own inner states, which interfere in the decision process. These states may integrate some components, like goals or values, which make the decision process much more complex and not solely stimulus-dependent. However, generally speaking, such components do not have a place in the brain and happen ethereally elsewhere. The number of components of the "organism" is open ended and their sequence and articulation may also be freely arranged. Of course S–O–R models cannot be implemented in simple neural systems. They require high processing abili-ties and have not been applied to species other than *Homo sapiens*. Nevertheless, this matter still is subject to dispute because some of the components, usually treated as exclusive to humans, are considered to exist in non-humans. For instance, cultures (Whiten & van Schaik, 2007) or semiotic ability (Savage-Rumbaugh et al., 1986), despite some expectations, were already mat-ters of controversy, like the putative existence of Theory of Mind in non-human primates (Call & Tomasello, 2008). In sum, S–O–R models may exist in thinking agents.

Marketers have known for a long time that S–R models work very well, for example trans-ferring status from celebrities by association with products and services (endorsement through classical conditioning), and S–O–R models work too. There is neural evidence for that. In an fMRI experiment, which is already a milestone in behavioral neuroscience, McClure et al. (2004) demonstrated that preference for sodas is a process determined more by cultural aspects, which are O, than by sensorial information, which is S. Specifically, when brand information was provided to subjects, they used a decision process that considered previously acquired brand meanings, a different situation from the one where brand information was not available and subjects therefore had to base their decisions just on sensory information. The two situations had distinct neural supports, and it is remarkable that cultural information overrode the information coming from stimuli. Hence, human behavior is not just a matter of exclusivity of S–R or of S–O–R, but, at least, a matter of S–R and S–O–R in coexistence.

To incorporate both models, it has been considered that the brain combines two distinct, but competing, decision processes (Evans, 2008): one grounded on intuition and automatisms, and the other relying on deliberative reasoning and pondering, which are summarized in panel c) in Figure 20.2.

This proposal largely corresponds to the work of Daniel Kahneman (Nobel laureate in 2002) and Amos Tversky, who postulated the System 1 and System 2 theory of human behavior (Kahneman, 2011). System 1 is fast to respond because it relies on automatic reactions learned during past experiences; however, it is rigid, because the behavioral responses were learned for a specific context, which may not be exactly reproduced; therefore, biases may result, reflect-ing the organism's response to the most similar situation, resulting in less-than-ideal behavior. System 1 is commonly connected to emotional responses and non-conscious decisions. System 2 is slow because it relies on flexible procedures, it is rule-governed, but requires time to perform calculations, and, sometimes, the optimization of the range of possible solutions; because of com-putational demands, it requires suitable hardware to implement it and can absorb all the faculties (e.g. attention); System 2 is commonly connected to reasoning and conscious decision-making.

Darlow and Sloman (2010) theorize about the two systems of reasoning and summarize thus (adapted from Table 1, p. 383):

- Intuition: product is conscious but process is not, automatic, driven by similarity and association, fast and parallel, unrelated to general intelligence and working memory capacity;
- Deliberation: agent is aware of both product and process, effortful and volitional, driven by more structured relational knowledge, slower and sequential, related to general intelligence and working memory capacity.

The parallels between System 1 and Intuition and between System 2 and Deliberation are obvious. Darlow and Sloman (2010) find different neural supports for each system, suggesting that the brain has more than one decision-making scheme, which means that System 1/ Intuition, represented by S–R, and System 2/Deliberation, represented by S–O–R, have separated neural supports. Further, Darlow and Sloman (2010) suggest that the two systems coexist, competing to make the decision; i.e. assuming that both receive the inputs simultaneously (e.g. sensorial information), they start working in parallel on the solution(s). Because System 1/Intuition is faster, it is likely to reach a decision earlier than System 2/Deliberation, although it is not certain that it would yield the best response. When System 2/Deliberation achieves a solution, it may be different, which can lead to regret. In this case, S–R and S–O–R process in parallel, in different neural supports, in different time frames, and probably with different results. One can choose to accept System 1/Intuition, or wait for System 2/ Deliberation, or even make System 2/Deliberation suppress the System 1/Intuition process (Darlow & Sloman, 2010). For example, it would not be advisable to buy a house, which is a big investment, relying only on System 1/Intuition. Some modulation of System 2/ Deliberation may exist to prevent such a *faux pas*.

The brain as a generating organ

The structure of any of these models resembles a pipeline, with more or fewer branches. Woodworth (1921) states that "Stimuli are necessary to arouse the activity of the organism. Without any stimulus whatever, it seems likely that the animal would relapse into total inactivity" (p. 42). At least for humans, this condition may be sufficient, but not necessary. Humans are not constrained to react to stimuli alone. However, Woodworth (1921) continues, "It should be said, however, that stimuli, such as that of hunger, may arise within the organism itself. The stimulus may be external or internal, but some stimulus is necessary in order to release the stored energy" (p. 42). It seems, then, that the problem is with the definition of stimulus. Usually, stimuli are external to the body, but Woodworth used it broadly, encompassing external and internal origins.

But where, when, and how does the stimulus "hunger" prompt? (In contrast to the questions that our students used to choose, this is a difficult one.) Probably there are no answers at all to this difficult question, at least if one assumes boundaries between the brain and the body, or between parts of the brain . . . or between mind and brain, or between psychology and biology . . . nevertheless, the idea that something may arise inside the organism to prompt reactions has to be retained.

Woodworth (1921) also adds that "The organism, animal or human, fully obeys the law of conservation of energy" (p. 41). The idea behind the law of conservation of energy could also be extended to better understand how the brain works. When chemical engineers calculate energy balances of a chemical reactor, they consider the following generic equation, which encompasses the principles of energy conservation (first law of thermodynamics):

Accumulation = Inputs − Outputs + Work + Heat

The interesting term here is Heat. It is not just about what enters and leaves the system; it is also about what the system can generate (create) or consume (make disappear). If one adds gaseous hydrogen and oxygen and a small amount of initial energy, it will result in liquid water and much more energy. Something new is generated. If that can happen in a chemical reactor, why not in a brain? Why shall brains be confined to process inputs (sensorial information from the environment) into outputs (motor interventions over the environment)? Where does creativity take place, i.e. produce something new from . . . the inner system?

This aspect was already stressed by Raichle (2009): the brain has intrinsic activity; it is not just about processing inputs into outputs; there is activity in the resting brain. The Default Mode Network (DMN), one of the Resting State Networks (RSNs), is a brain-wide network that is active when the brain supposedly is at rest, i.e. not processing inputs into outputs (Raichle et al., 2001). The DMN deactivates when the subject passes from a resting state into performing a task, and the task involves some conscious operation like reading, calculating, assessing, recognizing, etc., i.e. whether processing or at rest, the brain is always active, independently of whether the senses are introducing external information. Activity in the DMN supports the claim that the brain does not need external stimuli to generate and yield outputs. The brain can generate information.

Reason pervasiveness in the decision pipeline . . . and some criticism

Psychologists have proposed several behavioral models, summarized in the previous sections, although these models need to be integrated with biology and updated with regard to recent advances in neuroscience. However, economic and consumption studies largely have been building up theories stressing the rational decision-making scheme, emphasizing the cognitivist perspective of human behavior (see panel (b) in Figure 20.2), disregarding the remaining models. One immediate reason is the facility to conduct controlled experiments, simplifying the huge amounts of variables that settings introduce, especially in social contexts where individuals mutually influence one another. Economic and consumption studies are social disciplines, though.

In this framework, brain function has been interpreted much like computing machines, showing the decision-making process as a pipeline: first, variables declaration; second, inputs; third, processing following an established algorithm; and finally, outputs are yielded. This approach is not recent. It is the same considered by William James by the end of the 19th century. Østergaard and Jantzen (2002) identify and characterize this perspective on how consumers should be understood. They named it "Consumer Behavior" and, historically, it became the major perspective in the late 1960s. The consumer is metaphorically a computer, and the scientific foundation of this perspective is cognitive psychology. Data is mainly gathered using questionnaires because the assumption is that the respondent (consumer) behaves rationally, i.e. processes information like an electronic device. With more or less elaborated statistical analysis, much of the market research that is done still adopts this perspective.

In economic and consumption studies, this hypothetical consumer, considered to behave, mostly, as a rational being, who is in possession of calculus abilities sufficient to process huge amounts of data and do extensive optimization, maximizing expected utility (self-interest), without time restrictions, was named the *Homo economicus*. This perspective is flawed, however. Calculative abilities are limited in humans, rarely is all the necessary data available, individuals make sacrifices in the group interest, and time is a scarce asset, especially in postmodern contexts where fragmentation impedes deliberation, pondering, reflection, and all time-exigent processes (for a characterization of postmodernity, pertinent to marketing, see Firat and Venkatesh, 1993). Nevertheless, the rational pipeline still pervades economic and consumption studies.

Even so, Lee et al. (2009) sought the rational *Homo economicus* when studying consumer decision-making, but found instead a lack of consistency in the choices, more compatible with the involvement of emotions than with the assumed prevalence of cognition. Furthermore, these authors found that emotionally chosen products were consistently preferred, whereas products cognitively chosen had increased variance, which contradicts the straight computational procedures that *Homo economicus* would use during decision-making. Henrich et al. (2001) also looked for *Homo economicus* in 15 other cultures (in Africa, Asia, Oceania, and South America). In his/her place they found humans that give, reciprocate, and contribute to the mutual interest. Yamagishi et al. (2014) finally found *Homo economicus*. In a sample of 446 subjects, these authors found 31 individuals that exclusively made self-interested decisions. These subjects are characterized by having a high IQ and by using only deliberative decision-making.

At least three Nobel laureates have cast doubt on the rational decision-maker: Herbert A. Simon, awarded in 1978, Reinhard Selten, awarded in 1994, and Daniel Kahneman, awarded in 2002. Herbert A. Simon introduced two pertinent concepts: one is the concept of "bounded rationality", and the other is "satisficing" (Simon, 1956). Bounded rationality is the situation where the available information is limited and therefore uncertainty exists; the decision-maker has limited computation capabilities, and even so, has to decide. The concept of satisficing is in opposition to optimization. The latter requires assessment in parallel of the range of solutions to choose the one that maximizes the utility function, whereas satisficing is a sequential process that stops the search when a predefined threshold is reached. Satisficing is simple and requires limited computation and time, but optimization requires complex computation and time with increasing variables (and settings used to encompass lots of variables, mainly the social ones). Selten (2002) says:

> Modern mainstream economic theory is largely based on an unrealistic picture of human decision making. Economic agents are portrayed as fully rational Bayesian maximizers of subjective utility. This view of economics is not based on empirical evidence, but rather on the simultaneous axiomization of utility and subjective probability. (. . .) However, it is wrong to assume that human beings conform to this ideal.
>
> *(p. 13)*

One major concern is the lack of empirical support for such a computationally accomplished, fully informed, extremely selfish, and time-rich agent (for extensive criticism of this assumed perspective, see the contributions of Hertwig and Herzog (2009) and Gigerenzer and Gaissmaier (2011)). What can be said of theories built on such weak foundations? Cisek and Kalaska (2010) emphasize the lack of neural support for the information processing framework. The Perception → Cognition → Action framework and the S–O–R model are intrinsically the same. Both are present in linear computing devices, i.e. processing pipelines. However, it has not been possible to find these three stages in the brain. On the contrary, there is data that contradicts this theory. For example, it is assumed that the first stage, Perception, delivers representations "unified (linking diverse information into a common form available to diverse systems) and stable (reflecting the stable nature of the physical world) to be useful for building knowledge and making decisions" (p. 272) in the second stage. In fact, the visual system in the occipital cortex has specialized regions, e.g. for movement, or for colors, contradicting the assumption of unification, and attention is systematically challenging stability. So far, the existence of a cognitive processing unit in the brain has not been claimed. Nevertheless, the literature is full of references to an executive functions center, which, at best, is found dispersed through the frontal lobe. The brain should have a motor center for the execution of action plans. However, because the data do not support the existence of such a center, the ideomotor theory is proposed, where Perception and Action are represented by the same neural structures (Iacoboni, 2009). In support of this latter theory, the mirror neuron system was discovered in monkeys (Gallese et al., 1996; Rizzolatti et al., 1996). These are neurons that fire either when one is performing an action, or when that action is observed in conspecifics (Rizzolatti & Craighero, 2004). Hence, it seems that brain neurons perform both Perception *and* Action, the two extremes of the pipeline, ruining its linearity. It seems then that the sequential multistage computer-like processing brain does not find support from neuroscience.

Introducing the setting and drafting an alternative

To a large extent (but with exceptions; see the previous section), the models considered so far have misrepresented the environment where human behavior occurs. Such an anthropocentric approach gives the impression that the individual dominates the course of events through the process of deliberation, at the expense of other aspects of the situation. In contrast, ethologists study animal behavior in their settings, considering mutual interaction. The Behavioral Perspective Model (BPM) is a theory of consumer behavior that introduces the "consumer situation" (Foxall, 2001, 2010). The consumer situation represents the deciding consumer as being equipped with his/her previous learning about the world and, significantly, immersed in a specific setting, which constrains his/her decisions. In this case, humans do not decide independently of where they are. As in ethology, the settings' particularities mediate the processes in the brain.

At this point we would introduce some changes in the brain functioning model that reflect what has been said. Figure 20.3 includes a feedforward loop in the top that represents

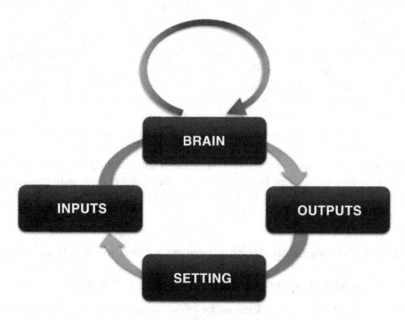

Figure 20.3 Figure of eight parsimonious model of human behavior. The top circle represents brain processes that were not prompted by input stimuli, but are generated by the brain itself. The bottom circle represents the interaction with the environment

non-stimuli-based brain productions. These are brain processes that do not depend on inputs. They are generated by the brain itself, as in reflective processes, for instance. The circle in the bottom represents the cyclic interactions that the subject has with his/her setting. The setting here is not just the things or the physical conditions that surround the individual, but his/her peers, family, friends, i.e. people that influence one's behavior.

Non-rational theories of decision-making

Inspired by the work of Herbert A. Simon and Reinhard Selten, Gigerenzer (2001) proposes non-rational decision-making theories, which are not to be confused with irrational choices. Non-rational decision-making theories are essentially non-optimizing and use instead concepts like satisficing or aspiration levels as stopping rules; they are fast, because they use little computation, and frugal, because they use limited information. Besides being non-rational, fast, and frugal, these heuristics have "ecological rationality", in the sense that environmental contingencies are determinant in selecting the heuristics more appropriate for the situation, i.e. the structure of the information of a certain setting is used to determine the heuristic more suitable for itself, so delivering precise predictions on it. With time and experience, the individual develops a repertoire of heuristics able to solve problems in a variety of specific situations, like a toolbox. It is by adaptation to environments that this non-rational, fast, and frugal toolbox is constructed.

Gigerenzer and Gaissmaier (2011) categorize these heuristics in four groups, recognition-based decision-making, one-reason decision-making, trade-off heuristics, and social intelligence, with many specific heuristics in each group. Social intelligence is a special case because it encompasses heuristics from the three previous groups. However, social heuristics may not be used in non-social situations. Examples of social heuristics are imitation, tit-for-tat, and the social-circle heuristic.

The non-rational, fast and frugal, adaptive heuristics fit well in S–R models, because they deliver fast behavioral responses to specific situations (though lacking flexibility), demand little computational ability (so can be easily implemented in simple systems), and require previous learning. Nevertheless, Gigerenzer and Gaissmaier (2011) decline to include these heuristics in dual-process systems, because the authors claim that they can be used consciously, or not. The dual-process system makes the separation between unconscious/S–R and conscious/S–O–R and, in fact, there are heuristics that can be applied consciously and others that are not. Perhaps the individual's specific situation may have a role here. We will return to this question later, when we consider the integration of the model with biological constraints, while retaining the above-mentioned commonalities with S–R models. It has to be emphasized that these heuristics incorporate an important innovation: the non-rational, fast, and frugal toolbox is built up in close interaction with the settings. In fact, the settings are critical in the selection process, which means the end of anthropocentrism, bringing humans to the same level as non-humans in their habitats, and adapting them to the environment.

Multithreaded, competing decision processes, and modulation in the rain

Setting-prompted and self-prompted actions in the S–R model

Cisek and Kalaska (2010) propose a model for brain functioning that is largely grounded in ethology, the affordance competition hypothesis. Animals, in the real world, behave in close interaction with their setting, using it, and being influenced by it, adapting behavioral responses accordingly. This is not a pipeline, with inputs, processing, and outputs, but a continuous cyclic interactive scheme. During this process, the brain integrates sensorial information, and also the previous experiences and knowledge that the organism has.

The visual system is split into two streams: the ventral stream and the dorsal stream (Goodale & Milner, 1992). The function of the ventral stream is vision-for-perception, identifying organisms and objects in the visual field, i.e. to answer the question "what?". It is sensitive to details and features, and relies on long-term representations for the process of *identification*. The function of the dorsal stream is vision-for-action, delivering spatial positioning for *actions*, i.e. to answer the question "how?". It is sensitive to spatial arrangement. It has to be noted, however, that the dorsal stream answers the question "how", not just "where", i.e. its role goes beyond the simple delivery of objects' coordinates in space to make a 3D reconstruction in the brain. The dorsal stream generates spatially defined possible actions, so answering the how question: "it [the dorsal visual stream] could be extended to other systems for a range of behavioral skills such as visually guided reaching and grasping, in which close coordination is required between movements of the fingers, hands, upper limbs, head and eyes" (Goodale & Milner, 1992, p. 20).

Fusiform gyri occupy a large portion of the ventral stream. It has been suggested that these brain structures have an associative function, which is necessary in identification processes. On the one hand, it encompasses a fusiform face area (FFA), which is supposed to be a region with the specific function of decoding human faces. On the other, decoding objects is supposed to be distributed in fusiform gyri (Hanson et al., 2004). In any case, the fusiform gyri are important brain structures in the identification process, i.e. answering the question "what?".

Nevertheless, the two streams are not independent of one another. They have complementary and interconnected workings (Milner & Goodale, 2008). Between the ventral and dorsal streams, there is the precuneus cortex. The functions attributed to this region include "visuo-spatial imagery, episodic memory retrieval and self-processing operations, namely first-person perspective taking and an experience of agency" (Cavanna & Trimble, 2006, p. 564). These functions are all pertinent to the model proposed by Cisek and Kalaska (2010), linking identification (based on one's own knowledge) and spatial arrangement to the directing of one's own behavior (based on one's own perspective and agency, i.e. the faculty of the individual to be accountable for his/her own actions, initiating them and controlling their unfolding).

It is also important to note that the precuneus cortex/posterior cingulate cortex is one important hub in the Default Mode Network (Andrews-Hanna et al., 2010). As previously noted (see section "The brain as a generating organ"), the DMN is a brain network active during resting periods that deactivates when the task requires cognitive effort. There are, however, some tasks, besides resting periods, that also make the DMN active. Andrews-Hanna et al. (2010) found evidence that the two hubs of the DMN are involved both in "present self" and "future self", i.e. "prospective, episodic decisions about one's self (*Future Self*) to be compared to self-referential decisions concerning one's present situation or mental state (*Present Self*)" (p. 551). Both situations, actual and future, are critical in one's navigation system, i.e. where I am and where I may go, and therefore the precuneus cortex/posterior cingulate cortex may represent the generating component that encompasses the "what" and the "how" questions.

This structure helps organisms in answering the questions that arise during interactions with the setting: what to do, and how to do it? According to Cisek and Kalaska (2010), the dorsal stream generates a range of possible actions that the organism can take. In principle, the organism performs one action at a time (to avoid possible conflicting or mutually confounding actions), and therefore the alternative actions compete with one another and, along the stream, the range is refined. The dorsal stream comprises then, from its beginning in the visual cortex until the motor output, a successively diminishing beam of potential actions. Supposedly, it is also responsible for the control of action execution in the posterior parietal cortex (Desmurget & Sirigu, 2009).

One may note that even very simple organisms need to eat, and that needs of this kind are powerful drivers of behavioral actions. The autonomic system/hypothalamus together with the basal ganglia, which have a determinant role in encoding habits and motor automacities (Ashby et al., 2010), account for generating, managing, and modulating hunger-like impulses.

Until this point the organism lives in close interaction with the setting, and responds and adapts to it, without needing high cognitive functions or complex computations. It does not need evaluation systems, or optimizing procedures, but copes well with Herbert A. Simon's concept of satisficing: if one intention reaches the threshold, then the individual should stop searching and the choice is made.

Introducing the O

Whereas animals, even non-primates such as rats, may be used to study brain processes such as the ones considered so far, which are restricted to S–R decision models, it is not acceptable to continue to use such animals to study functions which are not anatomically supported within the animal brain. In this respect, Craig (2009) warned that "a rat is not a monkey is not a human" (p. 466), emphasizing specific anatomical dissimilarities that exist among these brains, which necessarily indicate the possibility of different processes in the brain. Öngür and Price (2000) dissect in detail the differences that exist among these species in the prefrontal cortex. The differences are not negligible. On a complementary evolutionary perspective it was remarked that the prefrontal cortex is one part of the human brain that underwent "disproportionate increases" which may give anatomical support to some processes unique to humans (Schoenemann, 2006). We may include in this list value-based decision-making.

Value-based decision-making is probably one of the most studied themes in neuroeconomics (Montague et al., 2006; Rangel et al., 2008) and several areas in the prefrontal cortex have been found participating in the tasks. Grabenhorst and Rolls (2011) propose a decision-making model in this part of the brain, which develops in three tiers with the corresponding anatomical supports. The parallel between this three-tiered scheme and the sequential multistage computer-like processing pipeline (deliberation) is evident:

> Organization of cortical processing for computing value (in Tier 2) and making value-based decisions (in Tier 3) and interfacing to action systems. The Tier 1 brain regions up to and including the column headed by the inferior temporal visual cortex compute and represent neuronally 'what' stimulus or object is present, but not its reward or affective value.
>
> *(Grabenhorst & Rolls, 2011, p. 57)*

As deconstructed in previous sections, there are decisions that are already "made" when the process reaches the prefrontal cortex, namely those processed by S–R models. This is the main point of disagreement with Grabenhorst and Rolls's model. Nevertheless, we recognize that S–R models sometimes do not hold the necessary assumptions (e.g. existence of previous knowledge), or, because of the intrinsic particularities of the problem (e.g. high consequences in case of failure and no time restrictions, like buying a house), are not the best suited decision processes. English, and many other languages, have a long list of adjectives to describe the individual that proceeds to act on the decision prompted by an S–R model when an S–O–R is highly recommended. Such an individual may be called crazy, unwise, imprudent, impulsive, irresponsible, negligent, reckless, hasty, rash, impetuous, etc., and even considered a pathological case.

The prefrontal cortex is probably the part of the brain best equipped for computational intensive decisions, for example the ones that require the direct comparison of several alternatives (where satisficing does not work), or the ones that integrate future planning and long-term goals (McClure et al., 2004), or even those that include multiple alternative plans (Koechlin, 2011). In these cases the final goal must be present today and all the time until the objective is met, to influence immediate and further behaviors, i.e. the prefrontal cortex has to influence more caudal areas of the brain, probably in the dorsal stream, which may account, at least partially, for the refining process of possible actions that unroll in this path (Cisek & Kalaska, 2010). Hence, the O, accounted by the prefrontal cortex, is not part of the pipeline, but may have a modulating role instead.

Why do most neuroscientific studies in decision-making imply the participation of prefrontal cortex structures? Because these studies emphasize the participation of the O, i.e. prompt the computational pipeline: subjects are explicitly instructed to act in a certain manner, think, be collaborative and not answer randomly, to press buttons to record their decisions . . . and to decide displaced from the normal settings where the decisions are usually taken (shelves in the supermarket vs. virtual shelves in the scanner room).

To return to what was said concerning the dual-process system, there is evidence that both strategies coexist in the brain at the same time, competing with one another (Darlow & Sloman, 2010; Evans, 2008; Rangel et al., 2008). How to resolve conflicts and where is that done? The anterior cingulate cortex is a candidate supposed to do it. Allman et al. (2001) summarize its multiple roles: "Functions central to intelligent behavior, that is, emotional self-control, focused problem solving, error recognition, and adaptive response to changing conditions, are juxtaposed with the emotions in this structure" (p. 107). The specific functions of error recognition and adaptive response to changing conditions enable the anterior cingulate cortex (ACC) to manage the intervention of the O over the S–R. It controls unexpected results from the actions or even errors, and hence can exert some influence in the process, skewing behavior, through the extensive net of efferences. Lesions in the ACC may impair the ability to suppress automatic motor routines, as in akinetic mutism (Paus, 2001), i.e. such patients cannot control the S–R implementations, according to the theory here unfolded. In line with this, Miller and Cohen (2001) suggest that ACC is essential for control, signaling and avoiding possible conflicting processes, which enhances its suggested role in managing the influence of the O over the S–R.

The characteristics of the ACC also help to explain some differences in the *Primates* order, supporting an evolutionary perspective. The ACCs of *Hominidae* (humans and great apes) encompass spindle cell neurons, whereas monkeys' ACCs do not (Nimchinsky et al., 1999). Even in humans, such neurons appear after birth, by the age of four months, when the infants start to have motor coordination like holding up the head, smiling spontaneously, and tracking and reaching objects (Allman et al., 2001). This may explain why only humans, though not at all ages, can accurately perform complex behaviors that involve managing conflicting alternatives.

Imitative processes

What to do when the situation is novel, there is no previous knowledge, and the problem is complex to solve? This is a demanding situation because the organism cannot rely on previous learning to prompt a suitable heuristic to solve the circumstances where s/he is placed. In fact, S–R models are of little help here. One may use the computational pipeline: search for all necessary information, compute it and optimize the range of alternatives, and then act. But this is a slow process, there may not be enough information, the organism is eager for action . . . and the setting may change too quickly.

Pelzmann et al. (2005) give a timely example: how to choose a phone service provider? On the one hand, S–O–R models cannot solve this problem exactly because the choice of the best telecommunication provider mostly depends, today, on calls that will be made in the future. Therefore, the organism does not have all the information s/he needs to calculate the optimal solution. At most s/he will have to work with estimates, which introduce more complexity to the process and slow it even more. In any case, because of telecommunication providers' competition, the setting changes frequently, which means that the organism has to reinitiate the process over and over again, consuming lots of time. Who does that? Nobody. On the other hand, because of the changing competition setting, fixed heuristics are elusive and do not last. Here, operant conditioning is not effective since the reward/punishment schema changes too often. There is nowhere to repeat them successfully in the future and therefore, conventional S–R models also fail to provide useful answers.

Solution: imitate your peers. Imitation does not need knowledge, or previous learning, to yield suitable solutions. It is all about process, just process: do the same as others do, whatever they do, replicate it. In this respect, it is not like other S–R heuristics (which extensively rely on operant conditioning); it is quite similar to S–O–R models because its core is just process, but imitation is much faster, delivering immediate solutions. S–R heuristics are situation-locked, like a table entry: one situation prompts one heuristic. There are no arguments, or process. Although the process is very simple, imitation is like a function where the result depends on the arguments. In this respect it is similar to S–O–R, but without complex algorithms and optimization. Gigerenzer and Gaissmaier (2011) consider imitative heuristics within social heuristics, which is a special case of social intelligence. Social heuristics exist just in a social setting. Gigerenzer and Gaissmaier (2011) interpret moral behavior in the context of social intelligence, largely relying on imitation: moral behavior is not about rational conduct; on the contrary, it is unconsciously that one replicates what is agreed within the social group to gain acceptance by one's peers.

Supposedly, imitative processes have neuronal supports that, strikingly, are in the dorsal stream (superior and inferior parietal lobule) and in the prefrontal cortex (dorsal premotor cortex): the mirror neurons system (Iacoboni, 2009; Molenberghs et al., 2009). The mirror neuron system was already previously addressed in this chapter as one example of neurons that simultaneously do perception and action, i.e. a simple process to understand what is happening in the setting, which does not involve memory, projects the outcomes, and aligns one's own behavior with the environment by replicating the observed peers' conduct. The paradox is that the mirror neurons system was discovered in animals that are poor imitators: monkeys (Byrne, 2005).

At this point it is important to introduce a parenthesis and explore what imitation is. Imitation may be (pure) imitation . . . or may be emulation. For instance, whereas chimpanzees (*Pan troglodytes*) try to get the reward in the transparent puzzle-box independently of the action sequence, 3- to 4-year-old human children strictly follow the instructions (Horner & Whiten, 2005). In an emulative process the end is achieved irrespective of the means. The goal is the only thing that counts, blurring the steps that have to be taken. The organism only counts on his/her/its range of solutions (actions), which derive from his/her/its experience, to achieve the end. The instructions are disregarded. In purely imitative processes the composing stages, and their sequence or branches, and the goal, all matter. Urban and Bushman children both accurately replicate actions, even the redundant ones, in a process named "overimitation", which is exclusive to humans, and that is critical in the accurate transmission of complex behavioral plans, as in the case of culture formation and maintenance (Nielsen & Tomaselli, 2010).

To solve the paradox, Byrne (2005) suggests that the construct "imitation" should be split into two other constructs, apparently similar but different, which he named "social mirroring" and "learning by copying". Learning by copying is complex and recruits specialized brain structures that only humans and probably the great apes have, and consists in the faculty of deconstructing one full process into several components, extracting the intrinsic order, and reconstructing the whole process again, and so mastering it. Depending on the intelligence of the organism, learning by copying may be pure imitation or emulation, the former requiring sufficient brain structures, and the latter functioning in somewhat stripped systems. Social mirroring is not imitation, or emulation, it is just "matching the current behavior of another with similar-looking actions of one's own: and mutual identification requires synchrony, not creativity" (p. R499). Monkeys (and probably other social animals) perform social mirroring, like great apes and humans, which may be accomplished with the critical participation of the mirror neurons system in the superior and inferior parietal lobule and in the dorsal premotor cortex, which is then a network that implements imitative-based behavioral decisions.

Generalized model of decision-"making" in the brain

In this chapter, three different, but complementary and integrated, decision systems have been considered, each one relying on segregated, but integrated, neuronal supports: the fast intuitive system relying on previously acquired knowledge through experience where direct relations between stimuli and behavioral responses were coded; the slow deliberative system relying on working memory and computing abilities favoring processing; and the fast imitative system relying on a swift process that replicates other actions. These systems are depicted in Figure 20.4.

Starting in the most posterior areas of the brain and in the direction of the motor output (basal ganglia and motor cortex), the arrows represent the two streams originating in the visual cortex and the respective cross-talk between them. The intuition system is largely supported by this network: representation and identification of the particularities of the environment, acknowledging that during interpretation associations with previous experiences and the organism's state of knowledge are made; and generation of possible actions and their refinement according to the organism's actual state of knowledge and experience. At this point, behavioral (motor) responses can be executed, integrating the organism's physiological state, by the hypothalamus, basal ganglia, and the motor cortex. This is sufficient for the implementation of simple and fast S–R models of organisms interacting with their settings in an ongoing routine.

The slow modulation of deliberation comes from the more anterior areas of the brain, the prefrontal cortex and the anterior cingulate gyrus, and influences the intuition process, although with different time frames. It mainly originates in valuation systems (in the orbitofrontal cortex) and future planning (in the ventromedial prefrontal cortex), and its flow is in the direction anterior to posterior. This system functions not only during the period prior to the decision (in such cases it is non-optimal because the intuitive system is usually faster in reaching the decision threshold), but also after the decision is "made", either during the learning stage (when the outcomes are confronted with the previous expectations), or because of regret (when recently initiated behavioral responses are stopped and corrected according to new, better decisions). Nevertheless, its main role is when intuition fails because it does not have a ready solution, and the situation requires hard computations and optimization.

Strikingly, social mirroring neural bases (the dorsal premotor cortex and the posterior parietal cortex, i.e. the mirror neurons system) are located respectively in the anterior and posterior parts of brain, with the motor cortex in between. These two brain regions are connected by the superior longitudinal fasciculus, specifically the SLF I, which allows the swift exchange of information between both structures. Social mirroring delivers fast responses for

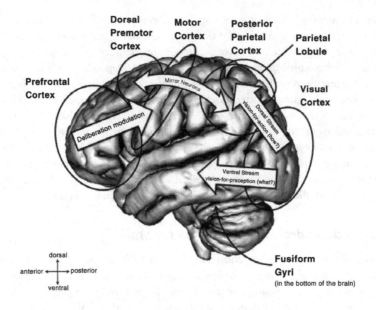

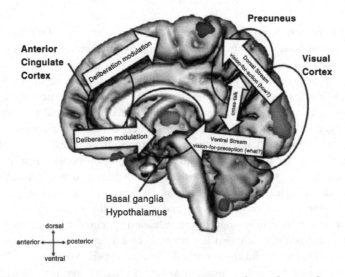

Figure 20.4 Generalized model of decision-"making". Refer to the text for an explanation of the decision systems and their flow in the brain. Top: the left hemisphere. Bottom: the left hemisphere was removed in order to make the medial brain visible

the sort of situations characterized by intrinsic multiplicity, which require specific responses for that particular set of circumstances, and for which previous learned intuitive plans cannot help. Social mirroring uses others as a pool of knowledge, reflecting their actions. Although social mirroring is flexible, like deliberation, it does not require long computations or optimizations. It is just about processing responses, constrained by the setting situation and inspired by actions observed in others.

These three decision systems have different neural supports but concurrently and complementarily contribute to the generation of behavioral responses for one organism immersed in and interacting with his/her/its setting. The decision system in the brain is not a contest between S–R and S–O–R, but involves the coexistence of several complementary systems acting, when appropriate, as a hybrid S–R × S–O–R, which equips the organism with systems that make him/her/it better adapted to respond in a broader range of settings and situations.

Shortcutting decision-making for ecological adaptation: the case of favorite brands

There is accumulating evidence that the decision schema proposed with the *Homo economicus* is not sufficient to account for and explain the decisions that humans perform when immersed in naturalistic settings. Although the model so far proposed is data grounded (behaviorally and neurally), how does it account for and explain other observations? We have been studying brands with neuroscientific techniques.

Before we analyze the brain bases of brand-elicited behaviors, we must consider faces. Faces convey information about the entity that lies behind them. The nature of the information may be social or emotional. Research has shown that brands' logos also convey social and emotional information (Santos et al., 2012; Santos et al., 2012). It has been proposed that faces have a special part of the fusiform gyrus, the fusiform face area (FFA), dedicated to their processing (Kanwisher et al., 1997; Sergent et al., 1992). Intriguingly, FFA is in the ventral stream and, although there are criticisms concerning the specificity or exact boundaries of this area, it is not unlikely that the human brain has structures or parts of structures dedicated to face processing (Weiner & Grill-Spector, 2012), given the importance that faces have in social navigation.

"With only a glance, humans instantly form impressions of another's face" (Freeman et al., 2014, p. 10573). Indeed, everyone has experience of this and knows that it is a compelling fact of everyday life. How does one make a decision about a face? By putting his/her sequential multistage computer-like processing pipeline to work on it? Freeman et al. (2014) bring evidence that humans can make a judgment about a face's trustworthiness even when that face is subliminally presented for 33 milliseconds, a glimpse too short for conscious perception. Even so, most humans perceive whether that face is trustworthy (or not) even in such a tight timeframe, a process that involves the amygdala according to these authors. Hence, outside of situations that are highly risky and are not time constrained, for instance buying a house, the most common decisions that one makes during the day exempt the computing pipeline. This is the case where decisions are needed for accurate social navigation, such as assessment of the information conveyed by human faces. Social decisions require fast processes like intuition or imitation. Otherwise, the process becomes slow and the situation awkward, which is typical of individuals with certain impairments, such as Asperger Syndrome, who supposedly have intrinsic synchronization problems between the frontal and posterior areas of the brain (Kana et al., 2009).

Social situations require fast processes, and social environmental restrictions (e.g. postmodern fragmentation) enforce the use of decision shortcuts. Studies that do not account for such environmental pressure bias the experiment, forcing deliberation instead of intuition or imitation. In our opinion, the bias is evidenced by the word used to name the process: decision-making. To make a decision implies planned participation and involvement, i.e. it requires deliberation. However, most social decisions do not follow such a scheme, missing out planning, for example. Mostly, they are reactive to environmental stimuli, depending on the situation, i.e. they are ongoing processes which call for fast behavioral responses. Because most human decisions are not really made during deliberation, we propose in the title of the present chapter that they are in fact decisions-"made".

Now, consider brands. Magnetoencephalography (MEG) is a neuroscientific technique that non-invasively measures, at the scalp level, the magnetic field generated by neuronal activity. Temporal resolution is one of its advantages (although with non-optimal spatial resolution), contrasting with fMRI, which has high spatial resolution and non-optimal temporal resolution. Braeutigam et al. (2004) used MEG with a choice task where subjects had to choose one among three products exhibited at the same time, on a virtual shelf. First, more salient products (whose choice was predicted) had faster response times than less salient products (whose choice was unpredicted), a result similar to the fMRI study that opened this chapter, where brands were exhibited one at a time (Santos et al., 2011). Second, where the neural activity flows from the posterior brain to the anterior:

1. at 100 ms there is evoked activity in the occipital cortex (vison);
2. at 150 ms there is bilateral activity in the inferior occipital-temporal cortices (visual stream);
3. at 250 ms the main activity is in the dorsal temporal lobe bilaterally;
4. in the range 350–700 ms there is increasing anterior prefrontal activity, with some flow back to parietal areas at 500 ms (with increasing activity until 1000 ms);
5. from this point, activity weakens and becomes dispersed throughout the brain.

Third, in the range 485–505 ms there is activity in the left inferior gyrus more intense for less salient products than for those mostly chosen; a similar pattern exists in the ranges 645–690 ms and 1255–1300 ms in the right prefrontal orbital cortex; in the range 860–950 ms there is activity in the right posterior parietal cortex more intense for salient products. Acknowledging that subjects made essentially explicit decisions, this pattern of brain activity is consistent and gives support to the model of decision-making herein advanced. It is important to note that the process flows backwards after reaching the anterior part of the prefrontal cortex, that less salient products recruit more time in the prefrontal cortex, and that more salient products generate increased activity in the posterior parietal cortex around 900 ms (mean reaction time is around 2100 ms).

Returning to Figure 20.1, it is possible now to suggest an explanation for the depicted data. Preferred brands had significantly faster decision times when compared with indifferent brands and fictitious logos. Probably subjects used intuition in reacting to the preferred brands' category of stimuli, i.e. subjects had previously coded their preferences in the early stages of the decision process, which prompted them to swiftly "make" their decisions. On the contrary, subjects used the deliberative system with indifferent brands and fictitious logos, either because it was the first time they had seen the logos (and therefore they had no previous experience to rely on), or because subjects were not certain how to make the assessment and therefore had to ponder, recalling information about the brand, and finally make an explicit decision. Importantly, the fine temporal data analysis reveals that the ventromedial prefrontal cortex participates more during the decision period for indifferent and fictitious logos than for preferred brands. After the decision moment, this pattern reverses: the ventromedial prefrontal cortex activates more for preferred brands than for the remaining (Santos et al., 2011). These observations cannot be explained with the sequential multistage computer-like processing pipeline, but the model proposed here accounts for them: the prefrontal cortex does not participate in deciding between familiar choices, but it is called on to participate when the decision requires deliberation.

One relevant aspect of the paradigm used in Santos et al. (2011) is that brands were assessed one at a time, whereas most studies on neuroeconomics and neuromarketing require that subjects prefer one among a set of two or three alternatives simultaneously exhibited (e.g. TAFC paradigm – two-alternative forced choice). Although the former study was carried out in a laboratory, its paradigm replicates more closely naturalistic decision settings (e.g. when buying groceries in a supermarket, the customer has in mind an idea, or even a list, of needs, supported by a personal consideration set – also known as an evoked set – helping in the search for the product/brand that s/he needs, i.e. corresponding more closely to Simon's notion of satisficing.

Some other studies and theories have involved the ventromedial prefrontal cortex in emotion-based judgments (Koenigs et al., 2007), with this brain structure being considered "a critical substrate in the neural system necessary for triggering somatic states from secondary inducers, although it can be involved in the emotions triggered by some primary inducers as well" (Bechara & Damásio, 2005, p. 340). A secondary emotional inducer is a stimulus that calls for past experiences and memories of something that was learned. Our model apparently contradicts this view. However, the ventromedial prefrontal cortex still may participate when the decision integrates information from several sources and this participation may happen before the decision (as in the case of indifferent and fictitious logos, i.e. deliberation), or may happen after the decision (e.g. for learning, or tracking long-term goals).

Studies with different data analysis approaches give extra support to the model. Hanson et al. (2004) used artificial neural networks to accurately classify faces, houses, cats, bottles, scissors, shoes, and chairs. The most interesting part is that they used data only from the fusiform gyri (the same structure that holds the fusiform face area), which belong to the visual ventral stream. Recently, Marques dos Santos et al. (2014) used artificial neural networks to extract information from two brain networks to classify, above randomness, faces, objects, and preferred and indifferent brands. The two brain networks contain voxels from the occipital and temporal occipital fusiform gyrus, the lateral occipital cortex, and the inferior temporal gyrus (temporooccipital part) all bilaterally, i.e. all brain structures that belong to the visual ventral stream. These results corroborate the suggestion that preference is already coded in early stages, in the visual ventral stream, probably in the fusiform gyri, which may explain the observed shortcuts in the decision process. In the brain, brand preferences, like human faces, exclude deliberation.

Cyclifying BPM and the regulation by reason

The Behavioral Perspective Model (BPM) is already implicitly cyclic, because of the interaction with the setting, which feeds back information that influences new behavioral responses. In this respect, the BPM and the model herein unfolded (see Figure 20.4) overlap, both acknowledging that contact with the setting is a crucial component of behavior. The individual does not exist in isolation from everything else. On the contrary, s/he/it is integrated in a setting, which encompasses the biological, sociological, and geological, institutions, and things, and the organism interacts with all of this world, and all of this world interacts with the organism, influencing and being influenced by his/her/its behavior in a continuously evolving cycle.

In the BPM, behavior is a consequence of the setting and individuals' learning history, and antecedents of reinforcements and aversion, either utilitarian or informational (cf. Foxall, 2001, 2010). Behavior outcomes contribute:

- changes to the setting, with consequences for the biology, sociology, geology, institutions and occupants (both animate and inanimate) of the space, with such interference leading to reactions;
- by enriching the individual's learning history, updating knowledge of the consequences of behaviors so they are available for integrating into future behavioral decisions.

Hence, the BPM is intrinsically cyclic, although its usual representation conceals this aspect. The individual acts, and the actions have consequences. Such consequences change the setting and also the individual encodes the relationship among actions and outcomes. The new framework will influence the next situation, and so on.

This behavioral schema has the same intuition and social mirroring (imitation) components of the decision-"making" model with their respective neural supports and constrictions. Intuition relies on the individual's learning history. It consists of the sets of fast responses encoded in the brain that the individual calls on in specific situations. Social mirroring is also a swift reaction to a setting's social content.

Deliberation, the sequential multistage computer-like processing pipeline, does not have a place in the BPM. This is because the BPM is a naturalistic model and a slow-acting deliberative model like the computational pipeline is ill-adapted to settings' evolutionary pressure where there is a need for immediate and continuous interaction with the setting. Simply, the setting does not wait.

Nevertheless, deliberation is useful during the updating stage. Deliberation monitors behavioral errors, when expectations have not been met. Deliberation may not be useful for ongoing interactions because of its intrinsic slowness, but afterwards, when the individual has time to reflect on the situation, probably in reaction to the frustration of having encountered the unexpected, the learning history may be re-encoded with the new outcomes to update the brain's repertoire of possible future behavioral decisions. In such cases, deliberation may be usefully integrated in the model, as situations where time is not critical and there is sufficient information available to make optimization possible are rare.

With all these considerations the parsimonious model of Figure 20.3 can be redrawn as in Figure 20.5, now incorporating the BPM's terminology and the tripartite decision-"making" model.

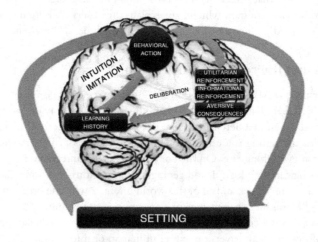

Figure 20.5 Integration of the BPM with the tripartite decision-"making" model in the brain. The diagram shows the situation of the brain interacting with its setting. Both information from the setting and the individual's history contribute to action behavioral plans, which can be made primarily by two means: intuition and imitation. The role of deliberation is residual so far, but it may be important during reflective periods after action is completed, when integrating the outcomes within the individual's history. The positioning of the constructs in the brain has to be considered parsimoniously

References

Allman, J. M., Hakeem, A., Erwin, J. M., Nimchinsky, E., & Hof, P. (2001). The anterior cingulate cortex. The evolution of an interface between emotion and cognition. *Annals of the New York Academy of Sciences, 935*, 107–117. doi: 10.1111/j.1749-6632.2001.tb03476.x

Andrews-Hanna, J. R., Reidler, J. S., Sepulcre, J., Poulin, R., & Buckner, R. L. (2010). Functional-anatomic fractionation of the brain's default network. *Neuron, 65*(4), 550–562. doi: 10.1016/j.neuron.2010.02.005

Ashby, F. G., Turner, B. O., & Horvitz, J. C. (2010). Cortical and basal ganglia contributions to habit learning and automaticity. *Trends in Cognitive Sciences, 14*(5), 208–215. doi: 10.1016/j.tics.2010.02.001

Bechara, A., & Damásio, A. R. (2005). The somatic marker hypothesis: a neural theory of economic decision. *Games and Economic Behavior, 52*(2), 336–372. doi: 10.1016/j.geb.2004.06.010

Braeutigam, S., Rose, S., Swithenby, S., & Ambler, T. (2004). The distributed neuronal systems supporting choice-making in real-life situations: differences between men and women when choosing groceries detected using magnetoencephalography. *European Journal of Neuroscience, 20*(1), 293–302. doi: 10.1111/j.1460-9568.2004.03467.x

Byrne, R. W. (2005). Social cognition: imitation, imitation, imitation. *Current Biology, 15*(13), R498–R500. doi: 10.1016/j.cub.2005.06.031

Call, J., & Tomasello, M. (2008). Does the chimpanzee have a theory of mind? 30 years later. *Trends in cognitive sciences, 12*(5), 187–192. doi: 10.1016/j.tics.2008.02.010

Cavanna, A. E., & Trimble, M. R. (2006). The precuneus: a review of its functional anatomy and behavioural correlates. *Brain, 129*(Pt 3), 564–583. doi: 10.1093/brain/awl004

Cisek, P., & Kalaska, J. F. (2010). Neural mechanisms for interacting with a world full of action choices. *Annual Review of Neuroscience, 33*(1), 269–298. doi: 10.1146/annurev.neuro.051508.135409

Craig, A. D. (2009). A rat is not a monkey is not a human: comment on Mogil (Nature Rev. Neurosci. 10, 283–294 (2009)). *Nature Reviews Neuroscience, 10*(6), 466. doi: 10.1038/nrn2606-c1

Damásio, A. R. (1994). *Descarte's Error: Emotion, Reason and the Human Brain.* New York: Penguin Putnam.

Darlow, A. L., & Sloman, S. A. (2010). Two systems of reasoning: architecture and relation to emotion. *Wiley Interdisciplinary Reviews: Cognitive Science, 1*(3), 382–392. doi: 10.1002/wcs.34

Desmurget, M., & Sirigu, A. (2009). A parietal-premotor network for movement intention and motor awareness. *Trends in Cognitive Sciences, 13*(10), 411–419. doi: 10.1016/j.tics.2009.08.001

Evans, J. S. B. T. (2008). Dual-processing accounts of reasoning, judgment, and social cognition. *Annual Review of Psychology, 59*(1), 255–278. doi: 10.1146/annurev.psych.59.103006.093629

Firat, A. F., & Venkatesh, A. (1993). Postmodernity: the age of marketing. *International Journal of Research in Marketing, 10*(3), 227–249. doi: 10.1016/0167-8116(93)90009-n

Foxall, G. R. (1990/2004). *Consumer Psychology in Behavioral Perspective.* London and New York: Routledge. (Reprinted 2004 by Beard Books, Frederick, MD.)

Foxall, G. R. (2001). Foundations of consumer behaviour analysis. *Marketing Theory, 1*(2), 165–199. doi: 10.1177/147059310100100202

Foxall, G. R. (2010). *Interpreting Consumer Choice: The Behavioural Perspective Model.* Abingdon: Routledge.

Freeman, J. B., Stolier, R. M., Ingbretsen, Z. A., & Hehman, E. A. (2014). Amygdala responsivity to high-level social information from unseen faces. *The Journal of Neuroscience, 34*(32), 10573–10581. doi: 10.1523/jneurosci.5063-13.2014

Gallese, V., Fadiga, L., Fogassi, L., & Rizzolatti, G. (1996). Action recognition in the premotor cortex. *Brain, 119*(Pt 2), 593–609.

Gigerenzer, G. (2001). Decision Making: nonrational theories. In N. J. Smelser & P. B. Baltes (Eds.), *International Encyclopedia of the Social and Behavioral Sciences* (Vol. 5, pp. 3304–3309). Oxford: Elsevier Science.

Gigerenzer, G., & Gaissmaier, W. (2011). Heuristic decision making. *Annual Review of Psychology, 62*(1), 451–482. doi: 10.1146/annurev-psych-120709-145346

Goodale, M. A., & Milner, A. D. (1992). Separate visual pathways for perception and action. *Trends in Neurosciences, 15*(1), 20–25. doi: 10.1016/0166-2236(92)90344-8

Grabenhorst, F., & Rolls, E. T. (2011). Value, pleasure and choice in the ventral prefrontal cortex. *Trends in Cognitive Sciences, 15*(2), 56–67. doi: 10.1016/j.tics.2010.12.004

Hanson, S. J., Matsuka, T., & Haxby, J. V. (2004). Combinatorial codes in ventral temporal lobe for object recognition: Haxby (2001) revisited: is there a "face" area? *NeuroImage, 23*(1), 156–166. doi: 10.1016/j.neuroimage.2004.05.020

Henrich, J., Boyd, R., Bowles, S., Camerer, C., Fehr, E., Gintis, H., & McElreath, R. (2001). In search of homo economicus: behavioral experiments in 15 small-scale societies. *American Economic Review, 91*(2), 73–78. doi: 10.1257/aer.91.2.73

Hertwig, R., & Herzog, S. M. (2009). Fast and frugal heuristics: tools of social rationality. *Social Cognition, 27*(5), 661–698. doi: 10.1521/soco.2009.27.5.661

Horner, V., & Whiten, A. (2005). Causal knowledge and imitation/emulation switching in chimpanzees (Pan troglodytes) and children (Homo sapiens). *Animal Cognition, 8*(3), 164–181. doi: 10.1007/s10071-004-0239-6

Iacoboni, M. (2009). Imitation, empathy, and mirror neurons. *Annual Review of Psychology, 60*, 653–670. doi: 10.1146/annurev.psych.60.110707.163604

Kahneman, D. (2011). *Thinking, Fast and Slow.* New York: Farrar, Straus and Giroux.

Kana, R. K., Keller, T. A., Cherkassky, V. L., Minshew, N. J., & Just, M. A. (2009). Atypical frontal-posterior synchronization of Theory of Mind regions in autism during mental state attribution. *Social Neuroscience, 4*(2), 135–152. doi: 10.1080/17470910802198510

Kanwisher, N., McDermott, J., & Chun, M. M. (1997). The fusiform face area: a module in human extrastriate cortex specialized for face perception. *The Journal of Neuroscience, 17*(11), 4302–4311.

Koechlin, E. (2011). Frontal pole function: what is specifically human? *Trends in Cognitive Sciences, 15*(6), 241; author reply 243. doi: 10.1016/j.tics.2011.04.005

Koenigs, M., Young, L., Adolphs, R., Tranel, D., Cushman, F., Hauser, M., & Damásio, A. R. (2007). Damage to the prefrontal cortex increases utilitarian moral judgements. *Nature, 446*(7138), 908–911. doi: 10.1038/nature05631

Lee, L., Amir, O., & Ariely, D. (2009). In search of homo economicus: cognitive noise and the role of emotion in preference consistency. *Journal of Consumer Research, 36*(2), 173–187. doi: 10.1086/597049

Marques dos Santos, J. P., Moutinho, L., & Castelo-Branco, M. (2014). 'Mind reading': hitting cognition by using ANNs to analyze fMRI data in a paradigm exempted from motor responses. Paper presented at the International Workshop on Artificial Neural Networks and Intelligent Information Processing (ANNIIP 2014), Vienna, Austria. http://dx.doi.org/10.5220/0005126400450052

McClure, S. M., Laibson, D. I., Loewenstein, G., & Cohen, J. D. (2004). Separate neural systems value immediate and delayed monetary rewards. *Science, 306*(5695), 503–507. doi: 10.1126/science.1100907

McClure, S. M., Li, J., Tomlin, D., Cypert, K. S., Montague, L. M., & Montague, P. R. (2004). Neural correlates of behavioral preference for culturally familiar drinks. *Neuron, 44*(2), 379–387. doi: 10.1016/j.neuron.2004.09.019

Miller, E. K., & Cohen, J. D. (2001). An integrative theory of prefrontal cortex function. *Annual Reviews in Neuroscience, 24*, 167–202. doi: 10.1146/annurev.neuro.24.1.167

Milner, A. D., & Goodale, M. A. (2008). Two visual systems re-viewed. *Neuropsychologia, 46*(3), 774–785. doi: 10.1016/j.neuropsychologia.2007.10.005

Molenberghs, P., Cunnington, R., & Mattingley, J. B. (2009). Is the mirror neuron system involved in imitation? A short review and meta-analysis. *Neuroscience and Biobehavioral Reviews, 33*(7), 975–980. doi: 10.1016/j.neubiorev.2009.03.010

Montague, P. R., King-Casas, B., & Cohen, J. D. (2006). Imaging valuation models in human choice. *Annual Reviews in Neuroscience, 29*, 417–448. doi: 10.1146/annurev.neuro.29.051605.112903

Nielsen, M., & Tomaselli, K. (2010). Overimitation in Kalahari Bushman children and the origins of human cultural cognition. *Psychological Science, 21*(5), 729–736. doi: 10.1177/0956797610368808

Nimchinsky, E. A., Gilissen, E., Allman, J. M., Perl, D. P., Erwin, J. M., & Hof, P. R. (1999). A neuronal morphologic type unique to humans and great apes. *Proceedings of the National Academy of Sciences of the USA, 96*(9), 5268–5273.

Öngür, D., & Price, J. L. (2000). The organization of networks within the orbital and medial prefrontal cortex of rats, monkeys and humans. *Cerebral Cortex, 10*(3), 206–219.

Østergaard, P., & Jantzen, C. (2002). Shifting perspectives in consumer research: from buyer behaviour to consumption studies. In S. C. Beckmann & R. H. Elliott (Eds.), *Interpretive Consumer Research – Paradigms, Methodologies & Applications.* Copenhagen: Copenhagen Business School Press.

Paus, T. (2001). Primate anterior cingulate cortex: where motor control, drive and cognition interface. *Nature Reviews Neuroscience, 2*(6), 417–424. doi: 10.1038/35077500

Pelzmann, L., Hudnik, U., & Miklautz, M. (2005). Reasoning or reacting to others? How consumers use the rationality of other consumers. *Brain Research Bulletin, 67*(5), 438–442. doi: 10.1016/j.brainresbull.2005.06.007

Raichle, M. E. (2009). A paradigm shift in functional brain imaging. *The Journal of Neuroscience, 29*(41), 12729–12734. doi: 10.1523/jneurosci.4366-09.2009

Raichle, M. E., MacLeod, A. M., Snyder, A. Z., Powers, W. J., Gusnard, D. A., & Shulman, G. L. (2001). A default mode of brain function. *Proceedings of the National Academy of Sciences, 98*(2), 676–682. doi: 10.1073/pnas.98.2.676

Rangel, A., Camerer, C. F., & Montague, P. R. (2008). A framework for studying the neurobiology of value-based decision making. *Nature Reviews Neuroscience, 9*(7), 545–556. doi: 10.1038/nrn2357

Rizzolatti, G., & Craighero, L. (2004). The mirror-neuron system. *Annual Reviews in Neuroscience, 27*, 169–192. doi: 10.1146/annurev.neuro.27.070203.144230

Rizzolatti, G., Fadiga, L., Gallese, V., & Fogassi, L. (1996). Premotor cortex and the recognition of motor actions. *Cognitive Brain Research, 3*(2), 131–141. doi: 10.1016/0926-6410(95)00038-0

Russell, J. A., & Mehrabian, A. (1977). Evidence for a three-factor theory of emotions. *Journal of Research in Personality, 11*(3), 273–294. doi: 10.1016/0092-6566(77)90037-X

Santos, J. P., Moutinho, L., Seixas, D., & Brandão, S. (2012). Neural correlates of the emotional and symbolic content of brands: a neuroimaging study. *Journal of Customer Behaviour, 11*(1), 69–94. doi: 10.1362/147539212X13286273975319

Santos, J. P., Seixas, D., Brandão, S., & Moutinho, L. (2011). Investigating the role of the ventromedial prefrontal cortex (vmPFC) in the assessment of brands. *Frontiers in Neuroscience, 5*(77). doi: 10.3389/fnins.2011.00077

Santos, J. P., Seixas, D., Brandão, S., & Moutinho, L. (2012). Neuroscience in branding: A functional magnetic resonance imaging study on brands' implicit and explicit impressions. *Journal of Brand Management, 19*(9), 735–757. doi: 10.1057/bm.2012.32

Savage-Rumbaugh, S., McDonald, K., Sevcik, R. A., Hopkins, W. D., & Rubert, E. (1986). Spontaneous symbol acquisition and communicative use by pygmy chimpanzees (Pan paniscus). *Journal of Experimental Psychology: General, 115*(3), 211–235.

Schoenemann, P. T. (2006). Evolution of the size and functional areas of the human brain. *Annual Review of Anthropology, 35*(1), 379–406. doi: 10.1146/annurev.anthro.35.081705.123210

Selten, R. (2002). What is bounded rationality? In G. Gigerenzer & R. Selten (Eds.), *Bounded Rationality: The Adaptive Toolbox* (pp. 13–36). Cambridge, MA: MIT Press.

Sergent, J., Ohta, S., & MacDonald, B. (1992). Functional neuroanatomy of face and object processing: a positron emission tomography study. *Brain, 115*(1), 15–36. doi: 10.1093/brain/115.1.15

Simon, H. A. (1956). Rational choice and the structure of the environment. *Psychological Review, 63*(2), 129–138. doi: 10.1037/h0042769

Weiner, K. S., & Grill-Spector, K. (2012). The improbable simplicity of the fusiform face area. *Trends in Cognitive Sciences, 16*(5), 251–254. doi: 10.1016/j.tics.2012.03.003

Whiten, A., & van Schaik, C. P. (2007). The evolution of animal "cultures" and social intelligence. *Philosophical Transactions of the Royal Society B, 362*(1480), 603–620. doi: 10.1098/rstb.2006.1998

Woodworth, R. S. (1921). *Psychology: A Study of Mental Life*. New York: Henry Holt & Company.

Yamagishi, T., Li, Y., Takagishi, H., Matsumoto, Y., & Kiyonari, T. (2014). In search of homo economicus. *Psychological Science, 25*(9), 1699–1711. doi: 10.1177/0956797614538065

Consumer behavior analysis

A view from psychoanalysis

John Desmond

Introduction

Imagine the chance conversation in Purgatory, when Rodrigo Borgia eventually runs into John Knox; what could they possibly say to each other once the introductions are over? Given their history and the ontological and epistemological gulf that separates them, it is perhaps unsurprising that this image sprang to mind as I pondered how possibly to write of a potential encounter between psychoanalysis and consumer behavior analysis. To begin with, all I could think of were their differences; for instance, the behaviorist imperatives of clear-cut observability, objectivity and indubitable proof against psychoanalytic tendencies towards the personal and speculative, which are reflected in the employment of different concepts to describe similar processes (Garvey, 2007). The conservative and parsimonious nature of behaviorism has produced a few firm concepts, while the conceptual profligacy of psycho-analysis has burgeoned from the, at times, antithetical schools of thought spun out from the Freudian mainstream over the years, including Ego Psychology, Object Relations, Lacanian psychoanalysis and Self-Psychology. Where behavior analysis traditionally eschews mental-ism, psychic determinism is a key tenet of psychoanalysis; where behavior analysis focuses on situational factors, psychoanalysis argues that subjective meaning is the only route to under-stand individual suffering.

As a long-time admirer of consumer behavior analysis, I am honored by the invitation to contribute to this work, although I am unsure of my credentials to do so. It shares with psy-choanalysis the aim to answer fundamental questions with respect to marketing and consumer behavior. Each perspective is similar too in arguing for the importance of environmental fac-tors and questioning assumptions about the volitional nature of behavior. The relatively recent move towards intentional behaviorism inspired by the work of Daniel Dennett (Foxall, 2007) opens up new possibilities for consumer behavior analysis which are interesting to discuss from a psychoanalytic perspective.

In this chapter, I first sketch out my understanding of the Behavioral Perspective Model (BPM) and intentional behaviorism. The relation of psychoanalysis to phenomenology is outlined prior to embarking on a brief discussion of the relations between psychoanalysis and science. The final section compares consumer behavior analysis and psychoanalytic accounts of addiction.

The Behavioral Perspective Model

The aim of consumer behavior analysis is clearly defined as being "concerned with the application of behavioral economics and behavioral psychology to the marketplace of human purchase and consumption activities", where research is conducted in natural settings (Foxall, personal communication). This project is pursued by a group of marketing scholars with Gordon Foxall at its fore, which aims to explain consumer choice and behavior by the three-term contingency, involving a discriminative stimulus, response and reinforcement, in naturalistic settings, in relation to everyday behavior and more extreme compulsions. This is summed in the BPM, which specifies that the rate of behavioral response is explained by discriminative stimuli in the behavior setting and by levels of informational and utilitarian, or hedonic, reinforcement (Foxall, 1990). In the consumption context behavior settings vary from open, as in a street market, to the relatively closed setting of, say, a car showroom. Utilitarian reinforcement relates to the technical and operational qualities of the product, its reliability and so forth, whereas informational reinforcement relates to the performance feedback, social status and prestige. Research consists in the main of studying molar processes, or patterns of response to the rate of reinforcement, identifiable from the relative frequencies at which responses are emitted and reinforcement is obtained, using consumer panel data rather than molecular, or single instances of responding.

The matching law, which is frequently referred to by theorists, was derived from observation of experiments using animals as subjects, to measure their responsiveness to concurrent variable interval reinforcements. Experimenters consistently found a pattern whereby pigeons allocated their behavior between the two options available according to the relative rate of reinforcement of the behavior received (Herrnstein, 1970). This was explained as "an efficient allocation of effort that extracts the most reward from a given piece of work" (Herrnstein & Prelec, 1992: 147). The law states that when given a choice, a subject will always match her response to the relative reinforcement provided; relative behavior, whether measured as a frequency or rate or time spent, will always match the relative consequences (frequency, magnitude, quantity or delay). In other words, we are most likely to choose that alternative that will yield us the most satisfaction or least dissatisfaction.

In the context of consumer behavior analysis the matching law explains that where two commodities, x and y, are taken as substitutes, a reduction in the price of x leads to an increase in the quantity of x demanded and as a consequence a decrease in the quantity of y demanded (Foxall, 2010: 189). Studies using consumer panel data confirm that responses to different brands are allocated in proportion to the relative rate of reinforcement (Foxall, 1999; Foxall et al., 2004; James & Foxall, 2010). I should mention that together with the work of the late Andrew Ehrenberg (e.g. Ehrenberg et al., 1990; Ehrenberg et al., 2004) I find that this work provides a useful counterpoint to mainstream assumptions of brand loyalty via the finding that the vast majority of consumers switch between brands within a small repertoire, depending on the consequential benefits yielded (Foxall et al., 2004), and are relatively impervious to point-of-sale messaging (Cavalcanti et al., 2013).

Another strategy, melioration, provides the basis of consumer behavior analysis' explanation of addictive behavior. Melioration argues that choice is always potentially suboptimal whenever tastes or values are affected by the rate of consumption. This involves the continual effort to keep on trying to improve the local or immediate level of reinforcement and thus discount the longer term. Rather than focus on substances, the emphasis is on the behavior, from watching television to gambling and exercise, all of which can be addictive. There are two explanations for melioration, based on exponential and hyperbolic discounting (Ainslie, 1991). The net effect is that as consumption of alcohol, exercise or television rises, so that of alternatives such as food declines, as does gratification from alternative sources such as family, friends and work.

Overall the BPM argument fits within a behaviorist explanation that adopts the contextual stance (Foxall, 2007: 9) to argue that behavior is predictable to the extent that it is environmentally determined, linked to a strict focus on observable behavior which can be objectively measured. In so doing it has introduced us to a number of useful concepts which carry the explanation of consumer decision making a good deal further than might be imagined by a reading of available textbooks, ranging from the nature of reinforcement (positive/negative; utilitarian/informational) – which still requires some care to teach – to the matching law and meliorating strategies.

Intentional behaviorism

The purview of the BPM has been extended since Foxall (2007) argued the need to incorporate the personal level into consumer behavior analysis, to provide explanations for the continuity of behavior. Daniel Dennett (1991) provides the model to enable discussion of personal, sub-personal and super-personal processes. Dennett acknowledged that his scheme, which involves different "stances; ranging from the physical stance to the intentional stance", was not novel, but effectively codified existing research in cognitive science, including "top down" and "bottom up" approaches (Marr, 1982).

I was intrigued to learn that the scheme developed by Daniel Dennett, albeit modified, would provide the basis for the development of intentional behaviorism; I should come clean and state that I am relatively unfamiliar with this work. I knew of Dennett's analogy between brain and computer and had also come across mentions of him in relation to the argument that algorithms developed during the Era of Evolutionary Adaptiveness (EEA), to solve recurrent adaptive problems in particular domains (Tooby & Cosmides, 1989). Relating to this, there was an interesting if limited encounter where Cosmides and Tooby (1996) critiqued Kahneman and Tversky (1979) on the basis that the latter mistakenly assumed rationality to be a domain-general ability to process social exchange problems. This is relevant to consumer behavior analysis because, given the link to environmental determinism, one might have expected it to be more open to a domain-general explanation than one based on domain specificity. John Bargh (2008) advocates a view that is similar to what I imagined to be the position adopted by consumer behavior analysis, which, while acknowledging the existence of domain-specific modules, argues also for domain-generality to the extent that humans are considered relatively open-ended systems, so allowing a greater role for the effect of culture in evolution. The domain-specific view is criticized on the basis that the computer analogy ignores the organic nature of the brain, which is more plastic than is acknowledged by those who assume that consciousness is constructed on such "hard-wired" computational principles (Panksepp & Panksepp, 2000). Additionally, the argument that domain-specific modules are adaptive is criticized as a form of Panglossianism (Gould & Lewontin, 1979); "just as Dr. Pangloss argued that the purpose of the bridge of the nose is to support spectacles, so the adaptationist seeks to explain all features of organisms by inference to the environment" (Roscoe, 2014: 97).

Given his acknowledgement that the *avoidance* of intentional language is the *defining characteristic* of radical behaviorism (Foxall, 2007: 4; my italics), by introducing intentional behaviorism to the world Foxall boldly proceeds to mix the oil of intentionality with the extensional water of behaviorism (Lacey, 2007). The intentional stance is alluring because this affords the opportunity to improve on behaviorism *and* on Dennett's scheme, each of which will be made more complete as a result. Behaviorism will benefit because as currently constituted, it simply isn't set up to deal with intentional language, such as remembering or intending as the basis for a personal-level explanation of the continuity of behavior (Foxall, 2008: 380). Using Dennett's heterophenomenological method exclusively to explain the patterning of behavior will improve intelligibility by providing a third-person account of beliefs, desires and motives. For instance, at a basic level a creature must "know" that a substance is food by being able to identify it from non-food, which implies that the "meaning" of what food is will likewise be important (Foxall, 2007: 21). He is especially keen on maintaining conceptual clarity and methodological dualism in maintaining a distinction between brain and mind and sub-personal and personal levels of analysis. This is for methodological reasons and to avoid the mereological fallacy, which, he argues, Dennett himself is prone to in his later works, by erroneously attributing properties of the whole to its parts (Bennett & Hacker, 2003), for instance by using the personal as a metaphor to discuss sub-personal processes as if they were intentional by ascribing desires and wants to them (Foxall, 2007: 27).

Phenomenology and psychoanalysis

Given the prominence accorded to heterophenomenology by intentional behaviorism, it is relevant, when discussing psychoanalysis, to sketch its grounding in phenomenology, not least to dispel the notion that this allows for introspection as a valid method. Dennett (1991) devised his neutral third-person "heterophenomenology" (Dennett, 1991: 40, 71) to scientifically account for subjective states as an antidote to the introspection he associated with classical phenomenology. However, it must be pointed out that phenomenologists object to Dennett's linkage between classical phenomenology and introspection as fundamentally mistaken, in that philosophers from Husserl to Heidegger, Sartre and Merleau-Ponty consistently argued *against* introspection (Zahavi, 2007).

The essential focus of phenomenology is the articulation of intentionality. Philosophers in this tradition elaborate the importance of the dispositional field, which makes the focal point of attention possible by receding into the background, as the object of consciousness is brought to focal attention. For Husserl, consciousness is not focal awareness, but is always accompanied by the margin which separates it from its surround. Heidegger dwells on the inauthentic tendency to separate the relation between thing and world, the thing being what it is by virtue of the world in which it is placed. Explained in relation to psychoanalysis, "afloat in a sea of indeterminate intuitions, the focus of consciousness is surrounded by an infinite expanse that bears upon and supports the central concern of consciousness but remains unavailable to it" (Boothby, 2001: 42). Like the background that must recede if one is to perceive the figure in Gestalt psychology, to facilitate the coming-to-presence of something within it, the field must withdraw into invisibility; must absent or negate itself. Every moment of revelation of a focal point is simultaneously a moment when something else, the dispositional field, which constitutes it, withdraws. In this sense the essence of psychoanalysis is the cogito and the unthought. Psychoanalysis is concerned to understand the realm of the "unthought" dispositional field (2001: 65).

It is interesting that Dennett refers to the virtual machine that gives rise to consciousness not as a Cartesian controller by Joycean machine, or mental operating system like Windows, that is implemented on the hardware of the human brain, which organizes homunculi into a stream of consciousness. The metaphor of the mind as a machine fitted out with algorithms devised to solve recurrent adaptive problems, which also contains an open-ended system equipped to download the current state of culture in its early years, is particularly powerful today. There are resonances, but also important differences, between the image of the Joycean machine conjured by Dennett and the formulations of Jonathan Lear (1999) and Jacques Lacan; Lear offers the vision of a restless mind as a machine that constantly interrupts itself. The Lacanian machine too is located in the unconscious, where metaphorical substitutions and metonymic displacements operate to prevent meaning from accessing consciousness. These preoccupations are pursued in Lacan's (1975/6) extensive reading of Joyce, from the *Portrait of the Artist as a Young Man*, to *Ulysses* and *Finnegan's Wake*.

Psychoanalytic explorations of the conditions of possibility for the intentional stance

Dennett does not enquire into the conditions of possibility for the "intentional stance", which he takes for granted (Carman, 2003: 113). This, on the other hand, constitutes a key question for developmental psychoanalysts (Fonagy & Target, 2003: 306). Intentionality is related to mentalization (Fonagy, 2002) insofar as it presumes one adopts the intentional stance by reacting to others as persons and not as objects. While Dennett employs the intentional stance as a vehicle to explain and predict behavior, he makes clear that it does not matter if there is a "real" agent at work; what looks like a human might be a zombie; indeed we are zombies.

Fonagy argues that attachment is best understood not as biological, but as an outcome achieved between caregiver and infant. One should not presume that the infant comes with a ready-made understanding of what separates internal from external reality, never mind the understanding that they are an intentional being. They must also come to take themselves as intentional by recognizing that they are treated as such by others who are. Self-ascription of intentionality is not primary but is created through the process of attachment, including gaze-following, mirroring of the caregiver's behavior and emotional mirroring (Brazelton et al., 1974). Given that attachment provides the conditions of possibility for intentional self-ascription, as mother and child come to take intentional stances towards each other, this project may fail in a number of ways, leaving the child with under- or over-regulated affects and an insecure sense of self detached from intersubjective relationship to others (Fonagy, 2002: 38–9). The consequence that psychological trauma leading to deficits in mentalizing can lead to severe mental character disturbance is of prime importance to psychoanalysis.

From the above, the attribution of intentionality to another translates into the achievement of real intentionality. Robbins and Jack (2006) discuss character formation in relation to Dennett's physical, design and intentional stances. Those high on the autism spectrum take the physical stance, excelling in tests of folk physics but especially poor in tasks requiring recursive mindreading. Psychopaths excel at taking the intentional stance, while demonstrably lacking in moral concern for the welfare of others and exhibiting poor behavioral control. Beyond the intentional stance the authors argue the phenomenal stance, "which autists are spared from and is absent in psychopaths" (ibid.: 70). The phenomenal stance requires more than mere role ascription, but rather a direct appreciation of their qualitative character; if you don't know what it is like to feel sad then you can't understand what it is like to feel sad. So while the intentional stance is an important aspect of personhood, it does not encompass all humans, such as those who are autistic, while psychopaths are superbly good at mentalization and constitute a perfect match with the intentional stance.

From the above, the conditions of possibility for the intentional stance are of major interest to psychoanalysts. But what do psychoanalysts make of the mereological fallacy, which Foxall takes such great pains to avoid (Bennet & Hacker, 2003; Foxall, 2007)? Freud often used psychological language to refer to unconscious processes and was thus assumed by some to understand the unconscious as something personal, which is claimed as an important difference between his theory and those of cognitive scientists This is the question addressed by Brian Garvey (2007: 37), who takes a more relaxed view than Foxall (2007) by applying the *metaphor* of intentionality to sub-personal processes, arguing that one should always retain the understanding that this *is* a metaphor (much in the same way as is argued by Solms & Panksepp, 2012, discussed below). Garvey argues that the same sub-personal processes linked to informational encapsulation, which signifies that a sub-system does not have all of the information available to the system as a whole, can be applied equally to the kind of illusion revealed by Müller-Lyer lines, where we "see" lines that are of different lengths, while simultaneously "knowing" in another part of our mind that they are of the same length; and to the denial that another person is dead, when one knows that they really are dead. While his exposition is quite different to the crisp exegesis of Foxall (2008), he too looks to the EEA to enquire what each system was designed to do.

Garvey argues that it is easily understood that the visual processing system which "believes" the lines to be of the same length was built to deal with a world that did not contain Müller-Lyer lines but did contain the features of linear perspective that make the illusion possible. Garvey then argues with respect to the situation where a person refuses to believe that another person is dead, that during the Pleistocene when survival was moment by moment, denial simply operated as a device to keep the person functioning (ibid.: 51). Not all beliefs are designed for the purpose of accurately describing the world. Instead some have been designed to make it easier to cope with the world. No matter; for each belief, the possibility of their operation in spite of contrasting evidence and contrary belief in another part of the mind, the conscious mind, involves a similar process of information encapsulation.

Towards psychoanalytic marketing science?

The clear and careful specifications of the BPM and intentional behaviorism encourage one to seek to consider the possibility of constructing a similar specification for psychoanalysis in relation to marketing and consumption. Dating to the early 1960s, there was little stomach for psychoanalysis in the marketing academy, as the unconscious amongst other concepts was ruled out of order, not least by behaviorists, as speculative (Bargh, 2008). There has recently been a revival of interest in unconscious processing and exploring the effects of environmental stimuli, including the use of subliminal and supraliminal primes (McFerran et al., 2010a; McFerran et al., 2010b; Martin & Morich, 2011). This has been accompanied by renewed interest in the sister disciplines of management and organizational behavior, where special issues of several prominent journals have been devoted to the contribution of Jacques Lacan, the "French Freud".

It is tempting to paraphrase Foxall in relation to the aims of consumer behavior analysis, to state simply that psychoanalytic marketing is concerned with the application of psychoanalytic theories and methods to the marketplace of human purchase and consumption activities. It could be argued that this is too general and should be related to the primary psychoanalytic enterprise, comprising the "talking cure", representing the attempt to translate bodily symptoms into speech and thereby to free the suffering subject from their grasp. In line with this conception, perhaps an evidence base can be constructed around a collection of ideographic case histories, which can then be related to theory to contribute better understandings for the persistence of human suffering in relation to marketing and consumption contexts.

The above raises the question of whether psychoanalysis *ought* to be considered a science. Past critics have argued against its use of case histories and the irrefutability of its constructs. In his early work, most notably the *Project for a Scientific Psychology* (1895), Freud, who trained as a neurologist, stressed his eagerness to construct a science of psychoanalysis, to the extent of mapping putative neuronal processes involved in repression. Later he moved distinctly away from this aim, leaving instructions that the *Project* should be burned (Boothby, 2001: 4). Freud was first dismayed by the narrow positivism of American scholarship (Roudinesco, 2001) and second, some of his fundamental insights changed through the course of his career. This second reason led Freud to devise a metapsychology as "a more speculative model that could account of concepts that were not directly linked to clinical experience" (ibid.: 107). By calling this a meta-psychology, Freud signaled the link to metaphysics, the speculative branch of philosophy. The concept of libido, or psychic energy, plays a key role in this formulation, as does his later fundamental reformulation, which includes the death drive. The philosophical approach is argued to be compatible with phenomenology (Boothby, 2001), which is distinctly not the heterophe-nomenology of Dennett, whose assertion that classical phenomenology is tied to introspection is argued to be incorrect (Zahavi, 2007).

The tradition of informed speculation in psychoanalysts is attractive to scholars who are principally concerned to generate novel insights and understanding, who would distance themselves from what they perceive as the narrow scientism that pervades social science today. On the other hand, there are others who are warmer to the idea of a scientific psychoanalysis. Given the variety of conceptual schemes and terms in psychoanalysis, there is a difficulty in devising a common base of assumptions. Peter Fonagy, who works in the object relations tradition and whose group is based at University College London, usefully defines some key concepts (Fonagy & Target, 2003: 3–6), which are useful for the purposes of this discussion:

a. Psychic determinism. While acknowledging the importance of biological and social factors, the individual's conscious and unconscious representation of past experience determine that person's relation to the external world and their capacity to adapt to it.

b. The genetic-developmental proposition, which states that all behaviors are understandable as sequences of actions developing out of earlier events. Whereas consumer behavior analysis argues that consumer choice occurs at the intersection of a person's behavioral history and the consumption setting, the psychoanalyst will also pay attention to that person's character. Key to this are structures of character development during childhood. This presumes certain regularities, depending on the nature of development, depending on whether the structure is neurotic, perverse or psychotic. Given the importance of culture and the symbolic, there is a dynamic relation between character formation and the society within which this develops.

c. Complex unconscious mental processes are assumed to be responsible for the content of conscious thinking and behavior. Unconscious fantasies around wishes for instinctual gratification or safety motivate and determine behavior and affect the ability to cope with the external environment.

In relation to consumer behavior analysis, I would add that the pleasure-unpleasure principle relates to the notion that behavior is a means to minimize psychic pain and maximize psychic pleasure. This is similar to the economic speculator envisaged by consumer behavior analysis, which assesses potential gains and losses in satisfaction in relation to alternative behaviors. However, Freud's (1920) later writing focuses on that which is *beyond pleasure* and in his work Lacan also refers to *jouissance*, which does not index the pleasure produced by the satisfaction of a need, but rather the quite different "enjoyment" produced by the function linked to a drive. Lacan (1960) illustrates this when discussing a story told by Kant. The king tells a man who is a sensualist that he can have the woman of his dreams if he so wishes, on the condition that this will be for one night only and that he will then be executed at first light. Where Kant uses the example to illustrate the point of a limit beyond which the sensualist will not go, Lacan to the contrary suggests that undoubtedly some will take up the bargain, if only for the unique experience of that unutterable "enjoyment".

Neuropsychoanalysis is perhaps that area of psychoanalytic investigation which best fits the agenda of intentional behaviorism (Solms & Turnbull, 2002). This accommodates Dennett's (1995) idea of reverse engineering and also provides a useful alternative reading of the basic emotions identified by Panksepp (1998) to that provided by Foxall (2008). There is no room to go into this in detail, but for instance, where Foxall links the SEEKING system to dominance, Solms and Turnbull assign this to Freud's libidinal drive (ibid.: p. 117) while the LUST sub-system, which relates to "pleasure", "reward" or "reinforcement", generates feelings of pleasurable delight. SEEKING is in turn linked by them to schizophrenia and bipolar disorder while PANIC and FEAR are related to anxiety disorders. The authors also widen and deepen understanding of key processes such as repression, by arguing that "any part of the brain's activity that is excluded from the overarching network of executive control exercised by the pre-frontal lobes is, in a sense, repressed" (1999: 287). If so, they argue that this means that "repression" refers to several different processes. Solms and Panksepp (2012) discuss several interesting and important issues and extend understanding of how certain forms of phenomenal experience can become unconscious through inhibition, by placing the "external" body as the subject of perception, or the "ego", and the "internal" body as the "id". They are also controversial by providing evidence that Freud mistakenly conflated cognitive unawareness of instinctual consciousness with an unconscious process. Their conclusion, which is that the "id" is conscious, has huge implications for psychoanalysis, some of which they discuss. Despite this, they conclude that Freud's overall insight stands up under scrutiny.

This discussion offers some initial conjectures based on my reading of the literature on intentional behaviorism, which need to be revisited in depth. Given that the overall nature of the discussion is relatively abstract, it may help to elucidate some of the similarities and differences between consumer behavior analysis and psychoanalysis by focusing on a specific issue that is important to consumer behavior. That is the aim of the final section in this chapter, which briefly compares and contrasts approaches to understanding and treating addiction.

Addiction

Addiction and consumer behavior analysis

If one includes Gary Becker's (1996) theory of rational addiction as essentially behaviorist, then behaviorism provides the most influential current account of addiction today. This explanation rests on melioration, which is a form of matching in relation to two variable interval schedules, where the option offering the higher immediate rate of reinforcement is chosen (Herrnstein & Prelec, 1992). In some recent papers, Foxall devotes a lot of space to discussion of exponential and hyperbolic discounting which he integrates into the BPM. Where Becker's explanation assumes a process of exponential discounting, Foxall (2008: 376) argues that hyperbolic discounting (Ainslie, 2001) provides a better explanation. This explanation, which is commonly referred to as the primrose path to addiction, results from the maximization of short-term rather than long-term utility, resulting in preferences being inconsistent over time due to hyperbolic discounting, where addiction leads to a lowering of overall utility (Ainslie, 1991, 2001; Herrnstein & Prelec, 1992; Rachlin, 2000). According to this explanation, I value a smaller immediate reward over a larger, future reward. The shape of the hyperbolic function shows that my preference for the present over the near-future is much stronger than my preference for the near-future over the distant future, so there is no point in my deferring present consumption. The primrose path to addiction thus describes the progressively slippery slope by which a person continues to maximize their short-term utility leading to lower overall utility. The only solution is to help the addict to bundle all the rewards of abstinence so that this weighs favorably over those proffered by immediate consumption (Foxall, 2008: 379).

Foxall (2008) mentions an alternative explanation which he says he does not find convincing, comprising the "two-systems" explanation, which argues that what looks like hyperbolic discounting is actually produced by the concurrent operation of two exponential brain systems, one of which operates according to a rational logic of discounting, while the other presses for more immediate rewards (McClure et al., 2007). It would have been useful to have learned some more of Foxall's reasons for rejecting this explanation.

Addiction is discussed within an integrated approach to consumer choice (see Foxall, 2008, Figure 8: 384). This argument is linked to an ultimate cause by Foxall (2010) where he provides a rationale for the emergence of temporal discounting during the EEA and additionally maps the addictive process, as it unfolds from routine consumption along the "primrose path" to addiction, then recovery, onto the scheme of operant classes of behavior (see also Foxall & Sigurdsson, 2011).

Read in conjunction with Foxall (2007), these papers convey an enviable breadth and depth of scholarship, clarifying issues that remained abstract in the former, weightier paper. While clearly influenced by Dennett, he makes clear his loyalty to Skinner (Foxall, 2008: 387). The question is, does the explanation in these papers provide a better explanation of addiction? As one moves along the primrose path to addiction, so neuronal firing of dopamine increases. Routine behavior generally involves "liking" and gives way to "wanting", related to compulsive behavior, which is arousing and pleasurable, but not dominant, while "craving" is linked to highly addictive behaviors that are highly arousing, unpleasurable and reduce dominance (see Foxall, 2008: 383–4).

Foxall's mention of the importance of craving suggests links to the visceral explanation of addiction, which made me wonder if he wishes to annex Loewenstein (1996) to his account. While Herrnstein and Prelec (1992) argue that addiction is a consequence of failure to notice the incremental negative effect of engaging in an addictive activity, in the visceral account, this results from a failure to appreciate the motivational force of future craving. Loewenstein (1996) argues that the primrose path explanation can be useful to explain addictions such as workaholism, where the dangers are not well published and where every extra hour worked has a small negative effect on the overall quality of life. However, he suggests that this explanation loses force when it comes to explaining crack cocaine or cigarette addiction, where the risks are well publicized and the process quite rapid (ibid.: 251). The visceral explanation advances two central premises. First, visceral factors crowd out all goals other than that of mitigating the effect of the visceral factor. Second, linked to the endowment effect, there is a pervasive tendency to consistently underestimate susceptibility to visceral factors and so although currently experienced effects are palpable, future states are discounted. Research on the effects of cheesecake, bacon and chocolate has found that these foods have a similar effect to addictive drugs, by disrupting the brain-stimulation reward system, leading to insensitivity to the adverse consequences of addiction (Johnson & Kenny, 2010). In line with the visceral hypothesis the authors wonder whether the availability of these foods has increased so quickly that, similar to addictive drugs, they stimulate brain systems more powerfully than we are evolved to handle, by signaling a false fitness benefit.

By seeking to integrate his explanation into a Darwinian framework, Foxall, by falling in with adaptationism, invites the criticism attracted by Dr. Pangloss (Gould & Lewontin, 1979). It could be argued that such speculation does not sit well with the otherwise conservative argument, and indeed there have been calls for a moratorium against the "idle speculation" which argues that this or that domain-specific module developed at some point during human evolution (Panksepp & Panksepp, 2000: 113). On the other hand, one wonders where we would be without such well-argued speculation. I am slightly more perplexed by the rather procrustean attempt to fit the seven core emotional states identified by Panksepp (1998) to the three terms of the BPM, where pleasure is equivalent to utilitarian reinforcement and arousal to informational reinforcement, and dominance is related to the setting (Foxall, 2008: 384–7).

Addiction and psychoanalysis

Addiction is not an ideal issue to discuss from a psychoanalytic perspective. This is because, as opposed to the psychoneuroses and even psychosis, it is known to be notoriously resistant to the "talking cure". However, addiction is interesting for psychoanalysis today, if only for the ubiquity of its presence in the therapeutic setting. Freud argued that masturbation is the model for addiction in the sense that it constitutes a means to access immediate gratification of the drives without the need to detour through potentially painful social interaction. The attraction of the object or behavior is that it provides the means for a drive to gain direct unmediated access to enjoyment through the body, without having to deal with real relationships. As the direct expression of a drive for enjoyment which is also the case in the actual neuroses, there is thus little scope for analysis. Theorists today acknowledge the difficulty in dealing with addiction, but argue that it can be analyzed. Although each psychoanalytic school has developed a perspective on addiction, two prominent explanations are provided by ego psychology and Lacanian psychoanalysis. While these are very broadly similar in some respects, for instance in taking into account the character of the individual, they also differ with respect to nomenclature and the role played by the analyst.

Ego psychology

American ego psychoanalysis pays particular attention to the adjustment of the individual to societal norms. The superego represents the set of internalized standards the person is expected to live up to and individuals are socialized to ego-ideal, which acts as a standard, based initially on the image of the parents that the person seeks to live up to. In traditional psychoanalytic terms the id is organized by the ego to conform according to the demands of the superego. Where repression has gone too far, there is a tendency towards neurotic behavior; on the other hand, where cultural proscription has not reached far enough, behavior begins to assume classic symptoms of psychosis.

Working within the ego psychology tradition, Albanese (2002) developed a personality continuum which describes a hierarchical arrangement of four distinct personality types, ordered according to the grip of superego and ego-ideal formations, ranging from normal to neurotic, primitive and psychotic characters. Each describes a qualitatively different kind of behavior. The normal consumer has transitive preference orderings and makes consistent choices over time. Their behavior is in the main prudential, instanced by self-control and delayed gratification. Neurotic consumers by comparison are indecisive and inhibited by feelings of guilt, being preoccupied with issues relating to self-control. The progressively loosened grip of the superego is apparent in the primitive level of development, where there is little coherence to preference structure, where the person is engaged in a constant struggle for self-control, experiencing a lack of impulse control where the strong presentist orientation would be produced by the use of hyperbolic discounting (Ainslie, 1991). In this explanation the addict is prone to splitting and so often will appear to have two selves, which is a behavioral manifestation of this primitive stage of personality development. Albanese's account shares similarities with Foxall (2008) to the extent that each argues that hyperbolic discounting plays a role in the process of addiction. The difference is that Albanese links this primarily to the compulsive character, who constantly experiences the need for self-control (Albanese, 2002: 14). Given that he wrote his piece before the publication of McClure et al. (2007), it would have been interesting to learn of Albanese's position on the explanation based on the existence of two systems.

Lacanian psychoanalysis

Lacanian psychoanalysis pays attention to how the demand of the id for pleasure is regulated and administered differently in different social contexts. Although substance use has the same physiological effect on users in traditional societies as in western contexts, in the former this acts as a support to social regulation, being codified through ritual and so integrated into society (Naparstek, 2011). Given this, it is argued that the fundamental question with respect to addictive behavior in western society is not so much to describe behavior, but to understand its role in society and why it is considered normal or deviant.

Analysts argue that the prevailing social organization of western societies produce a climate of "addictification" (Loose, 2011) by elevating values of advanced capitalism, such as individualism, competition and self-accountability, against a backdrop of the retreat of religiosity and other institutions which had previously underpinned social solidarity (Loose, 2011). The command in society today is not to defer gratification but rather to enjoy, now. This individualist value system pervades the understanding of addiction; for instance, while Goldstein (1994) argues that addiction rests on intense and impulsive decisions, he nonetheless maintains that individuals should be held accountable for their behavior as a matter of policy, as does Gary Becker (1996). Psychoanalysts also link illegal ingestion of drugs to their controlled regulation by medical practice, not just in terms of the legacy of addiction of millions of individuals to Valium and Librium through the 1960s and 1970s, but also the use of one drug to control another, as in the case of the use of methadone to regulate heroin, equivalent to fighting fire by pouring petrol on it (Loose, 2011: 3).

Although contending that there is a strong societal dimension to addiction, it is argued that society should not be held entirely responsible for the plight of the addict who makes a choice, between enjoying the "hard" way, by persevering with the ups and downs of relationships with other people and enduring suffering (the human lot), rather than turning to drugs or some other addictive behavior such as cutting or bulimia to relieve anxiety (Loose, 2011: 7). It is acknowledged that addicts are difficult to treat, being largely non-communicative and in search of instant solutions. In addiction there is no need for other people and so "a dire consequence is that there is increasingly less room for dissatisfaction, desire and the social bond" (Loose, 2011: 7). If treatment consists of opening up a space for anxiety to make its appearance and be reckoned with through the play of language, then therapies such as "twelve-step" programs can act negatively by providing a crutch for identity and thus a brake, constituting a stopping point for analysis.

There are similarities with ego psychology in that addiction is presumed to involve a dual diagnosis, first as an addict and second in relation to personality structure, as perverse, neurotic or psychotic. However, much depends too on the particularity of the individual. For instance, Svolos describes a woman analyzand addicted to alcohol, benzodiazepine and shopping, who used her addictions to prop up her participation in social and professional functions (Svolos, 2011: 79). The concept of jouissance, which features largely in the Lacanian explanation, is absent from ego psychology. Putting this very simply, jouissance describes an intensity of experience that is felt through the body as the consequence of the direct action of a drive. The "civilized" neurotic subject whose bodily experience of jouissance is clipped by culture experiences this most directly, when they can do so, in sexual orgasm. For them, addiction can involve a quest for a jouissance that is beyond pleasure as the only thing worth living for. On the other hand, the administration of addiction for those tending towards psychosis, on whose psychic organization culture has a much weaker grip, involves the quest for relief from a jouissance that is experienced as a constant source of pain. The challenge for the analyst in addressing this kernel of resistance to the symbolic is to enable the addiction to be translated into discourse.

There is a difficulty in relating Lacanian explanation to those based on temporal discounting or on the operation of visceral cravings, not least because this school of psychoanalysis has developed its own highly differentiated, some would say convoluted, language. The key when it comes to addiction is to enable whatever issues are at stake in the relation between the analyzand and others to be placed into discourse. Loose describes an analyzand's "(nearly) visceral and unlimited dependence on an object" (Loose, 2011: 34), in this case her mobile phone, not to justify a visceral explanation of addiction, but because he thinks the answer to her request should be "NO" (his capitals); a response that would no doubt provoke anxiety in her and have the potential to open up the play of her desire and who knows, fruitful enquiry.

Discussion and conclusions

The foregoing sections covered a fair bit of ground in relation to consumer behavior analysis and psychoanalysis, making some connections and also noting divergences. This section picks up on a few points for further discussion and reflection.

The first point refers to the importance of language. It is a truism that the behaviorism underpinning consumer behavior analysis constitutes a different language to psychoanalysis. Each constructs a radically different account of the human subject, which foregrounds environmental determinism in relation to the former and psychic determinism in relation to the latter. In translating between these different languages, the lot of the marketing academic seems to be that of jack-of-all-trades and master of none, thus courting the danger that one is not nearly as versed in the lore of specific domains as one ought to be.

Until recently, consumer behavior theorists have generally managed to avoid this problem of translation and achieved a good deal in the process, by adhering to the limited theoretical resources provided by behaviorism. Some argue that intentional behaviorism (Foxall, 2007) has gone too far (Hocutt, 2007; Lacey, 2007) and indeed this development represents a series of bold moves by Foxall who must convince even the converted on some points (Sigurdsson, 2013). Clearly this is a man on a mission, who wants to stamp out clearly defined territory which, in my view, is estimable. Intentional behaviorism is a more speculative enterprise than its predecessor, tying itself to an evolutionary, adaptationist account (Panksepp & Panksepp, 2000). Consumer behavior theorists are now expected to be conversant with developments in neuroeconomics, neuropsychology and evolutionary psychology.

By the standards of psychoanalysis the move to intentional behaviorism is conservative, representing a cautious extension of behaviorism, to include the ascription of beliefs and desires from a third-person perspective. This allows consumer behavior analysis to stick closely to the indubitable, and so avoid "apparently unlimited phenomenological speculation" (Foxall, 2007: 25). On first reading I found the elaboration of this in Foxall (2008) and Foxall (2010) shockingly reductive, especially when mapping "the primrose path" of addiction onto the consumer behavior continuum. This struck me as being about as useful in relation to addiction as using a world atlas to find a street in Glasgow city center. However, on closer examination I could not but be impressed by the depth of scholarship involved in the detailed discussion of issues such as the different sub-personal processes involved in "wanting", "liking" and "craving".

Consumer behavior analysis and psychoanalysis have equally benefitted from research in psychology and behavioral economics; the former from the recognition of the power of the environment and the latter in relation to regained recognition of the power of unconscious suggestion. Psychoanalysis, if one can conceive of it as one thing, is concerned to explain the intentionality of unconscious processes that work through us despite ourselves. Psychoanalysts use the metaphor of a restless mind (Lear, 1999), as opposed to that of an associative machine, to discuss the processes whereby what is repressed from consciousness can be recovered by means of the talking cure. The complexities of human language, which consumer behavior analysis is just beginning to open up, forms the basis of psychoanalytic explanation, where it is argued that the unconscious itself operates according to rules of metaphor and metonymy. Having said that, psychoanalysis is definitely not introspection. Rather, the analyst must look for those small irruptions in the flow of conversation which offer the potential of a break, of something new that can awaken anxiety and desire.

Where consumer behavior analysis concerns itself with the personal stance, psychoanalysis continues to be concerned speculatively to engage the soul of the individual, to address a subject who does not just take the personal stance but as a moral subject, subject of the phenomenal stance. From a scientific point of view one might rightly question the artfulness of a psychoanalytic account, which argues that there is not much point in asking for evidence of the death drive, or of jouissance, as these concepts arise in the context of a speculative metapsychology. On the other hand, consumer behavior analysis is not itself immune from speculation, just as it has never been truly free of intentional language. However, as discussed above, there is a potentially useful meeting of minds in relation to the developing science of neuropsychoanalysis (Solms & Turnbull, 2002; Solms & Panksepp, 2012) which addresses many of the same questions confronted by consumer behavior analysis in recent years. In this respect there is scope to evaluate the psychoanalytic claim that personality structure as well as environment can help explain behavior.

Consumer behavior analysis shares with psychoanalysis the idea that addiction can be linked to a choice. This runs against the grain of "folk" psychology, which links it to a disease model. The argument linked to hyperbolic discounting is compelling too, at least in some instances where it might be imagined that a person can sleepwalk into addiction. Here it is noteworthy that Albanese (2002) also uses exponential discounting as part of his reason. On the other hand, with intravenous cocaine, one-third don't like it the first time, one-third try it again without developing any problems, and one-third try it again and go on to ruin their lives, through lost jobs, lost families, legal troubles, lost savings, and so on (Elster, 1997). The finding that there is damage to areas of the frontal cortex which plays a role in inhibiting automatic sensory-driven formulas and attribution of primary salience to the drug of abuse at the expense of other available rewarding stimuli (Goldstein & Volkow, 2002) could be used to support hyperbolic discounting or a visceral account based on inability to control compulsion. On the other hand, and somewhat ironically given the focus on environmental determinism as opposed to psychoanalysis, it tends to place responsibility on the individual and not the social context. Overall it seems to me that many important questions remain to be answered in relation to addiction. However, Foxall (2008, 2010) has done much to provide a pretty convincing argument from intentional behaviorism, as the basis for further discussion and debate.

Given their provenance, there is more than a passing resemblance between utilitarian and information reinforcement and the psychoanalytic concept of the pleasure principle whereby erotic desire is propelled by the ego (which is not quite reducible to status) and sexual drives – although this also demarcates the gulf that separates them. Psychoanalytic authors stress what is over and above the pleasure principle, most notably written about by Freud in *Beyond the Pleasure Principle*, where he introduces the notion of the death drive as the process by which an organism strives to return to its original state. The beyond of pleasure is articulated in a different way by Lacan who argues that over and above what is pleasurable there is the direct expression of a drive which gives rise to jouissance, a term reflecting an intensity of experience that is on the other side of pleasure, which is either experienced as a "too-muchness" or a "not enough". This bears some comparison to Foxall's (2008) description of highly addictive behavior as involving low pleasure, low dominance and high arousal.

Finally, I should say that I have found the task of writing this chapter a challenging but not unrewarding activity. I have learned a lot and as a result I have more questions now than I had when I started out, which can be no bad thing!

References

Ainslie, G. (1987). Self-reported tactics of impulse control. *International Journal of the Addictions*, 22(2), 167–179.

Ainslie, G. (1991). Derivation of "rational" economic behavior from hyperbolic discount curves. *American Economic Review*, 81, 334–340.

Ainslie, G. (2001). A research-based theory of addictive motivation. *Law and Philosophy*, 19, 77–115.

Albanese, P. (2002). *The Personality Continuum and Consumer Behavior*. Quorum Books.

Albanese, P. (2005). Inside economic man. In: M. Altman (Ed.) *Foundations and Extensions of Behavioral Economics: A Handbook* (pp. 1–23). Armonk, NY: M.E. Sharpe.

Bargh, J. (2008). There is no such thing as free will. Chapter seven in: J. Baer, J. F. Kaufman & R. F. Baumeister (Eds). *Are we Free? Psychology and Free Will*. Oxford: Oxford University Press.

Baumeister, R. F. (2002) Ego depletion and self-control: An energy model of the self's executive function. *Self and Identity*, 1, 129–136.

Baumeister, R. F., Bratslavsky, E., Muraven, M. & Tice, D. (1998). Ego depletion: Is the active self a limited resource? *Journal of Personality and Social Psychology*, 74, 1252–1265.

Becker, G. (1996). *Accounting for Tastes*. Cambridge, MA: Harvard University Press.

Bennett, M. R. and Hacker, P. M. S. (2003). *Philosophical Foundations of Neuroscience*. Oxford: Wiley-Blackwell.

Boothby, R. (2001). *Freud as Philosopher: Metapsychology after Lacan*. London: Routledge.

Brazelton, T. B., Koslowski, B. & Main, M. (1974). Origins of reciprocity: The early mother-infant interaction. In: L. Rosemblum (Ed.). *The Effect of the Infant on its Caregiver* (pp. 49–76). New York: Wiley.

Carman, Taylor (2003). *Heidegger's Analytic Interpretation: Discourse and Authenticity in Being and Time*. Cambridge: Cambridge University Press.

Cavalcanti, P. R., Oliveira-Castro, J. M. & Foxall, G. R. (2013). Individual differences in consumer buying patterns: A behavioral economic analysis. *The Psychological Record*, 63, 259–276.

Cosmides, L. & Tooby, J. (1996) Are humans intuitive statisticians after all? Rethinking some conclusions from the literature on judgment under uncertainty. *Cognition*, 58, 1–73.

Csibra, G., Gergely, G., Biro, S., Koos, O. & Brockbank, M. (1999). Goal attainment without agency cues: The perception of "pure reason" in infancy. *Cognition*, 72, 237–267.

Dennett, D. (1991). *Consciousness Explained*. London: Penguin.

Dennett, D. (1995). Cognitive science as reverse engineering: Several meanings of "top-down" and "bottom-up". In: D. Prawitz, B. Skryms & D. Westerdahl (Eds). *Logic, Methodology and Philosophy of Science, IX*. New York: North Holland.

Ehrenberg, A. S. C., Goodhardt, G. & Barwise, T. P. (1990). Double jeopardy revisited. *Journal of Marketing*, 54, 82–91.

Ehrenberg, A. S. C., Uncle, M. D. and Goodhardt, G. J. (2004). Understanding brand performance measures: Using Dirichlet benchmarks. *Journal of Business Research*, 57, 1307–1325.

Elster, J. (1997). More than enough (Review of Gary S. Becker (1996) *Accounting for Tastes*, *The University of Chicago Law Review*, 64, 749–764.

Fonagy, P. (2002). *Affect Regulation, Mentalization and the Development of the Self*. London: Other Press.

Fonagy, P. & Target, M. (2003). *Psychoanalytic Theories: Perspectives from Developmental Psychopathology*. London & Philadelphia: Whurr Publishers.

Foxall, G. R. (1990). *Consumer Psychology in Behavioral Perspective.* London and New York: Routledge.

Foxall, G. R. (1999). The substitutability of brands. *Managerial and Decision Economics,* 20, 241–257.

Foxall, G. R. (2007). Intentional behaviorism. *Behavior and Philosophy,* 35, 1–55.

Foxall, G. R. (2008). Reward, emotion and consumer choice: From neuroeconomics to neurophilosophy. *Journal of Consumer Behavior,* 7, 368–396.

Foxall, G. R. (2010). Accounting for consumer choice: Inter-temporal decision making in behavioral perspective. *Marketing Theory,* 10, 315–345.

Foxall, G. R., Oliveira-Castro, J. M. & Schrezenmaier, T. C. (2004). The behavioral economics of brand choice: Patterns of reinforcement and utility maximization. *Behavioral Processes,* 66, 235–260. doi: 10.1016/j.beproc.2004.03.007

Foxall, G. R. and Sigurdsson, V. (2011). Drug use as consumer behavior. *Behavioral and Brain Sciences,* 35, 313–314.

Freud, S. (1895). *Project for a Scientific Psychology.* Standard Edition, 1, 281–387.

Freud, S. (1920). Beyond the pleasure principle. In: A. Richards (Ed.), *On Metapsychology: The Theory of Psychoanalysis.* Penguin: London, 275–338.

Garvey, B. (2007). Subdoxastic states and the "special characteristics" of the unconscious. In: C. Kerslake and R. Brassier (Eds), *Origins and Ends of the Mind* (pp. 37–57). Leuven: Leuven University Press.

Goldstein, A. (1994). *Addiction: From Biology to Drug Policy.* Oxford: Oxford University Press.

Goldstein, R. & Volkow, N. D. (2002). Drug addiction and its underlying neurobiological basis: Neuroimaging evidence for the involvement of the frontal cortex. *American Journal of Psychiatry,* 159, 1642–1652.

Gould, S. J. & Lewontin, R. C. (1979). The spandrels of San Marco and the Panglossian paradigm: A critique of the adaptationist programme. *Proceedings of the Royal Society of London,* B: Biological Sciences, 205 (1161), 581–598.

Greenaway, J. R. (1998). The "improved" public house, 1870–1950: The key to civilized drinking, or the primrose path to drunkenness? *Addiction,* 93, 173–181.

Henrich, J., Heine, S. J. & Norenzayan, A. (2010). The weirdest people in the world. *Behavioral and Brain Sciences,* 33, 61–135. doi: 10.1017/S0140525X0999152X. Epub 2010 Jun 15.

Herrnstein, R. J. (1970). On the law of effect. *Journal of the Experimental Analysis of Behavior,* 13, 243–266.

Herrnstein, R. J. & Prelec, D. (1992). A theory of addiction. In: G. Loewenstein & J. Elster (Eds), *Choice Over Time* (pp. 235–263). New York: Russell Sage Foundation.

Hocutt, M. (2007). Gordon Foxall on intentional behaviorism. *Behavior and Philosophy,* 35, 77–92.

James, V. K. and Foxall, G. R. (2010). *Retail Choice and Consumer Behavior Analysis: Further Analyses.* Presented at the Association for Behavior Analysis International Conference, May, San Antonio, TX.

Johnson, P. & Kenny, P. (2010). Dopamine D2 receptors in addiction-like reward dysfunction and compulsive eating in obese rats. *Nature Neuroscience,* 13, 635–641.

Kahneman, D. & Tversky, A. (1979). Prospect theory: An analysis of decision under risk. *Econometrica,* 47, 263–291. doi: 10.1016/0010-0277(79)90024-6

Kahneman, D. (2011). *Thinking, Fast and Slow.* New York: Farrar, Strauss & Giroux.

Lacan, J. (1960). The *Jouissance* of transgression. In: J-A. Miller (Ed.), *The Ethics of Psychoanalysis 1959–1960. Book VII,* Dennis Porter (Trans. with notes) (pp. 191–204). London: Routledge.

Lacan, J. (1975/6). *The Aeminar of Jacques Lacan, Book XXIII: Joyce and the Sinthome, 1975–1976.* (Cormac Gallagher, trans.). http://www.lacaninireland.com/web/wp-content/uploads/2010/06/Book-23-Joyce-and-the-Sinthome-Part-1.pdf

Lacey, H. (2007). Intentional behaviorism and the intentional scheme: Comments on Gordon R. Foxall's "Intentional Behaviorism". *Behavior and Philosophy,* 35, 101–111.

Lear, J. (1999). *Open Minded: Working Out the Logic of the Soul.* Cambridge, MA: Harvard University Press.

Loewenstein, G. (1996). Out of control: Visceral influences on behavior. *Organizational Behavior and Human Decision Processes,* 65, 272–292.

Loose, R. (2000). The addicted subject caught between the ego and the drive: The post-Freudian reduction and simplification of a complex problem. *Psychoanalytishce Perspectieven,* 41/42, 55–81.

Loose, R. (2002). *The Subject of Addiction: Psychoanalysis and the Administration of Enjoyment.* London: Karnac.

Loose, R. (2011). Modern symptoms and their effects as forms of administration: A challenge to the concept of dual diagnosis and to treatment. In: Y. Goldman, K. M. Baldwin & T. Svolos (Eds), *Lacan and Addiction: An Anthology* (pp. 1–38.) London: Karnac.

McClure, S., Ericson, K. M., Laibson, D. I., Loewenstein, G. & Cohen, J. D. (2007). Time discounting for primary rewards. *Journal of Neuroscience,* 5796–5804. doi: 10.1523/JNEUROSCI.4246-06.2007

McFerran, B., Dahl, D. W., Fitzsimons, G. J. & Morales, A. C. (2010a). I'll have what she is having: Effect of social influence and body type on the food choices of others. *Journal of Consumer Research*, 36, 915–929.

McFerran, B., Dahl, D. W., Fitzsimons, G. J. & Morales, A. C. (2010b). Might an overweight waitress make you eat more? How the body type of others is sufficient to alter our food consumption. *Journal of Consumer Psychology*, 20, 146–151.

Marr, D. (1982). *Vision*. San Francisco: Freeman.

Martin, N. & Morich, K. (2011). Unconscious mental processes in consumer choice: Toward a new model of consumer behavior. *Journal of Brand Management*, 18, 483–505.

Moore, J. (1981). On mentalism, methodological behaviorism, and radical behaviorism. *Behaviorism*, 9, 55–77.

Naparstek, F. (2011). New uses of drugs. In: Y. G. Baldwin, K. Malone & T. Svolos (Eds), *Lacan and Addiction: An Anthology* (pp. 39–59). London: Karnac.

O'Guinn, T. C. & Faber, R. J. (1987). Compulsive buying: A phenomenological exploration. *Journal of Consumer Research*, 16, 147–157.

Panksepp, J. (1998). *Affective, Neuroscience: The Foundations of Human and Animal Emotions*. New York: Oxford University Press.

Panksepp, J. & Panksepp, J. B. (2000). The seven sins of evolutionary psychology. *Evolution and Cognition*, 8, 108–131.

Rachlin, H. (2000). *The Science of Self-Control*. Cambridge, MA: Harvard University Press.

Robbins, P. & Jack, A. I. (2006). The phenomenal stance. *Philosophical Studies: An International Journal for Philosophy in the Analytic*, 127, 59–85.

Roscoe, P. (2014). Dr Pangloss and the best of all possible markets: Evolutionary fantasies and justifications of contemporary economic discourse. In: N. Campbell, J. Desmond, J. Fitchett, D. Kavanagh, P. McDonagh, A. O'Driscoll & A. Prothero (Eds), *Myth and the Market: Proceedings of an Interdisciplinary Conference* (pp. 96–111). 19–21 June, Carlingford.

Ross, D., Sharp, C., Vuchinich, R. E. & Spurrett, D. (2007). *The Picoeconomics and Neuroeconomics of Disordered Gambling*. Cambridge, MA: MIT Press.

Roudinesco, E. (2001). *Why Psychoanalysis?* (Tr. Rachel Bowlby). New York: Columbia University Press.

Sigurdsson, V. (2013). Consumer behavior analysis and ascription of intentionality to the explanation of consumer choice. *Marketing Theory*, 13, 133–134.

Solms, M. & Panksepp, J. (2012). The "id" knows more than the "ego" admits: Neuropsychoanalytic and primal consciousness perspectives on the interface between affective and cognitive neuroscience. *Brain Science*, 2, 147–175. doi: 10.3390/brainsci2020147

Solms, M. & Turnbull, O. (2002). *The Brain and the Inner World: An Introduction to the Neuroscience of Subjective Experience*. New York: Other Press.

Svolos, T. (2011). Introducing "the new symptoms". In: Baldwin, Y. G., Malone, K. & Svolos, T. (Eds) *Lacan and Addiction: An Anthology* (pp. 75–89). London: Karnac.

Thombs, D. (2006). *Introduction to Addictive Behaviors*. New York: Guilford Press.

Tooby, J. & Cosmides, L. (1989). Evolutionary psychology and the generation of culture, Part I. Theoretical considerations. *Ethology & Sociobiology*, 10, 29–49.

Zahavi, D. (2007). Killing the straw man: Dennett and phenomenology. *Phenomenology and the Cognitive Sciences*, 6, 21–24.

Ethnographical interpretation of consumer behavior

Employing the Behavioral Perspective Model

Paul M. W. Hackett

Introduction[1]

For many years prior to its incorporation within the market research industry, ethnography existed primarily within academia. The ethnographic research modus operandi, in its incarnation as consumer ethnography, filled a lacuna in consumer research by focusing upon the behavior of individuals or social groups situated where products and services are purchased and used. Consumer ethnography may be conceived as either a distinct discipline involving long-term participant observation or as a series of qualitative research techniques. Both formulations yield potentially rich understanding and insight in regard to consumers and their product and service purchasing/usage behaviors within the setting of their lived choices. However, a caveat must be issued as consumer ethnography faces the danger of producing fragmented and disparate insights that may be difficult to bring together to answer either theoretical or applied questions. Due to ethnographic research studies often being piecemeal and theoretically disjointed or bereft, this danger is most aggressive when researchers are attempting to amalgamate qualitative approaches within the specific auspices of understanding consumer behavior. Consequently, it may be argued that consumer ethnography is an approach, or series of techniques and methods, in need of a theoretical framework within which research design, techniques and findings may be assembled to reveal the deep insight which it is possible to garner through qualitative research.

I will consider how the Behavioral Perspective Model (BPM) of consumer choice (Foxall, 2010) provides such a potential framework and how this may be incorporated within ethnography. Moreover, using the BPM as a framework for conceptualizing consumer choice, along with ethnography as a research approach, facilitates knowledge development in a way that does not impose a structure upon data but allows knowledge to be assembled through the adaptable common framework that is provided by Foxall's BPM.

Three concepts that are intimately related to the juncture of the BPM and ethnography will run throughout this chapter: structural ontologies, the mapping sentence (MS) and mereology. Structural ontologies are expositions of how an individual or group conceives of the world around them. Mereology is the study of the relationships between parts of entities and the wholes from which they are drawn along with part-to-part relationships (see, for example, Calosi & Graziana, 2014). The MS provides a structured account of a specified mereology. All three are related to situated human experience and behavior, which is the subject matter of ethnography. Thus, the structural ontology (see Effingham, 2013) of consumer behavior present in the BPM will be considered as a mereological account of consumer activities and this will be modeled using mapping sentences and is shown to be particularly suited to ethnographic enquiry.

Category formation

Category formation is a fundamental human behavior (e.g. Aristotle, 2014, Haaparanta & Koskinen, 2012, Khalidi, 2013, Lowe, 2007, Poli & Seibt, 2010), which is equally rudimentary in consumer contexts where consumers and their actions are categorized to enable understanding and predic-tion (Hsu et al., 2013). For example, when describing consumer behavior we employ categorical words, phrases and ideas that describe consumers and their activities: consumer, user, customer, purchaser, adopter, buyer, browser, client, emptor, shopper, service-user, patient, product, etc. Each word and phrase has a specific meaning that differentiates consumer activity (I will represent these as CA). Similarly, we can comprehend and name the categories of objects (CO) or things we buy and use, for example merchandise, goods, consumer-durable, consumer items, services, and differentiate these in terms of their involving or being food, clothing, luxuries, necessities, a bargain, expensive. Other conceptual categories exist into which we readily assign an appreciation of the consumer process (CP): wasteful, thrift, retail, wholesale, aesthetic, market, buy-two-get-three, and many others. Categorically identifying components of what constitutes our behavior as a consumer does not therefore appear problematic.[2] A more complete understanding of being a consumer arises from integrating these different aspects along with an appreciation of the con-sumer context and culture as proposed in the BPM. It is useful if I define the key concepts I employ throughout this essay, as I use these in specific senses to demonstrate the appropriateness of melding the BPM with ethnographic consumer research. The word "proposition" has a vari-ety of pertinent meanings. As a noun a proposition is a theory, hypothesis, argument, concept or principle. As a verbal statement "propositional verbs" conveys an expression of a judgment, desire, opinion or belief. This latter sense is how I will be using the word whilst incorporating from formal logic the notion that a proposition expresses a statement, which may be true or false. A proposition may bear truth-value, which means either the truthfulness or falsity that is assigned to a proposition. Thus, a mental viewpoint held towards a proposition is a propositional attitude, which may have the value of true or false. Under these definitions the BPM embodies a theory of consumer choice that acts as a logical cartography for the concepts I listed above as CA, CO and CP along with the consumer environment (external environment "Ee") and other personal qualities of the consumer (internal environment "Ei"). Thus:

a person engages in CA in regard to CO that are CP within the context of Ei and Ee.

The BPM explicates the logic underlying propositions of consumer behavior by constituting a structured behavioral ontology realizing the major bearers of truth-value associated with under-standing overt and covert consumers' activities.

Ethnography

Ethnography embodies the systematic study of peoples and cultures, their customs and cul-turally located behaviors, with participant observation being the major research approach.

Ethnographic research necessitates those conducting the enquiry being intimately ensconced within the culture they are studying. This process often involves the researcher living amongst and being intimately involved in the activities of a culture over protracted time periods of typically a year. Systematic observation and experience in the form of diaries and field notes reflect significant events along with subjects' elucidations. When commencing participant observation the researcher gathers open-ended data about general aspects of cultural life to understand fundamental cultural norms. Frequently this includes learning the culture's linguistic peculiarities and traditions. After this initiation, researchers are better equipped to not impose their own norms of behavior and understanding upon their observations, to not transgress customs, but to establish rapport and acceptance in the culture. The researcher is now able to assess the appropriateness of the research questions and design. The data gathered is of directly observable behaviors and material objects and artifacts. Behaviors viewed include ceremonies, rites, conflicts and day-to-day events such as eating and working. As well as these overt behaviors, covert attitudes, values, beliefs, etc. are also of interest. Considering elements as parts of a semiotic system that both resides within a cultural milieu and forms a cultural context unites potentially disparate elements of behavior.[3] Within such systems, observations and enquiries are made into the actions committed and the meanings of these actions for the culture's residents.[4]

In a broader sense ethnography is a group of qualitative research techniques from psychology and anthropology. Along with participant observation, non-participant observation, interviews, dialogues and the collection of archival materials or artifacts are employed to reveal the behaviors, attitudes, beliefs, values and perceptions and how these form part of culturally related behavior. What I have so far commented upon is ethnographic research in a traditional, academic sense. I now turn to the application of ethnography as used in a consumer situation and how this may be employed within the structure of the BPM.

Consumer ethnography

I have introduced ethnography both as protracted participant observation and as a collection of qualitative research techniques. From this point I will call the former instantiation "big E ethnography" and the latter "little e ethnography" (Hackett, 2015b) (see Belk, 2012 and Hackett, 2015a for a review of these approaches). Consumer ethnography can be defined in a variety of ways (Hackett, 2015b) to include a lesser or greater array of mainly qualitative research methods. This assortment of approaches has been broadened from the observational and dialogic approaches employed in traditional ethnography to include: focus groups, projective techniques, autoethnographies and online versions of ethnographies (netnographies), in-depth and affinity group interviews, discovery groups, participant observation, video/visual ethnography/documentary, netnography, journal or diary keeping in many formats including video diaries, blogs, etc., and search approaches and creativity sessions. By using this wide array of research techniques consumer ethnography has been developed as a time-abbreviated commercial application of cultural anthropology, carried out surrounded by a setting that involves lived, real-world consumer experiences. Within consumer ethnographic studies researchers immerse themselves within a cultural setting and follow individuals over time periods of perhaps days or weeks. Researchers may attempt to become personally engulfed within the lives of their subjects and during this period of superficial intimacy, the researcher will interact with subjects and undertake direct observations of their commercially related everyday rituals.[5]

Within the consumer context, ethnography is particularly useful for unveiling insights into process-intensive scenarios or events where there is a large amount of consumer–retailer, consumer–product/service interaction. Examples of these forms of commercial behavior include grocery shopping, eating at restaurants or browsing and purchasing consumer goods. Research that uses ethnography is able to assemble a framework within which consumer behaviors may be understood in respect to the important psychological (thoughts, feelings) and socio-cultural-environmental influences in terms of consumers' reactions to products and services. The depth of knowledge gained from consumer ethnography may be employed to help develop and focus innovative marketing communications that are appropriate to the sector of interest. Ethnography is especially useful for resolving areas of provider inflexibility and redundant procedures or non-congruent client–provider behaviors and expectations, in situations such as point-of-sale locations and front desk settings where the actual behavior of clients and potential clients can be thoroughly investigated. Thus, consumer ethnography is able to provide organizations with a window that yields near direct insight into their clients' needs.

A characteristic that typifies ethnography in general and more specifically within the consumer context is that this research yields phenomenologically rich and insightful understanding in regard to consumers, their purchasing behaviors and their lived choices. Products and services are not experienced in isolation but within the contexts of work, recreation, family, education, etc. Ethnographic research makes available a more unified, in-situ view than many other research approaches. Focus group interviews, in-depth interviews and survey techniques, etc. depend upon the subject remembering and accurately reporting their attitudes and experiences, in research situations that are usually removed from the usage or purchase context. Ethnography employs some of these techniques but also uses participants' activities (participant observations, sort techniques, creativity sessions) to assist companies to develop insight into how clients experience their goods and to understand how changes in cultural circumstances may potentially affect product and service usage. In consumer ethnography, efforts are made to represent understanding from a user's perspective. Often the skilled observation and interpretation of service and product usage reveals surprising behaviors, leading to understanding of product usage and identifying areas for innovation. Commercial environments change rapidly. Consumer ethnography may help companies understand current markets and adapt to market changes.

An example of the usage, and the changing use, of commercial ethnography and its ability to help companies respond to changes in the social context of their product utilization is provided by exemplars from personal computers and hand-held communication devices. Two decades ago consumer ethnography in this market sector focused upon identifying new areas within which computers may be used and sold. Ethnography was used to reveal how consumers moved from using office computers to home computers, and from desktop computers to laptops. The questions that are now being asked within ethnographic studies have been adapted slightly to provide answers to questions about how entertainment and communication devices have and may continue to merge. Users have difficulties in verbally expressing what they want in such a changing environment, which presents a problem for a company attempting to innovate in such a market environment. Ethnography attempts to understand how people live and to predict potential future client needs. Variation in the usage patterns of different market segments may also be demonstrated through ethnography. For example, ethnographic research has identified how teens and baby boomers may respond differently to cloud applications. In this situation research approaches that rely upon directly questioning participants (such as surveys, interviews etc.) may produce inadequate or outdated research findings. However, consumer ethnographic approaches that employ direct observation (for example, ethnography, video diaries, etc.) may yield data that is able to demonstrate the important differences between the demographic and other characteristics of the consumer.

In recent years the approaches of autoethnography[6] (Chin, 2007, Muncey, 2010, Southerton, 2011) and netnography[7] (Kozinets, 2009) have entered the repertoire of the consumer researcher. The use of mobile technologies, for example, compiling video diaries using mobile phones or other hand-held devices, enables consumers to record and narrate their everyday activities as these activities happen. Using such technologies, consumers are able to record their own perspective of a given product or service, providing consumer researchers and market managers with first-hand unmediated experiences upon which they may build knowledge and understanding of consumer behavior. These approaches have the potential of facilitating business development and innovation. Having presented ethnography as an approach to consumer research, in the following section I turn attention to the BPM.

The Behavioral Perspective Model

Foxall develops his explanation of consumer behavior within the rubric of radical behaviorism where the observable rate of consumer response behavior is a behavioral response to environmental stimuli. The BPM comprises independent variables of 1) the degree to which a behavior setting is open or closed (a continuous variable); and 2) utilitarian and instrumental reinforcement (a bifurcated variable). These variables control the numerical rate of response behavior, identified as a generalized nomothetic action. The continuum of consumer location openness references the ease with which the outcomes of a behavior are controlled and the amount to which the consumer behavioral response rate may be attributed to the setting. At this and at other points in this chapter, I will be using a mapping sentence (MS) to illustrate how selected behavioral variables combine and exert an effect within a research area (Hackett, 2014). An MS is a mereological device that is formed by first identifying the major sub-domains of the content under scrutiny. These sub-domains are then divided into their pertinent features as defined by the topic of the investigation. I illustrate this procedure by formulating an MS of the BPM itself (Figure 22.1). In the BPM the major sub-domains are the two independent variables of setting and reinforcement type. A third sub-domain is present, which is the outcome or range over which the effects of the variables in the model are active: in this instance, this is the ensuing rate of consumer behavior. These components are then stated as a sentence that arranges and links the variables of concern using an everyday language sentence suggestive of the relationship between the sub-domains, their components and how this impacts upon the stated range of effect (see Hackett, 2014 for details of this procedure). The reason for developing an MS is to illustrate the operation of variables within a research setting in a clear, standardized and comparable format. Thus the MS for the overall structure of the BPM is:

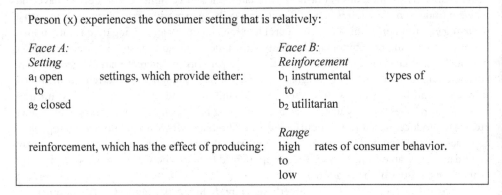

Figure 22.1 Mapping sentence for the BPM

Other MSs may be developed to illustrate the operational elements of the BPM's sub-components and the inter-relationships of these elements.

Open–closed settings

The openness of a setting depends upon the *availability of and access to reinforcement* and the *external control of the consumer situation*. The availability of reinforcement in any setting is determined by the number of available reinforcers, the number of ways of obtaining reinforcers and the need to perform certain tasks to attain the reinforcers. The external control of the consumer situation is determined by the extent to which marketers/providers control reinforcement, whether contingencies impact those that are imposing them and whether an alternate situation is readily accessible. This being the case, an MS for the openness–closedness of settings is stated in Figure 22.2.

The second of the BPM's two independent variables is that of utilitarian versus informational reinforcement.

Utilitarian and informational reinforcement

The type of reinforcement that a consumer situation provides can also be disassembled in the following manner. Overt consumer behavior that is subject to the control of reinforcement may see this effect instantiated through the elicitation of either informational or functional outcomes. Functional or utilitarian reinforcement is experienced by the person as positive feelings such as pleasure and satisfaction achieved through consumption, along with fantasies, happiness, fun, sensory stimulation, arousal, etc. Informational reinforcement exerts its influence by informing individuals about the appropriateness of their choices in attaining both economical reward and rewards derived from social prestige, status and acceptance as cognitively understood by consumers. Thus, behavioral consequences may be bifurcated to include the "outcome of a behavior" and the "consumer's understanding of this" where these are determined by the consumer's learning history. Learning history also determines the relative importance to an individual of either informational or utilitarian reinforcement to a given product or service. Utilitarian–informational reinforcement may therefore be stated as the MS in Figure 22.3.

Foxall claims his model is able to distinguish between different consumer environments and differences between consumers as these differences impact on consumer behavior. Furthermore, he claims the BPM achieves environmental discrimination independently of individual consumers. The BPM differentiates individuals independently of an environment, through: 1) accounting for the relative openness or closed nature of a consumer setting; and 2) the comparative valence of informational or utilitarian reinforcement as derived from learning history. The prediction that arises from the BPM has both immediate consequences in terms of browsing, purchasing, etc. and later consequences such as how the purchases or services are used.

Foxall exclusively combines all possible pairings of setting and reinforcement in a two-by-two table and identifies four operant classes and their consequent forms of consumer behavior. The combinations are as follows: high utilitarian and high informational reinforcement have a consequence of accomplishment; low utilitarian and high informational reinforcement have a consequence of accumulation; low informational and high utilitarian reinforcement have a consequence of hedonism; low informational and low utilitarian reinforcement have a consequence of maintenance. Foxall further develops the ability of the model to account for different types of consumer behavior by associating each operant class type with a specific schedule of reinforcement.

Person (x) experiences the openness of a consumer behavior setting as dependent upon

Fact A:
Availability
a1 many reinforcers
  to   being available to them, where there are
a2 few reinforcers

Facet B:
Obtainable
b1 many ways
  to
b2 few ways

Facet C:
Requisite Tasks
c1 need
of obtaining reinforcers, that   to   certain tasks performed to attain
c2 do not need

Facet D:
Situational Control
d1 great control
reinforcers, in situations where marketers/providers exert   to
d2 little control

Facet E:
Contingency Impact
e1 high impact
over reinforcement, where the contingencies have   to   upon those
e2 low impact

Facet F:
Accessible Alternative
f1 readily accessible
imposing them, in situations with accessible alternatives   to
f2 not readily

Range
regulate
with consequential levels of feedback that allow the person to   to
not regulate

their consumer behavior.

Figure 22.2   Mapping sentence for the BPM construct of openness of a consumer situation

I have briefly described both consumer ethnography and the BPM. In the next section I propose the merger of these and consider the results of such an amalgamation.

Integrating consumer ethnography and the BPM

Qualitative and ethnographic consumer research needs to be undertaken within, and to demonstrate commitment to, clear strictures imposed by a rational understanding of consumer behavior in conjunction with the needs and questions in a specific research project. Ethnographic research

---

Person (x) experiences the consumer behavior setting as providing:

Facet A:		*Facet B:*
Utilitarian		Informational
reinforcement		reinforcement
a1 high		b1 high
to	levels of utilitarian reinforcement, and	to
a2 low		b2 low

Range
high
levels of informational reinforcement, as causing them to feel   to
low

levels of positive affect, emotion or pleasure.

Figure 22.3 Mapping sentence for the BPM construct of utilitarian–informational reinforcement

is firmly rooted within the location and cultural significance of the observations being made. The BPM explicates an unrivaled understanding of consumers within consumption locations by incorporating the consumer setting as one of its two independent variables. For this reason alone the BPM has a design advantage that recommends it for guiding consumer ethnographic studies. Furthermore, the BPM reflects experiential affect as one of the components of its other independent variable of informational–utilitarian reinforcement: thus, the BPM provides an answer to the why questions found in consumer behavior. Ethnography, in particular, and qualitative research in general are especially adapted to yield answers that provide unique insight into human experience and expressions of pleasure and other emotions: Ethnography yields answers to the what, where, when and how questions in consumer behavior. For this reason, too, qualitative approaches to consumer research appear appropriate for use within the rubric of the BPM. Qualitative research is suitable for amalgamation with the BPM as both of its independent variables possess an intimate relationship with qualitative research orientations.

An example of how ethnography may be used in consumer research is that of washing detergent. When attempting to meet the needs of a low-income ethnic community, detergent manufacturers knew that a cleanly dressed family indicated a woman to be a good mother. In an attempt to strengthen appeal to this segment a concentrated detergent was produced that saved room through its smaller packaging. No ethnographic study was conducted and the manufacturer was unaware that the women associated a detergent's foaming when used with its ability to clean clothes well. Consequently, the product failed as the new detergent did not foam when used. If, however, a qualitative or ethnographic approach had been used, unexpected insights may have emerged not evidenced in quantitative research.

Understanding and prediction of consumer behavior is perhaps most acute when individual units of information are linked together in a way that is intelligible as a description of consumer behavior as a whole. Scientists call these linked systems ontologies[8] when they use them to classify natural science phenomena (see, for example, Hill et al., 2008). Heterogeneous data-gathering methods, across or even within studies, often lead to inconsistent or ambiguous results. When multiple research approaches are used or the results from multiple research studies are combined, there may be difficulties in identifying commonalities between data sets that are representative of respondents' behaviors. Furthermore, testing suppositions or building models from results can be similarly problematic. In qualitative research, investigators attempt to over-familiarize themselves with data and to thus draw connections between data. In science a similar problem was solved through the use of computer-based ontologies (Smith, 2013, Smith & Werner, 2010). Smith (2013, p. 102) claims that these ontologies should embody classifications "that are based on the established scientific understanding of the entities and relations in this domain". Within the sorts of ontologies scientists have employed to coordinate research, especially within biology, classifications comprise a specified domain; types of data and classes of entities represented by theoretical terms; and expressions to represent relations between entities. Ontology of this form can allow, according to Smith (2013), consistent depiction of research data and its expression often as a directed acyclic graph. The nodes of such a graphic ontology exemplify types or universals of the entity terms that are of interest. Nodes are connected to linguistically represent the ways in which entities with their respective subtypes are linked.

Biologists (Grenon & Smith, 2004, 2009, Smith & Grenon, 2004, Valore, 2009) use a specific domain-neutral architectural ontology, Basic Formal Ontology (BFO),[9] when they commence research. BFO embodies 34 very general terms and relations, for example process, object, function and other less common terms. The BFO has been extended and refined within several distinct approaches including that by Zemach (1970). Usefully for the current paper, Zemach distinguishes between two entities: events (occurrents) and things (continuants). The former of these entities is characterized by possessing both a spatial and temporal existence, whilst the latter is exclusively temporal. Foxall's BPM proposes a two-by-two categorical ontological square (Figure 22.4) reminiscent both of Aristotle's ontological square and BFO ontology. Foxall's occurrents are the rewards received from a given behavior. The continuants in the BPM are constituted by the location in which a behavior occurs.

In Figure 22.4 the following relationships exist: Instance and Independent Continuant – *instantiate* – Type and Independent Continuant (this consumer behavior is instantiated in consumer behavior); Instance and Independent Continuant – *exemplify* – Type and Dependent Continuant (this consumer behavior is exemplified in purchasing); Instance and Dependent Continuant – *instantiate* – Type and Dependent Continuant (this purchase is instantiated by purchasing); Instance and Dependent Continuant – *depends on* – Instance and Independent Continuant (this purchase depends on this consumer behavior).

Figure 22.5 presents a static depiction of the consumer behavior. However, consumer behavior is a changing process. Therefore, the ontological square needs extension to allow for such change.[10] Consequently, the category of event (change) is incorporated as an occurrent of both type and instance categories, resulting in the BPM ontological sextet (Figure 22.5) where the following relationships pertain: Instance and Independent Continuant – *instantiate* – Type and Independent Continuant (this consumer behavior is instantiated in consumer behavior); Instance and Independent Continuant – *exemplify* – Type and Dependent Continuant (this consumer behavior is exemplified in purchasing); Instance and Dependent Continuant – *instantiate* –

	Independent continuant	Dependent continuant
Type	consumer behavior	purchasing
Instance	this consumer behavior	this purchase

Figure 22.4 BPM in the format of Aristotle's ontological square

	Independent continuant	Dependent continuant	Occurrent
Type	consumer behavior	purchasing	course of purchasing changes
Instance	this consumer behavior	this purchase	changes in the course of this purchase

Figure 22.5 BPM ontological sextet

Type and Dependent Continuant (this purchase is instantiated by purchasing); Instance and Dependent Continuant – *depends on* – Instance and Independent Continuant (this purchase depends on this consumer behavior); Occurrent and Instance – *instantiates* – Occurrent and Type (changes in the course of this purchase depend on the course of purchasing changes); Occurrent and Instance – *depends upon* – Instance and Independent Continuant (changes in the course of this purchase *instantiate* this consumer behavior).

Having defined the ontological model of consumer behavior that the BPM exemplifies, and within which this chapter is written, I now turn to the incorporation with the BPM as a means for gathering consumer ethnography research data. In Figure 22.6, I blend the sextet of consumer behavior understanding present in the BPM with consumer ethnography.

The simple relationships shown in Figure 22.6 demonstrate that consumer behavior in general and the relationships of the BPM exist at the intersection of types, instances, independent continuants, dependent continuants and occurrents, and that these ontological categories are extant within the real-world situations of their occurrence. These relationships make ethnographic approaches to research revelatory *par excellence*, of actual and specific consumer behaviors and behavioral changes. Unique insight is therefore provided when ethnographic approaches are used in tandem with the structure inherent in the BPM. This conjoint usage facilitates knowledge development in a way that does not impose a structure upon data but allows insight to be assembled through a common adaptable framework. I am at present conducting research designed to assess the applied utility of this merger and further research is needed to support or refute these claims.

As with all approaches to research, there are problems and limitations and I now consider some of these before suggesting possible lines of mediation. Companies do not conduct research for academic reasons but to produce concrete findings that translate into commercial recommendations upon which organizational decisions may be based. Ethnographers use multiple approaches with multiple researchers to identify what may trigger or suppress client behavior, resulting in recommendations the company may directly act upon. Consumer ethnography research is therefore able to investigate propositional attitudes and illuminate the truth-values of propositional attitudes towards products and services by making these apparent in relation to in-situ consumer behavior. The challenge in consumer ethnography comes when attempting to use multiple research methods to reveal subtle commercially related meanings: Findings from consumer behavior research must be interpreted and blended with specific products or services along with the needs of the company commissioning the research.

	Independent continuant	Dependent continuant	Occurrent
Type	consumer behavior	purchasing	course of purchasing changes
Instance	ethnography of consumer behavior	ethnography of a purchase	ethnography of changes in the course of this purchase

Figure 22.6 Ethnographic ontological BPM sextet

Within this context there is a potential problem of the observer intruding into and interfering with the ethnography he or she is conducting. The act of being observed distorts behavior from the typical. This is a timeless source of error for all research with human subjects: When observed, subjects behave in ways that create the impression upon the researcher they desire, which may produce atypical behaviors, such as using a product more than they would usually, buying environmentally friendly products, etc. Awareness of being observed may also lead subjects to suppress typical behaviors that respondents do not wish observed, such as drinking excessive amounts of alcohol, driving too fast, etc. In protracted "true" ethnography, participant observation is conducted over a very long time period in the hope that the researcher will become accepted in the community and the effect of the observer's presence will be lessened, resulting in the observation of more realistic behavior. However, within consumer ethnography, such an elongated temporal span is unavailable and compromises must be made between a researcher becoming accepted over a longer time and gaining more valid data and the practical benefits of more speedy data collection which is more error prone. The BPM provides a structure to consumer behavior and that framework may be used to design ethnographic research that clearly addresses consumer behavior as it occurs in daily activity whilst imparting minimal distortion upon the observations made. By providing a common framework for qualitative research, the BPM allows the integration of multiple research approaches to answer the what, when, where and why questions of consumer behavior. The BPM manifests a framework for designing, conducting and interpreting consumer ethnography and also a format for communicating findings to a client.

In ethnographic approaches researchers may observe actual respondent behavior but this form of information tells us little about "why" a consumer committed the behavior observed: motivation and intention cannot be garnered through observation. A person may own a certain make of car because he or she liked the color, the price of the car, fuel economy, green features, the mp3 player, the celebrity in the internet advert for the car, for any combination of these or for other unknown reasons. Observation of car usage will not reveal a distinction between motives or purchase satisfaction levels. Ethnographic consumer research therefore describes culturally related behavior through data that has been collected using multiple methods in an attempt to identify consumer needs and to answer specific commercial questions.[11] It is my contention that the BPM may suitably be used to translate ethnographic findings in a manner that is in dialogue with the research context. When conducting quantitative research it is likely that a hypothesis or hypotheses are stated and investigations conducted within the comparatively rigidly defined setting of an experiment, quasi-experiment, survey, etc. When this is the case, the variables of interest to the researcher are clearly specified and related both to themselves and to an outcome measure or measures through experimental design. Analyses are predominantly statistical in character and are closely related to the design of the research and the hypotheses stated prior to data collection. In qualitative research, including ethnography, the design and investigation of a research question, or series of questions, are formally stated often without formal hypotheses. Frequently, the variables of interest are heavily embedded within the behavioral scenarios of interest. This complexity may make identification of separate variables and their discrete effects both problematic and meaningless. Instead, qualitative data is gathered over protracted periods of time, and is often in, or converted to, textual data, for some form of content analysis. This procedure seeks to establish super-ordinate categories of the data gathered in a manner that allows for the researchers to make rich and insightful comments about the questions that motivated the study. To sum up the potential weaknesses of consumer behavior research, I state that for me, the greatest potential failing of this type of research and its findings is that consumer ethnography is always in danger of producing a fragmented collection of disparate insights that are difficult to bring together to answer either theoretical or applied client questions.

If we accept my descriptions of ethnography and consumer ethnography, and the caveats I have issued about difficulties that may arise when trying to design and integrate multiple ethnographic techniques to answer applied research questions, it becomes apparent that consumer ethnography needs a theoretical framework within which research questions and findings may be assembled to reveal the unique and deep insights available. The criteria for selecting or devising a framework for consumer ethnographic research are as follows: 1) that the framework must form a generic template for the concept under investigation (allowing comparison between products within a product class and differently situated studies of the same product); 2) the framework is flexible enough to encompass and explicate a specific research area of interest (allowing a specific product in a specific situation to be clearly understood); 3) the possibility must exist to use the framework with multiple qualitative research approaches; 4) the framework must not impose unrealistic behaviors upon participants; and 5) the framework must not impose an unrealistic set of expectations upon those interpreting the data. The BPM has the potential to provide a structured framework for consumer ethnography and for theoretical perspectives of consumer behavior as the model meets these five criteria.

Notes

1 Consumer ethnography has the potential to avoid consumers' post-purchase rationalization to which many other methods fall. Later I will use the theoretical structure provided by the MS to provide a mereological account for the BPM related to ethnographic consumer research.

2 In addition to being able to supply and comprehend consumer-related verbs, nouns and adjectives, we typically have little difficulty in acting appropriately within retail, wholesale and service contexts without the aid of theoretical or academic input.

3 Semantic categories often emerge from these analyses. Anthropologists investigate ways in which we categorize our experiences. They employ different models to indicate what is worthy of classification within their research (Boster, 2005).

4 The observed behaviors are often most usefully interpreted as symbolic activities.

5 Consumer ethnography is not of a format that is strictly comparable with the academic study of a culture or society made at multiple locations within that community.

6 Autoethnography is a data-gathering technique and research findings presentation format in which the individual gathering data blends the approaches of writing a biographical account of a situation with the dispassionately rigorous outlook of an ethnographer. This results in an idiographic ethnographic consideration of a product or service. Insights from this research are likely to be focused upon the research questions but also form a potentially representative outlook that is not typical of consumers.

7 Over the last two decades a large amount of commercial activity that was until that time located in the high street has moved online. Consumers now interact online as consumer groups in relation to specific goods, services, companies, etc. Such interactions may be enthusiastic about the product and how this is used within a consumer's life, or the group discussions may be more critical of a product or service. A branch of consumer ethnography called *netnography* has been developed in which the researcher attempts to become a part of, and to gain understanding of, this online consumer culture through immersion within online consumer groups.

8 For philosophers, ontologies are the fundamental parts that compose our existence. Ontologies are typically sets of linguistic terms.

9 "BFO is an upper-level ontology framework encapsulating best practices in the development of ontologies to serve scientific research" (Ceusters & Smith, 2010). Barry Smith and colleagues, who formulated the formal ontological framework of BFO, comprising a series of different levels of sub-ontologies where each level forms a temporally determined exclusive inventory of entities, developed BFO out of a philosophical orientation. BFO addresses static/spatial and dynamic/temporal features of reality.

10 Theoretically, Odeberg suggests the incorporation of change.

11 The sample of respondents observed must be selected so they are able to provide the information needed through observations, diary-keeping, interviews, etc.

References

Aristotle (2014). *The Categories* (translated by E. M. Edgehill), Seattle, WA: CreateSpace Independent Publishers.

Belk, R (2012). *Qualitative Consumer and Marketing Research*, Thousand Oaks, CA: Sage Publications.

Boster, J. S. (2005). Categories and cognitive anthropology. In Cohen, H. and Lefebvre, C. (eds) *Handbook of Categorization on Cognitive Science* (pp. 91–118), Amsterdam: Elsevier.

Calosi, C. and Graziana, P. (eds) (2014). *Mereology and the Sciences: Parts and Wholes in the Contemporary Scientific Context*, New York: Springer.

Ceusters, W. and Smith, B. (2010). Foundations for a realist ontology of mental disease, *Journal of Biomedical Semantics*, 1:10 doi: 10.1186/2041-1480-1-10.

Chin, E. (2007). Consumer diaries or autoethnography in the inverted world, *Journal of Consumer Culture*, 7, 335–353.

Effingham, N. (2013). *An Introduction to Ontology*, Oxford: Polity.

Foxall, G. R. (2010). *Interpreting Consumer Choice: The Behavioral Perspective Model*, New York: Routledge.

Grenon, P. and Smith, B. (2004). SNAP and SPAN: towards dynamic spatial ontology, *Spatial Cognition and Computation*, 4, 69–103.

Grenon, P. and Smith, B. (2009). Foundations of an ontology of philosophy, *Synthese*, 182, 185.

Haaparanta, L. and Koskinen, H. J. (eds) (2012). *Categories of Being: Essays on Metaphysics and Logic*, Oxford: Oxford University Press.

Hackett, P. M. W. (2014). *Facet Theory and the Mapping Sentence: Evolution of Philosophy, Applications and Uses*, London: Palgrave.

Hackett, P. M. W. (2015a). *Qualitative Research Methods in Consumer Psychology: Ethnography and Culture*, London: Routledge.

Hackett, P. M. W. (ed.) (2015b). What is consumer ethnography: the big 'E' and little 'e' in consumer research? In Hackett, P. M. W. (ed.) *Qualitative Research Methods in Consumer Psychology: Ethnography and Culture*, London: Routledge.

Hill, D. P., Smith, B., McAndrews-Hill, M. S. and Blake, J. A. (2008). Gene ontology annotations: what they mean and where they come from, *BMC Bioinformatics*, 9 (suppl 5), S2. doi: 10.1186/1471-2105-9-S5-S2.

Hsu, G., Koak, Z. and Negro, G. (eds) (2013). *Categories in Markets: Origins and Evolution (Research in the Sociology of Organizations)*, Bradford: Emerald Group Publishing.

Khalidi, M. A. (2013). *Natural Categories and Human Kinds: Classification in the Natural and Social Sciences*, Cambridge: Cambridge University Press.

Kozinets, R. (2009). *Netnography: Doing Ethnographic Research Online*, Thousand Oaks, CA: Sage Publications.

Lowe, E. J. (2007). *The Four-Category Ontology: A Metaphysical Foundation for Natural Science*, Oxford: Oxford University Press.

Muncey, T. (2010). *Creating Autoethnographies*, Thousand Oaks, CA: Sage Publications.

Oderberg, D. S. (ed.) (2013). *Classifying Reality*, Oxford: Blackwell.

Poli, R. and Seibt, J. (eds) (2010). *Theory and Applications of Ontology: Philosophical Perspectives*, New York: Springer.

Simons, P. M. (1987). *Parts: A Study in Ontology*, Oxford: Oxford University Press.

Smith, B. (2013) Classifying processes: an essay in applied ontology. In Oderberg, D. S. (ed.) *Classifying Reality* (pp. 101–126), Oxford: Blackwell.

Smith, B. and Grenon, P. (2004). The cornucopia of formal-ontological relations, *Dialectica*, 58, 279–296.

Smith, B. and Werner, C. (2010). Ontological realism as a methodology for coordinated evolution of scientific ontologies, *Applied Ontology*, 5, 139–188.

Southerton, D. (ed.) (2011). *Encyclopedia of Consumer Culture*, Thousand Oaks, CA: Sage Publications.

Valore, P. (2009). *Topics on General and Formal Ontology*, Monza, Italy: Polimetrica, International Scientific Publisher.

Zemach, E. (1970). Four ontologies, *Journal of Philosophy*, 23, 231–247.

23

Collective intentionality and symbolic reinforcement

An investigation of Thai car-consumer clubs

Sumana Laparojkit and Gordon R. Foxall

Introduction

In this chapter, we make a case for how *collective intentionality*, which provides an ontological basis of human institutional society, should be assimilated into consumer research. There are growing numbers of brand communities in the virtual world, whose members appear to believe in their objective existence, and engage with those communities as if they were real, even though they have no actual presence in the physical world. Understanding better the underlying reasons for the behavior of club members in their brand communities is fascinating in itself as well as a necessary component of economic psychology.

The meanings and value of symbolic reinforcement (Foxall, 2013) rely considerably on collective intentionality among members of brand communities, enabling them to act together to recognize and assign status functions to the tangible and intangible objects and people who comprise their virtual surroundings. Many aspects of online brand communities are linguistically created and sustained, and provide symbolic reinforcers which shape and maintain their members' behavior. In this process, symbolic stimuli increase the value of reinforcement, acting as motivating operations within the consumer behavior setting, influencing consumer behavior through the learning histories in which they have participated as reinforcers. The behavior controlled by these antecedent verbal stimuli is rule-governed behavior. As a result, the system of symbols which takes control of consumer behavior is based on the collective intentionality that plays a significant role in societal development.

This chapter examines the integration of an intentional dimension into consumer behavior analysis by implementing the theory of collective intentionality to portray the case of the brand communities in Thailand. It also testifies to the usefulness of incorporating collective intentionality and symbolic reinforcement into the Behavioral Perspective Model (BPM). The chapter starts by reviewing the four constructs that are central to this endeavor: symbolic reinforcement, collective intentionality, rule-governed behavior and brand community. We will examine the case of car-consumer clubs in Thailand and explore the collective intentionality of members of the clubs. We then demonstrate how the account of collective intentionality could perform in consumer behavior and function in the brand community by applying the "counts as" formula. After connecting the particulars of consumer behavior in the brand communities to collective intentionality, we will examine the relationship of collective intentionality and symbolic reinforcement or rewards. The rationale for the rewards will be provided to complete the understanding of consumer behavior in the brand community.

Car-consumer clubs in Thailand typically formed as virtual communities, whose members come together via the Internet. The "web-board" is a communication center of the club in the virtual world where consumers can participate in the club's web-board at any time and from any place, at their convenience. However, the participants have to become members before they can interact with other members on the club's web-board. When the car-consumer clubs have become established in the virtual world for some time, there is a tendency for the members to extend their relationship into a real-life context. They begin to meet in the physical world via club activities (e.g. car meetings and social activities), which allow face-to-face contact. Such offline club activities can strengthen the intimacy of their relationships. These virtual consumer communities correspond to the notion of brand community in that the community is built around the consumption of a product or brand on a non-geographical boundary basis (Muniz & O'Guinn, 2001; O'Guinn & Muniz, 2005).

It is especially pertinent to study Thai car-consumer clubs in the context of brand communities in view of the criteria for brand community traits found in the literature (Muniz & O'Guinn, 2001; O'Guinn & Muniz, 2005). For example, the shared consciousness of "kind" is seen from the members' online interaction, such as comments and suggestions. Moreover, the clubs warmly encourage new members by stating "You are welcome to join us" on their website, thereby promoting inclusive "we-ness" feelings. The clubs also organize regular offline activities, prominent in the photographs posted on the website, representing their rituals and traditions. Furthermore, the clubs and their members also assume moral obligations to help one another, which is apparent from their responses to questions about car issues posted on the web-boards by other members. Therefore, the car-consumer clubs in Thailand are an example of brand communities which may illustrate how collective intentionality relates to symbolic reinforcement in the brand community.

The Behavioral Perspective Model

The Behavioral Perspective Model (BPM) is based on the three-term contingency approach. At the heart of the model lies the concept of a consumer situation that locates consumer behavior at the intersection of a consumer behavior setting and the consumer's learning history (Foxall, 1994; Foxall et al., 2006). The model also concentrates on the function of utilitarian (i.e. functional benefits of consumption that are mediated by the used-value of product) and informational consequences (i.e. symbolic benefits that are mediated by other persons) which have an impact on the consumer's learning history, thus creating a new consumer situation (Foxall et al., 2006; Foxall et al., 2011; Wells et al., 2011).

According to the BPM, discriminative stimuli that compose the behavior setting are antecedent stimuli which signal three kinds of consequence: utilitarian reinforcement, informational reinforcement, and aversive outcomes (leading, if they are accepted rather than avoided, to punishment) (Foxall, 1992, 1997a). However, this chapter will focus on the role of reward, which has an effect on members' continuing their membership and participation in the car-consumer clubs. Thus, the effect of punishment which terminates the membership status is excluded from the unit of analysis of this study. *Utilitarian reinforcement* refers to functional benefits which consumers derive from the functional outcomes of ownership and consumption (Foxall, 2010a). These functional benefits derive from intrinsic properties of the products and service; consequently, utilitarian reinforcement is mediated by the product or service from their use-value (Foxall, 1997a). Therefore, utilitarian reinforcement in this study describes the functional benefits which members will receive from their participation and that motivate them to maintain their participation in the brand community. We shall use the terms utilitarian reinforcement and functional reinforcement interchangeably from now on.

Informational reinforcement inheres in the social rewards an individual's performance receives, including social status, social esteem, prestige and acceptance (Foxall, 1997a). In terms of the BPM, it is not related to the usual definition of the word "information," but, following Wearden (1988), refers to the social significance of behavior and relies on the appraisal of one's behavior by one's community (Foxall, 2010b). Although, strictly speaking, it is a source of reinforcement that derives from social interaction, it may also be conferred by a consumer on him- or herself, as in self-esteem. Although there are individual differences in self-esteem, which may stem in part from personal and constitutional propensities to value oneself to a lower or higher degree, there may well usually be a social component to such valuation (Foxall, 2005). Informational reinforcement is, therefore, regarded as being mediated by socially inspired reactions rather than by the commodity itself. As discussed in Chapter 1 of this text, the inference of informational reinforcement shares with that of symbolic reinforcement a common ontology: the behaviors of both the consumer and his/her social community are identical, but while informational reinforcement belongs conceptually to the extensional model, BPM-E, symbolic reinforcement is a component of the intentional model, BPM-I. In this study, we are concerned with the interpretation of car-owner club members' behavior in terms of the symbolic benefits which members receive from their participation and that motivate them to maintain their participation in the brand community.

Both utilitarian/functional and symbolic reinforcement are independent variables in the BPM, which interact to form a pattern of reinforcement which strengthens consumer behavior, and most economic goods and services have both utilitarian and informational/symbolic effects (Foxall, 1997a, 2010b). Consequently, the interpretation of the meaning of reinforcers is dependent upon the situation under investigation (Foxall, 1997b). Furthermore, Foxall (1997b) suggests that the expressions of *pleasure* (denoting usefulness for biological fitness and/or survival) identify utilitarian (functional) reinforcement, whereas considerations of *arousal* identify informational (symbolic) reinforcement. Accordingly, the interpretation in this study considers functional and symbolic reinforcement from the context of an investigation based on interviews by looking for the pleasurable/usefulness and social/personal functions of reinforcers when identifying functional and symbolic reinforcers, respectively.

Brand communities

A brand community is defined as "a specialised, non-geographically bounded community, based on a structured set of social relationships among admirers of a brand" (Muniz & O'Guinn, 2001, p. 412). Three underlying markers characterize the brand community: consciousness of kind, rituals and traditions, and shared sense of moral responsibility (or sense of duty or reciprocity) (Muniz & O'Guinn, 2001; Cova & Cova, 2001; Quester & Fleck, 2010). Most research in this area interprets the brand community phenomenon in relation to social theories and cognitive approaches, such as the Theory of Reasoned Action (Mzoughi et al., 2010) and the Theory of Planned Behavior (Dholakia et al., 2004; Bagozzi & Dholakia, 2006). Little research on the topic of brand community has addressed the influence of environment consequences on consumer behavior in the community, particularly the rewards or benefits offered by the community and their effect on members' participation in the brand community. Therefore, we adopt the BPM to portray consumer behavior in this study.

Collective intentionality

The idea of collective intentionality, which has been used in the pursuit of understanding human society in contemporary philosophy, describes both cooperative behavior(s) and intentional states and intentions that are shared within groups (Searle, 1995). The account of collective intentionality by Searle seems the most appropriate to be integrated in the BPM, particularly regarding symbolic reinforcement, which consists of a system of symbols. This is because the system of symbols is in accordance with the ontological view of social reality as given by Searle (1995) in the philosophical sense. According to Searle, social reality is composed of two kinds of facts: brute facts and institutional facts. Brute facts are facts that already have an objective existence (such as the moon or a flower) while institutional facts refer to those facts which are created by and dependent on human social institutions for their existence. Examples of institutional facts include culture, class, money and government, all of which require language to portray their existence (Searle, 1995). In other words, institutional facts are generated by language. It is apparent that the view of institutional facts as given by Searle (1995) is in accord with the work of Foxall (2010b) in terms of the role of language in creating symbols which can reinforce one's behavior by the meaning attached to these symbols.

Furthermore, Searle (1995) notes those institutional facts which involve collective intentionality of two or more agents. According to Searle, three key elements lie in the structure of institutional facts, which are the assignment of function, constitutive rules and collective intentionality (Fitzpatrick, 2003). The assignment of function is in relation to status function. Status functions are created by humans and are a distinguishing mark to differentiate institution facts from social facts (Searle, 1995). People and objects can be assigned a status function by virtue of collective assignment by humans. In simplistic terms, people are able to impose function on material things (such as designating a piece of paper as money for transactions) and persons (such as designating a person to act as the leader of a society). It can be summarized that the collective assignment of function is involved with assigning a specified/agreed status to things and people, which Searle terms as "status functions" (Searle, 1995, 2010).

Searle (2010) remarks that persons and objects which have been assigned status functions will be able to perform certain functions on the condition that they have a collectively recognized or accepted status that allows them to perform those functions. To put it simply, for the status functions to work properly, they require a collective recognition or acceptance that the object or person has that status. Consequently, status functions are dependent on the collective intentionality of human institutions, which leads to shared desires, shared beliefs and shared attitudes as well as cooperative actions, and these make humans a distinct creature from other animal species (Searle, 1995, 2010). Another important aspect of status functions is that they carry "deontic powers" (Searle, 2010). Searle (2010: p. 9) states that "the deontic powers carry rights, duties, obligations, requirements, permissions, authorizations, entitlements, and so on." The status functions are considered to be the glue that holds society together because of the collective intentionality that created them and the deontic powers that carry their functions (Searle, 2010).

The meanings of such institutions are facts derived from constitutive rules. A constitutive rule is a logical form of the imposition of status functions (Searle, 2005). It is important to note that constitutive rules are different from general terms of rules, which often refer to an antecedent of behavior but which can also produce new forms of behavior. Searle (1995) distinguishes two kinds of rules: regulative rules and constitutive rules. Regulative rules are those rules that regulate existing forms of behavior which are antecedents of behavior. For instance, the rule "drive on the left" regulates driving in Thailand. Consequently, these regulative rules can be characterized in the form "do X" (Searle, 2010: p. 10). Constitutive rules have a more signifi-cant implication because they not only regulate behavior but also create the possibility of new forms of behavior that they also regulate (Searle, 2010). For example, the rules of a club not only regulate the actions needed to gain membership of the club but also regulate the necessity of other behaviors in conformity to other rules which constitute conditions for being in the club.

Constitutive rules are characterized by the formula "X counts as Y in context C" (Searle, 1995, p. 28). This formula is a basic representation of social interaction which creates the pos-sibility of institutional facts (Searle, 1995). It is a logical representation of the imposition of status functions (Searle, 2005). For instance, a piece of paper issued by the government in a specific form counts as a fifty-pound note in the United Kingdom because it has been given status functions. However, for the status functions to perform, they require collective recogni-tion and acceptance of that status. The example of the fifty-pound note also requires collective acceptance from people in the country for it to have the power of purchase. Moreover, the status functions are created by declarations where language is an essential tool to portray them. This happens because the human mind has the capacity to create symbolic representations, but it needs to convey meaning by language since otherwise there is a tendency to overlook the intentional states (Searle, 2010). Consequently, institutional facts only exist within human insti-tutions because of collective intentionality. Therefore, the collective assignment of functions to people and objects by the formula "X counts as Y in context C" is an essential application of collective intentionality which will be employed in the discussion to inform the phenomenon in car-consumer clubs in Thailand.

Research methodology

The lack of research and prior knowledge about car-consumer clubs in Thailand has led research-ers to adopt a qualitative approach because it is a suitable method to employ in a study where the researcher has little idea about the field (Creswell, 2003). The flexible style of a qualitative approach allows researchers to generate data and the meaning of phenomena (Carson et al., 2001). The nature of the research points toward a qualitative research technique which would allow the researchers to obtain rich, insightful and comprehensive data from the fieldwork.

The case study method is employed as a means of comprehending a particular setting where the focus is on a contemporary phenomenon within some real-life context (Schwandt, 2001; Yin, 2003). The cases were carefully selected on the basis of the following criteria. The first criterion, drawn from the literature, reflects the brand community traits specified by Muniz & O'Guinn (2001), which were adumbrated in the Introduction. The second criterion is directly concerned with the stability and reputation of the community in Thai society. Hence, the chosen communities should have been operating for at least three years and have at least 5,000 members (based on their website statistics). The final criterion is related to the accessibility of data. It must be possible to access the club leaders with the highest levels of administrative authority in the club to learn how the club had become established in Thai society. Seven car-clubs met all three criteria and served as case studies, a number deemed sufficient for the analysis on the basis of Yin's (2003) argument that between six and 10 case studies are generally consid-ered to provide effective results. The unit of analysis is current members of car-consumer clubs in Thailand and the sample of respondents from the seven clubs studied was 45.

Data collection initially involved interviews with those respondents' authority in the club, a leader who might be the webmaster, the administrator or the president depending on the structure of each club. Accordingly, purposive sampling was employed by selecting the respondents who, according to the researchers' judgment of appropriateness (David & Sutton, 2004), could answer the research questions (Marshall, 1996) and provide overall information about car-consumer clubs. Semi-structured interviews were conducted because of the flexibility they offer (Bryman, 2001; Al Qur'an, 2010), and the interview questions were developed from the literature (McCracken, 1988). Ten of the respondents were club leaders and each interview lasted for between 60 and 90 minutes.

The initial interviews with the club leaders provided several advantages for the subsequent interviews. First, connections, rapport and access were established between researchers and respondents. Second, the results showed that there are three categories of membership: Club Leader, Active Member and Non-active Member. Third, the semi-structured interview technique was confirmed as an appropriate method and the interview questions were refined for the next stage. Fourth, the feasibility of further investigation was established. Fifth, access was granted by club leaders or key members who could act as gatekeepers for the entrance to the research setting (Silverman, 2005).

The next step of the interview stage was targeted at current club members by employing a snowball sampling technique through personal connections. The initial stage of interviews indicated that this is a useful method of recruiting members to the research. As mentioned, the initial findings revealed the existence of both active and non-active members in the clubs, which rendered difficult the identification of engaged members. As a result, the Sense of Community Index (SCI) (Chavis et al., 1986) was administered to assess the cohesiveness of the club for members by suggesting their level of activity in club affairs. Thirty-two active and three non-active members among the respondents were identified in this way. The interviews lasted for between 30 and 60 minutes.

All of the respondents were contacted in advance and informed of the purpose of the research. Prior to each interview, the respondents were asked for their consent to recordings, photographs and notes being taken (depending upon their choice and comfort). The data are protected by an undertaking of anonymity. After each interview, the written notes and audio recordings were transcribed verbatim while the interview was still fresh in the researcher's mind (Grant, 2000). The interview and transcriptions were made in the Thai language to preserve the original context and the accuracy of the respondents' meanings and expressions. A back translation method was employed to reduce errors and improve the quality of translation. In practice, the data were translated from Thai to English by the researcher (who is a Thai native speaker). The translated data were checked by local translators (who were knowledgeable in English and have experience in research). Then the translated data were approved and verified by two native English speakers. The interviews were carried out until the data were saturated, which means that there was no further contribution to the analysis (Mason, 2010). When a stage was reached where new data appeared similar to that already gathered, showing no further ideas and components, this was taken as a signal to stop collecting data.

In the analysis of data, coding is vital to the meaningful analysis of the data and to the review of interview transcripts (Miles & Huberman, 1994). The theme and codes were drawn from the literature and checked by the researchers' team. They were predefined as start lists in the analysis. Nevertheless, the codes could be modified depending upon the circumstances to allow the data to express the real substance of the interviews in their context. These codes were modified from the interviews and then sent back to the respondents for them to confirm their agreement. Data from multiple sources of evidence such as the interview, the score on the SCI, photographs and the club's website were triangulated to increase the validity and minimize the chance of bias in the findings (Bryman, 2001; Rowley, 2002; Punch, 2005). Pattern matching techniques were implemented by which patterns of consumer behavior were drawn from the literature and pre-established to compare with the actual data. As Yin (1994) suggests, theories provide the predicted patterns of events in the early stage of the research which are then compared with the empirical data to determine whether they match the predicted patterns to predict the case study situation (Cao, 2007).

Each case was analyzed independently with the same set of propositions or within-case analysis (Yin, 2003). The results of each case were compared with the pattern of consumer behavior. As a consequence, all of the cases were compared for similarities or dissimilarities in a cross-case analysis. The cross-case analysis was implemented to enhance the insights into each individual case (Yin, 2009). Each case was analyzed individually prior to being combined into the overall framework. A respondent validation, in which the analyzed and reported data were reviewed by the respondents to refine the results (Silverman, 2001), was applied to increase the reliability and accuracy of the research.

Findings

Evidence of functional reinforcement

In the analysis of functional reinforcement, it is related to the functional benefits which the respondents received and which they mentioned in the interview. The examination of all case studies shows that the functional reinforcement found in the cases is composed of: car-knowledge, friends, cost savings and earnings from the club and business opportunities. (Note that friends can be categorized as sources of either functional or symbolic reinforcement depending on the context of friendship and closeness; careful interpretation of individual responses is therefore required.)

Car-knowledge in this study refers to a collection of related information and knowledge about the car in question. The accumulated information will eventually come to the attention of the members. This meaning covers all of the car-related news, details, information and knowledge to which the respondents referred, for instance:

> It is good. I like the club because it helps owners gain additional car-knowledge and save money.
>
> *(Non-Active Member)*

Cost-saving is considered a reward because club members can save money on their cars. Since a high maintenance cost is incurred when they purchase cars, they participate in the car-consumer clubs to reduce costs:

> I obtain data regarding the engine, wheels, stereo, and mileage checks because the Mercedes car engine is well-designed and complicated. Some accessories such as batteries can be found in general suppliers more cheaply than in the service center. The price is much lower. If you go to the car service center, you will have to pay a lot more.
>
> *(Active Member)*

Similarly, earnings from the club are among the rewards reported by the club leaders and the active members in all seven case studies. Because all of the clubs have created space on their web-board for commercial activity, members are not only able to buy the products but also sell their products to other members within the club. In the interviews, several of the active-member respondents who own a car-related business have reported that they are able to take advantage of the club to expand their business via a new sales channel which targets a very specific "right group" of customers. For example:

> I have obtained more information about the car. Besides, I have an opportunity to sell my products such as car spare parts to appropriate customers.
>
> *(Active Member)*

Business opportunities are the next noticeable benefit. Since the clubs provide opportunities for members to buy and sell products through the club, some members find that this is an opportunity to start running their own business in the club. Furthermore, it is likely that club members tend to support other members' businesses (such as shops, restaurants and non-car-related products), as in the following examples:

> First is friendship. Second is information which cannot be found in other places. . . . Finally is business. Based on familiarity, they trust me and use my company's service.
>
> *(Active Member)*

> Apparently, it is a business opportunity. If you sell clothes and want to sell in the club, members will buy your clothes before those from other shops. This is because people will buy a friend's products first.
>
> *(Club Leader)*

Friends can be categorized in terms of functional reinforcement when respondents declare that they only communicate with friends who drive the same car models and who can help them solve their car problems but who are not connected to their personal life, as in the following example:

> When I have any car problem, they will provide good support and answer my question in the web-board but I do not hang out with them.
>
> *(Non-Active Member)*

Effect of functional reinforcement

Analysis of the seven case studies reveals that the frequency of respondents' participation in the web-board is a response to the rewards, mainly functional reinforcement. The nature of the respondents' web-board participation is summarized in Figure 23.1. The bar chart compares the frequency of web-board participation by the different groups of members. As can be seen from the chart, all of the club leader respondents (n = 10) and most of the active member respondents (n = 26) visit the web-board daily. Three active member respondents visit the web-board twice a week, and three active member respondents visit the web-board once a week. It can be noted that all of the non-active member respondents visit the web-board only once a month. The frequency of their web-board participation shows that they are relatively reinforced particularly by the functional reinforcement. They still keep their membership status and visit the web-board, albeit at a low level, but they do not contribute as much to the clubs as the other types of membership respondents. In summary, it is clear that the frequency of web-board participation by the three types of member is particularly influenced/mediated by functional reinforcement.

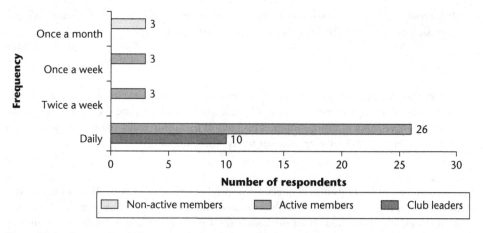

Figure 23.1 Respondents' frequency of web-board participation

Evidence of symbolic reinforcement

Symbolic reinforcement is evident from the feedback on one's performance and, consequently, it is usually mediated by society or other people (Foxall, 1997a, 2004, 2010a). In this study all the results indicate that symbolic reinforcement is composed of social recognition, social connection and mutual assistance. Surprisingly, however, there was no sign that symbolic reinforcement affected the behavior of the non-active members; in fact, they barely mentioned it, in sharp contrast to the responses of active members.

Social recognition derives from an individual's position in the club (positions in the club can include webmaster, consultants and senior members). These positions are established by members of the clubs in association with the club structure. Consequently, a member is accepted or respected by other members, or not, depending on their performance. The more a person contributes to the club, the more other members will respect that person; for example, in the interviews some of the club leader respondents said that:

> I have earned social respect from members because I have some knowledge about car engines. At that point, I have earned social recognition from members. When members have a problem, they will call me.
>
> *(Club Leader)*

> Ninety percent of members in the club have heard about me even though they never meet me in person.
>
> *(Club Leader)*

Friends or friendships in terms of symbolic reinforcement refer to friends or friendships that extend to personal life outside the club. In general, friendships formed while members were participating in the clubs are mainly based on cars; however, relationships in the club can further develop when they extend to their personal life and when they participate in club activities. As a consequence, they count each other as family members, demonstrating their friendship and cohesiveness, as in the examples that follow:

> It is about more than friends. It is about more than cars. We gain a whole family. We can approach everyone as a brother. We count each other as family.
>
> *(Active Member)*

> I have friends who can listen to me in everything. I can trust them. It seems that I trust them more than my old friends whom I have known for a long time. When I have a problem, they give me a perfect solution. This kind of friendship really exists. People may not believe. Hmm . . . I do not know what to say. It is fantastic.
>
> *(Active Member)*

A connection could be a business connection, a social connection or both. Both kinds of connections share common ground where they originate from friends/friendship in the club. Most of the respondents who talked about the connections repeatedly mentioned friends/friendship immediately before they mentioned the importance of connections during the interviews. The interview data empirically show that there is a relationship between the friends/friendship and connections, where the connections are a subsequent reward which results from friends/friendship; for example:

> I receive friendship and enjoyment. I have gained more social and business connections. We have made contact with other car-consumer clubs and other organizations. For example, our business partners who wish to participate in our club activities.
>
> *(Club Leader)*

Assistance is another reward arising from friends or friendships in the clubs, which is found in every single case. There were several interviews where respondents mentioned friends or friendships and their assistance beyond car-related issues. The empirical findings show that only two types of membership respondents (i.e. the club leaders and the active members) mentioned these rewards, and they are not mentioned by the non-active member respondents. The data suggest that this kind of reward derives from friends or friendship. When close friendships have developed, members tend to expand their interaction to topics beyond cars, as can be seen in the following examples:

> Assistance is always available here. We also have overseas members. It is a precious gift which is invaluable. We can get access to global assistance. Some members are located upcountry. When there is a car which is damaged, there will be members ready to help one another.
>
> *(Active Member)*

> We are close to each other. We help each other and extend our scope to personal matters and social affairs.
>
> *(Active Member)*

Effect of symbolic reinforcement

Analysis of the seven case studies reveals that most of the respondents assert the importance of the club activities which provide them with an opportunity to meet one another in person and to establish a relationship in the physical world. It is crucial to note that participating in activities is optional. The results from the seven case studies support the view that most of the respondents are willing volunteers who participate in the club activities whenever their time permits.

The frequency of participation in club activities by the respondents in the different types of membership is summarized in Figure 23.2. According to the interviews, all of the club leader respondents reported that they often participate in club meetings because they are in charge of the main club events and are willing to organize and participate in such activities. The results also show that all of the active member respondents frequently participate in the club activities. Most respondents reveal that they try to join in club activities as often as they can when they have free time. The results of the group of non-active member respondents show that they rarely, if ever, participate in the club activities. This result is valid if they characterize the rewards as functional rather than symbolic reinforcement. Therefore, they are not keen on the club activities, as shown by their behavior. The evidence clearly shows that symbolic reinforcement has an impact on the members' frequency of behavior, especially in club activities participation. In conclusion, it can be seen that the majority of the respondents in the case studies participate in club activities, and this recurring behavior is a result of symbolic reinforcement.

Characteristics of members of Thai car-consumer clubs

The findings from the cases are in line with the literature (e.g. Foxall, 1994; Foxall, 1997b; Foxall et al., 1998; Foxall, 2001; Foxall and Yani-de-Soriano, 2005; Foxall, 2010a; Wells et al., 2011) which shows that two types of reinforcement have an impact on behavior: the first is functional reinforcement (which is also known as utilitarian reinforcement), and the second is symbolic reinforcement. The rewards given by Thai car-consumer clubs appear to be both functional and symbolic reinforcement, which has an impact on the frequency of behaviors. The effects of both types of reinforcement strengthen one another. As illustrated in the case studies, the respondents have maintained or increased the frequency of participation in the web-board and club activities. On the basis of their participation and the types of rewards, the characteristics of members in the car-consumer clubs (see Table 23.1) can be divided into five main groups as follows:

The first is the *touch-and-go group*. This describes those members who seek information regarding the car they already have or which they are considering purchasing. They participate in the club only to gain car-knowledge and do not interact with other members or participate

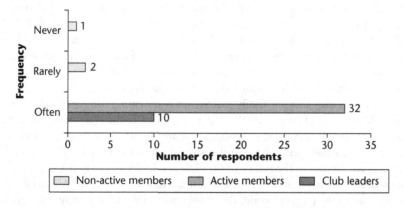

Figure 23.2 Respondents' frequency of participation in club activities

in club activities. The non-active members can be equated with the touch-and-go consumer. The recurring behavior of this type of consumer is mainly a result of functional reinforcement.

The second group is the *traders*. This describes those members who have participated in the club for business purposes. They may or may not participate in club activities. Their membership status is rather unpredictable and it varies depending upon their association with the club and other members. Consequently, they can be either potential active members or turn out to be non-active members. Similarly to that of the touch-and-go member, the recurring behavior of this type of consumer is also predominantly a result of functional reinforcement.

The third group is the *social networkers*. This describes those members who maintain their status owing to their relationship with other members. They habitually log in to the club web-board and keep up to date on information in the club. They are active members who often participate in the web-board and club activities. The recurring behavior of this type of consumer is mainly a result of symbolic reinforcement.

The fourth group is the *car-lovers*. This describes those members who maintain their status in the club because of car-knowledge. These people are in love with cars and car modifications. They are generally keen on discussion with club friends who have similar interests and also regularly participate in club activities. They are active members who often participate in both the web-board and offline activities. The recurring behavior of this type of consumer is a result of both symbolic and functional reinforcement.

The fifth and final group is the *club leaders*. This describes those members who have authority in club administration. They are persons who are at the core of the club, who take charge of club administration and who are responsible for the club's policy. The recurring behavior of this type of consumer is a result of both functional and symbolic reinforcement.

Discussion

Members' shared beliefs, desires and attitudes, and cooperative behaviors

The following interpretation is not intended to suggest that there is necessarily a sequential development from beliefs and desires to attitudes and behaviors in each and every car club member. It is not necessary for individuals to have shared beliefs, desires and attitudes in that order, or even to have all of them simultaneously. Nevertheless, it seems likely that each member will have at least one of these characteristics, since there is otherwise no reason for them to participate in the clubs' activities.

When individuals have shared beliefs, desires and attitudes, these can be expected to bring about cooperative behaviors, representing collective intentionality (Searle, 1995; Foxall, 2010b, 2013). The evidence can be observed from members' participation in club activities and their attaching of the club logo to their cars. With the cooperative behaviors of members, the car-consumer clubs achieve a status in society that sustains the club's existence in both the virtual and physical world.

Shared beliefs. Shared beliefs enhance the we-ness feelings among members of the clubs because they believe that they are family and friends representing the consciousness of kind, as indicated by Muniz and O'Guinn (2001). Moreover, status in the clubs, particularly membership status, relies considerably upon the members' shared beliefs. The status "membership" will be meaningful when members believe in the actual existences of their club. It is essential for members to share a belief in the reality of the club and its membership because car-consumer clubs are institution facts where members assign status functions to them. Although these clubs have no presence in the physical world, the members can still feel a sense of belonging and act as if the clubs are physically located in society. This happens because their shared belief in the

Table 23.1 Members' characteristics and types of reinforcement

Member characteristics	Reasons to continue membership status	Duration in the club	Member type	Type(s) of reinforcement
Touch-and-go	• To search for car-knowledge with regard to their cars. • To find information before purchasing a new car.	Short visit but likely to return when needed.	Non-active member	Functional
Traders	• To trade their products. • To promote their products in the clubs. • To find business partners.	Can be either a short visit or a long-term involvement in the club, depending on their rewards from the club.	Can be either non-active or active member	Functional
Social networker	• To meet friends who drive the same car brand and/or model. • To have a new social group of people who have like-minded tastes and lifestyle. • To interact with friends in the club via the club web-board and offline activities.	Most likely long stay in the club.	Active member	Symbolic
Car lover	• To discuss and exchange car-knowledge. • To interact with people who are in love with their cars. • To engage in activities in relation to cars with club friends.	Long stay in the club.	Active member	Functional and symbolic
Club leader	• To sustain a place for car-consumers to discuss and interact. • To manage and control the club. • To earn some revenue from the club's administration. • To have better social status and connections.	Long stay in the club.	Club leader	Symbolic and functional

club's existence develops a sense of community. Accordingly, the constitutive rule, X counts as Y in context C, plays a role as the "virtual communities" counts as the "car-consumer clubs" in the "car-consumer clubs communities," where the virtual communities = X, the car-consumer clubs = Y and the car-consumer clubs communities = C.

Once the clubs are established in the virtual world, for them to gain the status of "car-consumer clubs" requires collective acceptance from members in these communities. When the clubs have been collectively recognized as places by members or people involved, the clubs acquire the attributed status of reality. The empirical evidence that proves the members' belief in the existence of the car-consumer clubs is demonstrated when they compare their clubs to places such as home, school, library or community. Accordingly the car-consumer clubs are comparable to an imagined community (Anderson, 1983) where the brand community is brought into existence by members' feelings of shared belonging and participation as shown in the following examples:

This club is like a house where I am a father and live with my children.

(Club Leader)

We have a feeling of community because this is our home.

(Active Member)

Shared desires. When people have shared beliefs and collectively recognize that the clubs really exist, they are likely to share a desire to make their clubs visible to the public through their club symbols, rituals and traditions. Since most of the car-consumer clubs in Thailand have been formed in the virtual world, they have formulated an identity and then expanded out of the virtual community by creating club logos which represent that identity to the public. The club logo is another institution fact to which people collectively assign function. The value of the club logo is transmitted by the constitutive rule, X counts as Y in context C. "Symbol A" counts as the "club logo" in "Thai car-consumer clubs"; where "symbol A" = X, "club logo" = Y and "Thai car-consumer clubs" = C.

To assign a new status to symbol A, or status function of the club logo, requires collective acceptance and acknowledgment by both the individual club members and others in the wider community of car-consumer clubs. Once it is adopted and widely accepted by the public, the status function of the club logo engenders deontic powers (such as requirements and authorizations). To qualify to receive and display the club logo (which may be produced in the form of stickers and car plates, t-shirts, souvenirs and so on), one has to apply to become a member. In addition, everyone who displays the club logo in public (either as a sticker on their car or by wearing the club t-shirt) is expected to behave well and respect the club rules because their behavior will be assessed by people both inside and outside the club, reflecting on the club's image in society. Consequently, members' behavior is rule-governed and their behavior is mediated by other members and society. Thus, all of the respondents conform to the club rules due to the rewards they receive. Accordingly, the club logo becomes a very important asset in car-consumer club communities because it shows their identity and inclusiveness, and signals the codes of behavior for individuals (such as driving considerately, assisting one another and greeting each other) as stated by the club leaders of the two car brands:

The club logo is very important because if we have no symbol, there is nothing to indicate our identity to the public. Moreover, if there were no logo, our club would only exist in the virtual world. But when we have a logo in the form of stickers and t-shirts, it extends the club from the virtual world to the physical world and into public view. Then the public can identify us, perhaps by noticing our logo through their car mirror. Fellow members will also know that they are friends. There is a case where one club member's car broke down on the highway and our club logo sticker was noticed by another member who parked straightaway and helped that person even though they did not know each other before.

(Club Leader)

Nowadays almost all cars have their own clubs. We want to show that this is our own club and we belong and have a say in it.

(Club Leader)

Furthermore, the club logo represents belongingness (McMillan & Chavis, 1986). Other people who are in the car-consumer clubs communities recognize each other by noticing the club logo displayed on the car, t-shirt or elsewhere. Members may greet each other when they notice the club logo even though they do not know each other; this is consistent with the rituals and traditions as stated by Muniz and O'Guinn (2001). When a club's logo gains prominence, leading to recognition by the general public, this can attract new participants to the club. It can also lead to the power to negotiate with the car-company, car dealers and sponsors. Consequently, the logo becomes a symbolic reinforcer thanks to the positive public feedback that members receive from being associated with a prestigious club. The following examples show the importance of the logo in the views of the respondents:

It is necessary to have a club logo because it represents a community and members of the same club.

(Club Leader)

The logo makes me feel proud. When I drive and see others with the club logo, I feel that we are in the same club.

(Club Leader)

When I drive past other cars and see the club logo, I feel good because I have friends on the road.

(Active Member)

Shared attitudes. Once the feeling of community arises in members of the clubs, they are likely to share their positive attitudes with each other. When individuals have shared good feelings, cooperative behavior will appear, so in the Thai car-consumer clubs, members have a wide range of activities such as car meetings and social activities. These kinds of activities demonstrate the cooperative behaviors of members in the car-consumer clubs. The social activities can be organized either by the clubs or by the members themselves with the objective of making a positive contribution to society. These activities include charitable events and acts of social responsibility, such as visiting schools and temples (including making donations). Even though they have to contribute their personal investment, the findings reveal that they are willing to do so and cooperate with one another at the same time. The members do these acts without expecting anything in return. Rather, they only want to have a good time with other club members, while doing something good for the clubs and society. These social activities represent members' good intentions to society and in return they will make the members feel good about themselves. Furthermore, these kinds of activities can build a positive reputation for the clubs with the public. Eventually, they also create a position in Thai society for the club. Consequently, these shared attitudes lead to the members' cooperative behaviors. The following quotes, which are drawn from the interviews, are examples of the intentional language that reflects on the we-intentions which represent the collective intentions of the respondents to act:

> When we gather, we should make something good happen for other people. Therefore, we will see what we can do to help other people. Last year, we had a donation project making donations of clothes to children in the countryside.
>
> *(Club Leader)*

> It is a feeling that we should do something good for other people not just meet to make a car modification.
>
> *(Active Member)*

> Instead of gathering for fun, we want to do something good for society. . . . Since we will meet anyway to eat together, have a meeting, and talk about cars, we just insert other activities that make a contribution to the general social well-being rather than just meet.
>
> *(Active Member)*

Cooperative behaviors. The role of collective intentionality presents itself in the form of cooperative behaviors, and this lies at the heart of societal existence (Rakoczy, 2008). The outcomes of members' cooperative behaviors are determined by society in verbal form. In other words, the consequences of their actions are informed by societal feedback. All of the clubs have obtained positive feedback by achieving recognition and a good reputation from society, which can be considered as symbolic reinforcement to members of the clubs. When the clubs gain a high public reputation, members of the clubs will have pride and increased self-esteem from belonging to those clubs (which are considered as being private clubs) by having the status of "membership" (Foxall, 1997a). Consequently, symbolic reinforcement, reflecting status, has an important effect on members' cooperative behaviors by virtue of the collective intentionality of the people in car-consumer clubs communities.

The significance of rewards

Status, emerging from members' collective intentionality, is the key symbolic reinforcement in Thai car-consumer clubs. Simply applying to join a club confers a preliminary status, while the status of "membership" leads to the possibility of functional rewards (such as access to information and cost savings on car repairs). Members are able to receive additional rewards from their participation in the clubs, especially when they gain the status of "friend". The development of these clubs can be further promoted and sustained in Thai society because of the status "friend." It was apparent from our study that the majority of the respondents maintain their membership of the clubs because of friendship with club members because friends/friendship is an important source of symbolic reinforcement (such as connections and assistance from other members of the clubs). The members are willing to support and voluntarily help each other when close relationships have developed. This confirms the brand community literature which indicates that members' friendships allow them to share a sense of moral responsibility (e.g. Muniz & O'Guinn, 2001; McAlexander et al., 2002; O'Guinn & Muniz, 2005).

The reason why the reward "status" is meaningful to people in these car-consumer clubs is because they have shared beliefs, desires and attitudes which are the foundation of the club's existence in the physical world. Through their use of language the people in these clubs can assign meaning and functions to persons and substances that bestow new status on such entities (Searle, 1995); however, one cannot obtain this status unless it is given by others. Furthermore, this status requires collective acceptance and recognition from others, both of which are embedded in the collective intentionality of individuals to add meanings and value in respect of this status (Searle, 2010). This is the reason why status is socially mediated and is achieved through one's performance. Furthermore, status generally comes with a role, right and responsibility to act appropriately in the clubs (Searle, 1995, 2010). Hence, members' behavior in the clubs tends to be rule-governed, based on the instructions or prescriptions that derive from their allocated status, and this increases the value of their status by assigning meaning to it. They are controlled by both the formal rules of the club and the informal rules prescribed by society which are mediated by people in the clubs. These results are in agreement with Foxall (2010b) who stated that symbolic reinforcement controls behavior more firmly within structures of influence derived from social interactions and expectations.

In summary, the meaning and value of status relies on the collective intentionality of the people involved. When their status is significant to the members of the clubs, they will be affected as they strive to maintain this status, leading to cooperative behavior which represents collective intentions to act. The cooperative behavior of members results in the club's advancement because it will generate reciprocal rewards among members (Foxall, 2007a). A club's continued existence depends on members' interactions and expectations which are shaped and maintained by reciprocal rewards:

> The club is kept going by members themselves. The members' cohesiveness and contributions make the club progress and thrive in the society.
>
> *(Club Leader)*

> The club is maintained by members. If there are active members with us, we will continue to exist. If one day the club had no such members, it would have disappeared.
>
> *(Club Leader)*

> The club can be maintained in our society today by members. Members take care of the club. The club also takes care of members in return.
>
> *(Club Leader)*

> The club is maintained by members' contributions. Members give to members with generosity, sympathy and thoughtfulness. Members help one another by giving suggestions and solutions to problems. The contributions given by members are the most important reward which can maintain the club in the long run.
>
> *(Club Leader)*

The shared beliefs, desires and attitudes generate shared consciousness of kind, shared rituals and traditions and a shared sense of moral responsibility in the car-consumer clubs, which are key mechanisms of the brand community (Muniz & O'Guinn, 2001). Furthermore, the shared beliefs, desires and attitudes of members direct their collective intentions to act in the form of cooperative behaviors and bring about joint activity (Cova & Dalli, 2009). The members' cooperative behaviors enhance the club's development, and this reinforces the existence of the club in Thai society.

The emergence of successful car-consumer clubs results to a high degree from collective intentionality, where the value of symbolic reinforcement has an impact on members' cooperative behaviors which represent their collective intentions to act for the club to which they belong. The emergence of the car-consumer clubs is consistent with the emergence of social cooperation in that it relates to the facilitation of behavior by mutual rewards or reciprocal benefits, which relies on a system of symbols (Foxall, 2010b). The system of symbols is similar to the system of status functions that create facts (social facts) which exist in society. Once the status functions are assigned to people or objects by way of collective intentionality, then there will be a value attached that makes agents meaningful so that they turn into symbolic reinforcements through social assessment. This leads to individuals' desiring to possess that newly enhanced status or object for themselves. Therefore, when individuals have shared their beliefs, desires and attitudes, or collective intentionality, this results in cooperative behaviors that are at the root of societal development. Finally, the theoretical concepts from this study could be generalized to other consumer communities, and this also merits future study. These propositions are expected to be tested through further research in these areas.

Conclusions

This chapter has focused on the investigation of rewards and their effect on Thai consumers in the brand community. Since the clubs have provided benefits to members through their participation, members perceive such benefits as rewards (Watson & Johnson, 1972), which are reinforcements (Rachlin, 1976). These rewards are found in the forms of functional and symbolic reinforcement, or patterns of reinforcement, as indicated in the BPM (Foxall, 1994; Foxall et al., 2011), which have an influence on the frequency of behavior. As appeared in the case studies, the difference between the club leaders, the active members and the non-active members is their level of participation in both the web-board and club activities. We showed that non-active members with a low level of participation in the clubs are mainly motivated by functional reinforcement, whereas the club leaders and the active members with a higher level of participation are mostly motivated by both symbolic and functional reinforcement.

This study shows that most members join and use the clubs due to functional reinforcement; however, it is symbolic reinforcement that encourages them to remain in the clubs and increase their contributions to and participation in the web-board and club activities. Consequently, symbolic reinforcement has more effect on members' participation in the clubs (this is particularly true for club leaders and active members). Therefore, symbolic reinforcement augments functional reinforcement, encouraging members to continue their membership and participate in the clubs more often.

This chapter makes a contribution to the theoretical understanding of consumer behavior in the brand community. We address the role of rewards in relation to the patterns of reinforcement in the BPM (Foxall, 2010b) that have an influence on consumer participation in the brand communities. Our analysis also highlights three main types of membership in the brand community. Most of the literature is focused on the active members, and less focused on the managers of those communities, the club leaders (who are the key power-wielders in these communities) and the non-active members. This study fills a research gap because there are few studies which have employed a behavioral view to study brand communities in Asia. In addition, no previous study has investigated the kinds of rewards that have attracted different types of membership to participate and maintain their status in the communities, including club leaders and non-active members. This study reveals the potential rewards that persuade consumers to maintain their membership status in consumer brand communities. It is also the first attempt to integrate the SCI to distinguish the active members and non-active members in the brand community. Thus, the SCI from the literature of sociology is integrated into this study as a practical device to indicate the types of membership of the brand community.

The findings of this study have implications for marketers, practitioners and companies, who can all benefit from some of the guidelines it offers. Unlike previous research on brand communities, this study has examined three main different types of membership in the brand communities in relation to the rewards they receive from participation. The characteristics of members based on their participation in relation to both types of reinforcement have also been presented. Companies and marketers now have access to information which enables them to offer appropriate functional and symbolic rewards in response to the demands of members who support the communities.

Several issues arise from this study which would merit further research. One of the obvious extensions of this study is the degree of each reward that influences different types of membership. Although symbolic and functional reinforcement were both examined in this study, there was no assessment of their degree of influence on members' behavior. This could be investigated by changing the methodological approach from qualitative to quantitative analysis. A quantitative approach would enable researchers to test the initial findings of each reward and degree of influence of different kinds of rewards on different types of membership from those in this study. Furthermore, this study has employed only simple calculations of the SCI in categorizing the types of membership between active members and non-active members. Further studies may use factor analysis or other quantitative measures to investigate each factor and its degree of influence. It is also desirable that longitudinal research be undertaken to assess possible changes in consumers' sense of community and influential factors over time.

References

Al Qur'an, M. N. (2010). How to use multiple case studies in international business research: methodological aspects. *International Review of Business Research Papers*, 6(2), 104–119.

Anderson, B. (1983). *Imagined Community*. London: Verso.

Ardichvili, A., Vaughn, P. and Wentling, T. (2003). Motivation and barriers to participation in virtual knowledge-sharing communities of practice. *Journal of Knowledge Management*, 7, 64–77.

Bagozzi, R. P. and Dholakia, U. M. (2006). Antecedents and purchase consequences of customer participation in small group brand communities. *International Journal of Research in Marketing*, 23, 45–61.

Bryman, A. (2001). *Social Research Methods*. New York: Oxford University Press Inc.

Cao, G. (2007). The pattern-matching role of systems thinking in improving research trustworthiness. *Systems Practice and Action Research*, 20, 441–453.

Carson, D., Gilmore, A., Perry, C. and Gronhaug, K. (2001). *Qualitative Marketing Research*. Los Angeles, CA: Sage Publication, Inc.

Chavis, D. M., Hogge, J., McMilan, D. and Wandersman, A. (1986). Sense of community through Brunswick's lens: a first look. *Journal of Community Psychology*, 14, 24–40.

Cova, B. and Cova, V. (2001). Tribal aspects of postmodern consumption research: the case of French in-line roller skaters. *Journal of Consumer Behaviour*, 1, 67–76.

Cova, B. and Cova, V. (2002). Tribal marketing: the tribalization of society and its impact on the conduct of marketing. *European Journal of Marketing*, 36, 595–620.

Cova, B. and Dalli, D. (2009). Working consumers: the next step in marketing theory? *Marketing Theory*, 9, 315–339.

Cova, B. (1997). Community and consumption: towards a definition of the linking value of product or services. *European Journal of Marketing*, 31, 297–316.

Crane, T. (2001). *Elements of Mind: An Introduction to the Philosophy of Mind*. Oxford: Oxford University Press.

Creswell, J. W. (2003). *Research Design: Qualitative, Quantitative, and Mixed Methods Approaches*. 2nd ed. Los Angeles, CA: Sage Publication, Inc.

David, M. and Sutton, C. D. (2004). *Social Research: The Basics*. London: Sage Publications.

Dholakia, U. M., Bagozzi, R. P. and Pearo, L. R. K. (2004). A social influence model of consumer participation in network and small-group-based virtual communities. *International Journal of Research in Marketing*, 21(3), 241–263.

Dionisio, P., Leal, C. and Moutinho, L. (2008). Fandom affiliation and tribal behaviour: a sports marketing application. *Qualitative Market Research: An International Journal*, 11, 17–39.

Fitzpatrick, D. (2003). Searle and collective intentionality: the self-defeating nature of internalism with respect to social facts. *American Journal of Economics and Sociology*, 62, 45–66.

Foxall, G. R. (1990). *Consumer Psychology in Behavioral Perspective*. London and New York: Routledge.

Foxall, G. R. (1992). The consumer situation: an integrative model for research in marketing. *Journal of Marketing Management*, 8, 392–404.

Foxall, G. R. (1994). Behaviour analysis and consumer psychology. *Journal of Economic Psychology*, 15, 5–91.

Foxall, G. R. (1997a). *Marketing Psychology: The Paradigm in the Wings*. London & New York: Palgrave Macmillan.

Foxall, G. R. (1997b). Affective responses to consumer situations. *International Review of Retail, Distribution and Consumer Research*, 7, 191–225.

Foxall, G. R. (1998). Radical behaviorist interpretation: generating and evaluating an account of consumer behaviour. *The Behavior Analyst*, 21, 321–354.

Foxall, G. R. (2001). Foundations of consumer behavior analysis. *Marketing Theory*, 1(2), 165–199.

Foxall, G. R. (2003). The behavior analysis of consumer choice: an introduction to the special issue. *Journal of Economic Psychology*, 24(5), 581–588.

Foxall, G. R. (2004). *Context and Cognition: Interpreting Complex Behavior*. Reno, NV: Context Press.

Foxall, G. R. (2005). *Understanding Consumer Choice*. London and New York: Palgrave Macmillan.

Foxall, G. R. (2007a). Intentional behaviorism. *Behavior and Philosophy*, 35, 1–55.

Foxall, G. R. (2007b). Explaining consumer choice: coming to terms with intentionality. *Behavioural Processes*, 75, 129–145.

Foxall, G. R. (2007c). *Explaining Consumer Choice*. London and New York: Macmillan.

Foxall, G. R. (2008a). Intentional behaviorism revisited. *Behavior and Philosophy*, 36, 113–155.

Foxall, G. R. (2008b). Reward, emotion and consumer choice: from neuroeconomics to neurophilosophy. *Journal of Consumer Behaviour*, 7, 368–396.

Foxall, G. R. (2010a). *Interpreting Consumer Choice: The Behavioral Perspective Model*. New York and London: Routledge.

Foxall, G. R. (2010b). Accounting for consumer choice: inter-temporal decision making in behavioural perspective. *Marketing Theory*, 10, 315–345.

Foxall, G. R. (2013). Intentionality, symbol, and situation in the interpretation of consumer choice. *Marketing Theory*, 13, 1–23.

Foxall, G. R. and Yani-de-Soriano, M. (2005). Situational influences on consumers' attitudes and behavior. *Journal of Business Research*, 58, 518–525.

Foxall, G. R., Goldsmith, R. E. and Brown, S. (1998). *Consumer Psychology for Marketing*. 2nd ed. London and New York: International Thompson Business Press.

Foxall, G. R., Oliveira-Castro, J. M., James, V. K. and Schrezenmaier, T. C. (2011). Consumer behavior analysis and the behavioral perspective model. *Management Online Review*, 1–9.

Foxall, G. R., Oliveira-Castro, J. M., James, V. K., Yani-de-Soriano, M. M. and Sigurdsson, V. (2006). Consumer behavior analysis and social marketing: the case of environmental conservation. *Behavior and Social Issues*, 15, 101–124.

Glenn, S. S. (1987). Rules as environmental events. *The Analysis of Verbal Behavior*, 5, 29–32.

Grant, W. (2000). *Elite Interviewing: A Practical Guide*. Institute for Germany Studies discussion papers series no. 11. University of Birmingham: Institute for German Studies.

Hayes, S. C., Gifford, E. V. and Hayes, G. J. (1998). Moral behavior and the development of verbal regulation. *The Behavior Analyst*, 21, 253–279.

Heil, J. (2004). *Philosophy of Mind: A Guide and Anthology*. New York: Oxford University Press.

Hirschman, E. C. and Holbrook, M. B. (1982). Utilitarian consumption: emerging concepts, methods and propositions. *Journal of Marketing*, 46, 92–101.

Malott, R. W. (1989). The achievement of evasive goals: control by rules describing contingencies that are not direct acting. In: S. C. Hayes (Ed.) *Rule-Governed Behavior: Cognition, Contingencies, and Instructional Control* (pp. 269–321). Reno, NV: Context Press.

Marshall, M. N. (1996). Sampling for qualitative research. *Family Practice*, 13, 522–525.

Mason, M. (2010). *Sample Size and Saturation in PhD Studies Using Qualitative Interviews*. Forum: Qualitative Research, 11(3). Art. 8 [Online]. Available at: http://nbn-resolving.de/urn:nbn:de:0114-fqs100387 [Accessed: 13 April 2014].

McAlexander, J. H., Schouten, J. W. and Koeing, H. F. (2002). Building brand community. *Journal of Marketing*, 66, 38–54.

McCracken, G. (1988). *The Long Interview*. Los Angeles, CA: Sage.

McMillan, D. W. and Chavis, D. M. (1986). Sense of community: a definition and theory. *Journal of Community Psychology*, 14, 1–23.

Michael, J. (1982). Distinguishing between discriminative and motivational functions of stimuli. *Journal of the Experimental Analysis of Behavior*, 37, 149–155.

Miles, M. B. and Huberman, A. M. (1994). *Qualitative Data Analysis: An Expanded Sourcebook*. 2nd ed. London: Sage Publications Ltd.

Muniz, A. M. Jr. and O'Guinn, T. C. (2001). Brand community. *Journal of Consumer Research*, 27, 412–432.

Muniz, A. M. Jr. and O'Guinn, T. C. (2005). Marketing communications of consumption and brand communities. In: A. J. Kimmel (Ed.) *Marketing Communication: New Approaches, Technologies and Styles* (pp. 63–85). Oxford: Oxford University Press.

Mzoughi, P. M., Ahmed, R. B. and Ayed, H. (2010). Explaining the participation in a small group brand community: an extended TRA. *Journal of Business & Economic Research*, 8(8), 17–26.

Nilsen, R. D. (2005). Searching for analytical concepts in the research process: learning from children. *International Journal of Social Research Methodology*, 8, 117–135.

O'Guinn, T. C. and Muniz, A. M. (2005) Communal consumption and the brand. In: S. Ratneshwar and D. G. Mick (Eds.) *Inside Consumption: Consumer Motives, Goals, and Desire* (pp. 252–272). New York: Routledge.

Poppen, R. L. (1989). Some clinical implications of rule-governed behavior. In: S. C. Hayes (Ed.) *Rule-Governed Behavior: Cognition, Contingencies, and Instructional Control* (pp. 325–357). Reno, NV: Context Press.

Punch, K. F. (2005). *Introduction to Social Research: Qualitative and Quantitative Approaches*. 2nd ed. London: Sage.

Quester, P. G. and Fleck, N. (2010). Club Med: coping with corporate brand evolution. *Journal of Product & Brand Management*, 19, 94–102.

Rachlin, H. (1976). *Behavior and Learning*. San Francisco, CA: W. H. Freeman and Company.

Rakoczy, H. (2008). Pretence as individual and collective intentionality. *Mind and Language*, 23, 499–517.

Rowley, J. (2002). Using case studies in research. *Management Research News*, 25(1), 16–27.

Schau, H. J. and Muniz, A. M. Jr. (2007). Temperance and religiosity in a non-marginal, non-stigmatized brand community. In: B. Cova, R. V. Kozinets and A. Shankar (Eds.) *Consumer Tribes: Theory, Practice, and Prospects* (pp. 144–162). Oxford and Burlington: Elsevier.

Schwandt, T. A. (2001). *Dictionary of Qualitative Inquiry*. 2nd ed. Thousand Oaks, CA: Sage.

Searle, J. R. (1999). *Mind, Language and Society: Doing Philosophy in the Real World*. London: Weidenfield and Nicholson.

Searle, J. R. (1995). *The Construction of Social Reality*. New York: Free Press.

Searle, J. R. (2005). What is an institution? *Journal of Institutional Economics*, 1, 1–22.

Searle, J. R. (2010). *Making the Social World: The Structure of Human Civilization*. New York: Oxford University Press.

Silverman, D. (2001). *Interpreting Qualitative Data: Methods for Analyzing Talk, Text and Interaction*. Los Angeles, CA: Sage Publications, Inc.

Silverman, D. (2005). *Doing Qualitative Research: A Practical Handbook*. 2nd ed. London: Sage Publications Ltd.

Skinner, B. F. (1966). An operant analysis of problem solving. In: B. F. Skinner (Ed.) *Contingencies of Reinforcement: A Theoretical Analysis*. New York: Appleton-Century-Croft.

Szmigin, I. and Carrigan, M. (2006). Consumption and community: choices of women over forty. *Journal of Consumer Behaviour*, 5, 292–230.

Törneke, N., Luciano, C. and Salas, S. V. (2008). Rule-governed behavior and psychological problems. *International Journal of Psychology and Psychological Therapy*, 8, 141–156.

Watson, G. and Johnson, D. (1972). *Social Psychology: Issues and Insights*. Philadelphia, PA: J.B. Lippincott.

Wearden, J. (1988). Some neglected problems in the analysis of human operant behaviour. In: G. Davey and C. Cullen (Eds.) *Human Operant Conditioning and Behavior Modification* (pp. 197–224). Chichester: Wiley.

Wells, V. K., Chang, S. W., Oliveira, J. and Pallister, J. (2011). Market segmentation from a behavioral perspective. *Journal of Organizational Behavior Management*, 30(2), 176–198.

Yin, R. K. (1994). *Case Study Research: Design and Methods*. 2nd ed. Thousand Oaks, CA: Sage.

Yin, R. K. (2003). *Case Study Research: Design and Methods*. 3rd ed. Thousand Oaks, CA: Sage.

Yin, R. K. (2009). *Case Study Research: Design and Methods*. 4th ed. Thousand Oaks, CA: Sage.

Zettle, R. D. and Hayes, S. C. (1982). Rule-governed behavior: a potential theoretical framework for cognitive behavioral therapy. *Advances in Cognitive-Behavioral Research and Therapy*, 1, 73–117.

Zettle, R. D. and Young, M. J. (1987). Rule-following and human operant responding: conceptual and methodological considerations. *The Analysis of Verbal Behaviour*, 5, 33–39.

24

Consumer confusion

A Behavioral Perspective Model perspective

Ioanna Anninou, Gordon R. Foxall, and John G. Pallister

Introduction

The purpose of the Behavioral Perspective Model (BPM) of purchase and consumption has been to explore the possibility of a behavior analytical approach to consumer behavior and to ascertain the nature and status of the account it provides (Foxall, 1990; Foxall, 1993). The model offers an alternative, behavioral approach to the prevalent cognitive examination of consumer behavior and it remains a valid interpretive account and most importantly one which is strongly supported by relevant empirical evidence (e.g. Foxall, 1997b; Foxall & Greenley, 1999, 2000; Foxall & Soriano, 2005). Notwithstanding these empirical findings, the problematic areas of the specific model and behaviorism at large have also been identified. These areas mainly concentrate on hindering the explanation of some aspects of behavior. Specifically, aspects like the continuity of behavior, the personal level of explanation and the delimitation of behavioral explanation (Foxall, 2004; Foxall, 2007a, b) seem to require an alternative non-behavioral treatment and elucidation.

The main proposal for resolving these issues involves the addition of other kinds of psychological concepts, found in ordinary language, that have been avoided by behavioristic approaches. For example, it has been suggested that the model should consider intentional/dispositional concepts in general, which include, in addition to propositional attitudes, abilities, propensities, and personal emotions, or even personality traits (Foxall, 2007b). Considering that dispositional concepts and intentional idioms in general describe, imprecisely, what individuals have done and predict what they are likely to do under certain situations and conditions, they are good candidates to be included in the description of consumers' learning history (Oliveira-Castro, 2013). This is the reason that Foxall (2007a, p. 43) argues that intentional ascription can be perceived as the result of the intersection of the individual and the experiences in the specific situation.

This chapter will then act as an attempt to illustrate the way that the BPM can be expanded to include intentional idioms. In this attempt consumer confusion, a construct which has been treated very much in cognitive terms until recently, can now be extended to an interpretive account which allows its description based on both intentional and behavioral terms. It can then form part and be examined in terms of the BPM. The chapter will start by exploring the existing literature on confusion and the BPM, and will then describe the two different approaches to consumer behavior, the extensional and intentional framework, reaching the point where a novel suggestion for both confusion and the BPM will be examined.

Consumer confusion

In an attempt to summarize existing literature on consumer confusion, it is evident that a consensus on the state of confusion has not been reached; however, most psychology and consumer behavior researchers agree that confusion as a state can be meaningfully characterized by the following qualities (Ellsworth, 2003; Hess, 2003; Keltner & Shiota, 2003; Rozin & Cohen, 2003a and b; Schweizer, 2004; Walsh et al., 2007; Walsh & Mitchell, 2010):

- a state of not knowing/understanding;
- a sense of goal obstruction which in consumer behavior might equal either an inability to choose the preferred/best product or the impediment of an enjoyable shopping trip;
- perceived higher levels of effort, higher attention needed and possibly a sense of lack of control;
- intense uncertainty and/or impressions of overload, similarity, novelty etc., especially operationalized as such in consumer research and proposing the intense relationship between the state as an interaction between an individual and environmental conditions.

These characteristics are depicted in Table 24.1.

Based on the literature, the theoretical opportunities offered through the study of states like confusion have been established (Rozin & Cohen, 2003a). Confusion has been described as a state that holds both "affective and informational value." These entities have resulted in intense theoretical debates and for many years have been placed in the affect, the cognition or a mixed group of states. The requirement to further elucidate and understand such terms, to reveal their multiple characters and to discuss their role in theoretical and empirical undertakings has been stressed by previous researchers (Rozin & Cohen, 2003a, b).

The Behavioral Perspective Model

The fundamental proposition of the BPM is the "contextual stance" (Foxall, 1998), where consumer behavior is located at the intersection between the consumers' learning history and the behavioral setting. The analysis prompted by the BPM (Foxall, 1990) systematically relates known patterns of purchase and consumption to the situations in which they occur. The conceptual basis of the model is neo-Skinnerian (i.e., it is based on Skinner's operant conditioning principles). Further to that, the basic suggestion and a distinct concept of the BPM is a bifurcation of reinforcement, which is composed of utilitarian and informational reinforcement that are determined by consumers' learning history and previous experiences. As a result, the BPM proposes three formative components of consumer situations, which are: utilitarian reinforcement, informational reinforcement, and behavior-setting scope.

Table 24.1 A depiction of the main characteristics (or "qualia") of the state of confusion

A state of not knowing/lacking understanding		
Sense of goal obstruction	Inability to choose/ enjoy the shopping experience	Ambiguity/Similarity/Overload Variety/Novelty/Complexity/Conflict/Comfort/Reliability
	Higher levels of perceived effort and attention necessary	

Source: Anninou, 2013 (based on the characteristics attributed to confusion in previous theoretical and empirical papers)

According to the BPM, which is depicted in Figure 24.1, aspects of consumer behavior are then predictable from two dimensions of situational influence: (1) the consumer behavior setting; and (2) the utilitarian and informational reinforcement signaled by the setting as informed by the consumer's learning history.

The consequences of consumer behavior that stem from a consumer situation are of three kinds: utilitarian, informational and aversive consequences, which reduce the probability of future repetition (costs or utilitarian and informational punishment). Utilitarian reinforcement is defined as the functional benefits of consumption, while informational reinforcement includes the symbolic benefits like social status, self-esteem, pride and honor. Informational reinforcement can also be described as feedback on the level of performance of the consumer (Foxall, 1996; Foxall & Soriano, 2005). Thus, utilitarian reinforcements are the direct, functional benefits of being in a situation per se but they can also derive from owning and using products and services, while informational reinforcement is an outcome of socially and physically constructed aspects of the environment. According to the BPM, informational reinforcement does not derive from the typical explanation of the word "information," but it refers to the feedback-information an individual receives on the level of its performance (Foxall, 2010). The root of informational reinforcement lies in the notion of secondary reinforcement through status (see Foxall, 2007c for further details on reinforcements). Physical stimuli that can excite the senses like exciting packaging or colors, or situations that can enhance self-esteem like driving or owning an expensive car, are perceived as typical examples of informational reinforcement. Based on these general principles, the model identifies three interactive levels of interpretive analysis, namely the operant class, the contingency category and the consumer situation (Foxall, 2010).

The examination of the BPM until now has used "within-the-skin events" (Skinner, 1974) like emotions and approach-avoidance behavior and argues for the empirical interest of such terms. In this case, emotional and behavioral variables have represented the emphasis of radical behaviorism on the use of language as an indication of verbal behavior. This language, no matter if it is overt and public (as in conversations) or covert and private (as in thinking), can be representative of behavior (Foxall, 1990; Foxall, 1998). Thus verbal behavior in the way that has been used to explore the BPM until recently should be understood as a plain statement of the facts and a description of its functional relationships with environmental events, and particularly the relationship with its contingencies and consequences. Specifically, the dimensions of the BPM have been consistently found to be explained on the basis of the variables of the MR model

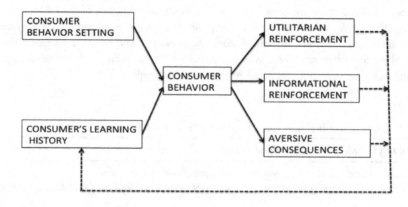

Figure 24.1 Summative Behavioral Perspective Model of consumer choice
Source: Foxall, 1996, p. 26

(Mehrabian & Russell, 1974), when applied in different situations. Specifically, *pleasure* has been described as an index of the utilitarian reinforcement signaled by the situations or by the usage of products and services implicated. This is so because utilitarian reinforcement consists of the benefits and satisfaction contingent in a situation. *Arousal* is a measure of the informational reinforcement which indicates the feedback on consumer performance, and finally *dominance* is predicted to increase with the degree of openness of the behavioral setting. Thus consumers are expected to feel more controlling, influential and important in an open rather than a closed setting (Foxall & Soriano, 2005). Regarding the behavioral measures, *approach behavior* is expected to increase with the total quantity and quality of reinforcement (utilitarian or informational) while *avoidance* is the expected outcome of lower levels of reinforcement.

The languages of explanation

Having illustrated the BPM as a model based on the principles of operant conditioning and behaviorism, the next section will move on to the determination of the two different languages that can be used to explain consumer behavior in general. The way these can find application in the determination of the BPM will be explored subsequently. As the aim of this chapter at large concerns the ways that the principles of both behaviorism and intentionality can be applied to the exploration of consumer choice when the main device of exploration is the BPM, part of this endeavor will be understanding the different languages that can be used to explore this model.

Lay people very often use language which attributes actions and intentions to other individuals' desires and beliefs, and researchers widely use this approach to understand and often predict human behavior. Behavioral science, on the other hand, deals with such an approach with circumspection due to the ease with which explanations of any behavior can be adduced by assuming that goals and dispositions from the behavior they are said to explain are used to explain that same behavior (Foxall, 2013). This has resulted in reaching a state resembling the chicken and the egg situation. On these grounds, the preferred approach for the investigation of the BPM until recently has been the use of an extensional language (in terms of simple verbal behavior), the avoidance of intentional or cognitive terms and at the same time the determination of the explanations that the extensional language can provide by observing the inadequacies of the intentional stance.

More specifically, the most important characteristic of extensional language is simply that it avoids intentional terms. In this kind of reasoning "a stimulus is a part of the environment which is consistently followed by a response" (Foxall, 2013, p. 108), and the idea that an organism expects, believes or desires something does not have a role in this explanation. At the other end, the intentional explanation exists exactly at the level of personal beliefs and desires and embodies terms that refer to or represent something other than themselves.

To properly mark the difference between the two languages, the defining characteristics that distinguish between the two can be exemplified as follows:

1. The extensional language is characterized by referential transparency while intentional idioms are referentially opaque. Referential transparency means that in any extensional sentence synonymous terms can be used to substitute one another without changing the value or meaning of the sentence. This is not valid in intentional idioms. One example used to indicate this property (Foxall, 2007a, b; Foxall, 2013) is the sentence, "That planet is Mars." In this extensional use of the language, "Mars" can be easily substituted by "the fourth planet from the sun." However, when saying "John *believes* that this planet is Mars," Mars cannot be substituted by "the fourth planet from the sun" simply because John might

not know or believe that Mars is the fourth planet from the sun and thus by substitution the meaning of the sentence might completely change and lose its original denotation.

2. Intentional language is characterized by intensional inexistence (while extensional language by physical existence). It means that an intentional sentence does not imply its true existence or non-existence. When an extensional sentence states that "John bought a BMW," this implies that both John and a car brand named a BMW exist. However, an intentional explanation which argues that "George thinks that John bought a BMW" does not imply the existence of either the action or the brand itself. This belief is inside the individual and it is not necessarily positioned in the actual word.

3. Finally, according to Brentano (1874/1973 as in Foxall, 2013) and based on both the above characteristics, it is difficult to translate intentional into extensional sentences. However, according to Searle items and constructs can be identified and described in the extensional – the physical level – but also in accordance to human intentionality. According to Foxall, 2013 (p. 118), rule-governed behaviors (in the form of tracks, plys and augments; Zettle & Hayes, 1982) are behaviors that carry this property. Rule-governed behavior (directed by self or other rules) can be explained both as responses to social and physical stimuli and as ideas expressed in accordance with human intentionality.

On these grounds and the overall understanding of the two accounts, it is safe to argue that intentionality does not provide the same kind of description as an extensional explanation, but it can be used to explain behavior whenever an extensional language no longer suffices (Foxall, 2007a and b, 2013). This is usual when the continuity or discontinuity of behavior, the personal level of explanation and the delimitation of behavioral interpretation is sought (Foxall, 2004). The consequences of this dichotomy are twofold: 1) a new philosophical framework, intentional behaviorism, has been proposed which can accommodate both approaches, and 2) two distinct models have been proposed to accommodate these explanations, the extensional (BPM-E) and the intentional (BPM-I) model (as in Foxall, 2013).

Intentional behaviorism

Following the above overview of the approaches to the languages of consumer behavior, it is essential to describe the way that the two main philosophical streams for explaining learning and behavior have been explored and used by consumer behavior researchers: radical behaviorism with its emphasis on operant conditioning and intentionality, an account that seeks to understand the internal thought processes and to explore their effect on behavior. Intentionality has been described as the power of the mind to be about, to represent something else (Crane, 2007); following this, logic systems are ascribed thoughts directed at something other than them – which is often referred to as the intentional stance. At the other end, the main characteristic of radical behaviorism and operant conditioning is its avoidance of intentional explanation and the use of a behavioral language which is based on situational/environmental influences – the contextual stance (Foxall, 2007a). These have until recently been presented as incommensurable theories of behavior.

Foxall, although an advocate of behavior analysis and the proponent of radical behaviorism in consumer behavior (Foxall, 1990), argues that the explanations provided by this stream of research are sufficient to predict behavior in experimental settings but when applied to real situations, they ultimately fail to give a complete explanation of behavior (Foxall, 2008). Several aspects of human behavior like the personal level of explanation, the continuity/discontinuity of behavior and the delimitation of human behavior can be better explained by adopting intentional terms, which can help to provide a more complete and accurate explanation of behavior.

Consequently, the imperatives of intentionality (what the use of intentional terms adds to behavior analysis) according to Foxall (2007a, b) are:

- The personal level of explanation – the distinct way each situation is experienced based on sensations and impressions.
- The continuity of behavior – an explanation of why a behavior which is followed by a particular reinforcing stimulus in a setting is re-enacted when encountering a similar setting.
- The delimitation of behavioral interpretation – the examination of open systems rather than focusing on closed/experimental settings only.

As a result, *intentional behaviorism* has been proposed (Foxall, 2004, 2007a and b) as a way to accommodate both ways of thinking, a novel way to conduct research and ultimately to facilitate the explanation of behavior. Based on behavior analysis and an a-ontological conception of intentional states grounded on Dennett's intentional stance (Dennett, 1987, 2007), new ways of conceiving and researching aspects of behavior can be crafted which can compensate for the shortcomings of the two aforementioned philosophical stances. The integration of the intentional and behavioral explanations compensates for the shortcoming of the cognitive/intentional explanation which taken alone results in the de-contextualization of human behavior. It can also help to overcome the shortcomings of behavioral analysis which, due to the lack of intentional explanation, when applied leads to the three aforementioned issues: a lack of the personal level of explanation, the continuity of behavior and the delimitation of behavioral interpretation.

Intentional behaviorism thus draws attention to the necessity of employing intentional mental language of beliefs and desires, intentions and propositional attitudes to account for what is happening at the personal level of explanation, and hence invokes an intentional explanation thereof. It can be used to explain operant behavior in experimental but more importantly in real settings where intentional explanation is imperative.

To support and extend the interpretation of intentional behaviorism, two issues related to the nature of intentionality and its role in the explanation of behavior should be clarified further. These two issues as deployed below are interrelated. The use of intentional language as described by Foxall (2007a, b) should be perceived as a linguistic convention that carries with it no ontological implications regarding its nature (Foxall, 2007a, 2008). Intentional objects hold then an a-ontological, linguistic nature. Subjects are attributed the formation of verbal rules which are manifest when the expected influence of contingencies is lost or altered (Foxall, 2008). However, this relationship is not enough to attribute causality to intentionality. It is merely to say that when an individual's actual rule-formulation coincides with the intentions we attribute to them, their behavior will be predictable in terms of behavior analysis. The causes of the behavior are still to be found in the contingencies, though the following questions remain to be answered: (1) whether the contingencies can consequently be modified by the person's rule-making, (2) just how initiating causes of overt and covert behavior private stimuli are, and 3) which are the areas that the contextual and the intentional stance are both found to hold (Foxall, 2000, 2008). The explanation for such behavior and the answer to these questions involve the ascription of intentionality and multiple theoretical and empirical endeavors (Foxall, 2007b).

Rule-governed behavior

In an attempt to specify the theoretical and empirical ways that intentionality should be related to behaviorism, the use of rule-governed behavior and especially rules has been proposed as a viable theoretical construct.

The interest in the distinction between contingency and rule-governed behavior can be traced to Skinner (1966) who argued that in humans, who are verbal creatures, reinforcement and consequently behavior could arise: 1) from the direct contact with environmental contingencies (contingency-shaped), or 2) from verbal descriptions of these contingencies provided by the individual or others, which he termed rules.

Verbal rules, which result in rule-governed or instructed behavior (RGB) (Skinner, 1969; Catania et al., 1990; Törneke et al., 2008), have been introduced, beyond their reinforcing power, in an attempt to explain complex human behavior which does not always follow the three-term contingencies. Rules can act as instructions and are effective as long as they are either specified in rules (in essence social rules or norms), or result from the verbal activity of a speaker or from rules or self-rules to which an organism has adhered throughout its history.

To date there is a debate over the actual role of those rules in behavior analysis because such rules may enter any kind of behavioral relationship (Cerutti, 1989). The most prominent functions suggested for the rules in question are those of reinforcers (Foxall, 1997a), those of verbal discriminative stimuli that can take the place of the contingencies themselves and strengthen or weaken behavior (Skinner, 1969; Baum, 1995; Okouchi, 1999), or those of function-altering contingency-specifying stimuli, which alter the function of other stimuli in a manner analogous to operant conditioning (Blakely & Schlinger, 1987; Schlinger & Blakely, 1987; Schlinger, 1993). This multi-functional nature explains why several authors have proposed that the terminology used to describe rules should always reflect the specificity of the phenomenon which is of interest each time (Brownstein & Shull, 1985; Michael, 1986). In a similar vein, Catania (1986) proposes that a rule should be judged and better defined based on the level of effect it has on behavior rather than on any other basis.

Functional units of rules and self-rules

Another central point in the debate of rule-governed behavior is the development of different functional units of rules for the speaker, the listener and also the formulation of self-based rules (Zettle & Hayes, 1982). Although speaker units of rule-governed behavior in the form of mands and tacts have been proposed by Skinner (1957), Foxall (2010, p. 82) describes how consumer behavior researchers should be mainly concerned with the verbal behavior of the listener (Zettle & Hayes, 1982; Schlinger, 2008), including cases where the listener is the same as the speaker. In this second instance, the rules are actually self-based (Barnes-Holmes et al., 2001) and have been described as being of importance (Foxall, 1997a; Kunkel, 1997; Foxall, 2010) because such self-rules can be formulated to guide habitual, everyday behavior.

On these grounds, three categories of listener rule-based behavior have been proposed and analyzed by the literature (Zettle & Hayes, 1982; Poppen, 1989). This account of listener-based units of rule-governed behavior is composed of pliance, tracking and augmenting.

Rule-following that is socially mediated is known as pliance. In this case, the listener's behavior is mediated by the rules of another individual, the speaker, who has the power to reward or punish subsequent behavior based on conformity or disobedience to the rule (Zettle & Hayes, 1982; Foxall, 2010). Foxall (2010) argues that a great deal of consumer behavior is actually pliance. Pliance can be found in cases when someone is doing what somebody else is saying to either comply with this person's rules as in a thief saying, "Your wallet or your life" (Zettle & Hayes, 1982), or to obtain another person's favor by following his rules (Törneke et al., 2008), or to comply with a rule that clearly states the reinforcing consequences of doing so (Foxall, 2010). A child conforms to spending his/her pocket money as instructed by a parent, following the rule "spending wisely, you can save more at the end of the week." Such rules are known as plys.

Another common category is the rule-governed behavior which arises from rules specified by another person, who is not in a position to reinforce or punish others' behavior (Foxall, 2010). This time the behavior is known as tracking, the rules are known as tracks and it is usually the physical environment that mediates the following of such rules. For example, when a passerby instructs a person the way to a store, the speaker is in no position to supply reinforcement or punishment for getting there or not. Success or failure to find the store depends upon progress in getting there and reinforcement is provided by finding the store, while punishment is failing to find the store (Foxall, 2010). According to Glenn (1987), tracks can function as antecedents to behavior and are expected to have a behavioral effect (Catania, 1989).

The third unit of rule-governed behavior is termed augmenting (Zettle & Hayes, 1982). This is rule-governed behavior which does not specify contingencies or consequences but rather states emphatically the reinforcing or punishing value of the consequences specified in the rule (Törneke et al., 2008). The rule itself has been termed an augmental. It is possibly the most difficult and advanced type of rule-governed behavior and is usually found in mixed form with either pliance or tracking (Zettle & Hayes, 1982). The results of augmentals are mainly evident when interacting with pliance or tracking and people act on an augmental usually where the consequences might be obvious at a subsequent time.

In addition to the rules which might govern listeners' behavior and are introduced by others, self-instructions or self-rules appear as a special kind of rule-governed behavior (Zettle & Hayes, 1982; Zettle, 1990; Kunkel, 1997). In this instance the speaker and the listener are the same individual. The main reason for the development of such self-rules has been described as "being personal" in the sense that an individual can react more effectively now or on a future occasion than when based on the contingencies alone (Zettle & Hayes, 1982). Such learned behavior may evoke appropriate actions in the future faster than the actual contingencies it describes (Vaughan, 1985). The rules the person formulates act then as a learning history (history of reinforcement or punishment) which the individual can rely on.

An interesting characteristic of self-rules is that due to the unclear distinction between the rule giver and follower, it is harder to distinguish among different kinds of functional units. Self-pliance and self-tracking range along a continuum rather than being two distinct categories (Zettle & Hayes, 1982). In analogy to listeners' units of rule-based behavior, self-tracking occurs when the rule is to be followed because this is a description of the state of affairs and self-pliance occurs when the rule is to be followed simply because it was formulated (Zettle & Hayes, 1982, p. 90).

A novel suggestion on the nature of confusion

The concept and especially the importance of rule-governed behavior (other or self-instructed) for the study of behavior have already been described. Rules are usually defined by social norms; however, self-rules are dictated when the speaker and the listener are the same, thus are dictated by the self. Self-rules act as instructions and are effective as long as they adhere to norms to which an organism has followed throughout its history (Foxall, 1997a). Based on the categories of rules developed by Zettle and Hayes (1982), especially the case of tracking is concerned with corresponding to a description of the state of affairs (Zettle & Hayes, 1982, pp. 79–92) or according to Foxall (2013, p. 118) it is a case of "responding to brute facts" like the arrangement of the physical environment. The arrangement of the physical environment indicates the state of affairs as the consumer is usually powerless to change it and needs to adhere to it. Tracking can be viewed as predominantly a contingency-shaped behavior and although most theorists (Zettle & Hayes, 1982; Foxall, 1997b; Törneke et al., 2008; Foxall, 2013) argue that it is a challenging task to clearly define and understand the different cases of rule-based behavior and discern among plys, tracks and augments, confusion can be understood as a case of a self-based tracking due to its special relationship with environmental conditions.

Confusion as "anomy"

In an attempt to further this understanding, the concept of anomy (or "anomie") will be brought to the fore. In its true meaning anomy comes from the Greek language and means the absence of law. The concept of anomy was initially introduced by the French sociologist Émile Durkheim and subsequently deeply analyzed by Merton (as in McClosky & Schaar, 1965). In sociology Durkheim used the term to describe a state of normlessness, deregulation and loss of social control usually produced by too sudden social change. Merton extended the concept to indicate (Merton, 1938; also Merton, 1957 as analyzed in Lowe & Damankos, 1968) that this deregulation is the result of the Western (USA) society's increasing emphasis on accumulation of wealth which is not accompanied by the relevant emphasis on the means to obtain these monetary goals. This is causing strain to the relevant social groups that do not have the means to attain the goals, leading to their isolation. In sociology, anomy is then a characteristic of social groups whose access to goals is blocked by social-structural barriers. Merton's approach to anomy is acknowledged as the pre-eminent sociological theory of deviant behavior.

In psychological research anomy has been portrayed as a state of mind rather than a state of the society or social groups (McClosky & Schaar, 1965). It has mainly been described in terms of the alienation and dis-institutionalization of the individual from others, the society or the goals that the social system approves, and it is usually measured by a relevant scale and conceptualization developed by J. L. Srole (Taylor, 1968). According to a more general definition and approach which is focused on an even less sociological and increasingly psychological perspective (as in McClosky & Schaar, 1965, p. 19):

> anomy is a state of mind . . . it is the feeling that the world and oneself are adrift, wandering, lacking in clear rules and stable moorings . . . for him (for the individual) the norms governing behavior are weak, ambiguous and remote.

Anomy, simply defined, is a rule for the lack of rules; it is a state where norms or rules are confused, unclear (complexity/ambiguity confusion) or absent (similarity confusion), and learning the norms is severely impeded due to all of these reasons (McClosky & Schaar, 1965). The case of confusion seems to correspond to this kind of reasoning. Different kinds of confusion can be characterized by the lack of market rules and norms which interfere with learning and impede behavior. Confusion can be characterized intensely by the sense of market anomy, this sense of disorientation, which can be defined as a rule characterizing the lack of other relevant rules.

Confusion as a self-based rule (or "a rule for the lack of rules")

Confusion can then be perceived as a case of self-tracking (self-based rule) and more specifically a "rule" suitable to describe the lack of other relevant rules. The role of self-rules as summarized by Zettle and Hayes (1982) has been "being personal" in the sense that a person can react more effectively now or on a future occasion than when based on the contingencies alone.

Extending further this theoretical reasoning, a fundamental faculty of rule-governed behavior according to Foxall (2013) is the capacity of being treated and expressed in both extensional and intentional terms. This logic follows Searle (as in Foxall, 2013) who concludes that items can be perceived in both an extensional account of "brute facts" and an intentional account based on "human intentionality". The meaning and application of this principle in the case of confusion will be described in the following sections. This study will then extend the understanding of confusion by placing it within the framework of extensional and intentional BPM and thus a novel understanding of the construct and application of the BPM will be offered.

Based on the underpinnings of the above theoretical understanding, the main proposition suggested by this chapter is: Confusion is a self-based rule (based on the propositions of rule-governed behavior). It is, more specifically, a rule for the lack of other rules (a case of market anomy). Due to its relationship with the state of affairs (environmental situations), it can be characterized as a self-based track and as such can be treated at two levels.

At the *extensional level*, it can be treated as a response to specific (discriminative) stimuli and can act along with verbal contingencies to predict behavior. In this case it represents verbal behavior; it is a plain statement of the facts.

At the *intentional level*, it is the result of the interplay between an individual and specific situations and in this case it can take the role of the consumer situation that signals consumer responses. By adopting this "less scientific" route, it can be assumed that confusion can have an impact on actual situational contingencies. Such an approach based on intentionality allows for the personal level of explanation to be examined.

In practical terms, when consumers enter retail/shopping environments they are faced at first instance with the surroundings. The formation of the environment (product assortment, for instance) is one of the factors that determines whether reinforcement or punishment will be received from the situation. In this context confusion can be described as a rule indicating the lack of environmental or market rules. Confusion further acts both as a punishment and as a learning history for future reference. In this context, confusion along with situational contingencies can ultimately act to determine consumer behavior. When market rules are unclear or too many, complexity confusion arises. When market rules are absent, this will result in what has been described as similarity confusion.

BPM-E and BPM-I

The extensional Behavioral Perspective Model (BPM-E)

The benefits of using the BPM have been described in previous research (Foxall, 1992 and all subsequent research). This model, which has until recently been depicted in the extensional language of stimuli, behavior and behavioral consequences (lacking reference to beliefs, desires or other intentional attitudes), has been introduced as an attempt to overcome the limitations of the cognitive portrayal of choice, especially the de-contextualization of theoretical models (Table 24.2). To start with, the model offers a relevant framework which accommodates the two main reinforcers innate in consumer situations, utilitarian and informational. It further

Table 24.2 The nature of confusion at the two levels (extensional and intentional) proposed by this chapter

BPM-E	Lack of (complex, weak or similar) market rules or norms that impede behavior; measured as plain facts and overall responses to consumer situations.
BPM-I	Individual perception of the lack of (complex, weak or similar) market rules or norms that impede behavior.

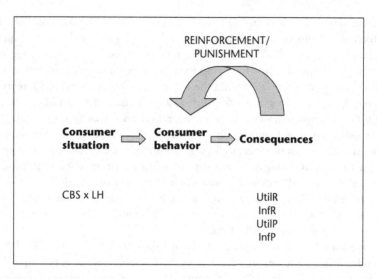

CBS = consumer behavior setting; LH = learning history; UtilR = utilitarian reinforcement; InfR = informational reinforcement; UtilP = utilitarian punishment; InfP = informational punishment

Figure 24.2   BPM-E

describes decision-making with respect to settings that range from the routine, habitual and everyday to the extreme. When using the model, several diverse situations have been described and categorized based on the reinforcers and behavioral setting. It places distinctive emphasis on the idea of *consumer situation*, which is the way that behavior is located in space and time by the extensional model.

Figure 24.2 depicts the model and explains its main constructs.

The variables are extensionally defined as responses to physical and social stimuli embedded in the consumer situation. The consumer situation (coterminous with the consumer behavior-setting scope) consists of the consumer behavior setting (discriminative stimulus, motivating operations and verbal rules) and the learning history. Reinforcement is composed of Utilitarian (UtilR) and Informational (InfR). Punishing or aversive consequences are also part of the possible consequences, conceptualized and examined in previous research mainly in terms of the cost of buying.

Following the extensive previous literature, these constructs have been conceptualized as the Pleasure (UtilR), Arousal (InfR), Dominance (consumer situation/behavior-setting scope) and the approach/avoidance behavior as the consumer behavior element. The way these have been used in the extensional construct has been in terms of *overall responses to stimuli*. These represent then *verbal behavior* (in accordance with Skinner, 1974) expressed with the help of an *extensional language* and should not be perceived as representing consumers' beliefs or attitudes. The language of radical behaviorism is very specific in this sense and very strict on the role of a discriminative stimulus. Thus a discriminative stimulus does not represent or signal utilitarian and informational reinforcers or punishers; it simply "sets the occasion" for them (Foxall, 2013, p. 111). It allows for neither personal nor group differences, disregarding in this manner the personal level of explanation.

In the boundaries of the BPM-E, confusion can then be defined as a rule-governed behavior (tracking) which is a "response to the physical and social environment". It is an

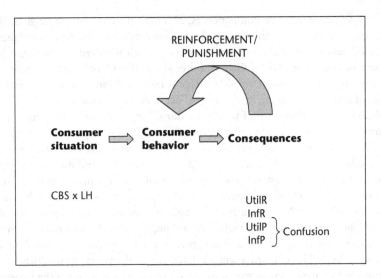

CBS = consumer behavior setting; LH = learning history; UtilR = utilitarian reinforcement; InfR = informational reinforcement; UtilP = utilitarian punishment; InfP = informational punishment

Figure 24.3 BPM-E

aversive, extensionally defined/objective consequence of environmental exposure to specific discriminative stimuli/markets. The role of the UtilR, InfR and confusion (which can have both UtilP and InfP implications) can facilitate the examination and establishment of overall differences in stimuli means (Figure 24.3).

It is also appropriate to argue that for the purposes of a relevant endeavor (which would deal with the nature, effect and addition of confusion in the BPM), the whole situational complexity of the BPM cannot find application. Consumers do not hold confusion for the range of operant classes (accomplishment, hedonism, accumulation and maintenance) and situations described by the model. Situations like being in a job-related seminar, driving an expensive car, being on a cruise or collecting loyalty card points (these are all situations used to describe the contingency categories of the BPM in previous research) are inappropriate for a relevant endeavor. Such situations have been specifically chosen and manipulated in previous research mainly to establish the measurement of the Mehrabian and Russell (1974) variables as good indicators for the aspects of the BPM.

To achieve the explanation of the contextual and intentional stance in the case of confusion, other specific choice/shopping-related situations need to be used. Thus the study of the integration of confusion should maintain the basic premises of the model on the importance of the reinforcers, the behavior-setting scope (proved to be conceptualized and measured in past research as the pleasure-arousal-dominance variables of the Mehrabian and Russell model) and approach/avoidance behavior and will extend the basic principles of the BPM beyond the original model in shopping situations where confusion is expected to pose an effect. In that sense a study based on these premises should allow for a free exploration of differing consumer situations by only hypothesizing the expected levels of the extensional value of the different variables.

A potential limitation of the BPM as presented above is that the model has been tested predominantly in terms of reinforcements – utilitarian (pleasure) and informational (arousal).

However, the effect of aversive consequences, although depicted in the original BPM (as a line connecting utilitarian and informational reinforcement with aversive consequences), has been examined mainly as the effect of monetary cost, which is indeed one of the main aversive consequences of consumer choices (Sigurdsson et al., 2010). Confusion can be described as a self-based rule, which in an extensional language is translated into "an aversive consequence/ punishment of shopping" and the extent of its effect needs to be examined.

An additional major limitation of this "extensional" approach and conception of the BPM and specifically confusion is that it removes the personal level of explanation (the level of personal rules in the form of beliefs/propositional attitudes) from the understanding developed. To examine this personal level, behavior should be reconstructed and discussed in terms of an intentional account. This account takes into consideration not only the environmental effect but also the consumer's perception of shopping, what the consumer has been led to believe in terms of their own experiences of other similar or dissimilar situations and what he/she actually desires. It is then possible that a consumer might find a complex environment more acceptable than another consumer who, based on a previous experience, was not able to buy the desired product based on unavailability. This consumer will act differently to the variety of products on offer than another consumer with different perceptions and experience. In this case of the personal level of explanation, we have no other resort than to turn to the language of intentionality, the language of beliefs and desires. By adopting the intentional language or stance we adopt a "less scientific" approach to the study of phenomena; but since the social world lacks the comfort of constant experimental conditions, where the complexity of the learning history of objects can be known, social scientists need to resort to such language to better explore phenomena (Foxall, 2013).

It is on these grounds that the inclusion of intentional terms and finally an intentional conception of the BPM (BPM-I) has been proposed (Foxall, 2004, 2007a and b, 2013). The flexibility that Searle offers on the multiple uses of terms allows us to employ the same constructs in both the extensional and intentional way and this rule will be followed here to indicate the ways that an intentional BPM can add to the understanding provided by the extensional BPM.

The intentional Behavioral Perspective Model (BPM-I)

To prove and describe the value of the intentional Behavioral Perspective Model (BPM-I), Foxall (2013) describes the importance of the concept of collective intentionality and explains the implications of this collective understanding for the model. The application of collective intentionality allows the application of one of the main principles of intentional behaviorism; through the use of intentionality, an individual's actual rule-formulation coincides with the intentions we attribute to them and in this case their behavior will be predictable in terms of behavior analysis. The remainder of this chapter will examine confusion in the form of a tracking self-based rule (confusion) to incorporate the personal level of explanation into the model. Figure 24.4 depicts the intentional BPM.

The intentional Behavioral Perspective Model. The central explanatory component of the BPM, the consumer situation, is redefined in this new understanding. Consumer situation in this intentional model can be found "in the complex of the representation and meaning which intentional construals" supply (Foxall, 2013, p. 107). Behavior is then transformed from reactions to presented stimuli into intentionality-directed behavior.

Rules and rule-governed behavior are capable of contributing to the two kinds of explanations as described above. These can be described in the extensional sense, as stimuli that come to have the same effect as non-verbal contingencies that can act to predict behavior. In addition, the alternative intentional explanation treats rules as representations of the three-term

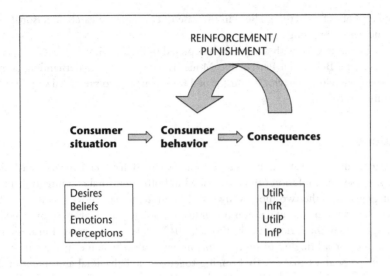

UtilR = utilitarian reinforcement; InfR = informational reinforcement; UtilP = utilitarian punishment; InfP = informational punishment

Figure 24.4 BPM-I

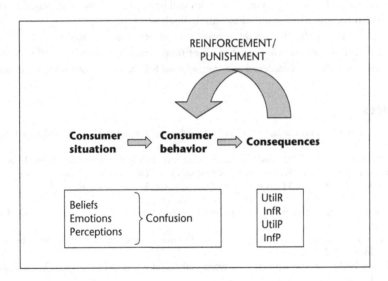

UtilR = utilitarian reinforcement; InfR = informational reinforcement; UtilP = utilitarian punishment; InfP = informational punishment

Figure 24.5 BPM-I

contingencies that act at the personal level and can be described using the *language of beliefs, the intentional language.*

On these grounds and as one of the least considered ideas in the psychology and consumer behavior realm, confusion can also have the characteristics of an intentional state, meaning that it can act at the belief/propositional attitude level. At this level confusion can be described as: a collective belief about something else – in the case of consumer research, a personal belief that a specific market is confusing.

Overall, the framework with confusion is depicted in Figure 24.5:

The intentional Behavioral Perspective Model is based on the understanding provided by rule-governed behavior. Behavior is transformed from reactions to presented stimuli into intentionality-directed behavior.

Conclusions

This chapter has dealt with an extension to the study of the Behavioral Perspective Model. More specifically, consumer confusion can be described in both behavioral and intentional terms and can be integrated into the two models suggested, the intentional (BPM-I) and the extensional (BPM-E). The addition and integration of confusion took the form of rule-governed behavior and more specifically the form of tracks (Foxall, 2013). The ideas expressed in this chapter lay the foundations for a bridging of diverse, incommensurable by some, paradigms of studying human psychology and behavior. By bringing together the behavioral and intentional understanding, this is not a way to advocate an "epistemological anarchism" (e.g., Feyerabend, 1993). Rules for the superior application of intentional behaviorism have been proposed in previous literature (e.g., Foxall, 2004, 2013). One of the central rules to be followed is that notwithstanding the use of intentional language, the focus and cause of behavioral control in both models is only to be found in the environment. Such rules will be better laid and understood in the future following the more extensive study of intentional behaviorism.

As a result of the application of these principles to other novel situations and constructs, a better understanding can be achieved. For all of these reasons, this chapter offers a theoretical framework that should be considered as a *starting point* for further theoretical endeavors.

References

Anninou, I. (2013). *Consumer Confusion: A Test of the Behavioral Perspective Model*. Unpublished PhD Thesis, Cardiff University.

Barnes-Holmes, D., Hayes, S. C. and Dymond, S. (2001). Self and self-directed rules. In S. C Hayes, D. Barnes-Holmes, and B. Roche (Eds.), *Relational Frame Theory: A Post-Skinnerian Account of Human Language and Cognition* (pp. 119–140). New York: Kluwer Academic/Plenum Publishers.

Baum, W. M. (1995). Rules, culture, and fitness. *The Behavior Analyst*, 18, 1–21.

Blakely, E. and Schlinger, H. (1987). Rules: function-altering contingency-specifying stimuli. *The Behavior Analyst*, 10 (2), 183–187.

Brownstein, A. J. and Shull, R. L. (1985). A rule for the use of the term, "Rule-governed behavior." *The Behavior Analyst*, 8, 265–267.

Catania, A. C. (1986). On the difference between verbal and nonverbal behavior. *The Analysis of Verbal Behavior*, 4, 2–9.

Catania, A. C. (1989). Rules as classes of verbal behavior: a reply to Glenn. *The Analysis of Verbal Behavior*, 7, 49–50.

Catania, A. C., Lowe, C. F. and Horne, P. (1990). Nonverbal behavior correlated with the shaped verbal behavior of children. *The Analysis of Verbal Behavior*, 8, 43–55.

Cerutti, D. T. (1989). Discrimination theory of rule-governed behavior. *Journal of the Experimental Analysis of Behavior*, 51, 259–276.

Crane, T. (2007). Intentionalism. In B. McLaughlin and A. Beckermann (Eds.) *Oxford Handbook to the Philosophy of Mind* (pp. 474–493). New York: Oxford University Press.

Dennett, D. C. (1987). *The Intentional Stance*. Cambridge, MA: MIT Press.

Dennett, D. C. (2007). Intentional systems theory. In B. McLaughlin and A. Beckermann (Eds.) *Oxford Handbook to the Philosophy of Mind* (pp. 339–350). New York: Oxford University Press.

Ellsworth, G. P. (2003). Confusion, concentration and other emotions of interest: commentary on Rozin and Cohen (2003). *Emotion*, 3 (1), 81–85.

Feyerabend, P. (1993). *Against Method* (3rd Edition). London: Verso.

Foxall, G. R. (1990). *Consumer Psychology in Behavioral Perspective*. New York: Routledge.

Foxall, G. R. (1992). The behavioral perspective model of purchase and consumption: from consumer theory to marketing practice. *Journal of the Academy of Marketing Science*, 20, 189–198.

Foxall, G. R. (1993). A behaviourist perspective on purchase and consumption. In W. F. Van Raaij and G. J. Bamossy (Eds.) *European Advances in Consumer Research*, Vol. 1 (pp. 501–506). Provo, UT: Association for Consumer Research.

Foxall, G. R. (1996). *Consumers in Context. The BPM Research Program*. London and New York: Routledge.

Foxall, G. R. (1997a). *Marketing Psychology: The Paradigm in the Wings*. London: MacMillan Press Ltd.

Foxall, G. R. (1997b). The emotional texture of consumer environments: a systematic approach to atmospherics. *Journal of Economic Psychology*, 18 (5), 505–523.

Foxall, G. R. (1998). Radical behaviorist interpretation: generating and evaluating an account of consumer behavior. *The Behavior Analyst*, 21, 321–354.

Foxall, G. R. (2000). The contextual stance in consumer research. *European Journal of Marketing*, 34(7), 768–779.

Foxall, G. R. (2004). *Context and Cognition. Interpreting Complex Behavior*. Reno, NV: Context Press.

Foxall, G. R. (2007a). Explaining consumer choice: coming to terms with intentionality. *Behavioral Processes*, 75 (2), 129–145.

Foxall, G. R. (2007b). Intentional behaviorism. *Behavior and Philosophy*, 35, 1–55.

Foxall, G. R. (2007c). *Explaining Consumer Choice*. London: Palgrave.

Foxall, G. R. (2008). Intentional behaviorism revisited. *Behavior and Philosophy*, 36, 113–155.

Foxall, G. R. (2010). *Interpreting Consumer Choice: The Behavioral Perspective Model*. New York: Routledge.

Foxall, G. R. (2013). Intentionality, symbol, and situation in the interpretation of consumer choice. *Marketing Theory*, 13 (1), 105–127.

Foxall, G. R. and Greenley, G. E. (1999). Consumers' emotional responses to service environments. *Journal of Business Research*, 46 (2), 149–158.

Foxall, G. R. and Greenley, G. E. (2000). Predicting and explaining responses to consumer environments: an empirical test and theoretical extension of the Behavioral Perspective Model. *The Service Industries Journal*, 20 (2), 39–63.

Foxall, G. R. and Soriano, M. Y. (2005). Situational influences on consumers' attitudes and behavior. *Journal of Business Research*, 58 (4), 518–525.

Glenn, S. S. (1987). Rules as environmental events. *The Analysis of Verbal Behavior*, 5, 29–32.

Hess, U. (2003). Now you see it, now you don't – The confusing case of confusion as an emotion: commentary on Rozin and Cohen (2003). *Emotion*, 3 (1), 76–80.

Keltner, D. and Shiota, M. N. (2003). New displays and new emotions: a commentary on Rozin and Cohen (2003). *Emotion*, 3, 86–91.

Kunkel, H. J. (1997). The analysis of rule-governed behavior in social psychology. *Psychological Record*, 47 (4), 698–716.

Lowe, M. C. and Damankos, F. J. (1968). Psychological and sociological dimension of anomie in a psychiatric population. *The Journal of Social Psychology*, 74, 65–74.

McClosky, H. and Schaar, J. H. (1965). Psychological dimensions of anomy. *American Sociological Review*, 30 (1), 14–40.

Mehrabian, A. and Russell, J. A. (1974). *An Approach to Environmental Psychology*. Cambridge, MA: MIT Press.

Merton, R. K. (1938). Social structure and anomie. *American Sociological Review*, 3 (June), 672–682.

Michael, J. (1986). Repertoire-altering effects of remote contingencies. *The Analysis of Verbal Behavior*, 4, 10–18.

Okouchi, H. (1999). Instructions as discriminative stimuli. *Journal of the Experimental Analysis of Behavior*, 72 (2), 205–214.

Oliveira-Castro, J. M. (2013). Comments on Foxall's "Intentionality, symbol and situation in the interpretation of consumer choice." *Marketing Theory*, 13 (1), 129–132.

Poppen, R. L. (1989). Some clinical implications of rule-governed behavior. In S. C. Hayes (Ed.) *Rule-Governed Behavior: Cognition, Contingencies, and Instructional Control* (pp. 325–357). Reno, NV: Context Press.

Rozin, P. and Cohen, B. A. (2003a). High frequency of facial expression corresponding to confusion, concentration and worry in an analysis of naturally occurring facial expressions of Americans. *Emotion*, 3 (1), 68–75.

Rozin, P. and Cohen, B. A. (2003b). Confusion infusions, suggestives, correctives, and other medicines. *Emotion*, 3 (1), 92–96.

Schlinger, H. D. (1993). Separating discriminative and function-altering effects of verbal stimuli. *The Behavior Analyst*, 16, 9–23.

Schlinger, H. D. (2008). Conditioning the behavior of the listener. *International Journal of Psychology and Psychological Therapy*, 8 (3), 309–322.

Schlinger, H. D. and Blakely, E. (1987). Function-altering effects of contingency specifying stimuli. *The Behavior Analyst*, 10 (1), 41–45.

Schweizer, M. (2004). *Consumer confusion im handel–Ein umweltpsychologisches erklärungsmodell*. St. Gallen: Rosch-Buch, Stresslitz.

Sigurdsson, V., Foxall, G. R. and Saevarsson, H. (2010). In-store experimental approach to pricing and consumer behavior. *Journal of Organizational Behavior Management*, 30, 234–246.

Skinner, B. F. (1957). *Verbal Behavior*. Englewood Cliffs, NJ: Prentice-Hall.

Skinner, B. F. (1966). An operant analysis of problem-solving. In B. Kleinmuntz (Ed.) *Problem Solving: Research, Method, Teaching* (pp. 225–257). New York: Wiley.

Skinner, B. F. (1969). *Contingencies of Reinforcement: A Theoretical Analysis*. Englewood Cliffs, NJ: Prentice-Hall.

Skinner, B. F. (1974). *About Behaviorism*. New York: Alfred A. Knopf.

Taylor, L. J. (1968). Alienation, anomie and delinquency. *British Journal of Social and Clinical Psychology*, 7 (2), 93–105.

Törneke, N., Luciano, C. and Salas, S. V. (2008). Rule-governed behavior and psychological problems. *International Journal of Psychology and Psychological Therapy*, 8 (2), 141–156.

Vaughan, E. M. (1985). Repeated acquisition in the analysis of rule-governed behavior. *Journal of the Experimental Analysis of Behavior*, 44 (2), 175–184.

Walsh, G. and Mitchell, V.-W. (2010). The effect of consumer confusion proneness on word of mouth, trust, and consumer satisfaction. *European Journal of Marketing*, 44 (6), 838–859.

Walsh, G., Hennig-Thurau, T. and Mitchell, V.-W. (2007). Consumer confusion proneness: scale development, validation, and application. *Journal of Marketing Management*, 23 (7/8), 697–721.

Zettle, R. D. (1990). Rule-governed behavior: a radical behavioral answer to the cognitive challenge. *The Psychological Record*, 40, 41–49.

Zettle, R. D. and Hayes, S. C. (1982). Rule-governed behavior: a potential theoretical framework for cognitive behavioral therapy. *Advances in Cognitive-Behavioral Research and Therapy*, 1, 73–117.

25

Consumer heterophenomenology

Gordon R. Foxall

> The challenge is to construct a theory of mental events, using the data that scientific method permits.
>
> *(Dennett, 1991, p. 71)*

Introduction

Dennett (1991, p. 72) describes heterophenomenology as

> the *neutral* path leading from objective physical science and its insistence on the third-person point of view, to a method of phenomenological description that can (in principle) do justice to the most private and ineffable subjective experiences, while never abandoning the methodological principles of science.

He argues, moreover, that we can study all there is to know about first-person consciousness at the level of third-person analysis without leaving a significant residue (Dennett, 2005, pp. 29–30). This chapter outlines the considerations of which an interpretation of consumer choice in the context of what I have called *consumer behavior analysis* (Foxall, 2002, 2010a) must be aware. The hallmark of Dennett's conception of scientific method, the use of third-person analysis which implies intersubjective agreement on terms and observations, is beyond the reach of attempts to investigate directly the conscious experience of human beings. Heterophenomenology is a methodology introduced by Dennett (1982, 1991) for obtaining such a third-person under-standing of the contents of consciousness which are directly apprehended only subjectively, i.e., in the first-person terms of the individual who is conscious of them. The essential character of this experience is its *privacy*. How are we to tap into this experience, given that the individual's account (say, in verbal expression) is not necessarily accurate? Dennett (2005) further charac-terizes heterophenomenology as a *bridge* between the subjective experience or consciousness of the individual and the physical sciences. At one end, the bridge must be securely affixed to the objective or third-person perspective pursued by the physical sciences in its conventional spheres of operation. The causation implied or invoked is that of standard conservative physics, or we might say, the extensional mode of explanation that is central to scientific explanation (Dennett, 1969).

The bridge between science and interpretation that I would like to argue for in the context of consumer heterophenomenology has two implications. First, a purely scientific approach to the analysis of consumer behavior, one that proceeds in third-person extensional terms, despite its value in aiding understanding of numerous facets of product and brand choice, consumer maximization, and the sensitivity of consumer behavior to the contingencies of reinforcement and punishment, cannot do full justice to aspects of consumer choice such as its cross-situational continuity. For this, it is necessary to turn to interpretation and interpretation requires rules if it is not to descend into undisciplined speculation. Second, therefore, a scheme of interpretation must rely on a standard of knowledge of consumer behavior founded on a third-person analysis.

My interest in heterophenomenological interpretation arises from my research program over the last thirty years. The Consumer Behavior Analysis Research Program came into being as a result of what I perceived to be the uncritical adoption of cognitive terms to "explain" whatever aspect of consumer choice happened to have been observed. Whatever consumers did could apparently be made intelligible by recourse to the mentalistic language of positive attitudes, beliefs and intentions, even though the measures of these artefacts seldom correlated beyond the low-level characteristic of almost any two variables in social science (Meehl, 1990) and failed to address many of the persistent facts of consumer choice identified by marketing scientists such as Ehrenberg and Goodhardt (e.g., Ehrenberg, 1988; Goodhardt et al., 1984). Despite these "inconveniences" for the cognitive analysis of the day, grand theories based on the prevailing paradigm of cognitive psychology held sway over most teaching and research. While I did not doubt that cognitive theory had an important role to play in explaining consumer choice, I doubted that so liberal an approach would yield useful consumer theories. The answer I proposed was to develop a parsimonious behavioral model of consumer choice which eschewed entirely cognitive and other structuralist terms. (The derivation of the model in contradistinction to the prevailing cognitive paradigm is described in Foxall, 1990/2004, 1997a, 2005.) The methodology of *establishing the boundaries of minimalism* or alternatively *the bounds of behaviorism* which I pursued involved testing this behaviorist model to destruction to ascertain the point at which the explication of consumer behavior in purely stimulus-reinforcer terms was no longer possible and resort had to be made to cognitive variables to make sense of the observed patterns of choice. Since then, the major question motivating my research has been how, once the need for cognition has been ascertained, it can be understood and legitimately ascribed.

In retaining the extensional analysis of behavior as my starting point, I aim to demonstrate when and how more interpretive approaches to understanding behavior ought to proceed if they are to avoid the charge that they consist in the undisciplined psychologizing of observed activity. This may not be standard ethnography, but it is surely what many ethnographers, and certainly many other social scientists, have been doing for decades. My aim is not to critically evaluate heterophenomenology (see, for example, the essays in *Philosophical Topics*, 22(1–2), 1994), or even to do so in the context of consumer behavior analysis: rather it is simply to set out a possible scheme for realizing its insights in this field, to introduce a substantive field of social inquiry to a methodological perspective.

The Behavioral Perspective Model

The parsimonious behaviorist model of consumer choice that underlies this research program, the Behavioral Perspective Model (BPM) (Foxall, 1990/2004), is a means of unifying the components of consumer behavior analysis, namely behavioral psychology, behavioral economics and marketing science. Radical behaviorism, the parsimonious model of human behavior on which my research program is founded, reflects the following observations. Behavior generates consequences, some of which are followed by an increase in the rate at which that behavior is performed; because these consequences seem to "strengthen" the behavior, they are termed *reinforcers*. Other consequences reduce the rate of responding and are known as "punishers." (My definitions are intended to avoid the circularity of reasoning to which some early statements of behaviorism were prone.) The BPM brings these guidelines for predicting behavior in the laboratory into the arena of consumer choice in the rough-and-tumble of real-world marketplaces.

It locates consumer behavior at the intersection of a learning history (more precisely, a nexus of learning histories both general and pertaining to previous patterns of consumption and their rewarding and punishing outcomes) and the rewarding and aversive outcomes of current consumption as signaled by the stimuli that make up the consumer's current behavior setting. The consumer behavior setting comprises two kinds of stimulus: discriminative stimuli and motivating operations. Discriminative stimuli are elements of the environment in the presence of which the consumer discriminates behaviorally, performing those acts that have previously met with rewarding outcomes and neglecting to perform those which have not. Motivating operations are also environmental stimuli that enhance the value of the reward promised by the setting variables as contingent on the performance of a particular behavior. An advertisement that asks, "Can't you just *taste* the difference?!" is an example.

The rewards so signaled are of two types: *utilitarian reinforcement* which refers to the functional benefits of purchasing, owning and consuming a product or service, and *informational reinforcement*, which is the feedback in the form of social status, prestige and self-esteem that follows these behaviors. Any laptop provides certain basic services such as enabling wordprocessing or designing presentations; in other words, all laptops provide a common degree of functional benefits (though some are more sophisticated than others, of course). But owning and displaying a particular leading brand that is acknowledged as the market leader may also confer additional benefits: the esteem provided by colleagues' appreciative statements or stares and the self-worth that accrues to the owner as a result of owning a superior product.

The BPM, summarized in Figure 25.1, elaborates the *three-term contingency* that is the explanatory building block of radical behaviorism:

$$S^D : R \rightarrow S^r$$

in which a discriminative stimulus, S^D, sets the occasion for reinforcement, S^r, contingent on the performance of a specific response, R (Skinner, 1953, 1974). The colon linking the S^D to the R indicates that the discriminative stimulus *increases the probability of* an appropriate response. The response, should it occur, is emitted by the organism rather than being elicited by the preceding stimulus as in classical conditioning. The $\rightarrow$ linking the R to the S^r indicates a necessary and contingent relationship in which the response is automatically followed by a consequence that subsequently alters the rate of behavior. Theoretically, this explanatory device could be extended into an *n*-term contingency, but it is sufficient to go only as far as four terms, including motivating operations (MO) as a pre-behavioral influence on choice. These elements and the relationships among them are defined entirely in extensional terms, i.e., without recourse to intentional terms such as *believes*, *desires* or *intends*. (For a philosophical treatment, see Smith, 1994; for development in the context of consumer behavior analysis, see Foxall, 2004, 2010b.)

The particular combination of utilitarian and informational reinforcement that consumers obtain by purchasing and using a product is known as its *pattern of reinforcement* and each broadly defined pattern of reinforcement gives rise to a particular pattern of consumer choice (Figure 25.2). Consumer behavior settings differ in the extent to which they compel a particular course of action. A (relatively)[1] *open setting* such as a café or bar provides numerous different

Gordon R. Foxall

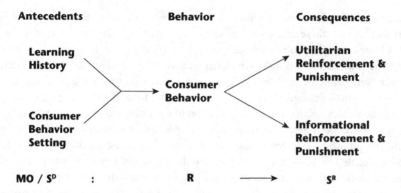

Figure 25.1 Summative Behavioral Perspective Model

Source: Foxall, G. R. (2010). *Interpreting Consumer Choice*. New York and London: Routledge. Reproduced by permission

Informational reinforcement

	Low	High
High	**Hedonism**	**Accomplishment**
Low	**Maintenance**	**Accumulation**

(vertical axis label: **Utilitarian reinforcement**)

Figure 25.2 Patterns of reinforcement and operant classes of consumer behavior

Source: Foxall, G. R. (2010). *Interpreting Consumer Choice*. New York and London: Routledge. Reproduced by permission

ways in which to behave, each reinforced uniquely by a particular pattern of reinforcement. By contrast, a (relatively) *closed setting* provides few, perhaps only one, behavior pattern or program: completing the paperwork necessary to purchase a home, for instance, or exercising at the gym, or undergoing dental treatment. This additional dimension of the *scope of the consumer behavior setting* is incorporated in Figure 25.3.

The BPM has generated a large volume of empirical research which indicates that it has the capacity to predict product and brand choice, the sensitivity of consumers' behavior to changes in price and value in relation to the pattern of reinforcement exhibited by the products they purchase, and that consumer behavior maximizes a utility function comprising a particular combination of utilitarian and informational reinforcement. In addition, the scope of the consumer behavior setting has been shown to be an important variable in actual consumer choice.

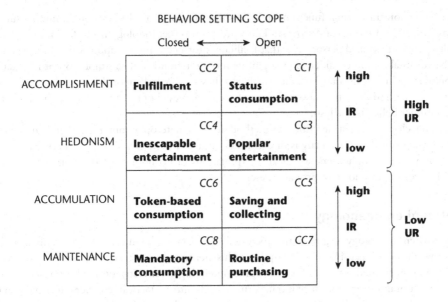

Figure 25.3 The BPM contingency matrix

Source: Foxall, G. R. (2010). *Interpreting Consumer Choice*. New York and London: Routledge. Reproduced by permission

The ascription of cognition

Despite these results, which indicate the efficacy of a purely extensional model of consumer choice, the search for the bounds of behaviorism has revealed three aspects of the explanation of human behavior for which the three-term contingency proves inadequate. In summary, these are to account for the continuity/discontinuity of particular patterns of behavior, to deal with the personal level of exposition, and to delimit the scope of behavioral interpretation (Foxall, 2004, 2007a). At these junctures, which denote the *imperatives of intentionality*, it becomes necessary to turn to intentional idioms to interpret the behavior.

The sole criterion for determining the point at which intentional interpretation becomes necessary is that the extensional language of radical behaviorism no longer suffices to explain the observed behavior. This is the case when the stimuli required are not empirically available: we cannot identify the reinforcers, for instance, that would be necessary to account for the persistence of a particular pattern of behavior. At this juncture, we have no alternative to accounting for the behavior in terms of what the subject believes or desires, perceives or feels. More difficult to arrive at are means of delimiting this intentional interpretation before it devolves into unnecessary psychologism, i.e. giving a ready-made "psychological" quasi-explanation of whatever behavior we happen to observe.

Because cognition is an unobservable, a theoretical creation aimed at making the observed more intelligible, its use owes more to *interpretation* than *explanation*. The relationship it proposes between the data language in which observation is described and the theoretical language in terms of which it is explicated is not amenable to the rigor of an experimental analysis in which behavior (the dependent variable) is a function of the environmental stimuli that precede and follow it (the independent variables). In experimental science such functional relationships can be demonstrated to hold; they can be so demonstrated to the satisfaction of an intellectual community; members of that community who wish to criticize the methodology of those who claim to have demonstrated such functional relationships can do so on the basis of common assumptions, criteria and modes of discourse. This third-person methodology is not foolproof but it is built upon standardized perspectives that facilitate informed criticism upon which progress may be based. Establishing confidence in cognitive interpretation is not so simple. But it is possible. Moreover, while consumer behavior analysis relies in this task upon heterophenomenology, Dennett's methodology may also make use of the basic model of consumer choice that is central to consumer behavior analysis.

In this chapter, I first describe the methodology of heterophenomenology and then show how it is applicable to the analysis of consumer choice. I then seek to establish criteria for the credibility of heterophenomenological interpretations of economic behavior, drawing on the BPM of consumer choice to provide these.

Heterophenomenology

Heterophenomenology begins with "recorded raw data." This means the transcribed verbal behavior of the subject. His/her description of his/her first-person thoughts, expressed in words and then transformed into data for heterophenomenological investigation. This transcription is itself an act of interpretation since it transforms sounds into syntactical sentences. It could also be that the subject responds to the investigator's instructions by means of key-presses (perhaps on a computer keyboard): these are then transformed into speech acts. However they are obtained, these speech acts constitute a *text* for further linguistic analysis, similar in principle to the text of a novel which is subjected to literary critique.

To clarify what are the fundamental data of heterophenomenology, it is useful to note Dennett's (2005) response to Levine's (1994) argument that these data ought to consist in actual conscious experiences rather than beliefs, judgments or other intentional expressions *about* those experiences. Dennett replies by tracing the levels from "raw data" to "heterophenomenological worlds": a. conscious experiences; b. beliefs about these conscious experiences; c. verbal expressions of these beliefs; and d. utterances. Dennett asks which of these represents the "primary data." For the heterophenomenologist, he says, they are the sounds or utterances, d. But these data can be interpreted via speech acts, c., to beliefs about experiences, b. These, he maintains, are the primary *interpreted* data, the QED, "organized into heterophenomenological worlds, for a science of consciousness" (Dennett, 2005, pp. 44–5). But it is not possible to go as far as a. to locate our primary data in conscious experience itself; for, if a. > b., indicating that I have conscious experiences I am not aware I have, these experiences are inaccessible to me exactly as they are to anyone else; and if b. > a., indicating that I believe I have conscious experiences that I don't in fact have, then the beliefs are what has to be explained rather than the non-existing experiences. Therefore, b., beliefs about one's subjective conscious experience, emerges as the "maximal set of primary data."

Given that conscious experience (a.) is ruled out as a datum for scientific analysis on the grounds that it is simply not empirically available for third-person analysis, the closest a scientific investigation of consciousness can get to the raw primary data is by reconstructing what the subject believes about his/her subjective experience (b.). This believing, when it is the unreconstructed mentalizing of the individual, is also a first-person occurrence, also not publicly available. But the subject is able to give it verbal expression (c.) and, in the course of a heterophenomenological investigation, to make utterances based on it (d.) The heterophenomenologist takes d., the basic recorded data, and employs the intentional stance to interpret them as expressions of beliefs and to infer the subject's beliefs themselves from the expressions. This is the heterophenomenological methodology. The subject describes what *seems* to be going on in his/her consciousness (on which he/she is the authority), not what is actually going on (on which he/she is not). He/she knows as no other what it is like to be him/her.

The intentional stance requires that to account for the behavior of an intentional system, the investigator ascribes to it the beliefs, desires and other intentions that enable the behavior to be predicted (Dennett, 1987). An intentional system is any entity the behavior of which is predictable by the ascriptions of such intentionality. The beliefs and desires that are ascribed for this purpose are those the system ought to have, given its history and its current circumstances: i.e., in the terms of the BPM, given its learning history and its current behavior setting. All there is to believing is to be predictable by the intentional stance. The point of the interpretive phase of the heterophenomenological enterprise is, therefore, to reconstruct the intentional structure that would be consistent with the utterances made by the subject. Dennett is careful to note that even in the process of transcribing these utterances into sentences (typified by but not limited to the work of an audio-stenographer transcribing a recorded voice) interpretation is taking place: the utterances are being organized into sentences that follow a particular syntactic logic; perhaps at some stage sentence structure is altered to make the utterances more intelligible (to whom?); perhaps the sentences themselves are later reordered to construct or preserve a narrative. But the application of the intentional stance requires another form of interpretation: the assignment of the beliefs and desires necessary to predict the behavior of the intentional system, beliefs and desires that are judged (by whom and by what criteria?) to be those the system "ought to have" (as determined by whom and on what basis?) given its history and circumstances. I propose here that the bases for the ascription of intentionality are twofold: a pattern of molar operant behavior and an underlying neurophysiological foundation. Before I say more about the rationale for this methodology, let me examine the form it would need to take.

Of course, if we were to know the precise operant learning history of a subject, together with his/her neurophysiology, we would have no difficulty in constructing an intentional framework within which to interpret his/her behavior. This is an unlikely prospect, however. Rather, we are thrown back on a general understanding of the kinds of behavior and its outcomes that the person is characterized by and its neurophysiological underpinning. In the case of the social and economic behavior of consumers, however, we have an advantage. We are aware of the general factors towards which such behavior is directed and the environmental stimuli that shape and maintain that behavior. They are the very subject of the BPM and the empirical research that it has inspired. We also have an understanding of the neurophysiological bases of these behavior patterns, the role of neuronal firing in the selection of behavior in regard to economic goals and behavioral norms. They are the subject of neuroeconomics. Knowing the potential and the limits of the methodology, we can now say more of its rationale. The point is not that we can pinpoint the exact causal texture of the consumer behavior the interpretation of which preoccupies us: rather, we can use behavioral science and neuroeconomics to delimit the scope of our intentional interpretations of behavior which otherwise might grow Topsy-like into the unfalsifiable generalizations of cognitive psychologism that brought the Consumer Behavior Analysis Research Program into being.

Consumer heterophenomenology

Dennett argues that the intentional stance is inevitable in transforming heterophenomenological data into interpretations. I would add that the content of such ascribed intentionality (in the context of consumer choice in which we are operating) is provided in the context of consumer choice by the structural variables of the BPM. Moreover, as the model proceeds from a purely extensional portrayal of consumer choice through the intentional and cognitive portrayals, it acquires more intentionally based constructs in terms of which the heterophenomenological interpretation should proceed such as that of the *symbolic consumer situation* and *symbolic reinforcement* (Foxall, 2013). The following account does not present a comprehensive example of consumer heterophenomenology but aims to show how such a study would need to adhere to the requirements of interpretive practice on the basis of consumer behavior analysis.

I should like to illustrate the distinctive mode of heterophenomenological interpretation by reference to research which sought to test the BPM by means of investigations of the emotional reactions elicited by descriptions of consumer situations based on the structural components of the model described above. A comprehensive analysis would require four stages of research, each of which would complement the others. These kinds of analysis are:

1. *A statistical analysis of aggregated results.* This would proceed in terms of a third-person investigation of the ways in which consumer-respondents react to written scenarios of consumer situations that reflect the levels of utilitarian and informational reinforcement and the scope of the consumer behavior setting as defined by the BPM. The responses would be cast in terms of answers to psychometric measures of the emotional dimensions appropriate to testing hypotheses about the consumer situations. The results would be interpreted according to the model's expectations of consumer choice in these various situations. Results for a large sample of consumers would be aggregated and subjected to statistical analyses.

   This I have done.[2] The responses to scenarios of consumer situations which embody sources of high vs. low utilitarian reinforcement, high vs. low informational reinforcement, and relatively open/closed consumer behavior settings in terms of the emotional reactions of consumer-respondents allow the process to be illustrated (Foxall, 1997b). The scenarios depict each of the eight contingency categories shown in Figure 25.3. The psychometric instruments employed to elicit consumers' reactions are the scales for the assessment of *pleasure, arousal* and *dominance* devised and tested by Mehrabian and Russell (1974). The working hypothesis of the studies we have conducted in several cultural contexts, two languages and for a wide range of consumer scenarios was that pleasure would be more strongly reported for situations embodying higher levels of utilitarian reinforcement, arousal for situations embodying higher levels of informational reinforcement and stronger dominance for more open settings. In the eight studies we have now conducted thus far, these hypotheses have been supported. Figure 25.4 shows the results.

2. *An individual-level analysis of a single respondent member of this sample.* This would still entail using the psychometric measure of emotional reactions. The verbal responses of this consumer would be interpreted according to the model from which the hypotheses in (1) were derived. Individual-level results could also be interpreted in terms of the results gained from (1).

3. *An individual-level interpretation of the verbal behavior of an individual requested to respond ad lib to each of the scenarios presented in (1) in terms of his/her first-person experience of the situations depicted.* This would enable a wider range of verbal responses to be sampled than those made available in the psychometric measures.

4. *An individual-level interpretation of the verbal behavior of an individual requested to respond ad lib in describing their subjective experience of whatever consumer situations they choose to speak about.* This is probably closest to the spirit of heterophenomenology since it imposes the fewest interviewer-defined categories on the respondent.

From the point of view of the heterophenomenological method, the verbal behavior provided by each respondent, when properly transcribed, provides a third-person account of the first-person feelings and experiences that that person felt on reviewing the stimuli presented in

BEHAVIOR SETTING SCOPE

Closed ←————————→ Open

	CC2	CC1
ACCOMPLISHMENT	**PLEASURE** **AROUSAL** dominance	**PLEASURE** **AROUSAL** **DOMINANCE**
	CC4	CC3
HEDONISM	**PLEASURE** arousal dominance	**PLEASURE** arousal **DOMINANCE**
	CC6	CC5
ACCUMULATION	pleasure **AROUSAL** dominance	pleasure **AROUSAL** **DOMINANCE**
	CC8	CC7
MAINTENANCE	pleasure arousal dominance	pleasure arousal **DOMINANCE**

Contingencies and emotions: research hypotheses and summary of findings. Studies show that: (i) pleasure scores for contingency categories (CCs) 1, 2, 3 and 4 each exceed those of CCs 5, 6, 7 and 8; (ii) arousal scores for CCs 1, 2, 5 and 6 each exceed those of CCs 3, 4, 7 and 8; (iii) dominance scores for CCs 1, 3, 5 and 7 each exceed those for CCs 2, 4, 6 and 8. Moreover, (iv) approach–avoidance (aminusa) scores for CCs 1, 2, 3 and 4 each exceed those for CCs 5, 6, 7 and 8; and (v) approach–avoidance (aminusa) scores for CCs 1 and 3 each exceed those for CCs 2, 4, 5, 6, 7 and 8

Figure 25.4   The BPM emotional contingency matrix

Source: Foxall, G. R. (2011). Brain, emotion and contingency in the explanation of consumer behaviour, *International Review of Industrial and Organizational Psychology*, 26, 47–92. Reproduced by permission

each scenario. The results summarized in Figure 25.4 are aggregated for statistical analysis and ease of presentation but the analyses to which methods (2)–(4) refer could be undertaken for each of the consumer-respondents in turn at the individual level. The pattern of responding revealed by the aggregate analysis (1) might provide a means of interpreting the verbal behavior of the individual respondent but the extent to which this is feasible or desirable is as yet an open question. Similarly, the information gained in the more interpretive analyses (2)–(4) might provide important insight into the actual experiences of consumers and allow the scope of the statistical patterns revealed by (1) to be more accurately assessed. The relationship between (1) and (2)–(4) is that of quantitative social science to qualitative.

Now the advantage of conducting this multi-stage research is that the quantitative stage (1) allows us to compare the content of the propositional attitudes employed by individual respondents in the later stages with that which a psychometric study imposes by regulating the range of responses the consumer is permitted. This is especially so with respect to the most nebulous stage (4) in which the consumer is seeking to reveal his/her beliefs, desires, emotions and perceptions in the context of any experience as a consumer he/she chooses to speak about. Are the categories on which the psychometric measures are based those in terms of which the consumer normally thinks when formalizing his/her prior behavior? Do the settings he/she chooses to speak of resemble those scenarios selected on the basis of the BPM's contingency categories (Figure 25.3)? Do consumers naturally think in terms of utilitarian and informational reinforcement, the functional and social/symbolic benefits provided, in describing their consumption experiences? Stages (2) and (3) facilitate a closer comparison of heterophenomenologically revealed consumer experience with the results of the psychometric work since they are based on greater situational continuity of the imagined scenarios. There is no ultimate need to confine the experimental stimuli to pre-written consumption scenarios, of course; the possibility arises of obtaining scripts that serve as texts for further analysis actually in the consumption situations populated by consumers.

The literary critique that is the methodology of the analysis of plays or novels or other written works is in my view not sufficient for the heterophenomenological analysis of texts produced by stages (2)–(4). In the case of consumer behavior, we can draw upon a much broader field of knowledge as our interpretive base, a functional model of consumer choice which can be subjected to empirical test by means of the third-person methodology of science, as well as a third-person description of the first-person experience of consumers that is as close as we are likely to get to the subjective mentality of consumption.

Heterophenomenology in the context of intentional behaviorism

The situations of explanation in which the imperatives of intentionality hold – where the continuity/discontinuity of behavior cannot be related appropriately to the discriminative and reinforcing stimuli required to fulfill the requirements of the three-term contingency, where the personal level of interpretation becomes necessary, and where behavioral interpretations must be delimited – are especially relevant to these heterophenomenological considerations. The extensional model of consumer behavior depicted in Figure 25.1 is insufficient to cope with these requirements and *intentional behaviorism* has been proposed as a methodology that can take them fully into account by responsibly ascribing intentionality. Although it is beyond the scope of this chapter to provide a complete account of the methodology of intentional behaviorism (see, for instance, Foxall, 2007a,b, 2008, 2009), I should like to illustrate the relevance to it of this discussion of heterophenomenology by reference to the derivation of appropriate intentional idioms.

The behavior of adults on matching tasks can be explained by the concurrent schedules of reinforcement in operation. If, in phase 1 of an experiment, pressing key A is reinforced every 10 seconds as long as at least one press has been made and pressing key B once every 20 seconds as long as at least one press has been made, then we can predict according to the matching law that the participant will allocate 66.6% of responses to key A and 33.3% to B. In addition, he/she will obtain similar proportions of reward, respectively, from each key. Similar results are obtained for human and nonhuman animals. But if, in phase 2 of the experiment, the schedules are modified so that different periods must elapse before responding receives reinforcement, nonhumans adapt quickly to the new schedule while human participants tend to retain the former response pattern. We cannot explain humans' insensitivity to the altered schedules by reference to the discriminative and reinforcing stimuli now in operation since their behavior is by definition not influenced by them. The sole explanatory factor within the scope of orthodox radical behaviorism is the private events (thoughts and feelings) that are a central, even defining, element in this philosophy of psychology. The rules that participants devise for themselves to comply with the schedules in force during phase 1 of the experiment and that are enshrined in their thoughts are held to be carried over to the new situation defined by phase 2 and to lead the individual to continue the behavior pattern that was reinforced in phase 1 but not phase 2.

An alternative strategy of explanation might be to maintain that it is the individual's learning history that carries over from phase 1 to phase 2, that he/she is constrained by previous reinforcement patterns to repeat the behavior under the new stimulus conditions.

Neither of these explanations is acceptable within a science of behavior because each deals in unobservables that cannot enter into either an experimental or correlational analysis. Any statements about the verbal rule-formulations that entered into the decision-making of an experimental participant are mere fabrications, untestable conjectures, explanatory fictions. Similarly, any appeal to a learning history that is not empirically available is not an entity that can enter into a scientific explanation. They are speculations the purpose of which is to save the theory on which the accompanying explanation of behavior rests. These are precisely the sorts of explanatory fiction that behaviorists such as Skinner sought to eliminate from scientific inquiry. The fact that they proceed in the terminology of behavior analysis may seduce the reader into thinking that they do not "appeal to events taking place somewhere else, at some other level of observation, described in different terms, and measured, if at all, in different dimensions" (Skinner, 1953, p. 193). In fact, they contravene Skinner's strictures on every count. Resort to private verbal behavior or to an unobserved learning history is necessarily an appeal to otherwise-located events, observed by who knows whom, and discriminable only in different dimensions. It would be intellectually dishonest to provide accounts of this kind simply to prop up the radical behaviorist ideology of explanation or to appeal to some form of "action-at-a-distance" to fill in the gaps that scientific observation is unable to fill. The fact of the matter is that the behavior cannot be explained in terms of the extensional language that is the hallmark of behaviorist psychology and perhaps its very raison d'être.

More satisfactory is to acknowledge the explanatory gap that arises when the stimuli responsible for a behavior pattern cannot be identified using intentional language to account for the behavior. But how is such an interpretation to be constructed and justified?

The construction of an interpretation in intentional terms depends on establishing how a pattern of behavior that *is* amenable to explanation in operant terms (because the antecedent and consequent stimuli that control the behavior and their relationships to the behavior can be identified) could be understood in terms of the putative desires, beliefs, emotions and perceptions that need to be ascribed to account for its emergence and persistence. So, the behavior of an adult human participant in a matching experiment could be interpreted in terms of his desire to achieve successful outcomes, his belief that this could be achieved by pressing keys A and B in a particular sequence, his feelings of pleasure, arousal and dominance on achieving a winning outcome, and his perception of the efficacy of the keys pressed in producing rewards at a particular rate. Yes, these desires, beliefs, emotions and perceptions amount to explanatory fictions but, faute de mieux, we have no alternative to employing them, given the absence of any means to ascribe the behavior to observable contingencies of reinforcement. To ascribe the schedule-insensitive behavior of the matching participant to the contingencies that were obtained in phase 1 would not square with the influence of the contingencies obtaining in phase 2 to which he/she is currently subject.

This strategy takes a pattern of behavior that is as close as can be achieved to the pattern to be explained and extrapolates an intentional interpretation from the former to the latter. The behavior that is the subject of the extrapolated interpretation must be consistent with selection by consequences at the levels of (A) natural selection, and (B) operant conditioning.

(A) The first criterion seeks a rationale for the interpreted behavior in the general neurophysiology of the individual. This is not the same as saying that his/her behavior is *caused by* neuronal activity: only that the organism would have evolved in such a way as to acquire a neuronal system that behaves consistently with the behavior pattern being interpreted. I have in mind here the formation and operation of reward prediction errors, the release of dopamine as a preparation for reinforced behaviors, the further reward of reinforced behaviors through the experience of emotion, and so on. An important demonstration in our work is therefore that the consumer behaviors we are investigating are rewarded by emotional feelings. Rolls's (1999) theory of emotion provides an underlying rationale for the necessary links between emotion and reinforcement. Rolls proposes that any reinforcing stimuli present in the extra-individual environment[3] can act as an eliciting stimulus to generate corresponding emotions (Foxall, 2011).

(B) To reach this level of corroboration it is necessary to determine that the behavior in question is amenable to reinforcement; hence, the requirement that selection by consequences be demonstrated by showing that the behavior is subject to operant conditioning. Operant conditioning is determined by applying the correlational law of effect (Baum, 1973) to the molar behavior pattern observed during the period when the contingencies of reinforcement can be ascertained (phase 1 in the matching experiment). The purpose of determining this is that an intentional interpretation of behavior that is under contingency control can be logically extended to that for which contingency control is not obvious, i.e. similar behavior that is interpreted because its explanation is not possible in view of the lack of observable contingencies.

This interpretation is broadly similar to that obtained in the case of consumers' emotional reactions to various consumption environments by means of psychometric analysis. At least it is as close as we can get to understanding the behavior of consumers in extensional terms and constructing an intentional interpretation that fits the "facts" so established. However, useful as this may be when extensional analysis is no longer possible, it is corrigible through the use of heterophenomenological methods (2)–(4). The possibility of reconstructing the consumer's actual experience of decision-making by eliciting his/her desires, beliefs, emotions and perceptions by heterophenomenology adds immensely to the warrant of assertibility we can assume as interpreters of behavior.

Moreover, this example of a behavioral situation requiring interpretation that goes beyond the explanation of which the three-term contingency alone is capable illustrates the three imperatives of intentionality: the fundamental problem is one of accounting for the continuity of behavior in the absence of supporting stimuli, be they antecedent or subsequent to the behavior; this necessitates a personal-level interpretation based on intentional language; finally, the range of interpretation invoked is limited by the scrupulous use of intentional language rather than explanatory fictions in the form of invented learning histories, private verbal behavior or rule-governance. Although this example is drawn from experimental analyses of behavior, its invitation to interpret behavior intentionally is also a common feature of consumer choice; e.g., when a new brand is incorporated into the consumer's consideration set in the absence of prior experience with it (Foxall, 2007b, 2008).

Conclusions

A third-person account is at the heart of science. But the methods of empirical confirmation to which it gives rise, e.g. experimentation and psychometrics, are not always sufficient to explain aspects of behavior e.g., cross-situational continuity, the personal level of experience and how behavioral interpretation is to be delimited so it does not descend into psychologism. Heterophenomenology allows us to access first-person accounts of experience and to translate them into the third-person statements of science. But how are such third-person transcriptions to be understood? I have argued that a framework supported by a more conventionally scientific approach to consumer choice allows the finer points of interpretation to be added to what is made available purely by heterophenomenological method in the abstract.

I must admit to being left wondering whether Dennett intends heterophenomenology to be taken up by the social and behavioral science community as a practical methodology for research or whether he is simply demonstrating that a third-person scientific account could be given of the first-person subjective experiences of human beings. (Just as I wonder whether Dawkins's 1976 introduction of *memes* into his discussion of the selfish gene was intended to be taken as a jumping-off point for a whole research program: but I digress.) Whatever, the exercise of examining the kinds of knowledge that could be gained through an examination of consumer experience from a variety of methodological standpoints is instructive. Nevertheless, as a stimulus to the systematic interpretation of consumer choice, the framework suggested in this chapter provides a means of comparing knowledge gained via a number of alternative perspectives, a means of triangulating our efforts to portray consumer behavior in its fullness. The usefulness of this multi-pronged approach will be revealed by further empirical investigation which will permit judgment of the extent to which stages (2)–(4) add to the knowledge gained by the purely quantitative analysis of stage (1), the ways in which that additional interpretation enhances and clarifies the relationships revealed by the psychometric approach, and the contribution to understanding made available by the interaction of these differing methodological avenues.

Notes

1 The openness and closedness of consumer behavior settings are always to be understood as relative, as are the levels of utilitarian and informational reinforcement that compose the pattern of reinforcement. It is tedious for both writer and reader to make this point repeatedly, however.
2 The range of scenarios investigated are itemized in Foxall (1997b) and Foxall and Yani-de-Soriano (2005). Details of the testing of the materials and establishment of intersubjective criteria can be found in Foxall (1999). Comprehensive analyses of the eight studies can be found in Foxall (2011) and Foxall et al. (2012). Further commentary and analysis is available in Foxall (2005), Yani-de-Soriano and Foxall (2006) and Yani-de-Soriano et al. (2013).
3 I employ the term "extra-individual environment" to make clear that the reinforcing stimuli exist outwith the organism in what we would normally call simply the environment. "Extra-individual environment" is a cumbersome locution intended to avoid confusion that could arise from Skinner's (1974) argument that a small part of the environment is enclosed within the skin. It is the "without-the-skin" environment to which I ascribe reinforcing stimuli. Within-the-skin are the emotion feelings that are the ultimate reward for behavior and that may be the final determinants of its rate of repetition.

References

Baum, W. (1973). The correlational law of effect, *Journal of the Experimental Analysis of Behavior*, 20, 137–153.
Dawkins, R. (1976). *The Selfish Gene*. Oxford: Oxford University Press.
Dennett, D. C. (1969). *Content and Consciousness*. London: Routledge and Kegan Paul.
Dennett, D. C. (1982). How to study consciously, or nothing comes to mind, *Synthese*, 53, 159–180.
Dennett, D. C. (1987). *The Intentional Stance*. Cambridge, MA: MIT Press.
Dennett, D. C. (1991). *Consciousness Explained*. New York: Little Brown.
Dennett, D. C. (2005). *Sweet Dreams: Philosophical Obstacles to a Science of Consciousness*. Cambridge, MA: MIT.
Ehrenberg, A. S. C. (1988). *Repeat Buying: Facts, Theory and Applications* (2nd ed.). London: Griffin.
Foxall, G. R. (1990/2004). *Consumer Psychology in Behavioral Perspective*. London and New York: Routledge. (Republished 2004 by Beard Books, Frederick, MD.)
Foxall, G. R. (1997a). *Marketing Psychology: The Paradigm in the Wings*. London and New York: Palgrave Macmillan.

Foxall, G. R. (1997b). Affective responses to consumer situations, *International Review of Retail, Distribution and Consumer Research*, 7, 191–225.

Foxall, G. R. (1999). The Behavioural Perspective Model: consensibility and consensuality, *European Journal of Marketing*, 33, 570–596.

Foxall, G. R. (2002). *Consumer Behaviour Analysis: Critical Perspectives in Business and Management*. London and New York: Routledge.

Foxall, G. R. (2004). *Context and Cognition: Interpreting Complex Behavior*. Reno, NV: Context Press.

Foxall, G. R. (2005). *Understanding Consumer Choice*. London and New York: Palgrave Macmillan.

Foxall, G. R. (2007a). *Explaining Consumer Choice*. London and New York: Palgrave Macmillan.

Foxall, G. R. (2007b). Intentional behaviorism, *Behavior and Philosophy*, 35, 1–56.

Foxall, G. R. (2008). Intentional behaviorism revisited, *Behavior and Philosophy*, 37, 113–156.

Foxall, G. R. (2009). Ascribing intentionality, *Behavior and Philosophy*, 37, 217–222.

Foxall, G. R. (2010a). Invitation to consumer behavior analysis. *Journal of Organizational Behavior Management*, 30, 92–109.

Foxall, G. R. (2010b). *Interpreting Consumer Choice: The Behavioral Perspective Model*. New York and London: Routledge.

Foxall, G. R. (2011). Brain, emotion and contingency in the explanation of consumer behaviour, *International Review of Industrial and Organizational Psychology*, 26, 47–92.

Foxall, G. R. (2013). Intentionality, symbol, and situation in the interpretation of consumer choice, *Marketing Theory*, 13, 105–127.

Foxall, G. R. and Yani-de-Soriano, M. M. (2005). Situational influences on consumers' attitudes and behavior, *Journal of Business Research*, 58, 518–525.

Foxall, G. R., Yani-de-Soriano, M., Yousafzai, S. and Javed, U. 2012. The role of neurophysiology, emotion and contingency in the explanation of consumer choice. In Wells, V. K. and Foxall, G. R. (Eds.) *Handbook of Developments in Consumer Behaviour* (pp. 461–522). Cheltenham, UK and Northampton, MA: Edward Elgar.

Goodhardt, G. J., Ehrenberg, A. S. C. and Chatfield, C. (1984). The Dirichlet: a comprehensive model of buying behaviour, *Journal of the Royal Statistical Society, A*, 147, 621–655.

Levine, J. (1994). Out of the closet: a qualophile confronts qualophobia, *Philosophical Topics*, 22, 107–126.

Meehl, P. E. (1990). Why summaries of research on psychological theories are often uninterpretable, *Psychological Reports*, 66, 195–244.

Mehrabian, A. and Russell, J. (1974). *An Approach to Environmental Psychology*. Cambridge, MA: MIT Press.

Rolls, E. T. (1999). *The Brain and Emotion*. Oxford: Oxford University Press.

Skinner, B. F. (1950). Are theories of learning necessary? *Psychological Review*, 57, 193–216.

Skinner, B. F. (1953). *Science and Human Behavior*. New York: Macmillan.

Skinner, B. F. (1974). *About Behaviorism*. New York: Cape.

Smith, T. L. (1994). *Behavior and its Causes: Philosophical Foundations of Operant Psychology*. Dordrecht: Kluwer.

Yani-de-Soriano, M. and Foxall, G. R. (2006). The emotional power of place: the fall and rise of dominance in retail research, *Journal of Retailing and Consumer Services*, 13, 403–416.

Yani-de-Soriano, M., Foxall, G. R. and Newman, A. (2013). The impact of the interaction of utilitarian and informational reinforcement and behaviour setting scope on consumer response, *Psychology and Marketing*, 30, 148–159.

Index

Note: page numbers followed by 'n' refer to notes

Printed in the United States
by Baker & Taylor Publisher Services